RS 2M03 Death and Dying in Comparative Religi
Janet Ross
Readings:

Part 1: How we Approach Death: Theory and Practice

A: Theory

B. Practice: Two Case Studies

Part 2: Chinese Religion

Part 3: Tibetan Buddhism

Part 4: Religions in Japan

Part 5: Religions in Africa

Part 6: Mexico: Day of the Dead

Part 7: Brazil

Part 8: Death in Hindu Traditions

Part 9: Indigenous North American Traditions

Part 1:
How we Approach Death: Theory and Practice

A: Theory

THREE

GOOD DEATH, BAD DEATH (I)

In Other Times and Places

Does it make any sense to think of a person as having either a "good" or a "bad" death? History suggests that it does. People in many times and places have developed strong preferences about ways to live and die that are deeply rooted in religious beliefs and cultural values. "The good (or bad) death" actually refers to the end phase of life. The latter term usually describes what medical people call terminal illness and the rest of us call dying. Death may also come suddenly, though: alive one moment, dead the next. Is it good or bad to die in a twinkling? Not everybody has the same opinion. But an even larger question seeks our attention: what is the relationship between how we die and (1) how we have lived and (2) how we fare after death? In this chapter we explore the anguish, inspiration, wisdom, and, perhaps, foolishness of societies in times and places other than today's mainstream North America. Particular attention will be given to the concepts of the deathbed scene and the moment of death. In the next chapter we work up the courage to look in the mirror to view the "good death" in our own lives.

I had spoken with Mr. Carter the previous morning. He didn't have much to say and not much breath to say it with. We didn't have to talk about death. That had become a worn-out topic. Life had been pretty much worn out, too, as can happen after more than ten years as a bed-and-chair resident in geriatric facilities. "Another day, another dollar," he had wheezed. Now I was standing in a cool, sparkling-clean room two doors down from the converted broom closet that had become my office as psychologist. The consulting pathologist was completing the postmortem exam. He commented that Mr. Carter probably had engaged in vigorous physical activity in his earlier years; he was still a strong and healthy man, allowing for his age and deadness. "The ward says he died in his sleep," I dutifully noted. Dr. Rimini produced one of his elegant snorts. "Or he died in the nurses' sleep. No matter. He died."

I felt sad that Mr. Carter had died, that Mr. Carter had to die, that anybody did. I also wondered what I would find in my studies of death and dying—did most people *want* to pass on in their sleep, or what? Later, another thought hit me as I met with students who had signed up for my strange new kind of class on death and dying at Clark University (in Worcester, Massachusetts) in the 1960s. Few had had direct experiences with the dying or the dead. Not many of these college students had lost a family member or close friend, and the deaths themselves had been processed and packaged by professionals. I might also have been isolated from the dying and the dead had I not embarked on what was then a beyond-the-fringe career of working with the aged and the life-threatened. Mr. Carter's life and death had been more instructive to me than any textbook on death (which did not exist at that time). If my office had not been so close to the morgue (a little joke on the part of the hospital administration), I would not have been acquainted with the unprocessed body of a person I had known.

My experiences with the dying and the dead did not come through everyday life in our society. We have succeeded more than most societies in reducing the presence of the dead. In part this has been accomplished by keeping people alive longer. In part, though, we have cultivated techniques for keeping not only the dead but also the dying from general view. For most people in other times and places, death and the dead were more a part of everyday life.

We begin with a visit to the Lugbara of Uganda and Zaire (now the Democratic Republic of the Congo). Our guide is anthropologist John Middleton, who studied the Lugbara during the 1960s.[1] The world has much changed since these observations, but they offer insights into a culture much different from the Euro-American mainstream. We step now into that time and place.

A MAN SHOULD DIE IN HIS HUT

Not much is hidden from view among the Lugbara. There are a lot of Lugbara families within small neighborhood areas. Everybody knows pretty much what's happening with everybody else. Death is the most important thing that happens, from the Lugbara standpoint, and it happens all too often. Illness and death become known quickly, and most of the community participates in funeral rites whether or not they are related to the deceased.

> The Lugbara have few rites to do with birth, puberty or marriage. But the rites of death are important, elaborate, and often long-lasting, and lead to the reorganization of local social relations of many kinds. A death is more than that of an individual family member: the dead person has also been a member of a lineage which is assumed to be perpetual . . . [the death] disturbs the continuity of the lineage and mortuary rites are performed in order to restore this continuity.[2]

There is something else to know about the meaning of death for the Lugbara before we focus on the deathbed scene itself. The dead continue to exist in some mysterious way, but no mortal can understand how and why. What the people can understand is that there is safety in the *akua* (the home, the village compound) and danger in the *amve* (the outside, literally "in the grass"). The forces of good are concentrated in the home compound; evil lurks outside.

Death raids the compound from the outside. Gods in a nasty mood or witch-women are responsible for each death: *nobody just dies*. The sexist nature of Lugbara belief cannot be ignored. Males are fully human. Females can be almost human if they accept male governance and make no trouble, but females have the potential to become witches and disrupt the order of things. Much of Lugbara life consists of trying to control or placate evil forces. Death, then, not only threatens social structure and continuity but also represents a victory for the forces of evil.

How can there be a good death within this belief system? And what, precisely, would be a bad death?

The Lugbara have a clear understanding of physical death. The person stops breathing; the body grows cold, and after a while it starts to smell. Like many other people, they believe the soul or spirit departs the body after the last breath but may still hover around for a while, making everyone feel uneasy. The newly dead are neither here nor there. Or, perhaps more accurately, they are both here with us, drifting and lurking, and there, seeking admittance to the spirit realm.

There is something else to consider as well: the person dies to society. The loyal dying person will accept disengagement from all the obligations and powers possessed during life. These obligations and powers will then be redistributed among the living according to established principles. Here we start to get an inkling of what a good death might entail. Middleton makes it clearer:

> A man should die in his hut, lying on his bed, with his brothers and sons around him to hear his last words; he should die with his mind still alert and should be able to speak clearly even if only softly; he should die peacefully and with dignity, without bodily discomfort or disturbance.

The when of dying is also important:

> He should die at the time that he has for some days foreseen as the time of his death so that his sons and brothers will be present; he should die loved and respected by his family. He should die physically when all these conditions have been or can be fulfilled and when he is expected to do so because he has said his last words and had them accepted by his kin, and especially by his successor to his lineage status.[3]

Obviously, the Lugbara have given a lot of thought to the deathbed scene. The dying person is not viewed primarily as a "medical case" or a "patient" or as a passive entity. The dying person has lines to speak and actions to perform. Dying happens to a person, but it is also something a person has to do—and do right.

The scene climaxes with the moment of death. Ideally, the dying person will have shed his social identity, powers, and responsibilities. The successor observes the final breath and then steps outside the hut to sound the dead man's *cere*.

> The *cere* is a falsetto whooping cry whose "melody" is that of certain words that make a phrase "belonging" to the "owner" and which is unique to a particular man or woman. It may never be called by anyone else than his successor on this single occasion. It then marks the death, physical and social, and the actual moment of succession.[4]

The moment of death, then, is the signal for a firm and public reorganization of social structure in the community. A person dies, and at the very next instant the community starts to make its adjustments (though preliminary adjustments have already been in progress).

That was a good death for the Lugbara. A person has died well when the community can persuade itself that the performance did not stray too much from the ideal. There was a little room for the fudge factor. A person might not be ready to die on schedule. The successor and others most closely affected are kept waiting. What to do? The community has the option to go ahead with the rites of mourning even though the recalcitrant fellow in his hut is still clinging to life. He becomes socially dead, and that helps to move things along. It will be concluded that he had a good death even though the schedule was a little off.

There is an important contingency here, though. The dying person should feel well disposed toward kin and community, well respected, well treated. The whole community will be at risk should the person die in bitter resentment. Spirits of the discontented or disconsolate dead are terribly malevolent. It is therefore in everybody's interest to provide the dying person with every comfort, whether physical or socio-ritual. We will want to look at this mutual obligation system again when we look at deathbed scenes in our own society.

The bad death for the Lugbara is very bad indeed. It's more than bad—it's downright dangerous. Sudden and unexpected deaths are bad; so are deaths that occur in the wrong place, such as far from home. What makes these deaths bad is that the deceased does not have the opportunity to prepare and enact a final scene. There may be nobody (or only inappropriate people) to hear the last words. The end of life is not firmly punctuated by the *cere* call, which restores social order while also respecting the death of the individual. Furthermore, the person who has died in the "out there" may yield up a confused spirit that has difficulty finding its way home. The wandering spirit is frantic. Wild with fear and rage, such a spirit is not pleasant to encounter when it tries to find its way home or to its next destination. A woman who dies in childbirth poses a special risk to others because this event has fractured the relationship between sexuality and fertility.

Whatever interferes with an orderly deathbed scene within the bosom of the community is likely to produce a dangerous ghost and at the same time interfere with social reorganization. It's pretty clear that how—

and how well—a person dies has postmortem implications for kin and community.

SETTING SAIL FOR DEATH

We are now far from the Lugbara of Uganda and Zaire. We set down in the rugged landscape of Papua New Guinea. Kaliai is a political district in West New Britain Province. The thousand or so Lusi-speaking villagers who live along the northwest coast are known locally as *the* Kaliai. These interesting people are slash-and-burn farmers who also hunt and fish. They had little or no contact with the outside world until the turn of the twentieth century. Most converted to Roman Catholicism but continued to keep pretty much to themselves. Our guides are anthropologists David R. Counts and Dorothy Ayers Counts, who explored Kaliai ways in the 1960s and 1970s.[5] Again, we will want to acquaint ourselves with the structure and strictures of a society's life before focusing on dying and death.

Theoretically, all are equal among the Kaliai. In practice, though, there is a decided advantage to being male, first-born, and of the senior generation. One thinks of George Orwell's four-footed character in *Animal Farm* who observes that all are equal, but some are more equal than others. Furthermore, not everybody is a person. To become a full-fledged person one must be integrated into the community. Young children are not yet part of the core social structure because they do not have command of the language and ways and are unable to distinguish between dreams and reality. Strangers and enemies (to the extent that these categories are differentiated) will never be enfranchised persons in the Kaliai scheme of things. Personhood among the Kaliai entails a complex network of perks and obligations. Count and Count tell us that "everyone in Kaliai society is debtor to some, creditor to others."[6] As with the Lugbara, death upsets the ongoing pattern of obligations, resources, and relationships. As death approaches, then, attention focuses on the resolution and distribution of the dying person's accounts. Ideally, an aging person of wealth and status in the community is expected to disengage somewhat from economic and social activity. In theory, this gradual withdrawal makes it easier to detach the person from society at death. In practice, though, few are so willing to step into the shadows any sooner than need be.

What of dying and death? To minds saturated in Western thought and traditions, there is a sharp divide between life and death. Indeed, "the moment of death" is salient in Euro-American culture, and we even expect time of death to be recorded fastidiously (if often erroneously). For the Kaliai and many other world cultures, though, death is a process. The Buddhist stages of death, for example, include four phases that occur while the person is still among the living and up to four additional phases beyond the point at which physical death is certified.[7] For the Kaliai, death is a process of separation that can—and should—begin while the person is still able to make decisions and perform socially significant actions. Separation continues through the dying process and as long afterward as might be necessary to free the deceased person and society from each other.

What is the good death, then? It is the death that the dying person has accepted, and it results in the proper and thorough severance of social relationships within a reasonable period of time. Again, as with the Lugbara, the bad death is the unprepared and the unresolved. The spirit of the deceased still has social power and obligations clutched in his hands. The complex network of social exchange cannot function effectively while the dead are still caught in the system. And, of course, the spirit cannot proceed toward its mysterious destiny while still entangled. The *incomplete death* is the worst kind because it disrupts basic patterns of interaction and obligation in the community and threatens to turn loose an unappeased ghost.

Assuring the good death is by no means simple. Furthermore, the Kaliai perspective can be quite different from our own. The following are examples of end-of-life scenes among the Kaliai.

An aged bigman dies. After a time, his widow asks other males in her family to kill her. The kin confer. If all agree, the widow will kneel on a mat. Her oldest son will strangle her with a garrote or break her neck at the base of her skull with a wooden club that was carved especially for that purpose. This is a good death. We see that it is prepared and acquiescent. The widow's request is rational: she enjoyed the prestige and comfortable life of a bigman's wife, and now she does not want to become a burden on others. Because the couple enjoyed an affectionate relationship, it is obvious that they will be rejoined in a spirit village. Suicide, it should be noted, usually is a bad death, because it is unnatural and leaves things in a jumble of unresolved obligations. Furthermore, a death by one's own hand is interpreted as homicide-at-a-distance, so the search begins for the "real" killer. A bereaved woman's assisted suicide is the exception; and most widows do not elect to end their lives in this way, nor are they under social pressure to do so.

Twins are born. This is unnatural. The infants are exposed to the elements until they die. This is neither a good nor a bad death: the babies have not become Kaliai persons.

An aged man falls ill and is taken to the mission clinic for treatment but soon judges that he will not recover. Despite protests from clinic staff and family, he insists on being moved to the beach not far from his home. There a sail is set up as a tent to provide protection from the elements, and word is sent to his relatives that Avel, the old man, is preparing to die. Because he has long been disengaged from the normal turmoil of shell money finance, the people who gather do so to comfort him and to say their farewells. He himself remains composed, his deepest concern being to cling to life until he can say good-bye to his children. Avel waits until all his children can arrive. Villagers and nurses expect him to die at any minute, but he holds on for two weeks, until his eldest daughter (a novitiate nun) reaches him via a small coastal vessel. Kumui is brought immediately to the tent where her father lies. Avel speaks only once, saying, "Ah, now that you are here I can die easily." He then closes his eyes, and within two hours he is dead.[8]

A sail fashioned into a tent, rippling slightly in the coastal breeze. Family in attendance. The dying person well reconciled and having no grievance or claim on the survivors. This was definitely a good death: it came at just the right time and had been so well prepared that all significant economic and social relationships had been resolved, save for that final visit from Kumui.

Another sail on the beach. Another person has returned from the hospital as quickly as possible, coming home to die. This return is the signal for erection of the sail shelter and the onset of mourning by relatives. The dying person is placed under the sail. Relatives minister to his or her needs. Others from the community also crowd around. What are they all buzzing about? They want to know who killed this person and why. What rules has this person transgressed, what enemies has he or she

made? All deaths, after all, are homicides, even though they may take such varied forms as illness or shark attack. Attention is also given to the financial implications: for example, has a widow been left wealthy or impoverished? Note that the gathering is carrying on lively discussions *about*, not *with*, the dying person. It is the significance of death for the community that matters most. (Incidentally, some of these "dying" people recover from their apparent fatal condition, and everybody goes about their business, unperturbed about the reversal of fortune. They have all acted prudently.)

REFLECTIONS ON GOOD AND BAD DEATHS IN BAND-AND-VILLAGE SOCIETIES

Time for an intermission. What we have learned about the Lugbara and the Kaliai has much in common with deathways in many other face-to-face societies around the world.[9] These are people who know they belong—belong to a culture with definite opinions about the world and their place in it, and belong to one another. When all goes as it should, they grow up within a framework of established rules and conduct their lives with familiar people in familiar surroundings. Not much is kept from others, and even that for not very long. People among us today who grew up in small towns beyond the reach of superhighways may feel a kinship with this kind of experience. Death, like life, is everybody's business, and it is a business that must be conducted properly. Private grief and loss are respected. In band-and-village cultures, the parents of twins or a deformed infant will experience personal pain and loss when they fulfill their communal obligation by exposing these "unnatural" births to death. Whatever one feels in private, though, is secondary to protecting the community against the ever-present risk from demonic powers.

There are examples of cross-cultural influence, but it is difficult to escape the conclusion that many peoples seem to have arrived independently at the same basic ideas about dying and death. The comm[illegible]lties I see as most prevalent are as follows: All or most deaths are c[illegible] hostile agencies, whether human, spirit, or god/demon. Death i[illegible] that includes, but goes beyond, what we call dying. *How* this [illegible] curs can be either good or bad—for the individual and for [illegible] nity. The "dying process," "deathbed scene," and "momen[illegible] important concepts in Western thought—must be considered within the totality of the flow of life for individual and community. The judgment that this is either a good or a bad death, then, cannot be limited to the experiences of the person in the last days and hours of life. The ideal death (1) requires some advance planning or awareness on the part of the individual and, if possible, kin; (2) requires acceptance by the individual; (3) takes long enough for kin and community to engage in both personal comforting and ritual observance but (4) does not take so much time that the waiting and rituals interfere with other community needs; and (5) has full and proper funerary and mourning rituals afterward to make sure the soul of the dead has headed off to its next destination instead of becoming a discontented or even a dangerous spirit. Finally, the ideal is just that. In practice, perfect deaths are rare, perhaps almost as rare as perfect lives. Nevertheless, the vision of the good death provides guidelines and inspiration.

THREE EXEMPLARY DEATHS: SOCRATES, JESUS, AND MARY

Not everybody today accepts the idea that there are better and worse ways to die. A fellow a few seats away at the ballpark replied to some comment by his friends that he did not care how or when he died. My ears automatically dialed up to eavesdrop (the baseball game itself seeming beyond rescue for the home team). He was going to eat what he liked to eat, drink what he liked to drink, and smoke what he liked to smoke. To make himself absolutely clear, he concluded: "When you're dead, you're dead. How you get dead—who the hell cares!" I will assume that others through the ages have held a similar opinion. Resistance to the idea of good and bad deaths is worth consideration, but not right here.

Our immediate concern is with deaths that have been taken as models for how we should live and die. The two most widely known and influential exemplary deaths come from antiquity: Socrates, the aged gadfly philosopher of Athens, and Jesus, an unknown miracle worker from a small town who had become disturbingly popular. It is not easy to find even a third example of a death with resonations so deep and wide. But the pages of history reveal that the mother of Jesus was once revered through all of Christianity for her death as well as her life. Much about Socrates, Jesus, and Mary will be left unsaid here in order to keep our focus on models for the good or ideal death.

The Fatal Cup

We know this of Socrates. At age seventy (and for many previous years) he was a luminary of intellectual life in Athens, attracting bright and inquisitive minds. He earned fame in his own time and for centuries thereafter through his introduction of what became known as the Socratic method. This is a form of adroit questioning and listening that lures knowledge from the inexperienced, hesitant, and inarticulate. So powerful was his impact on Western thought that the history of philosophy remains divided between the Pre-Socratic and the Socratic.

He entered the world theater of imagination, however, through the manner of his death. Athens had recently lost the Peloponnesian War, and the various political factions were in an ugly, blame-pinning mood. Socrates' conscience got him in trouble. He was chosen by lot to be presiding officer of a senate committee that proceeded to condemn eight commanders to death for having lost a critical naval battle. Socrates thought this condemnation was unjust and the punishment extreme: he did not sign off on it. Nevertheless, the commanders were condemned and executed. As Athenian power continued to deteriorate, Socrates became one of the more conspicuous scapegoats, although he had done nothing wrong. The story of the charges brought against him, his trial, and his defense has been told many times. We proceed directly to the execution of his death sentence in the year 399 B.C.

What we think we know about Socrates' death comes from the words of a man who wasn't there. Plato, one of the great names in the history of thought, was a disciple and friend of the condemned man and had visited him faithfully during his incarceration. On the appointed day, though, Plato said he was too ill to go—perhaps he meant too sick at heart. Plato did hear reports from his fellow disciples who had been with Socrates to the end. It was Plato who brought Socrates to future generations in a series of dialogues. In *Phaedo* he gives us the final scene, the last words of Socrates, spoken even as death crept through his body.[10]

There is a facade we have to get past to comprehend Socrates' death and its influence on posterity. Plato's description is almost certainly not an objective report of what actually happened. This was clearly understood in its own time. Readers would have expected Plato to cast the events as a moral lesson in the form of a dialogue. They would not have expected verbatim reportage. Instead they would have expected a coherent account with a satisfying beginning, a middle, and an end, an account that perfectly captures the mood and message without sweating the details. Socrates did end his life more or less as described by Plato, but it is probable that the surviving account also includes literary construction, selection, and invention.

What we have, then, is a moral story built around fact. We do not know precisely how fact and invention play together. Nevertheless, it is this literary take on the death of the great philosopher that has come down through the years to perplex and inspire: perplex because we are free to ponder why Socrates did not save his life while he had that option, and inspire because here was a man who remained true to his principles and looked Death in the eye.

The scene divides naturally into three sections. First is the period of his incarceration, when Socrates and his friends had wide-ranging discussions but always with his impending death well in mind. The jailer was friendly and respectful. He and the guards could have been bribed; they were not keen at being party to the execution of this wise and entertaining old man. Socrates was the one who wouldn't go along with such a plan. He would continue to be the law-abiding person even though dealt an injustice by the court. Socrates also knew that his escape would mean big trouble for his friends and was not about to let that happen. And so they waited together. Specifically, they waited for a ceremonial ship to return from its mission to Delos. This was an annual voyage that played a role in citywide purification rituals. No prisoner could be executed while the ship was away on its mission. Here was one of those little quirks of history that may have made all the difference in the turning of significant events. If the ship had still been in harbor, Socrates would have been given the fatal cup on the day he had been condemned. Now, however, there was time—time for Socrates to respond to all the questions and arguments his young friends could generate and, in so doing, to express for the last time his thoughts about death.

His friends believed the individual soul is immortal and that therefore everlasting happiness awaited them after death. Socrates did not rubberstamp these assumptions. Instead, he did what he did best. He drew out

their assumptions and subjected them to the light of critical reason. After exercising them through the labyrinth of thought, Socrates did affirm his belief in immortality. His reasoning is as ticklish as ever: the idea of life is imperishable, and since this idea dwells within us, we must be imperishable as well. His reasoning on the subject of immortality takes several other turns intended to pique and instruct his disciplines but not crucial to us here (a sigh of relief is permissible). His famous conclusion is that death should not be feared. It is the gateway to immortality, or, if not, then it is a kind of sleep, and who doesn't enjoy a nice long nap?

Peter J. Ahrensdorf believes that all this talk about death was intended as an instructional unit for Socrates' disciples.[11] Through contemplation of death we can best realize the importance of the examined life. And the world takes notice when a philosopher can philosophize lucidly on the verge of his own death.

This brings us to the remaining two scenes in the drama of Socrates' death: receiving the fatal cup and uttering the last words. By tradition, it was a cup of hemlock that the jailer reluctantly placed in Socrates' hands. This was a fraught moment: the hesitant executioner, the hushed and appalled friends, the philosopher still quite vigorously alive. Socrates tried to make it easier on everybody. He had already bathed "rather than give the women the trouble of washing me when I am dead."[12] Socrates also politely declined the invitation to give directions for what should be done after his death. Everybody wanted to please him. Socrates turned the decision back upon his friends. "Nothing new," he told Crito, "just what I am always telling you. If you look after yourselves, whatever you do will please me and mine and you too, even if you don't agree with me now. But if you neglect yourselves and fail to follow the [philosophical] line of life as I have laid it out for you both now and in the past, however fervently you agree with me now, it will do no good at all."

Crito agreed to this challenge, yet asked, "But how shall we bury you?"

"Any way you like," replied Socrates, "that is, if you can catch me and I don't slip through your fingers."

Now the time had come. Socrates accepted the cup without fuss or ostentation. A question for the jailer: was it permitted to offer a few drops as a libation to the gods? Sorry, but there was just enough for a lethal dose. Very well. Another question: what should he do after he had drained the cup? "Just walk about," replied the jailer, "until you feel your legs grow heavy, then lie down."

Socrates drained the cup. His friends, despite their resolve, broke into weeping. Socrates scolded them gently: we should end our lives in a peaceful state of mind. His listeners made a renewed effort to restrain their tears.

He did as instructed by the jailer, walking about until his legs felt heavy, then lay down on his back and covered his face. The jailer placed his hand on Socrates and a few minutes later examined his feet and legs. He asked Socrates if he had felt his foot being pinched. No, he hadn't felt a thing. The jailer's touch ascended upward, following the path of cold numbness. As the coldness moved above his waist, Socrates uncovered his face. He had one more thing to say:

> Crito, we ought to offer a cock to Asclepius. See to it, and don't forget.

With these words—asking his friends to offer a fee to the god of health, possibly a final quip—Socrates died.

But not of hemlock poisoning. *Or,* that was pure hemlock in the cup, but the description of his last moments has been scrubbed clean. The latter alternative seems most likely. The progressive numbness from lower to upper regions of the body is characteristic of hemlock poisoning. But where is the agonized gulping for air, the burning sensation in the mouth, the blue tinge of the skin, the tremors, the cramps, the convulsions? Hemlock is nasty stuff. It does not make for a tranquil deathbed scene. The dying person suffers, as would any compassionate witnesses. Medical historian William B. Ober asks and answers the logical question:

> What could have been Plato's motive for such a *suppressio veri?* The simplest answer is that he wanted to preserve the noble image of his friend and teacher, "the wisest and justest and best," and that he wanted no undignified details to obscure the heroic manner of his death.[13]

This celebrated philosophical death, then, depends at least as much on its telling as on its doing. We do not have to be ancient Athenians or trained philosophers to appreciate the way that Socrates mastered his final scene: the acceptance of an unjust verdict, the compassion shown to jailer as well as friends, the fearlessness in the face of death, and, above all, the very model of a person remaining true to his principles right up to the moment of death. This scene—as shaped by Plato—was so impressive that centuries later believers in a newly emerged religion could

also admire Socrates and judge that he had died in grace even though never baptized into Christianity.

Jesus: The Death of the Messiah

It happened a long time ago. A well-known man was unjustly condemned to death. The final scene in his earthly life resonated not only among his contemporaries but also through the corridors of time to this day. How we think of this man and his message has much to do with the way he died.

This general description applies to the deaths of both Jesus and Socrates. There are other similarities. Although both were executions, neither death was instantaneous. There was time for the condemned man to reflect on his situation and time for witnesses to observe. And there was suffering. The agonies of the crucified Jesus have been at the center of Christian faith since the beginning. Now we know that in all probability Socrates also suffered in his last moments even though this was concealed by Plato. On the surface of things, then, neither of these endings would seem promising candidates for the exemplary death, the good death that should inspire us throughout our lives. Obviously, there is a lot under the surface, something that has stirred us deeply.

One more similarity, and this is critical: how we know what we think we know about these deaths. Father Raymond Brown has placed us all in his debt with his magisterial studies *The Birth of the Messiah* and *The Death of the Messiah* (this in two lengthy and tightly packed volumes).[14] His command of scope and detail is crowned by a sophisticated perspective. Father Brown lays the situation out for us early on:

> Understandably there is a desire to know what Jesus himself said, thought, and did in the final hours of his life. Yet Jesus did not write an account of his passion; nor did anyone who had been present write an eyewitness account. Available to us are four *different* accounts written some thirty to seventy years later in the Gospels of Mark, Matthew, Luke, and John, all of which were dependent on tradition that had come down from an intervening generation or generations.[15]

Whatever eyewitnesses saw and heard and however they spoke about the death of Jesus have been lost to history. Brown notes that the pre-

Gospel tradition has not been preserved. The earliest sources accepted by the church, then, are at some distance from the actual events. There are additional cautions that Father Brown urges we keep in mind:

The evangelists had their own purposes, their own agendas, in preparing and disseminating the Gospel accounts of the passion of Jesus. Brown devotes much attention to elucidating these intentions because we are otherwise vulnerable to misunderstanding their messages.

The Gospels were intended for the audiences of the day. These listeners and readers would know some things that are unfamiliar to later generations, and they would have their own distinctive experiences, hopes, fears, and vested interests.

Even within these limits of knowledge and interpretation, there is much we do not, and in all probability will never, know about the circumstances of Jesus' death. Brown leads us through the available sources to note again and again that there are significant questions that simply cannot be answered.

Brown would also have us realize that we cannot well understand this "social and thought world quite different from our own."[16] It would be naive to assume that Jesus and his contemporaries thought about the world as we do today and that Jesus was speaking to us like some talking head on television. There is an enormous linguistic, cultural, and historical gap between us and the three crosses raised high on Calvary.

We don't like to hear things like this. We don't like to be told that what we think we know is not precisely and firmly what happened. Most often, we also don't like to have somebody coming along to shake our beliefs and assumptions—especially if that somebody is himself a man of faith who knows a lot more than we do about his subject matter.

With these qualifiers in mind, then, we focus on the received image of Christ on the cross and what centuries of believers have taken from this image. Jesus probably died on the day before the Sabbath, which would be a Friday, and probably in the middle of the month of Nisan in the religious calendar. This would have been either just before, or during, or just after the hours when thousands of lambs were being slaughtered for Passover. Years later a Gospel writer would speak of "the precious blood of Christ as of a lamb without blemish or spot" (1 Peter 1:19). We are reminded immediately that blood and slaughter were in the air. And we see that the image of Jesus as the paschal lamb is rooted in traditional events of the day.

I catch myself about to characterize this vein of thought as mystical. The man and the lamb are somehow one. Blood seems to be both actual and symbolic, a sanguine exchange between the sacred and the profane. And circling around the lamb and the man is the theme of sacrifice. I close my eyes and can envision Greeks of remote antiquity sacrificing grain and wine but also, most dearly, blood to their gods. I blink again and see Isaac on the verge of becoming a sacrifice to Jehovah. In my mind's eye I see a gallery of blood sacrifices by many people to many gods. The death of Jesus seems to ride on a long wave of mystical thought in which blood unites and lubricates the troubled relationship between gods and men. But then I do catch myself, with Brown's cautions in mind. Did Jesus as the sacrificial lamb seem at all mystical to the people of his own time? Or was it an auspicious event, but one which seemed quite in accord with their prevailing view of the world?

Do astounding events occur as Jesus dies? Yes and no, depending on sources. In Matthew, Jesus screams, *"Eli, Eli, lema sabachthani?"* "My God, my God, why have you forsaken me?" (Matthew 27:46). A moment or two later he screams again. Just then,

> . . . the earth was shaken, and the rocks were rent, and the tombs were opened, and many bodies of the fallen-asleep holy ones were raised. And having come out from the tombs after his raising they entered into the holy city; and they were made visible to many. (Matthew 27:51–53)

This miraculous event would surely have made the death of Jesus portentous. The earth itself trembled and marked his passage, the tombs opening to release their hostages.

Luke's version is different. Jesus cries out loudly but once and does not question God's intentions from the depth of despair. Instead: "Father into your hands I place my spirit" (Luke 23:46). The special effects in this version are limited to a solar eclipse (also mentioned by Matthew) and rending of "the veil of the sanctuary," presumably also by earthquake, but the tombs do not release their dead to mingle with the living.

Still different is John's account. Here there are no special effects in the form of eclipse, earthquake, or the dead emerging from shattered tombs. Instead, John offers one of the very few glimpses of Jesus as a son to his mother. He sees her in the crowd before the cross. "Woman, look: your son" (John 19:26–27). He then saw to it that his mother adopted one of his disciples, saying to him, "Look: your mother." In this version Jesus does not cry out in agony, although surely he is suffering, nor does he either question God or ask for safe passage. He simply bows his head and says, "It is finished" (John 19:30).

Mark gives us a version much like Matthew's, but here Jesus cries out only once and the tombs do not yield up their dead.

These descriptions agree on the basics: Jesus died on the cross after prolonged suffering. The Gospels are not quite in harmony about the occurrence of striking natural or supernatural events. There are also lingering and unresolved questions about two other salient matters. What should we believe Jesus actually said on the cross—and to whom? And what was the cause of death? No attempt will be made to answer these questions here. We simply note that scholars have been perplexed by these questions for a long time and have offered a variety of theories.

The most obvious discrepancy is between the last words of Jesus as given in three different versions. But there is also ambiguity regarding the listener to whom Jesus addressed his final utterances. If Jesus said, "It is finished," and only that, he might have been speaking to the witnesses and to himself. It is generally taken, however, that Jesus was either questioning or petitioning God. This interpretation is consistent with the subsequent belief that Jesus was the son of God. Yet the possibility has been raised that Jesus was addressing his final words not to God but to the prophet Elijah, who some people at that time expected to return soon to announce the end of days. Did Jesus actually call out to Eloi, Eli, Elias, Elahi, Eliyahu, or Eliya? We don't know, of course, and we don't know for sure how his original utterance might have been altered when his Aramaic language was translated into Hebrew, Greek, and Latin. The argument here is that Jesus considered either Elijah or John the Baptist (held by some to be the embodiment of Elijah) to be the representative of God on earth, not himself. This interpretation could make it a little more difficult to see Jesus as the Messiah.

The cause of death is a question that did not become of much concern until medical science in the twentieth century decided to try its hand at remote postmortem examination. Jesus died of asphyxiation, the lungs having filled with carbon dioxide, or of a lance thrust that pierced the right auricle of the heart, or of circulatory failure and loss of blood, or perhaps of a previously diseased condition of the heart muscle, or perhaps even of despair. Some medical theorists have suggested that several

of these causes were involved. Father Brown comments that all these explanations are based on a misplaced confidence in the descriptions offered by evangelists and Gospel writers, none of whom had any personal knowledge of the actual details.

Where does all of this leave us? Most believers through the centuries have focused on the basics: the suffering man on the cross. This is a vivid and affecting image. Discrepancies and ambiguities have been left to the disputing partisans and scholars. There has been an important divide, however, between those who build their faith around the passion of Jesus and those who make much of the natural and supernatural events said by some Gospel accounts to have accompanied his death.

Would the death of Jesus have become so engraved in hearts and minds if he had not been resurrected (as some believe)? This is another question for which we have no firm answer, but it is clear that the resurrection lit the torch for the dissemination and survival of Christianity in its early years and has remained at the center of the faith ever since. Jesus' death became increasingly compelling as it was woven into a larger fabric of belief over the years, much of it generated by Paul.

What became the traditional version was a triumphant message: "Death, where is thy sting?" (1 Corinthians 15:55). The man who died on the cross had now become a sacrifice. Through the death of Jesus others might live forever. Other religious cults had rituals in which a person became a sort of temporary god and was then sacrificed. Jesus' death has often been compared to these. In the public mind, though, God is often seen as having offered his own son in sacrifice, thereby forging a closer link with humanity. Victory over death was welcome news indeed. Historians conclude that death anxiety was rampant throughout the Roman Empire during those turbulent years. The new religion that called itself Christianity just might have provided the way out.

But—what precisely was the way? Should we follow to the letter the precepts of Jesus' own religion—the Hebrew? Should we emulate the compassion and mercy shown by Jesus, performing an "imitation of Christ"? Should we withdraw from the family circle and societal obligations to live a detached spiritual life, as Jesus had specified? Should we punish and mortify the flesh to overcome our inherent sinfulness and thereby gain entry into heaven—and escape the horrors of damnation? Should we live in a frenzy of anticipation because the end of days is at hand, the fiery apocalypse and the final reckoning as the Messiah returns?

Should we die as Jesus did and thereby prove our devotion and depart from our corrupt mortal shell to pure and everlasting glory?

People who regard themselves as Christians have sometimes taken one of these paths, sometimes another. The image of the suffering man on the cross and the assurance of everlasting life for true believers became the font of diverse rituals and ways of life. In the early years the suffering and death of Jesus held a fatal attraction. Roman authorities made martyrs of some Christians but soon found themselves annoyed by those who insisted on being put to death. The line between martyrdom and suicide became difficult to discern. Eventually church authorities would condemn suicide and attempt to restrain their more susceptible believers from imitating Christ by seeking painful deaths instead of living devout lives.

That people *should* suffer terribly and therefore identify with Jesus on the cross and expiate their own sins has remained a persistent theme even when overtaken by sociotechnological change. Progressive physicians in nineteenth-century Scotland introduced anesthesia and other measures to protect women in childbirth. This movement was hotly resisted by men of the cloth, who insisted that women were meant to suffer and, if needs be, die because of the carnal act that led to reproduction. In the twenty-first century there are still clergy and some physicians who believe that terminal agony is a test of character that should not be remedied. Not many dying people agree, however. Few of the terminally ill cancer patients interviewed in the National Hospice Demonstration Study considered suffering to be a spiritual value.[17]

Through succeeding centuries the image of the man on the cross would continue to inspire not only devotion but also a variety of responses to the challenges of living and dying.

The Beautiful Sleep of the Virgin

In the first thousand years that passed after Christ's death, Christianity expanded its domain, although not without both martial and spiritual combat. The Catholic Church still reigned, though convulsed by serious difficulties of its own. In later medieval years there was a persistent need that could no longer be denied. The people had Jesus, the pope (or, for a while, the popes), and the church fathers. But where was woman? Who could truly understand the prayers and tears of a mother with a sick child? Who could comfort the widow? Who among those most sacred to God embodied the female principle?

The Virgin Mary, Mother of God, was the obvious person to fill this void. Cults of the Virgin continued to develop. She became a popular figure in literature and song, the worship-worthy mother of the Holy Infant. She knew what it was like to bear a child and then to see this child die. Mary understood sorrow. Mary was the brave and loving mother—and she was the personal link to comfort and salvation for every anxious woman in Christendom. People wanted to know more about Mary's life than the sparse information offered in Scripture. How had she lived after the infancy of Christ—and how had she died? Philosopher Donald F. Duclow explains how a woman finally became an exemplar of the good death.[18] By the seventh century the Roman church had entered the Feast of the Assumption into its calendar, celebrating the ascension of Mary to heaven (despite the lack of support for this event in the writings accepted for inclusion in the Bible). Artists started to depict the Dormition (literally "sleep," but here referring to Mary's death) in the tenth century. Gothic churches were dedicated to Mary, and her imagined likeness appeared in stained glass, paintings, and manuscript illuminations.

The story of Mary's death and ascension was greatly enhanced in the thirteenth century when Jacobus de Vorgaine wove apocryphal materials into *The Golden Legend*.[19] This account provided the basis not only for art and literature but also for the intensified worship of Mary. Actually, two narratives are given by de Vorgaine, and, as with the Gospel accounts of Jesus' death, they differ in some details. What do they agree on? Mary has been revisiting the places where Jesus was baptized, suffered, died, was resurrected, and ascended. She weeps with longing to be with her son. One day an angel appears: "Hail, blessed Mary!" He presents her with a palm branch from paradise. She is told she will die within three (or forty) days. Several miracles occur involving apostles and unbelievers. In the more popular version, Mary arrays herself in funeral clothes, bids farewell, takes to bed, and dies peacefully—then ascends to heaven in soul and body.

This story inspired a great many works of art, often depicting the deathbed scene and the flight of her soul to Christ at her death. Visitors to Massachusetts can view a late-thirteenth- or early-fourteenth-century panel at Harvard University's Fogg Museum, and other examples have survived from this period when Mary's deathbed scene first became a powerful image throughout at least Western Christianity. Dormition iconography is all about a woman, a mother, a bereaved mother. Other women can relate. It's also a reconciliation—the lost son who abandoned his family and hometown people in favor of an extremist mission has now opened his arms to his mother. Mothers can be appreciated. They are not used up, worn out, and thrown away after they have served their men. Death, in fact, is renewal, rejuvenation: the iconography often depicts the soul of Mary as an innocent babe rising to heaven. The deathbed scene is really important. It is the crucible for miracles, where the last mortal breath becomes the first taste of immortality. The ideal deathbed scene is serene and confident, well prepared by knowledge and acceptance of the mortal move. And there is something more: blessed Mary, ascended to heaven, might also bless our own lives and deaths. In our fear and doubt we can pray to her for merciful deliverance.

Duclow reports that the popular books of the hours often included *obsecro te,* a prayer addressed to the Virgin:

> At the end of my life show me your face, and reveal to me the day and hour of my death. Please hear and receive this humble prayer and grant me eternal life.

Duclow comments:

> Like the dormition itself, this prayer suggests the ideal death as one foreseen, consecrated, and leading to salvation. That the Virgin's intercession may confer such a death is a medieval commonplace . . . a model for dying.[20]

Prayers, works of art, and theatrical enactments of the last beautiful sleep of the Virgin combined to make this the most influential example of the good death in the later medieval years.

What Was Good about These Deaths?

Socrates died while he was still at the top of his game. Philosophers often have lived a long time, continuing to cerebrate impressively. Jesus was at that glorious season of life where youth and maturity complement each

other. A charismatic person who seemed to have already done wonders, Jesus might have graduated to the rank of exalted elder, a treasured resource to his people. Mary had other children to cherish and protect. She could also have become a person venerated in life, an embodiment of the wise and loving crone. None of these people really had to die when they did. They were not physically or mentally deteriorated. From this standpoint their deaths were not so good, since they were deprived of further experiences, and the world of their continuing contributions.

Socrates died in pain (if we believe medicine rather than myth), and Jesus much more so. According to one Gospel account, he also died in doubt and despair. Most people regard suffering as a bad thing. Indeed, some choose death to avoid further suffering. It goes against common experience to praise or emulate a death that is ravaged by pain. Socrates and Jesus also died in disgrace with the establishment, although supported by others. Other things being equal, the prospect of meeting one's death as punishment and rejection is not what most of us would consider ideal.

Whatever was good about the deaths of Socrates and Jesus had to be powerful enough to overcome the formidable negatives. And apparently this is just what happened. The gadfly philosopher and the man hailed as prophet or messiah ended their lives in ways that spoke deeply to others. There was a message too important to ignore—even if we would not necessarily agree on the specifics of that message. Their deaths were *meaningful.* Therefore, should our deaths not also be meaningful? They died *for* something, something they had also lived for. Should we not also live and die for something? And both showed us it was possible to look death in the face, to accept and perhaps to transcend it. Should we not also embrace death as part of life?

It was different with Mary. Good men die heroically in military or spiritual battles. Good women lie down, close their eyes, and sleep the sleep of the innocent. Mary's successors include Briar Rose, Sleeping Beauty, and the many other representations of the beautiful, innocent, and passive woman who must be animated by the warming breath of a gallant man (dark, handsome lover or gentle comforter).

We know that these great exemplary deaths owe much to literary license and invention (which can be said without denying those historical facts that have been reasonably well established). We also know that such deaths have been out of range for most people, whether in ancient or in modern times. Not that many of us will be condemned to death, nor do we have Mary's privileged access to angelic intercession. We must step closer now to visions of the good and the bad death in the hopes and fears of ordinary people, and to the church's response to their final passage.

ORDO DEFUNCTORUM: DEATH BECOMES CHRISTIAN

The Christian leadership in the first millennium A.D. had its hands full. Evangelists sallied forth to spread the good word throughout the world. This was a daunting task, considering the hazards of travel, the multitude of languages, the competition from entrenched local religions, and the bellicose response to strangers. Furthermore, not everybody agreed on the precise nature of the good word. The Christian message diversified as it melded with local cultures. Attempting to forge the one true canon of belief was a difficult and fractious effort. There was a lack of consensus on who was the authentic standard bearer and who the dangerous heretic. This engendered confusion in the regulation of life and death. What rituals are appropriate when? And just what do these rituals mean? To understand the rituals surrounding death, we will also need to become familiar with other ceremonies and customs, especially communion or the Eucharist.

We now have a better idea about the Christian approach to dying and death in the first millennium, thanks to advances made by recent scholarship. Our primary guide here is Frederick S. Paxton. *Christianizing Death* is the apt title of his integrative contribution.[21] There had been rites devoted to the dying and the dead before Christianity split itself off from Judaic tradition. The "Christianizing" of these rites started right away, and not surprisingly so. Salvation and eternal reward were the lure of Christianity for most of the new disciples. Tracing the development of death rituals over a millennium has produced a lot more information than can or should be stuffed into these pages. The following are what's really important to us:

The early Christian church responded to sickness with prayer and ritual. A passage from James (5:14–15):

> Is any among you sick? Let him call for the elders of the church, and let them pray over him, anointing him with oil in the name of the Lord; and the prayer of faith will save the sick man; and the Lord will raise him up; and if he has committed sins, he will be forgiven.

Prayer and ritual enhance each other. Anointing with oil for both medical and ritual reasons was already a long-established tradition in the Mediterranean. Not mentioned by James in this passage was another important ritual: the laying on of hands. These basic elements of prayer and ritual have continued to be called upon to the present day.

The primary purpose of prayer and ritual was to cure the sick and return them to the community. These performances were not specific for the dying. Instead, they were inspired by the cures that Jesus had wrought when he was among the living.

Yes, as implied by James, there was a connection between sickness and sinfulness. Purification rituals could rinse away the sin, hence restore health. This belief had been held by many religious communities prior to Christianity and was criticized by Jesus. Nevertheless, as Paxton notes, Jesus himself performed healing miracles that included forgiveness of sins. So, then—sickness is caused by sin and cured by forgiveness and ritual purification. Why wouldn't that also work for dying and death?

Feasting for the dead continued as a popular, though non-Christian, practice. Pagans excelled in commemorative services for their dead. The phrase "Roman banquet" has come down to us through the years for good reason. They liked to eat and to eat again. Paxton tells it thusly:

> The first of many meals served in honor of the dead was eaten at the grave on the day of the funeral. Others were eaten on the ninth and fortieth days, on the anniversary of the dead person's birth, and during the festivals of the dead, especially the Parentalia. The centrality of eating in these commemorative acts links them with similar rites of incorporation observed in many societies around the world, for eating symbolizes the re-establishment of the integrity of the family in the wake of the death of one of its members as well as the incorporation of the dead into their new home in the tomb or into the society of the other world.[22]

Fill the platters again! The more we eat, the more we help the dead (a possible marketing ploy not yet discovered by McDonald's). It was also useful to illuminate funerals with torches so the dead could find their way. (Abandoned lovers today who "carry the torch" for their fickle flame might be emulating this tradition. Or maybe not.) Roman Christians continued to participate in these torchlight banquets for the dead with the tacit approval of the church until about halfway through the first millennium, when Augustine of Hippo proved the spoilsport. Douse those torches, curb that appetite! Augustine sounded a modern note in saying that making such a do was simply a way for the living to satisfy themselves; it didn't do a thing for the dead—better that the funereal bread and meats be given to the poor.

The road to distinctively Christian death rites was paved by the establishment of special cemeteries for the special dead. Little attention had been given to the earthly remains of the average person. The martyred dead, though, deserved something better. Cemeteries for the sainted dead were established throughout Christian lands. Did this really matter? Yes, very much so. These holy sites are credited with stimulating an enhanced sense of community. The powerless and the poor, who were otherwise excluded from ritual care, could feel embraced by the loving strength of the sleeping martyrs.

The final Eucharist enabled the dying Christian to journey from this world to the next in a state of grace. It was, in effect, a second baptism. Ritual had welcomed the infant into the Christian community, and ritual would again confirm this membership at exit. This practice had been foreshadowed by the Greek practice of placing a coin in the mouth of the dead as payment to Charon, the ferryman on the River Styx. The dying Christian—or, sometimes, his corpse—would receive instead the body and blood of Christ. The Roman Christian *ordo defunctorum* encompassed rituals for both the dying person and the corpse. Here is what was done for the dying:

> As soon as they see him approaching dying he is to be given communion even if he has eaten that day, because the communion will be his defender and advocate at the resurrection of the just. It will resuscitate him. After the reception of communion the Gospel accounts of the passion of the Lord are to be read to the sick person by priests or deacons until his soul departs from his body.[23]

The good death, then, was one that passed through Christian ritual. A crucial facet of that ritual was the identification of the dying person with Jesus in the form of the Eucharist and the Gospel readings. One died with Christ.

In this ritual we see purification, blessing, and safe conduct from life

through death. Although there are parallels with other religious customs of the time, the passion of Jesus the Redeemer provided the dying Christian with a special state of grace.

One problem, though: precisely what happened after death? Salvation, of course, if all had gone well. But salvation *when?* Not just yet. Not until the end of time, when the graves yawn open and final judgment is meted. In the meantime, defunct Christians subsisted in the *refigerium interim,* cooling their heels while many another generation birthed, bred, and died. Dying and death were just not that simple. And another problem: as already noted, the blessings of deathbed communion were not equally accessible throughout the population during the early Christian years or thereafter. Diligent priests would attempt to comfort the most humble members of society and even to convert pagans to the true faith before the last breath. Nevertheless, it would be a continuing challenge for the Christian message of brotherhood to overcome entrenched prejudices based on social status, hierarchy, and discrimination against out-grouped peoples.

The foundational *ordo defunctorum* would lend itself to variations and refinements throughout the first millennium of the Christian era. Setting aside the differences, though, we can see that the human race had divided itself on the deathbed: there were those who died in Christian grace, swathed in reassuring ritual, and those who went to earth without the benefit of baptism into the truth faith.

What happened as we moved well into the second millennium?

ARS MORIENDI: THE ART OF DYING WELL

We may find it difficult today to imagine a time when death was the prevailing object of thought and emotion. But by the fifteenth century the religious establishment was relentlessly directing attention to the day of our demise. We wake but to sleep. We live but to die. And what is the bed but a grave? Money, power, fame, even mortal love are vanities. All will perish. Who embraces the hollow things and empty pleasures of earthly life also embraces damnation. Even children were taught to prepare themselves for death. We must live in keen anticipation of our death. The prize we can wrest from the snares and deceits of earthly life—and it is the only prize worth having—is to die well.

The deathbed is more than the last stop on the mortal journey: it is the beginning of either surpassing joy or agony everlasting. Death is with us every step of the way from the toddler to the striding knight, from the dignified cleric to the shuffling elder. Unlike early Christians buoyed by hope, the later Christians were expected to realize that they lived every moment in death.

This was the message of the *Ars moriendi* movement at its high tide. Images and representations of death were everywhere—in art, theater, song, dance, literature, and, perhaps most chillingly, in stone. Sculptures had taken to showing the illustrious dead suffering graphic postmortem decay. Somehow the joyful message of Christian triumph over death had taken a dark turn. Why? Recall the origins of Christianity. Jesus had lived, had died, had lived again. Big things were sure to happen right away. The Messiah would return. Sinners would be punished. The righteous would be rewarded. The dead would rise from their tombs and the valley of bones. What hope! What excitement!

Disappointment! Dismay! Doubt! The world continued much as it had been. The nascent theologians now had a lot of explaining to do. Many persevered in the belief that the big bang was still coming any time now and that we should continue to look for the signs and portents. Others held that the master plan was still unfolding. We had not understood perfectly. We must be patient. Still others proclaimed that we had been misled by the deceits and dissemblings of Satan, that we miserable sinners did not yet deserve the Messiah. Argumentation became more subtle, disputes more arcane.

The common people did not find solace in the ever-growing thicket of theological speculation and assertion. What they observed was that people kept dying and the dead stayed dead. Absent the foretold transformations, faith had to rely ever more on faith.

And so it continued year after year, century after century. Hope flickered, nursed along by exhortation and ritual and nourished by the occasional beatific vision. Miracles were eagerly seized upon as proof that the Lord had not forsaken them: the deal was still on. A thousand years and more had passed since Jesus had walked on this earth, and there was still unfulfilled yearning in Christian hearts.

The heritage did furnish striking images of the tormented death of Jesus and the newly invented peaceful Dormition of the Virgin. Perhaps if one could die in a state of grace? Perhaps if one could die as a true Christian even if one had lived as a sinner? Perhaps salvation depended on one's own state of soul at the last moment of life? Perhaps it was really up to each of us as individuals?

The game plan for a Christian life and death was changing. There would still be an end of days, a final reckoning for all. But now the fate of the individual had become more salient. *I* will be saved, or *I* will be damned. This exposure of the individual was in consequence of a long, slow wave of social and economic transformations. Most people still perceived themselves primarily as members of a kinship network and a small community. Individuality was starting to break loose from its moorings, however. History started to have more names and faces. People were going to more places and doing more new things. As lives became more conspicuously individual, so did deaths. And with the liberating winds of individualism came also the intensified anxieties of choice and personal responsibilities. *I* must learn how to live well, and *I* must learn how to die well.

Learning how to die was the essential goal of the *Ars moriendi* movement. Instructional tracts were created for this purpose and snatched up by those who could read. (Many tracts were flamboyantly illustrated for the benefit of the illiterate majority.) These books, in turn, were influenced by the popularity of mystery plays—theological dramas, not whodunits. Deathbed scenes were enacted in which the dying person was either raised to heaven or dumped into hell as angels and demons fought over the departing soul. We have already touched on the crowning literary achievement, Jeremy Taylor's *Rules and Exercises of Holy Dying*. Now we take an instructive sample from the first generation of tracts that appeared around the turn of the fifteenth century. These were brief books that much resembled one another in content and tone. The passages quoted here come from a rare-document collection edited by Frances M. M. Comper.

SAMPLE A

> As then the bodily death is the most fearful thing of all other things, so yet is the death of the soul as much more terrible and reproachable, as the soul is more precious and noble than the body.[24]

This is not good! Dualism was supposed to give us two lives; here it makes us vulnerable to two deaths. Furthermore, anxiety is heightened by passages such as this because we in the medieval period know plenty about the loss of the body, especially through memories of the recent Black Death. We are invited to become nervous wrecks, then, when informed that the death of the ever-elusive soul is even more catastrophic. And we can hardly miss the reminder that body and soul are somehow in competition with each other, and it is up to us to favor the latter over the former.

SAMPLE A, CONTINUED

> And the death of sinners is right cursed and evil; but the death of just and true people is precious before God for the dead men be well happy that die in our Lord.[25]

Just as body and soul are sharply divided, so are the ranks of sinners and the righteous. Dying is not just the natural end of life. The Old Testament expected people to come to terms with the withering away: "For all flesh is as grass" (Isaiah 40:6); "To all things there is a season" (Ecclesiastes 3:1). But now dying is presented as *judicial*—punishment for the guilty sinner. And as *paternal rejection*—kicked out of the house with Father's curses stinging like a swarm of hornets. Perhaps it is almost as much a strain to envision the radiant alternative. Men (and it's men, men, men; rarely if ever a mention of women in these tracts) should joyfully anticipate becoming dead men. Death is supposed to make men, well, happy. This is a mental strain because it is so difficult to associate the miseries of dying and the silence of death with great happiness. We may ardently wish to immerse ourselves in the vision of happy death, but it does rub against the grain of everyday experience.

So—what to do? This question is answered by passages such as the following.

SAMPLE B

> I purpose me to learn to die. And I hope by God's grace to amend my life . . . for I am made so sore afeared. Wherefore now do away for me the softness of bedding, and the preciosity of clothing, and the sloth of sleep, and all that letteth me from my Lord Jesu Christ.[26]

Good dying must be learned. The motivation here swings to the side of being "so sore afeared" rather than the spiritual ecstasy of salvation. There are occasional passages in which the joys of dying have the upper hand, but as the *Ars moriendi* gained its footing we more often encountered fear-driven impetus. We also see that the snug routines of life, all that comforts body and mind, must be cast aside. Interestingly, Heinrich Suso (quoted above by Comper), who wrote a very early tract in the fourteenth century, has chosen sleep as his main example. A person following this example to the letter would become sleep deprived and, eventually, mentally and emotionally unhinged. This would enhance a mind-set that tunes out everyday life. It is difficult to see how society could function if all or even most or many people deliberately deprived themselves of "the sloth of sleep" and withdrew from their tasks and obligations.

Must learning to die be reserved for the elite? Should everybody else toil in the fields and raise the children, only to die a miserably ignorant death while the spiritually elite prepare their souls for that auspicious moment?

The following sample, by a Richarde Hampole, has a statistically tinged cost-effectiveness message.

SAMPLE C

> [Consider] the measure of thy life here; that is so short that unnethes it is nought; for we live in a point—that is the least thing that may be—soothly our life is less than a point if we liken it to the life that lasteth forever.
>
> Another is the uncertainty of our ending; for we wit never when we shall die, nor how we shall die, nor wither we shall go when we be dead; and that *God will that it be uncertain to us, for He will that we always be ready to die.* [italics added][27]

Let's use our heads: why cherish this mere point in time that we call our earthly lives when all of eternity balances on our righteousness? And why delude ourselves into thinking that death will come in some distant time and circumstance when the next moment could be our last? We must always be on the ready to trade this life for the next. How foolish it would be to imagine that we can predict, let alone control, the future. It's God's game, and he holds all the cards.

Now—to the deathbed scene itself.

SAMPLE D:
THE COMPLAINT OF THE DYING CREATURE TO THE GOOD ANGEL

> O my Good Angel, to whom our Lord took me to keep, where be thee now? Me thinketh ye should be here, and answer for me; for the dread of

> death distroubleth me, so that I cannot answer for myself. Here is my bad angel ready, and is one of my chief accusers, with legions of fiends with him. I have no creature to answer for me. Alas it is an heavy case![28]

Perhaps the most vivid expression of the *Ars moriendi* centered on the cosmic struggle around the deathbed. Bad angels (Satan, his demons, imps, and familiars) contested with angels for the dying Christian's soul. How many people of the time believed this to be a literal and how many a symbolic or allegorical conflict? This we do not know. But we do know that theology was transformed into high drama (which did not exclude low comedy) with the soul of the Dying Creature at stake.

The bad angels or demons usually represent temptations. The good angels represent inspirations that strengthen us against yielding to temptation. Although wicked to the core, the temptations present themselves in an orderly manner. First, the Evil One attempts to lure the dying Christian into doubt and heresy. The resolute Christian will recite or listen to Scripture in order to affirm faith. Next comes one of Satan's most powerful temptations—despair. The dying person has been such a sinner that there can be no last-minute rescue. The Evil One presents a list of the dying person's sins so there can be no doubt about them. "You did fornicate with that woman!" accuses the devil, having at that moment produced that woman at the head of the bed. "You did stab that man!" he continues (a splash of red blood might be added to the pages of the tract at that point). Even more tellingly, "You ignored those in need. Because you gave no mercy, you will receive no mercy!" If the devil has his way, the dying person will collapse in despair, having lost faith and confidence in God.

But—inspiration to the rescue! Recite or listen to a penitential psalm: for example, "O Lord, deliver my soul: oh save me for thy mercies' sake. For in death there is no remembrance of thee: in the grave who shall give thee thanks?" (Psalm 6:4–5).

The Seven Deadly Sins were whipped into an official list in the sixth century. Pride, Envy, Avarice, Wrath, Lust, Gluttony, and Sloth would trigger the finger of divinity to strike the eject button and hurl the miscreant into the bottomless pit of despair (later, purgatory became an option). Furthermore, each sin carried its specific torment. Pride, the root of all other sins, was punished by the sinner's being broken on the wheel. Envy? Encased in freezing water. Avarice? Boiled in oil. Wrath? Torn

Figure 6 The triumph of the virtuous Christian over temptation was a dominant theme, as depicted in this image from a German edition of the *Ars moriendi* (Augsburg: 1471).

Figure 7 The angry are dismembered in this scene of infernal punishment for the Seven Deadly Sins. Woodblock print from *Le grant kalendrier et compost des Bergiers* (Troyes: printed by Nicolas Le Rouge, 1496).

apart, limb from bloody limb. Lust? Roasted by fire and brimstone. Gluttony? Forced to eat live rats, snakes, spiders, and toads. Sloth? Into the snake pits! These sins were deadly not because they might be responsible for termination of earthly life, but because they endanger the soul after death.[29]

And so the battle rages. The bad angel tries to provoke the dying per-

Figure 8 The lustful are smothered in fire and brimstone in another scene of punishment for a deadly sin. Woodblock print from *Le grant kalendrier et compost des Bergiers* (Troyes: printed by Nicolas Le Rouge, 1496).

son into impatience, pride, and avarice. Prayer and ritual are available to overcome each of these temptations. If all goes well, the Dying Creature passes this final test and confirms trust in "none other thing [than] His passion and in His death wrap all myself fully."[30] Meanwhile there should be abundant witnesses to the scene, pulling as hard as they can for the imperiled soul. The deathbed scene is not a passive tableau: everybody has work to do. Furthermore, this cosmic drama is public. Every person's death concerns everybody else, as John Donne would later say more elegantly in one of his devotions.[31] In one popular illustrated *Ars moriendi* instruction, ten prayers are sent to heaven by the witnesses. This sequence is crowned by an image of the good death itself. A priest offers the dying man a candle, and an angel receives his soul in the form of a child. Off to the side is a Crucifixion scene featuring Mary and a selection of notable saints. Bad losers that they are, demons at the foot of the bed fuss and fume.

Aries makes a telling point about this new intensified way of conceiving the deathbed scene:

> All that used to take place at the end of time now happens at the hour of death, in conjunction with the traditional rites—no longer in the explosive world of the Apocalypse, but instead . . . in the bedchamber, at the bedside.[32]

The death of the individual and the ultimate day of judgment for humankind become merged at the final moment.

Another significant observation is offered by Paul Binski.[33] He reminds us that the dead body was an object of dread for most people in the Holy Land prior to Christianity. (This fear was also shared by many other societies throughout the world. Into modern times anthropologists have found many examples of the fear of contamination by contact with the dead.) Christian belief went counter to these deeply entrenched beliefs. The last rites, then, have a function that has sometimes escaped notice: purifying the corpse, making it not only safe but sacred. Those busy little demons hopping around the deathbed scene might be regarded as the evil spirits of folk cultures who have been deprived of their prize by the more powerful force of Christian piety.

Binski also notes that the good death has a significant structural value for society. The Dying Creature is at the center of things in this drama, but the survivors benefit greatly, too. Discontinuity and disorder threaten society when a full-fledged member of the community dies. We have already seen this problem and how it is addressed among the Kaliai of Papua New Guinea. It is, in fact, a common source of concern practically everywhere. The good death does a lot to keep the game going, to lessen conflict and dysfunction at the loss of an important person. Re-

lieved that this person has died in spiritual grace and that they have all done their part, the survivors can start the process of grief recovery and restored function with a clear conscience. There can be little doubt that how we die (or how we are *perceived* to have died) has significant implications for the living.

Nevertheless, some people had still another temptation to deal with—to play the deathbed scene for even more than what it was worth. Bernardino of Siena (1380–1444) caught them at it. Bernardino was a celebrated Franciscan priest who attracted many disciples and left enough of his own words to fill nearly twenty volumes of sermons. Franco Mormando distilled and commented on Bernardino's message. Most relevant here was Bernardino's critique of slothful and wobbling Christians who believed that all would be forgiven and the gates of heaven open to them if they pulled off a convincing deathbed scene.[34]

Don't count on it! First, there is the practical matter of being sufficiently in possession of one's physical and mental faculties as the fatal moment nears. Racked with pain and anxiety, the sinner may be in no condition to repent. Second, fear is not enough to win salvation. Of course, one might become sincerely afraid as the Infernal Pit yawns open for an eternity of torment. At this moment the wayward Christian finally gets the message—but it's too late. A charitable word or gesture is also insufficient. Heaven doesn't come that cheap. Bernardino takes the trouble to specifically undermine an ace-up-the-sleeve that many people of his time assumed they could bring to the deathbed scene. Yes, the "Good Thief" crucified next to Jesus did win his way to heaven because he spoke a word of compassion to his companion in suffering. But, no, such an easy redemption is not in the cards for the everyday sinner. In fact, the Good Thief is the only fellow who got away with it.

We must bring a credible track record to the deathbed scene. Prayer, ritual, and the mercy of Mary and Jesus can pull through the truly repentant Christian who has made a few errors along the way. But a desperate deathbed conversion may not cancel out a life etched in sloth and sin. Live the good life and we have a fighting chance for a good death, even though we have stumbled now and then.

We cannot close even this brief book on the *Ars moriendi* without acknowledging a sisterhood whose humane ministrations to the dying not only provided comfort in their own time but also set an example for palliative care today. The Beguines first appeared more than half a century before the Black Death. There was already more than enough dying and death and not nearly enough hands to offer personal services. Christine Guidera tells us that the Beguines came forth from France, Germany, and the Low Countries.[35] They were pious women who had no official status in the church hierarchy. Their good works reached into many spheres of life but were perhaps most distinctive and welcome in care of the ill, the dying, and the dead. Unfortunately, little is known about the specifics of their practice with the dying. It is reported, though, that the Beguines incurred suspicion and hostility from some quarters because they provided intimate care to the dying. Were they seducers? Sorcerers? In all probability the Beguines were just what they seemed to be: compassionate women who ventured across the threshold to provide care for the dying that others were unable or unwilling to provide.

DEATHBED SCENES AFTER THE DEPARTURE OF ANGELS AND DEMONS

Angels and demons left the deathbed scene only with considerable reluctance and have returned for numerous encore appearances since the heyday of the *Ars moriendi*. But, just as people in the late medieval period reconstructed the mysteries of dying to accord with their changed circumstances, so subsequent generations have experienced deaths as influenced by their own altered circumstances. History in general has unearthed more information (and misinformation) about the lives of movers and shakers than the lives of other individuals. This bias holds true with their deaths as well. We will join this parade by reviewing the fairly well-reported exits of several eminent people that bear on our exploration of good and bad deaths. The royal deaths we visit here have been collected by historian Olivia Bland.[36]

Queen Elizabeth I had been in robust health most of her seventy years. What proved to be her fatal illness, in 1603, was preceded by two and possibly three stressful events. Upon her inauguration forty-five years earlier, the queen had announced that her marriage would be to the kingdom. As a token of this union, she had placed her coronation ring on her finger in lieu of a wedding band and had never removed it. But now it had grown painfully into the flesh, and she had to have it filed off. Af-

terward the queen brooded—did this presage her complete severance from the mystical union with her kingdom? Two months later her closest friend, Lady Nottingham, died. The queen responded with despair. Her legendary energies had evaporated. Only Elizabeth's habit of resolve kept her going at all. Later a story circulated that has never been either confirmed or dismissed conclusively. Supposedly, Lady Nottingham made a deathbed confession that devastated Elizabeth: Elizabeth had given her true love, Essex, a ring in their younger days, and he had later given it to Lady Nottingham with an urgent request to rescue him from the Tower of London and his imminent execution. Instead, Lady Nottingham had hidden the ring, and Elizabeth—after self-tormenting hesitations—had signed the execution order. (The lovers' ring sent by Essex should not be confused with the coronation ring that had burrowed itself into the queen's finger.) Favoring the authenticity of this dramatic episode was the intensity of the queen's despair during the interim between robust health and terminal illness. If the story was true, Lady Nottingham could not die in grace with the weight of that terrible betrayal of her friend Elizabeth. To spare herself a disgraceful death, she had to confess—but this, in effect, passed the trauma on to the queen.

Reports agree that Elizabeth was in low spirits before showing signs of physical illness. As her health failed she complained mostly of her sad and heavy heart. She refused nourishment and medicine. Only the closest and most persuasive people in the royal circle could persuade her to take a few sips of broth. Those who assured her she would live many more years were waved off; more of this life was not appealing. Respiratory infection and pneumonia were bringing her down.

When the aged archbishop and his retinue attended her for the last time, the queen answered all his ritualistic questions promptly and firmly. She was in the faith, had always been in the faith.

> After he had continued long in prayer, 'till the old man's knees were weary, hee blessed her, and meant to rise and leave her. The Queene made a sign with her hand [desiring] he would pray still. He did so for a long halfe houre after, and then thought to leave her. The second time she made signes to have him continue in prayer. He did so for halfe an houre more, with earnest cries to God for her soul's health, which he uttered with that fervency of sprit, as the Queene to all her sight much rejoiced therat, and gave testimony to us all of her christian and comfortable end.[37]

The queen fell asleep. A few hours later she was dead.

Was this a stereotypical good death? Not quite. Actually, not close. The central element was there: passing in a state of grace embroidered by extended prayers from the archbishop himself. She had also carried out her final obligation, signifying that the crown should be given to King James VI of Scotland. There was something missing, though: the resistance, the fear. It was almost a conspiracy, as though Elizabeth had opened the door a bit so Death, like a secret lover, could slip in. A state of depression robs this world of its joys. It could hardly be a good death, pure and simple, if one were sad and heavy of heart, no longer desirous of life. Earthly temptations to overcome, there were none. Faith was supposed to overcome fear. But should one actually invite death?

This question became salient when, as we recall, some early Christians rushed to martyrdom. The church came down on both sides of the issue. On the one hand, suicide was a grave sin: the dead sinner could not then repent of any sins and thereby earn salvation. On the other hand, martyrs often became revered saints. Circumstances are often more subtle and ambiguous than this, however. Elizabeth did not arrange for her own execution, nor did she lift a hand against herself. At that point in her long and eventful life, though, she seemed ready enough for death that she yielded almost gratefully when the opportunity presented itself. In general, deathbed scenes after the *Ars moriendi* seemed to become less formulaic and more tinged with ambiguities and conflicts. The goodness of a death became more relative to circumstances.

Consider, for example, the Stuart monarch Charles II. It is the evening of February 1, 1685. Here is an abridged version of Bland's account:

> The King had dined heartily that night, but unusually included two goose eggs in his menu which may have accounted for the restless night he passed. . . . the King, who always slept like the dead, tossed and muttered all night. . . . When the King woke . . . he felt very ill. . . . His countenance was pale as ashes. [His doctors] persuaded the king back to his bedchamber where it became apparent his speech was affected. Then . . . he was seized with a violent convulsion and fell back with a terrible cry into the arms of Bruce.[38]

Charles II recovered! A robust man, he seemed on the road to full recovery, but the doctors insisted on doing their bit. He was pierced with lancets, the better to bleed. "Physicks" purged his bowels repeatedly. Additionally he was administered tinctures of white vitriol in peony water, juleps of prepared pearls, sneezing powders of white hellebore root, emetics of orange, infusions of metals in white wine, blistering agents, and spirits of sal ammoniac in antidotal milk water. But the doctors, in their onslaught of remedies, had by no means exhausted their bag of tricks. Now it was time for the more exotic: Peruvian bark, and Oriental bezoar stone from the stomach of an eastern goat, augmented by spirits of human skull, and more herbs and spices than anyone was able to catalog. Nobody could accuse the royal physicians of standing by and doing nothing—even though doing nothing might have been a much better plan, leaving recovery to nature and the king's hearty constitution.

The more odious or painful the procedure, the more it was deemed likely to work a cure. A dose of catharides, a pseudoaphrodisiac irritant, made his urine scalding hot. Speaking of heat, the king's head was shaved and red-hot irons and plasters applied to his scalp and to the soles of his feet. The king endured these medical assaults with remarkable patience. When, despite everything, Charles II again showed signs of recovery, the physicians renewed their attacks on the royal personage with purges, enemas, emetics, cuppings, and bleedings. Even a strong man with an ardent will to live could not long withstand so much medical assistance.

Now occurs not only the drama of a king's death but a bizarre sideshow as well. His passing would reflect the crises of the times, particularly the sharp division of faith between Catholic and Protestant claims on the immortal soul. Prayers for the sick were offered in both chapels day and night, followed by the bedside services for the dying. This was just as it should be in the Protestant kingdom ruled by Charles II. The king did not follow the approved script, however. He was not comforted by prayer and, worse, refused to take the Sacrament. At this point, then, both the soul of the sovereign and the safety of his realm were compromised by the prospect of a bad death. If the king should die unrepentant (not that he had been a wicked fellow), this could only make the kingdom increasingly vulnerable to the forces of disorder. What to do?

Imagine this sequence, if you will. First we have the duchess of Portsmouth whispering in the ear of the French ambassador. In turn he quietly seeks audience with the duke of York and whispers in the ducal ear. York now betakes himself to the king's bedside, and a whispered message is again imparted. The plot is now on the kettle. A Catholic priest is smuggled into the palace (a risky covert operation for all concerned). The disguised priest enters through a secret door. He performs the *ordo defunctorum* for the grateful king, who declares his sins and tries to rise in order to receive the Holy Communion. The dying monarch is much relieved when the priest assures him that Almighty God will accept his good intentions. Now the priest slips away through the secret passage. The king? He has become calm and serene. When he lasts through the night, he apologizes to his attendants for having imposed on them by "so long a-dying." Assured of forgiveness and salvation, he is ready for death.

The story should end here. But both bishops and doctors keep after him. He is repeatedly besieged by clergy to receive the Protestant version of the Sacrament (they don't know about the priest). The physicians—by now numbering fourteen!—are still concocting treatments. Despite all these impositions, Charles II remains tranquil and focused. He bids a tender farewell to Catherine; they had been a rare example of a truly loving regal couple. He then embraces all his legitimate children and sees to their continued education and well-being. Later he asks for the curtains to be opened so he may once more see the day—and reminds his attendants that the eight-day clock needs to be rewound. About an hour later he experiences difficulties in breathing and struggles unsuccessfully to arise. This gives his crowd of physicians another opportunity to bleed the king and force stimulants into his mouth. This time the king foils them. He dies. Unable to try any further remedies on the royal personage, the physicians return to their lengthy and learned discussions: "You should have given the Whatchamacallit before the Whoknowswhat!" "You failed to diagnosis the Blippitybop properly!" "You should have allowed me to use more hot plasters!" and so on.

This eventful, moving, and flawed deathbed sequence tells us much about the conditions of life in late-seventeenth-century England and, to some extent, elsewhere in Europe as well. The good death envisioned in the past had emerged within a monolithic religious structure. For most Christians, there had been only one church and one set of doctrines and rituals (heretics were inviting violent death). The black comedy of disguised priest and secret passage was a product of the schism within Christianity and, at that time, one fraught with peril for those who were perceived as being on the wrong side. Charles II could not

accept the wrong good death, but there would be hellacious consequences for the regime and his family if his Catholic allegiance were to become known.

Another source of stress had also become increasingly pernicious. Physicians were less humble, though not spectacularly more effective, than their medieval predecessors. Physicians were advancing their own claims for power and prestige. Many brought ignorance, arrogance, and rivalry to the deathbed scene, more often adding to the torment than working a cure. It was Charles II's misfortune to suffer from three demonstrations of medical ineptitude. First, excessive, unnecessary, and wrong-headed interventions deprived the king of his best opportunity to recover naturally from his illness. Second, the royal physician refused to acknowledge later that the king was on the brink of death, resulting in additional exhausting and painful measures. *He,* reassured by ritual and aware of his condition, could accept death. *They* could not or would not. There had always been circumstances in which the impulse to rescue a person from death had conflicted with the impulse to provide comfort in the last hours. Now, however, physicians were feeling sufficiently empowered to fight the battle to the very last breath, if not beyond. Ritual and comfort for the dying—or a full-court press to restore life? The deathbed scene was becoming more complicated. And third, only the wealthy few were so tormented. The numerous and anonymous poor died too soon after too deprived and stressful a life, but at least their demises were not aggravated by the painful and useless interventions of a swarm of physicians. Overall, there were advantages to medical care, which is one of the reasons the wealthy enjoyed a significant edge in life expectancy. But, then as now, many physicians hated to say die.

The deathbed was becoming a contested zone between the claims of the church and those of the physician, while political considerations (such as succession to the Crown) also were influential for "important" people. But what about deaths without beds? We will take just one example here. Back we go some years to 1649 and another British monarch, Charles I. He had been convicted of high treason and murder and denied the opportunity to address the court after his death sentence had been passed. When the time came, the king said his farewells and gave various personal objects to his children and faithful attendants. The drums rolled. The crowds gathered for the execution. He marched faster than the drumbeat in the procession to the palace and then, after an interval, to the scaffold. According to reports, he conversed cheerfully with the bishop and guard by his side.

At this point, can we speak of his impending death as good or bad? Today we might think of a death as bad—or, at least, unfortunate—if it comes while the person would still have had many years ahead. This, however, was not the decisive consideration in the time of Charles I. A lot of people died young; this had come to be expected. Furthermore, in some quarters the death of the very young did not count for much from a societal standpoint: infants and children consumed resources and contributed little. The king, however, was a mature adult; he had had a life. Next, we recall that tribal peoples have emphasized the importance of being well prepared for death. The person who dies by sudden violence becomes a risk to the community as a disconsolate spirit. Readiness for death was a core element in the *Ars moriendi* and, indeed, in the sacraments for the sick and the dying. Purification from sin should precede death.

In this regard Charles I was well served. He accepted Holy Communion from the bishop and announced that he was relieved of sin and prepared for all that he would have to undergo. Charles I knew that his head would be severed from his body within about an hour. To this fate he was philosophically resigned and at peace with himself and his God. Perhaps this was a good death emerging from difficult circumstances. The victim was prepared, and the nation had decided upon regicide after what it considered to be due process in court, so the death itself should affirm rather than weaken the spirit of the land. "We chopped off the bloody head of the bloody king, but we did it the right way!"

Nevertheless, the scene would not play out quite as devised. The king, the executioner, and the mob had to wait hour after hour. The stroke of the ax could not be delivered until the stroke of the pen on the death warrant, and the commissioners were dillydallying. It was one thing to grandly condemn a king to death in the name of the people; it was something else actually to sign one's name to the document just before the blood began to flow. The impending death no longer seemed so justified, so desirable to those who had condemned the king. Finally, the administrative deed was done.

We come to the final scene. The king is quite in command of himself and cooperative with the proceedings. A cloak accidentally flaps against the blade of the ax. Cautions Charles I: "Hurt not the ax that may hurt me." He has a few words to say to his people:

> Sirs, it was for the liberties of the people that I am come here. If I would have assented to an arbitrary sway, to have all things changed according to the power of the sword, I needed not to have come hither; and therefore I tell you (and I pray God it be not laid to your charge) that I am the martyr of the people. I die a Christian according to the profession of the Church of England, as I found it left me by my father.[39]

Charles I removes his coat and presents it to an attendant, saying, "Remember." He adds, "I go from a corruptible to an incorruptible crown, where no disturbance can take place." Still in command, the king instructs the executioner: "I shall say a short prayer, and when I hold out my hands thus—strike." The hooded ax man replies: "I shall wait for it, sir, with the good pleasure of Your Majesty!" He intends no irony.

The ax is raised. A thud is heard. The severed head, held aloft by the regal hair, is shown to the crowd.

At this moment the crowd is given its opportunity to judge. It was something amazing—to see a king get his head lopped off. Every grudge against the Crown could now be given voice in a thunder of vengeful roar and mockery. That response would have stamped the decapitation of Charles I as a good death for the people, if not for the victim. Instead: a rumble, a groan, a cry of grief from the crowd. No, this was a wrongful death. During the last moments they had seen in their monarch a brave and reasonable man who was perhaps the best Christian of all. They surged forward to dip their handkerchiefs in his precious blood but were driven back by mounted troops.

Many an ax had fallen on many a neck in not-entirely-merry Olde England. These had been entertaining spectacles as well as warnings to other potential miscreants. The crowds had jeered, not wept. This was different. This was a death that hit home to them, a death that made them feel more than a little guilty themselves.

The Puritan Struggle

Charles I had a good death *if*—if being prepared is good, if receiving safe passage through ritual is good, if continuing to act as a responsible member of the community until the last breath is good, and if touching the hearts of others is good. And he also had a good death in a more distinctive way. Unlike many others, the king had the opportunity to speak his mind to attentive listeners, his last words being duly recorded for posterity. The drama was further intensified because these words were uttered against the stark stage set of a scaffold with a small crowd of guards, dignitaries, and, of course, that hooded fellow with the ax. Somehow he had managed to make this death his own. Three centuries later there would arise a movement in England that was quickly taken up in North America, and later throughout the world. This movement was predicated on the value that the good death should be one's own, not the standardized demise doled out by the establishment. We will consider "the appropriate death" and the hospice/palliative care movement in the next chapter. For now we allow ourselves one more memory image of Charles I as he bows his head for the blow. He is still a king, still a Christian, and still very much himself. In fullness of life he is ready for death.

We cross the Atlantic now, taking the seventeenth century with us. Here, *too*, salvation was an urgent issue. The Puritans, struggling to survive in a literal wilderness, also faced a wilderness within, a tangle of fears, desires, and imperatives. One must live the good life. This must be accomplished over and again each day, fighting off temptation, pride, and sloth. Even so, the good life does not necessarily beget the good death. In other words, the Puritans were imbued with the Calvinistic philosophy of predetermination. God has already selected the Select. But who has been chosen, who rejected? Only God knows. All we can know is that doubt is necessary. Why? Because we should live in faith, not require proof, not demand guarantee. Eschew false hope and test thyself severely lest thee discover the hypocrite beneath thy respectable visage. Puritans therefore became their own inquisitors. Daily the diligent Puritans examined themselves for evidence of impurity while lamenting the inherent depravity of the entire deplorable human race.

Historian David E. Stannard tells us that people could and did crack under this pressure. For example, the notable John Winthrop spoke of a Boston woman who was so desperate about her spiritual estate that

> one day she took her little infant and threw it into a well, and then came into the house and said, now she was sure she would be damned, for she had drowned her child.[40]

Doing good did not necessarily win heaven, but doing evil assured hell: the certainty of a dismal fate might be preferred over prolonged uncertainty.

To the deathbed now. The fleeting pilgrimage through the imperfections of earthly life would now be transformed into a beautiful flight to heaven. All one had to do was die. A passage from 2 Corinthians (5:6–8) was frequently cited:

> Being therefore always of good courage, and knowing that, whilst we are at home in the body, we are absent from the Lord (for we walk by faith, not by sight); we are of good courage, I say, and we are willing rather to be absent from the body, and to be at home with the Lord.

Life without or death with the Lord? The true believing Puritan would not hesitate. And yet—dying was an ordeal, a severe test for body and soul. Furthermore, death was punishment because it had entered into the world by sin. Talk about ambivalence! Death was agony and punishment but also the gateway to redemption and heaven. Furthermore, unlike Elizabeth and the two Charleses, the Puritan could not be assured of salvation by ritual and prayer. Absolute faith was demanded, but doubt ever gnawed at even the most stalwart.

Consider, for example, two of the most devout of the devout Puritans. Increase Mather and his son Cotton have remained durable exemplars of the creed. The long tide of the *Ars moriendi* had very nearly subsided, but the Mathers told all who would listen that we should die daily and always have foremost in our minds that each strike of the clock brings us an hour closer to our blessed release. Cotton even wrote several books on the subject, including *Death Made Easie & Happy.* Increase declared, "How glad should I be, if I might dye before I stir out of this pulpit!"[41]

In practice, though, it was the doubt, the dread, and the horror that had a death grip on the Puritan soul. Stannard concludes:

> The Puritans were gripped individually and collectively by an intense and unremitting fear of death, while *simultaneously* clinging to the traditional Christian rhetoric of viewing death as a release and relief for the earth-bound soul.[42]

When the desired and dreaded moment came, Increase was wracked by doubt. Cotton, at his bedside, heard his father speak about the Dark

Vapors that assaulted him, the Great Wrath that might be unleashed at the Last Judgment. Perhaps despite everything, despite his severe self-criticisms, despite his relentless effort to live the saintly life, the dying man had been deceiving himself all along, a gullible fool misled by the Serpent. The phrase "fear and trembling" occurs repeatedly in Cotton's report of his father's death. A devout life could still end in a state of doubt and anxiety.

CONCLUDING THOUGHTS

What precisely is the connection between how we live, how we die, and how we fare after death? Can we get away with a dissolute life if we manage a deathbed conversion? Does even the most devout life end in anguish and uncertainty on the deathbed? Are prayer and ritual enough to see us through, or can other circumstances alter the outcome? Does the deathbed scene belong to God (perhaps in competition with the demons) or to the physician fascinated by an "interesting" case? These are among the questions that remain ponderable after two millennia of Christianized death.

What *can* be said with confidence? We can say this: the passage from life to death became central to the Christian experience by the end of the first millennium. The good death required dying in a state of grace, and this in turn required preparation, ritual, and, when possible, community participation. We can also say that the good death was a powerful tool for arousing the complacent: "This is how it should be done. Can you do the same?"

The bad death was experienced by those who departed unprepared. This included unrepentant sinners and heretics and also those who had procrastinated. It was the responsibility of every devout person, then, to remind others of their mortality, to guide them along the path of redemption before it was too late. Nevertheless, many people perished without either pastoral or medical care. These were mostly the anonymous, the poor, the marginal. John McManners speaks, for example, of the gap between theory and practice in eighteenth-century France.[43] Here there was an unusually strong emphasis on paying last respects to dying people and their families: this was a demonstration of piety and charity. It was good to be seen at a deathbed as a sympathetic and consoling citizen. Even here, though, people died alone, untended, unconfessed, and unsanctified. Devout and socially responsible citizens suffered from their inability to prepare every Christian soul for the passage.

The *ordo defunctorum,* with all its ancient associations and resonances, would find itself in a strange new context as industrialism took hold in the nineteenth century. There were increasing signs that both the dying and the dead were losing their special status, perhaps even within the church. Slowly but steadily arising was the image of the aged and dying person as a failed machine. What, then, of the soul? Christianity responded, but with various voices. The Marists formed themselves and, as noted in chapter 2, renewed the gravity and intensity of the deathbed scene. For those touched by the Marist endeavor, the dying person was once again engaged in a cosmic struggle. The inspirational death had returned—but this time it was available to peasants as well as to the high and mighty.

Others, though, practiced a degraded form of deathbed ministry. Elsewhere I have offered a sample of the spiritual comfort meted out by a nineteenth-century English doctor of divinity. The Reverend Dr. Warton specialized in hectoring and humiliating dying people and their families, all supposedly in the service of redeeming their immortal souls.[44] It is clear, though, that he thoroughly enjoyed the opportunity to bully the lower class at their most vulnerable moments and to score points through his clever rhetoric. The deathbed scene attracted both the most ardent and the most self-serving ministers as Christianity rallied against the machine and the pitiless cities.

A formidable new challenge would appear a generation later: Darwin, with his specimen and his theory. Science now threatened to demote mankind to the animal kingdom. The special arrangement with God was called into doubt. And, perhaps worst of all, humans seemed consigned to die like other creatures rather than rejoice in salvation. As the century lengthened, the prime battleground shifted from the deathbed scene per se to the defense of immortality. Ghosts, phantasms, and other spirit visitors were frequently called upon to testify. Rituals for safe passage of the dying became less salient than the emerging shadow rituals for contacting the dead through seances and other mysterious procedures.

Meanwhile, in Uganda, Papua New Guinea, and very many other places, the traditional beliefs were proving resilient. Even as missionaries accomplished their work, the native peoples for the most part continued to think of life and death as part of a flow rather than as the radical dichotomy that had become installed in Western thought. Some were learning—with difficulty—to think of death as punishment for original sin. It was even more difficult to think of the dying person and especially the corpse as sacred: everybody knew how dangerous the dead could be!

A general pattern can be discerned through the many variations: the passage from life was deeply embedded in beliefs and practices regarding how one should live and what occurs after death.

So—how about us? What is the good death for us today, and how does this accord with our media-massaged lifestyles and our expectations for what happens after the doctor signs our death certificate? Next chapter, please.

CHAPTER 4

Living with the Dead, Exiting Gracefully

Death is greeted with an outlay of ritual that far exceeds that of birth. More time, money, and resources are spent on funerals than on birth rites. Whereas few cultures have explicit birth ceremonies, many have elaborate death rites. Globally considered, having negligible or sparse death rites is exceptional. Even in urbanized North American countries where funerary sparseness is the reigning ideology, the decorum of death is sufficiently strong to command a temporary suspension of ordinary behavior. Whereas most of us have not experienced a birth rite, everyone knows what a funeral is. Funerals of important people are sometimes televised; births never are. Even if we in the technologically preoccupied West avoid talking about death, it is obligatory to respect the necessity of funerals. Failure to provide a decent funeral for a parent or mate is a ritual insult.

A few people such as the Mbuti of Zaire, the Hadza of Tanzania, the Baka of Cameroon, and the !Kung of Botswana and Namibia display little ritual activity at death. Christians in the Appalachian Mountains occasionally forego funerals, or they "funeralize," that is, put a dead body in the ground with no ceremony, waiting several months to have one when a preacher arrives.[216] The Navajos of the American Southwest expend few of their extraordinarily rich ritual resources on conducting death rites; strictures against touching or even speaking about the dead are exceptionally strong. Ritually resourceful in the face of illness, Navajos are nevertheless happy to turn deaths over to others, even white people.

Funerary sparsity in Europe and North America is often associated with memorial societies, most of which are consumer organizations. The Funeral and Memorial Society of America is a federation of nonprofit societies.[217] The aim of memorial, or funeral, societies is to facilitate funerals that are affordable, meaningful, and dignified. They provide scanty resources on ritual but rich lodes of consumer information and practical advice.

Not only do death rites have a higher profile than birth rites, they

also have left a more obvious historical residue than either birth or marriage. No other rite of passage inscribes such extensive markings on the landscape. Births, weddings, and initiations do not ordinarily leave enduring archaeological monuments. The Egyptian pyramids and the tomb of Chi'in Shih-huang-ti, China's first emperor, are visually impressive and rich sources of information about past practices, but birth, marriage, or coming-of-age rites leave few such remains.

I am often asked, "What sorts of things do people do around death, and why do they do them?" It is a simple, important, and difficult question to answer. There is infinite variation in the world's mortuary customs, but the motives for engaging in them are limited. As a result, the funerary gestures of others are largely recognizable to us, even though a few of them may seem bizarre if we do not grasp their meanings. Listed below are some of the most obvious motives for engaging in death rites, followed by examples of actions used to accomplish those aims. I refer to these actions as gestures rather than rites, because, even though they are stylized and convey meaning, some would not be considered formal rites.

anticipating death: listening to stories or sermons about death; contemplating or imagining one's death; learning to glorify, fear, or rationalize death; promulgating death wishes

segregating, observing taboos: wearing special clothing, for example, black "widows weeds"; using symbolic colors—black or white, for instance; not saying bad things about the deceased; refraining from public activities

mourning: weeping; wailing aloud; looking sad; avoiding laughter; walking slowly in processions; refusing to eat

marking an end to mourning: holding an end-of-mourning ceremony after a specified lapse of time; disinterring, cleaning, and redepositing bones; wearing regular clothes; remarrying

protecting survivors from the dead: verbally dismissing the soul; sending the spirit on its way; closing doors and windows; uttering protective spells to keep away ghosts; confining the dead to a specific, closed space

publicizing or announcing a death: publishing death notices; calling friends and kin; announcing a death; setting special times for observances

congregating, comforting: visiting or contacting the bereaved; coming together to enact a death rite; partying or orgiastic behavior; appealing to tradition, for example, by reading sacred texts or using religious leaders

showing gratitude, respect, or sympathy: attending a funeral; paying functionaries with gifts or money; sending messages of sympathy and condolence; offering to help; giving food; delivering or listening to a eulogy

demonstrating kinship or status, ensuring succession: being properly notified of a death; not remarrying too soon or at all; playing the role of widow or widower; writing wills; designating heirs; assuming roles—for instance, that of chief mourner, therefore, primary heir; being seen, being on display

dramatizing death's finality: making good-bye gestures such as touching or kissing the dead; putting the corpse on display; allowing signs of decay to be witnessed

maintaining and reconstructing social order after a death: placing limits on the expression of grief; displaying normalcy; demonstrating that "life goes on"; placing bereaved children in the care of relatives or guardians

denying death's finality: embalming; disguising the smell of putrefaction with perfume or incense; dressing up the corpse; using circumlocutions, for instance, "at rest" rather than "dead," the "deceased" rather than the "dead person"; believing in life after death; providing the dead with food, equipment, and clothing for their journey

releasing, integrating, embracing death's finality: laying a person on the earth to die; carrying ashes or bones to a final resting place; exposing a corpse so birds of prey may have their fill; pouring out water; breaking something, for instance, a pot or the skull of the dead person; burning, burying, exposing, or immersing the corpse; destroying clothing or possessions of the deceased; hugging or touching the bereaved; giving away possessions; speaking to the dead; saying good-bye

commemorating: making donations in the name of the deceased; conferring the name of a dead relative on a newborn child; retaining keepsakes—for example, locks of hair and photographs; erecting monuments, installing tablets, and setting up gravestones; lighting candles for the dead; honoring or praying to ancestors; visiting cemeteries; attending annual commemoration rites

In North America we place little emphasis on anticipating our own deaths. In fact, we avoid doing so with notable consistency. We observe few formal taboos at death and look askance at protracted mourning; therefore, it seldom occurs to us that we should formally mark its cessation. Since our public worldview does not include disgruntled ghosts,

mainstream funeral rites assume little need to protect the bereaved from the recently deceased. When a death occurs, we announce it in newspapers, expect people to pay their respects, and congregate to garner comfort. At the funeral, the closest of kin receive special treatment, but there are no pronounced demonstrations of kinship status except perhaps at the reading of wills, an action normally separated from the funeral and burial. We have mixed feelings about the finality of death. On the one hand, we believe in its finality and urge each other to "get on with life"; on the other, we deny its finality by concentrating time, money, and energy on embalming, a way of denying death's finality. We believe in the private release of grief but not in the public or metaphysical release of souls. Even though funeral oratory often refers to "the other life," funeral rites de-emphasize gestures for sending souls elsewhere. On occasion we commemorate the dead, but we seldom regard them as ancestors whose advice and presence should be actively courted.

However many facts science has accumulated concerning death as a biological event, we in the West avoid occasions that would force us to contemplate death. We do not keep close company with the Grim Reaper. No matter how many murders lace the late-evening news or how many wars have been waged in the past fifty years, Old Death is not welcome at after-dinner conversations. With death held at bay, most of us expire unprepared, relying on professionals to do the work; they do it *to* us and *for* our families. In contemporary North America, death knowledge is professional knowledge, not personal knowledge.

Not only are we spiritually unprepared for whatever hereafter there may be, most of us know little about what happens at death in what our forbears used to call "this" world. Even the mundane actions surrounding death—embalming a body, building a casket, cremating a corpse, adapting a funeral rite—are foreign to us. Even though media and movies traffic in death, only a few of us preplan funerals. Not only do we ponder life insurance with circumspection and anxiety, we also postpone writing our wills.

Good Ways to Die

The dying process is implicit in being born. To be born is not only to be in the process of growing up but also to be on the road to death. But for most of us dying only slowly reveals itself as distinct from maturing. The curvature of life from ascent to descent is gradual. At least we would prefer it that way, so we organize much of our cultural and religious life to stave off the anticipation of death. But because we can anticipate our own deaths, even apart from a threatening attack, both the anticipation and the avoidance of death condition the ways we act. A culturewide refusal to imagine a good death tends to ensure that we will not experience one.

Death rites is a broader term than *funeral*. Death rites include memorials, exhumations, reburials, and even predeath ceremonies. The Bena Bena of Papua New Guinea have funerals for the very old before, not after, they die.[218] Narrowly defined, a funeral is only the most formal, liturgical portion of a postdeath rite. In funeral-home parlance, a funeral is the "service" that takes place after viewing and before burial. In popular speech the term *funeral* sometimes refers to all mortuary behavior from visitation through burial. Even the broad usage of the term *funeral* is still too narrow, since it excludes ritualized anticipations of death, preparation of the body, and commemorations of the dead.

In *Western Attitudes toward Death* Philip Ariès, a French cultural historian, bemoans the loss of the *ars moriendi,* the art of dying.[219] Trained in such an art, people presided over their own deathbed scenes. Ariès claims that doctors, not the dying, now preside over deathbeds. Some would argue that doctors more characteristically abandon deathbeds. In any case, dying people become largely passive and are no longer primary actors. Before the twentieth century, dying in Europe and North America was more consciously embraced and publicly performed. A dying person's deathbed scene was saturated with explicit death rites as well as ritualized social drama. Dying was a family, if not a public, occasion. Deathbed utterances were given special credence. To listen to someone straddling the great divide was considered an opportunity for spiritual growth.

In earlier times, says Ariès, not only did believers hear about death in sermons and daily discourse, they also actively contemplated the possibility of their demise. Not that our forebears looked forward to dying, only that they knew there were better and worse ways to face the inevitable, so they cultivated a good death, or perhaps more accurately, images of a good death. In prescribed ways they prepared themselves and their families.

Ariès's portrait is perhaps romanticized, a depiction of the exemplary rather than the average death. Not everyone achieved a good death. Some were lost at sea or dismembered. Others expired violently, accidentally, unexpectedly, or prematurely. Many died afraid and angry

rather than speaking oracularly or departing at peace with their maker and neighbors. Nevertheless, people knew how exiting *ought to happen.* As with sex, so with death; they were ambivalent about talking too openly and frankly, but to avoid the powerful and inevitable was foolish. A good death, then, was one contemplated and prepared for. A bad death was the outcome of refusing to face your mortality until it was too late.

In the Middle Ages living a life permeated by awareness of death was most intense in monasteries, where certain religious orders encouraged their members to dwell on images of putrefying flesh and skeletal remains. The aim of monastic meditations on death was not to sadden or depress but to heighten your sense of urgency, your appreciation for the preciousness of life. You lived fully in the present because you had an eye trained on your ultimate destiny. Pondering death, far from being life denying, was meant to be life enhancing: "Stop and smell the roses today, for tomorrow, they—and you—die."

As late as the mid twentieth century, children were ceremoniously instructed in death awareness: "Now I lay me down to sleep, I pray the Lord my soul to keep. If I should die before I wake, I pray the Lord my soul to take." Perhaps the ritualizing of death's immediate possibility contributed to its routinization, but the intention was the opposite. Ritual preparation of the spirit was supposed to be a goad to readiness, a stimulant of spiritual alertness.

The notion that a death can be good may strike some as macabre. A death can be easy or hard perhaps, but good? The idea confuses us because we are prone to think of goodness in too moralistic a way. The idea of a good death is less about morality than it is about ritual practice. Dying a good death is a ceremonially stylized way of exiting gracefully. By ritualized means a grim necessity is transformed into a dignified and exemplary demise.

Because death is death, after all, the idea of a good or bad one may seem strange. But we still discriminate among kinds of death, even if we do so informally. We regret premature deaths and those of the promising young. We deplore mass deaths, suicides, and murders as well as deaths that take so long that they drain a family of its economic and emotional resources. We prefer deaths in ripe old age and deaths that appear peaceful rather than painful or regret filled.

Not just in early modern Europe and North America was preparing for death ritualized. Preparing to die is practiced in other traditions, even highly developed, in Buddhism, for instance. Buddhists not only tell enlightenment stories about awakening to the true nature of the self, they also recite tales about the deaths of masters. A master's death is exemplary. True mastery is not merely a matter of studying scriptures or teaching meditation. It is not even the supremely important art of living fully; it is the art of dying well.

Buddhist meditation is in one sense a death rite, although it is seldom called that. Meditation practice is about sitting attentively on the abyss between life and death without clinging to life as if it were good or fleeing death as if it were bad. Masterful dying, in meditative traditions such as Hinduism and Buddhism, is supposed to be harmonious with ritual meditation practice. As one practitioner puts it, "Die a little bit each day in meditation."[220]

Although the Soto Zen Buddhist dictum "Die sitting, die standing" is a metaphoric counsel of mindfulness, there are many stories about masters who died literally standing or sitting in meditation posture or who exited on cue at the strike of a meditation bell. The point of such narratives is not so much that Buddhists should imitate this way of dying as it is that people should live in ways that will eventuate in such a death. In Buddhism one's exiting is a summary, a grand metaphor, of one's life. Although meditation is primarily about living this life—here, now—life is inextricably wed to death. So it is that meditation becomes a ritualized way of preparing to die.[221]

Some Hindu and Buddhist dying stories are miracle tales, illustrating the spiritual prowess of the protagonist or legitimizing a teacher's successors. Others are parables meant to illustrate proper attitudes such as detachment or presence to the moment. Whether or not dying masters actually perform concluding ritual dramas, intending their deaths to be instructive, students nevertheless search their teachers' deaths for messages. Ritualizing, then, emerges from two sources: the ways in which masters perform their deaths and the ways in which disciples gather, invent, consume, stylize, and repeat stories about their teachers: "Sensing that death was near, Master Razan called everyone into the Buddha Hall and ascended the lecture seat. First he held his left hand open for several minutes. No one understood, so he told the monks from the eastern side of the monastery to leave. Then he held his right hand open. Still no one understood, so he told the monks from the western side of the monastery to leave. Only the laymen remained. He said to them: 'If any of you really want to show gratitude to Buddha for his compassion to you, spare no efforts in spreading the Dharma. Now, get out! Get out of here!' Then, laughing loudly, the master fell over dead."[222]

The good Buddhist death is sensed from afar. In traditional stories, death does not sneak up on the master unaware, since he is too well attuned for such an oversight. He neither shrinks back nor tips forward in anticipation. The master's death culminates in a posture, literal or figurative, that epitomizes the tradition. In this tale he falls over, consumed by laughter, but he could just as easily have died sitting in meditation posture or reclining Buddha-like on his side.

For the enlightened person, death happens; that is all. And one is in perfect accord with the event. Like breath, people come and go, but with practice, ritualized and regular, Buddhists determine *how* they go. Those who witness a master's death, usually disciples, are at once liberated (in this story, kicked out) and obligated (go teach; show your gratitude). The dying scene is simultaneously instructive and opaque. After it concludes, witnesses have something obvious to do, yet they will return again and again, peering into mysterious aspects of the demise in search of their meaning. A disciple's death ritual, then, does not begin when he or she dies but upon witnessing a teacher's death or hearing a graceful exit story that strikes home.

Do people actually die this way—laughing, instructing, quipping, sitting in full lotus position? Perhaps a few do. But these stories are myths of dying, stories told to inspire. The tales are not photographs of what masters do but portraits of what students imagine that masters, if they live consistently with their teachings, are capable of doing. The ritualizing of dying emerges not only from how "great beings" perform in their last hours but also from the telling and retelling of death narratives that bolster courage, evoke compassion, and instigate community. Dying myths are primarily about aspirations, secondarily about achievements. The question is less whether to believe such stories than it is whether their teachings permeate the lives of practitioners.

Even in the West we speak of one's "last breath," sensing the connection between living and breathing. In Asian meditation traditions, breathing is deliberately ritualized. Inhalations and exhalations are counted or imagined as having weight and color; the spaces between them are contemplated. Each breath is attended to as if it were one's last. Since one aim of practice is to extend meditative consciousness to everyday life, it is no exaggeration to say that breathing, simple inhalation and exhalation, is ritual preparation for death.

The possibility of an exemplary death worthy of emulation implies the possibility of a bad death. Zen Buddhists talk little about ways *not* to die, since doing so would imply "discriminating," clinging to distinctions that feed the illusion that life is good and death bad. Even so, an aspiring student would have to be dense to miss the point that a mindless, distracted, clinging way of dying should be avoided.

The Vajrayana Buddhism of Tibet is explicit about the terrors of dying badly. In this branch of Buddhism the art of dying is called *phowa*. *Phowa* is not a mere matter of bodily comportment and style—dying in lotus position rather than sprawled, mouth gaping open, on a hospital bed. Rather, it is a skill for negotiating the various levels of *bardo*, which one enters upon dying. The *Tibetan Book of the Dead* is not only a depiction of horrific scenes in the afterlife but a manual on how to survive the disorientation inevitable both during and after dying. This guide is not about funerary decorum but liberation. Whereas Zen Buddhist stories concentrate on the dying moment in the here and now, the *Tibetan Book of the Dead* focuses on the cycle of dying and being reborn. In both traditions death myths serve a preparatory function. Hearing and reading them ritualizes a practitioner's life so it can be lived with a heightened awareness of death.

In some traditions the enduring images are positive: Die like this if you can. In others, the more compelling images are negative: Whatever you do, don't go like Coyote. Coyote, or some other version of the native trickster, brings death into the world. Although death is an obvious necessity (otherwise, the world would be overrun with people), you do not want to imitate Coyote or Raven. You do not want to die as he does—self-preoccupied, oblivious of your connections to other people or the earth. He's a good example of what you should avoid.

It seems that North Americans of European ancestry have few compellingly good or disgustingly bad examples, that the medicalization and professionalization of death has neutered it. Not only does death lack a face or name, it is also neither good nor bad nor paradoxical like Coyote. We may have few compelling images or long-standing, powerful cultural myths about dying, but we do have values.

In *How We Die: Reflections on Life's Final Chapters*, Sherwin Nuland, a teacher of surgery and the history of medicine, describes death by cancer, heart failure, Alzheimer's Disease, and AIDS—ways of dying we would like to evade. He concludes with a chapter called "Lessons Learned." Eighty percent of Americans now die in hospitals, and he worries about the scene he sees repeated there, that of the solitary

death. Nuland tells the story of his Aunt Rose's death and confesses his collusion in keeping from her the diagnosis of aggressive lymphoma. "We knew—she knew—we knew she knew—she knew we knew—and none of us would talk about it when we were all together," he admits.[223] Nuland questions what he calls the "rescue credo" of his own profession and weighs it against the patient's right to die. He wonders whether the physician's art of saving life should always assume the upper hand over the patient's art of dying.

In summarizing the lessons he has learned, Nuland proposes a credo of his own: "When my time comes, I will seek hope in the knowledge that insofar as possible I will not be allowed to suffer or be subjected to needless attempts to maintain life; I will seek it in the certainty that I will not be abandoned to die alone; I am seeking it now, in the way I try to live my life, so that those who value what I am will have profited by my time on earth and be left with comforting recollections of what we have meant to one another."[224]

As Nuland envisions it, a good death in contemporary America has several features. It is based on diagnostic truth but not dominated by medicine's need to be in control. It is devoid of needless suffering, and it is talked about openly, not weathered in loneliness. The aspiration, though compassionate, is bereft of ritual.

This picture is not, of course, how things actually transpire, but how Nuland would like them to happen. This contemporary credo is not quite a *vision* of the good death, since it lacks compelling imagery. It is not underwritten by a particular religion or even by the American Medical Association, and it is not the basis of a ritual system such as the medieval Christian or contemporary Buddhist one. So it is, rather, a *philosophy* of death that exercises prescriptive force.

There is no good reason why we should have either a single vision or a single philosophy of death. In fact, in societies as complex as ours, a multiplicity of images of the good death and the proper funeral are a necessity. Whether we think rites mask death or facilitate it, and whether we are inspired by visions or philosophies, we need occasions and places in which to contemplate death before it arrives.

Dying Scenarios

Most popular writing on death seems at first glance to be about how we *in fact* die and not about how we *ought* to die. In 1969 Elisabeth

Kübler-Ross's *On Death and Dying* popularized the notion that people negotiate the terms of their deaths in stages: First there is denial. Then one moves through anger, bargaining, and depression. Finally, one arrives at acceptance. Kübler-Ross's book was so popular that it became impossible to say simply "death"; one had to say "death and dying." But no one, Kübler-Ross included, has ever demonstrated that most people do in fact go through such stages, although no one denies that they *might* do so or that they *sometimes* do so. The notion of stages has been so influential that it sometimes functions like a talisman, drawing attention away from the actuality of dying and focusing instead on a scheme for analyzing a dying person's progress.

The fivefold scheme is occasionally useful for coping with death, because it conjures order in the midst of bewilderment, and it offers the possibility of a more or less happy ending, acceptance. Though radically different in intent and worldview, the Tibetan Buddhist idea of *bardo* and Kübler-Ross's scenario can take the edge off the fear and chaos that can make dying a terrible conclusion in the human life cycle. But like the threefold rites-of-passage scheme, this dying scenario can also distort the process.

Because they were named, schematized, and popularized, Kübler-Ross's stages have had considerable popular and therapeutic impact. The scheme has gone the way of most developmental scenarios, from description to prescription. It has became a tool for prodding dying people along the correct path. One *is permitted* to start with denial because one *ought* eventually to arrive at acceptance. Inspired by Kübler-Ross's phases, spiritual advice is tendered in the form of a supposedly nondirective question, "Don't you think you are in denial, dear?" But the interrogative mode hardly disguises the imperative lurking beneath the surface: "Hurry up and get through this phase; it is not good to die in a state of denial." Not only do others expect a dying person to follow the ceremoniously prescribed course, the dying themselves also expect their deaths to follow this course. If the trajectories of dying deviate, people may feel they have failed, died a bad death.

Is the application of credos and schemes ritual? Not exactly. But ritual action is prescribed (even though not all prescribed action is ritual). Ritual action is also sometimes based on mythic narratives or cultural values and the images that convey them. So in this respect, living a life calculated to eventuate in a proper death is ritualized. And when a particular kind of death is elevated to heroic proportions, held up for emulation, death is also mythologized. That such mythologizing and ritual-

izing may operate outside religious institutions does not dampen their effect.

Wouldn't it be better to approach dying naturally, without ritualizing, schematizing, and mythologizing it? Why is a ritualized way, riddled with oughts and traditions, any better than an unritualized way? Isn't there something artificial, even dehumanizing, about all the customs that crowd like vultures around a poor dying soul?

Protesting funeral rites is part of the American way of death. In the beginning of its nationhood the United States was infused with a Protestant ritual sensibility, one inclined to trim away liturgical excesses. First the frontier experience, then the experience of high mobility enhanced the American tendency toward funerary minimalism. But is it really "natural" to approach death without ambivalence—the attitude that drives much human ritualizing? Or to dispose of the dead without protracted mourning? What seems natural to us may seem anomalous to others.

In many societies death preparation is communal, distinctly religious, and laced with overt rites and explicit myths. In our culture, neither doctors nor funeral directors actively help us anticipate death, but their control during and after the moment of death is almost complete. Educators and psychologists now carry much of the burden once assumed by families and religious institutions. Since the 1970s the so-called death-awareness movement has attempted to educate the public.

Death education has become a legitimate topic, and there are journals devoted to the study of death such as *Omega* and *Death Studies.* The study of death now has a formal, academic-sounding name: thanatology. Like being suspicious of ceremony, preferring education to ritualization is part of the American way. Unlike, say, the Buddhist way, the American way places heavy emphasis on death research and therapy. Both are means not only of building cultural consensus and garnering support but also of mapping the terrain of death, insofar as it is knowable, and of advising travelers how best to walk it.

Every society has its avoidances—words you don't say, places you don't go, things you don't do. When sufficiently ritualized, we call these avoidances taboos. A taboo is not only something to steer clear of, it is also something charged and dangerous—potentially transformative, but also latently destructive. Most societies stigmatize certain ways of dying, so the death rites in which they culminate usually reflect these cultural judgments. Among the ways of dying we treat as taboo are death by murder, suicide, execution, torture, or lynching. Also, we do not want to go too soon or too painfully. More recently, Alzheimer's and AIDS have been placed on the list of stigmatized ways of dying, thus displacing older ways such as leprosy.

Certain ways of dying are borderline—sometimes tabooed, sometimes sanctified. A thin line separates martyrdom and suicide, for instance. In T. S. Eliot's play *Murder in the Cathedral,* Thomas Beckett struggles with the problem of doing "the right thing for the wrong reason." Deliberately getting himself killed could be an effective form of revenge against King Henry. But to die in this calculated way would not really constitute martyrdom, even if others were to interpret the event as if it were. Although we in the West find Japanese *sepuku* (better known as hara-kiri) baffling, we countenance heroic deaths on battlefields, even though running across a bullet-riddled zone in wartime can be suicidal rather than heroic.

To contemplate death in North America requires attention not just to the passive experience of dying but also to the active delivery of death, to killing. Because of the power of the media industries, we are most familiar with death in this form. Movies regularly proffer bad deaths as if they were good entertainment. Executions and lynchings, however devastating, are also theatrical; they are performed, witnessed, and consumed. In addition, they are riddled with the dynamics of scapegoating, a ritual process in which "others" are regarded as evil and therefore sacrificed to relieve "us" of our own burden of guilt. Although witnessing actual hangings is no longer fashionable, capital punishment and murder trials still draw media attention. We avoid thinking about our own mortality, on the one hand, but are drawn to the spectacular deaths of others on the other. The nightly witnessing of television deaths may not be a rite, but it is certainly ritualized.

It Took Two Funerals to Bury My Brother

If deaths can be good or bad, so can funerals. A good funeral is one that celebrates a life, comforts the bereaved, and facilitates working through grief. Some traditions accomplish this goal by making death seem the most natural thing in the world. Others do it by admitting death's absurdity and expressing the hope that it can be overcome. Whatever the strategy, some funerals are more effective than others. A funeral can stifle, amplify, formalize, or facilitate grief. The relation between the ebb and flow of human emotion and the forms and rules of ritual is complex, as Bill Myers's story shows:

When I woke up in this world, I was five years old and nobody else was there but my four-year-old brother, Terry. Nobody else mattered except Richard and Fox, our dogs. Terry and I were inseparable; he followed me everywhere. I was always going somewhere to fight somebody who had messed with him. Fighting was not in his nature. He loved life, loved things, loved everything, loved me. Nobody loved me unconditionally, without equivocation, like Terry. I loved him and protected him as if I were his father. I had to, because we had no mother or father to take care of us, just a mean old lady who hated us.

Then at thirty-four he was dead, shot in the head by a woman he was living with. And I wasn't there to protect him. Why wasn't I? I had always been there to protect him. During beatings in the middle of the night, I had covered him with my body. When others jumped him because he would not fight, I fought for him. When he was put in jail for something he didn't do, I bailed him out. I was always there to protect him.

I was eleven and Terry was ten when we abandoned that mean old lady in Mississippi. We moved to Cleveland to live with our mother, whom we had just met. We landed in a rat- and roach-infested tenement in the ghetto. But it was paradise compared to what we had left.

We met a man who would change our lives, the Rev. Cary McCreary. He wasn't looking for us; he was looking for a piano player for the storefront church he had just started. As providence would have it, he found us instead. He was a big man with a fast gait, a consecrated, old-style Baptist preacher who tried every day of his life to be like Jesus, a man who could predict future events in minute detail. He was not just our pastor and friend, he was the father we never had. He taught us hard work, love instead of hate, survival instead of self-destruction, respect instead of violence, education instead of hopelessness.

Rev. McCreary picked up Terry and me in his Cadillac and took us to Sunday school. He gave us work, loaned us money, baptized all three of us, ordained me, performed my first wedding, baptized and christened every one of my children, attended all my graduations. Then he preached Terry's funeral.

McCreary, God rest his soul, had always said that anyone missing more than ninety days of church without a "legal excuse" such as sickness or work and without putting some money in the collection plate could not have a church funeral. He declared that even if his mother belonged to this church and she broke that rule, he would not allow her funeral to be held in the church. Her body, he declared, would be sent to the funeral home.

On that cold February night in 1984, when Terry was shot, he died instantly. So the detective said. I went to my brother's apartment to gather up his things. There was blood on the wall, broken glass on the floor. I hadn't even given him his birthday gift.

When McCreary informed me the funeral would not take place in the church, I was shocked, then angry, embarrassed, and depressed. Terry and I had been like his very own sons. What would my students, some of them pastors, think? What would church members think? How would I act? How would a funeral-home burial affect the fate of my brother in the afterlife? Did McCreary, with his ability to predict the future, know more about running churches and conducting funerals than I did with all my training? When my children, students, colleagues, and friends asked me how I could be so calm during the funeral and trial, they didn't know how completely these questions consumed me. The pain was too deep, too theological, to be merely personal.

My oldest brother and a half sister I had never met came to the funeral. I was numb through it. I remembered that a colleague of mine had held the funeral of Count Basie and Moms Mabley in his church, and they didn't even belong to a church. I was trying desperately not to let anyone know what I was thinking or feeling. Despite my anger and embarrassment, I appreciated the eulogy. Rev. McCreary loved my brother and mourned his death greatly and openly. At the grave, McCreary allowed my friend Leroy to commit the body to the ground.

We returned to the church dining hall. Black Baptists have a long tradition of gathering to eat after a funeral. The meal is supposed to signal the end of mourning and the beginning of a celebration of a Christian life. Christians should not mourn like others, because their loved ones are better off being with Jesus than being here.

I wanted to go home. I preferred the other eating ceremony, the one in which people bring food to the house, the one that allows you to eat when and if you want, the one not disturbed by everyone coming up to you and saying the same thing over and over again, muttering how sorry they are and hurling some useless or misinterpreted scripture at you. I wanted to go to my mother's house. It was a stone's throw away from the church. But, no, to be respectful, I went to the dining hall.

Rev. McCreary was not a man to be delayed when it was time to eat. When he sat down, it was time for food to be on the table—right then. The family sat in a cramped space on hard seats as people streamed by our table to console us. I didn't want consoling or food; I wanted to be alone.

Finally, I couldn't stand the scene any more, so I did the unthinkable: I refused to eat, a clear sign that I was not celebrating in the way a Christian should. I stood, thanked Rev. McCreary, the church members, and all the others who had come. After I admitted I couldn't eat, McCreary displayed his anger by announcing in a loud and angry tone, "Let's eat."

I fled to mother's house, leaving the rest of the family behind. No one followed me. People were so stunned by such an audacious act that they didn't know what to do. Later, Leroy said that after I left, he couldn't eat either. So shortly thereafter, he left. So did a few others.

In the privacy of my mother's house I fell to mourning. My brother was gone—never to be seen again in this life. I would never hear his laughter, never hear him call me Bubba, never hear him ask me for a couple of dollars for gas. A part of me went to the grave with him, so I did in private what I couldn't do in public: I cried.

Thirteen years later, when my daughter Robin died, after years of struggling with lupus, she was the same age as Terry had been. Like my brother, she died within a week or so of her birthday. Robin had been my daughter Teresa's protector, just I had been Terry's. However, in Robin's last years, as her health failed, the roles reversed and Teresa became Robin's protector.

Robin's funeral was held in our church, where she had been baptized. Due to an illness, Rev. McCreary couldn't talk; therefore, he allowed me to run the funeral as I chose. I asked Leroy, who had known Robin since childhood, and he conducted the service in the way I wished. Colleagues, students, and friends commented on how beautiful the funeral was.

At the grave site, Teresa cried fervently, just as she had at her uncle's funeral. Then she asked, "Daddy, isn't this where Uncle Terry is buried?"

"Yes, it is," I replied.

"Well then," she said, "Robin is with Uncle Terry, and I know she's all right."

At that very moment I knew the final chapter of my brother's funeral had been written and concluded. After thirteen years, a funeral done right helped me find closure and peace, enabled me to gather my footing while standing on the slippery banks of the Jordan.[225]

The story of one funeral becomes the story of two. By telling the events in this way, Bill leaves us wondering, When does a funeral *really* end? If a funeral can be unfinished, requiring a second to complete it, why not a third or fourth? What if there is no end at all to the ripples created by a death? What if there is an insatiable need for sacred acts with which to resolve unfinished business left over from the past?

Terry's funeral is not hermetically sealed in the jar of ceremony. It is extended by means of Bill's memory and that of his daughter Teresa. Robin's funeral completes, even redeems, Terry's funeral. And Bill's telling extends the pair of rites even further. Even though death rites do their work by imposing definite limits in time and space, a ceremony's boundaries are permeable to the social forces surrounding it. A funeral rite is but a slender thread woven into a much larger social and spiritual fabric.

The second funeral, Robin's, brings closure. We are relieved when Bill lays claim to peace. But he is not naive, and we should not be either. His feeling of resolution notwithstanding, Bill knows he has not died and gone to heaven, where, we are told, problems are permanently resolved. Bill is standing, still, on the slippery banks of the Jordan, where things regularly slide back into indeterminancy.

There is, after all, the unfinished business of the Rev. McCreary's rule that determines who can and cannot have church funerals. The refusal of Bill's mentor to sanctify fully the death of one who didn't pay the expected Christian dues, along with McCreary's insistence that Bill demonstrate his faith by eating properly, sticks in the gullet. We have little choice but to believe this powerful preacher when he announces that he would refuse his own mother a church funeral if she failed to abide by the rules, his rules. So Bill's story of closure also opens up a new question, one about a third funeral, McCreary's. When he dies, what will his funeral resolve, and what will it leave dangling? Rites of passage do not always accomplish the tasks we assign them, and sometimes they accomplish others we do not anticipate.

What funerals actually do, or should do, is less obvious than we may think. Globally considered, there is a range of aims. Psychologically considered, there is a variety of consequences. Ritually considered, the official public ceremony may not be the most interesting or important one. So we do well to be cautious about overgeneralizing. Westerners sometimes reduce the work of funerals to facilitating personal grief. Our attitude is predictably psychological. Regardless of the otherworldly rhetoric of some funerals, we are certain that funerals are for the living, for comforting them and helping them work through grief. As a matter of fact, our funerals may suppress grief more often than they facilitate it. We leave serious crying for the home or the psychiatrist's office, not for funerals. Even though we conventionally say funerals do grief work, they are rarely cathartic.

Cross-culturally considered, the major aims of funerals are to sup-

port and protect the living; honor the dead; facilitate their exit from the society of the living; and initiate, if not complete, their incorporation into whatever level of existence or nonexistence the dead inhabit. Death rites may have other aims as well as other effects both intentional and unintentional. The effects do not necessarily coincide with the aims. Royal funerals typically become vehicles of state propaganda. Postfunerary meals afford families a chance to visit and hungry people something to eat. Sometimes the side effects and tributary events upstage the official performances:

About 1984, when I was a monk in the monastery of Entsuuji in the town of Imari in Kyuushuu, Japan, I became involved in the many memorial services and funerals that the monastery performed for the local families. One of the first funerals I conducted as the head monk of Entsuuji was for an elderly woman who had lived in a small farming village near the town of Imari. She must have been around eighty when she died. At a Japanese funeral there is a *chouji* instead of a eulogy. At *chouji*, a good friend of the deceased speaks, not directly to the assembled people, but to the deceased person. Of course, all the assembled people overhear, as they are meant to. Usually, the family arranges for someone to give an appropriately dignified and eloquent *chouji*, but anyone may come forward to say a final good-bye.

The funeral of this elderly lady was held at the farmhouse in which she and her family lived. The sliding partitions and exterior windows had been removed, so the interior of the house was completely open to the guests who gathered in the garden area outside. At *chouji*, an old man who had been sitting at the back of the assembled guests came forward. He wobbled on his cane as he approached. He sat down facing the coffin, and after a while, he started to sing in a low voice. I did not know the song and could not make out the words. After a few minutes, he finished and returned to his seat. I noticed then that a few of the women were crying. I did not know what to make of this scene.

A week later, I was back at the farmhouse to do the weekly chanting that follows a funeral for forty-nine days. After I finished and was drinking tea with the deceased woman's children and grandchildren, I asked about the old man and heard this story:

Both the old man and the deceased lady had been born in that little village. When young, they had fallen in love. But marriages then were strictly arranged by parents. And each was married off to someone else. Since the marriages had taken place in the village, they had lived within a short distance of each other for all of their lives. They saw each other constantly. Both had children and grandchildren. Then as they grew old, her husband died. A little later his wife died. In their old age they were single again, but since they were old, they no longer cared what anyone said about them. When she was not around, her children knew she was visiting him at his place. If he was not around, his children knew he was drinking tea at her place. The entire village knew the story.

The scene I had witnessed but not understood was that of the old man sitting before her coffin, singing a song to her. This was the first and only time he had been able to declare his love publicly.

Victor Hori, a Japanese Canadian and Buddhist monk, explains, "A *chouji* is not a eulogy. In a eulogy, the speaker addresses the audience. Everyone gathers to construct an ideal image of the departed person. People do not speak of the problems, the difficulties, the unfinished business they had with the deceased. Strangely, the deceased is lying there hearing this speech about him- or herself and is not really part of the conversation. In *chouji,* however, speakers come forward to finish unfinished business. Usually *chouji* express gratitude but quite often feelings that were never expressed while the person was alive. Some rites make the private into the public. A wedding stamps public recognition onto a love relationship which, before the ceremony, was private. The old man and the old lady in my story never got that chance while alive, so the old man made his love public at the *chouji.*"[226]

To the Western ear this funeral has something of a matrimonial undertone, since it makes space for a love story. One passage can echo another. A wedding can feel like a funeral. Initiation can seem like a new birth. Birth can be a veritable initiation. Besides echoing one another, rites of passage sometimes piggyback. A parent's unfinished grieving over the death of a child can be finished at the funeral of someone else's child. Things left unsaid at one's own wedding can be uttered twenty years later at an anniversary celebration or while gossiping about someone else's wedding.

A Coffin Lined with Paper

Death rites serve several functions. For the dead, a funeral completes a life and facilitates a transition. A rite, however filled with personal remembrances, also depersonalizes the deceased, transforming a human

into something else—a corpse, an ancestor, a god. For survivors, death rites offer consolation, garner support, facilitate grief, display loyalty, test the net of kinship, and declare hope in the face of meaninglessness. For the larger society, death rites are a patch stitched across a rip in the social fabric. Such ceremonies assert social control, reestablish equilibrium, and display social, economic, and political status. For professionals such as health-care workers, grave diggers, clergy, and undertakers, death rites provide work and remuneration. For religious traditions and institutions, death rites are an occasion on which to assert their relevance and confirm their privileged access to ultimate sources of meaning.

It is impossible to say with certainty whether funerals affect the destiny of the deceased. Despite myths of an afterlife, the promises of sacred texts, and the hopes of the faithful, none of us really knows *what* continues, and if it does, *where* it goes or *how* it gets there. People imagine life after death variously: as purgatory, as a final reckoning, as arrival in a longed-for paradise, as eternal suffering, as final liberation, as continual reincarnation into other forms, as reintegration with the elements, as entry into a world of shadows and shades, as becoming one with all that is. But in the end, what death is a transition *to* is unknown. Our knowledge about what's "over there" is a gaping void that we fill with imaginings or fears. Either that, or we resolutely determine to dwell in the middle of the void, refusing to imagine its contents.

Imagining is fundamental to the dying process, even if all we imagine is the final disintegration of a body. After an initiation, the community can watch to see if a girl behaves like a woman. After a wedding, people can observe whether the groom acts as husbands should. But after a funeral, one has to imagine the deceased as an ancestor or saint or devil or dust.

Death rites are squeezed between what we can imagine and what weighs upon us. A poverty-stricken Danish mother advised her son, "Poor people don't belong in heaven; they have to be thankful if they can get into the earth."[227] Not only is there a right way to prepare for death, there is also a proper way to be treated when you die. If death preparation is a sign of spiritual readiness, receiving a decent farewell is a symbol of a person's social standing. Even though we know that a proper funeral does not necessarily prove either love or respect, most of us act as if funeral rites accomplish or demonstrate things of considerable importance. A decorous send-off is as necessary for those who give little thought to heaven as it is for those who are certain about their postmortem destiny. However little a funeral may mean in the light of things eternal, most societies have not dispensed with them. However heaven tends its own gates, if those who tend cemetery gates won't admit you, you are less than human.

In Alto do Cruzeiro, a Brazilian shantytown in Bom Jesus da Mata, death is not the great equalizer; it is the great signifier of status: Poor in life, poor in death.[228] At one time the rallying cry of peasants there was, "Six feet under and a coffin of one's own."[229] Such modest requirements hardly seem to warrant rallying, but only from the point of view of the privileged who can take for granted the bare minimum.

People of the Alto cannot assume a burial of sufficient depth to prevent bones from working their way to the surface. Nor can the poor take for granted that their bodies will be left to rest in coffins. Coffins, unlined and hard, will be returned so they can be used again by another person too poor to purchase one.

The residents of Bom Jesus know well enough that as living people they have no land rights. Still, they would appreciate being granted tenure over the bit of soil in which they are buried. But the chances are slim; most will lack the resources to control even a postage stamp's worth of turf. Buried without coffins, they will be exhumed in a year if they are adults, six months if children. Their bones will be tossed unceremoniously into the municipal bone yard—ossuary we would call it, if our desire to be sensitive were allowed to override our knowledge of the indignity it is to land there. Even worse than having no plot is being unable to afford a decent coffin. Residents find it deeply shameful to have no proper coffin of their own. Some labor in abusive circumstances to ensure that enough money remains to buy a coffin. More often than not, their meager wages are insufficient to ensure they will be properly disposed of.

The people of Bom Jesus have a great fear of being dumped, without liturgical attention, into a dark hole. The rich are entombed, ensconced above ground rather than buried. They escape the rats, or so they imagine. The poor remember stories from the time of cholera, when people were buried so quickly that some were still alive. Driven by this historic memory, residents insist that a person not be buried on the day of his or her death. But to rules there are always exceptions. The rule is often overlooked in the case of infants. The children of the poor are at the bottom of the social order, less likely to have marked graves or sturdy coffins and to evoke elaborate ceremony or protracted mourning.

Dona Amor, almost ninety, tells Nancy Scheper-Hughes the story of her mother's death:

My mother, may Jesus and His angels embrace her, lost a bunch of children. Only a few of us survived. We suffered a lot in growing up, until everyone left and there was only me working to keep my mother housed and fed in her old age. . . .

Well, it turned out that it was only a week before my mother suffered this terrible fall that was to claim her life. . . . She called me to her side and said, "My love, I am not going to escape death this time, so don't forget about the little brass box where I have hidden away the money for my funeral." She wanted me to go and order her coffin and her *mortalha* [burial clothes and coffin decorations]. "My God," I thought, "what will I do now?" You see . . . , I had to spend a long time nursing Mama after the fall, and during that time I could not work. So from time to time I had to take out a few notes and coins from the brass box. I took out only what was needed, not a penny more. I could recognize the value of the bills from their colors. After all, was I going to let her and me die of hunger, *querida*, knowing all along that there was money set aside . . . ?

I felt very bad after this, and I walked the streets all that afternoon. When I came home my mother was very, very weak. I said to her, "Mama, I am not going to be seeing you very much any more." And we both cried. And all I could think of was that mother would die without anything put aside for her burial. But I lied to her: Don't worry, Mãe. I will go down into the street and order your funeral things."

"That's a good girl," she said. My mother was a simple person. It never would have entered her head that I could have spent the money from her special brass box.

I went to my old boss's house. "What is it?" he said. "Has your mother died?"

"Not yet," I said, "but she is at the portals of death, and I'm here to borrow the money I need so I can arrange her funeral."

"I don't have any money here," he said. Imagine that! And he was the manager of a big bank! But he said, "Just take this check, and with it you can buy what you need." Well, *minha santa,* ignorant race that I am, did I understand anything about bank checks? I thought my patron was tricking me, and so I took the check from him, but outside I tore it up and threw it away.

[When Dona Amor's mother finally dies, she does not know the money in the brass box is gone. Dona Amor has successfully hidden the truth from her mother and now has to bury her in "a piece of crap," a charity coffin decorated in paper rather than fabric and ribbons. By borrowing, improvising, and rationalizing, Dona Amor succeeds—more or less. She comforts herself by recalling that her mother had said she wanted to be buried in the same way as her husband. That much she gets. Dona Amor concludes the story of her mother's death by invoking a sacred story, one that relieves her of some of her guilt as well as the heavy burden of an expensive coffin.]

So I am content. If our sweet Savior could come into this world in a manger lined with hay, then my mother can surely leave this world in a coffin lined with paper.[230]

Few funerals escape compromise. One advantage in having strict traditions is that they relieve us of the burden of exercising choice. But for those who cannot live up to customary expectations, traditions are no relief. In fact, death rites may add to, rather than soften, the hard blow of death. Dona Amor, torn between the desire to feed and care for her ailing mother and the obligation to bury her properly, does what she has to do, even if some of her siblings are unhappy when they find out. The interests of the dead must be weighed against those of the living, the interests of one survivor against those of another, the interests of individuals against those of family and state. The necessities of the other, supposedly more real world have to be weighed against the requirements levied upon life in this one.

A Cloud of Earth for a Pillow

Subverting the wishes of a dying woman is dangerous, but death does not ensure that the danger is past. Even when dead, people clamor for attention, sometimes looming menacingly if the living do not pay it. In pre-Communist imperial China, the primary purpose of funerals was not mainly to comfort bereaved individuals but to enhance filial piety.[231] Death rites were not performed primarily for the sake of purging personal grief. Rather, mourning existed for the sake of cultivating enduring relationships between children and their parents. A child owed a dead parent at least three years of active mourning and, following that, less intensely focused ancestral veneration. It was popularly held that these years were repayment for the initial three years of the child's life, during which she or he was completely dependent on the parent.

Chinese death practices percolated up from a grassroots level to the

imperial courts, but they also trickled from the top down, from rulers to peasants. Even when there is an imposed and accepted ritual pattern based on a widely read ritual text, as was the case in China, there can still be great local and regional variation in the way rites are performed. Ritual tradition and creativity are not mutually exclusive. The history of any mortuary practice, even in so-called traditional societies, is replete with debate and reform, cycles of ceremonial elaboration followed by movements toward simplification.

Before the twentieth century the pattern of Chinese funerals was widely standardized, having been propagated by the state and prescribed in ritual manuals such as the *Li Chi,* a copy of which was in many households.[232] Traditional death practices followed a pattern.[233] Death was announced by wailing and sometimes supplemented by pasting white banners on the house of the deceased. White was associated with death in China much as black is associated with it in Europe and North America. Although white clothing symbolized mourning, degrees of kinship were indicated by the kind of clothing put on.

In south China the corpse was bathed ritually with water purchased from the guardian deity of a well. The dead person was presented with play money, incense, and food, especially pork and rice. A soul tablet was inscribed with the deceased's name and installed on the altar of the family home or, in the case of the wealthy, in an ancestral hall. Specialists, funeral priests, were hired to manage the complex rites, since without monetary exchange the corpse could not be safely exported from the community. Piping and drumming typically accompanied the dead during crucial transitions. The deceased, packed so as not to move around, was sealed into a coffin with caulk and nails hammered in ceremonial order by the chief mourner. Finally, the coffin was carried in procession out of the city or village, concluding the formal part of the ceremony.

In Confucian China, *li* ("ritual") governed relationships between children and parents as well as between the people and the emperor and between the emperor and Heaven (one of the constitutive forces of the cosmos). Since ritual linked the cosmic and social orders, the proper way of behaving at death was, naturally, ritualistic. Chinese sages did not intend ritual forms to displace personal grief. Instead, they were supposed to facilitate it by providing form, without which only *luan,* chaos, would reign. *Luan,* the sages taught, was the natural consequence of a death, but it was potentially destructive. A ritual form without filial feeling could be empty, but bare feeling, unabashed grief without ritual form, could eventuate in mental disorder and social anarchy. In the Chinese view, ritual action, moral behavior, and one's mental state were integrally related. Each reflected, and was reflected by, the other.

Before the Sung dynasty (960 to 1279 C.E.), ancestor rites, including those that marked death, were the purview of rulers and privileged classes. Access to the gods was the exclusive right of such people. After this period, however, peasants gained access to death rites. In fact, they were sometimes punished if they did not observe them or if they practiced unorthodox, which is to say, Buddhist or Taoist, rites. Participation in mortuary rites was a privilege in one era, an obligation in another.

Eventually, sponsoring elaborate and costly funerals became a means of climbing the social ladder. The rules of decorum were elaborate, prescribing even the bodily details of feeling and demeanor that we think of as private and psychological. Mo Tzu, a Chinese sage who lived around 470 to 390 B.C.E., complains about, and caricatures, the expectations: "We are told that he [the mourner] must wail and cry in a sobbing voice at irregular intervals, wearing hemp mourning garments and with tears running down his face. He must live in a mourning hut, sleep on a straw mat, and use a clod of earth for a pillow. In addition he is urged not to eat so as to appear starved, to wear thin clothes so as to appear cold, to acquire a lean and sickly look and a dark complexion. His ears and eyes are to appear dull, his hands and feet lacking in strength, as though he had lost the use of them. And in the case of higher officials we are told that during a period of mourning they should be unable to rise without support or to walk without a cane. And all this is to last three years."[234]

Mo Tzu complains that contemporary rulers believe they need outer and inner coffins, jewels, weaponry, horses, musicians, and a long list of other "necessities." He imagines that ancient sage kings were more modest, their grave goods simple and their funerals short. Today's officials, he complains, "confuse what is habitual with what is proper, and what is customary with what is right."[235] Mo Tzu's conclusion is that the family and state suffer unless funerals are conducted with more moderation.

Moderate or extravagant, funerals were of utmost importance to the Chinese. Adhering to Chinese mourning customs became so essential that it sometimes served as a key identifier of who was *really* Chinese. Chinese death rites were more determinative symbols of Chinese identity than North American funerals are of our identity.

Living with the Dead

North American popular psychology places a great deal of emphasis on "working through" grief. The phrase does not quite imply forgetting, since forgetting would constitute repression, and repression is considered unhealthy. Still, "working through" connotes getting on with your life, not dwelling too long on those you loved: "Come on, Mom, why don't you try dating? Dad's been gone for a year."

When social scientists speak of "corpse disposal," we are reminded that we live in a society with a serious disposal problem, but should we speak of corpses, fetuses, or the senile in the same way we talk about atomic waste or urban refuse? All these topics are hedged by taboos, but they are of differing moral and spiritual orders. If the dead become merely part of our disposal problem, then our dilemma is not just practical but moral and imaginative as well. If we imagine the dead as "things," then hurried or truncated funerals designed to save time and cut through grief make sense. But if we imagine the deceased as people making a profound and mysterious transition, then we will construct funerals that take their time, becoming occasions for dwelling with the dead. If death is a quick commuter flight, we behave one way. If it is a picnic among relatives, some of whom have come on long journeys from afar, we act another.

Twenty-five miles southwest of Mount Olympus sons do not urge their mothers to get on with their lives by dating:

At the sound of the church bell calling the village women to vespers, I went out into the bright sunlight. A few minutes later a woman entered the graveyard dressed entirely in black, with a black kerchief covering her forehead, hair, and neck. She carried one large white candle and a handful of small yellow ones. After crossing herself three times she lit the white candle and one yellow one at the grave of the person she had come to mourn. Then she went up and down the rows of graves placing candles in the sand-filled containers at the foot of several other graves. Finally she returned to the first grave and began the elaborate procedure of preparing and lighting the oil lamp by the headstone.

Soon the graveyard was alive with activity, and a forest of candles burned at the foot of each grave. About ten women, all dressed in shades of black, brown, or blue, busied themselves lighting lamps and sweeping around the graves. Several women began hauling water in large buckets from the faucet in the church courtyard nearby. After watering the flowers on the graves they were caring for, the women began to wash the marble headstones with sponges and detergent kept in little plastic bags hidden carefully in the grass by the graveyard wall. So attentive was their care for the graves that some women would sift through the sand-filled containers throwing out clumps of melted wax or scrape old wax off the marble slabs with small knives kept just for that purpose.

After fifteen or twenty minutes, when most of this housecleaning had been completed, the atmosphere in the graveyard once again turned somber and quiet. Each woman sat on the grave of her husband, parent, or child, tending the candles and talking quietly with women at nearby graves. They discussed the crops, the weather, or the long-awaited summer visits of their children working far away in Athens, Germany, and the United States. Often their conversations dealt with matters closer at hand—funerals in neighboring villages, the expense of renting a cemetery plot in a large city, or the circumstances surrounding the deaths of their relatives who lay buried beneath them.

One woman stood near the head of a grave, staring at a photograph of a young woman. She rocked gently back and forth, sobbing and crying. Suddenly she began to sing a lament in a pained, almost angry tone of voice. Before she finished the long, melismatic line of the first verse she was joined by other women. The intensity of emotion in the women's voices quickly increased. The verses of the lament, sung in unison by the chorus of mourners, alternated with breaks during which each woman shouted a personal message addressed to her own dead relative.

"Ah! Ah! Ah! My unlucky Eleni."

"Nikos, what pain you have caused us. You poisoned our hearts."

"Kostas, my Kostas, the earth has eaten your beauty and your youth."

These cries were interrupted by the next verse, as the singing resumed. When the first lament ended, a woman sitting in the far corner of the graveyard immediately began a second. Finally, after singing three or four laments lasting perhaps fifteen minutes in all, the women stopped. The loud songs and cries were followed by quiet sobbing and hushed conversations.[236]

With minor variations this scene is performed once, often twice, a day in the Greek village of Potamia.[237] In 1974 Eleni was twenty years old when she died after a hit-and-run automobile accident. Because she had not yet married, she was buried in a white wedding gown, making her funeral—at least symbolically—her wedding. After the death, Irini, Eleni's mother, formally entered into mourning. She did not leave home

to see people, attend church services and baptisms, or visit her own mother. She did not attend the wedding of another daughter. For five years, she left her house twice daily to visit the graveyard. Eleni's father not only mourned openly at his daughter's funeral, he also sang laments while herding sheep and goats in the hills.

Greek laments are not laced with sugar-sweet comfort. Some of them are extraordinarily graphic, depicting the earth and its creatures as consumers of buried bodies. Just as the living once ate off mother earth, so mother earth eats us. "Mother," complains a dead child, "here in the underworld where I have come / I found snakes twisted like braids and vipers curled like ribbons. / One snake, mischievous and smaller than the others, / came and built a nest above my head. / He ate my eyes, with which I saw the world. / He ate my tongue, with which I sang like a nightingale. / He ate my hands, with which I did my chores. / And he ate my feet, with which I used to come and go."[238]

The rural Greek cemetery is a primary space for carrying on relationships with both the living and the dead. Irini and Maria become neighbors by virtue of the fact that Maria's son Kostas is buried in the grave beside Eleni. At home Maria laments as she hugs her son's clothes. Neither woman is behaving abnormally. Both are acting in accord with tradition, so no one advises them to get on with their lives. At the cemetery the women share their grief and converse daily. The cemetery is a place for socializing, like coffee shops, malls, or city squares in other parts of the world.

North Americans fear emotional display at funerals almost as much as death itself. Distaste for funerals arises for two contradictory reasons: on the one hand, suspicion that ceremonial formalities stifle genuine feeling and, on the other, fear that funerals will not succeed in stifling emotional display.

The problem of managing the relation between ritual form and the onrush of feeling is persistent, but the relation among death, emotion, and ritual is not straightforward. We cannot be certain that ritualized mourning behavior is cathartic or even that such mourning is the direct expression of emotion. In some traditions there are professional mourners who are paid for their ability both to control and to let go of their emotions. The fact that their emotions are "theatrical" rather than "natural" reminds us that emotions of all kinds, not just grief, can be stylized, performed as expected. Likely most of us have been in ceremonial situations that required us to perform with solemnity or dignity or joy when we felt nothing of the kind. But in some cultures performed grief is standard ritual behavior, not hypocrisy.

Under the influence of Western romanticism, we sometimes imagine emotion as following a more or less causal sequence. Emotion is a wellspring rising up spontaneously from the heart. Emotion lodges in the throat, contorting facial contours and producing tears. The "heart strings" are tied directly to those we love, and when they die, their "downward" motion tugs at those strings, eliciting strong feelings. In this model the connection between the beloved's death and our emotional upsurge is direct.

Ritualized emotion, however, works differently. Weeping and wailing are not just personal expressions of affection but also social obligations: Greek women are *expected* to grieve. It may even be that the basic funerary emotion is not sorrow but togetherness or some other feeling such as relief. There is no reason to assume that emotion, on the one hand, and obligation or stylization, on the other, are mutually exclusive. It may be that a mourner, under social obligation, at first *performs* grief only to find that the performance itself elicits *felt* grief. My point is not that ritual mourners never feel grief but that we should not assume a one-to-one correspondence between what someone feels and what he or she expresses in mourning. We should be cautious about inferring either feelings or the lack of feelings from ritual performances.

After five years, as tradition requires, Eleni is exhumed, putting a formal end to mourning and releasing the mother from her tenure at the grave site:

> Eleni's two brothers, who had started to dig down through the gravel and sandy soil, were soon overcome with emotion, as the intensity of the lamenting increased. When they began to cry, two young women took their shovels and continued digging. Eleni's brothers withdrew to the outside of the circle of women, where they stood quietly and awkwardly, men out of place in a women's world of death.
>
> The loud chorus of laments could not mask the sharp ring of the shovels against the earth, nor could it blot out the increasingly violent cries and shouts of Irini and Maria. As the gaping hole in the middle of the grave grew deeper, Irini leaned farther over the place where her daughter lay, until she had to be pulled back by her sister. Eleni's father, much more restrained in the expression of his grief, though no less intense, would occasionally cry out: "You didn't live to accomplish anything, Eleni, anything at all."
>
> When the earth in the grave turned a much darker color, and fragments of rotten wood appeared, the singing grew louder. The young women with shovels were replaced in the grave by an older widow with a small hoe. Some women shouted instructions to her, telling her to dig carefully: "More to the right. Find the skull first, then the ribs. Don't break anything." When she struck something solid with her hoe, she put it down and began to dig with her hands. The singing grew weaker; the melody was carried now by only a few voices. Irini, Maria, and the other close relatives continued their wild, angry shouting.
>
> When the widow uncovered the skull, she crossed herself and bent down to pick it up. People threw flowers into the grave. All singing stopped, while the screaming, shouting, and wailing reached a new peak. The widow tried to wipe what looked like hair off the back of the skull before she wrapped it in a white kerchief. She crossed herself again and placed some paper money on the skull outside the kerchief. Then she kissed the skull and handed it to Irini.
>
> Irini cradled her daughter's skull in her arms, crying and sobbing uncontrollably. The women behind her tried to take it from her but she would not let go. She held Eleni's skull to her cheek, embracing it much as she would have embraced Eleni were she still alive. Finally she placed more paper money on the skull and wrapped another kerchief around it, a kerchief which had been embroidered by Eleni as part of her dowry. Irini kissed the skull and touched it to her forehead three times before she handed it to Maria, who did the same. Irini and Maria embraced the skull together for several minutes, shrieking and wailing. Then they handed it across the open grave to Eleni's father, who greeted his daughter's skull as the others had before him. It was then passed down the side of the grave to be greeted by sisters, brothers, cousins, and others.
>
> As more bones were uncovered, they were placed in the metal box by the headstone. Irini took the photograph of Eleni, which had stood for five years in the glass case at the head of the grave, and placed it in the frame on the front of the box. Women tossed small coins into the box as it slowly filled with bones. Eleni's skull was returned to Irini, who held it in her lap for the remainder of the exhumation. Some women commented on the blackness of the bones and on how well preserved Elenis's shoes, stockings, and dress were. Others offered advice as to where to find the small bones of the hands and feet. Irini reached into the metal box and picked up a severed bone from one of Eleni's legs, which had apparently been broken when she was fatally injured. She dropped it back into the box, crying: "You were a beautiful young partridge, and they killed you."
>
> The widow was still sifting through the earth, in search of a ring, a cross, and a gold tooth. The lamenting gradually ceased, and women began to ex-

change fatalistic comments about human mortality and the inevitability of death: "That's all we are, a pile of bones. We are born, and we will die. Then we'll all come here." Two women counted the bones in the box and discussed the best way to arrange them. At last Irini was persuaded to let go of her daughter's skull and place it in the box on top of the other bones.

Suddenly all the women stood up and crossed themselves. The graveyard was filled with silence and the smell of incense. The village priest had arrived. . . . He poured a bottle of red wine over the bones, forming the shape of a cross three times. He continued to recite from the funeral service: "You shall sprinkle me with hyssop and I shall be clean. You shall wash me and I shall be whiter than snow. The earth is the Lord's and the fullness thereof, the world, and all that dwell therein. You are dust, and to dust you will return."[239]

These villagers are Greek Orthodox Christians, but their beliefs and practices are a mixture of Orthodoxy and traditional folk beliefs. A description of the official Orthodox rites that follow the events recounted above by Loring Danforth would present only a fraction of rural Greek death ways. The mortuary process in this part of rural Greece is complex, involving home, church, and cemetery, and there are several phases: preparation and laying out the body at home; procession to the church; the Orthodox funeral service; and memorial services on the third, ninth, and fortieth days after death and two more, six months and one year, respectively, after the death. Exhumation, the final rite, occurs five years after death.

In rural Greece, if rites are not properly performed, the deceased cannot be fully incorporated into paradise. The state of the bones at exhumation is indicative of the state of the soul.[240] If, on the one hand, the flesh has decomposed and the bones appear clean and white, the soul has completed its journey. The relatively permanent nature of bone symbolizes the eternal nature of the soul. If, on the other hand, hair and flesh continue to cling to the bones, the transition process is unfinished and the bones are reburied. Prayer, additional memorials, and more time are necessary. Flesh symbolizes the transient nature of the body. If the deceased died violently, unforgiven, or under the influence of a curse or excommunication, the decomposition will be tellingly incomplete. Although a few people, mostly men, insist that decomposition is the natural result of soil and climactic conditions, others hold that morality rather than nature determines the state of the bones.

Once bones are exhumed and deposited in an ossuary, the deceased gradually becomes part of the anonymous dead. This secondary burial

more or less completes the funerary process. I say more or less because even after exhumation there are memorials and remembrances for the collective dead. They are held on Soul Saturdays. Each year several such ceremonies are held, and the names of the past few generations of dead are recited.

Except in the Orthodox funeral service, at which a male priest officiates, women are the primary actors around death. Between the first of the memorial services and the exhumation, bereaved women make one or two visits a day to the cemetery. Cemetery ritual is determined by customary practice rather than formally mandated by a ritual book. The more formal aspects of it consist of laments, many of which are conversations with the dead. The following example stitches together specific biographical details with general mythological themes and characters: "Eleni, you didn't cry out so that we could rescue you." / "How could I cry out? How could I answer your call? / My mouth was gagged. There was a kerchief around my neck. / And that vicious Haros [death personified, an angelic messenger] was raining blows down on me."[241]

Another lament takes up the widespread theme of death as a process of being eaten: "Tell me, tell me, my darling: How did Haros receive you?" / "I hold him on my knees. He rests against my chest. / If he is hungry, he eats from my body, / and if he is thirsty, he drinks from my two eyes."[242] By means of ritual laments death is made graphic and real, but at the same time the harsh split between life and death is momentarily overcome.

The Greek dead, like the living, desire human company, hence the importance of grave visiting. The dead have needs that resemble those of the living. Graves are homes, and candles provide light for the inhabitants. Food consumed by mourners feeds the dead. As one woman put it, an elaborate funeral sends a husband off "well fed and pleased."[243] A variety of symbolic foods and ceremonial meals are connected with the funerary process. Eating and being eaten are major themes linking women's activities in death to those in ordinary life.

Women bear the burden of washing, feeding, and caring for the dead, just as they do for the living. Because of Greek marriage and work patterns, wives regularly outlive their husbands, resulting in what one might call a widow culture. In a widow culture, death is a central fact. Death does not prevent women from carrying on relationships with one another or with the dead; if anything, death amplifies their relationships. Women typically bury their husbands, but widowers have no parallel responsibility for burying their wives or tending their graves. Instead, these responsibilities usually fall to a daughter-in-law, the wife of the youngest son.

The ritualizing of death in graveyards is carefully watched and overtly criticized by villagers. Proper grave tending is an obligation implied by the right to inherit. The primary activities are grave visitation and musical lamentation, but dreaming about the dead, naming children after the deceased, and hoping for the resurrection also keep the dead alive. Caring for the dying and dead is one way to repay an obligation; naming one's children after a grandparent is another. By preserving his or her name, the deceased will be remembered. Dead people feel joy at having their names passed as gifts to young people. In effect, the dead are resurrected by means of, or into, ritualized behavior.

Yet, these same rites also depersonalize the dead. The deceased are made more fully dead by the drama of a funeral liturgy and exhumation rite, so the ceremonial victory over death is only short-term. In the long run, even the Greek dead fade, becoming less and less individualized as time passes. Greek women learn to hold two paradoxically related attitudes. On the one hand, in their graphic laments they imagine the dark and dreary aspects of afterlife; they are blunt in expressing their pessimism about the future. On the other hand, they believe in, or at least hope for, eternal life by way of their participation in the resurrection-centered liturgies enacted by the Greek Orthodox Church.

In North America the dogged, long-term care of the dead by Greek women would be labeled denial, a refusal to come to terms with the finality of death. Some might wish the women spent their time caring for the sick, or even the dying, rather than chanting to and chatting up those already dead. There is an enormous difference, after all, between the five-year Greek mourning period and the typical three-day bereavement leave granted by American and Canadian employers.

But from the point of view of a Greek widow, the North American haste to get on with life is a blatant refusal to assume responsibility or act in a caring way. In one lament the speaker says of her grief, "I will go to a goldsmith and have it gold-plated. / I will have it made into a golden cross, into a silver amulet, / so that I can worship the cross and kiss the amulet."[244] Grief is not to be vetted but cherished; keeping grief alive is one way of knowing that you yourself are not dead. Cemetery visiting is a way of achieving catharsis, a method of purging grief, and a way of cultivating it. The culture of these rural Greek women is largely a culture of death, but their dead are alive. Although exhumation is

supposed to incorporate the deceased into the world of the dead, grief, particularly that of a mother, is "a wound that never heals."

The Release of a Hungry Ghost

But what about those who die without healing? Like all rites, those surrounding death condense a people's cosmology, their most fundamental, taken-for-granted images and assumptions about the nature and destiny of human life. The European American West is comparatively dogmatic in believing that the line between life and death is clear and definite and that the dead do not require the ritual efforts of the living. Even though an occasional individual may be stranded, having been rendered a "vegetable" by mishap or medical error, we nevertheless cling to the clear distinction between the living and the dead with the tenacity of faith. An occasional smudge of the boundary line does not squelch confidence in its basic clarity.

Even reports of near-death experiences do not threaten the public's confidence that there are only two sorts of human beings, the quick and the dead, and that the latter are less than human. Ghosts, the restless and hungry dead, even though they are objects of contemporary popular fantasy, are considered figments of the imagination. They inhabit Gothic novels and horror films but not real life. Like figures of speech, these figures of the imagination fascinate but have not earned the right to be considered primary actors in Western funeral rites.

Faith in the distinction between the living and the dead is buttressed by the split between the self and others. A key Western dogma is that of the singular self. In our cosmology spirits neither "inhabit" nor "ride" the living by possession, reincarnation, or any other means. Except in fiction and in the gushy rhetoric of weddings, a person is definitely one—not two.

Or so it would seem. Even in the West we sometimes talk as if the self is divisible into a mortal part (the remains) and an eternal part (the soul or spirit). However we put it, or avoid putting it, death raises questions about the nature of reality and the constitution of the self, and death rites are predicated on the answers we give to such questions. It also works the other way around: Rites teach us the expected answers to such questions.

In any case, religions exist in which intermediate zones are interleaved between life and death, leaving human identity with fuzzy rather than clear boundaries. In such traditions, the work of death rites is not restricted to funerals or even ceremonies enacted close to time of death. Death rites may be retroactively performed:

Fifteen years ago, I was leading a meditation program at Rocky Mountain Dharma Center (RMDC), a retreat facility high up in the mountains near Red Feather Lakes, Colorado. We were conducting the program in a group of buildings owned by the Girl Scouts. One night, a participant heard someone cry out in a high, sharp-pitched, mournful voice. On subsequent nights, others heard it.

A woman who worked at RMDC said it wasn't unusual to hear this sound and that people had been hearing such cries for the past couple of years. She then told the story of a little girl, perhaps ten years old, who had been killed here a number of years before. She had been climbing on some rocks that tower up behind the camp. Her parents had been battling each other for years. The family, in tremendous disarray, was disintegrating. The girl's parents had finally decided to divorce, so they had sent her away for the summer to remove her from the situation. She was beside herself with anxiety, loneliness, and fear.

One day, the girl fell from the rocks and was gravely injured. Brought into a nearby cabin, she died there. After this tragedy, use of the camp by the Girl Scouts tapered off. There were even thoughts of selling the place.

The Tibetan teacher Trungpa Rinpoche, informed of this story, said the sound was probably a hungry ghost who was stranded, attached to this physical locale, unable to move on to a better rebirth. He suggested planning a Sukhavati ceremony for the little girl. The Sukhavati is a traditional Buddhist ceremony performed for people after they die to encourage them toward a favorable rebirth. It is also done to help a hungry ghost, stuck in a state of attachment and unfulfillment, on its way to better rebirth.

Those of us participating in the retreat, most of whom had been Buddhists for many years, decided that now was the time to perform the Sukhavati. One of my friends, well acquainted with the story, took me into the cabin and up to the room where the little girl had died. The air of sadness and grief in the room was palpable. It was upsetting to sit on her bunk and feel it.

I didn't lead the ceremony. In fact, I thought, "Well, maybe this is real and maybe it's a collective fantasy." I had my doubts. Whenever you are in this "flat world," you always have doubts. The only part you can prove is the flat part; the rest you cannot prove. The part that is not flat is accessible only through intuition.

I was sitting there with all my doubts, but I was paying attention because I was curious. At a certain point in the ceremony, the officiant snaps his or her fingers to release the trapped ghost. When the woman officiating snapped her fingers, I saw a being rush off to the east. A sudden sense of joy filled the room. I was taken completely by surprise and felt as if I had been hit by lightning. In that moment, I was sure that the notion of hungry ghosts had something objective to it, that it was not just a way of talking about a human state of mind. I understood why Tibetans feel so strongly about ceremonies that make connections with beings in other realms. For Tibetans, we humans are in a unique position to help beings in other realms who may be suffering terribly and are otherwise without recourse. I realized why Tibetans become so upset when Western Buddhists want to jettison any belief in realms of existence other than this flat, immediately visible, human one. When one is dealing with other realms, flat-world instruments don't apply.

Subsequent to our performance of the Sukhavati ritual, the air of sadness that hung over the room where the little girl had died dissipated completely. The mournful cries were no longer heard at night. People at RMDC stopped talking about the tragedy. The Girl Scouts began using the camp more frequently and a new board decided against selling the property.

The people who now manage the camp do not seem to be familiar with the incident of the little girl's death.[245]

Contemporary views of ritual would have us believe that rites exist for the sake of their psychological and social effects. Ritual is a flat-world device, but it can also be a way of interacting with the multidimensional world. Performers use it to connect with powers and entities on other planes, those that, although they exceed the human grasp, are tangible if approached attentively and with due ceremony.

In Reggie Ray's story above, *sukhavati* is not performed to make participants feel better about themselves, to consolidate group feeling, or even to inculcate the Buddhist moral value, compassion, even though the rite accomplishes all these. Its aim rather is to straighten out a warped state of affairs; to unhook a sentient being hanging from a shard at the edge of the universe. The *sukhavati*'s removal by several years from the time of the girl's death divests the rite of what we Westerners normally consider the usual funerary motive, that of comforting a family in its loss and of paying respects to the dead.

"Was a ghost actually trapped, and did the performance of a mere ceremony release her?" This is a flat-world question, to which the flat-world answer must be, "Who knows?" Reggie's doubts authorize us to articulate our own doubts if we are so inclined. But his conclusion also encourages us to consider the possibility that there may be more than two dimensions, or even three. Across the world it is a widespread view that the dying and deceased are susceptible to influence by ritual means, perhaps *only* by ritual means. How else could we humans even imagine assisting a dead, but still wailing, ten-year-old girl?

It would be ethnocentric to build into the definition of "rites of passage" the conviction that a funeral is the "last rite" or to require allegiance to a credo declaring that, after death, there are no further passages to be made. Our definition of death rites must be large enough to include not only ritualized preparation for death and rites performed near the time of a death but also ritual activities that follow long after the occasion of a person's death.

Dancing with the Dead

So far we have been considering rites of passage that mark the deaths of individuals. But not all death rites are rites of passage, ceremonies that mark a moment in a person's life cycle. Some are occasioned not by the event of a specific death but by a seasonal, or calendrical, recognition of the dead.

In the Christian world November 2 is known as All Souls' Day. Although part of the Christian liturgical calendar, this day is not widely celebrated in English- or French-speaking North America. The preceding day, All Saints' Day, is slightly better known. More widely observed than both is the evening of October 31, All Hallows' Eve, popularly called Halloween.

The Mexican counterpart of this festival is called *el Día de los Muertos*, the Day of the Dead. All over Mexico, even in rural areas, Day of the Dead symbols are bandied about for political, commercial, and artistic purposes, as well as religious ones. The day has become a national symbol of Mexico itself. Not merely a rite dutifully observed, the Mexican Day of the Dead is festive even though it celebrates death. Canadians and Americans have few occasions on which death and festivity, tears and laughter, publicly coincide, so to them the atmosphere of this Mexican fiesta is incongruous but intriguing.

The appearance of skeletons on Halloween as well as on *el Día de los Muertos* is an obvious iconographic link between the Mexican observance and that of Mexico's Anglicized neighbors to the north. But Halloween is child focused and rarely an occasion for contemplating

the dead, death, or even horror, despite the masks that herald its arrival. In contrast, the Mexican Day of the Dead is about tending and nurturing the links of extended families with their ancestral dead.

On the Day of the Dead, Mexicans visit the graves of friends and relatives. The living picnic among the deceased, cleaning and decorating their earthy abodes, the graves. The living chat with neighbors and relatives, exchanging stories about the dead. The deceased—some sainted, most not—are, ritually speaking, an integral part of society.

Although names of the dead may be remembered for several generations, personalities of dead people begin fading after their funeral. But the anonymous collective, "all souls," continues its existence, requiring ritual attention from the living.

The Day of the Dead, although part of the Christian calendar, incorporates attitudes and images that are unique to Mexico, with its confluence of Spanish and indigenous symbols. The day triggers an avalanche of folk-art forms: toys, food, grave decorations, statues, paintings, songs, and poems. Families build domestic altars on which to display pictures of the dead, to whom are made offerings of drinks, incense, candles, flowers, water, and food (even if, in popular lore, disembodied souls can only smell, not actually eat, the food). Marigolds, chrysanthemums, and other brightly colored flowers are everywhere. Places are set at dinner tables for deceased family members, their empty chairs trumpeting their absence. Special foods are prepared: red or blue corn tamales, mole (meat cooked in a sauce made of cocoa, chili, and ground peanuts), pulque (a cactus liquor), and *pan de muerto,* "bread of the dead." One is especially favored if she or he bites into a piece of bread containing a tiny skeleton. Death toys are distributed to children, dead ones in their graves as well as living ones in their homes. Skulls and other reminders of death made of sugar are consumed with gusto. Eating death is at once a way of defying and submitting to it.

The Mexican relationship with death is not only respectful and somber but jocular, ironic, even defiant. *Calacas,* skeletons representing the Grim Reaper, are ubiquitous. *Calaveras,* "skull" verses, are satirical lines, often in the form of obituaries written by dead authors: "This gay skull invites mortals today / To go to visit the infernal regions. / There will be special trains as amusements during this trip, / And there won't be any need to wear a new outfit."[246] In cities as well as rural areas, *calaveras* lampoon the living—the town drunk or even the mayor—with ironic eulogies.

Day of the Dead iconography is less informed by heavenly bliss than it is by infernal irony. So statues of skeletons not only wear wedding dresses or ride bulls, they smoke and fall, bottle in hand, into drunken stupors. Hell bound, they forget their clothes and are less than modest.

Although there is probably some truth in the claim that the Day of the Dead arises from a unique convergence of native and medieval Spanish Christian elements, the contemporary forms became recognizable only during the Mexican revolution, between 1910 and 1930, a period when death was, in fact, at everyone's elbow. *Corridos,* ballads, were written to prepare people for the necessity of death in combat. So the first use of Day of the Dead death imagery was propagandistic and nationalistic, not mystical and religious. After the revolution, the media continued the iconographic tradition, putting the imagery to commercial use.

The Day of the Dead has had its literary and artistic popularizers. Octavio Paz, whose book *The Labyrinth of Solitude* was translated into English and widely read by English-speaking North Americans and Europeans, popularized the romantic view that many of us now hold of the Mexican love affair with death: "To the inhabitant of New York, Paris, or London," wrote Paz, "death is a word that is never uttered because it burns the lips. The Mexican, on the other hand, frequents it, mocks it, caresses it, sleeps with it, celebrates it; it is one of his favorite toys and the most permanent lover. It is true that in his attitude there is perhaps the same fear that others also have, but at least he does not hide this fear nor does he hide death; he contemplates her face to face with impatience, with contempt, with irony."[247]

But not all Mexicans are so happy with a portrait that casts them as death's lover. Aunt Guadalupe died in squalor on the Day of the Dead, 1962. Guadalupe's niece Consuelo Sánchez had prayed just two days before, on All Souls' Day, to San Martín de Porres for a miracle. If she was not to be granted a miracle then, please, at least a chance to see her aunt before she died. Consuelo got no such chance. Word of her aunt's death arrived before she could pay her a visit:

Then I looked directly at Saint Martín on his marble pedestal surrounded by lighted candles and I said to him, "Brother Martín of Porres, if it is true that you can perform miracles, I challenge you to heal my aunt—overnight. That is the only thing that will make me believe in you."

Saint Martín didn't take up my challenge and now I scolded him, "You are bad. I don't love you. You revenged yourself. Why? Why? I prayed so hard."

What can I say to express the pain that has drained away the last drop of joy from my heart? I have never been able to accept death the way it comes to people in my class. We are all going to die, yes, but why in such inhuman, miserable conditions? I've always thought there was no need for the poor to die like that. Their struggle is so tremendous . . . so titanic . . . no, no, it isn't fair. They can be saved. I refuse to resign myself to death in that tragic form.

There are authors who have written that the Mexican cares nothing about life and knows how to face death. There are jokes and sayings and songs about it but I would like to see those famous writers in our place, undergoing the terrible, hideous sufferings we do, and then see if they are able to accept the death of any one of us with a smile on their lips, knowing that the person didn't have to die. It's all a big lie. The way I see it, there's nothing charming about death nor is it something we have become accustomed to because we celebrate *fiestas* for the dead or because we eat candy skulls or play with toy skeletons. . . . No, the death of a loved one is not accepted, anyway you look at it.

. . . Why do we insist on carrying on that absurd masquerade, the gigantic lie that hides the real truth here in this "republic" of Mexico? "We, the Mexicans," amid "this prospering beauty with its politically strong, economically solid foundation . . . " Oh yes, we are making progress. We are advancing in technology and science; the steel structures are rising over the corpses.[248]

Here, Consuelo is still grieving for her aunt, but her grief does not authorize one to dismiss her anger. She knows there is a contradiction between *el Día de los Muertos* and the experience of dying in poverty. She reminds us that however willing death is to play the butt of verbal and pictorial jousting, and however well it receives jests and tolerates ironies, death is still not a loved one. Celebrations of death, even if they do remind us of our mortality, should not be allowed to cover up the fact that dying is neither cute nor acceptable, especially if you are poor. The story that Consuelo and her brothers tell Oscar Lewis, who recorded the narrative, reminds us of the distance between Day of the Dead coffee-table books, with their array of gloriously colored, taunting, playful images and the harsh realities of dying Mexican, female, and penniless.

Death rites never provide answers. In fact, celebrations often spring up around questions that are by their very nature unanswerable. Ritual is a way of performing, thereby becoming identified with, our most troubling questions.

The American Way of Death

In some respects scholarship on death is better informed about the rites of other cultures than it is about our own. Although there is an enormous amount of literature, much of it recent, on "the American way of death," it pays scant attention to death rites, focusing instead on general beliefs and attitudes toward death, grief counseling for the bereaved, or the economics of funerals. So not only is the general population distanced from the dead, but scholarly knowledge about death rites in the United States and Canada is scant.

One of the most widely used and respected textbooks on death is Robert Kastenbaum's *Death, Society, and Human Experience.* Originally published in 1977, the book is now in its sixth edition, and it is as near as one can get to a comprehensive survey of death trends and thanatological research in contemporary America. Kastenbaum introduces the idea of the death system, defining it as "the interpersonal, sociophysical and symbolic network through which an individual's relationship to mortality is mediated by his or her society."[249] He understands well the complex network in which death occurs. The people, places, times, objects, and symbols of a death system work together to achieve several aims: warning about and predicting death, preventing death, caring for the dying, disposing of the dead, consolidating groups after a death, making sense of death, and delivering death, which is to say, killing.

A death system, then, includes much more than death rites. But since our concern here is with death ritual, it is revealing to note the space Kastenbaum allots to it. Only one of his fifteen chapters is devoted to the funeral process. Within this chapter, half a page is spent on the funeral service, even though Kastenbaum calls it is the "centerpiece of the entire process."[250] If this authoritative textbook's representation reflects either the state of American thanatology (the study of death) or the state of American attitudes toward death, then death rites are of minor importance to both the American way of death and to American research on death. The American way of death is more focused on emotions, relationships, and ethical issues than on ritual processes.[251]

The popular avoidance of the topic of death, coupled with the intellectual focus on nonritualistic issues, makes it difficult to paint a full or accurate picture of American death rites. Our only alternative, then, is to understand the construction the "American way of death" and to pay close attention to how it works in the literature.

In 1963 Jessica Mitford's book *The American Way of Death* popularized the notion that there is a distinctively American way of dying. This idea is seldom challenged or even questioned. In her characterization, the most telling feature of the American way is its commercialization, the sale of expensive caskets and costly embalming services to the bereaved, who, in their moment of vulnerability, naively sign on the dotted line without reading the fine print. Writing in the tradition of journalistic muckraking, Mitford exposed manipulative schemes perpetrated by undertakers and railed against their overcharging. She counseled better planning and wiser spending. She said little about the structure and content of funerals. In the wake of her book's publication, burial societies were formed to resist the well-organized cadre of professional funeral directors, who are largely responsible for creating the "American way of death." Mitford's exposé did not substantially change American practice, which remains heavily determined by the funeral industry. And the alternative rites inspired by her criticism were not more elaborate or more effective, just shorter and cheaper.

Despite—or perhaps because of—the American tendency to avoid talking about or preparing for death, the "American way of death" and "death and dying" became popular topics, selling books and spawning university courses. Even so, there are few sustained descriptions of specific funeral rites in Canada, Mexico, or the United States. Not only are the ethnographic data scant, but sources that provide long historical views of death practices are in short supply too. Most of the writing on death consists of reportage and analysis of social trends, or it is psychologically oriented self-help literature. So describing a typical American funeral is not easy unless one is content to speak anecdotally.

From one point of view, it may not matter that no one has closely observed and fully documented death rites in America. Who, after all, needs a description of what everybody knows? Such a description would be a boring repetition of the obvious, wouldn't it? But suppose "what everybody knows" about the American way of death is wrong or a cliché? What if there is no such thing as *the* American way of death? After all, the bewildering variety of religious and ethnic groups in America should make it impossible to identify a single template as *the* American way of death. Surely, anthropologists with their penchant for cultural distinctiveness are capable of dispelling too homogenous a picture of American mortuary practices.

In *Celebrations of Death,* one of the most reputable cross-cultural treatments of death rites, Richard Huntington and Peter Metcalf complain about the lack of American data; there are richer, more plentiful descriptions of, say, Indonesian death rites than of American ones.[252] American death ways, they claim, are homogeneous. In view of the large population, as well as the ethnic and religious diversity of the United States, one would expect the range of funerary options to be great, but in fact, they argue, the range is small. From coast to coast, the funerary pattern is uniform. Predictably, it has three steps: embalming, display, and burial. A person dies in the hospital. The body is rapidly removed to the funeral parlor, where it is embalmed (even though embalming is not a legal requirement). After it is publicly viewed or visited, the body is buried.[253]

In the American way of death, the most important of the three phases is that of the wake, the ceremonial viewing of the craft of professional death workers.[254] Compared with other peoples, say Huntington and Metcalf, Americans have a pronounced tendency not to confront mortality. The primary expression of American avoidance is extensive embalming, which is nowhere else in the world practiced with the intensity that it is in the United States.

The apparent uniformity of American mortuary practice and the removal of death rites from the public eye make it hard to identify a coherent set of beliefs that undergird the rites. Americans show a pronounced vagueness of belief, an "indeterminate ideology."[255] Americans, despite their predominantly Christian upbringing, are unsure what they believe about death and life after death.

Huntington and Metcalf find in American mortuary culture several ironic reversals, if not contradictions. One is that in a country whose rhetoric emphasizes the family, little of the dying process actually occurs at home. Another is that a nation that so rigorously avoids contemplating death would let funerals hold a privileged place in its system of civil ceremonies.[256] A third irony is that a society stressing individual achievement prescribes so passive a role for the dying person. Funeral directors and doctors, both highly organized groups, are the primary actors in the dying process. Dying people are objects, not subjects, of action. Clergy, kin, and the dying play bit parts. "In the Middle Ages men and women made themselves masters of their own deaths. In America, the archetypal land of enterprise, self-made men are reduced to puppets."[257]

Huntington and Metcalf's summary of the American mortuary sequence is revealing for what it excludes: the funeral rite itself. Like Kastenbaum's portrait, their depiction excludes the obvious, the service at

the local synagogue, temple, or church and the meal that often follows it. Even though the two scholars discuss the informal and unwritten codes of decorum that dictate who should be called first after a death, when to visit a bereaved family, and how to approach a corpse on display, they omit the most obviously and explicitly ritualized actions, those of the funeral itself. Such an oversight would be unimaginable if these social scientists had been reporting on a society other than their own. They do not explain their omission, perhaps do not even notice it.

The omission of the funeral liturgy is consonant with the assertion that American attitudes toward death are not shaped primarily by religious institutions, that is, by organized, denominational religion. The uniformity of American mortuary practices, say Huntington and Metcalf, is the result of the power and omnipresence of American civil religion.[258] By "civil religion" the two writers do not mean only Fourth of July celebrations or the religious rhetoric that laces inaugural ceremonies and state-of-the-nation addresses. Civil religion also includes American "faith" in medicine, the media, and the professions, especially funeral directing. American civil religion is death centered, even though it includes Christmas, Thanksgiving, and other holidays not focused on death. This civil religion has no proper name, so the "American way" will have to do. But this no-name religious complex has actual rites. Huntington and Metcalf present two specific examples of death rites in American civil religion: the funerals of Presidents Washington and Lincoln.

Even though I do not consider American death practices to be as uniform as Huntington and Metcalf claim, or as exclusively linked to the deaths of politicians as they imply, I agree that death rites in the United States are not contained or controlled solely by American religious institutions. In my view American funeral rites arise from the confluence of public civil ritual, religious death liturgies, and the embalming procedures of professional funeral directors. But a historical perspective is necessary if we are to understand this configuration.

Dead, He Presides Over Us

In *The Sacred Remains* Gary Laderman offers a historical perspective on the American way of death. He subtitles his book *American Attitudes Toward Death, 1799–1883,* but the book is really about northeastern, white Protestant attitudes. The dates of the subtitle are revealing: 1799 is the date of George Washington's funeral, 1883 of the second annual meeting of the Funeral Directors' National Association. Laderman tells what transpired between Washington's funeral and that of Abraham Lincoln, in 1865, as a way of explaining how embalming became an American "article of faith."[259]

Like Huntington and Metcalf, Laderman considers embalming and gazing ceremonially at the "restored" corpse the centerpiece of American death ways. As a historian of American religions, his question is, How did embalming and "viewing," or "visitation," come to be the dominant American practice? His answer is complex, as any good historical answer must be. It hinges on the convergence of several factors. The two central ones were the problem of disposing of the Civil War dead and the effect of Abraham Lincoln's death rites.

American Puritanism was heavily invested in contemplating death. In sermons the horrors of bodily decay—worms, rottenness, and putrefaction—were reminders of the reality of sin.[260] Actual corpses, in contrast to homiletically imagined ones, were buried quickly with little ceremony. The Puritan emphasis was not on the deceased or the memories of survivors but on the actions of God.

However, by the nineteenth century, Puritan theology, with its austere, sometimes harsh, attitude toward death, was giving way to a more romantic, sentimental one preoccupied with imagining "beautiful" deaths. Death was no longer a punishment for sin but a natural event. This newer theology emphasized the feelings of mourners, remembrance of the dead, and spiritual bliss in the next world.[261]

The deathbed scene, an emotional spectacle, assumed center stage, at least in the popular literary imagination. The proper homiletical aim was no longer that of frightening congregations into embracing salvation but that of consoling people. There arose a consolation literature, written largely by women with the support of liberal male ministers and replete with inspiring death stories. Such narratives constituted a new way of caring for the dead, one less overtly ritualistic and more imaginative or literary. However literary, this sensibility had its ritual moments, though, for instance, in the giving and taking of locks of hair from the deceased's head.

During the pre–Civil War period the northeastern Protestant way of death had three phases: the preparation of the body, transportation of it to the site, and burial. But like most tripartite summaries of rites of passage, this one is an oversimplification. Laderman's account actually implies other phases.[262] For instance, he describes a stopover at the church

during the procession to the grave site, as well as a deathbed scene in which the dying person was surrounded by family, friends, and neighbors. The scene often involved an inquiry into the dying person's physical conditions and spiritual readiness.

Before the Civil War, death in the white Protestant northeastern United States typically occurred in the home, so the body was prepared there. It was laid out, washed, dressed in a winding sheet or sack, and put in a coffin, usually by women. Local cabinet makers or carpenters took measurements and built the pine coffin. Family and friends kept a vigil over the deceased for one or two nights—partly to ensure that the corpse was, in fact, dead and also to protect the body from being stolen, used for anatomical dissection, or otherwise treated with disrespect. Where ice was available, chunks were placed beneath the body to slow decomposition.

The funeral procession led from the home to the cemetery. It was marked by prayers at the beginning, then by a sermon at a church or meeting house on the way. Clergy were common but not essential. At the stopover, the larger community joined the primary mourners. Sometimes participants were afforded an opportunity to view the corpse. Afterward, the procession, now more ritually elaborate, continued. At the grave site, the body was either interred or entombed, the latter being mainly an upper-class option. For most families neither cremation nor embalming was conceivable. The final act of burial was accompanied by prayers and discourses briefer than those offered at the stopover.

Before the Civil War, urbanization was already precipitating changes in mortuary practice. Fewer people were being buried on their farms. An increasingly mobile population could not assume that their descendants would live on the premises and thus be able to tend their graves. The city was not a good place for burial either. With city space at a premium, and with growing fear that decaying corpses might spread disease, cities became less hospitable to the dead. The so-called rural cemetery movement emerged, advocating the establishment of space for the dead on the outskirts of urban areas rather than in churchyards. Suburbia originated as a way of distancing the dead from the living.

The dead were being distanced metaphorically as well as literally. The medical profession was young, attempting to establish itself as scientific. Anatomical dissection was crucial to its future. For research purposes it required cadavers. But first, says Laderman, the self had to be conceptually disaffiliated from the body, leaving it a mere corpse, an object. There was much Christian resistance to objectifying the body in this way. It was the temple and image of God, therefore difficult to divest of religious significance. There was also the matter of the doctrine of the resurrection of the body; God alone should reconstitute the dead body. Consequently, it took time to render the dead body theologically meaningless. It also required the Civil War to produce a surplus of corpses and thus disrupt the usual funerary routine.

Eventually, Christian theology and the new medical science succeeded in stripping the human body of its religious meaning. The body became "only" the body, mere remains, so its fate had no effect on the destiny of the soul. Then, and only then, did it seem natural for the body to be cut open or to reside in a grave that no family member tended.

The carnage of the Civil War was a national trauma in which one out of sixteen white northern males died.[263] The usual funeral—death at home surrounded by loved ones, a stately procession, burial in a marked grave—was no longer possible for many young men. Bodies were left unburied by the enemy, or they were heaped into poorly marked mass graves. A few corpses were mutilated; trophies were taken. Baby rattles made from enemy bones were sent home; skulls became drinking cups.

The horror of a civil war was great enough, but it was compounded by the absence of the dead from funerals. Some families went to look for the bodies of kin, or they paid others to retrieve them. When bodies were found, how might they be transported home for a decent burial?

Previously, embalming had been a repulsive notion to Christians; its purview had been strictly medical, a means of preserving corpses for dissection. But now, embalming came to be regarded as a practical necessity for transporting the war dead across great stretches of time and space.

This necessity was supported by a powerful example. When President Abraham Lincoln was killed, a decision of major ritual importance was made: to embalm him, put him on a train, and let citizens greet their dead president on the long journey from Washington, D.C., to Springfield, Illinois, his home. The Civil War, over which he had presided, and his assassination, which traumatized the national psyche, required desperate measures. There was no gentle death at home, no washing by his wife Mary Todd, rather, embalmers, professionals, prepared him in quite another way. They sawed off the top of his head, performed an autopsy, and removed not only the bullet but the brain itself. They flushed the blood from the man's veins, replacing it with embalming fluid.

Reduced from a man to a puppet, Lincoln was nevertheless dramatically elevated into something more than a man. He was "sacredly preserved" and in this state became the "father of his country." As Laderman wryly puts it, Lincoln hollowed became Lincoln hallowed.[264] The president's paraded body was deified, a source of healing for a wounded nation (even though it began decomposing and had to be repaired on the journey). The train trip, much longer than the usual procession to the cemetery, was so successful that within a few years embalming had become desirable, *the* preferred, the *American,* way of death.

Laderman argues that the crux of the transition to embalming was short, concentrated into the five years of the war that culminated in Lincoln's death.[265] In a brief time, public attitudes shifted from revulsion and disgust to sentimental acceptance of embalming. Lincoln's death journey was a watershed, after which dissection and embalming lost the power to provoke public moral indignation.

Lincoln's death contrasted considerably with George Washington's in 1799. Washington had been buried on the grounds of his home. His body belonged not to the nation but to his family. His corpse was absent from the many ceremonies that marked his demise, and his survival of death was largely portrayed in heroic narrative and mythic art. Ritually, his presence and absence were simultaneously symbolized by a riderless horse, but he was never a preserved corpse presiding over the nation from a chair.

By 1882 entrepreneurial death workers had organized themselves into the National Funeral Directors' Association. They began lobbying and publicizing to convince consumers that embalming was essential, not just for lab use in anatomical studies but for "home" use. Eventually, their place of work would become a funeral "home" and embalming a ceremonial way of creating a "loving memory." Embalming would not have been saleable for long if its only value had been that of preserving medical cadavers or transporting war-torn corpses from the South.

Embalming would not have become widespread if bodies had retained their value to organized religion. Churches had to be willing to abandon the body as a site of religious meaning if funeral homes were to exercise squatters' rights over them. The doctrine of the resurrection of the body had to be displaced by an exclusive interest in the fate of the soul. But if bodies lost *all* their sentimental value, people would not pay to make their loved ones viewable.

At its outset funeral directing required a delicate balancing act. Quasi-religious ritual concerns had to be played off quasi-scientific and esthetic ones. "Undertakers," priests of a peculiar sort, became "funeral directors." They had to become, and to sell themselves as, experts. Whereas American communities had previously entertained a mild curiosity about viewing dead bodies, now the public would learn to desire a final, almost pornographic gaze at a body in repose, a body not decaying or in pain but "at rest," "natural."

In addition, embalming promised to curb the much publicized, often exaggerated danger to public health posed by decaying corpses. Public desire and salesmanship, rather than theological correctness or ritual sensitivity, colluded to shape the American way of death. Intimacy with the bare bones and naked reality of death was no longer the American way.

Mortuary photography, like embalming or wedding photography, might have become a ritual necessity. Photographs of Civil War battlefield scenes, before the dead were removed, became popular items. Some of these scenes, replete with close-ups, were even staged. The worth of these photos was not mainly utilitarian, that of helping families identify their unlocated dead, but of satisfying the curiosity of a people increasingly removed from their dead. The real money was in casket making and embalming. As a way of preserving memories, embalmed corpses were more successful than photographs of them. Photographing the violently killed continues in photojournalism, but photographing those embalmed and "at rest" in funeral "homes" has largely disappeared.

The picture Laderman paints is a powerful one but, I believe, too enamored of wars and heroically mythologized presidents. It is striking that he does not examine specific funerals rites other than those of presidents. The ordinary ones transpiring in either religious sanctuaries or funeral homes hardly appear in his account. Of course, Laderman is studying American *attitudes* toward death, not American death *practices*. But rites reveal attitudes, and rites often leave substantial traces, for instance, in ritual texts that instruct people on what to do and say. Historical data on American funeral rites do exist, and Laderman largely ignores them as a source of understanding American attitudes toward death. Like Kastenbaum's important textbook on death or

Huntington and Metcalf's reputable cross-cultural study of death, Laderman's history marginalizes death rites and overemphasizes death attitudes.

The best we can do, therefore, is to conclude that we know much about the American way of death, but little about American funerals. We know that Americans have explicit death rites in a way that they do not have explicit birth rites. We know that during some periods in American history, death rites have been more elaborate than in others. We know it is not true that Americans have gone from much death ritual to little. The shift from the Puritan era to the present is in the direction of increasing, not decreasing, ritual. It is also clear that the American dead, once in the hands of women, are now largely in the hands of professionals, mostly men. Also, it is obvious that neither families nor religions play the role they once played in caring for the dying and the dead, their place having been taken by medical professionals and mortuary institutions. It seems fairly certain that Americans, who once stared death more or less hard in the face, began in the nineteenth century to sentimentalize it, cover it up, distance themselves from it, and then in the twentieth century to become intensely interested in reading about it.

There is a pronounced tendency in the research to claim or imply that the American way of death has little to do with religion, ethnicity, or region. African American ways, Jewish ways, Sikh ways, the New Orleans way, the Hispanic Catholic way—all such configurations fade into mere background for scholars who write on the topic. I have little doubt that the professionalization and medicalization of death have influenced, and in some cases, displaced other practices. But I also have no doubt that death rites in North America are poorly understood because they are so seldom explicitly and carefully studied. If we attempt either a global or an American perspective, we should regularly ground ourselves in the local, stubbornly particular stuff of actual deaths and their attendant ceremonies. The problem with concentrating on *attitudes* toward death or the funerals of *presidents* is that we seldom descend from such altitudes to ground level, where most people die. At ground level, there is, I believe, both more tradition and more experimentation than standard portraits of the American way of death would lead us to believe.

The dearth of detailed ethnographic studies on death rites in North America prevents us from drawing reliable conclusions about funerals. However, the research does support a broad-stroke portrait of contrast-

Simple or minimal rites	Elaborate or protracted rites
Single disposal of the corpse	Double or multiple disposal patterns, e.g., burial/exhumation/reburial
Emphasis on the expression of personal feeling	Emphasis on the adherence to social or ritual form
Optional or minimal mourning	Required or protracted mourning
Minimum philosophical or mythological attention paid to the afterlife	Elaborate conceptions of life after death
Minimal interaction with the dead	Active veneration of ancestors
Little fear of the dead displayed; death not regarded as polluting	Considerable fear of the dead displayed; death regarded as polluting
Death avoided; hands-off approach	Death embraced; hands-on approach
Emphasis on the preservation of the remains	Emphasis on the destruction of the remains
Ways of dying not fully or clearly distinguished	Clearly identified "good" and "bad" deaths
Death rites that "level," de-emphasizing hierarchy and status	Death rites that emphasize hierarchy and status

Figure 3. Polarities in Responding to Death and the Dead

ing attitudes. Figure 3 summarizes the major contrasts in mortuary practice found in the world's religions and cultures. These are not all the alternatives, only major ones that distinguish one tradition or group from another.[266] In general, the left column more nearly summarizes mainstream North American practices. The usual rites are relatively simple; they do not take days or years to complete. We bury once and would consider exhumation a horror unless it were for forensic purposes. As a society, we emphasize the expression of personal feelings but not the public expression or sadness or grief. So, although we are suspicious of formalities, our rites, in fact, emphasize form as well as feeling. We do not require mourning, although the absence of tears can be taken to signal denial in someone especially close to the dead person. We pay only a little attention to myths and ideas of the afterlife. We interact minimally with the dead, having buried them in places removed from centers of commerce and residence. Too much speaking of or with the dead is considered deviant. Although we fear death and it is considered impolite or morbid to talk much about it, we have little fear of the dead. Although we do not think of death or the dead as polluting, we nevertheless have

a hands-off approach to death and hire professionals to handle the dead for us. Although we are uncertain about the fate of the dead, we place strong emphasis on the preservation of their remains. Informally, we distinguish kinds of death, for example, the timely from the untimely, the suicide from the nonsuicide. A certain amount of display separates rich from poor or lower-class from upper-class funerals, but too much display or emphasis on status evokes gossip or criticism.

It is dangerous to summarize what we do, not only because there is great variation in who "we" are but also because what we "do" is not necessarily what we did or will do. Death rites can change. Ritual is reputed to be the most conservative cultural activity in which humans engage. Death rites are said to be the most conservative kind of ritual, the most stubbornly resistant to innovation. In contrast with funerals, European American weddings are sites of experimentation. Somehow, ritual creativity seems more consonant with the promise of marital bliss than with the somber duty of laying our dead to rest.

It not easy for people to marshal the energy to reinvent rites when they are racked with grief. But we have seen how American funerary practice did, in fact, turn on a dime (or maybe a silver dollar—the death, after all, was Lincoln's), so mortuary change is not impossible. Despite their reputation, funeral rites, in North America and elsewhere, have histories, and they are marked by the kind of substantive changes that require significant reimagining.

Before 1949 China had a rich history of death rites and ancestor veneration, but after that date, in the hands of the Communist Party, Chinese death rites underwent a major revolution. The cautious reinstatement of a few traditional practices in more recent times has not negated or reversed that ritual revolution.

North American mortuary history, too, continues. It did not end with, or even culminate in, the introduction of embalming and professional death workers. Two of the most visible mortuary innovations in recent decades, the growing acceptance of cremation and the establishment of hospices (places dedicated to caring for the dying), are evidence that death rites, like other rites of passage, evolve.

The Western debate over cremation lasted for almost two millennia. During that time Christian burial gradually displaced cremation, the usual pagan practice. By the late eighth century, Charlemagne made cremation a capital offense. Burial became *the* Christian, thus *the* European, way of disposing of the dead. By the seventeenth century, however, the wheel of history was turning again. French republicans and other Europeans began promoting cremation as the more enlightened way to dispose of bodies. Within the last half century we have witnessed the doubling of the life expectancy of middle-class North Americans. This fact and the crisis of overpopulation have helped cremation gain ground despite the long history of religious strictures against it.

In 1963, the year of Jessica Mitford's attack on the American way of death, the Roman Catholic Church, in its *Instruction with Regard to the Cremation of Bodies,* relaxed its absolute ban on cremation (although it still prefers burial). For centuries the change was slow, but in the mid twentieth century the pace became rapid. By 1997 the cremation rate in England was over 70 percent. In the United States, in 1995, it was 21 percent and still rising.[267] In China, in 1983, 90 percent of city dwellers and 15 percent of rural people were being cremated, resulting in a national average of 30 percent.[268] The near-global shift from burial to cremation, as simple as it may seem, is having an enormous impact. Cremating rather than burying transforms land use, changes the employment demands for funerary specialists, and precipitates fundamental shifts in one's image of the self, family, and afterlife. So it is possible, whether by legislation, imagination, or some combination of both, for death rites to be reimagined, reconfigured, or reinvented.

Mortal Acts

Social, economic, and political forces only partly account for shifts in death ways. Rites also emerge or decline when a people's way of imagining a passage changes. How death is imagined in America depends on who is doing the imagining. For instance, funeral directors paint death as a kind of restful sleep. Filmmakers portray it as a dramatic event replete with guns; death is delivered to "others" who deserve it. Clergy mythologize death as a preliminary step in a long journey, rendering death not so much a cessation as a transformation.

More recently, therapists have tendered other ways of reimagining death. Just as initiatory fantasy is driven by images from movies, novels, and stories, just as weddings are pressured by fashion-magazine imagery, so funerals are conditioned by doctrines, myths, and images of life after death. Death rites are occasions for performing fundamental cosmological tenets—for asserting what a self is, counting out what a life is worth, speculating about our origins as a people, guessing where

we are going, declaring who we are. We do not have the whole view of things until a life is finished, so when we bury or burn our dead, we often do so in a setting adorned with ultimate postulates.

An ultimate conviction of many Americans is that individuals are sacred. Accordingly, Americans continue to individualize and privatize death and its ritualization. *Mortal Acts: Eighteen Empowering Rituals for Confronting Death,* a book by David Feinstein and Peg Elliott Mayo, is based on a guided-imagery technique in which a reader guides a relaxed listener's imagining. This approach does not depend on templates for designing your own funeral rites but rather on exercises for coming to terms with your mortality. The intent is preparatory rather than funerary. Feinstein and Mayo refer to their exercises as "therapeutically informed rituals" and "internal rites of passage." When the authors talk about "postmortem life," they are not referring to life after death but to living after imaginative and emotional acknowledgment of one's own mortality.

Feinstein and Mayo are convinced that Americans are no longer well prepared to meet death. What these two guides offer are not cultural or religious alternatives but personal growth–oriented ones. American culture, they assert, no longer provides a way of dying, so individuals must now find it for themselves. They claim that their "personal rituals" are also universal.[269] Their treatment implies that cultural differences regarding the great themes—birth, maturation, bonding, decline, and death—are insignificant in comparison to the commonalities. This tactic, which equates the personal with the universal, thus bypassing the local, ethnic, and national, is a familiar American New Age conceptual move.

The aim of the book's eighteen "mortal acts" is therapeutic. It is to facilitate self-examination of one's "death-denial system" and to transcend it. In an early guided-imagery exercise, Feinstein and May direct us:

> When you were a child, you had many fears about death. You may remember the terror of a nightmare or of a monster that you imagined had crawled under your bed or into your closet. . . . Pull yourself back to being very young and feeling your fear. (Pause.) Feel yourself moving back in time now to this early experience of your fear of death. (Pause.) Where are you? What is occurring? Who is there? (30-second pause.) You are about to find a symbol of these fears. Focus on a sensation in your body that relates to this early experience. . . . This symbol represents your fear of death, and you will be able to remember it so you can, in a little while, draw it on your shield.[270]

[In a later exercise, having concretized our fears, we have now faced, incorporated, and overcome them. We are at peace. Our guides encourage us with the power of positive thinking:] From this heightened awareness, your appreciation of life is amplified, along with a sense of peace about death. You can feel yourself, now, moving forward in time. You are moving forward to the occasion of your own death. In this death scenario, precisely the atmosphere you would desire for your last moments on earth already exists. (Pause.) As you survey the situation, you can vividly see or sense yourself in the scene, along with any others who are there. People are relating to you and to one another just as you might wish. (Pause.) You are about to imagine a ceremony or ritual to maintain or heighten the mood. It may be performed by you alone or with others. (Pause.) In the following silence, you will experience the entire ceremony. (45-second pause.) As the moment of death approaches, you begin to recite your death chant. Start to use it now and continue it as you imagine your consciousness moving out of your body. In your imagination, allow your death chant to be the bridge as you leave your body and come into a space from which you will be able to view your funeral or memorial service. . . . Again, the atmosphere is exactly as you would like it to be.[271]

Just as we would like it to be. . . . This vision is a far cry from the Puritan hell, a place where one would *not* have wanted to be. No longer sinners in the hands of an angry God dangling our feet over the fires of hell, Americans can now soar on the power of positive thinking, taking comfort from their spirit guides and death chants.

Funeral rites can take days, months, or even years to prepare, execute, and finish, yet here we are given a forty-five-second pause. Perhaps other people's imaginations are more concise than mine. Or maybe the authors have no experience with, or faith in, rites that require heavy outlays of time. I am not an advocate of the Puritan vision, but if I had to choose, I would opt for it. For the Puritan vision had courage and integrity. This one is not only a far cry from the realities of hell but also from those of dying. Placed beside the Mexican and Brazilian death scenes described earlier, this kind of fantasy is self-indulgent, luring us into the future with positive, personal, mood-enhancing armchair fantasy.

Do the exercises work? Perhaps some people are comforted by them, but the emphasis is on "comfort." I am disturbed not by the idea of imagining death or personifying someone's fears of it but by the lack of irony and humor as well as by the utter failure to recognize how ethnocentric these supposedly universal ritual exercises are. The images are stereotypical and the plots predictable. If in reimagining death, we domesticate it, we have failed.

Cyber Ritual and Death on the Web

All the major rites of passage are making their appearance on the World Wide Web, but none with such persistence and verve as death. There is much talk these days about "cyber ritual" and the revolution it promises to precipitate in our conception and practice of ritual. Aficionados insist that cyber ritual is real, not merely imaginary, ritual. Virtual reality is its own kind of reality.

The question is not *whether* cyber ritual is real, but *how* it is real. How does it work, and what does it do that is different from "normal," embodied ritual? Just as there are similarities and differences between the real and imagined, there are continuities and discontinuities between virtual and embodied rites. Virtual ritualizing is not completely disembodied: Someone sits at a keyboard; someone else stares at a monitor.

Actually embodied rites are not without their virtual dimensions. Some rites, when they are not being enacted, have what we might call a virtual, or latent, reality; a ritual text is, we might say, a virtual rite. Virtual reality is not the invention of computers but of ritual, literature, art, and theater. These are the original multimedia that enabled the appearance of gods, demons, and other hyperrealities. As-if, or subjunctive, realities are nothing new to ritual. What is new is the solitude and anonymity with which cyber ritualizing can be enacted. A couple can now be married without even being in each other's presence.

A prominent feature of death ritualizing on the Web is imagery. What meets the Web surfer are first of all the images—not the words or enactments. Even the words are images.

Behind the images are the persons, places, companies, and groups that create and maintain them. However much we may celebrate virtuality, reveling in images for their own sake, one is inevitably forced to ask what is behind them. Are their signatures and facts to be trusted? Will their downloads infect my files? How might I contact the designers and writers? It is the net-linked computer's promise of a person coupled with the absence of a face and tone of voice that gives cyber ritualizing its peculiar quality.

The cyber world is as important for the "places" you can "visit" as it is for the things it enables you to "do." In this sense, it is a better substitute for a cemetery than for a funeral. The World Wide Cemetery, established in 1995, contains "monuments," entries concerning persons who have died.[272] They are listed alphabetically as well as by region and year of death. Many include not only the usual facts of death (birth and death dates, name, and so on) but also photos, eulogies, and stories. Each "monument" costs between ten and twenty dollars, depending on what you want it to contain.

"Flowers" are notes of consolation left by "visitors." Flowers can be left in response to the dead in general, to specific dead people, or, more often, to their survivors. The site also has "memorials," deaths grouped into categories: World War II, Vietnam, AIDS, cancer, organ donation, and suicide.

The World Wide Cemetery site bills itself as a permanent marker and boasts that unlike real cemeteries it is accessible from anywhere in the world. Not only is it eternal and virtually omnipresent but it does not weather with time. At least that is what the site writers tell us. Writers of the World Wide Cemetery's statements are enthusiastic about the possibility of creating hypertext links among family members. They imply that using these links constitutes a new, virtual form of kinship. Furthermore, the cemetery is open to all faiths; there are no spatial markers of religious discrimination here.

On the same page as the claim to permanence, the site's managers solicit sponsors to help keep the site alive. This site, then, like most others on the Web, has about it both the illusion of permanence and a distinct feeling of ephemerality.

Do the World Wide Cemetery and sites like it help people ritualize death? What are the ritualistic implications of virtual-passage sites? There are testimonials illustrating that the World Wide Cemetery can have real effects. On March 7, 1998, one person wrote, "I surfed into this site just for a curiosity, but now I feel a great commotion. I remember all my deads, and I ask my grandpas and granma to watch over me. . . . "

Another person posted this in December 1996: "This site is strangely moving . . . that one of the unanticipated uses for electronic communications has turned out to be a digital columbarium is, to me, quintessentially human."

Another, identified only by a numerical code, left on Sunday, June 18, 1995, a simple note: "A bouquet of yellow roses, always fresh."

It is, I suppose, no more bizarre that we should remember our "deads" while searching the Web than remembering them while wearing masks or reading tombstones. Electronic roses, despite their lack of fragrance, are perhaps no stranger than the plastic or stone ones left in Mexican cemeteries or etched into medieval edifices.

Even so, the further disembodying of death that is possible on the Internet is, especially in a society already distanced from death, potentially dangerous. Virtual, like fictional, realities always work both ways, as substitutes, on the one hand, and as feeders back into lived life on the other. In my view we already have too many ritual substitutes. So the question is, What ways of reimagining death lead us closer to, rather than farther away from, a death that not only entertains but stings?

Reinventing Death Rites

It would be easy to make the World Wide Cemetery look silly and superficial by setting it alongside the death of Dona Amor's mother or Bill Myers's brother. So I will resist the temptation and turn instead to a funeral with a significant virtual dimension. Media, with their as-if qualities, are here to stay, and the ritually minded will not be able to avoid them.

When Princess Diana died in 1997, a news commentator referred to it as the funeral of the century, and a colleague labeled it the best example she knew of a truly postmodern ritual. It not only overshadowed Mother Teresa's last rites, it also successfully undermined traditional rules of decorum that governed English royal ceremony.

The day of the funeral my daughter asked, "Dad, did you know her?"

"No, not really," I replied.

"I don't mean did you *know* her. I mean did you know much about Princess Diana before she died?"

"Only a little. I saw her on TV occasionally."

"Well, I didn't know who she was or anything about her until last night and today, but, still, it makes me sad, really, really sad," she confided earnestly.

"She was a princess. I guess that would be enough to make a nine-year-old girl sad," I said.

Not about to let me explain away her feelings, much less with a stereotype she's already learned to criticize, Caillcah set me straight:

"No, I don't mean that kind of stuff. I mean all these things they are saying and doing make me sad." Then she added, almost as an afterthought, "And that she died, of course."

Sunday morning, the day after the funeral, Michael Enright of CBC Radio pronounced in his sagely manner, "We kept distracting ourselves with ceremony."

Enright was half right. Funerals do distract. In the midst of chaos and loss, they construct a countervailing order—in the British case, one marked by a slow and stately rhythm. After a high-speed chase through the streets of Paris, what could be more comforting than a slow-speed walk through the streets of London behind a gun carriage accompanied by Welch guards? Funerary decorum is hard to break in public and difficult to criticize openly. The distraction it provided was tranquilizing. Like any rite of passage, a funeral erects a safety net, allowing participants to fall—but only so far. After that, the net of ceremony yanks us up, just short of hitting hard ground at too high a velocity. Perhaps it is true that Diana's funeral rite, cobbled together—it was part tradition, part invention, part adaptation—helped to anesthetize grief and pain.

But Enright was also wrong. What the princess's funeral did for my daughter and for millions of others who knew little of the person Diana was not only to distract them from pain but also to take them to a place where it hurt, even if it did not need to, even if they never knew the woman.

Among television and radio commentators, it sometimes seemed as if there were only two possibilities: Either you cried for Diana or you distracted yourself. If you distracted yourself, you had two options. You could wrap yourself in the soft blanket of the funeral, or you could put your face to the hard wall of reality by pondering Diana as a collectively imagined media creation. We all know—at least we were told repeatedly—that Diana was a creation of the media, that she used the media and the media used her. So it was obvious that not only did Diana make us weep, but that the media made us weep as well. Without TV sets, fewer would have cried.

On the day of, and day after, the funeral you could not buy blank videotapes in Westmount, Quebec, where we were living for the year. People in this English-speaking enclave on the French-speaking island of Montreal were at home. Not just watching, they were taping so they could relive the funeral until their grief was fully spent. I know of people who've watched the funeral half a dozen times now. By making videotapes, not only could they take a souvenir of a historic event, witness a spectacle, peek at royalty and aristocracy stumbling in public, they could also wail—privately, with the public. Diana was not necessarily the only object of our keening, but she—rather, her funeral—was its occasion.

The afternoon of Diana's funeral my son, Bryn, and I walked through a large department store in downtown Montreal. An elderly bag lady had come in from the street. She sat on the floor eclipsed by three large-screen television sets and her array of plastic grocery bags. From Montreal, she was leaning into Westminster Cathedral, her face flushed, her eyes swollen, her cheeks wet with weeping.

For a while there were two camps. In the camp of the softhearted, we cried shamelessly in our innocence, British or not. The tears, I believe, were genuine, heartfelt. They needed no justification. They made perfect sense of Diana's physical beauty, regal bearing, candid observations, premature death, and obvious humanity toward those less fortunate than herself. She was saintly, or if not that, then a warm human being and a good mother. So why shouldn't we weep at such a loss?

In the camp of the hard-hearted, where critics huddled around their television sets, Diana was an empty cipher, the algebraic X, a mirror devoid of content. Never really knowable, because she had no real self, this Diana was a creation of the media. Bereft of cameras, she was nothing—less than a squashed pumpkin at midnight lying on a cobblestone road leading away from the ballroom. Why weep any more at this loss than at the loss of any other human being? What kind of mourning is virtual mourning anyway?—just another form of sentimentality, not at all like real grief. "Sad she died," the cynical said, "but that's life; no TV, no tears."

The way of innocence would have us pretend there was no camera between Diana and us. The calculatedly innocent would require that we ignore the obvious: Most of us hardly knew the woman or cared about her life before the funeral. The way of naïveté would make Diana a saint and her death a revelation, the appearance of absolute being.

The way of cynicism would make of Diana's life, death, and funeral a show, or worse, a sham. This way tempts one to forget there was a real human life on the other side of the cameras and to believe that the emotions of those on this side of the cameras do not matter.

The skeptical eye, I remind myself, would do the same to my daughter's life if the cameras were turned on her. So do we really have to choose between theatrical sham and revelatory purity? Only if we forget the ceremony; it mediated between the extremes. That Diana's funeral was a media event no one doubts. But it was also a ritual event, and this utterly basic fact went almost unrecognized and certainly unanalyzed.

During the televised funeral proceedings, the network anchors were accompanied by specialists in British politics, royalty, and society but no one who knew much about ceremony. The commentary on the ceremony was banal and uninformed, whereas the analysis of media performance was reflective and debate filled. In contrast to media analysis, the analysis of ritual was nonexistent. Commentary took the form: "And now here is so-and-so, the duke of . . . " "There go the guards." "This is Westminster Cathedral where such-and-such is buried." What little discussion there was of the ceremony took the form of an inquiry about which actions and objects and places were typical of a royal funeral and which were innovative. But even this kind of analysis was sporadic and piecemeal. Recognition of the elements of the ceremony, explanation of the ways rites work (or fail to)—this kind of analysis was utterly missing. After the ceremony, commentators dwelled on the content of Diana's brother's eulogy and the emotional impact of Elton John's "Candle in the Wind." The commentary was, functionally speaking, "protestant." Word and song were treated as the real stuff; the rest, the gestures, the movements, was window dressing—great to shoot but not worth analyzing.

In one sense it was a relief to have so much dead air time; silence is rare on television. The silence arose mostly from ignorance, not from reverence. Although it may not be appropriate to hear analysis *during* a funeral, afterward surely someone needs to think about the cadence of the walk, the tones of voice, the mediation of public and sacred space, the effect of dressing up and dressing down, the relationship between ceremonial traditions and spontaneous actions. For instance, what should we make of the fact that applause arose outside and rippled from the periphery through the doors of Westminster Cathedral, where, instead of being ignored, it was taken up by those most privy to the mortuary proceedings? No mere breach of decorum, applause, a performative gesture, overtook a liturgical one. Another kind of question that we should raise is, Where does the rite end? After the ceremony in Westminster Cathedral? After the private burial on an island? When the condolence registers are finally closed? When the last flower is laid at

the tunnel in Paris? Or when the last person weeps while watching a video rerun of the funeral?

Deaths do not make most of us cry unless we are closely related to the deceased. But perhaps it is good to mourn those we don't know. One of the reasons we human beings enact funeral rites is to train ourselves in the art of grieving. It is better to grieve than not, and some grieve with more facility than others. Grief is learned, thus taught, and funerals are one means of instruction. To say that grief is learned is to say that it is cultural. But saying that something is cultural doesn't mean that it isn't also biological, psychological, or spiritual. Some of us learn not to grieve or at least to minimize grieving. Some are taught not to display grief (even to themselves). It is a widespread ritual, therefore cultural, convention for men to control or suppress grief and for women to have the cultural obligation or freedom to display it. None of this is to deny the reality of the human experience of grief. It is just to say that almost every physical activity from breathing to eating to defecating to weeping is choreographed. However natural (or supernatural) all these actions are, they are also canvases on which traditions put their stamp.

Did Diana's funeral work? If so, for whom? And how? What does it mean to say a funeral "works"? What are funerals supposed to do? The current, popular answer is that a funeral's job is to expedite grief. With what sounds like very Protestant rhetoric, we like to talk about "grief work." With the British weeping openly in the streets (a scene never witnessed by most of us before), Canadians, and even some nonroyalist Americans, crying in front of their TVs, you could say that Diana's funeral "worked." In fact, it worked better than expected. What we expected was the stiff upper lip, cold formality; what we got was weeping in the streets, anger at the queen and the media expressed inside Westminster Cathedral, and applause outside the cathedral. What we got was ritually framed social drama. With the help of television, the funeral was global, overshadowing even that of Mother Teresa, who was perhaps more deserving but less in need of a global funeral that somehow redeemed a troubled life.

However much poor ceremonies stifle grief, effective ones liberate us to the gift of tears—if not in public, then in private. Funerals help us find our grief, even if that grief is left over from some other death and our mourning for someone other than the deceased. Even if you didn't know the woman, even if you couldn't have cared less, it felt good to feel so bad watching Diana's funeral. It was good to grieve with the world, the one that includes our daughters and sons who pry us with questions when Old Death arrives. Princess Diana's funeral rite did not just distract people from pain, it conjured pain.

Because Diana was divorced and not quite a princess, elements of her death rite had to be invented. The ceremony was partly royal, partly not. The recasting and performance of a popular song by Elton John, the critical speech by Diana's brother, and the outbreak of applause all signaled some remarkable ceremonial revisions and inventions. In addition, the worldwide broadcast of the ceremony led not only to its global extension but also to its reconstruction. Literally, before our very eyes, a funerary tradition was being reinvented.

A major question that bedevils death rites more than the other passages is that of belief. *Chouji,* the Japanese practice of addressing the dead (illustrated in the story told by Victor Hori), may or may not imply a belief in the continuing presence of the dead. But the death rites of rural Greeks and Chinese, as well as of Brazilian Catholics like Dona Amor, assume a belief in life after death or at least a conventional compliance with the notion that the dead persist, either as venerated ancestors or as vaguely troubling shades. Even Reggie Ray, in telling about the performance of *sukhavati* to put to rest the restless spirit of a deceased girl, resists foreclosure on the belief question, since doing so would amount to a premature, "flat-land" pretension.

As the veneration of both Abraham Lincoln and Princess Diana illustrate, it is possible to participate in death rites and to commemorate the dead without necessarily implying belief in their metaphysical persistence. For ritual purposes it is enough that the dead persist in memory, imagination, or in the form of visual icons and that we approach them with empathy or respect. Belief, it seems, is not an absolute requirement.

In all likelihood Bill Myers, who shared his account of his brother's funeral, is a believer. But his story does not invoke articles of Baptist faith or depend on the acceptance of Protestant dogma. Whether or not there is "another side," and whether or not funerals are necessary for the dead to make it to that other side, the rites in Bill's story matter. Either they facilitate grief or they obstruct it. Whereas Reggie Ray's narrative suspended the question of belief, Bill Myers's story circumvented it. Ritual effectiveness does not depend on literal belief.

Several other attitudinal possibilities emerge from the descriptions and narratives we have considered. For example, Feinstein and Mayo, in the exercises from *Mortal Acts,* render death and the human con-

frontation with it in purely imaginative terms; the rites they offer are only "in the head." Another variation appears among Mexicans, some of whom greet death not only "beliefully" but playfully and ironically. A final example of alternative funerary attitudes: From Jessica Mitford's scathing attack in 1963 until the present no other rite of passage has been approached with a more critical attitude than the European American funeral. Ceremonial effectiveness is not undermined by sustained critique.

So the moment of passage that would seem to demand the most metaphysical credulity turns out to have generated the most interesting array of alternative ritual attitudes. People may participate in death rites not only feeling grief or expressing belief but also critically, ironically, playfully, imaginatively, pragmatically, or in a state of suspended disbelief.

Reinventing death rites, like reclaiming birth, requires not only experimenting with less conventional ritual attitudes but also a wrestling match with the institutions that control them. We are more fundamentally out of touch with the dead than with the newborn. At least the newborn, when carried home, swamp us with their utter tactility and ever-demanding presence. The dead, on the contrary, continue to recede, so there is urgency for us to lay hands upon them. The dead do not come home with us but are driven to the edge of town and laid to rest at a considerable remove from where we reside. Certainly, the dead should be laid to rest, and the bereaved deserve to be comforted, but the great haste with which we turn our backs on the deceased is one of our major ritual difficulties.

We are in dire need of doing hands-on work—at the very least, washing, dressing, and burying, perhaps also coffin building and grave tending. Otherwise, death itself becomes ethereal and abstract, prolonging grief and severing our felt connections with the earth in which they rest or with the sky in which they float as particles. As long as we pay funeral directors to shield us from the smells, touch, and sight of death, there is little hope that the so-called final passage will be any more than an exercise in decorum. If death rites are to become celebrations, there must be not only space and time for dwelling with the dying and the dead but also myths and images that support communication with the dead. I am not talking about seances, which are far too literal for most of us but about what we might call "subjunctive" communication: talking and eating with the dead *as if* they had presence and counsel to offer.

A truly reinvented funerary sensibility would require us to imagine the dead in a much more serious way than we do, and it would lead us to enact rites based on such imagining. In effect, we need a renewed mythologizing of death and the dead, one that does not require naive belief but depends on dramatic storytelling and bold, performed images of Old Death. I am no advocate of a women's cemetery culture like that of rural Greece, but we must overcome excessively pristine and falsely hopeful images of death. We need funerary, not cinematic, images as stark and compelling as that of Eleni's mother holding her daughter's exhumed skull or that of the lament in which the dead daughter is made to say of Haros (the death figure), "I hold him on my knees. / He rests against my chest. / If he is hungry, he eats from by body, / and if he is thirsty, he drinks from my two eyes."[273] We need graphic myths rooted in tactile rites and passionate engagement without the requirement of literal belief.

207. Boswell, *Marriage of Likeness,* 111.
208. Boswell, *Marriage of Likeness,* 178 ff.
209. Searle and Stevenson, *Documents of the Marriage Liturgy,* 239–51.
210. Ross-Macdonald, *Alternative Weddings,* v–vi.
211. See the materials posted at www.weddingcircle.com/ethnic.
212. *Sposa: The Magazine for the Discerning Bride* (spring/summer 1998).
213. Lalli and Dahl, "Ethnic Customs." See also McGrath and English, "Intergenerational Gift-Giving."
214. See Anderson and Foley, *Mighty Stories, Dangerous Rituals;* Anderson and Foley, "Wedding of Stories."
215. Butler, *Ceremonies of the Heart,* 55–69.
216. Crissman, *Death and Dying,* 84.
217. See the materials posted at vbiweb.champlain.edu/famsa/.
218. Langness, "Hysterical Psychosis."
219. The term was popularized in 1491 by William Caxton of Westminster; he published a little treatise called *Ars Moriendi, That Is to Say the Craft for to Die for the Health of Man's Soul.*
220. Blackman, *Graceful Exits,* 148.
221. In some strains of the Western theistic traditions (Judaism, Christianity, Islam), worship occasionally sounds a similar preparatory note.
222. Blackman, *Graceful Exits,* 42.
223. Nuland, *How We Die,* 244.
224. Nuland, *How We Die,* 257.
225. William H. Myers, personal communication, August 1997. Bill is a Baptist and a professor of New Testament and Black Church Studies.
226. Victor Hori, personal communication, August 1997. Born in Canada in 1944, Victor earned a Ph.D. in philosophy at Stanford University in 1976. From 1977 to 1990 he was a Rinzai Zen monk. Currently, he is a member of the Faculty of Religious Studies at McGill University in Montreal.
227. Lewis, *Death in the Sanchez Family,* x. The son was novelist Martin Nexo of Copenhagen.
228. The account that follows is based on Scheper-Hughes, *Death Without Weeping.*
229. Scheper-Hughes, *Death Without Weeping,* 253.
230. Scheper-Hughes, *Death Without Weeping,* 255–58.
231. The following account is based on Rawski, "Chinese Death Ritual," 26.
232. For the full text prescribing Chinese funerals, see Ebrey, *Chu Hsi's Family Rituals.*
233. This summary is based on Watson, "Chinese Funerary Rites."
234. Watson, *Mo Tzu,* 68.
235. Watson, *Mo Tzu,* 75.
236. Danforth, *Death Ritual,* 11–12.
237. Pseudonym for a village in Greek Macedonia. The names of all the participants are also pseudonymous.
238. Danforth, *Death Ritual,* 101–2.
239. Danforth, *Death Ritual,* 19–21.

240. This connection between the treatment of remains and the state of the soul is articulated in a theory developed by Hertz, *Death and the Right Hand.*
241. Danforth, *Death Ritual,* 129.
242. Danforth, *Death Ritual,* 129, 101. The kerchief is a strip of cloth used to tie up the lower jaw of a corpse.
243. Danforth, *Death Ritual,* 127.
244. Danforth, *Death Ritual,* 143.
245. Reginald A. Ray is a faculty member at Naropa Institute in Boulder, Colorado. He teaches Buddhist studies, specializing in the Buddhism of Tibet and India, and he is the author of the award-winning book *Buddhist Saints in India* (Oxford University Press, 1994).
246. Fort Worth Art Museum, *El Día de los Muertos,* 11.
247. Quoted in Monsivais, " 'Look Death, Don't Be Inhuman.' " Monsivais wryly complains that Octavio Paz codified a "vision of the internal and external tourism" that is "subject to the intensities of Kodak."
248. Lewis, *Death in the Sanchez Family,* 35–36.
249. Kastenbaum, *Death, Society, and Human Experience,* 59.
250. Kastenbaum, *Death, Society, and Human Experience,* 353.
251. In a personal communication of October 3, 1998, Kastenbaum wrote, "Students in my death classes and others who come by to see me almost never bring up the core death rites. Most often they do not feel a close connection with these rites and have responses to the entire funeral process that are more psychological than anything else. I don't think 'death educators' discourage discussion of funeral rites; other concerns and experiences seem to come up more often and more forcefully."
252. Huntington and Metcalf, *Celebrations of Death,* 186.
253. Huntington and Metcalf, *Celebrations of Death.* Notice the discrepancy between the two different summaries of the pattern. On page 187 the pattern is fourfold; on page 198 it is threefold.
254. Huntington and Metcalf, *Celebrations of Death,* 209.
255. Huntington and Metcalf, *Celebrations of Death,* 187.
256. Huntington and Metcalf, *Celebrations of Death,* 210.
257. Huntington and Metcalf, *Celebrations of Death,* 203.
258. Huntington and Metcalf, *Celebrations of Death,* 209.
259. Laderman, *Sacred Remains,* 8. Laderman's perspective is the classic Americanist stance, one that views American history as emanating from New England and its environs. In this view the Puritan way of death becomes root and soul of the American way of death. From such a perspective, Boston, Philadelphia, and New York loom large on the map. Not only are Los Angeles and Santa Fe, Atlanta and New Orleans missing, so are Detroit, Cleveland, and Minneapolis, much of the upper midwestern north.
260. Much of the following account is based on Laderman, *Sacred Remains.*
261. Laderman, *Sacred Remains,* 55.
262. For this reason, we should be skeptical of all three-phased patterns that researchers "find" in rites of passage.
263. Maris Vinovskis, cited in Laderman, *Sacred Remains,* 97.
264. Laderman, *Sacred Remains,* 162.

265. Laderman, *Sacred Remains,* 153.

266. Although it is tempting to think of the two columns as representing types of "death cultures," for example, secular and sacred or technological and traditional, it is dangerous to do so without issuing several caveats.

267. Prothero, "To Bury or to Burn?" 14.

268. White, "People's Republic of China," 304.

269. Feinstein and Mayo, *Mortal Acts.*

270. Feinstein and Mayo, *Mortal Acts,* 38–39.

271. Feinstein and Mayo, *Mortal Acts,* 103.

272. Available at www.cemetery.org.

273. Danforth, *Death Ritual of Rural Greece,* 129, 101.

274. Sheehy, *New Passages,* 5.

275. See, for instance, the section on "Celebratory Centenarians" in Sheehy, *New Passages,* 427.

276. I served as its content adviser.

277. Feinstein and Mayo, *Mortal Acts,* 5–6.

278. Herdt, *Sambia,* 141–44.

279. For a fuller discussion of the topic see Grimes, *Ritual Criticism.*

280. Kratz, *Affecting Performance,* 114, 121, 125.

281. Kratz, *Affecting Performance,* 347.

282. See especially Hoffman, *Covenant of Blood.*

283. Much of the following discussion of sati depends on Sharma, *Sati.*

284. Majumdar, *Age of Imperial Unity,* 567–68.

285. The full account is available at www.religioustolerance.org.

286. The estimate is proffered by Ross, *Satanic Ritual Abuse,* 71.

287. See the data gathered by the Ontario Consultants on Religious Tolerance and posted at www.religioustolerance.org/sra.htm.

288. Ross, *Satanic Ritual Abuse,* 99.

289. Ross, *Satanic Ritual Abuse,* 20–123.

290. For example, see Milloy, *National Crime.*

291. Ross, *Satanic Ritual Abuse,* 145.

292. Materials on her practice may be found at weddingcircle.com/gioia. All subsequent quotations concerning Joyce Gioia are from this Web site.

293. See their materials at www.ozemail.com.au/~jimbos/.

294. Devereux, *Abortion in Primitive Societies.*

295. Hardacre, *Marketing,* 251.

296. Hardacre, *Marketing,* 248.

297. Hardacre, *Marketing,* 158–59.

298. LaFleur, *Liquid Life,* 6–9.

299. LaFleur, *Liquid Life,* 155.

300. Hardacre, *Marketing,* 251.

301. Hardacre, *Marketing.*

302. Hardacre, *Marketing,* 26.

303. See also Smith, "Buddhism and Abortion."

304. Kluger-Bell, *Unspeakable Losses.*

305. Marie Snyder, thirty-three, is a single mother of two young children, a high school teacher, and an ecofeminist with no religious affiliation.

306. Ted Tollefson is a Unitarian Universalist minister who lives with his wife, Kristen, at a research and retreat center in Frontenac, Minnesota. He is director and cofounder of Mythos Institute (freenet.msp.mn.us/org/mythos/mythos.www/mythome.html), a nonprofit organization devoted to the study of mythology, dream work, and creative ritual. He teaches at Metro State University and United Theological Seminary near Minneapolis, MN.

307. One can see the rite enacted in Littman, *In Her Own Time.*

308. Sandra Woolfrey.

309. Oscar Cole-Arnal.

310. Kay Koppedrayer.

311. Larry Toombs.

312. Delton Glebe.

313. Jen Alboim, O. J. Poulsen, and Dax Thomas.

314. Harold Remus.

315. Harold Remus.

316. Kleinman, *The Illness Narratives.*

317. Laird, "Women and Ritual in Family Therapy," 342–45.

318. O'Connor and Hoorwitz, "Imitative and Contagious Magic," 152–54.

319. The following account is based largely on Richard Katz et al., *Healing Makes Our Hearts Happy.*

320. Katz et al., *Healing Makes Our Hearts Happy,* 107.

321. Katz et al., *Healing Makes Our Hearts Happy,* 113.

322. Axel, *Babette's Feast.*

Rites of Passage

Rites of passage are ceremonies that accompany and dramatize such major events as birth, coming-of-age initiations for boys and girls, marriage, and death. Sometimes called "life-crisis" or "life-cycle" rites, they culturally mark a person's transition from one stage of social life to another. While these rites may be loosely linked to biological changes like parturition and puberty, they frequently depict a sociocultural order that overlays the natural biological order without being identical to it. Birth rites are not necessarily celebrated when a child emerges from the mother's body, and many initiation rites do not neatly coincide with the hormonal changes that usher in fertility and young adulthood. Marriage ceremonies may precede or follow adulthood or even first intercourse, while funeral rites may continue to be celebrated years after a family member has died—or, sometimes, before death. Indeed, life-cycle rituals seem to proclaim that the biological order is less determinative than the social. Physical birth is one thing; being properly identified and accepted as a member of the social group is another. Likewise, the appearance of facial hair or menses does not make someone an adult; only the community confers that recognition, and it does so in its own time. Some scholars have theorized that there is a deep human impulse to take the raw changes of the natural world and "cook" them, in the words of Lévi-Strauss, thereby transforming physical inevitabilities into cultural regularities. This impulse may be an attempt to exert some control over nature or to naturalize the cultural order by making physical events into elements of an embracing conceptual order of cognition and experience. In any case, the tension between the natural and cultural that is sometimes recognized and sometimes disguised in life-cycle rituals appears to be integral to the values and ideas that shape personal identity, social organization, and cultural tradition.

Arnold van Gennep interpreted all rituals as rites of passage with a three-stage process. In this ritual process, the person leaves behind one social group and its concomitant social identity and passes through a stage of no identity or affiliation before admission into another social group that confers a new identity. Such rites of passage from one stage of life to another, van Gennep went on to argue, provide the model for initiations into special groups whose membership is not closely tied to any formal stage of life.[4] For example, even though the practice of adult baptism is not necessarily linked to becoming an adult, it evokes the distinct framework of initiation into a new community and spiritual stage of life. Clubs, fraternities, and secret societies have traditionally put neophytes through ritual ordeals that culminate in acceptance into the new community—all independently of life-cycle transitions. The logic of these rites creates symbolic stages and passages that redefine social and personal identity. For this reason, it is not surprising to find symbolic and experiential similarities in the initiation of neophytes into the 19th-century Chinese secret society known as the Triads, basic training at a U.S. Marines Corps boot camp, and the three-year seminary program for new monks at a Zen monastery.[5] In these cases a series of ritual passages define a "before," a period of training that is "betwixt and between," and finally an "after" in which the transformation of the person is complete. They all orchestrate a physical removal from the rest of the world, physical changes of appearance (through shaved heads and identical, utilitarian clothing), and basic conceptual changes in one's sense of self (through physical challenges, lessons in submission, and new achievements). When this progression into a different framework for identity is thought to have established a new way of seeing and acting, the recruit is officially confirmed and socially recognized by others as having a new identity and community.

In most cultures, social life is a series of major and minor ritual events. While predominantly secular cultures may have just a few rites to mark birth, marriage, and death, more traditional or religious societies may envelop one in a nearly endless sequence of ritual obligations. Birth rituals, for example, are frequently an extended set of activities invoking fertility, the purification of birth pollution, the sexual identity of the fetus, the safety of mother and child, and the conferral of social status when the baby is named and introduced to the larger community. Whether one thinks in terms of van Gennep's pattern of passage (separation, liminality, reincorporation) or Lincoln's pattern of female transformation (enclosure, metamorphosis, emergence), birth and birth rituals appear to provide some of the most basic models and metaphors for all sorts of ritual processes, as well as religious experience in general.[6]

The traditional Chinese birth rituals still found in agricultural villages in Taiwan and mainland China are a complex orchestration of customs and concerns.[7] To begin with, marriage usually brings a young woman to live with her husband's family, where she is apt to be considered an outsider of little account until she gives birth to children, particularly sons to carry on the family line. The importance of childbearing is such that both the new wife and her mother-in-law might undertake the presentation of offerings in supplication for a son to special maternal deities, such as the Buddhist goddess Guanyin or other folk deities associated with children and childbirth. In Chinese culture as elsewhere, these fertility rites are part of a distinct female ritual culture focused on bearing and protecting children, which men tend to ignore or dismiss. One 1936 rural magazine urged young wives to visit older women in the village who had raised many sons to ask them for advice.[8] An earlier account of customs in Beijing at the turn of the century describes a "baby tying ceremony" passed on to a young wife by the experienced mothers of the neighborhood. In hopes of becoming pregnant, the young wife is told to undertake a pilgrimage to a temple renowned for its connections to childbearing. There, in the usual fashion, she should light a bundle of incense sticks and place them in a burner before the image of the main deity. However, on entering the Hall of the Goddess of Sons and Grandsons, she should select a paper image of an attractive baby boy from among an array of such figures, tie a red thread around its neck and pray that the "child" will come home with her to be born as her son. If she subsequently gives birth to a son, the new mother should return with offerings to thank the goddess.[9]

In Taiwanese reckoning, a child is created from the mother's blood and the father's semen.[10] The mother's blood requires the "seeds" in the father's semen in order to turn itself into flesh and bone. Once a child is conceived, menstrual blood collects in the mother's womb to form the child's body. Any excess is discharged at birth. Beliefs about this blood are related to the important god Taishen (or Thai Sin), whose name can be translated as either the God of the Placenta or the God of the Pregnant Womb. Taishen is thought to come into existence when a child is conceived and functions as a type of soul for the child. Not confined to the developing fetus or womb, however, the god is free to roam about the mother's bedroom and is particularly apt to do so about midway through the pregnancy. Taishen is treated like a temperamental guest who should not be disturbed. Even cleaning the room is thought to risk disturbing him, resulting in harm to the fetus or even a miscarriage. If disturbances do occur, especially any accompanied by unusual pain for the mother, a professional medium is summoned to try to appease the god. Since Taishen can reside in the birth fluids, they must be disposed of very carefully after birth in order to keep the child from falling ill.

Undisturbed, Taishen remains in the room until the mother and child formally end their seclusion some 30 to 40 days after birth, although in some areas Taishen may be "ushered" under the child's bed to reside there until the baby reaches young adulthood. In the secluded postpartum period, a woman is not supposed to wash her hair, body, clothes, or dishes. She must also avoid contact with drafts and "cold food," that is, foods associated with damp places and other yin qualities. The bedroom in which she stays during this time not only protects her from many such threats but also protects others from her, since she is considered polluted and dangerous throughout the pregnancy, birth, and recovery. Those who enter the room during or after the birth are affected by this pollution and may not attend weddings or enter temples, where they would offend the gods. Although her husband stays away throughout this period, the new mother is taken care of by a female companion, usually her mother-in-law.[11]

After giving birth, the process of postnatal recuperation is socially marked by a variety of small rites that gradually reincorporate mother and child into the family and then the larger village community. These include several purifying herbal baths and culminate in a ceremony known as the "full month ritual" that ends the thirty days of seclusion. In the case of a baby boy, he is bathed, his hair and eyebrows are shaved except for a tuft in the front and back of his head, his scalp is oiled, and he is

dressed in a new, bright red outfit. He is formally shown off to guests at a luncheon celebration at which his name (*ming*), one of several conferred in his lifetime, is officially announced. The mother's room is thoroughly cleaned, and she is free to resume normal domestic life with her husband and family. However, she and the baby are still sufficiently polluted and vulnerable that they must stay quietly at home for another sixty days, altogether about one hundred days after the birth. By that time it is thought that Taishen, as the child's soul, will be sufficiently attached to the child that disturbances in the vicinity of the child no longer threaten to disturb it.

Traditionally, this rather standard ritual sequence has differed significantly in mood and elaborateness depending upon whether the baby is a boy or girl. If it is a girl, both mother and baby receive a great deal less attention. In fact, an old custom of disguising a boy baby with a girl's clothes or name in order to fool any gods or ghosts who might want to steal such a precious bundle clearly demonstrates the relative value of girls. The birth of a boy usually generates more excitement and festivities in patrilineal cultures, where social and personal identity is defined in terms of the father's family line. In these systems, women may have little social identity outside their roles as wives and mothers. While both boys and girls are given a name after thirty days, these names are rarely used, and family nicknames are preferred. Yet by middle age, a boy will usually have acquired four or five formal names, corresponding to a social and ritual process by which a man develops a progressively more individuated social identity. Women, in contrast, traditionally remained nearly nameless, losing their early name at marriage and thereafter known almost exclusively by kinship terms or impersonal labels like "auntie" or "old woman."[12]

Despite the male dominance seen in the importance of sons over daughters and in the concern for the pollution of pregnancy and childbirth, ceremonies like the full month ritual bring about an important change in the mother's domestic and social status. In giving birth and taking up the role of mother, a woman has made a dramatic and indispensable contribution to the prosperity of the family. This is true even for a baby daughter but fully appreciated most in regard to sons. The mother receives gifts, even from her own relatives, and the preparation of special foods to restore her strength testifies to the importance of her new maternal role. Her new responsibilities include continued recourse to rituals in order to safeguard her child, such as various offerings to ancestors and deities, bribes to ghosts, and protective devices, foods, and spells.

A fuller interpretation of the details of these childbirth rites would necessitate a long discussion of Chinese cosmology, customs and social organization. However, some general features of the Chinese example are echoed in birth rituals in many other cultures. Particularly widespread is the idea that pregnancy is a time of great vulnerability and the mother must not be disturbed in any way. Her activities, diet, and social contacts are often severely restricted. Equally common is the imposition of seclusion and greater restrictions during and after birth, since the blood, birth waters, placenta, and umbilical cord are considered highly polluting, dangerous to others, and a source of vulnerability for the child. In many cultures, these materials must be disposed of in careful accordance with traditional rules—usually by burial. Prior to this century, it was not uncommon for there to be a separate room or village hut used just for birth and nothing else. Scholars analyzing Chinese pregnancy and childbirth practices have pointed to different reasons for beliefs in the mother's pollution. Some stress how these ideas relate to an embracing cosmological and social system in which pollution ideas attend any major event that disturbs the boundaries of the family, especially the events of birth, death, and sex.[13] Others stress how such beliefs are used primarily to maintain a system of social relations that subordinate women in roles rendered as ambivalent as they are indispensable.[14] These themes also appear in analyses of childbirth procedures in American hospitals. R. E. Davis-Floyd argues that medical necessity cannot explain the highly symbolic ways in which childbirth is institutionally handled. She finds that values of family and mothering are ritually affirmed over and against those of individuality and sexuality in modern hospitals. Obstetrical procedures that include "preps, enemas, shaves, [and] episiotomies," she argues, are designed to be rites of passage that transform a woman as a sexual person into an asexual mother and custodian of the values of the culture.[15]

Many religious traditions go on to orchestrate the whole of human life as a series of ritual passages and obligations. Eastern Orthodox and Roman forms of Catholicism, for example, identify seven sacraments that span the course of a person's life. The rite of baptism removes the stain of the original sin of Adam and Eve and brings the child (or adult convert) into the community of those "reborn" both in the name of Jesus Christ and in the same manner that Christ himself was baptized by John. Baptism is followed by the rite of reconciliation (penance) at about seven years of age when the child confesses and makes restitution for his or her sins. Following closely is the rite of first communion (the eucharist, Lord's Supper) in which the child consumes a wafer of bread consecrated as the body and blood of Jesus Christ. The rite of confirmation (chrismation) takes place at about twelve years of age, signaling transition to a more adult stage marked by the indwelling of the Holy Spirit, the third person of the Christian godhead. Rites of marriage or holy orders may follow, while at death a priest performs the anointing of the sick (extreme unction), more commonly known as the "last rites," in which the dying person confesses his or her sins and is anointed with oil. While one performs some of these rites only once to make major transitions, others are repeated constantly throughout one's life.

Judaism lays out a series of ritual passages beginning with the *berit milah* or "covenant of circumcision" on the eighth day after the birth of a male child, which initiates him into the community governed by the covenant between God and Abraham. The bar and bat mitzvah, meaning son and daughter of the commandments, respectively, are celebrated at about thirteen years of age, initiating the young person into adult responsibilities for observing the laws binding on the Jewish community. A boy traditionally participates in the public reading of Torah in the synagogue, which is followed by a festive family celebration. Although the bat mitzvah for girls has been incorporated into most nonorthodox Jewish congregations (i.e., Conservative, Reform, and Reconstructionist) since the 1950s, its format still differs widely, although it can be an exact duplicate of the bar mitzvah for boys.

Marriage also marks a major life passage in Judaism, originally accompanied by separate rites of engagement, betrothal, and wedlock that have gradually merged. Jews ritualize death with communal activities and the observation of distinct mourning periods. Since embalming is eschewed, burial tends to take place as soon as possible, entailing a synagogue ceremony, a procession to the cemetery that stops seven times

along the way to recite Psalm 91 ("O thou that dwellest in the covert of the Most High"), and graveside prayers that include the famous doxology known as the Kaddish, a prayer invoking the sanctity of God's name, the glory of his kingdom, and the coming of the Messiah.[16] During the initial seven-day period of mourning that follows, the family "sits shivah," that is, they stay at home; sit on low chairs or stools; refrain from sex, shaving, washing, or grooming; and eat special foods brought by family and friends, who are obliged to visit. Traditionally, a minyan, the group of ten men minimally needed to recite Jewish prayers, gathers twice a day during this week for prayer services in the home. The first-year anniversary of the death is observed with prayers and a memorial lamp.

Hindu life-passage rites known as *saṃskāras* (purifications) can number from ten to forty, varying with geographic, linguistic, or caste differences, although the system as a whole has traditionally been open only to males of the upper castes. The word "samskara" not only means to purify, but also to make over or transform, and ritually it denotes a series of actions that progressively refine and prepare the inner and outer person for the ultimate goals of Hinduism—better rebirth and final release from the cycle of life and death in this world.[17] A set of prenatal rites address fertility, physical well-being, and the goal of having a male child. Other samskaras are performed in early childhood and include rites for naming the child, leaving the birth room, first bites of solid food, first haircut for boys, ear piercing for girls, and so on. Rites during adolescence further prepare the maturing child for taking up his or her social role in the world. The most important of these is the *upanayana* initiation for upper-caste boys (eight to twelve years old) by which they are "reborn" into their caste identities through instruction in the ancient scriptures known as the Vedas. Prior to this critical rite, even upper-caste boys are seen as low caste (*Sudra*) and are not allowed to study the Vedas. The boy's transition is depicted in a series of actions that separate him from his former identity. After a night spent alone in silence, he eats a last meal at his mother's side, bathes, has his head shaved, and dons new clothes. Then he is formally presented to his new teacher, whom he takes as his guru. The teacher drapes a sacred thread (*yajnopavita*) over the boy's left shoulder and under his right arm. Then, laying a hand on the boy's heart, the teacher recites the sacred *Savitri* prayer, which is understood to give symbolic rebirth to the young man.[18]

Other samskaras mark the conclusion of the boy's period of studies and his return to the social community in readiness to marry. Marriage is considered to be the most important samskara since it is the basis of the family and the whole social order. It is also thought to effect a particularly extensive transformation of those involved. According to Bengali custom, writes Ralph W. Nicholas, marriage "completes the body of a male," bringing him into the formal status of a householder and therein able to make offerings to the gods. For the woman, the marriage rites are thought to transform her physical identity, remaking her into a member of her husband's family and, indeed, into his "half body." As the last samskara while one is alive, marriage joins "together into a single body what were previously two separate bodies.[19] Marriage rites differ from one locale to another in India, but they generally include a Brahman priest who guides the couple through the ceremony and builds a sacred fire to which offerings are made. The bridegroom takes the hand of the heavily veiled bride and leads her in circling the fire three times; in some places she is carried around him seven times. As each circle is completed, he has her step on a grinding stone and vow to be like a stone in firmness and resolve. In some places, their clothing may be knotted together; in other places, the bride may take seven steps in a northeast direction, each step symbolizing qualities sought in married life, such as fertility, wealth, and devotion. The groom paints on the bride's forehead the vermilion dot (*bindi*) that signifies a married woman.[20]

Traditionally, the fire from the wedding ceremony was taken back to the couple's home and kept burning for the duration of the marriage. At death, this fire could be used to light the funeral pyre on which the body is committed for yet another act of sacrificial purification (destruction of the corporal body) and rebirth into a further stage of existence (release of the subtle body). As in many religious traditions, smaller rites around the corpse and its cremation are followed by offerings of various sorts to appease the spirit of the dead, which is considered somewhat tentative and even dangerous until it has fully joined its ancestors. This latter transition is the object of the final samskara, the postmortem rites (*śrāddhā*) in which "pure" offerings of rice, water, and prayers are made to the deceased, usually every month for a year and then on the anniversary of the death.

There is another stage of life defined as a traditional ideal in Hinduism, that of the *sannyāsī*, one who renounces family, career, personal identity, and even standard ritual obligations in order to abandon all earthly attachments and seek salvation.[21] The sannyasi lives as a homeless wanderer, begging for food and seeking a total spiritual release from the cycle of death and rebirth. The ritual transition to this stage is marked by legal declarations in which the renouncer sheds all assets, debts, and obligations and then performs his own funeral ceremony. With the same purifying preparations used for a corpse, he shaves his head, clips his nails, and bathes. Then, performing his household ritual obligations for the last time, the renouncer burns all of the ritual implements, mentally internalizes the external fire, and finally lays his sacred thread in the flames. In effect, he renounces ritual itself.[22] With the words, "To me belongs no one, nor do I belong to anyone," the renouncer completes his death to the world. With this separation from the human community, the renouncer's subsequent life is lived in the most liminal fashion, awaiting the final incorporation into the great ultimate.[23]

In American society, as in other highly industrialized countries, rites of passage tend to be less highly organized and far from routine outside small communities or subcultures. While many people turn to familiar religious institutions to observe the traditional rites of birth, marriage, or death, others use more secular rituals, some of which are built into the legal and bureaucratic processes of the state, such as marriage by a justice of the peace. In small American subcultures, coming-of-age rites may still be quite formal, as seen in the debutante balls sponsored by the social elite of major cities or the high school graduations enthusiastically celebrated in midwestern farming towns. For less tightly knit communities, informal and ad hoc ritualizations tend to stand in as symbolic markers of the passage into adulthood. Owning a car, registering with the draft board, beginning to date, getting a first job, leaving home, or simply celebrating one's eighteenth birthday may all function as semiritualized markers of passage.

It is often suggested that the lack of clear life-passage rites in American culture has contributed to the loss of community and a growing sense of social alienation.[24] Some scholars and social critics have even argued that without formal testimony to their passage into adulthood, young people are pressured to prove themselves, both personally and publicly, in rash displays of daring or excess. Yet it is far from clear whether the loss of formal rites of passage is a cause or a symptom of the breakdown of small traditional communities, or that American life is so lacking in rituals. At particular times in history, however, such as the late 19th century until the Great Depression of the 1930s, American life clearly was much richer in ritual. In the Victorian period, for example, many of the domestic and public rituals we take for granted were devised and popularized, such as the elaborate domestic Christmas celebration with a decorated tree, stockings, gifts, and carolers. That period also saw an explosion of men's fraternal organizations dedicated primarily to elaborate series of secret initiations and ceremonies. The need to define and formally achieve gender identity, in this case masculine identity, in the rapidly changing social and economic conditions of the times appears to explain, in part, the "solace and psychological guidance" provided by fraternal rituals in a passage that Victorian America came to be see as fraught with problems.[25]

It is now generally recognized that cultures construct models of masculinity and femininity, subtly pressuring people to conform to them. To be a "real" man or a "real" woman, therefore, socially means much more than an anatomically correct body and mature sensibility. In fact, in most societies manhood and womanhood are not usually thought of as a natural or spontaneous process but a matter of socially orchestrated training that is learned and mastered despite difficult obstacles. As the profile of the Mukanda initiation demonstrated, this process can range from the fairly benign to the traumatic. Controversial initiatory practices—from forced drinking in fraternity hazings in America to female genital circumcision (clitoridectomy) in many parts of the world—suggest that fairly complex processes are involved in the way a society or subculture defines its men and women.[26] In a study of cultural constructions of masculinity, David Gilmore finds "a constantly recurring notion that real manhood is different from simple anatomical maleness." He compares a number of cultural models of manhood and asks "why people in so many places regard the state of being a 'real man' or 'true man' as uncertain or precarious, a prize to be won or wrested through struggle, and why so many societies build up an elusive or exclusionary image of manhood through cultural sanctions, ritual, or trials of skill and endurance."[27] Hazing rites that vary from the yucca whippings of the Tewa to the psychophysical rigors of the traditional British boarding school suggest that the purpose of cultural gender constructions and the rituals that reinforce them is to distinguish and polarize gender roles as the most fundamental form of cultural "ordering" that human beings attempt to impose on nature.[28] The more fundamental such constructions come to seem, the more natural and incontestable.

Psychologists and mythologists like Otto Rank, Carl Jung, and Joseph Campbell have used the model of Van Gennep's three-stage process of initiation, with its echoes of older myth and ritual theories of the dying and rising god, to analyze the structure of hero myths and, by extension, the process of human individuation that leads to the achievement of a mature sense of self.[29] These theories support the idea that rites of passage not only effect transitions in the social sphere but also concomitantly in the psychological sphere. Van Gennep's model has also been applied to the ritual-like, even initiatory, nature of pilgrimage and some of its more recent analogs. Setting out from home and a familiar world, the pilgrim endures the trials and tribulations of the journey, passes through strange lands to which he or she does not belong, and finally arrives at a place considered holier than others, a sacred center where wisdom or grace or gifts are dispensed. Securing a token of that dispensation, the pilgrim returns home bearing the transformed identity of one who has made the journey, touched the sacred objects, and received heavenly boons for the effort. These themes are visible in literary accounts of pilgrimage, from Chaucer's *Canterbury Tales* and John Bunyan's *Pilgrim's Progress* to the Chinese classic novel, *Journey to the West*, which recounts the journey of the 7th-century pilgrim Xuanzang to India to secure Buddhist scriptures, and to Malcolm X's decisive trip to Mecca as recounted in his autobiography.[30] Setting off on a journey has always evoked aspects of an initiatory ritual transition to a new identity, and in both fictional and historical versions the pilgrim is apt to find it hard to fit back into the old life afterward. Religious pilgrimage has continued to thrive amid the transportation developments of the 20th century, while its more secular counterpart, tourism, is apt to invoke very similar images of transformation and renewal, whether the destination is Paris, Gettysburg, or Disneyland.

Territorial Passage and the Classification of Rites

ARNOLD VAN GENNEP

Facts of publication: *van Gennep, Arnold. 1960 (1909).* The Rites of Passage, *10–13, 15–25. Edited by Monika B. Vizedom and Gabrielle Caffee. Chicago: University of Chicago Press.*

In this brief excerpt from Arnold van Gennep's classic work The Rites of Passage *we are introduced to his threefold enumeration of ritual phases: separation (preliminal), transition (liminal), incorporation (postliminal). Van Gennep makes clear that by "rites" of passage he does not mean whole rituals but rather phases, gestures, or other parts of some greater whole. Here he also articulates the basic metaphor that is the basis of his theory, namely, territorial passage across an international frontier or physical passage through a doorway (in Latin, a* limen*). On the basis of this one kind of ritualized action, van Gennep then treats societies as if they were rooms separated by doorways, portals, or passageways. Transition from one social status (or "room") to the next requires means of negotiating them, namely rites of passage.*

For an application of van Gennep's views see Thomas Leemon, The Rites of Passage in a Student Culture *(New York: Teacher's College, 1972).*

About the author: Dates: *1873–1957, French, born in Ludwigsburg, Germany.* **Education:** *École Pratique des Hautes Études (France); École des Langues Orientales (France).* **Field(s)**: *anthropology; ethnography; folklore.* **Career:** *Ministry of Agriculture, Paris; Professor of Ethnology, University of Neuchâtel (Switzerland), 1912–1915.* **Publications:** Mythes et legendes d'Australie *(E. Guilmoto, 1906);* Religions, mours et legendes *(Société du Mercure de France, 1908–14);* Le Folklore *(Stock, 1924);* Essai sur le culte populaire des saints fransciscains en Savoie *(J. Vrin, 1927);* Manuel de folklore français contemporain *(A. Picard, 1937–1958);* The Rites of Passage, *(University of Chicago, 1960 [1909]);* The Semi-Scholars *(Routledge, 1967);* Culte populaire des sainte en Savoie *(G.-P. Maisonneuve & Larose, 1973). See also* Bibliographie des oeuvres d'Arnold van Gennep *(Paris, 1964).*

I have tried to assemble here all the ceremonial patterns which accompany a passage from one situation to another or from one cosmic or social world to another. Because of the importance of these transitions, I think it legitimate to single out *rites of passage* as a special category, which under further analysis may be subdivided into *rites of separation, transition rites,* and *rites of incorporation.* These three sub categories are not developed to the same extent by all peoples or in every ceremonial pattern. Rites of separation are prominent in funeral ceremonies, rites of incorporation at marriages. Transition rites may play an important part, for instance, in pregnancy, betrothal, and initiation; or they may be reduced to a minimum in adoption, in the delivery of a second child, in remarriage, or in the passage from the second to the third age group. Thus, although a complete scheme of rites of passage theoretically includes preliminal rites (rites of separation), liminal rites (rites of transition), and postliminal rites (rites of incorporation), in specific instances these three types are not always equally important or equally elaborated.

Furthermore, in certain ceremonial patterns where the transitional period is sufficiently elaborated to constitute an independent state, the arrangement is reduplicated. A betrothal forms a liminal period between adolescence and marriage, but the passage from adolescence to betrothal itself involves a special series of rites of separation, a transition, and an incorporation into the betrothed condition; and the passage from the transitional period, which is betrothal, to marriage itself, is made through a series of rites of separation from the former, followed by rites consisting of transition, and rites of incorporation into marriage. The pattern of ceremonies comprising rites of pregnancy, delivery, and birth is equally involved. I am trying to group all these rites as clearly as possible, but since I am dealing with activities I do not expect to achieve as rigid a classification as the botanists have, for example.

It is by no means my contention that all rites of birth, initiation, marriage, and the like, are only rites of passage. For, in addition to their over-all goal—to insure a change of condition or a passage from one magico-religious or secular group to another—all these ceremonies have their individual purposes. Marriage ceremonies include fertility rites; birth ceremonies include protection and divination rites; funerals, defensive rites; initiations, propitiatory rites; ordinations, rites of attachment to the deity. All these rites, which have specific effective aims, occur in juxtaposition and combination with rites of passage—and are sometimes so intimately intertwined with them that it is impossible to distinguish whether a particular ritual is, for example, one of protection or of separation. This problem arises in relation to various forms of so-called purification ceremonies, which may simply lift a taboo and therefore remove the contaminating quality, or which may be clearly active rites, imparting the quality of purity.

In connection with this problem, I should like to consider briefly the pivoting of the sacred.[1] Characteristically, the presence of the sacred (and the performance of appropriate rites) is variable. Sacredness as an attribute is not absolute; it is brought into play by the nature of particular situations. A man at home, in his tribe, lives in the secular realm; he moves into the realm of the sacred when he goes on a journey and finds himself a foreigner near a camp of strangers. A Brahman belongs to the sacred world by birth; but within that world there is a hierarchy of Brahman families some of whom are sacred in relation to others. Every woman, though congenitally impure, is sacred to all adult men; if she is pregnant, she also becomes sacred to all other women of the tribe except her close relatives; and these other women constitute in relation to her a profane world, which at that moment includes all children and adult men. Upon performing so-called purification rites, a woman who has just given birth re-enters society, but she takes her place only in appropriate segments of it—such as her sex and her family—and she remains sacred in relation to the initiated men and to the magico-religious ceremonies. Thus the "magic circles" pivot, shifting as a person moves from one place in society to another. The categories and concepts which embody them operate in such a way that whoever passes through the various positions of a lifetime one day sees the sacred where before he has seen the profane, or vice versa. Such changes of condition do not occur without disturbing the life of society and the individual, and it is the function of rites of passage to reduce their harmful effects. That such changes are regarded as real and important is demonstrated by the recurrence of rites, in important ceremonies among widely differing peoples, enacting death in one condition and resurrection in another. These rites are rites of passage in their most dramatic form.

The Territorial Passage

Territorial passages can provide a framework for the discussion of rites of passage. Except in the few countries where a passport is still in use, a person in these days may pass freely from one civilized region to another.[2] The frontier, an imaginary line connecting milestones or stakes, is visible—in an exaggerated fashion—only on maps. But not so long ago the passage from one country to another, from one province to another within each country, and, still earlier, even from one manorial domain to another was accompanied by various formalities. These were largely political, legal, and economic, but some were of a magico-religious nature. For instance, Christians, Moslems, and Buddhists were forbidden to enter and stay in portions of the globe which did not adhere to their respective faiths.

It is this magico-religious aspect of crossing frontiers that interests us. To see it operating fully, we must seek out types of civilization in which the magico-religious encompassed what today is within the secular domain.

The territory occupied by a semicivilized tribe is usually defined only by natural features, but its inhabitants and their neighbors know quite well within what territorial limits their rights and prerogatives extend. The natural boundary might be a sacred rock, tree, river, or lake which cannot be crossed or passed without the risk of supernatural sanctions. Such natural boundaries are relatively rare, however. More often the boundary is marked by an object—a stake, portal, or upright rock (milestone or landmark)—whose installation at that particular spot has been accompanied by rites of consecration. Enforcement of the interdiction may be immediate, or it may be mediated by frontier divinities (such as Hermes, Priapus,[3] or the deities represented on the Babylonian *kudurru*). When milestones or boundary signs (e.g., a plow, an animal hide cut in thongs, a ditch) are ceremonially placed by a defined group on a delimited piece of earth, the group takes possession of it in such a way that a stranger who sets foot on it commits a sacrilege analogous to a profane person's entrance into a sacred forest or temple.

The idea of the sanctity of a territory so delimited has sometimes been confused with the belief in the sanctity of the entire earth as the Earth Mother.[4] In China, according to the most ancient documents, the deity was not the earth as such, but each plot of ground was sacred for its inhabitants and owners.[5] It seems to me that the ease of Loango,[6] the territory of Greek cities, and that of Rome,[7] are all analogous.

The prohibition against entering a given territory is therefore intrinsically magico-religious. It has been expressed with the help of milestones, walls, and statues in the classical world, and through more simple means among the semicivilized. Naturally, these signs are not placed along the entire boundary line. Like our boundary posts, they are set only at points of passage, on paths and at crossroads. A bundle of herbs, a piece of wood, or a stake adorned with a sheaf of straw may be placed in the middle of the path or across it.[8] The erection of a portal,[9] sometimes together with natural objects or crudely made statues,[10] is a more complicated means of indicating the boundary. The details of these various procedures need not concern us here.[11]

Today, in our part of the world, one country touches another; but the situation was quite different in the times when Christian lands comprised only a part of Europe. Each country was surrounded by a strip of neutral ground which in practice was divided into sections or marches. These have gradually disappeared, although the term "letter of marque"[12] retains the meaning of a permit to pass from one territory to another through a neutral zone. Zones of this kind were important in classical antiquity, especially in Greece, where they were used for market places or battle-fields.[13]

The same system of zones is to be found among the semicivilized, although here boundaries are less precise because the claimed territories are few in number and sparsely settled. The neutral zones are ordinarily deserts, marshes, and most frequently virgin forests where everyone has full rights to travel and hunt. Because of the pivoting of sacredness, the territories on either side of the neutral zone are sacred in relation to whoever is in the zone, but the zone, in turn, is sacred for the inhabitants of the adjacent territories. Whoever passes from one to the other finds himself physically and magico-religiously in a special situation for a certain length of time: he wavers between two worlds. It is this situation which I have designated a transition, and one of [my] purposes . . . is to demonstrate that this symbolic and spatial area of transition may be found in more or less pronounced form in all the ceremonies which accompany the passage from one social and magico-religious position to another.

* * *

With this introduction we now turn to some descriptions of territorial passages. When a king of Sparta went to war, he sacrificed to Zeus; if the prognostication was favorable, a torchbearer took fire from the altar and carried it in front of the army to the frontier. There the king sacrificed again, and if the fates again decreed in his favor he crossed the frontier with the torchbearer still preceding the army.[14] The rite of separation from one's own land at the moment of entering neutral territory was clearly acted out in this procedure. Several rites of frontier crossing have been studied by Trumbull,[15] who cites the following example: when General Grant came to Asyut, a frontier point in Upper Egypt, a bull was sacrificed as he disembarked. The head was placed on one side of the gangplank and the body on the other, so that Grant had to pass between them as he stepped over the spilled blood.[16] The rite of passing between the parts of an object that has been halved, or between two branches, or under something, is one which must, in a certain number of cases, be interpreted as a direct rite of passage by means of which a person leaves one world behind . . . and enters a new one.[17]

The procedures discussed apply not only in reference to a country or territory but also in relation to a village, a town, a section of a town, a temple, or a house. The neutral zone shrinks progressively till it ceases to exist except as a simple stone, a beam, or a threshold (except for the pronaos, the narthex, the vestibule, etc.).[18] The portal which symbolizes a taboo against entering becomes the postern of the ramparts, the gate in the walls of the city quarter, the door of the house. The quality of sacredness is not localized in the threshold only; it encompasses the lintels and architrave as well.[19]

The rituals pertaining to the door form a unit, and differences among particular ceremonies lie in technicalities: the threshold is sprinkled with blood or with purifying water; doorposts are bathed with blood or with perfumes; sacred objects are hung or nailed onto them, as on the architrave. Trumbull, in the monograph which he devoted to "the threshold covenant," bypassed the natural interpretation, although he wrote that the bronze threshold of Greece "is an archaic synonym for the enduring border, or outer limit, of spiritual domain."[20] Precisely: the door is the boundary between the foreign and domestic worlds in the case of an ordinary dwelling, between the profane and sacred worlds in the case of a temple. Therefore to cross the threshold is to unite oneself with a new world. It is thus an important act in marriage, adoption, ordination, and funeral ceremonies.

Rites of passing through the door need be stressed no further at this point. . . . It will be noted that the rites carried out on the threshold itself are transition rites. "Purifications" (washing, cleansing, etc.) constitute rites of separation from previous surroundings; there follow rites of incorporation (presentation of salt, a shared meal, etc.). The rites of the threshold are therefore not "union" ceremonies, properly speaking, but rites of preparation for union, themselves preceded by rites of preparation for the transitional stage.

Consequently, I propose to call the rites of separation from a previous world, *preliminal rites,* those executed during the transitional stage *liminal* (*or threshold*) *rites,* and the ceremonies of incorporation into the new world *postliminal rites.*

The rudimentary portal of Africa is very probably the original form of the isolated portals which were so highly developed in the Far East,[21] where they not only became independent monuments of architectural value (for example, porticoes of deities, of emperors, of widows) but also, at least in Shintoism and Taoism, are used as ceremonial instruments.[22] This evolution from the magic portal to the monument seems also to have occurred in the case of the Roman arch of triumph. The victor was first required to separate himself from the enemy world through a series of rites, in order to be able to return to the Roman world by passing through the arch. The rite of incorporation in this case was a sacrifice to Jupiter Capitoline and to the deities protecting the city.[23]

In the instances cited thus far the efficacy of the ritual portal has been direct. But the portal may also be the seat of a particular deity. When "guardians of the threshold" take on monumental proportions, as in Egypt, in Assyro-Babylonia (winged dragons, the sphinx, and all sorts of monsters),[24] and in China (in the form of statues), they push the door and the threshold into the background; prayers and sacrifices are addressed to the guardians alone. A rite of spatial passage has become a rite of spiritual passage. The act of passing no longer accomplishes the passage; a personified power insures it through spiritual means.[25]

The two forms of portal rituals mentioned above seldom occur in isolation; in the great majority of cases they are combined. In the various ceremonies one may see the direct rite combined with the indirect, the dynamistic rite with the animistic, either to remove possible obstacles to the passage or to carry out the passage itself.

Among the ceremonies of territorial passage those pertaining to the crossing of mountain passes should also be cited. These include the depositing of various objects (stones, bits of cloth, hair, etc.), offerings, invocations of the spirit of the place, and so forth. They are to be found, for instance, in Morocco (*kerkour*), Mongolia, Tibet (*obo*), Assam, the Andes, and the Alps (in the form of chapels). The crossing of a river is often accompanied by ceremonies,[26] and a corresponding negative rite is found where a king or a priest is prohibited from crossing a certain river or any flowing water. Likewise, the acts of embarking and disembarking, of entering a vehicle or a litter, and of mounting a horse to take a trip are often accompanied by rites of separation at the time of departure and by rites of incorporation upon return.

Finally, in some cases the sacrifices associated with laying the foundation for a house and constructing a house fall into the category of rites of passage. It is curious that they have been studied in isolation, since they are part of a homogeneous ceremonial whole, the ceremony of changing residence.[27] Every new house is *taboo* until, by appropriate rites, it is made *noa* (secular or profane).[28] In form and dynamics, the lifting of this taboo resembles those pertaining to a sacred territory or woman: there is washing or lustration or a communal meal. Other practices are intended to insure that the house remains intact, does not crumble, and so forth. Scholars have been wrong in interpreting some of these practices as survivals and distortions of an ancient custom of human sacrifice. Ceremonies to lift a taboo, to determine who will be the protecting spirit, to transfer the first death, to insure all sorts of future security, are followed by rites of incorporation: libations, ceremonial visiting, consecration of the various parts of the house, the sharing of bread and salt or a beverage, the sharing of a meal. (In France, a housewarming is given, called literally, "hanging the pothook.") These ceremonies are essentially rites identifying the future inhabitants with their new residence. When the inhabitants—for instance, a betrothed man or a young husband and his family or his wife—build the house themselves, the ceremonies begin at the very start of construction.

Rites of entering a house, a temple, and so forth, have their counterpart in rites of exit, which are either identical or the reverse. At the time of Mohammed, the Arabs stroked the household god when entering and when leaving,[29] so that the same gesture was a rite of incorporation or a rite of separation, depending on the case. In the same way, whenever an Orthodox Jew passes through the main door of a house, a finger of his right hand touches the mezuzah, a casket attached to the doorpost which contains a piece of paper or a ribbon upon which is written or embroidered the sacred name of God (Shaddai). He then kisses the finger and says, "The Lord shall preserve thy going out and thy coming in from this time forth evermore."[30] The verbal rite is here joined to the manual one.

It will be noted that only the main door is the site of entrance and exit rites, perhaps because it is consecrated by a special rite or because it faces in a favorable direction. The other openings do not have the same quality of a point of transition between the familial world and the external world. Therefore thieves (in civilizations other than our own) prefer to enter otherwise than through the door; corpses are removed by the back door or the window; a pregnant or menstruating woman is allowed to enter and leave through a secondary door only; the cadaver of a sacred animal is brought in only through a window or a hole; and so forth. These practices are intended to prevent the pollution of a passage which must remain uncontaminated once it has been purified by special ceremonies. Spitting or stepping on it, for instance, [is] forbidden. But sometimes the sacred value of the threshold is present in all the thresholds of the house. In Russia I saw houses in which little horseshoes, used to protect the heels of boots, were nailed on the threshold of every room. In addition, every room in these houses had its own icon.

In order to understand rites pertaining to the threshold, one should always remember that the threshold is only a part of the door and that most of these rites should be understood as direct and physical rites of entrance, of waiting, and of departure—that is, as rites of passage.

NOTES

1. This pivoting was already well understood by Smith (see *The Religion of the Semites*, pp. 427–28 and discussion of "taboo," pp. 152–53, 451–54, etc.). Compare the passage from sacred to profane, and vice versa, among the Tarahumara and the Huichol of Mexico as described by Karl Sofus Lumholtz, *Unknown Mexico: A Record of Five Years' Exploration among the Tribes of Western Sierra Madre* (London: C. Scribner's Sons, 1903), *passim.*
2. [It should be remembered that van Gennep wrote in the first decade of the twentieth century.] (Vizedom & Caffee note)
3. Here is my interpretation (as yet to be fully demonstrated) of the almost universal association between landmarks and the phallus: (1) There is an association of the stake or the upright rock with the penis in erection; (2) the idea of union associated with the sexual act has a certain magical significance; (3) pointed objects (horns, fingers, etc.) are believed to protect through their power to "pierce" the evil influences, the wicked jinn, etc.; (4) *very seldom* is there the idea of the fecundity of the territory and its inhabitants. The phallic symbolism of landmarks has almost no truly sexual significance.
4. Several interpretations by Dieterich (in *Mutter Erde*), which I believe to be incorrect, will be discussed with reference to birth and childhood.
5. "In the ancient Chinese religion there was a god of the soil for each district (no doubt for twenty-five families); the king had a god of the soil for his people and one for his own personal use; the same was true for each feudal lord, each group of families, each imperial dynasty. Those gods presided over war, which was created us a punishment; they were fashioned from a piece of wood and associated with gods of the harvest. It seems to me that the earth goddess came later as a result of several syncretisms" (Eduard Chavannes, "Le dieu du sol dans l'ancienne religion chinoise," *Revue de l'histoire des religions*, XLIII [1901], 124–27, 140–44).
6. Cf. E. Dennett, *At the Back of the Black Man's Mind: Or Notes on the Kingly Office in West Africa* (London: Macmillan, 1906), and Eduard Pechüel-Loesche, *Volkskunde von Loango* (Stuttgart: Strecher & Schroeder, 1907).
7. Cf. W. Warde Fowler's interesting discussion titled "Lustratio" in *Anthropology and the Classics*, ed. Robert R. Marett (Oxford, 1908), pp. 173–78. My readers will, I hope, accept the view that *lustratio* is nothing more than a rite of territorial separation, cosmic or human (e.g., return from war).
8. To the references given by H. Grierson in *The Silent Trade* (Edinburgh, 1903), pp. 12–14, n. 4 (where, unfortunately, the rites of appropriation and the taboos of passage have been confused), add: Dennett, *At the Back of the Black Man's Mind*, pp. 90, 153, n. 192; Pechüel-Loesche, *Volkskunde von Loango*, pp. 223–24, 456, 472, etc.; J. Büttikofer, *Reisebilder aus Liberia* (Leiden, 1890), II, 304; van Gennep, *Tabou et totémismo à Madagascar*, pp. 183–86 (taboos of passage); J. M. M. Van der Burght, *Dictionnaire français Kirundi: Avec l'indication succincte de la signification swahili et allemande augmente d'une introduction et de 196 articles ethnologiques sur les Urundi et les Warundi* (Bar-le-Duc: Société d'Illustration Catholique, 1904), s.v. "Iviheko," etc. The custom of planting a stake surmounted with a sheaf of straw to prohibit the entrance into a path or field is very widespread in Europe.
9. Paul B. du Chaillu (in *L'Afrique sauvage: Nouvelles excursions au pays des Ashongos* [Paris: Michel Levy Frères, 1868], p. 38, from the English; *Journey to Ashango Land* [New York, D. Appleton Co, 1867]), mentions a portal with sacred plants, chimpanzee skulls, etc. (in the Congo). Portals formed by two stakes driven into the ground with a pole running between them, on which hang skulls, eggs, etc., are often found on the Ivory Coast as taboos of passage and protection against the spirits (oral report by Maurice Delafosse); Pechüel-Loesche, *Volkskunde von Loango*, figures on p. 224, 472, etc.
10. See among others for Surinam, K. Martin. "Bericht uber eine Reise ins Gebeit des oberen Surinam," *Bijdragen tot de Taai-Land on Volkekunde von Nederlands* Indie (The Hague). XXXV (1886), 28–29. Figure 2 shows a statue with two faces which I compared to *Janus bifrons* in an article of the same title in *Revue des traditions populaires*, XXII (1907), No. 4, 97–98. It confirms Frazer's theory in *Lectures on the Early History of the Kingship*, p. 289.
11. Occasionally in Loango a palisade is erected across the road (Du Chaillu, *L'Afrique sauvage*, p. 133) to prevent diseases from entering the territory of the villages; Büttikofer (*Reisebilder aus Liberia*, p. 304) mentions a barricade of straw matting used to prevent access to sacred forests where initiation rites take place; perhaps the barriers made from branches and from straw matting found in Australia and in New Guinea serve this purpose, rather than simply that of hiding from the profane what is going on there, as is usually thought.
12. Letters of marque originally constituted a license from a sovereign authorizing a subject to seek reprisals against subjects of a hostile state for injuries inflicted by that state. In later times these letters enabled privateers to commit acts against a hostile nation which otherwise would have been considered piracy. In Europe, letters of marque were abolished by the Congress of Paris in 1856. (See *Oxford English Dictionary*.)]

13. On the subject of sacred zones and bands of neutral territory, see Grierson, *The Silent Trade*, pp. 29, 56–59; and on frontiers and signs of sacred frontiers in Palestine and Assyro-Babylonia, see H. Gressmann, "Mythische Reste in der Paradieserzählung," *Archiv für Religionswissenschaft*, X (1907), 361–63 n. On the feast of the Terminalia in Rome, see W. Warde Fowler, *The Roman Festivals of the Period of the Republic* (London: Macmillan, 1899), pp. 325–27. It seems likely that the Capitoline Hill was originally one of those neutral zones of which I speak (Fowler, p. 317), as well as a frontier between the city of the Palatine and that of the Quirinal: see also *Roscher's Lexikon*, s.v. "Jupiter," col. 668, and W. Warde Fowler in *Anthropology and the Classics* pp. 181 ff. on the subject of the pomerium.
14. See Frazer, *The Golden Bough*, I, 305.
15. H. Clay Trumbull, *The Threshold Covenant: Or the Beginning of Religious Rites* (New York: Charles Scribner's Sons, 1896), pp. 184–96. I wish to thank Mr. Salomon Reinach for lending me this book, which is difficult to find.
16. *Ibid.*, p. 186. Trumbull's thesis is that the blood which was shed is a symbol, if not an agent of union.
17. A collection of these rites has been published in *Mélusine: Recueil de mythologie, littérature populaire, tradition, et usages* (Paris: Gaidoz & Rolland, 1878–1912). A few imply the transfer of a disease, but what are commonly called rites of purification suggest the idea of a transition from the impure to the pure. All these ideas, and the rites to which they correspond, often form a single ceremonial grouping.
18. For details on the rites of passage pertaining to the threshold, I refer you to Trumbull's *The Threshold Covenant*. Some prostrate themselves before the threshold, some kiss it, some touch it with their hands, some walk upon it or remove their shoes before doing so, some step over it, some are carried over it, etc. See also William Crooke, "The Lifting of the Bride," *Folk-lore*, XIII (1902), 238–42. All these rites vary from people to people and become more complicated if the threshold is the seat of the spirit of the house, the family, or the threshold god.
19. For a detailed list of Chinese practices with reference to doors, see Justus Doolittle, *Social Life of the Chinese with Some Account of the Religious, Governmental, Educational, and Business Customs and Opinions with Special but Not Exclusive Reference to Fuhchau* (New York: Harper, 1865), I, 121–22; II, 310–12; Wilhelm Grube, *Zur pekinger Volkskunde* (Berlin, 1902), pp. 93–97. On magical ornamentation pertaining to the door, see Trumbull, *The Threshold Covenant*, pp. 69–74, 323.
20. I cannot share Trumbull's view that the threshold is a primitive altar and the altar a transplanted threshold, nor can I attribute a greater importance to the presence of blood in rites pertaining to the threshold than to the use of water or simple contact. All these are rites of incorporation or union.
21. [This statement appears to be primarily speculative.]
22. For China, see Gisbert Combaz, *Sépultures impériales de la Chine* (Brussels: Vromant & Co., 1908), pp. 27–33; Doolittle, *Social Life of the Chinese*, II, 299–300. For Japan, see W. E. Griffis, in Trumbull, *The Threshold Covenant*, Appendix, pp. 320–24; B. H. Chamberlain, *Things Japanese: Notes on Various Subjects Connected with Japan for the Use of Travellers and Others* (London: Paul, 1891, p. 356, s.v. "torii"); N. Gordon Munro, "Primitive Culture in Japan," *Transactions of the Asiatic Society of Japan*, XXXIV (1906), 144.
23. For the order of rites of triumph, see Le Père Bernard de Montfaucon, O.S.B., *Antiquités expliquées et représentées en figures* (Paris: F. Delaulne, 1719), 2d ed.; IV, 152–61.
24. Regarding these divinities and the rites pertaining to them, see Eugène Lefebure, *Rites égyptiens: Construction et protection des édifices* (Paris: E. Leroux, 1890); for the Assyrian winged bulls, see p. 62.
25. Regarding the divinities of the threshold, see (in addition to Trumbull, *The Threshold Covenant*, pp. 94 ff.): L. R. Farnell, "The Place of the Sonder-götter in Greek Polytheism," in *Anthropological Essays Presented to E. B. Tylor*, p. 82; and Frazer, *The Golden Bough*. In China they are ordinarily Shen-Shu and Jü-Lü (see Jan M. de Groot and Eduard Chavannes, *Les fêtes annuellement célébrées à Emouy* [Paris, 1886], pp. 597 ff.) but in Peking also Ch'in-Ch'iung and Yü-chih-Kung (see Grube, *Zur pekinger Volkskunde*). For Japan see Isabella L. Bird, *Unbeaten Tracks in Japan: Travels in the Interior, Including Visits to the Aborigines of Yozzo and the Shrine of Nikko* (London: J. Murray, 1905), I, 117, 273; Revon, "Le shinntoisme," pp. 389, 390; Munro, "Primitive Culture in Japan," p. 144, etc.
26. See among others H. Gaidoz, *Étude de la mythologie gauloise*, Vol. I: *Le dieu gaulois du soleil et le symbolisme de la roue* (Paris: E. Leroux, 1886), p. 65; I recall the ceremonies of construction and of the opening of bridges (cf. "pontifex"). As for rites of passing between or under something, they have been collected in *Mélusine* and by almost all folklore students. They should all be discussed again, but it will be impossible to do so at this time. Therefore I will cite only the following, taken from Stepan Petrovitch Kraŝeninnikov, *Histoire et description du Kamtchatka*, trans. from the Russian by M. de Saint Pré (Amsterdam: M. M. Rey, 1760), I, 130–31, and see p. 136: "Soon afterward, they brought birch branches into the yurt, according to the number of families represented. Each Kamchadal took one of these branches for his family, and after bending it into a circle he made his wife and children pass through it twice; as they emerged from this hoop, they began to spin around. Among them this is called being purified of one's faults."

    It is apparent from the detailed descriptions by Kraŝeninnikov that the birch is a sacred tree for the Kamchadals and that it is used ritually in most of their ceremonies. Two interpretations are possible: direct sanctification may occur under the influence of the birch, which is considered *pure*, or a transference of impurity from the people to the birch may take place. The latter seems to be in keeping with the rest of the ceremony: "When all had been purified, the Kamchadals came out of the yurt with these small branches through the *župan*, or the lower opening, and they were followed by their relatives of both sexes. As soon as they were out of the yurt, they passed through the birch circle for the second time and then stuck the little branches in the snow, bending the end towards the east. After throwing all their *tonŝič* on this spot and shaking their clothing, the Kamchadals re-entered the yurt by the ordinary opening and not by the *župan*." In other words, they rid themselves of the sacred material impurities which had accumulated in their clothes, and of their most important ritual object, the *tonšič* (which together with "sweet grass," etc., comprises their category of sacra). The branches, which had been endowed with the sacred, are thrown away.

The passage through the sacred arcs automatically removes from the celebrants the sacred characteristics which they acquired by performing the complicated ceremonies that this rite terminates. These circles form the portal which separates the sacred world from the profane world, so that, once they have entered the profane, the performers of the ceremony are again able to use the big door of the hut.

27. Regarding construction sacrifices, see Paul Satori ("Über das Bauopfer," *Zeitschrift für Ethnologie*, XXX [1898], 1–54), who did not see that a few of them are rites of appropriation. For French rites, see Paul Sébillot, *Le folk-lore de la France* (Paris: E. Guilmoto, 1907), IV, 96–98; and for various theories, see Trumbull, *The Threshold Covenant*, pp. 45–57, and Edvard Alexander Westermarck, *The Origin and Development of Moral Ideas* (London: Macmillan, 1906–8), I, 461. Those rites fall into a wider category which I call the "rites of the first time." The charm 43, 3–15, of the Kausika-sutra (W. Calland, *Altindisches Zauberrei: Darstellung der altindischen Wunschopfer* [Amsterdam: J. Muller, 1900], pp. 147–48) not only is connected with construction and with entering but also is mentioned in people's and animals' changing of dwellings.
28. For a typical ceremony, see W. L. Hildburgh, "Notes on Sinhalese Magic," *Journal of the Royal Anthropological Institute*, XXXVIII (1908), 190.
29. Smith, *The Religion of the Semites*, pp. 461–62.
30. Trumbull, *The Threshold Covenant*, pp. 69–70, with reference to Syria. [Van Gennep evidently relied on Trumbull for this information. According to *The Jewish Encyclopedia*, ed. Isidore Singer (New York and London: Funk & Wagnalls, 1916), the prayer at the door is translated as "may God keep my going out and my coming in from now on and evermore." The inside of the mezuzah contains the words of Deuteronomy 6 : 4–9 and 11 : 13–21, both of which exhort the Jews to love and obey God, and which command them to write God's name on their doors and gateposts. "Shaddai" is written on the outside of the mezuzah, which is touched and kissed in passing through the door.]

3

Liminality and Communitas

FORM AND ATTRIBUTES OF RITES OF PASSAGE

In this Chapter I take up a theme I have discussed briefly elsewhere (Turner, 1967, pp. 93–111), note some of its variations, and consider some of its further implications for the study of culture and society. This theme is in the first place represented by the nature and characteristics of what Arnold van Gennep (1960) has called the "liminal phase" of *rites de passage*. Van Gennep himself defined *rites de passage* as "rites which accompany every change of place, state, social position and age." To point up the contrast between "state" and "transition," I employ "state" to include all his other terms. It is a more inclusive concept than "status" or "office," and refers to any type of stable or recurrent condition that is culturally recognized. Van Gennep has shown that all rites of passage or "transition" are marked by three phases: separation, margin (or *limen*, signifying "threshold" in Latin), and aggregation. The first phase (of separation) comprises symbolic behavior signifying the detachment of the individual or group either from an earlier fixed point in the social structure, from a set of cultural conditions (a "state"), or from both. During the intervening "liminal" period, the characteristics of the ritual subject (the "passenger") are ambiguous; he passes through a cultural realm that has few or none of the attributes of the past or coming state. In the third phase (reaggregation or reincorporation),

the passage is consummated. The ritual subject, individual or corporate, is in a relatively stable state once more and, by virtue of this, has rights and obligations vis-à-vis others of a clearly defined and "structural" type; he is expected to behave in accordance with certain customary norms and ethical standards binding on incumbents of social position in a system of such positions.

Liminality

The attributes of liminality or of liminal *personae* ("threshold people") are necessarily ambiguous, since this condition and these persons elude or slip through the network of classifications that normally locate states and positions in cultural space. Liminal entities are neither here nor there; they are betwixt and between the positions assigned and arrayed by law, custom, convention, and ceremonial. As such, their ambiguous and indeterminate attributes are expressed by a rich variety of symbols in the many societies that ritualize social and cultural transitions. Thus, liminality is frequently likened to death, to being in the womb, to invisibility, to darkness, to bisexuality, to the wilderness, and to an eclipse of the sun or moon.

Liminal entities, such as neophytes in initiation or puberty rites, may be represented as possessing nothing. They may be disguised as monsters, wear only a strip of clothing, or even go naked, to demonstrate that as liminal beings they have no status, property, insignia, secular clothing indicating rank or role, position in a kinship system —in short, nothing that may distinguish them from their fellow neophytes or initiands. Their behavior is normally passive or humble; they must obey their instructors implicitly, and accept arbitrary punishment without complaint. It is as though they are being reduced or ground down to a uniform condition to be fashioned anew and endowed with additional powers to enable them to cope with their new station in life. Among themselves, neophytes tend to develop an intense comradeship and egalitarianism. Secular distinctions of rank and status disappear or are homogenized. The condition of the patient and her husband in *Isoma* had some of these attributes—passivity, humility, near-nakedness—in a symbolic milieu that represented both a grave and a womb. In initiations with a long period of seclusion, such as the circumcision rites of many tribal societies or induction into secret societies, there is often a rich proliferation of liminal symbols.

Communitas

What is interesting about liminal phenomena for our present purposes is the blend they offer of lowliness and sacredness, of homogeneity and comradeship. We are presented, in such rites, with a "moment in and out of time," and in and out of secular social structure, which reveals, however fleetingly, some recognition (in symbol if not always in language) of a generalized social bond that has ceased to be and has simultaneously yet to be fragmented into a multiplicity of structural ties. These are the ties organized in terms either of caste, class, or rank hierarchies or of segmentary oppositions in the stateless societies beloved of political anthropologists. It is as though there are here two major "models" for human interrelatedness, juxtaposed and alternating. The first is of society as a structured, differentiated, and often hierarchical system of politico-legal-economic positions with many types of evaluation, separating men in terms of "more" or "less". The second, which emerges recognizably in the liminal period, is of society as an unstructured or rudimentarily structured and relatively undifferentiated *comitatus*, community, or even communion of equal individuals who submit together to the general authority of the ritual elders.

I prefer the Latin term "communitas" to "community," to distinguish this modality of social relationship from an "area of common living." The distinction between structure and communitas is not simply the familiar one between "secular" and "sacred," or that, for example, between politics and religion. Certain fixed offices in tribal societies have *many* sacred attributes; indeed, every social

position has *some* sacred characteristics. But this "sacred" component is acquired by the incumbents of positions during the *rites de passage*, through which they changed positions. Something of the sacredness of that transient humility and modelessness goes over, and tempers the pride of the incumbent of a higher position or office. This is not simply, as Fortes (1962, p. 86) has cogently argued, a matter of giving a general stamp of legitimacy to a society's structural positions. It is rather a matter of giving recognition to an essential and generic human bond, without which there could be *no* society. Liminality implies that the high could not be high unless the low existed, and he who is high must experience what it is like to be low. No doubt something of this thinking, a few years ago, lay behind Prince Philip's decision to send his son, the heir apparent to the British throne, to a bush school in Australia for a time, where he could learn how "to rough it."

Dialectic of the Developmental Cycle

From all this I infer that, for individuals and groups, social life is a type of dialectrical process that involves successive experience of high and low, communitas and structure, homogeneity and differentiation, equality and inequality. The passage from lower to higher status is through a limbo of statuslessness. In such a process, the opposites, as it were, constitute one another and are mutually indispensable. Furthermore, since any concrete tribal society is made up of multiple personae, groups, and categories, each of which has its own developmental cycle, at a given moment many incumbencies of fixed positions coexist with many passages between positions. In other words, each individual's life experience contains alternating exposure to structure and communitas, and to states and transitions.

Part 1:
How we Approach Death: Theory and Practice

B: Practice: Two Case Studies

Introduction · Grief and a Headhunter's Rage

IF YOU ASK an older Ilongot man of northern Luzon, Philippines, why he cuts off human heads, his answer is brief, and one on which no anthropologist can readily elaborate: He says that rage, born of grief, impels him to kill his fellow human beings. He claims that he needs a place "to carry his anger." The act of severing and tossing away the victim's head enables him, he says, to vent and, he hopes, throw away the anger of his bereavement. Although the anthropologist's job is to make other cultures intelligible, more questions fail to reveal any further explanation of this man's pithy statement. To him, grief, rage, and headhunting go together in a self-evident manner. Either you understand it or you don't. And, in fact, for the longest time I simply did not.

In what follows, I want to talk about how to talk about the cultural force of emotions.[1] The *emotional force* of a death, for example, derives less from an abstract brute fact than from a particular intimate relation's permanent rupture. It refers to the kinds of feelings one experiences on learning, for example, that the child just run over by a car is one's own and not a stranger's. Rather than speaking of death in general, one must consider the subject's position within a field of social relations in order to grasp one's emotional experience.[2]

My effort to show the force of a simple statement taken literally goes against anthropology's classic norms, which prefer to explicate culture through the gradual thickening of symbolic webs of meaning. By and large, cultural analysts use not *force* but such terms as *thick description, multivocality, polysemy, richness,* and *texture.* The notion of force, among other things, opens to question the common anthropological assumption that the greatest human import resides in the densest forest of symbols and that analytical detail, or "cultural depth," equals enhanced explanation of a culture, or "cultural elaboration." Do people always in fact describe most thickly what matters most to them?

The Rage in Ilongot Grief

Let me pause a moment to introduce the Ilongots, among whom my wife, Michelle Rosaldo, and I lived and conducted field research for thirty months (1967–69, 1974). They number about 3,500 and reside in an upland area some 90 miles northeast of Manila, Philippines.[3] They subsist by hunting deer and wild pig and by cultivating rain-fed gardens (swiddens) with rice, sweet potatoes, manioc, and vegetables. Their (bilateral) kin relations are reckoned through men and women. After marriage, parents and their married daughters live in the same or adjacent households. The largest unit within the society, a largely territorial descent

group called the *bertan,* becomes manifest primarily in the context of feuding. For themselves, their neighbors, and their ethnographers, head-hunting stands out as the Ilongots' most salient cultural practice.

When Ilongots told me, as they often did, how the rage in bereavement could impel men to headhunt, I brushed aside their one-line accounts as too simple, thin, opaque, implausible, stereotypical, or otherwise unsatisfying. Probably I naively equated grief with sadness. Certainly no personal experience allowed me to imagine the powerful rage Ilongots claimed to find in bereavement. My own inability to conceive the force of anger in grief led me to seek out another level of analysis that could provide a deeper explanation for older men's desire to headhunt.

Not until some fourteen years after first recording the terse Ilongot statement about grief and a headhunter's rage did I begin to grasp its overwhelming force. For years I thought that more verbal elaboration (which was not forthcoming) or another analytical level (which remained elusive) could better explain older men's motives for headhunting. Only after being repositioned through a devastating loss of my own could I better grasp that Ilongot older men mean precisely what they say when they describe the anger in bereavement as the source of their desire to cut off human heads. Taken at face value and granted its full weight, their statement reveals much about what compels these older men to headhunt.

In my efforts to find a "deeper" explanation for headhunting, I explored exchange theory, perhaps because it had informed so many classic ethnographies. One day in 1974, I explained the anthropologist's exchange model to an older Ilongot man named Insan. What did he think, I asked, of the idea that headhunting resulted from the way that one death (the beheaded victim's) canceled another (the next of kin). He looked puzzled, so I went on to say that the victim of a beheading was exchanged for the death of one's own kin, thereby balancing the books, so to speak. Insan reflected a moment and replied that he imagined somebody could think such a thing (a safe bet, since I just had), but that he and other Ilongots did not think any such thing. Nor was there any indirect evidence for my exchange theory in ritual, boast, song, or casual conversation.[4]

In retrospect, then, these efforts to impose exchange theory on one aspect of Ilongot behavior appear feeble. Suppose I had discovered what I sought? Although the notion of balancing the ledger does have a certain elegant coherence, one wonders how such bookish dogma could inspire any man to take another man's life at the risk of his own.

My life experience had not as yet provided the means to imagine the rage that can come with devastating loss. Nor could I, therefore, fully appreciate the acute problem of meaning that Ilongots faced in 1974. Shortly after Ferdinand Marcos declared martial law in 1972, rumors that firing squads had become the new punishment for headhunting reached the Ilongot hills. The men therefore decided to call a moratorium on taking heads. In past epochs, when headhunting had become impossible, Ilongots had allowed their rage to dissipate, as best it could, in the course of everyday life. In 1974, they had another option; they began to consider conversion to evangelical Christianity as a means of coping with their grief. Accepting the new religion, people said, implied abandoning their old ways, including headhunting. It also made coping with bereavement less agonizing because they could believe that the deceased had departed for a better world. No longer did they have to confront the awful finality of death.

The force of the dilemma faced by the Ilongots eluded me at the time. Even when I correctly recorded their statements about grieving and the need to throw away their anger, I simply did not grasp the weight of their words. In 1974, for example, while Michelle Rosaldo and I were living among the Ilongots, a six-month-old baby died, probably of pneumonia. That afternoon we visited the father and found him terribly stricken. "He was sobbing and staring through glazed and bloodshot eyes at the cotton blanket covering his baby."[5] The man suffered intensely, for this was the seventh

child he had lost. Just a few years before, three of his children had died, one after the other, in a matter of days. At the time, the situation was murky as people present talked both about evangelical Christianity (the possible renunciation of taking heads) and their grudges against lowlanders (the contemplation of headhunting forays into the surrounding valleys).

Through subsequent days and weeks, the man's grief moved him in a way I had not anticipated. Shortly after the baby's death, the father converted to evangelical Christianity. Altogether too quick on the inference, I immediately concluded that the man believed that the new religion could somehow prevent further deaths in his family. When I spoke my mind to an Ilongot friend, he snapped at me, saying that "I had missed the point: what the man in fact sought in the new religion was not the denial of our inevitable deaths but a means of coping with his grief. With the advent of martial law, headhunting was out of the question as a means of venting his wrath and thereby lessening his grief. Were he to remain in his Ilongot way of life, the pain of his sorrow would simply be too much to bear."[6] My description from 1980 now seems so apt that I wonder how I could have written the words and nonetheless failed to appreciate the force of the grieving man's desire to vent his rage.

Another representative anecdote makes my failure to imagine the rage possible in Ilongot bereavement all the more remarkable. On this occasion, Michelle Rosaldo and I were urged by Ilongot friends to play the tape of a headhunting celebration we had witnessed some five years before. No sooner had we turned on the tape and heard the boast of a man who had died in the intervening years than did people abruptly tell us to shut off the recorder. Michelle Rosaldo reported on the tense conversation that ensued:

> As Insan braced himself to speak, the room again became almost uncannily electric. Backs straightened and my anger turned to nervousness and something more like fear as I saw that Insan's eyes were red. Tukbaw, Renato's Ilongot "brother," then broke into what was a brittle silence, saying he could

make things clear. He told us that it hurt to listen to a headhunting celebration when people knew that there would never be another. As he put it: "The song pulls at us, drags our hearts, it makes us think of our dead uncle." And again: "It would be better if I had accepted God, but I still am an Ilongot at heart; and when I hear the song, my heart aches as it does when I must look upon unfinished bachelors whom I know that I will never lead to take a head." Then Wagat, Tukbaw's wife, said with her eyes that all my questions gave her pain, and told me: "Leave off now, isn't that enough? Even I, a woman, cannot stand the way it feels inside my heart."[7]

From my present position, it is evident that the tape recording of the dead man's boast evoked powerful feelings of bereavement, particularly rage and the impulse to headhunt. At the time I could only feel apprehensive and diffusely sense the force of the emotions experienced by Insan, Tukbaw, Wagat, and the others present.

The dilemma for the Ilongots grew out of a set of cultural practices that, when blocked, were agonizing to live with. The cessation of headhunting called for painful adjustments to other modes of coping with the rage they found in bereavement. One could compare their dilemma with the notion that the failure to perform rituals can create anxiety.[8] In the Ilongot case, the cultural notion that throwing away a human head also casts away the anger creates a problem of meaning when the headhunting ritual cannot be performed. Indeed, Max Weber's classic problem of meaning in *The Protestant Ethic and the Spirit of Capitalism* is precisely of this kind.[9] On a logical plane, the Calvinist doctrine of predestination seems flawless: God has chosen the elect, but his decision can never be known by mortals. Among those whose ultimate concern is salvation, the doctrine of predestination is as easy to grasp conceptually as it is impossible to endure in everyday life (unless one happens to be a "religious virtuoso"). For Calvinists and Ilongots alike, the problem of meaning resides in practice, not theory. The dilemma for both groups involves the practical matter of how

to live with one's beliefs, rather than the logical puzzlement produced by abstruse doctrine.

How I Found the Rage in Grief

One burden of this introduction concerns the claim that it took some fourteen years for me to grasp what Ilongots had told me about grief, rage, and headhunting. During all those years I was not yet in a position to comprehend the force of anger possible in bereavement, and now I am. Introducing myself into this account requires a certain hesitation both because of the discipline's taboo and because of its increasingly frequent violation by essays laced with trendy amalgams of continental philosophy and autobiographical snippets. If classic ethnography's vice was the slippage from the ideal of detachment to actual indifference, that of present-day reflexivity is the tendency for the self-absorbed Self to lose sight altogether of the culturally different Other. Despite the risks involved, as the ethnographer I must enter the discussion at this point to elucidate certain issues of method.

The key concept in what follows is that of the positioned (and repositioned) subject.[10] In routine interpretive procedure, according to the methodology of hermeneutics, one can say that ethnographers reposition themselves as they go about understanding other cultures. Ethnographers begin research with a set of questions, revise them throughout the course of inquiry, and in the end emerge with different questions than they started with. One's surprise at the answer to a question, in other words, requires one to revise the question until lessening surprises or diminishing returns indicate a stopping point. This interpretive approach has been most influentially articulated within anthropology by Clifford Geertz.[11]

Interpretive method usually rests on the axiom that gifted ethnographers learn their trade by preparing themselves as broadly as possible. To follow the meandering course of ethnographic inquiry, field-workers require wide-ranging theoretical capacities and finely tuned sensibilities. After all, one cannot predict beforehand what one will encounter in the field. One influential anthropologist, Clyde Kluckhohn, even went so far as to recommend a double initiation: first, the ordeal of psychoanalysis, and then that of fieldwork. All too often, however, this view is extended until certain prerequisites of field research appear to guarantee an authoritative ethnography. Eclectic book knowledge and a range of life experiences, along with edifying reading and self-awareness, supposedly vanquish the twin vices of ignorance and insensitivity.

Although the doctrine of preparation, knowledge, and sensibility contains much to admire, one should work to undermine the false comfort that it can convey. At what point can people say that they have completed their learning or their life experience? The problem with taking this mode of preparing the ethnographer too much to heart is that it can lend a false air of security, an authoritative claim to certitude and finality that our analyses cannot have. All interpretations are provisional; they are made by positioned subjects who are prepared to know certain things and not others. Even when knowledgeable, sensitive, fluent in the language, and able to move easily in an alien cultural world, good ethnographers still have their limits, and their analyses always are incomplete. Thus, I began to fathom the force of what Ilongots had been telling me about their losses through my own loss, and not through any systematic preparation for field research.

My preparation for understanding serious loss began in 1970 with the death of my brother, shortly after his twenty-seventh birthday. By experiencing this ordeal with my mother and father, I gained a measure of insight into the trauma of a parent's losing a child. This insight informed my account, partially described earlier, of an Ilongot man's reactions to the death of his seventh child. At the same time, my bereavement was so much less than that of my parents that I could not then imagine the overwhelming force of

rage possible in such grief. My former position is probably similar to that of many in the discipline. One should recognize that ethnographic knowledge tends to have the strengths and limitations given by the relative youth of field-workers who, for the most part, have not suffered serious losses and could have, for example, no personal knowledge of how devastating the loss of a long-term partner can be for the survivor.

In 1981 Michelle Rosaldo and I began field research among the Ifugaos of northern Luzon, Philippines. On October 11 of that year, she was walking along a trail with two Ifugao companions when she lost her footing and fell to her death some 65 feet down a sheer precipice into a swollen river below. Immediately on finding her body I became enraged. How could she abandon me? How could she have been so stupid as to fall? I tried to cry. I sobbed, but rage blocked the tears. Less than a month later I described this moment in my journal: "I felt like in a nightmare, the whole world around me expanding and contracting, visually and viscerally heaving. Going down I find a group of men, maybe seven or eight, standing still, silent, and I heave and sob, but no tears." An earlier experience, on the fourth anniversary of my brother's death, had taught me to recognize heaving sobs without tears as a form of anger. This anger, in a number of forms, has swept over me on many occasions since then, lasting hours and even days at a time. Such feelings can be aroused by rituals, but more often they emerge from unexpected reminders (not unlike the Ilongots' unnerving encounter with their dead uncle's voice on the tape recorder).

Lest there be any misunderstanding, bereavement should not be reduced to anger, neither for myself nor for anyone else.[12] Powerful visceral emotional states swept over me, at times separately and at other times together. I experienced the deep cutting pain of sorrow almost beyond endurance, the cadaverous cold of realizing the finality of death, the trembling beginning in my abdomen and spreading through my body, the mournful keening that started without my willing, and frequent tearful sobbing. My present purpose of revising earlier understandings of Ilongot headhunting, and not a general view of bereavement, thus focuses on anger rather than on other emotions in grief.

Writings in English especially need to emphasize the rage in grief. Although grief therapists routinely encourage awareness of anger among the bereaved, upper-middle-class Anglo-American culture tends to ignore the rage devastating losses can bring. Paradoxically, this culture's conventional wisdom usually denies the anger in grief at the same time that therapists encourage members of the invisible community of the bereaved to talk in detail about how angry their losses make them feel. My brother's death in combination with what I learned about anger from Ilongots (for them, an emotional state more publicly celebrated than denied) allowed me immediately to recognize the experience of rage.[13]

Ilongot anger and my own overlap, rather like two circles, partially overlaid and partially separate. They are not identical. Alongside striking similarities, significant differences in tone, cultural form, and human consequences distinguish the "anger" animating our respective ways of grieving. My vivid fantasies, for example, about a life insurance agent who refused to recognize Michelle's death as job-related did not lead me to kill him, cut off his head, and celebrate afterward. In so speaking, I am illustrating the discipline's methodological caution against the reckless attribution of one's own categories and experiences to members of another culture. Such warnings against facile notions of universal human nature can, however, be carried too far and harden into the equally pernicious doctrine that, my own group aside, everything human is alien to me. One hopes to achieve a balance between recognizing wide-ranging human differences and the modest truism that any two human groups must have certain things in common.

Only a week before completing the initial draft of an earlier version of this introduction, I rediscovered my journal entry, written some six weeks after Michelle's death, in which I made a vow to myself about how I would return to writing anthropology, if I ever did so, "by writing Grief and

a Headhunter's Rage . . ." My journal went on to reflect more broadly on death, rage, and headhunting by speaking of my "wish for the Ilongot solution; they are much more in touch with reality than Christians. So, I need a place to carry my anger—and can we say a solution of the imagination is better than theirs? And can we condemn them when we napalm villages? Is our rationale so much sounder than theirs?" All this was written in despair and rage.

Not until some fifteen months after Michelle's death was I again able to begin writing anthropology. Writing the initial version of "Grief and a Headhunter's Rage" was in fact cathartic, though perhaps not in the way one would imagine. Rather than following after the completed composition, the catharsis occurred beforehand. When the initial version of this introduction was most acutely on my mind, during the month before actually beginning to write, I felt diffusely depressed and ill with a fever. Then one day an almost literal fog lifted and words began to flow. It seemed less as if I were doing the writing than that the words were writing themselves through me.

My use of personal experience serves as a vehicle for making the quality and intensity of the rage in Ilongot grief more readily accessible to readers than certain more detached modes of composition. At the same time, by invoking personal experience as an analytical category one risks easy dismissal. Unsympathetic readers could reduce this introduction to an act of mourning or a mere report on my discovery of the anger possible in bereavement. Frankly, this introduction is both and more. An act of mourning, a personal report, *and* a critical analysis of anthropological method, it simultaneously encompasses a number of distinguishable processes, no one of which cancels out the others. Similarly, I argue in what follows that ritual in general and Ilongot headhunting in particular form the intersection of multiple coexisting social processes. Aside from revising the ethnographic record, the paramount claim made here concerns how my own mourning and consequent reflection on Ilongot bereavement, rage, and headhunting raise methodological issues of general concern in anthropology and the human sciences.

Death in Anthropology

Anthropology favors interpretations that equate analytical "depth" with cultural "elaboration." Many studies focus on visibly bounded arenas where one can observe formal and repetitive events, such as ceremonies, rituals, and games. Similarly, studies of word play are more likely to focus on jokes as programmed monologues than on the less scripted, more free-wheeling improvised interchanges of witty banter. Most ethnographers prefer to study events that have definite locations in space with marked centers and outer edges. Temporally, they have middles and endings. Historically, they appear to repeat identical structures by seemingly doing things today as they were done yesterday. Their qualities of fixed definition liberate such events from the untidiness of everyday life so that they can be "read" like articles, books, or, as we now say, *texts.*

Guided by their emphasis on self-contained entities, ethnographies written in accord with classic norms consider death under the rubric of ritual rather than bereavement. Indeed, the subtitles of even recent ethnographies on death make the emphasis on ritual explicit. William Douglas's *Death in Murelaga* is subtitled *Funerary Ritual in a Spanish Basque Village;* Richard Huntington and Peter Metcalf's *Celebrations of Death* is subtitled *The Anthropology of Mortuary Ritual;* Peter Metcalf's *A Borneo Journey into Death* is subtitled *Berawan Eschatology from Its Rituals.*[14] Ritual itself is defined by its formality and routine; under such descriptions, it more nearly resembles a recipe, a fixed program, or a book of etiquette than an open-ended human process.

Ethnographies that in this manner eliminate intense emotions not only distort their descriptions but also remove potentially key variables from their explanations. When anthropologist William Douglas, for example, announces his project in *Death in Murelaga,* he explains that his objective

is to use death and funerary ritual "as a heuristic device with which to approach the study of rural Basque society."[15] In other words, the primary object of study is social structure, not death, and certainly not bereavement. The author begins his analysis by saying, "Death is not always fortuitous or unpredictable."[16] He goes on to describe how an old woman, ailing with the infirmities of her age, welcomed her death. The description largely ignores the perspective of the most bereaved survivors, and instead vacillates between those of the old woman and a detached observer.

Undeniably, certain people do live a full life and suffer so greatly in their decrepitude that they embrace the relief death can bring. Yet the problem with making an ethnography's major case study focus on "a very easy death"[17] (I use Simone de Beauvoir's title with irony, as she did) is not only its lack of representativeness but also that it makes death in general appear as routine for the survivors as this particular one apparently was for the deceased. Were the old woman's sons and daughters untouched by her death? The case study shows less about how people cope with death than about how death can be made to appear routine, thereby fitting neatly into the author's view of funerary ritual as a mechanical programmed unfolding of prescribed acts. "To the Basque," says Douglas, "ritual is order and order is ritual."[18]

Douglas captures only one extreme in the range of possible deaths. Putting the accent on the routine aspects of ritual conveniently conceals the agony of such unexpected early deaths as parents losing a grown child or a mother dying in childbirth. Concealed in such descriptions are the agonies of the survivors who muddle through shifting, powerful emotional states. Although Douglas acknowledges the distinction between the bereaved members of the deceased's domestic group and the more public ritualistic group, he writes his account primarily from the viewpoint of the latter. He masks the emotional force of bereavement by reducing funerary ritual to orderly routine.

Surely, human beings mourn both in ritual settings *and* in

the informal settings of everyday life. Consider the evidence that willy-nilly spills over the edges in Godfrey Wilson's classic anthropological account of "conventions of burial" among the Nyakyusa of South Africa:

> That some at least of those who attend a Nyakyusa burial are moved by grief it is easy to establish. I have heard people talking regretfully in ordinary conversation of a man's death; I have seen a man whose sister had just died walk over alone towards her grave and weep quietly by himself without any parade of grief; and I have heard of a man killing himself because of his grief for a dead son.[19]

Note that all the instances Wilson witnesses or hears about happen outside the circumscribed sphere of formal ritual. People converse among themselves, walk alone and silently weep, or more impulsively commit suicide. The work of grieving, probably universally, occurs both within obligatory ritual acts and in more everyday settings where people find themselves alone or with close kin.

In Nyakyusa burial ceremonies, powerful emotional states also become present in the ritual itself, which is more than a series of obligatory acts. Men say they dance the passions of their bereavement, which includes a complex mix of anger, fear, and grief:

> "This war dance (*ukukina*)," said an old man, "is mourning, we are mourning the dead man. We dance because there is war in our hearts. A passion of grief and fear exasperates us (*ilyyojo likutusila*)." . . . *Elyojo* means a passion or grief, anger or fear; *ukusila* means to annoy or exasperate beyond endurance. In explaining *ukusila* one man put it like this: "If a man continually insults me then he exasperates me (*ukusila*) so that I want to fight him." Death is a fearful and grievous event that exasperates those men nearly concerned and makes them want to fight.[20]

Descriptions of the dance and subsequent quarrels, even killings, provide ample evidence of the emotional intensity involved. The articulate testimony by Wilson's informants

makes it obvious that even the most intense sentiments can be studied by ethnographers.

Despite such exceptions as Wilson, the general rule seem to be that one should tidy things up as much as possible by wiping away the tears and ignoring the tantrums. Most anthropological studies of death eliminate emotions by assuming the position of the most detached observer.[21] Such studies usually conflate the ritual process with the process of mourning, equate ritual with the obligatory, and ignore the relation between ritual and everyday life. The bias that favors formal ritual risks assuming the answers to questions that most need to be asked. Do rituals, for example, always reveal cultural depth?

Most analysts who equate death with funerary ritual assume that rituals store encapsulated wisdom as if it were a microcosm of its encompassing cultural macrocosm. One recent study of death and mourning, for example, confidently begins by affirming that rituals embody "the collective wisdom of many cultures."[22] Yet this generalization surely requires case-by-case investigation against a broader range of alternative hypotheses.

At the polar extremes, rituals either display cultural depth or brim over with platitudes. In the former case, rituals indeed encapsulate a culture's wisdom; in the latter instance, they act as catalysts that precipitate processes whose unfolding occurs over subsequent months or even years. Many rituals, of course, do both by combining a measure of wisdom with a comparable dose of platitudes.

My own experience of bereavement and ritual fits the platitudes and catalyst model better than that of microcosmic deep culture. Even a careful analysis of the language and symbolic action during the two funerals for which I was a chief mourner would reveal precious little about the experience of bereavement.[23] This statement, of course, should not lead anyone to derive a universal from somebody else's personal knowledge. Instead, it should encourage ethnographers to ask whether a ritual's wisdom is deep or conventional, and whether its process is immediately transformative or but a single step in a lengthy series of ritual and everyday events.

In attempting to grasp the cultural force of rage and other powerful emotional states, both formal ritual and the informal practices of everyday life provide crucial insight. Thus, cultural descriptions should seek out force as well as thickness, and they should extend from well-defined rituals to myriad less circumscribed practices.

Grief, Rage, and Ilongot Headhunting

When applied to Ilongot headhunting, the view of ritual as a storehouse of collective wisdom aligns headhunting with expiatory sacrifice. The raiders call the spirits of the potential victims, bid their ritual farewells, and seek favorable omens along the trail. Ilongot men vividly recall the hunger and deprivation they endure over the days and even weeks it takes to move cautiously toward the place where they set up an ambush and await the first person who happens along. Once the raiders kill their victim, they toss away the head rather than keep it as a trophy. In tossing away the head, they claim by analogy to cast away their life burdens, including the rage in their grief.

Before a raid, men describe their state of being by saying that the burdens of life have made them heavy and entangled, like a tree with vines clinging to it. They say that a successfully completed raid makes them feel light of step and ruddy in complexion. The collective energy of the celebration with its song, music, and dance reportedly gives the participants a sense of well-being. The expiatory ritual process involves cleansing and catharsis.

The analysis just sketched regards ritual as a timeless, self-contained process. Without denying the insight in this approach, its limits must also be considered. Imagine, for example, exorcism rituals described as if they were complete in themselves, rather than being linked with larger processes unfolding before and after the ritual period. Through what processes does the afflicted person recover or continue

to be afflicted after the ritual? What are the social consequences of recovery or its absence? Failure to consider such questions diminishes the force of such afflictions and therapies for which the formal ritual is but a phase. Still other questions apply to differently positioned subjects, including the person afflicted, the healer, and the audience. In all cases, the problem involves the delineation of processes that occur before and after, as well as during, the ritual moment.

Let us call the notion of a self-contained sphere of deep cultural activity the *microcosmic view,* and an alternative view *ritual as a busy intersection.* In the latter case, ritual appears as a place where a number of distinct social processes intersect. The crossroads simply provides a space for distinct trajectories to traverse, rather than containing them in complete encapsulated form. From this perspective, Ilongot headhunting stands at the confluence of three analytically separable processes.

The first process concerns whether or not it is an opportune time to raid. Historical conditions determine the possibilities of raiding, which range from frequent to likely to unlikely to impossible. These conditions include American colonial efforts at pacification, the Great Depression, World War II, revolutionary movements in the surrounding lowlands, feuding among Ilongot groups, and the declaration of martial law in 1972. Ilongots use the analogy of hunting to speak of such historical vicissitudes. Much as Ilongot huntsmen say they cannot know when game will cross their path or whether their arrows will strike the target, so certain historical forces that condition their existence remain beyond their control. My book *Ilongot Headhunting, 1883–1974* explores the impact of historical factors on Ilongot headhunting.

Second, young men coming of age undergo a protracted period of personal turmoil during which they desire nothing so much as to take a head. During this troubled period, they seek a life partner and contemplate the traumatic dislocation of leaving their families of origin and entering their new wife's household as a stranger. Young men weep, sing, and burst out in anger because of their fierce desire to take a head and wear the coveted red hornbill earrings that adorn the ears of men who already have, as Ilongots say, arrived (*tabi*). Volatile, envious, passionate (at least according to their own cultural stereotype of the young unmarried man [*buintaw*]), they constantly lust to take a head. Michelle and I began fieldwork among the Ilongots only a year after abandoning our unmarried youths; hence our ready empathy with youthful turbulence. Her book on Ilongot notions of self explores the passionate anger of young men as they come of age.

Third, older men are differently positioned than their younger counterparts. Because they have already beheaded somebody, they can wear the red hornbill earrings so coveted by youths. Their desire to headhunt grows less from chronic adolescent turmoil than from more intermittent acute agonies of loss. After the death of somebody to whom they are closely attached, older men often inflict on themselves vows of abstinence, not to be lifted until the day they participate in a successful headhunting raid. These deaths can cover a range of instances from literal death, whether through natural causes or beheading, to social death where, for example, a man's wife runs off with another man. In all cases, the rage born of devastating loss animates the older men's desire to raid. This anger at abandonment is irreducible in that nothing at a deeper level explains it. Although certain analysts argue against the dreaded last analysis, the linkage of grief, rage, and headhunting has no other known explanation.

My earlier understandings of Ilongot headhunting missed the fuller significance of how older men experience loss and rage. Older men prove critical in this context because they, not the youths, set the processes of headhunting in motion. Their rage is intermittent, whereas that of youths is continuous. In the equation of headhunting, older men are the variable and younger men are the constant. Culturally speaking, older men are endowed with knowledge and stamina that

their juniors have not yet attained, hence they care for (*saysay*) and lead (*bukur*) the younger men when they raid.

In a preliminary survey of the literature on headhunting, I found that the lifting of mourning prohibitions frequently occurs after taking a head. The notion that youthful anger and older men's rage lead them to take heads is more plausible than such commonly reported "explanations" of headhunting as the need to acquire mystical "soul stuff" or personal names.[24] Because the discipline correctly rejects stereotypes of the "bloodthirsty savage," it must investigate how headhunters create an intense desire to decapitate their fellow humans. The human sciences must explore the cultural force of emotions with a view to delineating the passions that animate certain forms of human conduct.

Summary

The ethnographer, as a positioned subject, grasps certain human phenomena better than others. He or she occupies a position or structural location and observes with a particular angle of vision. Consider, for example, how age, gender, being an outsider, and association with a neocolonial regime influence what the ethnographer learns. The notion of position also refers to how life experiences both enable and inhibit particular kinds of insight. In the case at hand, nothing in my own experience equipped me even to imagine the anger possible in bereavement until after Michelle Rosaldo's death in 1981. Only then was I in a position to grasp the force of what Ilongots had repeatedly told me about grief, rage, and headhunting. By the same token, so-called natives are also positioned subjects who have a distinctive mix of insight and blindness. Consider the structural positions of older versus younger Ilongot men, or the differing positions of chief mourners versus those less involved during a funeral. My discussion of anthropological writings on death often achieved its effects simply by shifting from the position of those least involved to that of the chief mourners.

Cultural depth does not always equal cultural elaboration. Think simply of the speaker who is filibustering. The language used can sound elaborate as it heaps word on word, but surely it is not deep. Depth should be separated from the presence or absence of elaboration. By the same token, one-line explanations can be vacuous or pithy. The concept of force calls attention to an enduring intensity in human conduct that can occur with or without the dense elaboration conventionally associated with cultural depth. Although relatively without elaboration in speech, song, or ritual, the rage of older Ilongot men who have suffered devastating losses proves enormously consequential in that, foremost among other things, it leads them to behead their fellow humans. Thus, the notion of force involves both affective intensity and significant consequences that unfold over a long period of time.

Similarly, rituals do not always encapsulate deep cultural wisdom. At times they instead contain the wisdom of Polonius. Although certain rituals both reflect and create ultimate values, others simply bring people together and deliver a set of platitudes that enable them to go on with their lives. Rituals serve as vehicles for processes that occur both before and after the period of their performance. Funeral rituals, for example, do not "contain" all the complex processes of bereavement. Ritual and bereavement should not be collapsed into one another because they neither fully encapsulate nor fully explain one another. Instead, rituals are often but points along a number of longer processual trajectories; hence, my image of ritual as a crossroads where distinct life processes intersect.[25]

The notion of ritual as a busy intersection anticipates the critical assessment of the concept of culture developed in the following chapters. In contrast with the classic view, which posits culture as a self-contained whole made up of coherent patterns, culture can arguably be conceived as a more porous array of intersections where distinct processes crisscross from within and beyond its borders. Such heterogeneous

processes often derive from differences of age, gender, class, race, and sexual orientation.

This book argues that a sea change in cultural studies has eroded once-dominant conceptions of truth and objectivity. The truth of objectivism—absolute, universal, and timeless—has lost its monopoly status. It now competes, on more nearly equal terms, with the truths of case studies that are embedded in local contexts, shaped by local interests, and colored by local perceptions. The agenda for social analysis has shifted to include not only eternal verities and lawlike generalizations but also political processes, social changes, and human differences. Such terms as *objectivity*, *neutrality*, and *impartiality* refer to subject positions once endowed with great institutional authority, but they are arguably neither more nor less valid than those of more engaged, yet equally perceptive, knowledgeable social actors. Social analysis must now grapple with the realization that its objects of analysis are also analyzing subjects who critically interrogate ethnographers—their writings, their ethics, and their politics.

5

DEATH RITUALS AND LIFE VALUES: RITES OF PASSAGE RECONSIDERED

LIFE THEMES IN DEATH

Death is a transition; but it is only the last in a long chain of transitions. The moment of death is related not only to the process of afterlife, but also to the process of living, aging, and producing progeny. Death relates to life: to the recent life of the deceased, and to the life he or she has procreated and now leaves behind. There is an eternity of sorts on either side of the line that divides the quick from the dead. Life continues generation after generation, and in many societies it is this continuity that is focused on and enhanced during the rituals surrounding a death. The continuity of the living is a more palpable reality than the continuity of the dead. Consequently, it is common for life values of sexuality and fertility to dominate the symbolism of funerals.

Let us carry our comparison of the variety of Southeast Asian funerals to the westward limits of the Malayo-Polynesian culture area: to the island of Madagascar (see Figure 6). The forebears of the Malagasy inhabitants of the island sailed their outrigger canoes from Borneo and Indonesia thousands of miles across the Indian Ocean more than a millennium ago. Over the centuries in Madagascar, these Indonesians mixed with peoples of Arab and African descent to form the unique Malagasy culture and language. Even after centuries of mixing and blending, and after long isolation from the East, the Indonesian and Bornean ele-

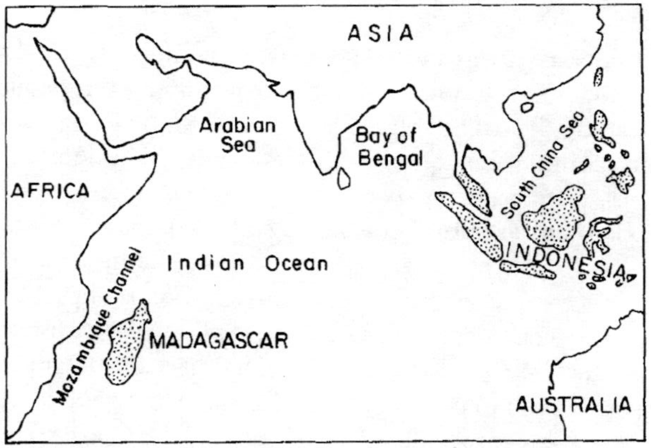

Figure 6. Countries bordering the Indian Ocean, showing as the shaded area the Malayo-Polynesian culture area.

ments still dominate Malagasy culture. The linguistic evidence suggests that the Malagasy are most closely related to the Ma'anyan of Borneo (Dahl 1951).

The cultural diversity within Madagascar is almost as great as that in island Southeast Asia. The variety of funeral rites and tomb design is also great; some people construct large showy tombs, where other groups dispose of their dead in secret and camouflaged caves. Yet, despite the variation among the eighteen major ethnic groups that comprise the Malagasy people, the ritual of exhumation and reburial is of great importance in almost all regions of the island. For instance, the Merina people open the family tomb ever few years, bring out the skeletons, rewrap them in new cloths, add the newly exhumed relics of those who have died since the last general tomb opening, and then replace all the relics and close the tomb. As the dominant ethnic group, the Merina have moved away from their homeland near the capital city and spread throughout the island. For these general exhumation ceremonies, kin from all regions converge on their ancestral hamlet as an expression of family solidarity and to arrange practical matters such as marriages (Bloch 1971). Among the Sakalava of the western region, only the relics of royalty receive this sort of periodic attention. The royal ancestors belong, in one sense, to everyone. Commoners do not exhume and rebury their own dead, but rather they attend the annual ritual treatment of the "national ancestors."

Among the Bara people of the South, the focus of this chapter, everyone is eventually exhumed and placed in a family tomb. Details of secondary treatment of the dead are not available for all the Malagasy peoples, and so it is difficult to chart all the variations with accuracy. But it is clear that secondary treatment of the skeletal remains is an important custom that is called on to give expression to various social and political values among the different ethnic groups.

These funeral rituals are the most important cultural institutions in traditional Malagasy societies. The expenditures of time and resources for death rituals and the maintenance of tombs are considerable, especially in light of the often meager economic base. The conspicuous entombment of the dead is the central activity in Malagasy systems of religion, economics, and social prestige. Even a casual visitor to Madagascar quickly becomes aware of the large role burial customs play in the lives of the people. In many parts of the island, tombs, whose elaborate and solid construction far exceeds the care given to the houses of the living, dominate the landscape. During the cool season, one finds the roads full of people traveling to their family reburial ceremonies. Even in the taxicab on the way from the international airport, the visitor reads on the official list of cab fares that the rental rate for exhumations is negotiable.

Let us contemplate for a moment the implications of this centrality of death in Malagasy culture, for most of us belong to a society in which death is kept on the periphery of our experience. In order to begin to understand the death rituals of the Malagasy, or of many of the other peoples considered in this study, it is necessary to see that the social and cultural context of funerals is utterly different from that in our society. Death rituals, especially the seasonal reburials, are, in much of Madagascar, as normal and as pervasive as is Christmas or the Fourth of July in the United States. The Malagasy funeral-related institutions are both private and public affairs of religious as well as social significance, and they are a great expense to individual families and a stimulus to the general economy. These activities are closely associated with positive and central familial, social, and political structures, and their connection deprives them of that sense of abnormality and near indecency that seems to hover around funerals in most Western societies.

There is in most Malagasy funerals the sort of emphasis on life and vitality that Wilson described for the Nyakyusa, and which he suggested

may be a universal aspect of death rituals. Certainly the themes of rebirth, love, and sexuality as symbols transcending death have been explored by countless poets and dramatists. If people feel the need to confront death with an emphasis on life, then, nonetheless, the theme will be uniquely implemented in societies that put death and the dead at the center of their social and moral system.

In our society, both sexuality and death belong somewhat outside the normative and public values pertaining to the family and the community. Hence love and death, sex and death, rebirth and death provide symbols whose great power is partly derived from the fact that they oppose everyday institutions. The relationships are very different in Madagascar, where death and funeral customs pertain to the ancestral order that is at the heart of the normative social system. Furthermore, this ancestral system directly requires the birth of new generations, and the ancestors themselves are seen as the most important agents encouraging virility and fertility. Funerals, social order, fertility, and all that these entail are naturally and positively related in Madagascar. The combination of themes of death and sexuality contains little of the antisocial power that these themes evoke in our cultural tradition.

PROBLEMS WITH THE APPROACHES OF HERTZ AND VAN GENNEP

Both Hertz and van Gennep were familiar with the funeral customs of Madagascar and both made important use of the Malagasy data in their studies (Hertz 1960: 47–8; van Gennep 1960: 148–9). Van Gennep in particular was a leading authority on the religion of Madagascar, and the author of a major monograph on the topic (1904). Although the examples he cites in *The Rites of Passage* have a worldwide distribution, the elaboration of his theory is strongly influenced by his long familiarity with Malagasy ethnography.

There are, however, problems in the application of the theories of van Gennep and Hertz to the ritual data of Madagascar. Both viewed such rituals as a symbolic representation of the ambiguous liminal state of the deceased while in passage from life toward some fixed eternal condition. But, in spite of the widespread custom of secondary treatment of the dead in Madagascar, the emphasis on beliefs about the afterworld present in our Indonesian examples is lacking in Madagascar. There are few concepts of a journey of the soul, or of a land of the dead off somewhere in the distance. The dead reside in the tomb. This is not to say that eschatological concepts are entirely lacking. It is just that they are not important enough, explicit enough, or central enough to the culture to provide a basis for such elaborate rites of burial and reburial. Bloch (1971) noted this difficulty in his study of the secondary burial rituals of the Merina. He asked about the world of the dead and received scant information.

Hertz identified a metaphorical relationship between corpse and soul that makes sense of the rituals, large and small, of death in Borneo. The same is not true in Madagascar. There, a different significance is placed on the separation of bone and flesh that is celebrated in the rites of secondary treatment. In view of the discussion of cultural universals in Chapter 3, it comes as no surprise that there are symbolic uses of the corpse that achieve considerable generality without becoming universal even within a particular culture area. How these differential symbolic elaborations arose is a matter for speculation. Meanwhile, it is interesting to note that there are echoes of Malagasy notions about death in Bornean funerals, just as eschatological ideas are not entirely absent in Madagascar.

Van Gennep's notion that a funeral ritual can be seen as a transition that begins with the separation of the deceased from life and ends with his or her incorporation into the world of the dead is merely a vague truism unless it is positively related to the values of the particular culture. The continued relevance of van Gennep's notion is not due to the tripartite analytical scheme itself, but to the creative way it can be combined with cultural values to grasp the conceptual vitality of each ritual. In following this theoretical approach, it is necessary not merely to apply an old formula to new rituals, but in a sense to create anew the rites of passage in a dynamic relationship among the logic of the schema (transitions need beginnings and ends), biological facts (corpses rot), and culturally specific symbolizations.

The most striking aspect of Malagasy funerals is the bawdy and drunken revelry enjoined on the guests. Malagasy participants state that these lively events are necessary because the deceased is in transition. He or she is isolated and lonely and needs to be amused and entertained. But such an explanation is obviously incomplete. It fails to tell us why

these particular forms of entertainment are seen as the appropriate amusement for the spirit of a recently departed relative. Why drunkenness, sexual liaisons, and bawdy songs? Why not respectful hymns of praise or a decorous show of family morality and solidarity? To answer this, and provide an analysis of the specific symbolic content of Malagasy funerals, one must look away from beliefs about ghosts and the hereafter and examine basic values and concepts about the nature and meaning of life.

BARA LIFE VALUES: ORDER AND VITALITY

We focus the rest of this chapter on one ethnic group of Madagascar, the Bara, sedentary pastoralists of the island's southern plains. Only by looking at one situation in some detail can we evaluate the several analytic aspects that have been discussed so far in this book. In a single case, we can view the complex interplay of the expression of emotion, ritual action, specific beliefs, the universal rite-of-passage schema, and the phoenix theme of rebirth with those basic values and categories that are pervasively important to Bara social life. The Bara, of course, cannot stand as a substitute for any other society either within or outside Madagascar. But they can stand as a demonstration of how people of one culture face squarely the fact of death.

A difficulty in the analysis of Bara funerals stems from the fact that although the rite-of-passage approach stresses the ambiguous and transitory aspect of dying, important Bara values stress that it is life that is transitory, and dying that is tragically unambiguous. In terms of the Bara phenomenology of the person, life is maintained by a tenuously balanced combination of what can be referred to as "order" and "vitality." As a biological being, a person is formed when the fertile blood of the mother's womb is ordered and arranged by the sperm of the father during sexual intercourse. To be socially and economically successful, an individual must balance out his or her relationships with his mother's and father's families. A person's life is seen as a journey leading gradually from mother's womb to father's tomb. Bara kin groups, if they are to maintain themselves, must balance their members' desire for agnatic solidarity against the need to maintain affinal alliances. Dying, tombs, ancestors, father, and social order are explicitly associated by the Bara. Keeping this in mind, we seek to explain Bara funeral behavior with the hypothesis that they view death as an excess of order upsetting the life-sustaining balance, and that much of the funeral behavior is an attempt to redress the imbalance through a symbolic increase in vitality.

By formalizing these Bara notions of order and vitality into a table of oppositions and extensions, it is possible to begin to understand how such conceptions articulate with the ritual behavior.

Order	*Vitality*
male	female
father	mother
semen	blood
bone	flesh
sterility	fecundity
dying	birth
tomb	womb

However, oppositions include relationships of many different natures.

> Consider the pairs black and white, and odd and even. . . . The first pair admits intermediates (grey and other colors), but the second pair does not. It is not the case that all colors are either black or white, but every whole number is either odd or even. [Lloyd 1966: 87]

Additionally, some terms admit only one opposition, whereas others may be opposed to several terms. The obvious term to pair with "male" is "female"; but "father" can as easily be opposed to "son" or "mother's brother" as to "mother," depending on the context. By examining the list of opposed pairs in terms of the varying natures of the oppositions, it is possible to begin to see in what ways the notion of death as a transition relates specifically to Bara culture.

As one moves down the columns, the relationships of opposition become more and more extreme. The upper pairs are each complementary, with the two poles combining to produce viable existence (male/female, father/mother, semen/blood, bone/flesh). But for the other three pairs, this complementarity is replaced by a profound antagonism. In fact, this antagonism is so pronounced as to be almost inexpressible, for as the one column progresses toward the maximal order of the tomb, the other column progresses toward maximal vitality and chaos. We have

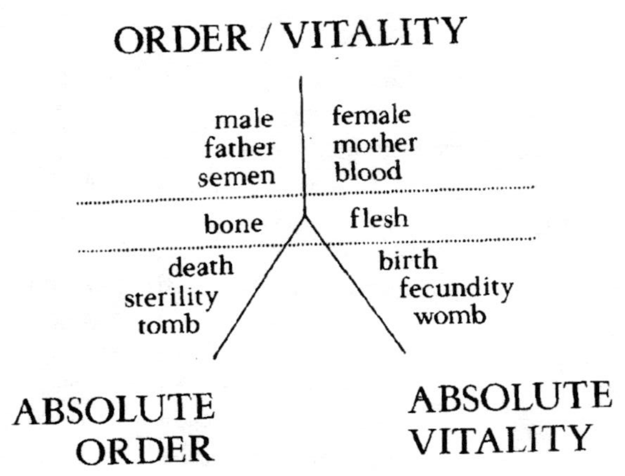

Figure 7. Bara concepts of the person.

used the terms "fecundity," "birth," and "womb" merely to indicate the sorts of attributes the Bara view in opposition to death. But actually, the opposite of pure order cannot be expressed in an orderly fashion. Reconsidering the list of symbolic oppositions and extensions, it is clear that there are two different relationships of opposition represented, one complementary and one antagonistic. The pair flesh/bone partakes of both these forms of opposition. Bone and flesh are complementary in the human body but become antagonistic when breath has ceased. The two columns of the list can be elaborated to express the change in the nature of the symbolic opposition that accompanies dying.

The corpse clearly occupies a liminal state between that conjunction of bone and flesh that is considered "life" and that separation of these substances that is considered "death." As Hertz and van Gennep explained long ago, an understanding of the liminal nature of the corpse does much to explain the rites of burial, exhumation, and reburial. The sexual aspects of these rituals relate to the mortal consequences of liminality: the dead, sterile order of bone takes dominion over the ebbing vitality of the decomposing flesh. A state of mediated equilibrium between order and vitality has become a state of pure, fatal order. This extreme aspect of order cannot be mediated, but can only be opposed by the most extreme aspects of vitality. The sex and sex-related activities of the funeral nights are symbolic ammunition in the open warfare between the extreme ends of the polar continuum of the human condition (see Figure 7).

THE BARA FUNERAL SEQUENCE: BURIAL, GATHERING, REBURIAL

Let us bring this abstract interpretation down to earth and see how the opposition between male orderliness and female vitality is worked out in the activities of the funeral-goers. The Bara perform a series of three ceremonies in the process of providing final disposition for each person. There are (1) the burial, which takes place in the first few days after death; (2) the gathering, which is a great feast celebrated after the harvest following the death; and (3) the exhumation and reburial after the corpse has completely dried and the flesh rotted away. This is the sequence for the deceased, but the living experience these rituals somewhat differently. Death and burial are often shocking events that disrupt the normal flow of village activity. But the gathering and reburial events are experienced as an annual season of festivities during which families go first to one gathering, and then, perhaps the following week, to another, or to a nearby reburial celebration. It is partly in this sense that we suggested that funeral ritual in Madagascar is somewhat like Christmas to Western Christians. It is a seasonal event, which is highly sociable, but also deadly serious. We will consider these rites in order – burial, gathering, reburial – and, in so doing, we can observe the relevance of van Gennep and Hertz's insights.

Burial The radical separation at death of the "male" and "female" components of the person is dramatically established in the first few moments after breath has ceased. The death is not immediately acknowledged or announced, but the preparation of the body and houses are quickly and silently begun. A male and a female house are selected. The corpse will rest in the female house for three days. Here women will gather and keep a long vigil punctuated with periods of loud ritual weeping. For this reason, the female house is also called "the house of many tears." In the "male house," the men of the stricken family will receive male visitors from whom they accept stylized expressions of condolence. The formality in the "male house" is striking with regard both to seating patterns and

verbal exchanges. Here also the men will keep a vigil and organize the logistics of burial. At first, while these two houses are being cleared and arranged, all are enjoined to silence, and weeping is forbidden. The most important task is the preparation of the body. The eyelids and jaw are closed. The limbs are straightened and the body is placed on its back. The jaw and limbs may be tied in place until the postmortem stiffening sets in. Directly after breathing ceases, the person is divided in two, as it were. The male aspect, deriving from the soon-to-be-joined ancestors, is represented in one house, from which the burial is directed. Yet the corpse remains with the living, with the women, for a little longer.

The rigid separation of males and females is broken during the nighttime festivities. Girls must leave the "house of many tears" to sing and dance in the courtyard. The young men come out to watch, and gradually join in. Rum and food are served, a musician is hired, and, little by little, the funeral generates an orgy of sorts. These festivities exhibit a close, almost licentious relationship between males and females that is most unlike the normal cross-sex behavior patterns. All in all, the burial is a ritual of extremes. The sexes are almost absolutely separated by day and enjoined to an obscene, boisterous togetherness by night. There is also an extreme contrast in sound: Funeral activities are separated from the preceding normality by total silence at the time of death, which is then followed by loud wailing, singing, shouting, and gun shooting.

On the third day, the men enter the "house of many tears," put the body in a coffin, and take it outdoors over the tearful protests of the women. The coffin is covered with a cloth, which must be new and in an unsewn, unfinished state. At this point the coffin is carried around and around the "house of many tears" while unhusked, fertile rice is sprinkled in its wake. Several gunshots may be fired and the procession heads toward the burial mountain several miles away. The funeral procession stretches out over the countryside with the youths and young girls quickly leading the way with the coffin, followed at a distance by adult men, then women and children, and finally the family cattle herded at the rear. The youths with the coffin, the so-called "strong birds," pull farther and farther in advance, running all the way, carrying the coffin in relays. Only youths who have had sexual experience can take part in this episode, which is represented as a sexual contest between the girls and the boys for possession of the corpse.

The procession halts and regroups at a prearranged place about halfway to the mountain. At this point, the cattle are brought up and stampeded around and around the coffin while the young men vie with one another in the somewhat risky sport of cattle wrestling, which consists of leaping up onto the hump of one of the members of the stampeding herd and holding on as long as possible. Finally, the young men and girls go on with the coffin to the burial cave, accompanied by two or three older men to ensure a proper burial. The remainder of the people sit and wait for the party's return.

At the tomb, an elder acting as "owner of the death" approaches, sprinkles rum on the entrance, and announces the presence of the mourners to the ancestors. The rocks sealing the cave entrance are taken away, and the principal workers are served rum. The coffin is slid head first into the small opening of the tomb-cave, but most of the assistants feel safer entering the tomb feet first, in contrast to the corpse. After the coffin is properly placed inside, and the assistants have come out, the entrance is carefully closed again. The elder then addresses the ancestors within:

> Here is your grandchild.
> Born here. Do not push him
> away, even from here.

Then the elder picks up a green branch and raps the entrance to the tomb several times, addressing the newly deceased:

> There you are, brother.
> If someone has bewitched you,
> then look for this tree.
> If it is God [Gods] who has taken you,
> who can command God, brother?
> But if it is merely a person
> who has bewitched you,
> Then you take him, you bewitch him.

People say that the branch is like the new corpse, cut off but still wet, and that before either is dry, the witch too will die.

Gathering The gathering is the biggest, most important and most elaborate event in Bara social life. Whereas at the burial ceremony there may

be 50 to 100 people, as many as 500 people may attend a gathering. Whole families walk ten, twenty, or thirty miles and then move into the host village for several days. A hundred liters of rum are considered very adequate for a burial ceremony, but at a gathering there are often 500 liters. Ten or twelve cattle are slaughtered, providing abundant beef for all. The gathering is essentially a conspicuous display of wealth. The rum is paraded before the people to be admired, and anticipated, likewise the cattle. Girls dressed in their finest clothes parade before the crowd. All expenditures are announced to the public: the fee for the dance specialists, the amounts of money given to the wrestlers and cattle riders, the number of slaughtered cattle, and most important, the amount of rum. Normally, the Bara are quite modest about their material success, and they never boast of, or even admit to, the size of their herds or the success of their harvests. But a gathering is not a time for modesty.

Although these activities are largely a grand extension of the earlier burial ceremony, the gathering does not exhibit the extreme polarities that characterize the burial. In particular, the relations between the sexes are more normal. There is a women's hut and a men's hut as at the burial, but now women and men often enter the opposite hut for a variety of reasons. The young men and girls dance together at night, form liaisons, and couple discreetly; but their public demeanor is somewhat reserved. Bawdy songs and sexual taunts are notably absent. Also, the paradox of extreme grief and great celebration is diminished with the passage of time. Death and burial are sudden, unplanned-for, shocking, events. Gatherings, on the other hand, are prepared, organized celebrations that occur each year at the same season. So, in spite of the huge consumption of resources and its association with the activities surrounding death, the gathering partakes of a regularity and normality that clearly distinguish it from the burial ceremony.

There is, however, a dark side to the gathering, which is due to the danger of witchcraft. A witch causes illness or death by deftly slipping a minute amount of evil medicine into rum or food while serving it to the victim. Rum is considered especially dangerous in this regard, and I have seen Bara order that a liter bottle of valuable rum be poured out because its cork seemed to have been disturbed. Also witchcraft medicine is transferred from one person to another by being placed on the genitals before sexual intercourse. In cases of adultery, incest, and witchcraft, the victim suffers from a similar malady: a grotesque and fatal swelling of the stomach. It is no wonder, given this analogy between witchcraft, sexual excess, and gluttony, that a ceremony at which hundreds of people eat, drink rum, and copulate should generate a degree of inquietude regarding witches. Additionally, it is the dry season; the "wet branch" and the corpse are drying out fast. If the man was killed by witchcraft, time is running out for the responsible party. A gathering, then, is particularly dangerous, both because it is a perfect opportunity for witches in general, and because it is seen as the logical time for specific witchcraft attacks in retaliation for the death that has already occurred.

In summary, the gathering is characterized by multiple but related dangers. The standard entertainments of wrestling, cattle riding, and specialized dancing are all believed to be dangerous to the practitioners, who must carry protective charms and observe numerous taboos. The risks of witchcraft, sex, incest, and adultery have already been explained. Rum is considered extremely dangerous, not only as a vehicle for witchcraft, but also because of its power of intoxication. I have seen gatherings that ended in large-scale fighting or individual hatchet attacks. Often, all the spears, clubs, walking sticks, and rifles, which Bara men always carry to these affairs, are collected and placed in a large pile some distance away before the rum is served. The occasion is beset by what a Western observer would classify as both natural and supernatural dangers, but the Bara do not seem to make such a distinction. They are concerned with the danger of unrestrained, excessive, and destructive vigor, whether it comes as a hatchet attack or a witchcraft attack.

Reburial At the first burial ceremony, the deceased is placed in an individual coffin and put in the family tomb or in some other temporary location. After the flesh has decayed, the body is exhumed and the bones are cleaned and then put in the final resting place in the tomb. This reburial ceremony, which like the gathering takes place during the dry season following the harvest, is referred to by several names and euphemisms such as "doing the corpse," "dropping the tree or branch," and "moving the dried-out one." The rite lasts only one day and, although there is usually rum, beef, music, and dancing, it is a smaller affair than the gathering. It is, however, ritually more important than the gathering. Although reburial can be delayed for many years, it is an absolute obligation of the descendants toward the deceased.

Inside the tomb are numerous large, decorated, communal caskets, each containing the dried bones of perhaps ten persons. The number of caskets varies, but the tomb of a well-established family may contain between ten and fifteen of these caskets. To the north are grouped the caskets containing the bones of all the male ancestors. Each skeleton is placed in its rightful position with that of its father. At the south, by the door, are grouped the caskets holding the bones of the female agnates. The bones of a woman are grouped with those of her sister, father's sister, and brother's daughter. Also in the female casket are the bones of young children of female agnates. These skeletons properly belong to the tomb of the father, but are given to their mother's family as an affinal prestation. Women are always buried in the tomb of the father, never with the husband. This common custom, "dividing the children," is the only way a woman can be buried with immediate kin. Otherwise a woman is cut off in death from her father (with whom she shares a common tomb but not a common casket), mother, husband, and children. The male caskets embody a lineal order of grandfather, son, and grandson; the female caskets are like collection boxes for the skeletal residue of this agnatic system.

If a corpse is to be moved from another location to the official tomb, then the "strong birds" leave early in the morning to exhume the body. The composition of the group of "strong birds" is very much like that at the burial, but now there are more senior male relatives of the deceased. At the opening of the temporary tomb (usually another cave), the "strong birds" take care to announce themselves, sprinkle a little rum on the rocks, and then drink the remainder. The old coffin is pulled out and opened and then the bones are scraped clean, rubbed with cow grease, and placed in a new cloth. All signs of grief are forbidden during these preparations, just as they are forbidden during the preparations immediately following death. The return down the mountain is also much like the burial procession, with everyone running and the boys carrying the remains in relays. They do not return to the village, but join the rest of the people already gathered at a prearranged location out on the savannah. There is one last wailing scene with both male and female kin joining in, and then the "strong birds" pick up the remains, perhaps a new casket, as well as clothing for the deceased, and start on the merry run up to the final tomb.

The tomb is opened with the usual rum sprinkling and drinking; the remains and other objects are taken inside and arranged. At reburial, new clothing is placed near the corpse to replace the now rotted unfinished cloth in which he or she was originally buried. The clothes are his or her "best," and often include Western items such as long trousers, shoes, used military uniforms, and even an occasional umbrella. One additional item brought to the tomb is a pair of horns from a newly slaughtered ox to be placed with those from previous reburials. At some tombs, there are as many as 100 pairs of ox horns placed in front of the wall opposite where the male caskets are grouped. When these arrangements are completed, the "strong birds" rejoin the group down in the savannah for a celebration, with more beef and rum.

Bara reburial rites are much like the burial and gathering ceremonies. But in spite of the similarity of the feasting, drinking, dancing, running, and general merrymaking, there are important differences. The reburial activities take place entirely by day and entirely out of the village. There is little of the extreme polarity and paradox of the original burial, and little of the dangerous element so conspicuous at the gathering. Bawdy songs, professional dance troupes, wrestling matches, and cattle-riding contests would all be out of place at a reburial. Not surprisingly, the reburial signals a return to normality, one important aspect of which is that the deceased's spouse is finally free to remarry.

SYMBOLIC GENERATION OF "VITALITY"

The full funeral sequence is long and complex. Let us now focus our attention on the symbolism of one brief phase leading up to the initial burial. Dying, to the Bara, involves an imbalance in the components of human life. As we have indicated, the extreme and fatal dominion of "male" order must be countered by a radical increase of "female" vitality. Vitality is represented in songs, dances, and contests that express the interrelated themes of sex, birth, life, disorder, incest, danger, war, and fertility.

Songs These powerful themes are most explicitly presented in the lyrics of the girls' songs that continue throughout the preburial nighttime festivities. New songs come into fashion every year and the most popular songs of even recent years are rarely heard. Like popular music in much

of the world, new songs rapidly replace old, but the themes remain the same from year to year. The most popular funeral song of 1970 was a clever and rousing piece of ribald double entendre.

Now hide it
Now hide it, boys
Now hide it because there is a death
Together let us copulate
Together let us copulate, boys
Now hide it
Now hide it because there is a death

"Brroo" flies the quail
To perch at the head of the *sely* tree
The eye wants to sleep?
They eye wants to copulate

"Brroo" flies the quail
To perch on a bump of a *sakoa* tree
The eye wants to copulate
The eye wants to ejaculate

"Brroo" flies the quail
To perch at the head of the mud
Hide it!
Hide it boys!
Now hide it because there is a death
Together let us copulate
Together let us copulate
Whether big
Whether little
Now hide it!

The onomatopoeic "brroo" of the quail is an expression commonly used to refer to ejaculation in sexual intercourse. The word for quail is also the word for belly. The word for eye also refers generally to any center, hole, circle, or vortex, in this case, the vagina. The vagina is also suggested by the word for mud, which refers generally to any wet slime or slipperiness. And the quail, according to the Bara, is quite incapable of perching either at the top or the lower branches of a tree. There is the suggestive image of the quivering quail looking for the appropriate place to hide. First it tries the head of a tree, then a lower knob, and finally settles into the stickiness below. The comparison between these Bara songs and the long funeral travelogues of the Berawan elders discussed in Chapter 4 is interesting. Playful sexual themes are also present in the Berawan song cycle, but they play a subordinate role to the songs pertaining to the land of the dead. By contrast, the sexual theme dominates all the funeral singing of the Bara.

Another popular funeral song takes up a serious related theme as the girls sing a lament on the difficulties of childbirth. This song, like all these funeral songs, is sung at funerals and at no other time.

O bright red
O I am hurting now
O bright red
I am hurting from this birth
O bright red
My breasts have fallen heavily
O I hurt, mother
Massage my stomach
Make it easier

Energy When referring to participation in these preburial vigils, the Bara say they are going to await *faha*. The word *faha* is difficult to translate, but its various usages and connotations include: nourishment, ration, a live prestation to a visitor, rifle cartridge, the winding of a clock, elasticity, rebound, resiliency, and energy. Bara most commonly use the word in referring to a thin cow (lacks *faha*) and as a name for those curing ceremonies that aim to strengthen one who has been weakened by illness. In general, *faha* signifies vitality, but the emphasis is on a potential, stored-up vitality rather than on the dissipation of energy in activity.

Here again there are parallels with Berawan practices. At Berawan funerals, there is an emphasis on lively, even tumultuous, socializing and play. In Chapter 3 we described several energetic games in connection with the making of noise. Horseplay among young people is common at funerals and is encouraged by the older folk. Frequently this involves an element of flirtation, as when a teenage girl attempts to rub pot black on the face of a young man. Often such ambushes result in chases up

and down the longhouse, and melees involving dozens of people. During this skylarking more body contact between the sexes is allowed than would normally be tolerated, and young people think of funerals as an opportunity to initiate new sexual liaisons. Although themes of vitality play a less conspicuous part in Berawan than in Bara funerals, Berawan do express the sentiment that displays of exuberance are proper in order to offset the presence of death. The sleepy and the comatose are fair game for all manner of practical jokes.

Dance The concept of storing up vitality is perhaps evident in the mode of dancing associated with Bara funeral activities. The meaning of a dance style is less explicit than that of the lyrics of a song and perhaps less amenable to analysis. However, there is a definite contrast in style between funeral dancing and all other Bara dancing. In addition to the three funeral ceremonies, Bara also dance at circumcision and spirit-possession ceremonies. On these occasions, the dancing is wild and unrestrained, with dancers individually showing off their skills. At funerals, the girls dance in a slow, tight circle in front of the "house of many tears." One by one, the boys join so that there are often two or three circles, one inside another. The dancers in the innermost circle move slowly forward, dancing in a tense double-time, while those in the larger outer ring come down hard on the beat. Often one or two preadolescent boys dance at a languid half-rhythm very quickly around the outside of the other circles. Each succeeding circle (from outside) is tighter, faster rhythmed, and slower moving. The dance gives the appearance of winding a human clock spring. It is this dancing combined with the girls running (while singing) around and around the hut containing the body that are seen by the Bara as the epitome of *faha*, vitality.

Cattle Cattle play important roles in Bara funeral events in two ways. First, there is the little cattle wrestling at the burial and gathering ceremonies. This sport of stampeding the herd around and around resembles a bovine version of the funeral dances (see Figure 8). When describing the event, Bara boys always emphasize the snorting, panting, and bucking of the cattle as signs of intense vitality. This sport is practiced at only one other occasion and that is at the sowing of the rice fields when the trampling hooves perform a plowlike function. The association of cattle

Figure 8. Cattle wrestling at a Bara funeral.

with the fertility of the earth is also clear in a number of Bara legends. In one such tale, the cow states:

> When I die do not bury me in a tomb but your stomachs shall be my tomb. My head you shall not eat. Bury it in the earth. After one week corn sprouts and rice, manioc, and sweet potatoes. And the herd too shall give you life. And this is why you must offer up the First Fruits in thanksgiving. [Faublée 1947: 381]

Another legend recounts how God was once about to give all the animals a potion of life so that death would be eradicated. The cow accidentally drank the entire supply and because there was no more to be had God advised the other animals to kill the cow during times of danger and eat of its flesh, which contains the force of life. This relates to the second role of cattle in the funeral events, namely the slaughter of numerous cattle to provide for the feasting. The killing of the cattle is done differently at funeral events than at all other ceremonies. Whereas in other ceremonies cattle are carefully sacrificed to facilitate communication with

the ancestors, at funerals cattle are slaughtered en masse so that the living can protect themselves by absorbing the force of life inherent in beef.

Chaos: incest and war An important aspect of the representation of vitality is the idea that it is chaotic, as opposed to the order of the ancestor cult. In one of the songs, the girls call on the boys to act crazy, unrestrained, and shameless during the funeral fete. It is in this regard that rum takes on special significance. Rum is served not merely because intoxication is pleasant, but because disorderly conduct is essential.

The most dramatic aspect of the generation of disorder is manifest in the tolerance of incest. For the neighboring Betsileo funerals, Father Dubois describes what he considers "the moment of horror," when everyone copulates incognito with a total disregard for incest regulations (1938: 666). The Bara do not tolerate unexpiated incestuous intercourse, not even at funerals; but the songs, dances, and bawdy remarks exchanged among kin at a funeral would at any other time require the sacrifice of a cow in expiation. An actual attempt at intercourse with a relative at a funeral celebration constitutes a wrong and must be expiated. But the attitude of the Bara toward such incest is that it is an inevitable part of the funeral fetes and the offender should pay the penalty (one cow, bony) with good humor. The incestuous behavior of the participants in the burial and the gathering celebrations is in opposition to the fundamental Bara principle of moral and social order.

Dance troupes are also viewed as possessing dangerous and asocial qualities. They are hired for virtually every gathering and occasionally for a burial, if the family can afford it, but they are prohibited from singing or dancing at any other function. Should such performers sing to a sick person, it is said that the patient will die. At the gathering celebration, the dancers perform only during daylight to stimulate and amuse the guests. At night, with the occasional exception of early in the first evening, it is considered far too dangerous to have them performing. They may not enter the village before the start of the gathering celebration and must be out of the village before the final closing ceremony. They dress outrageously. The men wear their hair in long braids entwined with coins and bells. They are explicitly dressed in the symbols of warriorhood, and no dancer ever dances without his elaborate spear. The dancing is wild and sexual, with particularly energetic dances being done to entice even more money from members of the audience. The dancers do not merely have low status, but are seen as being, in a sense, outside the system of social and moral order.

RESOLUTION: INTERCOURSE AND REBIRTH

During the time following death, vitality is generated through the various excesses of the funeral celebration, in an effort to counterbalance the excessive order of death. The instability of the situation derives from the antagonism between the bone and the flesh of the corpse, the resolution depends on removing the corpse from the world of the living. For as long as the corpse, in which bone is taking dominion over flesh, remains in the village, the life-giving balance is impossible. In another Bara legend, a man with ten cows asks the king for advice because his cows are barren. The king says this is because the man did not bury his father, who died when he was young. The man then holds a funeral, builds a tomb, kills cattle, and buries his father. Soon there are many new calves and his wife also gives birth.

The actual burial takes the form of a double metaphor of sexual intercourse and birth. The funeral procession resembles a "burial by capture," as the men enter (for the first time) the "house of many tears" and take away the coffin over the tearful protests of the women. The young men then run, carrying the coffin in relays, toward the mountain of the ancestors. A group of young girls, often with their hair and clothes disheveled, run to catch up to the coffin bearers, and to distract and detain them from their task. Often the girls intervene physically to stop the journey to the tomb and there ensues a tug-of-war over the coffin as the girls try to pull it back to the village. When this fails, the girls may run ahead and line up across the boys' path. The boys then charge, using the coffin as a battering ram to penetrate this female barrier.

This sexual symbolism is continued at the tomb itself as the coffin is poked head first into the small hole at the mouth of the cave. But the symbolism shifts as attention focuses on the arrival of the deceased among his ancestors. The dominant theme becomes that of birth, with the deceased entering the world of the ancestors head first like a fetus. When asked to comment on the meaning of burial, the Bara invariably use the metaphor of birth. This theme is evident as well in the song cited earlier and in the tomb-side address to the ancestors: "Here is your grand-

child, born here. Do not push him away, even from here." Just as one must be born into the world of the living, so must one also be born out of it and into the world of the dead.

Bara burial is indeed concerned with transition, but the Bara recognize only one mode of transition that is adequate for changing the state of being for a human: sexual intercourse and birth. Not unexpectedly, the process of being born into the world of the dead is the inverse of the process of entering the world of the living. Biological conception begins with the chaotic fecundity of the mother's womb and menstrual blood, to which must be added the ordering power of the father's semen. Order is added to fertile vitality. Entering the tomb, however, is quite the reverse. The cessation of life and breath in the deceased has created a situation of sterility, which must be offset to accomplish the difficult birth into the world of the ancestors. It is not enough merely to bury someone, merely to dispose of the body. The survivors must bring about the renewed conception and rebirth of their deceased kin into the world of the ancestors. This process is as difficult and risky as childbirth. Should it fail, the consequence is nothing short of catastrophic infertility, with the deceased remaining like a dead fetus in the womb of the survivors' world.

TRANSITION AND LIFE

Among the Bara, the familiar phases of the rite of passage are expressed through a unique configuration of values relating to the opposition between flesh and bone. Because the notions of flesh and bone are closely associated with ideas of male and female, father's line and mother's line, ancestors and affines, and the ultimate human problem of reconciling unchanging order with the disruption of necessary renewal, the corpse is a powerful symbol relating the fate of the individual to the ongoing moral order of society. The imbalance of the male and female components of the corpse threatens the balance of the very same components in the Bara social and moral universe, and only through their symbolic manipulation can the corpse be removed.

The burial is only the first rite, however. Each of the three Bara funeral ceremonies concentrates on liminality of a different sort. The burial is largely concerned with the transition of the corpse. The gathering is distinguished from the other ceremonies by the concern shown toward the reordering of social relationships that have been altered by the loss of a kinsman. This is manifest in the witchcraft fears and accusations that concern the settling of old scores, especially with regard to the death of the person in whose honor the gathering is held. The affair closes with the granting of new names to the deceased and to some of the living, followed by a short speech stating that it is time to leave off yearning for the departed.

The reburial focuses on the transition of the remains from the individual coffin to the final resting place in the communal coffin containing the bones of agnatic kin. The ritual itself is a miniature and subdued replication of the original burial. The exhumation is marked by the same mandatory silence and prohibition of weeping that mark the moment of death itself. There is a festive procession between the temporary burial place and the family tomb, ending with the placement of the bones in their proper place and the closing of the tomb. Separation, transition, incorporation. It is a rite of passage concerned with arranging the ambiguities that death creates in the organization of the ancestors. The proper relationship between the worlds of the ancestors and the living is reestablished.

Additionally, one can view the whole funeral sequence as a single rite of passage, seeing the original burial as a rite of separation, the gathering as a period of liminality, and the reburial as the ceremony of reintegration. It is a question of how wide a perspective one takes. There are transitions within transitions. For the Bara, all of life is ultimately a transition and only a perspective wide enough to include birth allows an understanding of death.

The deepest Bara value is vividly expressed in one of their legends about the origin of death. God gave the first man and woman a choice between two kinds of death. They could die like the moon, being reborn over and over. Or they could die like the tree, which puts forth new seeds and, although dying itself, lives on through its progeny. It was a difficult decision, but the first man and woman chose to have children even at the cost of their own lives. And which of us, asks the storyteller, would not make the same choice today?

Part 2:
Chinese Religion

ONE

The Structure of Chinese Funerary Rites: Elementary Forms, Ritual Sequence, and the Primacy of Performance

James L. Watson

In one important respect this collection of essays is the sequel to an earlier volume entitled *Popular Culture in Late Imperial China.*[1] The popular-culture conference (held in 1980) considered the general theme of Chinese cultural diversity and uniformity, looking specifically at the question What held Chinese society together? There were, of course, many institutions and social processes that led to the creation of a unified, centrally organized culture in late imperial China. One of the most obvious was control over the written word as expressed in literature and religious texts;[2] equally important was the subtle manipulation of oral performing arts, notably opera and public storytelling.[3] The authors of *Popular Culture* approached the problem of diversity within unity from many angles, but conference discussions made it clear that one important dimension was missing, namely, ritual.

If anything is central to the creation and maintenance of a unified Chinese culture, it is the standardization of ritual. To be Chinese is to understand, and accept the view, that there is a correct way to perform rites associated with the life-cycle, the most important being weddings and funerals. By following accepted ritual routines ordinary citizens participated in the process of cultural unification. In most cases they did so voluntarily,

1. David Johnson, Andrew Nathan, and Evelyn Rawski, eds., *Popular Culture in Late Imperial China* (Berkeley and Los Angeles: University of California Press, 1985).

2. David Johnson, "Communication, Class, and Consciousness in Late Imperial China," in Johnson et al., *Popular Culture*, pp. 34–72; James Hayes, "Specialists and Written Materials in the Village World," in Johnson et al., *Popular Culture*, pp. 75–111.

3. Tanaka Issei, "The Social and Historical Context of Ming-Ch'ing Local Drama," in Johnson et al., *Popular Culture*, pp. 143–160; Barbara E. Ward, "Regional Operas and Their Audiences," in Johnson et al., *Popular Culture*, pp. 161–187; and "Not Merely Players: Drama, Act, and Ritual in Traditional China," *Man* n.s. 14 (1979): 18–39.

without the necessity of enforcement by state authorities. What we accept today as "Chinese" is in large part the product of a centuries-long process of ritual standardization.

This volume, therefore, is more than a set of essays about death and mortuary ritual: It is a study in cultural homogenization as expressed in performance, practice, and beliefs regarding the dead. The essays that follow demonstrate that there was a uniform structure of funerary rites in late imperial China. The elements of this structure are outlined below. It is my contention that the proper performance of the rites, in the accepted sequence, was of paramount importance in determining who was and who was not deemed to be fully "Chinese." Performance, in other words, took precedence over belief—it mattered little what one believed about death or the afterlife as long as the rites were performed properly. The polemical tone of this essay is deliberate. It is hoped that others will take up the cause of belief, thereby leading to an exchange of views regarding the role of ritual in Chinese society.

RITUAL: THE TRANSFORMATIVE ASPECT

Given that this volume focuses on funeral rites and mortuary practices, it seems appropriate to begin with a general discussion of ritual. There is, of course, a vast literature on this problem, and I do not propose to review all aspects of the topic here. Suffice it to note that anthropologists have long debated the meaning and definition of ritual; unfortunately, little agreement has been reached among contending schools, and there is still no generally accepted definition.[4] However, in all studies of the subject it is generally assumed that ritual is about transformation—in particular it relates to the transformation of one being or state into another, changed being or state. Most anthropologists would agree that it is this transformative aspect that sets ritual apart from other social actions. That which is merely repeated is not necessarily ritual. Rather, rituals are repeated because they are expected to have transformative powers.[5] Rituals change people and things; the ritual process is active, not merely passive.

4. Victor Turner, *The Ritual Process* (Chicago: Aldine, 1969); Jean La Fontaine, ed., *The Interpretation of Ritual* (London: Tavistock, 1972); Clyde Kluckhohn, "Myths and Rituals: A General Theory," *Harvard Theological Review* 35 (1942): 45–79; S. J. Tambiah, "A Performative Approach to Ritual" (Radcliffe-Brown Lecture, 1979), *Proceedings of the British Academy* 65 (1979): 113–169; Sally Falk Moore and Barbara Myerhoff, eds., *Secular Ritual* (Assen, Netherlands: Van Gorcum, 1977); Edmund Leach, *Culture and Communication* (Cambridge: Cambridge University Press, 1976); Ronald Grimes, "Ritual Studies: Two Models," *Religious Studies Review* 2, no. 4 (1976): 13–24.

5. Fred W. Clothey, *Rhythm and Intent: Ritual Studies from South India* (Bombay: Blackie and Son, 1983), pp. 1–5.

One of the most insightful studies of ritual to appear in recent years is Gilbert Lewis's *Day of Shining Red*.[6] This study is a minute "unpacking" of a puberty rite practiced by New Guinea villagers. The author works his way through the received definitions of ritual only to find them wanting. He concludes: "What is clear and explicit about ritual is how to do it—rather than its meaning."[7] The people he worked among knew how to perform rites, and they knew when something was performed incorrectly, but they could not provide ready explanations (in words) for what was being expressed, communicated, or symbolized. This, of course, is a familiar problem to all fieldworkers, not just those who work in New Guinea.

Lewis raises a fundamental question that, at one time or another, has haunted most scholars who attempt to analyze rituals: How can we go beyond what we are told by informants, texts, or documentary sources?[8] Many anthropologists try to create meaning by reassembling symbols, metaphors, and actions into a coherent set of messages—thereby engaging in structural analyses of various types. Lewis is not alone in questioning such procedures.[9] Whose meaning are we constructing when rituals are interpreted: our informants' or our own? Nor is it possible, as some have suggested, to present "value free" or "pure" descriptions of ritual, devoid of contaminating interpretations by the observer. The very act of description involves multiple judgments regarding the behavior being performed. Even the most detailed description demands that one isolate certain actions as being more significant than others.

Films and photographs of ritual present equally complicated problems of analysis. During the conference that preceded this volume participants observed nearly twenty hours of slides and films dealing with Chinese funerary ritual. It was fascinating, and enlightening, to learn that everyone present "saw" something different in the visual records of Chinese rites. Historians and anthropologists, in particular, did not even appear to be witnessing the same events, to judge from their comments (the historians were preoccupied with written messages and texts evident in the slides or films, whereas anthropologists tended to treat these messages as peripheral or at least secondary to the actions of ritual specialists; see Evelyn Rawski's observations on this matter, chapter 2). I might add that such variation in interpretation is also true for those who actually participate in funerals and perform the rites portrayed in ethnographic films or slides. Among Cantonese villagers in rural Hong Kong, for instance, there is no generally

6. Gilbert Lewis, *Day of Shining Red: An Essay on Understanding Ritual* (Cambridge: Cambridge University Press, 1982).

7. Ibid., p. 19.

8. Ibid., p. 24.

9. See, e.g., Roger M. Keesing, *Kwaio Religion: The Living and the Dead in a Solomon Island Society* (New York: Columbia University Press, 1982), pp. 3–5, 181–187.

accepted agreement regarding the signification or symbolism of rituals. When I asked about the meaning of an act or a symbol I was usually told, "I'm not clear about that. We do it this way because that's how it has always been done."

Rituals must be routinized and conventionalized before they can be accepted as part of the standard repertoire at a Chinese funeral. But this does not mean that they are immutable. In fact, several chapters in this volume focus on cases of ritual variability and modification to suit changing political circumstances (see especially chapters by Rawski, Wakeman, R. Watson, and Whyte). These changes are always made, however, within a recognizable framework of cultural convention; modifications are never arbitrary, given that they must conform to general notions of "Chineseness."

Closely associated with the problem of convention are notions of performance and audience. All rituals must have an audience to judge the quality and conventionality of the performance. When considering Chinese funerary ritual the question of audience becomes very complex. Who judges, and thereby validates, the performance? the deceased? the community? the gods, ancestors, and guardians of hell? or the performers of the rites themselves? Among rural Cantonese all of these interested parties represent the audience or separate audiences. But most villagers make it clear by their actions that the general community, represented by neighbors and kin, constitutes the most important audience. It is the community that determines convention and affirms that a funeral has been performed properly (a botched funeral can have disastrous consequences for everyone involved; see chapter 5). As with Lewis's informants, Cantonese villagers know what is correct and what is not; they represent a hypercritical audience even though they may not be able to articulate the reasons for their strongly held views about ritual propriety. Lewis nicely summarizes these issues: "In ritual as in art, he who devises or creates or performs is also spectator of what he does; and he who beholds it is also active in the sense that he interprets the performance. The value of ritual lies partly in this ambiguity of the active and passive for creator, performer and beholder."[10]

At Chinese funerals the general audience plays an active role, together with paid professionals, in creating a ritual performance. Community members are both the observed and the observers; they play a leading part in performing the rites while at the same time acting as audience. It is the proper performance of the rites—by specialists, mourners, and community members—that matters most to everyone concerned. As I shall argue below, the internal state of the participants, their personal beliefs and predispositions, are largely irrelevant.

10. Lewis, *Day of Shining Red*, p. 38.

THE STRUCTURE OF RITES, I: THE IDEOLOGICAL DOMAIN

One of the central themes emerging from this study, as was noted earlier, is the view that there was a *uniform* structure of funeral rites in China during the late imperial era. This structure is still very much alive in Taiwan, Hong Kong, and some overseas Chinese areas, but it no longer dominates the ritual life of modern China as it did in the past. This is particularly true of Chinese cities, although it is evident that traditional rites are reemerging in many parts of rural China (see Whyte's discussion in chapter 12).[11] Prerevolution burial practices are evident throughout rural Kwangtung, and in 1985 the ritual paraphernalia for traditional funerals were readily available in rural markets.[12] However, in comparison with Taiwan and Hong Kong, contemporary China seems peculiarly devoid of *public* rituals that have a religious content (i.e., festivals and collective displays of devotion). There is, of course, a great deal of public ritual activity in China, but it is strictly controlled by the party and is directly related to the political goals of the central administration.[13] The deritualization, and possible reritualization, of Chinese religious life is a subject that deserves a full-scale, interdisciplinary study by a team of scholars familiar with the traditional system. It is difficult to determine whether China, in the late 1980s, now has a uniform structure of funerary rites. Whyte suggests (chapter 12) that there is a growing dichotomy between rural and urban sectors in the People's Republic, with different rites emerging in city and countryside. The implications of this will be discussed below.

During the late imperial era (approximately 1750 to 1920)[14] rituals associated with marriage and death constituted a kind of "cultural cement" that helped hold this vastly complex and diversified society together. There are several ways to approach the problem of structural uniformity: It is not a simple matter of assembling a check list of ritual acts and routines, nor is it of particular concern that elements of the structure may be found in other societies. Rather, it is the unique *configuration* of ritual elements that makes a funeral acceptably Chinese. It was, in other words, a coherent package of

11. See also William L. Parish and Martin K. Whyte, *Village and Family in Contemporary China* (Chicago: University of Chicago Press, 1978), pp. 260–266.

12. Author's field investigations, Kwangtung province, summer 1985.

13. Martin King Whyte, *Small Groups and Political Rituals in China* (Berkeley and Los Angeles: University of California Press, 1974); Richard Madsen, *Morality and Power in a Chinese Village* (Berkeley and Los Angeles: University of California Press, 1984).

14. The year 1920 might be accepted as a rough "cutoff" date for the late imperial era, although for certain features of cultural life (e.g., lineage organization, ancestor worship, folk religion) 1940 or even 1950 may serve as well. This is a matter of some debate among anthropologists.

actions, routines, and performances which constituted the structure of Chinese rites.

There are two domains within which the processes of ritual standardization can be analyzed. The first might be called the ideological domain, given that it is concerned with abstract notions regarding the relationship between life and death. Many of the essays in this volume deal specifically with the ideological aspects of mortuary rites (see chapters by Cohen and Martin). Among Chinese, there was a strong belief in the continuity between this world (life) and the next (death). Both worlds were governed by bureaucratic principles that mirrored the imperial bureaucracy.[15] There was, as Thomas Laqueur pointed out during conference discussions, no radical dualism in Chinese thought—separating body from soul—similar to the central concern that governed European notions of life and death. In other words, the "moment of death," whereby body and soul were forever parted, did not have the same meaning among Chinese as it had among Europeans.[16] One of the primary goals of Chinese funeral rites, in fact, was to keep corpse and spirit together during the initial stages of death; separation prior to the ritualized expulsion from the community was thought to bring disaster (see chapter 5).

Another key feature of Chinese ideology regarding the afterlife was the belief that one's social status remained largely unaffected by death. In particular, both worlds were dominated by kinship, and it was believed that death did not terminate the relationships between agnatic kinsmen (the status of women is more problematic and deserves further study).[17] It is important to note that, for most Chinese, it was patrilineal kinship that survived beyond death; matrilateral ties (through one's mother) and affinal links (through marriage) were generally terminated upon death. Ancestor worship was the concrete expression of this preoccupation with the patriline.

The ideological domain of late imperial China was also dominated by the notion that the soul, or spirit, was composed of several parts. There is considerable debate regarding the exact configuration of the soul,[18] but most observers accept a dual (*hun* versus *p'o*) or a tripartite (grave, domestic

15. Arthur P. Wolf, "Gods, Ghosts, and Ancestors," in *Religion and Ritual in Chinese Society*, ed. Arthur P. Wolf (Stanford: Stanford University Press, 1974), pp. 131–182; Emily Martin Ahern, *Chinese Ritual and Politics* (Cambridge: Cambridge University Press, 1981).

16. Philippe Ariès, *The Hour of Our Death* (New York: Knopf, 1981).

17. On the ambiguous status of women in the afterlife, see James L. Watson, "Of Flesh and Bones: The Management of Death Pollution in Cantonese Society," in *Death and the Regeneration of Life*, eds. Maurice Bloch and Jonathan Parry (Cambridge: Cambridge University Press, 1982), pp. 178–180.

18. Stevan Harrell, "The Concept of Soul in Chinese Folk Religion," *Journal of Asian Studies* 38 (1979): 519–528.

shrine, hall tablet) division.[19] The origin of the *hun/p'o* dichotomy is the subject of an important essay by Ying-shih Yü.[20] Associated with this ideological complex was a preoccupation with controlling, managing, and placating the dangerous aspects of the spirit of the deceased. Much of the ritual at funerals is aimed specifically at settling the volatile and disoriented spirit of the recently dead. There is, in other words, a need for social control in the nether world; ideally no one should be allowed to wander at will, outside the constraints of kinship and community, in life or in death. To bury a person without proper attention to ritual details is to create a hungry ghost who will return to plague the living. The analogy between ghosts and bandits is a conscious one in Chinese society.[21] Both exist outside the constraints of family, kinship, and community.

Another uniform feature of the ideological domain is obvious to those who are familiar with Chinese mortuary practices. This is the idea that there must always be a balance between the sexes, even in death. The notion of gender, a cultural construction, survives in the Chinese afterlife (this is not the case in all societies). If it is at all possible, married people are reconstituted as couples in death, usually by burial in close proximity. Posthumous unions, often referred to as "ghost marriages,"[22] are sometimes arranged for unmarried people, for it is considered unnatural, in life and in death, to be without a spouse.

Closely associated with these ideas of social continuity is the final, and some might say the most important, feature of the Chinese ideological domain: the idea of *exchange* between living and dead. Death does not terminate relationships of reciprocity among Chinese, it simply transforms these ties and often makes them stronger. A central feature of Chinese funerals and postburial mortuary practices is the transfer of food, money, and goods to the deceased (see Thompson's discussion in chapter 4). In return the living expect to receive certain material benefits, including luck, wealth, and progeny.

This notion of continued exchange between living and dead is the foundation of late imperial China's ideological domain. In other words, all rituals associated with death are performed *as if* there were a continued relationship between living and dead. It is irrelevant whether or not participants actually *believe* that the spirit survives or that the presentation of offerings

19. See e.g., Maurice Freedman, "Ancestor Worship: Two Facets of the Chinese Case," in *Social Organization: Essays Presented to Raymond Firth*, ed. Maurice Freedman (London: Frank Cass, 1967), pp. 85–103.

20. Ying-shih Yü, "O Soul, Come Back: A Study of the Changing Conceptions of the Soul and Afterlife in Pre-Buddhist China," *Harvard Journal of Asiatic Studies* 47 (1987): 363–395.

21. Robert Weller, "Bandits, Beggars, and Ghosts: The Failure of State Control over Religious Interpretation in Taiwan," *American Ethnologist* 12 (1985): 46–61.

22. Wolf, "Gods, Ghosts, and Ancestors," pp. 150–152.

has an effect on the deceased. What matters is that the rites are performed according to accepted procedure.

The ideological domain in China, in other words, does not assume universal belief or unquestioned acceptance of "truth."[23] Here is where China may have been unique among centralized societies. There was, of course, a close relationship between the ideological domain and what I shall call the performative domain (i.e., ritual; see below) in late imperial China. But, unlike the common pattern one finds in Christian Europe and Hindu India, the two Chinese domains do not seem to be totally dependent upon each other. There was a noticeable disjuncture between the requirements of ritual standardization (which were absolute) and the maintenance of a centralized belief system (loosely organized at best and rarely enforced).

In dealing with religious cults among peasants, Chinese imperial authorities were content to control and legislate actions, not beliefs.[24] Much the same was true for funerary ritual. As long as the rites were performed according to standardized and generally accepted sequence, it was of little consequence what people actually thought about the efficacy of those rites. As Jonathan Parry and Thomas Laqueur (Indianist and Europeanist respectively) noted in conference discussions, a radical distinction between belief and practice was never a central feature of Hindu or Christian social orders. In early Christendom, for instance, it was belief that carried more weight than practice, and in later eras debates regarding the proper performance of the Eucharist focused on ideological concerns underpinning practice.[25]

It is my contention that this was not the case in late imperial China. The standardization of ritual practice almost always took precedence over efforts to legislate or control beliefs. This, I would argue, had profound consequences for the creation of a unified cultural system. By enforcing orthopraxy (correct practice)[26] rather than orthodoxy (correct belief) state officials made it possible to incorporate people from many different ethnic or regional backgrounds, with varying beliefs and attitudes, into an over-

23. The concept of belief, its definition and cross-cultural applicability, has been the subject of considerable debate among anthropologists; see, for example, Rodney Needham, *Belief, Language, and Experience* (Oxford: Basil Blackwell, 1972).

24. James L. Watson, "Standardizing the Gods: The Promotion of T'ien Hou (Empress of Heaven) Along the South China Coast, 960–1960," in Johnson et al., *Popular Culture in Late Imperial China*, pp. 292–324.

25. Charles Gore, *The Body of Christ: An Inquiry into the Institution and Doctrine of Holy Communion* (London: Murray, 1901); A. M. O'Neill, *The Mystery of the Eucharist* (Dublin: M. H. Gill, 1933); Rudolf Bultmann, *Theology of the New Testament*, vol. 1 (London: SCM Press, 1952); Richard A. Watson, "Transubstantiation among the Cartesians," in *Problems of Cartesianism*, eds. Thomas Lennon, John Nicholas, and John Davis (Montreal: McGill-Queen's University Press, 1982), pp. 127–148.

26. Judith A. Berling, "Orthopraxy," in *Encyclopedia of Religion*, vol. 11, ed. Mircea Eliade (New York: Macmillan, 1987), pp. 129–132.

arching social system we now call China. Had this not been the strategy (conscious or unconscious) of state officials, Chinese culture could never have reached such heights of uniformity and coherence as it did during the late imperial era.

Before moving to a consideration of the performative domain, a clarification seems in order. I am *not* suggesting that belief and ideology are somehow irrelevant to the processes of cultural integration in China. Given the obvious uniformity of beliefs just surveyed, it would be absurd to make such a contention. Rather, I would argue that the Chinese state had no effective means of controlling beliefs regarding the afterlife in the absence of a unified church. There was, in other words, no centralized hierarchy of specialists charged with the responsibility of dispensing religious truth, as in Christendom. The closest equivalents would have been imperial bureaucrats, but these were relatively few in number,[27] and they were concerned primarily with good governance, not religious beliefs. What is truly intriguing about the Chinese case, therefore, is the fact that there *was* such a high level of uniformity in beliefs, attitudes, and conceptions regarding the dead. The creation of a unified culture obviously involved more than the conscious manipulation of the ideological domain by agents of the state, as some scholars have suggested.[28] I shall return to this point in the conclusion of this essay.

THE STRUCTURE OF RITES, II: THE PERFORMATIVE DOMAIN

A survey of ethnographic sources on Chinese funerals,[29] together with conference discussion, films, photographs, and the results of my own field research, leads me to conclude that there was indeed a prescribed set of ritual

27. On this point, see G. William Skinner, "Rural Marketing in China: Revival and Reappraisal," in *Markets and Marketing*, ed. Stuart Plattner (Lanham, Maryland: University Press of America for the Society of Economic Anthropology, 1985), pp. 7–8.

28. See, e.g., Kung-chuan Hsiao, *Rural China: Imperial Control in the Nineteenth Century* (Seattle: University of Washington Press, 1960), p. 225.

29. The Cantonese sequence is outlined in J. Watson, "Of Flesh and Bones." On ritual sequences in other parts of China, see Emily Ahern, *Cult of the Dead in a Chinese Village* (Stanford: Stanford University Press, 1973); J. J. M. de Groot, *The Religious System of China*, vol. 1 (Leiden: Brill, 1892); Henry Doré, *Researches into Chinese Superstitions* (Shanghai: T'usewei, 1914); Bernard Gallin, *Hsin Hsing, Taiwan: A Chinese Village in Change* (Berkeley and Los Angeles: University of California Press, 1966), pp. 219–230; Sidney D. Gamble, *Ting Hsien: A North China Rural Community* (Stanford: Stanford University Press, 1954), pp. 386–393; Francis L. K. Hsu, *Under the Ancestors' Shadow* (Garden City, N.Y.: Anchor Books, 1967), pp. 154–166; and Arthur P. Wolf, "Chinese Kinship and Mourning Dress," in *Family and Kinship in Chinese Society*, ed. Maurice Freedman (Stanford: Stanford University Press, 1970), pp. 189–207.

actions that had to be performed before a corpse could be expelled from the community and buried. These actions are perhaps best referred to as the elementary structure of funeral rites, in the sense that they were performed, with minor variations, throughout China during the late imperial era, irrespective of class, status, or material circumstance. It is important to distinguish between *funerary rites* and *rites of disposal*.[30] The former involve actions undertaken from the moment of death to the formal expulsion of the deceased (in a sealed coffin) from the community. Rites of disposal are distinct from funeral rites in that the procedures of burial, cremation, or coffin storage are not governed by universally accepted norms. In fact, once the corpse is removed from the community almost any form of disposal is permitted. More will be said below about variations in burial practices.

What were the main features of funeral ritual in late imperial China? It appears that by Ming and Ch'ing a uniform structure had emerged, based roughly on classical models outlined in the *Li chi* and later simplified by Chu Hsi and others (see Rawski's account in chapter 2). The standardized rites required the following actions:

(1) Public notification of death by wailing and other expressions of grief. Women of the household, in particular, announced the death to neighbors by high-pitched, stereotyped wailing. Such actions were required by survivors; they were not voluntary. Formal notification of death was also given by pasting white banners on the house of the deceased and hanging blue lanterns from the eaves (these actions were optional in some parts of China, whereas the wailing was not).

(2) Donning of white clothing, shoes, and hoods (made of sackcloth or hemp) by mourners. The degree of kinship between the deceased and the mourner was often coded in the style of dress.[31] There were, of course, many regional variations in color symbolism and garment ensemble, but the use of white as an unambiguous symbol of mourning was a key feature of Chinese funerary ritual.

(3) Ritualized bathing of the corpse. This act was often accompanied by a final change of clothing deemed to be suitable for the journey to the otherworld. The provision of new or special clothing was optional and may not have been common among the poor, but the bathing of the corpse was an essential feature of the rites. In south China the water was often purchased (for a token sum of real money) from the deity of a well or a stream; this rite is called *mai-shui* (lit. "buying water").[32] The bathing of the corpse varied from a full, vigorous scrubbing to a ritualized daubing of the forehead.

30. Rubie S. Watson (chapter 9) notes that there is also a fundamental distinction between *funeral rites* (which are prescribed) and *grave rites* (which are fluid and subject to political manipulation).

31. Wolf, "Chinese Kinship and Mourning Dress."

(4) The transfer of food, money, and goods from the living to the dead. Mock money and paper models of items to be used in the afterlife (e.g., houses, furniture, servants, vehicles, etc.) were transmitted by burning. Food was presented in the form of offerings, whereby the essence of the gift was consumed by the deceased while the remnants were often eaten by the mourners. It appears that there was an element of symbolic communication implicit in these prestations, with pork and rice being the irreducible food gifts (see chapter 4 by Thompson). In addition to food, the basic set of material offerings to the deceased included mock money and incense[33]—all other offerings were thus optional. This elementary feature of the rites was a concrete expression of the continuing relationship between living and dead.

(5) The preparation and installation of a soul tablet for the dead. All deceased Chinese, save those who died as infants or as wandering strangers, had to have a written tablet to serve as a repository for one aspect of their soul. This feature of the rites required the services of a literate person, usually a ritual specialist. The finished tablet of most married people was installed in the domestic altar of the deceased's household (tablets in ancestral halls—outside the home—were not an essential part of the rites but an option few could afford).[34] Unmarried women and other people who were not deemed to be members of households sometimes had their tablets placed in temples, convents, or institutions that provided such services for a fee. In considering funerary ritual as a mechanism of cultural standardization it is highly significant that the soul was represented as a written name (usually a posthumous *hao*) on a tablet; the repository of the soul did not take the form of icons, statues, or pictures.[35] It is surely no coincidence that the written script, a primary instrument of Chinese cultural unification, played a central role in the formal structure

32. J. Watson, "Of Flesh and Bones," pp. 161–162.

33. Strict codes govern the number of incense sticks offered; see, e.g., Stephan Feuchtwang, "Domestic and Communal Worship in Taiwan," in *Religion and Ritual in Chinese Society*, ed. Arthur P. Wolf (Stanford: Stanford University Press, 1974), p. 107.

34. Rubie S. Watson, *Inequality Among Brothers: Class and Kinship in South China* (Cambridge: Cambridge University Press, 1985), p. 41.

35. Among Hong Kong boatpeople small wooden statues of ancestors were sometimes kept on boat altars. It is significant, however, that the boat people (mostly illiterate) also maintained written ancestral tablets; see Eugene N. Anderson, Jr., *The Floating World of Castle Peak Bay*, Anthropological Studies no. 4 (Washington: American Anthropological Association, 1970), pp. 149–150.

of funerary rites. In order to follow the prescribed rites one had to have a Chinese written name—irrespective of social background,[36] education, or general level of cultural assimilation (for those of non-Han origin).

(6) The ritualized use of money and the employment of professionals. The proper conduct of Chinese funerary rites required the services of specialists who performed ritual acts in exchange for money. It was not possible, given the complex structure of rites, for mourners or untrained neighbors to perform all of these essential services. The payment of money to specialists was more than a simple monetary exchange; it was a required feature of the rites (see chapter 5). Someone, in other words, had to accept money from the mourners (or the deceased's estate or a public charity) before the corpse could be safely expelled from the community. The implications of this exchange have yet to be thoroughly analyzed, but it is evident that monetary exchange, in numerous forms, permeates Chinese funerary ritual.[37] This is testimony, perhaps, to the extent that money—as a universal medium of exchange—had penetrated into the cultural domain of late imperial China. Even in death one continued to engage in monetary exchange.[38]

(7) Music to accompany the corpse and settle the spirit. Two forms of music seem to have played a key role in the structure of funerary rites: high-pitched piping (from an oboe-like instrument) and percussion (particularly drumming). The sound of piping and drumming accompanied the corpse during critical transitions in the ritual, most notably when physical movement was required.

(8) Sealing the corpse in an airtight coffin. This action was considered by many Chinese to be the most important feature of the traditional funerary ritual. The use of coffins, usually constructed of wood, has

36. There are some interesting gender distinctions that might be pursued in future research. For instance, a deceased Cantonese woman is represented in writing by the surname of her father—not her own, personal name. Males, on the other hand, have their full posthumous names on soul tablets, tombstones, and funeral banners. This symbolic negation of female names suggests that Cantonese women are not perceived as complete human beings, at least in the context of mortuary ritual; see Rubie S. Watson, "The Named and the Nameless: Gender and Person in Chinese Society," *American Ethnologist* 13 (1986): 619–631.

37. Discussed in chapter 5; see also Hill Gates, "Money for the Gods: The Commoditization of the Spirit," *Modern China* 13 (1987): 259–277.

38. Among Cantonese in the Hong Kong New Territories, the dead sometimes continue to make annual prestations to popular deities. The offerings are made possible by the profits of the benefactor's ancestral estate, established during his lifetime. The offerings are often elaborate, and the benefits are said to accrue to the spirit of the deceased. In one case the benefactor has been dead for over four hundred years, but he continues to worship T'ien Hou (Empress of Heaven) every year on the occasion of her "birthday."

been common in China since at least the Neolithic.[39] Settling the corpse in the coffin and packing it so no movement was possible were tasks often assigned to paid specialists. Securing the lid, with nails and caulking compounds, ensured that the coffin was airtight. The ceremonial hammering of nails to seal the coffin was a centerpiece of the ritual sequence; this act was usually performed by the chief mourner or by an invited guest (i.e., someone of high social status relative to the mourners).

(9) Expulsion of the coffin from the community. When the coffin had been sealed, it was ready for removal from the village, town, or neighborhood of the deceased. This expulsion was the last formal act in the sequence of funerary rites,[40] but it need not be accomplished immediately. In fact, high-status families (including the imperial household; see Rawski's discussion in chapter 10) often kept the coffin in the domestic realm for months—even years—as a mark of respect for the deceased. But, in the end, the coffin must be expelled from the domain of the living.

As was noted earlier, there were no generally accepted guidelines—applicable everywhere in China—for the conduct of burials, cremations, and other means of disposal. In contrast, the formal expulsion of the coffin was orchestrated with considerable uniformity. At a precise moment chosen in advance by a specialist, the coffin was carried quickly out of the community by a team of pallbearers (often paid professionals). A procession of mourners and neighbors was formed to accompany the coffin to the point of disposal. When the procession had passed beyond the boundaries of the deceased's village, town, or city (often symbolized by walls and gates), the formal sequence of funeral rites had been completed.

VARIATION AND UNIFORMITY: RITES OF DISPOSAL

By isolating these nine acts as the elementary features of Chinese funerary ritual I do not mean to imply that there was no variation in performance. So long as the acts were accomplished in the approved sequence, there was room for infinite variety in ritual expression. For instance, the bathing of the corpse and the sealing of the coffin were performed differently in almost

39. David N. Keightley, "Dead But Not Gone: Cultural Implications of Mortuary Practices in Neolithic and Early Bronze Age China," paper presented at the conference on Ritual and the Social Significance of Death in Chinese Society, Oracle, Arizona, January 1985.

40. The implication of this act is that the deceased can no longer be treated (in ritual) as a member of the community once the coffin has been formally expelled. The dead retain their membership in (patrilineal) kinship organizations, but neighbors and other non-kin cease engaging in exchange with the dead at this point. The funeral, therefore, also serves as a rite of severance from the community.

every Chinese community. In my own experience of two closely related Cantonese villages (only six miles apart) there were striking contrasts in the conduct and organization of funerals, but the overall structure of the rites was similar.[41]

Herein lies the genius of the Chinese approach to cultural standardization: The system allowed for a high degree of variation within an overarching structure of unity. The rites of disposal constitute an excellent example of this principle (variation within unity). As long as the sealed coffin was removed from the community in the accepted fashion, mourners were free to dispose of the corpse according to local custom. Research on Chinese burial customs (as opposed to funerary rites) is surprisingly underdeveloped; there are whole regions of China for which we have little information on final disposal of the dead.

Most of our data derive from the south, notably Fukien, Kwangtung, Hong Kong, and Taiwan. Secondary burial is practiced in these areas, and it is intriguing to see how local people have accommodated to the standardized rites. Briefly summarized, Chinese secondary burial involves an initial burial of the coffin for approximately seven to ten years, followed by an exhumation of bones, which are placed in a large pot and eventually reburied in a permanent tomb (see R. Watson's discussion in chapter 9 for details). As was outlined above, one of the fundamental features of Chinese funerary ritual is the evacuation of the corpse in an airtight coffin. This procedure is diametrically opposed to the requirements of secondary burial, which puts a premium on the rapid decomposition of the flesh (thereby allowing for the retrieval and reburial of bones).

Peasants in south China had no difficulty following the standard rites, given that the prescribed actions of a proper funeral ended when the coffin left the community. In Taiwan, Hokkien villagers sometimes bash in one end of the coffin with an axe just prior to burial; in another part of Taiwan a specialist is hired to drill holes in the coffin.[42] Among Cantonese the seal around the coffin lid is often broken before interment. All of these practices, of course, are designed to hasten the decomposition of the flesh.

In north China, secondary burial is not practiced, and in fact northerners are often revolted when they first learn about southern customs. But northerners do things that shock southerners, such as storing coffins above ground, sometimes for decades, until the death of a spouse or a parent—thereby allowing family reconstitution by simultaneous burial (see Naquin's summary in chapter 3).

41. For instance, in one village attendance at funerals depends upon neighborhood (hamlet) affiliation, whereas in the other funerals are organized by voluntary associations.

42. Photographic slides presented at the 1985 Death Ritual Conference by Emily Martin and Stuart Thompson respectively.

In the borderlands of Szechwan where Han and non-Han have interacted for centuries, many who consider themselves Han do not bury their dead at all; instead, coffins are left in hillside caves that serve as family sepulchers.[43] And finally, when considering methods of disposal, we must not forget that cremation was practiced in many parts of China, even though it was condemned by Neo-Confucian scholars and regularly banned by the state.

What is significant about these diverse practices is that they could all be accepted as "Chinese" customs. By excluding disposal from the standard set of funeral rites, state officials implicitly condoned the cultural expression of ethnic and regional differences. This may have been the consequence of a conscious policy, given that any attempt to control burial practices would have been disastrously expensive and impossible to enforce (as Communist authorities were to discover during the 1950s and 1960s). Following the standard funeral sequence, on the other hand, did not impinge very deeply into regional sensitivities, and it was a small price to pay for the privilege of being accepted as proper Chinese. Those who chose not to perform funerals according to standard procedure were marked as non-Chinese or, worse yet, as dangerous sectarians.[44] This is why it was in everyone's interest to embrace the funeral rites as an expression of cultural identity and as an affirmation of loyalty to the imperial state.

The Chinese cultural system thus allowed for the free expression of what outsiders might perceive to be chaotic local diversity. The performative domain of ritual, in particular, gave great scope for regional and subethnic cultural displays. The system was so flexible that those who called themselves Chinese could have their cake and eat it too: They participated in a unified, centrally organized culture and at the same time celebrated their local or regional distinctiveness.

The imperial state, of course, was intimately involved in the standardization of funerary ritual, but it would never have been possible to *impose* a uniform structure of rites on a society of such vast size and complexity. More subtle means were required. There is good evidence that imperial officials were engaged in the promotion of a standardized set of funeral and mourning customs throughout the empire. These norms were enshrined in county gazetteers and in ritual manuals,[45] available throughout the empire (see Naquin's discussion in chapter 3). Given what we know about the distribution of power in late imperial China, it is probable that local elites

43. See, e.g., Shih Chung-chien 石鍾健, "Ssu-ch'uan hsuan-kuan tsang" 四川懸棺葬 [Szechwan hanging burials], *Min-tsu hsueh yen-chiu* 民族學研究 [Ethnological Research] 4 (1982): 100–118.

44. J. J. M. de Groot, *Sectarianism and Religious Persecution in China* (Taipei: Ch'eng-wen Reprints, 1976 [original 1901]), pp. 231–241.

45. Manuals (printed from wood blocks) outlining the sequence of funeral ritual, with crude illustrations, can still be found in Cantonese villages, Hong Kong New Territories.

subscribed to the accepted customs and enforced a kind of ritual orthopraxy in the communities under their control. Unacceptable rites were gradually suppressed or modified to conform to centralized models.

This may well have been the mechanism for the superimposition of a standard ritual structure, but we still know little about the process of acceptance. Is the standardization we now perceive a consequence of state-sponsored social engineering carried out over a period of many centuries? Or is it the result of voluntary adoption by the general populace? Need we assume that these processes are mutually exclusive? It is obvious that there must have been some strong incentives for people of all classes and regional backgrounds to cooperate in the cultural construction of a standarized set of rites. Much more work needs to be done before we can even begin to answer these questions. What is clear, however, is that the preoccupation with performance—rather than belief—made it possible for imperial authorities, local elites, and ordinary peasants to agree on the proper *form* for the conduct of funerals.

The fact that all Chinese, irrespective of personal circumstance, appear to have been subject to the same basic set of rites is an interesting commentary on the traditional Chinese class system. This uniformity of ritual structure is not found in all class-based societies. In nineteenth-century England, for instance, paupers were treated very differently from property-owning citizens. As Laqueur notes, England was changing rapidly during this period, and notions of what constituted a minimally acceptable funeral (i.e., the basic ritual form) were changing as well.[46] Ariès, in his now classic study, *The Hour of Our Death,* documents similar changes in European mortuary customs and attitudes toward death.[47]

It is probable that China has also undergone transformations in funerary ritual over the centuries. There is some evidence, for instance, that a major change in mortuary customs occurred during the T'ang–Sung transition, corresponding to changes in the Chinese kinship system.[48] Furthermore, we may be witnessing a radical transformation in China's ritual structure today, with a new sequence of rites inspired by socialist ideology replacing the old (see Whyte's survey in chapter 12). Can we expect to find something characteristically "Chinese" in these emerging rites, or are they basically

46. Thomas Laqueur, "Bodies, Death, and Pauper Funerals," *Representations* 1 (1983): 109–131.

47. Ariès, *The Hour of Our Death*, pp. 559–588.

48. See, e.g., David G. Johnson, *The Medieval Chinese Oligarchy* (Boulder, Colo.: Westview Press, 1977), pp. 94, 108; Patricia B. Ebrey, *The Aristocratic Families of Early Imperial China* (Cambridge: Cambridge University Press, 1978), p. 91; and Patricia Ebrey, "The Early Stages in the Development of Chinese Descent Groups," in *Kinship Organization in Late Imperial China, 1000–1940*, eds. Patricia B. Ebrey and James L. Watson (Berkeley and Los Angeles: University of California Press, 1986), pp. 20–29.

indistinguishable from socialist forms practiced in other parts of the world?[49] Whyte's account makes it clear that the ritual structure that helped hold China together as a coherent culture for so many centuries no longer has meaning to millions of Chinese (particularly in the cities). One wonders whether a new set of rites, together with new categories of ritual specialists, will emerge to fill the void.

49. Christel Lane, *The Rites of Rulers: Ritual in Industrial Society, the Soviet Union* (Cambridge: Cambridge University Press, 1981); Christopher A. Binns, "The Changing Face of Power: Revolution and Accommodation in the Development of the Soviet Ceremonial System, Parts 1 & 2," *Man* n.s. 14 (1979): 585–601, and 15 (1980): 170–187.

Stephen F. Teiser

GHOSTS AND ANCESTORS IN MEDIEVAL CHINESE RELIGION: THE YÜ-LAN-P'EN FESTIVAL AS MORTUARY RITUAL

The yü-lan-p'en festival has long been considered a prime example of the mix of Chinese and Buddhist ideas; it synthesizes ancestral sacrifices and the Chinese value of filiality with Indian notions of karma and offerings to monks. Yü-lan-p'en ritual practice as well as the myths associated with it exemplify the multifaceted process whereby China was made more Buddhist and Buddhism made more Chinese. This blend is evident in one of the earliest accounts of the festival, contained in Tsung Lin's (ca. 498–561) *Record of Seasonal Observances in Ching-ch'u:*

On the fifteenth day of the seventh month, monks, nuns, religious, and lay alike furnish bowls for offerings at the various temples and monasteries. *The Yü-lan-p'en Sūtra* says that [these offerings] bring merit covering seven generations, and the practice of sending them with banners and flowers, singing and drumming, and food probably derives from this.

The sūtra also says, "Mu-lien saw his departed mother reborn among the hungry ghosts. He filled his bowl with rice and sent it to his mother as an offering, but before the food entered her mouth it changed into flaming coals, so in the end she could not eat. Mu-lien let out a great cry and rushed back to tell the Buddha. The Buddha said, 'Your mother's sins are grave; there is nothing that you as a single individual can do about it. You must rely on the

0018-2710/86/2601-0003$01.00

mighty spiritual power of the assembled monks of the ten directions: for the sake of seven generations of ancestors and those in distress, you should gather [food] of the one hundred flavors and five kinds of fruit, place it in a bowl, and offer it to those of great virtue of the ten directions.' The Buddha decreed that the assembly of monks should chant prayers on behalf of seven generations of ancestors of the donor, that they should practice meditation and concentrate their thoughts, and then receive the food. At this time Mu-lien's mother gained release from all of her sufferings as a hungry ghost. Mu-lien told the Buddha, 'Future disciples of the Buddha who practice filial devotion must also carry out the yü-lan-p'en offering.' The Buddha said, 'Wonderful.'"

Based on this, later generations [of our time] have expanded the ornamentation, pushing their skillful artistry to the point of [offering] cut wood, carved bamboo, and pretty cuttings [of paper] patterned after flowers and leaves.[1]

The story of Mu-lien (Sanskrit Maudgalyāyana) invoked in this passage provides the origin myth for the festival of "yü-lan-p'en," popularly understood to mean "the bowl (*p'en*) filled with offerings to save ancestors from hanging upside-down (*yü-lan*) in purgatory."[2] The events and themes described in this myth were recounted and embellished in several literary forms during the T'ang dynasty (618–906), when the practice of the festival spread throughout Chinese society.[3] Three canonical and apocryphal sūtras, including *The Yü-lan-p'en Sūtra* cited by Tsung Lin, were recorded (probably written)

[1] Translation from the annotated text of Moriya Mitsuo, *Chūgoku ko saijiki no kenkyū* (Tokyo: Teikoku shoin, 1963), pp. 359–61. Tsung Lin titled his work *Ching-ch'u chi.* Tu Kung-chan (ca. 581–624) edited Tsung Lin's text and named it *Ching-ch'u sui-shih chi.* Characters for Chinese and Japanese names and terms are listed in the Glossary at the end of the article.

[2] Hui-ching's (578–645?) commentary on *The Yü-lan-p'en Sūtra, Yü-lan-p'en ching tsan-shu,* in *Taishō shinshū daizōkyō,* 100 vols. (1924–34; reprint, Taipei: Hsin-wen-feng, 1974; hereafter abbreviated as T.) no. 2781, 85:540a; Tsung-mi's commentary, *Yü-lan-p'en ching shu,* T. no. 1792, 39:506c–507a. Scholars of Buddhism since the T'ang dynasty have offered numerous explanations and Sanskrit, Central Asian, and Iranian etymologies for the term; for a summary of the opinions, see Kenneth K. S. Ch'en, *The Chinese Transformation of Buddhism* (Princeton, N.J.: Princeton University Press, 1973), pp. 61–64; and Victor Mair, *Tun-huang Popular Narratives* (Cambridge: Cambridge University Press, 1983), p. 224.

[3] For a general introduction to the literary sources of the Mu-lien story, see Ch'en Fang-ying, *Mu-lien chiu-mu ku-shih chih yen-chin chi ch'i yu-kuan wen-hsüeh chih yen-chiu,* History and Literature Series, no. 65 (Taipei: Taiwan National University, 1983). Ch'en omits mention of an important noncanonical source, the *Ching-t'u yü-lan-p'en ching;* this is Pelliot MS no. 2185 of the Fonds Pelliot Chinois in the Bibliothèque Nationale in Paris, transcribed and translated by both Jan Jaworski, "L'Avalambana sūtra de la terre pure," *Monumenta Serica* 1 (1935–36): 82–107; and Iwamoto Yutaka, *Bukkyō setsuwa kenkyū,* vol. 4, *Jigoku meguri no bungaku* (includes *Mokuren densetsu to urabon*) (Tokyo: Kaimei shoten, 1979), pp. 25–32. Of the many Japanese studies of the Mu-lien myth in Chinese literature, see esp. Iwamoto, *Jigoku meguri no bungaku;* Ogawa Kan'ichi, *Bukkyō bunkashi kenkyū* (Kyoto: Nagata bunshōdō, 1973); Okabe

in China between the fifth and seventh centuries.[4] The Mu-lien myth was elaborated at its greatest length in the oral storytelling traditions popular among the illiterate in the T'ang. These vernacular *chantefables* or "transformation texts" (*pien-wen*), discovered in Tun-huang in the first decade of this century, reveal the high repute accorded Mu-lien by the popular imagination.[5] *The Transformation Text on Mu-lien Saving His Mother from the Dark Regions* follows Mu-lien in his shamanic journeys to all reaches of the cosmos, painting a terrifying picture of the tortures of hell. They illustrate the karmic fruits produced by Mu-lien's mother's actions in previous lifetimes and emphasize the point that filiality can be fulfilled only by Buddhist ritual means, by making offerings to the Sangha.

Festival activities were carried out in a broad range of cultic centers: homes of laypeople and popular shrines, state-sponsored temples and the imperial chapel. In lay religious life the yü-lan-p'en festival had, by T'ang times, become part of the cycle of ancestral sacrifices, thus assuming an important place in family religion and mortuary ritual. By drawing participants from all walks of life to community temples for a day of festivities during the seventh lunar month, the festival joined the round of calendrical celebrations that punctuated the Chinese year. Yü-lan-p'en also marked an important juncture in the monastic life cycle. Having sequestered themselves in the monastery for three months, monks ended their retreat on the fifteenth day of the seventh month. Monks freed themselves from the stricter rules in force during the summer meditation session, welcoming lay donors into temples and preparing large feasts. Further, by the seventh century yü-lan-p'en practice was made a part of Chinese state religion: state functionaries were ordered to present offerings at officially sponsored temples throughout the empire, and ceremonies were frequently performed in the imperial chapel for the benefit of imperial ancestors.[6]

Kazuo, "Urabon kyōrui no yakkyō shiteki kenkyū," *Shūkyō kenkyū* 37, no. 3 (March 1964): 60–76; and Sawada Mizuho, *Jigoku hen: Chūgoku no meikaisetsu* (Kyoto: Hōzōkan, 1968).

[4] They are *Pao-en feng-p'en ching,* T. no. 686; *Yü-lan-p'en ching,* T. no. 685; and *Ching-t'u yü-lan-p'en ching,* Pelliot MS no. 2185.

[5] For an introduction to *pien-wen* as a genre, see Pai Hua-wen, "What Is Pien-wen?" trans. Victor H. Mair, *Harvard Journal of Asiatic Studies* 44, no. 2 (December 1984): 493–514. *The Transformation Text on Mu-lien Saving His Mother* is collated in *Tun-huang pien-wen chi,* ed. Wang Ch'ung-min et al., 2 vols. (Peking: Jen-min wen-hsüeh ch'u-pan-she, 1957), pp. 714–55. For a listing of all manuscript sources of various *pien-wen* concerning Mu-lien, consult Victor Mair, "Lay Students and the Making of Written Vernacular Narrative: An Inventory of Tun-huang Manuscripts," *Chinoperl Papers,* no. 10 (1981), pp. 5–96.

[6] The celebration of yü-lan-p'en in the year 692 by Empress Wu is particularly well known, largely because of the "Yü-lan-p'en Rhapsody" (Yü-lan-p'en fu) composed by Yang Chiung (650–ca. 694); see the *Chiu t'ang shu* (Peking: Chung-hua shu-chü, 1975),

Consonant with the more syncretic character of popular religion after the T'ang, a number of diverse elements enter into yü-lan-p'en celebrations in later times. Taoist elements loom large in some yü-lan-p'en celebrations, since in fact Taoists had long held a festival called "*chung-yüan*" on the fifteenth day of the seventh month, in which the "Grand Emperor, Officer of Earth" (*ti-kuan ta-ti*) descended to judge people's actions, and participants performed repentance rituals and made sacrifices to ancestors in hell.[7] New liturgies associated with Tantric Buddhism also came to be used in yü-lan-p'en celebrations in later times.[8] Vocabulary deriving from yü-lan-p'en was also incorporated into the general language of popular religion. The motif of Mu-lien's descent to hell, for example, became part of the masses for the dead held at irregular intervals during the year. These later elements are evident in the ethnographic treatments of the festival written in the eighteenth, nineteenth, and twentieth centuries.[9]

The interest of the yü-lan-p'en festival to historians of religion, of course, is that it provides an excellent lens through which to construe the interaction of Buddhism with indigenous social and cultural systems, in this case those of China. An analysis of the festival—like

p. 5001. Yang's rhapsody is contained in numerous medieval encyclopedias; see, for instance, *Ch'u-hsüeh chi*, by Hsü Chien (659–729) (Peking: Chung-hua shu-chü, 1962), pp. 79–80. The *T'ang liu-tien* preserves a description of the government office in charge of supplying offerings during yü-lan-p'en; see *T'ang liu-tien* (639), Chang Chiu-ling, ed., Ssu-k'u ch'üan-shu chen-pen, series 6, vols. 117–19 (Taipei: Commercial Press, 1976), *chüan* 22, p. 10b.

7 See Yoshioka Yoshitoyo, *Dōkyō to bukkyō* (Tokyo: Toshima shobo, 1959, 1970), 1:369–432; 2:231–85.

8 See, e.g., Tsun-shih's (964–1032) liturgy for the "Mass [for offerings to spirits] of the Water and Land" (*shui-lu hui*), *Chih-sheng-kuang tao-ch'ang nien-sung i*, T. no. 1951, 46:978–82; and Ferdinand Lessing, "Skizze des Ritus: Die Speisung der Hungergeister," in *Studia Sino-Altaica: Festschrift für Erich Haenisch zum 80. Geburtstag, in Auftrage der Deutschen Morgenländischen Gesellschaft*, ed. Herbert Franke (Weisbaden: Franz Steiner Verlag GMBH, 1961), pp. 114–19. For a general overview, see Makita Tairyō, "Suirikue shōkō," *Tōhō shūkyō*, no. 12 (July 1957), pp. 14–32.

9 See the collation of notices from local gazetteers in *Ku-chin t'u-shu chi-ch'eng* (completed 1725), 100 vols. (Taipei: Wen-hsing shu-tien, 1964), 3:692–94. De Groot's account of the festival, replete with historical background and a discussion of terms and symbolism, remains the classic study; see Jan Jakob M. de Groot, *Les fêtes annuellement célébrées à Émoui*, trans. C. G. Chavannes, 2 vols., Annales du Musée Guimet, vols. 11, 12 (Paris: Ernest Leroux, 1886), 12:403–35. For de Groot's even more detailed treatment of irregularly held ancestral rites, see his "Buddhist Masses for the Dead in Amoy," *Actes du sixième congrès international des orientalistes* (Leiden, 1885), pt. 4, sec. 4, pp. 1–120, and *The Religious System of China*, 6 vols. (Leiden, 1892–1910), vols. 1–3. Of the many twentieth-century reports, see esp. Suzuki Mitsuo, "Bon ni kuru rei," *Minzokugaku kenkyū* 37, no. 3 (1972): 167–85; Karl Ludwig Reichelt, *Truth and Tradition in Chinese Buddhism: A Study of Mahayana Buddhism*, trans. Katharina van Wagenen Bugge (Shanghai: Commercial Press, 1927), pp. 77–126; and Claude Lombard-Salmon, "Survivance d'un rite bouddhique à Java: La cérémonie du *pu-du* (*avalambana*)," *Bulletin de l'Ecole Française d'Extrême-Orient* 62 (1975): 457–86.

studies of tales of karmic retribution popular in ninth-century Japan[10] and of local spirit-cults in contemporary Thailand[11]—should cast light on the mutual accommodations made between Buddhist symbols, myths, and rituals, on the one hand, and indigenous forms of ritual, explanations of evil, and conceptions of society, on the other. The Chinese were not alone in melding the concerns of a strong and pervasive ancestral cult with the institutionalized presence of world renouncers, and the Chinese adaptation of Buddhist cosmology provides an interesting case for cross-cultural comparison. All of these facets of the relation between Buddhism and indigenous traditions are evident in yü-lan-p'en myth and ritual. My treatment of the festival also shares many points of departure with recent studies of the role of ancestral cults in various societies and with the continuing effort to place Buddhism within society, rather than beyond it.[12]

In narrower terms, the yü-lan-p'en festival appears particularly apt as a frame of comparison in East Asia. It shares many affinities with the Korean ritual for lost souls, the *manghon-il*. And in Japan the celebration of the festival currently thrives under the name of "*Obon,*" having undergone numerous changes since its introduction from China in the seventh century.[13]

Previous studies of the festival have treated it in the context of Chinese literature and in the history of the translation of Buddhist scriptures. While building on this scholarship, I shall view the festival in a different context, that of Chinese religion and Chinese society. Specifically, I shall explore the significance of yü-lan-p'en as *ritual.*[14]

10 See Kyoko Motomochi Nakamura, trans., *Miraculous Stories from the Japanese Buddhist Tradition: The "Nihon ryōiki" of the Monk Kyōkai*, Harvard-Yenching Institute Monograph Series, vol. 20 (Cambridge, Mass.: Harvard University Press, 1972).

11 See Stanley J. Tambiah, *Buddhism and the Spirit Cults in North-East Thailand*, Cambridge Studies in Social Anthropology, no. 2 (Cambridge: Cambridge University Press, 1970).

12 See Helen Hardacre's review of Robert J. Smith, *Ancestor Worship in Contemporary Japan* (Stanford, Calif.: Stanford University Press, 1974), in *History of Religions* 15, no. 4 (May 1976): 388–92; and Roger L. Janelli and Dawnhee Yim Janelli, *Ancestor Worship and Korean Society* (Stanford, Calif.: Stanford University Press, 1982). For a good overview of the second issue, see Stanley J. Tambiah, "Buddhism and This-Worldly Activity," *Modern Asian Studies* 7, no. 1 (January 1973): 1–20.

13 Feasts held on the fifteenth day of the seventh month and the eighth day of the fourth month (the traditional observance of the Buddha's birthdate) were held as early as the year 606; see *Nihon shoki*, Nihon koten bungaku taikei, vols. 67–68 (Tokyo: Iwanami shoten, 1967, 1965), 2:187. On the fifteenth day of the seventh month in 659, government officials were ordered "to encourage and expound the *Urabon kyō* [*Yü-lan-p'en Sūtra*] so as to repay [the kindness bestowed by] seven generations of ancestors"; see *Nihon shoki*, 2:341.

14 A brief article by Takenaka Nobutsune draws on anthropological analyses of ritual to explore the significance of funerary rites in Buddhism, focusing on the concept

Placing the festival in the cycle of mortuary rites casts new light on the mixing of Chinese and Buddhist themes in yü-lan-p'en celebrations and helps to resolve some conundrums of traditional scholarship. Drawing upon van Gennep's analysis of the structure of rites of passage, I shall first explore what yü-lan-p'en *does,* how it effects the passage of individuals from life through death to rebirth. The ritual functions to carry the marginal figures of the Chinese underworld (ghosts and the recently deceased) to a secure, postliminal state. Turning to the social group defined by participation in yü-lan-p'en, I shall then examine the ritual community and its values. The values expressed in the festival—what yü-lan-p'en *says*—affirm the place of the individual not only in the family and the community but within the cosmological rhythms of nature as well. Third, I shall draw attention to the dichotomy usually assumed to exist between wandering ghosts as recipients of yü-lan-p'en offerings and settled ancestors as recipients. Far from reflecting the opposed values of Buddhist impermanence and Chinese social solidarity, these elements are part of a broader and more unitary process. I shall argue, then, that the ritual process surrounding death provides a more comprehensive framework in which these seemingly dichotomous elements assume a coherent and complementary place.

YÜ-LAN-P'EN AS A RITE OF PASSAGE

In his classic work, *The Rites of Passage* (1909), Arnold van Gennep proposed to analyze various sets of rituals from a broad range of cultures, not in terms of their content or the beliefs on which they rested but in terms of their formal structure. He found that many rituals surround and make possible the passage of the individual from one social group or status to another. Such rites de passage mark the great transitions of social life: movement from one territory to the next, the entry of the infant into social life at birth, the adolescent's coming of age and assumption of adulthood, initiation into secret societies and clubs, betrothal and marriage, and the transition from life to death. In each of these transitions, the individual leaves one group or "world" and joins another, with a liminal period in between. Thus, for van Gennep each rite of passage consists of three subrites marking three substages: "I propose to call the rites of separation from a previous world, *preliminal* rites, those executed during the transitional stage *liminal (or threshold) rites,* and the ceremonies of

of purgatory in Buddhism and on the funeral rites performed for the historical Buddha. See Takenaka Nobutsune, "Sōsō no gireiteki ichi," in *Bukkyō to girei: Katō shōichi sensei koki kinen ronbunshū,* ed. Bukkyō Minzoku Gakkai (Tokyo: Kokusho Kankōkai, 1977).

incorporation into the new world *postliminal rites.*"[15] A few years prior to van Gennep's study, Robert Hertz had reached similar conclusions: "Each promotion of the individual implies the passage from one group to another: an exclusion, i.e., a death, and a new integration, i.e., a rebirth. . . . To the social consciousness, death is only a particular instance of a general phenomenon."[16]

Chinese rites of passage surrounding death (probably beginning with the system of double obsequies in evidence in the fourth millennium B.C.) generally conform to this pattern.[17] In the Chinese view, death occurs when the lighter, more refined components of the person (the *hun*) float upward, leaving behind the coarser, more corporeal components (the *p'o*), which will constitute the physical remains.[18] This process completed, rites of *separation* are performed during the few days immediately following death. The body of the deceased is separated from the living in a process that ends with the encoffining and first burial. As the deceased is separated from the everyday world of the living, so too are those who have been touched by death.

[15] Arnold van Gennep, *The Rites of Passage,* trans. Monika B. Vizedom and Gabrielle L. Caffee (Chicago: University of Chicago Press, 1960), p. 21; see also pp. 11, 191.

[16] Robert Hertz, *Death and the Right Hand,* trans. Rodney Needham and Claudia Needham (Glencoe, Ill.: Free Press, 1960), p. 81.

[17] The description of the cycle of mortuary rituals in this section is general enough to include most mortuary practice for almost two millennia. Structurally similar rites in other cultures include the Hindu ritual of Sapiṇḍīkarana, which transforms "the vulnerable, disembodied spirit (*preta*) of this world into the secure *pitṛ* [ancestor, literally "Father"] of the other world" (David M. Knipe, "Sapiṇḍīkarana: The Hindu Rite of Entry into Heaven," in *Religious Encounters with Death,* ed. Frank Reynolds and Earle Waugh [University Park: Pennsylvania State University Press, 1977], p. 111). Compare also celebrations of the Day of the Dead in most Latin American countries, such as All Souls' Day in Bolivia, described by Olivia Harris, "The Dead and the Devils among the Bolivian Laymi," in *Death and the Regeneration of Life,* ed. Maurice Bloch and Jonathan Parry (Cambridge: Cambridge University Press, 1982), pp. 45–73; and the Cool Funeral Beer ceremony of the LoDagaa in Northwestern Ghana described in Jack Goody, *Death, Property, and the Ancestors* (Stanford, Calif.: Stanford University Press, 1962).

[18] For overviews of Chinese concepts of the "souls," see Michihata Ryōshū, *Chūgoku bukkyō shisō shi no kenkyū* (Kyoto: Heiryakuji Shoten, 1979), pp. 102–71; Daniel L. Overmyer, "China," in *Death and Eastern Thought: Understanding Death in Eastern Religions and Philosophies,* ed. Frederick H. Holck (Nashville, Tenn.: Abingdon Press, 1974), pp. 198–225; and Walter Liebenthal, "The Immortality of the Soul in Chinese Thought," *Monumenta Nipponica* 8, semi-annual no. one-half (1952): 327–97. Tao-shih (ca. 600–668), a Buddhist scholar-monk of broad interests, includes the traditional Chinese soul concepts in his section on mortuary ritual in *Fa-yüan chu-lin,* T. no. 2122, 53:998c–1000b, after noting that "the cycle of birth and death is not separate from conventional [or secular] truth [*su-ti, saṁvṛti-satya*]" (T. 53:998c). His point is that while Buddhism may include a level of ultimate truth, which relativizes any concept of a substantial soul, nevertheless to the same extent that everyone else does, Buddhists also have *hun* and *p'o* components that disperse upon death and that are dealt with in mortuary rituals.

Mourners distinguish themselves from nonmourners by abstaining from work and by adopting different patterns of dress, diet, and comportment. During this phase the corpse and often the dead person's spirit are considered to be extremely polluting, which suggests a strong desire on the part of the living to avoid death, in a situation where the physical and cultural demands of disposal make this impossible.

Next, liminal rites are performed during the period of *transition.* Here, the spirit of the deceased travels through various hells and meets with the bureaucrat gods of the underworld (notably King Yama) on the way to rebirth and/or ancestorhood. In the scheme that became popular even before T'ang times, this intermediary period was deemed to last forty-nine days and was marked by a set of seven rituals lasting seven days apiece. In these rituals, and in the less identifiably Buddhist rituals of popular religion since the Sung dynasty, chants and prayers are recited, priests are called in to mourners' homes to preach, and paper money and paper items are burned to help the dead negotiate their way through difficult passages. The living also assist the dead by lighting lamps to guide them through the dark, and by providing bamboo versions of the attendants and bearers needed for official journeys. Betwixt and between, the deceased has left the world of the living but has not yet made the final transition to individual or corporate rebirth.

Mu-lien's mother is most often pictured in this liminal condition in yü-lan-p'en literature, and yü-lan-p'en ritual is meant to carry her—and the ancestors generally—beyond this state of limbo. Mu-lien first tries the usual ritual methods for securing her safe passage: he sends his mother a food offering.[19] This transaction is foiled, though, due to the mother's avarice in her previous lives: the food bursts into flames as it reaches her lips, or other hungry ghosts come to steal it. In the popular tales, Mu-lien further offers to stand in for his mother, to suffer the fruits of her evil actions in her place.[20] This too is impossible, as each person must suffer his or her own karma and liminality. The usual methods for ferrying the dead through this tortuous period simply do not work: as a group of hungry ghosts explains to Mu-lien: "Though there be a thousand kinds of food placed in our grave-mounds / How can they alleviate the hunger in our stomachs?"[21]

19 In the *avadāna* tale related in *Ching-t'u yü-lan-p'en ching,* Mu-lien places the offering on her "spirit altar" (*ling-ch'uang*); text in Jaworski (n. 3 above), lines 97–98.

20 *The Transformation Text on Mu-lien Saving His Mother* (n. 5 above), p. 735; translation following Mair, *Tun-huang Popular Narratives* (n. 2 above), p. 110.

21 *The Transformation Text on Mu-lien Saving His Mother,* p. 719; translation following Mair, *Tun-huang Popular Narratives,* p. 193.

Yü-lan-p'en rituals are usually associated with the final phase of *incorporation* in the cycle of mortuary rituals: they mark the successful transition of the individual from the world of the living to the world of the reborn. Yü-lan-p'en rituals succeed in effecting this transition where the traditional mortuary rituals have failed: only when Mu-lien follows Buddhist ritual practice—giving gifts to monks at the end of their summer retreat—is his mother released from the torments of purgatory. In the yearly celebration of the yü-lan-p'en festival and the myths associated with it, the dead are incorporated into the community of ancestors, and it is this established group that receives the merit transferred by descendants. In many yü-lan-p'en offerings, descendants burn paper servants and paper houses for use by the ancestors who have achieved rebirth in Amitābha's Pure Land. Settled in their new abode, the dead assume a familiar and hence familial existence. In cases of corporate rebirth, then, the festival marks the assumption of the status of ancestor by the dead.

The yü-lan-p'en festival also marks the end of a transitional period in cases where rebirth is individual rather than corporate, when the deceased is incorporated directly into the realm of the living forty-nine days after death. A colophon to a tenth-century manuscript of the *The Yü-lan-p'en Sūtra,* for example, states that Chai Feng-ta, auxiliary secretary of the Ministry of Public Works, commissioned the copying of the sūtra for the memorial service following the one-hundredth death-day anniversary of his wife, née Ma.[22] Since rebirth was assumed to take place forty-nine days after death, this indicates that the sūtra was associated with the postliminal period, when the dead person has been reincorporated into the world of the living. The yü-lan-p'en festival is integrating for descendants as well: by coming together as a group for services and banquets, family members display their achievements to the community at large, inspire filial sentiments, and generally reaffirm the solidarity of the kinship organization composed of the living and the dead.[23]

THE RITUAL COMMUNITY AND ITS VALUES

As I have suggested, the yü-lan-p'en festival may profitably be viewed as a part of the cycle of rites of passage marking the transition from

22 *Catalogue des manuscrits chinois de Touen-Houang* (*Fonds Pelliot chinois*), vol. 1, nos. 2001–2500 (Paris: Bibliothèque Nationale, 1970), pp. 39–40; citing P. no. 2055r.

23 For an extended analysis of ancestral rites as functional glue holding together and sanctioning the kinship system, see C. K. Yang, *Religion in Chinese Society: A Study of Contemporary Social Functions of Religion and Some of Their Historical Factors* (Berkeley: University of California Press, 1961), pp. 28–57; and Hugh D. R. Baker, *Chinese Family and Kinship* (London: Macmillan Press, 1979), pp. 71–106.

life, through death, to rebirth. In this cycle yü-lan-p'en rituals facilitate the transition from the liminal phase to the phase of incorporation: the dead assume their status as ancestors or as sentient beings in the six paths of existence. But in addition to this functional aspect, rituals also have an expressive role. Rituals say things with actions as much as they do things with words.

Symbols of rebirth are often prominent in rituals marking the incorporation of the individual into a new social group.[24] Yü-lan-p'en rituals, coming at the end of the mortuary cycle, are no exception to this general phenomenon. One school of thought has accounted for the dominance of symbols of rebirth in mortuary practices by appeal to the Durkheimian concept of society as the transcendent creator and sustainer of the individual's life and values. In this view, death presents the greatest possible threat to society. Death not only strips the individual away from the group, but it radically calls into question the stability and immortality necessary for collective life:

> Indeed society imparts its own character of permanence to the individuals who compose it: because it feels itself immortal and wants to be so, it cannot normally believe that its members, above all those in whom it incarnates itself and with whom it identifies itself, should be fated to die. . . . Because it believes in itself a healthy society cannot admit that an individual who was part of its own substance, and on whom it has set its mark, shall be lost for ever. The last word must remain with life; the deceased will rise from the grip of death and will return, in one form or another, to the peace of human association.[25]

More recently, anthropologists with less faith in a transcendent or reified society have wedded this global explanation to the distinctive tonalities of various cultures. They have suggested that the specific element that is revitalized through funerary ritual is the resource deemed most essential to the reproduction of the social order of the particular culture. Different cultures define this resource variously as agricultural fertility, human fecundity, property, and the like.[26] As communities vary in social organization, so do the values expressed by their mortuary rituals.

In the case of Chinese Buddhist mortuary ritual, themes of integration, social solidarity, and cosmic regeneration are prominent in yü-

24 See Mircea Eliade, *Birth and Rebirth: The Religious Meanings of Initiation in Human Culture*, trans. Willard R. Trask (New York: Harper & Row, 1958).

25 Hertz (n. 16 above), pp. 77–78.

26 See Maurice Bloch and Jonathan Parry, "Introduction: Death and the Regeneration of Life," in Bloch and Parry, eds. (n. 17 above), pp. 7–9; and Goody (n. 17 above).

lan-p'en celebrations. Yü-lan-p'en combines death and decay with rebirth and fertility. Not only human life but plant life too follows the patterns of *yang* and *yin,* expanding and contracting, blooming and dropping. I shall explore these themes by examining the ritual communities defined by those who participate in yü-lan-p'en ritual and by assessing the specific values shared by community members.

By moving the liminal dead into ancestorhood, yü-lan-p'en rituals replace the individual into the dominant group in Chinese socio-religious life, the family. By presenting gifts to Buddhist monks, descendants are able to ensure the continued prosperity of the kinship group, comprising ancestors going back seven generations. As an ancestor, the recently deceased person reenters not only a social network but a cultural or ideological one as well, since he now receives veneration and plays an important role in sanctioning core values. Yü-lan-p'en rituals reaffirm the family as a group and the mutual obligations that invigorate it, in part by drawing on a network of exchange. For ancestors and descendants, gifts presented in the yü-lan-p'en sustain bonds and recapitulate the relationships that constitute the kinship group. In short, one ritual group defined by yü-lan-p'en is the family, its values summed up by the notion of filiality.

Another ritual group defined by yü-lan-p'en is the local community. In the progression of mortuary rituals, the yü-lan-p'en rite differs from those that preceded it not only in form and function—as a rite of incorporation it ends the stage of liminality—but in locale as well. Unlike the rites of corpse preparation, mourning, one-hundred-day anniversary of death, and first- and third-year anniversaries, which were usually celebrated just in the home, the yü-lan-p'en festival was also celebrated in temples and marketplaces. These centers were the locus of festival life, and they integrated a broad range of communal, economic, theatrical, diversionary, and religious functions.[27] The yü-lan-p'en festival thus drew together both the living and the dead in those *lieux de culte* central to the development and spread of Buddhism among the masses in medieval China.[28]

27 See Kenneth K. S. Ch'en, "The Role of Buddhist Monasteries in T'ang Society," *History of Religions* 15, no. 3 (February 1976): 209–30. For an elaboration of the concept of "cultic centers" in a Japanese context, see Allan G. Grapard, "Japan's Ignored Cultural Revolution: The Separation of Shinto and Buddhist Divinities in Meiji (*shimbutsu bunri*) and a Case Study: Tōnomine," *History of Religions* 23, no. 3 (February 1984): 240–65.

28 See Jacques Gernet, *Les aspects économiques du bouddhisme dans la société chinoise du Ve au Xe siècle* (Saigon: Ecole Française d'Extrême-Orient, 1956), esp. pp. 191–224, 240–50.

The community of monks makes its own special contribution to the renewal and regeneration characteristic of yü-lan-p'en celebrations. Coming at the end of their summer retreat, the yü-lan-p'en ritual allows monks to release the ascetic energy built up during retreat, tapping their potency for the benefit of the ancestors. Critics have traditionally charged that monks are asocial and that the Sangha institutionalizes otherworldliness. But in yü-lan-p'en, monastic renunciation ultimately affirms the values of regeneration and rebirth, and the participation of those who have left the householder's life is essential for the health and well-being of the ancestors.

The celebration of yü-lan-p'en is regenerative in the broadest sense in that it harnesses the dead to the reproduction of all life by incorporating them into the cycle of seasonal festivals.[29] This recognition forces us beyond the Durkheimian paradigm assumed thus far. That is, the model of ritual I have assumed thus far—ritual functioning to mediate and make congruent social organization, on the one hand, and cultural values, on the other—must now be revised because the ritual community is not merely a social group. As I have suggested, the yü-lan-p'en festival marks a social passage: it reintegrates the deceased into the social groups of family and community and reinforces the values of these communities. But in addition, it marks a *cosmic* passage: it is celebrated every year in the middle of the seventh lunar month when crops begin to ripen. It links the dead to cosmic rhythms by making them an integral part of the seasonal festivals that come near the end of the summer growing season.

As noted above, the festival has long been associated with sacrifices to Ti-kuan, "Officer of Earth," the god who presides over the vital force of the earth and who controls the ripening of crops.[30] Scholars have long recognized and theorized a connection between the family cult and agricultural production.[31] My suggestion is that the dead, as ancestors, are drawn into the agricultural cycle of fertility through yü-lan-p'en ritual. A thirteenth-century work describing life in and around Hangchow, the *Meng-liang lu,* makes the connection between ancestors and fertility explicit. It notes that offerings are given to ancestors on this day with the aim of "responding to autumn ripening [*pao ch'iu-ch'eng*]."[32] People repay their ancestors' fructifying influence on agriculture with offerings of food.[33] In this view, through yü-lan-p'en the dead are not simply drawn into the circle of ancestors and thereby incorporated into the human web; the dead, in their rebirth as ancestors, are placed at the very center of the natural cycle of fertility.

29 Compare Bloch and Parry, "Introduction," p. 10.

30 See de Groot, *Les fêtes* (n. 9 above), pp. 445–46 for an analysis of the fertility symbolism.

31 See, e.g., Bernhard Karlgren, "Some Fecundity Symbols in Ancient China," *Bulletin of the Museum of Far Eastern Antiquities* 2 (1930): 1–65.

32 *Meng-liang lu,* by Wu Tzu-mu, in *Tung-ching meng-hua lu, wai ssu-chung* (Shanghai: Ku-tien Wen-hsüeh Ch'u-pan-she, 1957), *chüan* 4, p. 160.

The integrative, affirming tendencies common to most forms of death ritual are evident in yü-lan-p'en rituals as well. Seen in this light, mortuary ritual guarantees the rhythms of nature as much as it stabilizes society. The yü-lan-p'en festival provides a good example of what Granet has said in more lofty terms about the Chinese worldview: "Man and Nature do not form two separate domains, but a single *society*. . . . In place of a Science having for its object the knowledge of the World, the Chinese conceived a *Ritual* of life [*Etiquette de la vie*] which they considered efficacious enough to establish a total Order."[34] Ritual does not simply hold together society and express its cultural values, but it articulates the larger order in which individual, society, and culture are harmonized and given meaning.

GHOSTS AND ANCESTORS

Treating yü-lan-p'en celebrations as rites of passage, I have explained their function as rites of incorporation and have suggested that they express social and cosmological themes of regeneration. Adopting this perspective also helps resolve several traditional problems in the interpretation of yü-lan-p'en and related mortuary practices. These problems have arisen largely because scholars and apologists have focused on only one side or the other of a dual yet integrated phenomenon. My analysis, however, has shown that the yü-lan-p'en complex of myth and ritual expresses both the danger of the liminal stage in rites of transition and its resolution in rites of incorporation. Put differently, in yü-lan-p'en attention is drawn both to ghosts in a marginal state and to ancestors in a settled group. Viewed in the context of mortuary ritual, then, both factors are seen as necessary aspects of a unitary process.

Some scholars have attempted to answer an unfruitful question: who receives the offerings in the yü-lan-p'en rite, wandering ghosts or ancestors? Stated in this fashion, the question betrays a skewed,

33 Compare Lien-sheng Yang, "The Concept of 'Pao' as a Basis for Social Relations in China," in *Chinese Thought and Institutions,* ed. John K. Fairbank (Chicago: University of Chicago Press, 1957), pp. 291–301. See also Marcel Mauss, *The Gift: Forms and Functions of Exchange in Archaic Societies,* trans. Ian Cunnison (New York: W. W. Norton & Co., 1967).

34 Marcel Granet, *La pensée chinoise* (Paris: Albin Michel, 1968), pp. 25–26.

because partial, view of the significance of the yü-lan-p'en festival. The Japanese ethnographer, Yanagita Kunio, for example, claims that the Japanese festival of Bon, like the New Year celebration, originally was a festival for welcoming one's ancestors back into the home. He interprets the rites of Bon as directed essentially to ancestors and not to wandering ghosts. This latter class of non-kin *muenbotoke,* a later Buddhist import, was merely grafted on to indigenous ancestral sacrifices.[35] Concerning yü-lan-p'en practice in China, Hugh Baker summarizes the view of most sociologists: "Other people's dead were of little concern: the only dead to be worshipped were one's own dead, one's ancestors."[36] The sociologist's insistence on the significance of the kinship group in the yü-lan-p'en festival accords well with the traditional Confucian view. For traditionalists and defenders of native traditions like Yen Chih-t'ui (531–91) and Yao Ch'ung (650–721), only one portion of the yü-lan-p'en celebrations is valid, that side emphasizing the solidarity of the ancestors. The bestowal of posthumous blessings or merit (*chui-fu*) on the deceased as individual, and the offerings intended to appease the hunger of wandering ghosts, were not legitimate in their eyes.[37]

Others have answered the same question by insisting that wandering ghosts, not ancestors, are or ought to be the sole recipients of yü-lan-p'en offerings. They assert that the idea of making offerings to *preta* has logically and historically been the basis of the yü-lan-p'en festival and that the concern with ancestors so obvious in the Chinese, Japanese, and Korean cases is simply a function of the willingness of Buddhists to adapt their religion to dominant but ultimately nonessential cultural values.[38] For other Buddhist apologists and historians, the ritual is a contradictory mix of elements that should be kept

35 See Yanagita Kunio, "Senzo no hanashi," in *Yanagita Kunio shū,* Kindai nihon shisō taikei, vol. 14 (Tokyo: Tsukuma Shobō, 1975), pp. 164–281; and the excellent study by Suzuki (n. 9 above).

36 Baker (n. 23 above), p. 75.

37 For Yen Chih-t'ui's view, see Teng Ssu-yü, trans., *Family Instructions for the Yen Clan: Yen-shih chia-hsün,* T'oung Pao Monograph no. 4 (Leiden: E. J. Brill, 1968), p. 211. In a testamentary statement to his sons, Yao Ch'ung wrote: "[Among the corrupt Buddhist practices of the day] people also make statues for the sake of the dead. This is called 'posthumous blessings [*chui-fu*].' Although there are many good grounds for this teaching of expedient means, merit [*kung-te*] must issue from one's own mind—how can the help of others [living descendants] call forth a positive response?" (*Chiu t'ang shu,* p. 3028). Knowing that his sons would follow popular practice in holding services after his death, he allowed only *his own* personal possessions to be given as offerings, since using family wealth for prestations would constitute seeking "posthumous blessings"; see *Chiu t'ang shu,* pp. 3028–29; cf. Gernet (n. 28 above), p. 202.

38 See, e.g., Michihata Ryōshū, *Haka to bukkyō: Sono rekishi to bosō hihan* (Kyoto: Hyakkaen, 1977), esp. chap. 10; and Jean Przyluski, "Les rites d'avalambana," *Mélanges chinois et bouddhiques* 1 (1931–32): 221–25.

separate, the stress on family being opposed to the higher goals of Buddhist deliverance from the six paths of rebirth.[39]

Most interpreters have insisted on one or the other, either ancestors or ghosts. Buddhist apologists have tried to explain away the ancestors, while Confucian apologists have ignored the ghosts. In the end, these opposed interpretations reflect the interests and presuppositions of the cultural and academic traditions out of which the main schools of scholarship have grown and demonstrate how a unitary phenomenon can be carved into two distinct parts by traditions of scholarship unaware of their own dichotomizing analysis.[40]

The historical record clearly shows that yü-lan-p'en offerings were made to both ancestors and ghosts. *The Yü-lan-p'en Sūtra,* dating from the fifth century, is perfectly ambiguous on this point. In this sūtra the Buddha instructs Mu-lien to undertake offerings on behalf of both non-kin ("those in distress") and kin: "The Buddha told Mu-lien, 'On the fifteenth day of the seventh month, when the assembled monks of the ten directions release themselves, for the sake of seven generations of ancestors, your current parents, and those in distress, you should gather food of the one hundred flavors and five kinds of fruit, basins for washing and rinsing, incense, oil lamps and candles, and mattresses and bedding; take the sweetest, prettiest things in the world and place them in a bowl, and offer it to the assembled monks, those of great virtue of the ten directions.'"[41] Contemporary accounts of actual observances describe food offerings being given not simply to ancestors and monks but to hungry ghosts as well. An eighth-century source notes that "only on the fifteenth day of the seventh month, at the great feast attended by the assembly of monks, do all sinners in the six paths of rebirth get any food to eat. This is why people send food offerings on this day."[42] And other medieval sources

39 See, e.g., Tsuda Sōkichi, *Shina bukkyō no kenkyū* (Tokyo: Iwanami Shoten, 1957); and Michihata Ryōshū, *Bukkyō to jukyō* (Tokyo: Daisan Bunmei Sha, 1976).

40 It seems that Buddhists and Buddhologists have typically stressed the liminal side of the yü-lan-p'en festival, while sociologists have emphasized the postliminal side. Given their training in impermanence, Buddhists stress transition and process. And with their schooling in philology and philosophy, Buddhologists usually stress the pan-Asian, noncontextually bound character of Buddhism, considered as a single tradition. They naturally focus on the liminal state, in which the dead belong to no group at all. Accordingly, Buddhist apologists have usually stressed the universality of salvation, concern for sentient beings regardless and outside of any social group, as the key function of yü-lan-p'en ritual. Nor is the opposite case surprising. Long accustomed to defining the boundaries of social groups and the cultural values that hold them together, sociologists have looked for the bonds uniting the living and the dead in one corporate group. They have thus identified the strengthening of social solidarity as the key function of yü-lan-p'en ritual.

41 Translation from *The Yü-lan-p'en Sūtra,* T. no. 685, 16:779b.

42 *Chin-ku-yüan chi,* by Li Yung (d. 746), in Moriya (n. 1 above), p. 443.

establish that offerings to hungry ghosts were a regular part of most Buddhist feasts.[43]

Recognizing the presence of both ancestors and ghosts, some scholars use a historical framework to explain the seemingly dual nature of yü-lan-p'en ritual. Prior to the entry of Buddhism into China, festivals at the beginning of autumn included sacrifices to the ancestors, the celebration of harvest, and the conjunction of decay and regeneration. Buddhism as an institutional religion was thus able to popularize yü-lan-p'en practice simply by providing a new form for an old practice. In de Groot's view:

> If in fact Buddhist masses for the dead were celebrated throughout China in the seventh month, and if then all the inhabitants of the Middle Kingdom vied to celebrate the festival of offerings in honor of their deceased ancestors, then these ceremonies, however Buddhistic they may have become in ritual, already existed in China before Buddhism penetrated there. The priests of the doctrine of Shakyamuni, when they began to invade China in the first two centuries of our era, erected an exotic edifice upon this base, which was provided them by the religion of a people who always showed extreme concern for the destiny of the dead.[44]

This historical explanation still leaves a dichotomy puzzling to some, since there appears to be no logic tying the two sides together except for Chinese "practicality." Holmes Welch writes:

> Like the Aryans, the Chinese preserved the cult of ancestors as though rebirth had never been heard of.
>
> Their approach, while it might seem to be inconsistent, was actually that of a prudent man dealing with the unknown. There was no way to be sure which version of the afterlife was correct. On the chance that it was the Chinese version, the filial son made regular offerings at his father's tablet, reported all important family news, and thanked him for help received. On the chance that it was the Buddhist version, he had rites performed immediately after his father died to help him toward a better rebirth in forty-nine days.[45]

Western scholars since Frazer have further galvanized the distinction by making it a logical one. Writes Baker: "In many ways Buddhism and ancestor worship were contradictory. . . . The idea of re-birth is clearly contrary to the concept of a continuing ancestral spirit. Could one logically go on worshipping an ancestor who had been reborn as

43 See *Fo-tsu t'ung-chi,* T. no. 2035, 49:320b, 322a; and *Fa-yüan chu-lin,* T. no. 2122, 53:753b–755b.

44 De Groot, *Les fêtes* (n. 9 above), pp. 405–6.

45 Holmes Welch, *The Practice of Chinese Buddhism: 1900–1950* (Cambridge, Mass.: Harvard University Press, 1967), p. 183.

TABLE 1

YÜ-LAN-P'EN AS A RITE OF PASSAGE

Ritual state	Liminal; transition	Postliminal; incorporation
Recipients	Non-kin (ghosts)	Kin (ancestors)
Mode of rebirth	Individual in six paths	Corporate as ancestor
Temporal value	Change	Permanence
Symbolic value	Polluting; avoided	Pure; honored

an animal or as another person?"[46] Yet there are interpretive options open to us aside from saying that one side ought not to be there, or that natives commit a logical mistake by "worshipping" the dead as both ancestor and reborn sentient being. Since the fifth century both sides have been present in Chinese mortuary ritual and yü-lan-p'en celebrations. Further, construing the dead simultaneously as a ghost in limbo, as an ancestor, and as a reborn sentient being conforms to a general pattern in the history of religions. David M. Knipe writes, "This simultaneity of presence of the deceased in varied, even contradictory situations appears to be more the norm than the exception in the history of religions."[47]

Instead of being a logical contradiction with which our interpretation or explanation ends, this multilocality should provide the starting point for our analysis. My thesis is that by interpreting the yü-lan-p'en festival in the context of mortuary ritual, both sides of the ritual may then be seen as coherent and necessary parts of a greater whole: they are related aspects of a single process marking the passage from life to rebirth. Ritual, then, provides a context that encompasses several polarities, a broader scheme in which these polarities make sense. In van Gennep's terms, the yü-lan-p'en festival marks the transition between the state of liminality or transition and that of postliminality or incorporation. Accordingly, elements from *both* of these ritual states are present in yü-lan-p'en rites (see table 1 for a schematic view).

As *recipients* of offerings, ghosts and ancestors represent two sides of the same process, the process whereby society ritualizes the passage of its members from one group (the living) to another (the reborn). This process comprises an intermediary period during which the dead exist as ghosts and a postliminal period in which the dead have been incorporated into a social group as ancestors. Both sides are often

46 Baker (n. 23 above), p. 98.

47 Knipe (n. 17 above), p. 114. See also Mircea Eliade, "Mythologies of Death: An Introduction," in Reynolds and Waugh, eds. (n. 17 above), p. 19.

included within the same ritual structure; while different, they are in no way contradictory. As anthropologists have often noted, the *yin* and *yang* aspects of the dead (corresponding to ghosts and ancestors) are two sides of the same phenomenon.[48] Both ghosts and ancestors are included and ranked within the compass of Chinese banquets as well as mortuary rituals: de Groot reports that in the first evening of yü-lan-p'en celebrations, people first invite deceased family members to partake of the banquet set out in front of each home, and after they are done the remainder of the meal is offered to non-kin ghosts.[49]

As a ritualized means of dealing with death, the yü-lan-p'en festival further encompasses two *modes of rebirth:* individual and corporate. Addressing the liminal state of the dead, festival offerings secure for them a better rebirth as provisionally existing sentient beings. Affirming the postliminal state of the dead, offerings enrich the corporate group of ancestors, portrayed in most texts and prayers as stretching back for seven generations. One side recognizes the individualizing character of death and sees rebirth as an affair of the individual, while the other side resocializes the individual and stresses corporate rebirth.

In general terms, death forces people to recognize the ephemeral nature of existence as well as to affirm that life continues after all. The *temporal values* seen in mortuary ritual thus include impermanence as well as permanence.[50] The impermanent side of death is seen in the practice of setting out lamps to illuminate a path for the return of the soul and providing paper boats to ferry the departed back to his family for the yü-lan-p'en banquet.[51] The soul is unstable; it occupies no fixed position; it is in transit. These symbols highlight the mortality of the individual and the impermanence of the group. Furthermore, yü-lan-p'en practice reaffirms the permanence of the group in the face of death: as an ancestor the deceased is made an integral part of the structurally unchanging kin group, and all of its members, living and dead, gather for a communal meal. One side of the festival thus highlights the change and disruption that death inevi-

[48] See, e.g., Göran Aijmer, "A Structural Approach to Chinese Ancestor Worship," *Bijdragen tot de Taal-, Land- en Volkenkunde* 124, no. 1 (1968): 91–98; and Arthur P. Wolf, "Gods, Ghosts, and Ancestors," in *Religion and Ritual in Chinese Society,* ed. Arthur P. Wolf (Stanford, Calif.: Stanford University Press, 1974), pp. 131–82.

[49] De Groot, *Les fêtes,* p. 421.

[50] Compare Hy Van Luong, "'Brother' and 'Uncle': An Analysis of Rules, Structural Contradictions, and Meaning in Vietnamese Kinship," *American Anthropologist* 86, no. 2 (June 1984): 304.

[51] See, e.g., de Groot, *Les fêtes,* pp. 421, 428–29.

tably brings, the other side emphasizes the solidarity and permanence of the social group as it reconstitutes itself after a loss.[52]

As a rite of passage, the yü-lan-p'en ritual assumes as a context the delineation of a boundary, that between life and death, and it effects the crossing of that boundary. Anything that crosses the boundary is in a liminal state, falling outside the ordered categories of life and rebirth. To the extent that the yü-lan-p'en ritual assumes both a classificatory grid and its contravention, then, the *symbolic values* attaching to various symbols include both purity and pollution.[53] Death offends, yet it must ultimately be accepted for life to continue. In their liminal state, the dead are threatening: *preta* are disorderly and indeed need a higher authority to keep them in line, such as the god, Ta-chung yeh, "Old Fellow [who rules] the Great Crowd [of ghosts]."[54] Ghosts are dangerous, and their pollution is to be avoided: they are shunned as well as placated by offerings of food and money lest they visit maladies upon the living.[55] Yü-lan-p'en offerings to wandering ghosts reflect at the same time that they attempt to reduce this polluting presence of death. Conversely, the dead as ancestors have crossed back into a settled condition. They are not simply orderly but symbolize and enforce the highest principles of social order. As ancestors, the dead are honored and welcomed to family meals, their purity affirmed in the regenerative role they play in family, communal, and agricultural life.

CONCLUSIONS

Interpreting yü-lan-p'en as mortuary ritual offers several advantages. Many studies, for instance, attempt to explain yü-lan-p'en practice as based on certain key beliefs—fear of the dead, belief in spirits, universal salvation, and so on. I have tried to reverse the direction of explanation by first placing beliefs in their ritual setting. By stressing the ritual context, we also gain a greater appreciation of the plural functions of the festival and the multivocality of the symbols upon which it draws. Yü-lan-p'en celebrations are carried out in the home, in the village, in the temple, and in the cosmos, serving to invigorate

[52] Compare Eliade, "Mythologies of Death," p. 21, who writes of "man's paradoxical nostalgia of being fully immersed in life, and concurrently partaking of immortality— yearning to exist alike in time and in eternity."

[53] For the general notion of pollution, see, after the works of Durkheim and Mauss, the recent work of Mary Douglas, esp. *Purity and Danger: An Analysis of Concepts of Pollution and Taboo* (London: Routledge & Kegan Paul, 1966).

[54] See, e.g., de Groot, *Les fêtes* (n. 9 above), pp. 426–28; Suzuki (n. 9 above), p. 172.

[55] Suzuki especially emphasizes this aspect of yü-lan-p'en offerings; see Suzuki, esp. p. 175.

these overlapping structures and the cultural values that permeate them. In this view, ritual is not simply seen as a static reflection of social structure or a coded substitute for cosmology. Rather, it is viewed as a dynamic way of creating and sustaining structures of meaning that keep individual, society, and nature in harmony.

Further, the recipients of yü-lan-p'en offerings have been identified as both kin and non-kin, without reducing one to the other. The analysis of ritual helps to show why both are present at yü-lan-p'en celebrations, without erasing the tensions between them. They are both part of the ritual structure marking the passage from life, through death and liminality, to rebirth. These ambiguities, often seen as exclusive or even logically contradictory, are necessary aspects of a near-universal ritual structure. Within the unifying field of ritual, they are separate yet complementary foci of symbolic action.[56]

Most broadly, using ritual as a frame of analysis assists in reformulating the general issue of the relation between Buddhist and indigenous traditions. While attention has been drawn to the Buddhist background and the Chinese precedents for some elements of yü-lan-p'en ritual, my interpretation has not assumed their exclusivity. "Buddhism" and "Confucianism," ghosts and ancestors, liminality and incorporation are helpful sets of explanatory concepts. But they lose their value when they become unchanging essences or when the interpretive task comes to center on explaining the separateness of Buddhist "transcendence" and an indigenous "this-worldly" orientation. The distinction between great and little traditions was made, after all, not for the purpose of reifying them, but with the intention of showing their interrelation, how they "are dimensions of one another."[57] The ritual field provides a context in which both liminal and postliminal elements may be recognized as distinct but not opposite aspects of a coherent religious system.

Middlebury College

[56] Compare Tambiah, *Buddhism and the Spirit Cults in North-East Thailand* (n. 11 above), esp. pp. 337–50.

[57] Robert Redfield, *Peasant Society and Culture: An Anthropological Approach to Civilization* (Chicago: University of Chicago Press, 1956), p. 87.

GLOSSARY OF NAMES AND TERMS

Chai Feng-ta 翟奉達
Chang Chiu-ling 張九齡
Ch'en Fang-ying 陳芳英
chui-fu 追福
chung-yüan 中元
Hsü Chien 徐堅
Hui-ching 慧淨
hun 魂
Iwamoto Yutaka 岩本裕
kung-te 功德
Li Yung 李邕
ling-ch'uang 靈牀
Ma 馬
Makita Tairyō 牧田諦亮
manghon-il 亡魂日
Michihata Ryōshū 道端良秀
Moriya Mitsuo 守屋美都雄
Mu-lien 目連
muenbotoke 無縁仏
obon おぼん
Ogawa Kan'ichi 小川貫弌
Okabe Kazuo 岡部和雄
pao ch'iu-ch'eng 報秋成
pien-wen 變文
p'o 魄
Sawada Mizuho 沢田瑞穂
su-ti 俗諦
Suzuki Mitsuo 鈴木満男
Ta-chung yeh 大衆爺
Takenaka Nobutsune 竹中信常
Tao-shih 道世
Ti-kuan ta-ti 地官大帝
Tsuda Sōkichi 津田左右吉
Tsun-shih 遵式
Tsung Lin 宗懍
Tsung-mi 宗密
Tu Kung-chan 杜公瞻
Wang Ch'ung-min 王重民
Wu Tzu-mu 吴自牧
Yanagita Kunio 柳田国男
yang 陽
Yang Chiung 楊炯
Yao Ch'ung 姚崇
Yen Chih-t'ui 顏之推
yin 陰
Yoshioka Yoshitoyo 吉岡義豊
yü-lan-p'en 盂蘭盆

Part 3:
Tibetan Buddhism

CLAES CORLIN

The Journey Through the Bardo

Notes on the Symbolism of Tibetan Mortuary Rites and the Tibetan Book of the Dead

Partir, c'est mourir un peu
C'est mourir e ce qu'on aime.
On laisse un peu de soi-même
En toute heure et dans tout lieu.
(Edm. Haraucourt)

Introduction

Ever since Orpheus entered Charon's boat to search for his beloved Eurydiche, the theme of death as a journey has fascinated the Western audience. In different variations it is illustrated by innumerable stories, plays, and folktales. Similar conceptions and speculations may be found in many other cultures throughout the world. The Egyptian Book of the Dead, to mention one well-known example, depicts the journey of the deceased person through the underworld of the Egyptian cosmos. The cultural tradition of Tibet is no exception in this regard. Being Buddhists the Tibetans believe in reincarnation, but the period from a person's demise to his subsequent rebirth is conceived as a journey through the *bardo*, a liminal state which is neither "here" nor "there". The aim of this paper is to analyze some interrelations between the mortuary practices of Tibetans and their beliefs about the *bardo* state, as testified by a remarkable ritual text. This will lead to a discussion of some basic concepts of death and the hereafter in Tibetan culture.

One early translation of a Tibetan work into a Western language was Evans-Wentz' edition of the *bardo thos-grol* (pronounced as "bardo thödol"), or "Tibetan Book of the Dead" in English in 1911. Introduced by the famous psychologist C.G. Jung, this work aroused attention not only as a testimony of an exotic culture but also as an account of a "spiritual journey" into the unconscious depths of man. The recent popular interest in Eastern religions and the occult has led to reprints of this work which can be found in many bookstores. Its rather cryptic account of the progress of the "soul" of the deceased in the *bardo* before becoming reborn, has been subjected to various more or less scientific interpretations. (See e.g. Lauf 1977.)

For centuries this book has been used by Tibetan monks and lamas as a psychopomp's manual the reading of which serves to guide the dead person's consciousness which would otherwise be wandering perilously about, facing demons and dangers that are in reality products of the person's karma. Thus it is simultaneously a didactic work, aimed at understanding and eventual liberation as well as it is a magic formula that through mystic channels affects the progress of the deceased person's consciousness. Like Tibetan religion in general, the Tibetan Book of the Dead is a mixture of scholarly Buddhism and magical beliefs.

Buddhism in Tibet can be aptly described as a varnish that spread over, adapted to and transformed a wealth of local beliefs and cults, that were more or less of a shamanistic nature. There are still marked differences between the more esoteric speculations of the Buddhist Great tradition on the one hand, and on the other, the ritual practices and beliefs of lay Tibetans. This difference is generally recognized and it is referred to as *Lha chos* ("religion of the gods") and *Mi chos* ("religion of men") respectively. In some aspects there are even marked contradistinctions between the tenets of the Great tradition and popular beliefs. Both are involved in the mortuary practices of Tibetans.

The Ritual

Below I will describe the ritual actions surrounding a death in Tibet. There is considerable variation according to the age, status, and economical standing of the deceased, but certain themes and practices are common to most death rites. The following description treats the procedure at the death of an adult layman of medium status.[1]

When someone has died his family and close relatives (*spun*) gather to take care of the corpse. This is carried into the chapel of the house (*chos-khang*) where it is placed in a sitting position. The backbone of the body is broken, in order to prevent it from becoming a spook or "rising corpse" (*ro-langs*). Some monks from the village or a nearby monastery are summoned to the house where they read a text called *Klong-rgyas*. An astrologer lama is also consulted to make divination regarding the cause of the death, and to decide a suitable day for the funeral—generally on the third day after the death. Also, a *rtogs-ldanpa* or "undertaker" is selected to assist with the cutting-up of the corpse and to perform other tasks in connection with the rites. In central Tibet, this person was a member of a certain "caste", the corpse-cutters, while in the peripheral regions any man could volunteer to perform this duty.[2]

On the day appointed by astrology, a wooden bier is constructed and the corpse is placed on the bier. Over this, an effigy (*sob*) is made out of the dead person's clothes and a ball of wool representing the head, wearing a *rigs-lnga* "crown"[3] if it is a man, or a *rgyan-cha* (noble hairdress) if it is a woman. The face is represented by a drawing on a paper. This effigy is placed on the bier in a sitting position, with the corpse inside.

Before the procession starts for the dismemberment site, everyone present is purified by a lama who sprinkles the participants with sacred water, using a juniper twig. In some areas all people in the house also rub themselves with small pieces of dough, which are then thrown away (Brauen, pp. 78 f). This procedure takes away pollution and is performed not only at deaths but at all occasions where pollution is risked, e.g. childbirth. It is not clear how this pollution affects the polluted person, but the state is contagious and the affected person must remain isolated until purification rites are completed.

The bier with the *sob* is carried by four or eight men, whose birth-years should be astrologically compatible with that of the deceased. The procession is led by a monk who carries a juniper incense (*bsangs*), and preferably accompanied by some monks who play religious music. Another monk immediately preceding the bier carries a long white scarf, one end of which drags on the ground to "show the way" (*lam-ston*).

As the procession reaches the dismemberment site (*dur-khrod*) which is situated outside and to the east of the village or town, the corpse is taken out from the effigy and placed on a flat rock. The "undertaker" proceeds at once to chop the corpse into pieces small enough to be eaten by the vultures, that often linger around these places. The bones are pounded together with the brain to make sure that nothing will be left from the meal. Only one small piece of bone from the top of the skull (where the "Brahma aperture" is situated; see below) is laid aside and taken back. Meantime, the *sob* is dismantled later to be carried back and washed in the river. Conches are blown to summon the vultures and the people watch at a distance as the birds complete their meal. Nothing must be spared.

Afterwards the group return by exactly the same path as they arrived since any deviation would bring misfortune. Before entering the house they are purified by sacred water and by passing through the smoke of a *bsangs* fire.

On the third day after the death—regardless of the date of dismemberment—the monks congregate in the village sanctuary to perform a rite called "third day" (*zhag sumpa*). The *sob* effigy is reassembled and placed facing the altar, and offerings consisting of an odd number of cups with various drinks are placed in front of the effigy, the liquids later being poured onto a *bsangs* fire. The essence of the liquids is said to be consumed by the deceased.

The third day is also the first of the deceased one's forty-nine day long sojourn in the *bardo*. A large earthenware jar is coated with white clay and suspended from a roof-beam in the deceased's house. The jar is dressed in a headgear resembling that of the *sob* and adorned with necklaces around its neck. Every morning and evening offerings are made by the house-people—the consciousness of the deceased is believed to take residence in the jar, which is called "spirit-place" (*thugs-sa*).

Seven days later the first of seven ceremonies intended to guide the deceased's consciousness through the *bardo* is performed. One or several monks gather in the house to read a part of the Tibetan Book of the Dead. In some areas, this is followed by a general distribution of grains to the villagers by the family of the deceased.

A main ceremony, the merit-making ceremony (*dgeba*) is performed on an astrologically suitable date, no less than three to four weeks after a death, sometimes much later. This is organized and paid for by the family of the deceased, if need be also by the *spun* group (close consanguine relatives). All the villagers together with as many monks as one can afford, are invited to the village sanctuary, where they are fed lavishly with good food and beer. The *sob* effigy is again reassembled and placed in front of the altar, with similar offerings.

On the same day, a block-print representing the deceased is made on paper, and his or her name and sex is written on it. The consciousness of the deceased is magically transferred from the earthen jar to this "purification picture" (*sbyang-bar*). The jar is later taken out and destroyed, while the paper print is placed on the altar opposite the *sob*. According to Ramble (p. 340), the *sob* represents the body of the deceased while the *sbyang-bar* represents the consciousness of the deceased. At the end of this ceremony, the *sob* is carried out from the temple, the wailing women embrace it to take farewell of the deceased, and the undertaker carries it out of the village where it is destroyed.

At the final ceremony on the 49th day the consciousness of the deceased is believed to be ready for a new rebirth. The officiating lama now takes the print between his hands and, holding it in the flame of a butter-lamp, pronounces that the sins of the deceased are annulled as the flame consumes the paper. The consciousness of the deceased departs from the fire on its way to rebirth. The ashes of the print are spared and the piece of bone that was kept from the dismemberment is ground and mixed with the ashes and clay or tsampa dough, forming small cones (*tsha-tsha*), which are then placed in various "clean places" outside the village, such as caves, streams or trees.

One year later, a merit-making ceremony is held in the sanctuary, which is often followed by another general distribution of food. I will not discuss this ceremony in the present context.

The Text

"Buddhists and Hindus alike believe that the last thought at the moment of death determines the character of the next incarnation. As the *bardo Thödol* teaches, so have the Sages of India long taught, that the thought-process of a dying person should be rightly directed, preferably by the dying person if he or she has been initiated or physically trained to meet death, or, otherwise, by a *guru* or a friend or relative versed in the science of death." (Evans-Wentz, p. xviii).

Such is the basic belief behind the efficacy of the Tibetan Book of the Dead. Yet to understand this we must extend the notion of "dying" to the entire period from the state of dying in our sense of the word, until some 52 days after clinical death (that is, 3 days of "unconsciousness" and 49 days of *bardo*, or liminal period until the next rebirth). "... the last thought at the moment of death" is just one, although important, stage in the process of dying. This book is a manual in "the science of death" that is intended to be recited in front of the dying or deceased person, to be attended to by his spirit and directing his consciousness towards liberation or, at the least, a good rebirth. This is clearly reflected in the disposition of the book, which is divided into sets of "instructions to the Officiant" chronologically arranged to correspond with the different stages of passage in the *bardo*, and commentaries on the state of the deceased's consciousness and what he will experience during the period of transition.

The authorship of this work is attributed by the Tibetans to the great yogi Padma Sambhava (c. A.D. 750). Be that as it may, the book is certainly of ancient origin (an early version has been found in the Tun-Huang caves), and it has been used throughout Tibet for centuries. The several editions differ much, but the overall structure is common to all of them. In the following, the translation by lama Kazi Dawa-Samdup as edited by W. Y. Evans-Wentz will be used. Page numbers within square brackets refer to the third edition (Oxford U.P. 1957).

The process of dying and death, as described in the Tibetan Book of the Dead, is concisely the following:

When the dying person becomes unconscious he enters the first of the three *bardo* states, the *Chikhai Bardo*. Death is experienced as a bodily sensation of pressure: "earth sinking into water", a bodily sensation of clammy coldness which gradually merges into heat: "water sinking into fire", and a feeling as though the body were being blown to atoms: "fire sinking into air". Thus the elements making up the body[4] are merged as life leaves it. [93]

The very moment of death is also the moment of the greatest possibilities and freedom of choice for the deceased. For a fleeting moment his consciousness is entirely free of the karmic weight (that is, independent of the destiny that is created by one's earlier actions), and he experiences an intense colourless light, which is called the Clear Light of Reality. Now or never is the time to enter Nirvana, provided that the dying person is able to master his intellectual capacities to overcome the cycle of rebirths. Much of the psychic training of the Tibetan monastic schools is designed to meet this moment, and this is also the reason why the last thought of the dying person is very important in affecting his future. [92 ff]

If this immediate liberation be not achieved, the consciousness of the deceased is then believed to be "numb" during the first 3 days after death (which may be the reason for the break in mortuary rites during this period). Then, the consciousness will "awake" into the second stage of the death *bardo* (*Chönyid Bardo*) which is also the "birth" of the *bardo* body. [101]

This body is radiant but otherwise alike the physical body. It is capable of unlimited motion as directed by the desires of the consciousness (hence it is also called "desire body"). The deceased will possess this body right up to his entering a womb for rebirth. [155 f] In the *Chönyid Bardo* that will last for two weeks he will now travel around in the *bardo* state, perceiving both the physical world (such as his own body being carried away to dismemberment, etc) but also experiencing sounds, lights and visions of a paranormal and often frightening nature. The pantheon of the Tibetan cosmography will appear in front of him—somewhat alike the "poor man's bible" on the frescoes of medieval churches—but in this case the visions will appear real, alive and often terrifying. [104–151]

The purpose of the text is now to inform the deceased that these visions are unreal, products of his imagination, and symbolic reflections of his past deeds and sins. They serve as an initiation experience, are reminders that he has now passed on from the realm of absolute reality (the clear light of the first *bardo*) to the world of forms and duality, dragged there, as it were, by the karmic gravitational forces. As Jung remarked in his psychological commentary to the Tibetan Book of the Dead, the *bardo* experience is a kind of initiation in reverse, from the highest forms of existence into progressively more earth-bound forms, serving as a preparation for rebirth.

This tendency is strengthened as the deceased enters the third and final *bardo*, the *Sidpa Bardo*. At this stage his intellect will be driven hither and thither by the ever-moving wind of Karma in a grey, twilight-like light, seeking rebirth. His spirit can rest at temples, stupas and other sacred places and he is fed by the offerings made in front of the effigy or the earthen jar that represents his consciousness (see above). Visions of the six worlds of existence (gods, titans, humans, animals, ghosts and hells) and of the continents of this world will appear in front of him. At a later stage the deceased will even be able to see the wombs amongst which he can chose to be reborn, and foresee the life careers springing out from these alternatives. [160–165]

But his free will and power to chose is always limited by his Karma. *Sidpa Bardo* is also the place of Judgement where the Lord of Death will appear in a terrifying vision. The past good and evil deeds of the deceased will be represented by white and black pebbles, the balance deciding which kind of rebirth that he will be entitled to. Then he will be subjected to an experience of dismemberment:

> "Then ... the Lord of Death will place round thy neck a rope and drag thee along; he will cut off thy head, extract thy heart, pull out thy intestines, lick up thy brain, drink thy blood, eat thy flesh, and gnaw thy bones; but thou wilt be incapable of dying. Although the body be hacked to pieces, it will revive again." [166]

This experience may be interpreted as the symbolic rebirth as a new human being that marks the end of many initiation ceremonies (Turner 1969); in this case preceding the physical rebirth. But it also reminds one strongly of the ecstatic dismemberment experience that is part of the shaman's initiation in many cultures, as exemplified by the Tibetan *gcod* rite (Eliade p. 384, Nebesky-Wojkowitz p. 550).

The text ends with technical instructions concerning the closing of the womb-door (to avoid undesirable rebirth) and how to transform the chosen womb into a "celestial mansion". [175–193]

To sum up, the instructions that are given in the text throughout underline two things: that the visions experienced, however "real" and painful, are always imaginary, and that the deceased has considerable means to influence his passage in the *bardo* and thus to enhance his rebirth. In this state "the intellect becomes ninefold more lucid" than in life, and past learning as well as the influence of the mortuary rites correctly performed, helps the deceased to adopt the right attitude and seek the best out of his situation. Not just faith alone but knowledge and the help of the living are necessary. In this context there is a warning regarding the dangers of incorrectly performed rites:

"... (on) the sight of (the funeral rites) being conducted in an incorrect way, mixed up with sleep and distraction and non-observance of the vows and lack of purity (on the part of any officiant) ... thou wilt be extremely depressed ... This affecting the psychological moment, thou wilt be certain to be born in one of the miserable states." [171]

And again:

"That the performance of funeral rites should be efficacious is, likewise, because of that reason (i. e. the deceased person's ability to percieve what is happening). Therefore, the perseverance in the reading of the Great *Bardo Thödol* for forty-nine days is of the utmost importance." [183; my parentheses]

Time and Space

It is clear from what has been told that Tibetan mortuary practices aim at transferring the deceased person's consciousness from the living world through the intermediate state of the *bardo* (let us for the moment disregard the internal divisions of this) to subsequent rebirth, or directly to Liberation (the latter is however an exception and the privilege of those few who master the yogic technique). This has to be done in an orderly fashion, in a sequence that is largely cosmologically determined.

I have elsewhere described the Tibetan concept of *chos* (the word can be roughly translated as "world view" or "religion" in its widest sense) as a kind of space-time continuum that is regulated in time by successive phases of creation, development, decline, and destruction. According to this view, the world is re-created with the appearance of a Buddha and religion and "the good" is spread but subsequently corrupted by the increasing appearance of evil, in the end leading to a topsy-turvy world where the servants will become masters, etc. Only with the inevitable coming of another Buddha, will chaos be averted and the social order restored. (Corlin 1975).

The concept of the life-span of the individual (understood as the cycle from birth to rebirth) seems to be symbolically equivalent to this cosmic rhythm, and the 49 day period in the *bardo* is hence homologous to the transition between the cosmic eras. Closely connected to this time sequence in both cases is the moral state of the world and of the individual respectively, and the same goes for the medicine for improvement, which is knowledge and understanding (every Buddha spreads knowledge, not conversion) as a way to liberation from evil. Likewise, the deceased is purified from his earlier sins and symbolically reborn through the Judgement and dismemberment experiences, before becoming reborn as a new physical person.

Though the *bardo* transition proceeds in an orderly way, as regulated by the 49 day sequence, the deceased himself is not well aware of time and space. His *bardo* body is staying in a twilight world, being blown around by the karmic wind, but also gradually transformed back to humanity—to the womb. Though his powers of perception and cognition are abnormal, he is in the state of "betwixt and between" (Turner 1969), in a liminal state where ordinary rules of time and space do not apply. Things can happen in the time of "snapping a finger" or of "completing a meal", all depending on the karmic influences.

Cosmic time influences mortuary rites on yet another level. Tibetans believe strongly in astrology and astrological calculations are made before every important decision or turn of life. In the death rites, astrology and divination influence the proceedings heavily, as described. *The Astrology for the Dead* is a Tibetan work, in many versions, for determining the appropriate time, place, and method for the disposal of the corpse, and the after-death realm to which the deceased is destined and the land and condition in which he will be reborn on earth. [193 note]

The Nature of the bardo

bardo means literally "between two", intermediate, transitional state. [28 note 1] Tibetans count six kinds of *bardo* not all of which are related to death. One refers to the embryonic state in the mother's womb, the second to the dream state in sleep, the third to meditation and trance, and the remaining three refer to death. Common to all of them is that they refer to abnormal or suspended states of mind, set apart from "everyday reality". Four of them refer to liminal periods within the life cycle (in our extended sense of the word). One refers to the daily cycle, and only one—that of meditation—is volutionally induced.

Common to the six forms of *bardo* state is that they—exactly by being removed from the normal state of mind and behaviour—convey messages about the transcendental world and in some cases even a certain amount of control over this. Tibetans regard dreams seriously, as omens and premonitions of events to come, and more than often a bad dream will prevent someone from a planned undertaking. Meditation is a well-known and accepted means of spiritual achievement and deepened understanding. Also, as in the case of the Tibetan State Oracle (*Nechung*) and other such oracles, the *bardo* of trance establishes direct communication with the supernatural world. As to the concepts about the foetal state I have no information, but in a way this may be seen as a continuation of the death states.

Most important for the fate of the individual are the three death *bardo* states. They are decisive for the individual's place at the moment of conception (Tibetans are well aware of the nature of conception, but add a third element:

the *rnam-shes*, or consciousness principle, being added to the union of sperm and ovum) and hence for his future. These three liminality states form a series of initiations into a descending order of reality: the *Chikhai Bardo* offers a flash of insight into and possibility of immediate liberation in Nirvana; the *Chönyid Bardo* again introduces the world of forms, but still with good chances of liberation for those adequately trained; and the *Sidpa Bardo* serves as a "last rescue", where the common man might at least improve his rebirth somewhat.

The succession of *bardo* states after death thus bear the mark of a true passage rite: a dramatic separation from the world of the living, a liminal phase which is subdivided into successive stages but apart from the time and space of everyday reality, and eventual reintegration into society by rebirth. The difference from a common passage rite is that there are "special exits" in the form of possibilities of liberation from the cycle of rebirths.

The Nature of the "Soul"

Tibetan concepts about "soul", spirit, consciousness and life substance are very complex and vary through history (for general information see Stein 1969: 223–229). I will confine myself to those relevant for the discussion of death: *srog* ("vital force"), *rnam-shes* ("consciousness"), *sems* ("mind, spirit"), and *yid lus* ("mental body").

When the expiration has ceased, the vital force *srog* will have sunk into the psychic nerve-center of Wisdom (located in the heart). The cognizing functions of the mind (*rnam-shes*) will travel from the brain to the heart to unite with the vital force and will then move upwards through the "Brahma aperture" on the top of the skull, and out. Part of the mortuary rite is designed to facilitate the correct exit of the "soul", as in case of exit through another bodily orifice it would have a difficult rebirth. [90]

srog is in fact "... the life principle which does not exist independently of the physical body, and when it is withdrawn death results" (Ramble p. 339 note 13). *rnam-shes* is "consciousness" and "cognition" as a result of our sensory experiences, which survives in the *bardo* as a sensible entity. But behind this apparent faculty of experiencing and knowing, there is according to Buddhist psychology the mind or "transcendent consciousness" (*sems*).

The Tibetan concept of *sems* is different from Western notions about mind or soul. *sems* as "mind" is not subject to birth or death,[5] but it is always (except for brief periods of liminality in the *bardo*) to be found in a body. The destiny of one's *sems* in existences to come is regulated by Karma. For most people (except for the *sprul-sku* or "incarnate lamas", who by virtue of their status as emanations of bodhisattvas stand at the threshold of Nirvana) there is little possibility to terminate the cycle of rebirths. All one can strive for is an improved social position in future lives.

This transcendent consciousness (*sems*) emanates from a mental body (*yid lus*), which travels from life to life, driven by its karmic inheritance. The yogi can transform this *yid lus* into a body of transcendent cognition through meditation and experience. In sleep and at the moment of death a vibratory power which is the same as the "cosmic breathing" of *sems* produces the *yid lus* (Tucci pp. 59–63).

This might be an explanation for what was noted in the preceding section—that the *bardo*-states in general make possible contact with the transcendental world. Because of the lack of ordinary sensory experiences that accompany such states (dreams, meditation, trances, the foetal state, and death), the *yid lus* is "produced" and tunes in the individual with the cosmic respiration. It is like a sophisticated version of the shaman's spirit travelling to the spiritual realms to seek knowledge.

The Significance of the Death Rites

What was said above about *sems* and *yid lus* refers to the philosophy of the Buddhist Great tradition; to lay Tibetans, not well versed in these esoteric speculations, the matter is more pragmatic: the deceased person's corpse must be disposed of, his "soul" be transferred to rebirth, death pollution must be averted and the dead person must be prevented from haunting the living.

Such practical considerations partly tune in with the instructions given in the Tibetan Book of the Dead, while some actions are not prescribed in the latter and probably represent local beliefs (*mi chos*). The sequence of ritual actions roughly follows the time schedule of the text. Hence, the *Klong-rgyas* ritual[6] is performed as soon as possible after death, when the consciousness of the deceased has just entered the *Chikhai Bardo*.

Three days later, when the deceased passes to the *Chönyid Bardo*, the *Zhag sumpa* ("third day") ritual is performed and this is followed by seven rituals when the *bardo thödol* is read—one for each week during the 49 day passage. The *dge-ba* merit-making ceremony roughly corresponds in time to the Judgement-phase in the *Sidpa Bardo*, where the moral merits of the deceased are on trial. And the final ceremony is performed on the 49th day when his consciousness has passed the *bardo*, being ready for rebirth.

Meantime, the spirit of the deceased is represented in one way or another amongst the living and is fed by offerings. But this representation of the deceased changes shape several times in a sequence that leads towards greater abstraction. The most visible evidence of death—the corpse—is destroyed after a few days, but before that some of its "life" has been transferred to a human-shaped effigy (*sob*) that will play a role in several of the subsequent rites. At the *Zhag sumpa* ritual, the consciousness of the deceased (being in the *bardo* liminal state—both in this world and the other) is transferred from the *sob* to the *thugs-sa* or "spirit-place" that is quasi-human (a jar dressed in headgear and jewellery). Later, at the *dge-ba* ritual, the consciousness is again transferred from the jar to a "purification picture" (*sbyang-bar*) where the deceased is no more represented *in corpore*. Instead he is represented by an abstract but still personalized symbol: his name and sex on a printed paper. And lastly this print is burned and mixed with his skull-bone to form a purely abstract and anonymous symbol: a cone (*tsha-tsha*) which is placed at a spiritually pure place together with other such symbols. Thus there is a process of transformation from the most tangible evidence of death (the corpse) to a fully abstract and general symbol.

Related to this process of transformation is the symbol of the bone. The Tibetan word *rus* means both bone and patrilineage (*rus-rgyad*), as well as the male essence in the body, as opposed to flesh, *sha*, which is the female essence in the body. As the bones of the corpse are split and pounded at the dismemberment site, so the continuity of the patrilineage is symbolically broken. Only one piece of bone, from the "Brahma aperture" at the top of the skull is set aside later to be pounded and mixed with the ashes of the "purification picture" and made into *tsha-tsha*. Thus the body and "soul" of the deceased are finally unified again, but now in the form of a purified, abstract symbol which is placed outside the habitat of the living.[7]

Another feature of the death rites is the concern with protection against ghosts and death pollution. The physical corpse is the most polluting object and the living who take care of it must undergo several purification procedures. Hence the special status of the "undertakers" (*rtogs-ldanpa*) caste. The succession of more abstract representations seem less polluting, and the final result, the *tsha-tsha*, are placed at "clean" places. Breaking the backbone of the corpse as well as the care taken to guide the soul along the right path, are all attempts to avoid the possibility of the dead one coming back to haunt the living.

In section 3 I pointed out the symbolic correspondence between the passing of ages in the cosmos and the passing of lives in the individual cycle. On another level of analysis much the same seems to apply to the society of the living in case of a death. Hertz (1960) has pointed out that every death creates an emotional turbulence in society and is perceived as a threat to the social order.

As the demise of an individual symbolically reflects the destruction of the world, so the society is threatened by the chaos pertaining to the appearance of death and destruction in the midst of society. Chaos has to be avoided by excessive adherence to order. The minute regulation of the mortuary rituals, the procession with a white scarf to "show the way" and the care to return by exactly the same path are, I think, symptoms of this striving to re-create cosmos and order in the face of death. This apart from the explicit aim, as testified by the Tibetan Book of the Dead, that a correct performance of mortuary rites is efficacious in improving the future of the deceased one.

Conclusions

In the introduction to this essay I pointed out the almost world-wide distribution of concepts about death as a journey. Now we are in the position to single out some characteristic features of the Tibetan variation on this theme. First, the cosmological dimension. Unlike for example the Christian belief, Tibetans do not split their cosmos into wholly separate domains (heaven, hell, the physical world). Rather, as might be expected from an mentalistic creed that focuses on the individual's spiritual achievement, these cosmological regions are more aptly described as being different states of mind. The voyage of the deceased person is not directed towards heavenly spheres or subterranean hells, like Dante told, nor is it undertaken in an entirely physical landscape like that of the near-by Garo tribe, as described in Professor Burling's contribution to this book. Instead, the *bardo* state is literally "between two", a liminal state of mind that presents features of this world and the "other" alike.

It would be tempting to regard the *bardo* state as a "mediator" between the physical and the metaphysical worlds. But this would be to impose binary oppositions on a cosmos where there seems to be no such dualism. The six different *bardo* states (dreams, meditation or trance, foetus and death states) are regarded by the Tibetans as periods of exceptional mental abilities and possibilities of improving one's karma. From their point of view, these states would be closer to reality than would the normal state of mind. This "latent power of reality" is approached and even controlled by means of what might be called the "*bardo* techniques". The Tibetan Book of the Dead describes (and by its performance also accomplishes) one of these techniques: "the science of dying".

This ego-centered view of the universe is also reflected in the function of the death rites. These rites do not aim at propitiating deities but indirectly, through the medium of the deceased person by influencing his consciousness. The outcome of the process is his, and only his responsibility. The living can only help him to find the best way on his journey.

To us in the West, believers or not, death is like a "black hole"; "To die—to sleep—No more" (Hamlet, 3.1). Fear of death is created not only by the impossibility of knowing what happens next, but also by the feeling of losing control, no more to be able to influence one's circumstances. In contrast to this helplessness, the Tibetans are provided both with a thorough "introduction to death" and with the means to control their destiny to a fair degree. This serves as a powerful psychological tool to diminish the fear of death, and to make this ultimate event intelligible, if not tolerable.

Notes

1. In Tibet there were several alternative forms of disposing of the corpse. "Air burial" (as described here) was the most common one. Stillborn infants could be thrown into a river, while those who had died of infectious diseases were often buried. Cremation was used in some peripheral areas, e. g. Ladakh (See Brauen 1980). As to the mummification of holy lamas, see note 7. Ramble has provided an excellent account of the different forms of disposing of the corpse as related to social status (Ramble 1982).

2. See e.g. Ramble, pp. 336 f. The "caste" of corpse-cutters that was despised by other Tibetans has been mentioned by several early travellers. It

seems that it became less stigmatized in modern times.
3. Such a "crown" is also worn by lamas and oracles during trances—another kind of *bardo*!
4. The elements are Earth, Air, Water, Fire, and Ether. These play an important part in the Tibetan creation myth, and four of them are represented in the human body: "In the body of man ... there are four kingdoms of living creatures [sic]: (1) those of the Element Fire, (2) those of the Element Air, (3) those of the Element Water, and (4) those of the Element Earth." (Evans-Wentz, pp. 9f.) The fifth Element, ether, is associated with the transcendental consciousness (*sems*). (Ibid., my parentheses).
5. It is noteworthy that present-day Tibetan conceptions of the continuity of mind or ego differ considerably from the original teachings of the Buddha. "... Buddha ... recognized no immortal soul. The ego (*atman*) or individuality is only a conglomeration of life factors, the so-called *dharmas*, and at death their bond is released. However, if *Nirvana* is not realized before death, the nonquiescent *dharma* impulses produce a new life. Thus it is not the ego which is immortal, but only the sorrowful process of development and decline..." (Hoffman 117 f).

The concept of a transcending *sems* principle (which should not be confounded with the Christian concept of an immortal soul) seems to have appeared with the doctrine of the *Yogacara* school in the fourth century. "'Store consciousness' is defined by Asanga as an overpersonal consciousness which is the foundation of all our acts and thoughts. The experience of past occurrences is stored in it, which means that it is, so to say, impregnated by all our deeds and their results. Thus 'Store consciousness' is not a permanent soul monad, but it is rather like a river which changes as a result of constantly receiving and giving water. This idea goes very well with the teaching of Karma ... The old 'non-ego' teachings of Hinayana seemed no longer satisfying; and the new doctrine therefore accounts on the one hand for the sense of the personal identity of the empirical ego (which, strictly speakingp is wrong), and on the other hand it lasts until *Nirvana* is realized." (Hoffman p. 121)
6.The name *Klong-rgyas* means "to widen the expanse [of consciousness]" which alludes on the experience of "absolute reality" that is part of this *bardo*.
7. The corpse of a *sprul-sku* (incarnate lama) or other holy person is not dismembered but mummified and placed inside a reliquary, because the sanctity of that person is still active after death, like a catholic relic.

References

Brauen, M. (1980), *Feste in Ladakh*. Graz: Akad. Druck und Verlagsanstalt.

Corlin, C. (1975), *The Nation in Your Mind. Continuity and Change among Tibetan Refugees in Nepal.* Doct. diss., Gothenburg University.

Dante, *Divina Commedia*.

Eliade, M. (1951), *Le chamanisme et les techniques archaiquesde l'extase*. Paris: Plon.

Evans-Wentz, W.Y. (1957), *The Tibetan Book of the Dead.* Oxford University Press (3rd ed.)

Hertz, R. (1960), Contribution to the Study of the Collective Representation of Death. *Death and the Right Hand.* Aberdeen.

Hoffman, H. (1980), *Tibet—a Handbook*. Bloomington: Indiana University Publications.

Lauf, D. I. (1977), *Secret Doctrines of the Tibetan Books of the Dead.* London: Shambhala Press.

Nebesky-Wojkowitz, R. de (1956), *Oracles and Demons of Tibet.* s'Gravenhage: Mouton.

Ramble, Ch. (1982), Status and Death: Mortuary Rites and Attitudes to the Body in a Tibetan Village. *Kailash*, Vol. IX No. 4: 333–360.

Stein, R. A. (1969), *Tibetan Civilization.* London: Faber.

Thargyal, R. (1985), *A Traditional Estate in Eastern Tibet: Pastoral Nomads in Zil-phu-khog*. MA Thesis, Oslo University.

Tucci, G. (1970), *The Religions of Tibet.* London: Routledge & Kegan Paul.

Turner, V. (1969), *The Ritual Process. Structure and Antistructure.* Hammondsworth: Penguin.

Echoes of a Yolmo Buddhist's Life, in Death

Robert Desjarlais
Sarah Lawrence College

Ethnosemiotics

Shi mandi mareko hoina. Sareko ho. I hear these words as I drive south along Interstate 84, gliding past Worcester and Hartford and a world of unknown places as the magnetic trace of a voice recorded months before sounds through an unreliable tape deck set on the seat beside me. Time and again during these weekly commutes from Boston to New York and back again, I listen to the voice and try to soak up the sounds and grammars of the sentences heard. I wonder about the welfare of the speaker, hoping that the old man is alive and well and talking still while asking myself why there isn't more of an anthropology of voice, of the histories of voicings in their many particulars as they are heard and echoed by others who speak or write in turn.

Shi mandi mareko hoina. . . . "Dying does not mean dying."[1] The voice belongs, if a voice can ever belong to its speaker, especially once it is recorded and resounded electronically, to an elderly man often called "Meme Lama" or Grandfather Priest by other members of his community, many of whom identify themselves as "Yolmo wa" or "Yolmo people," an ethnically Tibetan Buddhist people who for two centuries or so have lived in hamlets and villages along the upper ridges of the Yolmo or Helambu Valley of north-central Nepal. Meme (pronounced "mhem-ē") lived in a village on the southwestern ridge of this valley until some twenty years ago, when, in seeking a more comfortable life in the city, he moved with his second wife and daughter to Chabahil, an ethnically mixed neighborhood on the eastern outskirts of Kathmandu, about one mile west of the Tibetanesque neighborhood of Boudhanath. Born in 1916, the second son of a respected priest from a prestigious Nyingma lama lineage, Meme raised a daughter and three sons with his first wife, who died in 1964. He remarried two years later, and his second wife soon gave birth to a daughter, as yet unmarried and living still with her parents. Much of his life had been spent either farming or practicing "the lama work," with the former taking priority in his youth and the latter gaining importance as he grew older, in part because his weakening body prevented him from working as he once did and in part because he wanted, as many Yolmo men and women do, to prepare well for death. "Now the most important thing to do is to die," he told me.

. . . *Sareko ho.* Dying "means moving." Meme took his death to be quite imminent when I came to know him well, in the summer of 1997, when he was in his early eighties, his body seemingly composed then of frail bones, a weather-lined face, and steady, gentle eyes: he felt that the "burning flame" he knew to be lodged in his forehead was slowly dimming and that, with his *tshe* or "life" expiring, he had not much "time" left. For several months that summer and again in the winter and spring of the following year, I worked with the old man to elicit and record his "life story" (n. *jīvan kathā*). Much of this work entailed traveling from Boudhanath, where I was staying at the time (in the home of his first son, in fact), to Meme's house in Chabahil and visiting and talking with him and his family. Often at first I was accompanied by Meme's grandson Norbu, a 23-year-old man who had lived and studied in India until he was 18, when he returned to Nepal with his parents and siblings to set up a home in Kathmandu. Norbu, who speaks Nepali and English fluently, helped me to explain to his grandfather what I hoped to accomplish and then joined me in my initial conversations with him. Several months after I left Nepal in 1997, Norbu himself traveled to New York with the help of a "sponsor letter" I wrote on his behalf. When I returned in 1998, Nogapu, a Yolmo friend, agreed to help me understand Meme's use of Yolmo, a Tibetan language that most Yolmo wa consider their native language. Meme took an immediate liking to Nogapu, in part, I think, because Nogapu, like Meme but unlike Norbu, grew up in Yolmo, spoke Yolmo fluently, and knew village life well.

Dying does not quite mean dying. Fair enough. But does the same principle hold for a society and culture that has changed substantially in the past two decades? This was a question on the minds of many Yolmo wa living in Kathmandu in the 1990s, when youths and (usually wealthier) families continued to migrate from the Yolmo region to the city in search of employment, better educations for their children, and more "comfort" (n. *sukha*) than could be found in any village. People spoke often of the consequences of these "dispersals": houses in Yolmo were being boarded up; mostly elderly people and impoverished farmers remained in the villages; the forests were growing wild again; children studying in Kathmandu were learning Nepali rather than Yolmo as their first language; and many youths were, like Norbu, leaving Kathmandu to look for better paying jobs in places like New York City. Many I spoke with, young and old, were concerned that "traditional" Yolmo culture was eroding away, with the histories and lifeways of "the old days" soon to be lost with the passing of the most senior Yolmo wa. In response to these concerns, several organizations had been created with the aim of cultivating and preserving aspects of Yolmo society. "If we don't collect the stories, if we don't know the history, everything will be lost," one member of a Yolmo student association told me in speaking of the work he and other students sought to do in their free time. Given that many Yolmo wa would agree that a death is often "the death of memory" (Behar 1996:42), my plans to record the life histories of elderly Yolmo men and women were well

Cultural Anthropology 15(2):260–293.

received by acquaintances when I returned to Nepal in 1997 after an eight-year absence. And while neither Meme nor I put it in so many words when I introduced the subject to him, I believe he also found that our work together could substantiate something of his life and "time," especially if we conversed not in Nepali but in Yolmo, a language that, he felt, embodied so much of Yolmo culture. "We should not leave the Yolmo language," he once said pointedly to Norbu, who, to Meme's chagrin, knew but a few words. To later insist, after Norbu had left for the States, that our conversations take place in Yolmo was therefore to make a political statement about the value of this language and the need to preserve it as well as the cultural heritage encoded within it.[2]

What is "dying," what is "moving," and how does a culture shape the makings of a life or the meanings of a death? What does it mean to generate a life story in a place where people often advance the idea that a life is, by nature, impermanent, ephemeral, perhaps ultimately illusory, and yet also highly consequential? Through a polyphonic mix of Nepali, Yolmo, and English, profoundly co-constructed, multiauthored traces of a life took form: while Yolmo wa do have some culturally patterned ideas of biographies and life histories as the oral or written recounting of an individual's significant doings and travels while alive, I soon realized that Meme would not be talking extemporaneously and at length about his life as though recounting an artfully formed story without prompting. Rather, much like others who told me something about their lives, he seemed to expect that our conversations would build on a protocol of questions and answers whereby he would respond, sometimes concisely and sometimes at length, to specific questions that I posed: perhaps he had gleaned from previous observations that this was how I sometimes went about my research; or he had spotted mike-wielding reporters interview people on television; or, alternately, a complex set of motives and expectations led us to proceed in this manner. In any event, as his daughter Maya served us cup after cup of salt-butter tea and the tape recorder, set on a rickety chair between us, quietly "picked up" traces of our words, my companions and I asked Meme a range of questions about his life, from memories of childhood to his thoughts about the fate of Yolmo culture. Meme, usually relaxing cross-legged in the center of his bed with his wife and a small tin box of snuff by his side, tried to answer these queries, sometimes with a simple nod of his head and sometimes with great intensity.

What interests me most here are less the specifics of the man's biography than what he understood was going on when I came to talk to him and his words took form on paper—what, in effect, the act of inscribing his life on paper meant for him. The likes of such an inquiry are seldom to be found in life history research in anthropology. While detailed narrations of non-Western lives are commonly generated, as are reflective essays that examine in sophisticated ways how ethnographers came to regard those lives or engaged dialogically with their informants, rarely have anthropologists seriously examined how life history informants themselves make sense of the act of setting their lives to paper.[3] Nor have they considered the potential consequences of such an act or, significantly, the personal sensibilities or cultural metaphysics that shape the act and its

consequences as perceived by those involved. I would like to try something along these lines by mulling over a few of Meme's words and the meanings apparently implicit in those words. My aim is to convey what I think he in part thought our engagements were about in order to detail the various ways in which a written account of his life might come to "echo" in his life or after his death. By tracing the possible trajectories of a few such echoes, we can, I think, gain some sense of what it means for Meme and other Yolmo wa to speak about a life or to incise elements of it onto paper, especially when that paper is understood to be potentially more durable than the life itself. Yolmo ideas about the epistemic and ontic nature of speech, writing, biography, duplication, remainders, reminders, and other acts-in-time must therefore be considered here.

Such an inquiry also requires an attempt to understand something of the pragmatic import of people's engagements with one another. It requires an attempt, that is, to estimate the potential social significance and real world effects of various utterances and actions—how people do things with words, as well as how words and actions do things on their own, in particular social worlds. Anthropological inquiries of this sort usually investigate how certain actions, such as a lengthy pause, a laugh, or a sigh, build to certain identities or understandings, with conscious intention or not, in the course of a conversation or two in order to understand more precisely how discursive meanings take form through social engagements.[4] Here, the focus is broader and more diffuse, concerned as it is with the meanings that emerged, in the span of a year and beyond, with meanings that are emerging still, out of the heteroglossic invocation of a life. And because what I have come to know of this invocation is similarly tied to the emergence of meanings in time, my writing reflects, in some ways, my shifting awareness of what is at stake, and what my responsibilities might be, in the writing of that life.

As for such meanings, it strikes me that in order to make sense of what my work with Meme meant for him, one first needs to consider *how* things mean for him and other Yolmo wa. This is to say that anyone who lives outside the folds of Yolmo culture must try to suspend her or his own notions about how signs signify and explore something of the ethnosemiotic sensibilities of these people and how those sensibilities contributed to the ways in which Meme thought of his life and the textual inscription of that life. To do this effectively, one needs to attend to how he and other Yolmo wa think of the interrelated workings of such matters as language, time, bodiliness, personhood, life, and death and what it meant for an aged man to tell something of his life at a time when he thought that life to be ending.

A Logic of Echoes

One rainy afternoon in the spring of 1998 Meme used a word whose multiple, intershading connotations have greatly influenced how I have come to think about his life and the meanings he and I have invested in his life story. In trying to elicit Meme's thoughts on good ways to die, Nogapu and I had asked if it was better if family members kept quiet in the presence of a dying person, which is something I heard other Yolmo wa speak of. "It's good, for sure," he said in response and then continued: "If no noises are made, it's good. If it's quiet, we can die well. . . . If it's quiet, we can get the way easily. If the noisy sounds come, then the dead person becomes confused. He gets confused, the poor man *[nyingjua]*. If he dies and is lost, what can we do?"

He then went on to describe what happens to a dead person during the *bardo* or "intermediate" state between one life and the next. He ended by detailing what the soul encounters when it tries to leave the deceased's body—namely, amplified features of that person's body as perceived by the itinerant soul as it journeys through it:

> We need not go somewhere else, far away. After we die, if we have long hair, we can see lice and a bear and tiger. The hair appears like a jungle. We can see a bear and a big tiger. The forehead appears like a plain, and the nose appears like a big hill. When they say the soul goes out, it's our own body that frightens us. Our shadow *[tip]* frightens us. Whatever we do, our shadow does the same thing. That's called an echo *[bhaja]*. When we make a loud sound, an echo is heard. If we say, "Wey!" it also says, "Wey!" That's called bhaja. "Good echo" *[bhaja zangbu]* is said: if we've done good, good comes. If we've done bad, bad comes.

After a pause, he continued, "Bhaja is like imagining. After we die, if we imagine good things, they echo in what we see. If we make a loud noise, a bad echo [bhaja] comes. If we pray, 'Om mani-padme hūm,' a good echo comes. If people are crying and fighting and making a lot of noise, then it's no good. If one dies when it's very quiet, it's good. Noises are no good."[5]

A cluster of subtly overlapping meanings infused Meme's uses of the Yolmo word *bhaja*. Meme first used the word in speaking of echoes. *Bhaja* in this sense means very much what *echo* does in English: the repetition or reverberation of a sound. Its 19th-century Tibetan equivalent, *brag-cha,* which also translates as *echo,* appears to have literally meant "rock-noise" or "rock-clamor" (Jäschke 1995:138, 380). As Meme observed, "When we make a loud sound, an echo is heard. If we say, 'Wey!' it also says, 'Wey!' " But for Meme and other Yolmo wa, visual echoes of sorts can also occur; as the soul tries to journey beyond its corporeal abode, features of the deceased's body (hair, forehead, nose) "appear like" elements of a landscape (jungle, plain, hill). An element of mimesis is therefore at work here, for echoes, be they acoustic or visual in nature, simulate the phenomenon they re-sound or re-vision. From this perspective, as Meme noted, a person's shadow can be seen as a bhaja or illusory visual echo of that person, and the thoughts of the dying person or the cries of grief-stricken family members can reverberate in the liminal, phantasmagoric world encountered in the hours after a death. As he put it, "Bhaja is like imagining. After we die, if we imagine good things, they echo in what we see. If we make a loud noise, a bad echo comes." For this reason, bereaved family members should not mourn a loss too vocally because their cries will be heard as noises by the deceased, with the din of any noises sounding in direct proportion to the intensity of the cries: "How many tear drops, that much rain comes. The

sound of crying brings thunder," Meme explained. The voicings of others help determine the nature of a dying person's afterlife.

Such mimetic acts mesh well with the "homological" or "analogical" thinking of many South Asian and Himalayan peoples, in which images and objects are understood to resemble or ritually stand for other, often sacred, images or beings.[6] Aspects of Meme's world often involved such homologies, and mimesis was for him a common, but by no means the only, means of thought and being. He and other lamas tried, for instance, to meditatively imagine their bodies as resembling the divine forms of great bodhisattvas—the king's palace, he told us, was but "a very small model" of a deity's palace in heaven; and, like other Yolmo wa, he said he learned how to do things largely by watching others and then copying what they did. It is important to note, however, that a strong temporal dimension often inhered in the mimetic echoes of which Meme spoke. Certain acts or images repeated or were repeated in turn. In general, then, it is not simply a question of copies or simulations, as many modern Western discussions of mimesis suggest, but, rather, one about repetitions and re-presentations in time.[7] When it comes to such repetitions, any copies are like the original, but not quite—much as, for Meme, dying is like dying, but not quite. Arne Melberg seems to be getting at much the same thing in a very different context—in his study of mimesis as repetition in Western literature—when he notes that "repetition repeats what has been, but turns it into something else: repetition re-presents and overcomes its origins" (1995:37). Intrinsic to ideas of repetition, especially among Yolmo wa, are ideas of death and rebirth. In its most basic configuration, a logic of echoes implies a logic of change, loss, and death, in that one sound or form replaces another in time and earlier forms dissolve in time. To repeat is to occasion a death in some way. An echo can therefore signify a loss; it can indicate the absence of something once present, something that can only be represented through a reverberation of some sort.

Yolmo wa understand an echo to be something immaterial and unreal. One hears the echo "as though" one is hearing the actual sound but usually while knowing well that it is not the actual sound. Because the repeated sound is secondary to the original, it is commonly taken to be an illusory, insubstantial trace of the original. *Bhaja,* then, can also mean "illusion," and Meme and others use the word in this sense as well.[8] "That is only the heartmind [*sem*] imagining," Meme once said of phenomena encountered by a deceased person soon after dying: "There's not really a body. It's only an illusion [bhaja], for sure." Meme might have had this connotation in mind as well when he observed that "bhaja is like imagining," for, as a good Buddhist, he would at times understand and encourage his interlocutors to realize that much of life, including a person's body and self-perceptions, is illusory apparitions. Echoes, then, are on a par with other illusory phenomena, such as mirages and hallucinations, in that, despite their differences, they all involve perceptual phenomena that are understood to be not materially real. As a Yolmo lama put it one day when explaining to me the illusory nature of bhaja, "We say from our Tibetan books, 'Bhaja tabu, gyuma tabu, migyug tabu' [Like an echo, like an illusion, like a mirage]." One such book, read often by Yolmo lamas, relies on similar thinking in advising its listeners to recognize all phenomena of waking life as being "like a dream, a magical illusion, an echo, a fairy city, a mirage, a reflection, an optical illusion, the moon in water, lacking even a moment's truth-status, definitely untrue, and false" (Thurman 1994:185–186). For Yolmo wa, bhaja can be understood as an "as though" phenomenon: as an apparition that appears, but only appears, to be real.[9]

In fact, Yolmo lamas like Meme advise, as do their Tibetan counterparts, that the images perceived in the hours and days after a person dies are best understood as apparitions of this sort. Meme, like other Yolmo lamas, often reads a Tibetan text called the *Bardo thos grol* (usually pronounced *Bardö thödöl* in Yolmo), a title that can be translated as "Liberation through Hearing/Understanding in the Between," although the text is more famously known in the West as "The Tibetan Book of the Dead" (Thurman 1994). One of the main reasons for reading this text to oneself while alive, or to others when they are dying or have already died, is that readers or listeners can gain a better understanding of the nature of the apparitions encountered during the "between" and so not be so frightened by or attracted to them when encountering them in the liminal dream world after dying. One passage, for instance, encourages any recipients of its instructions to develop and affirm an understanding that all sights and sounds perceived are one's "own":

> May I know all sounds as my own sounds!
> May I know all lights as my own lights!
> May I know all rays as my own rays!
> May I know the between's reality as mine! [Thurman 1994:111]

Elsewhere the text advises its readers to recognize that all visions encountered in the "death-between" are "but empty images," the product of one's "own creations," with one's body itself "born by apparition" (Thurman 1994:112, 114, 167).

For Meme and other Yolmo wa, such selfsame manifestations are a kind of bhaja, in that they entail mimetic apparitions of a person's thoughts, utterances, or perceptions. Yet the presence of such manifestations points to the fact that a logic of echoes also implies a logic of traces, of lingering consequences, in that something of an original sound or phenomenon can carry on in subsequent reverberations. An element of mimesis still applies with any echo, for the secondary phenomenon simulates, in some respect, an initial phenomenon or action. An echo contains traces of its predecessor. To repeat is to continue living in some way. Dying does not quite mean dying.

All this helps to explain why the word *bhaja* among Yolmo wa can also refer to a "residue" or "trace" of some sort, particularly of something that no longer exists. The residuum left in an empty teacup, for instance, can be said to be a bhaja or "remainder" of the tea that once filled that cup. A ghostly presence, in turn, can be thought to entail a bhaja of the person that once inhabited a household, and Yolmo wa often worry that a family member might leave such an

unwelcome remainder behind, for such a ghostly trace can have harmful effects on the living. A good death, consequently, is one in which a deceased person does not leave a dangerously strong "echo" behind. When speaking to the spirits of the deceased at funerals, for instance, bereaved family members will often tell them not to "give a bhaja" in death or not to "leave a bhaja behind." In voicing such concerns, they have in mind the possibility that the deceased might remain attached to his or her former life circumstances and, in effect, "cling" to cherished loved ones or possessions. "His bhaja is left behind with his youngest daughter," a sentence I once heard, suggests that a father's ghostly presence was clinging to his daughter; the attachment was threatening to pull the daughter into death as well. Apparitions of the deceased are fitting exemplars of bhaja: they occur after the fact, as ghostly traces of beings once alive, as illusory afterimages of former presences, like the original, but not quite.

Invested in Meme's understanding of the physics of echoes, then, were two somewhat opposed but characteristically Buddhist messages: the understanding that everything is impermanent, that nothing lasts forever, that life is transient, shifting from form to form; and the idea that traces remain, residues linger, rebirths occur, and actions have consequences long after the actions themselves are completed. Life is impermanent and, some say, ultimately illusory, yet the actions a person undertakes in life can effect powerful reverberations. Milarepa, the great 11th-century Tibetan saint, sang of similar notions in a song of his:

> All that which manifests
> Is unreal as an echo,
> Yet it never fails to produce
> An effect that corresponds.
> Karmas and virtues therefore
> Should never be neglected. [Chang 1977:511]

Manifestations of a life, unreal as echoes, produce further, corresponding echoes.

Something of Meme's understanding of the consequential force of human actions in the world can be heard in his statement, cited above, that " 'good echo' is said: if we've done good, good comes. If we've done bad, bad comes." That is, if people act in morally good ways, good will result, whereas if they harm others, misfortune will plague them sooner or later. In more general terms, and as Milarepa reminded his audience, this is the principle of karma (or *le*, "work"), as basic and commonsensical to Buddhist peoples as the law of gravity is to others, in which, quite simply, any moral act, good or bad, brings about a correspondingly positive or negative result, either in this or in a future lifetime. The principle, central to Yolmo notions of time and causality, resounded in many aspects of Meme's life, in his understanding of the moral consequences of actions in a sequence of lives, and in his assumption that good comes of good and bad results from bad: a person who gives alms, he explained, will later "prosper"; crippled or disfigured bodies were the result, he said, of previous sinful actions; and a person who did not repay loans in one life would need to work as a servant in the house of his or her lenders "after being born again." The consequences immanent in certain actions entail a kind of temporal mimesis, of "results" echoing in time, for many deeds entail *corresponding* effects later on—what one Nyingma text revered by Yolmo lamas identifies as "effects similar to the cause": "Sometimes babies die at birth as an effect similar to the cause of having killed in a past life. . . . To have stolen will make us not only poor, but also liable to suffer pillage, robbery or other calamities" (Patrul Rinpoche 1994:112–113). As Meme once said of people fated to die at the hands of others, "Before they did this to [murdered] others, then later the same thing comes." The force of karma sometimes involves a mimetic economy of meaning and action.

For Meme and many other Yolmo wa, karmic principles intensify when a person dies. The shadowy images that a recently deceased person encounters in the intermediate state between lives are often held to be manifestations of that person's karmic and psychic dispositions. Both of the key features of Yolmo echoes—reverberation and illusion—thus pattern what a recently deceased person perceives. The nature of a person's rebirth, in turn, is profoundly conditioned by the way in which that person lived in previous lives. In fact, much of Meme's talk with me seemed to be concerned with what had happened while he was alive and, by implication, what might happen when he dies—how, in effect, his life might echo in his death. Such musings, along with the way in which he went about his life, led me to conclude that his world was very much shadowed by an anticipatory consciousness; his thoughts and actions were geared toward anticipating and preparing for the future and, in particular, for his death. "This is work for later, not for now. This is work for the time of dying," he once told Norbu and me of the religious texts he read daily in order to augment his spiritual merit and so increase the chances of a good fate after dying: "One reads as much as one can. If one reads more, one reaches heaven." And yet, despite all his preparations, all his spiritual practices, and all his efforts to develop a spiritually pure heart, he still feared immensely what might happen. "Dying means something very bad," he said on several occasions:

> We can't get this life the next time. That's why we should think, "Don't commit sins," and that's why we should have a pure, "bodhicitta" heart *[jang chup sem ba]*. If one thinks about the pure heart all the time, it [that thought] will take him to the Buddha [Sange] after he dies. "He's the bodhisattva," [the gods will say].[10]
>
> . . . What can be done? Dying means the worst thing, for sure. It's good now, we can do anything. With this king [the king of Nepal], if we do something wrong, we can run away and hide. But when we meet the Lord of Dharma [Che Gyalbu], we cannot hide. He can see us.
>
> . . . Dying does not mean dying. It means moving [n. *sareko*]. If someone dies, his soul goes inside another person [in the womb of his next mother]. Then later he needs to call those people "father and mother."

In our conversations, Meme's words often quietly designated him as a spiritual teacher of sorts. I think such a role made a lot of sense to him while talking

with us, given that many Yolmo wa knew him foremost as a lama, as "one who knows," and given that one of the main forms of biographical representation known to him were the *nam-thar* or "full liberation [stories]" of Tibetan Buddhist lore, in which the spiritual development and fruition of a spiritually great person's life are portrayed in writing with the intent that the portrait will serve as a supreme example for others also seeking liberation (see Gyatso 1997:6, 103, for instance). While Meme never said that his imminent life story would in fact be like a nam-thar, I do believe he sincerely wanted to teach us and others something, and much of what he conveyed to us, about his life or life in general, could indeed be heard as a primer on meritorious ways to live a life, with his words and deeds exemplifying, perhaps, a good life in modern, spiritually flawed times. So it was with the first set of words quoted above, voiced when Meme was detailing certain principles of death and rebirth to Nogapu and me in the spring of 1998: one should maintain a pure "bodhicitta heart" and avoid thoughts of wrongdoing. Yet what his next life might entail, where and in what sentient form he might be reborn, and what might happen when he met up with the Lord of Dharma after dying were unknowns that troubled him a great deal.[11] At the same time, Meme, I believe, was also trying then to think of death, his death in particular, in terms that did not involve the complete loss of the "I" known to him or the end of life in a world of familiarity and loved ones from which he did not wish to part. To die, he therefore held, did not entail a complete annihilation but, rather, meant a rebecoming, another echo, or, more prosaically, a "move" into a new life.

Afterimage

Shadowy echo, trace or illusion, reverberation and manifestation, remainder, reminder, afterimage—*bhaja* carries these many connotations. Any "life story" told by Meme or written about him, I slowly came to understand, would imply a similar whirl of echoes. Put most simply if not most subtly, an account of his life, as rendered into print, would work as an "echo" of that life as many Yolmo wa might understand that term: as a secondary, illusory trace of something that existed prior to that trace. Much like an acoustic echo repeats a sound, Meme's words as presented in these pages reiterate his words as uttered. When speaking of his life in general, we have echoes upon echoes upon re-echoes: any words I write about Meme's life repeat, in a greatly translated and edited fashion, his words as heard and recorded on tape, which in turn speak of the actions that make up his life, as remembered.

Yolmo uses of the word *bhaja,* I have noted, sometimes carry with them the sense of a "residuum" or "remainder" of some sort, especially of something that no longer is fully present, like the drops of tea left with the tea leaves after a cup of tea has been consumed. Within the imaginal spirit of this same logic, a biography could very well serve at times as a shadowy remainder of the life it indicates. The idea that, through the making of his life story, some trace of his life would remain after he died was apparently a powerful one for Meme, and he clearly appreciated the staying power of the "talk" that was being put into print.

When Norbu and I were concluding our taped conversations with his grandfather in the summer of 1997, we wanted to make sure that our interlocutor was satisfied with our engagements, especially because he had earlier said that thoughts about the past sometimes troubled him and made sleep difficult.

"Meme, how have you liked this process?" Norbu asked. "We've asked many personal questions, perhaps this offended you?"

"No," Meme quickly replied. "I can understand what he's doing."

"Perhaps it's been painful to remember such memories?"

"No, I would say. Now, I won't be staying after I die. But this talk/matter [n. *kūra*] will be staying after I die. Isn't that a good thing?"

And then, nine months later, another set of last words took form. "Meme," Nogapu said in the course of a conversation, "your grandchildren and your grandchildren's grandchildren might be able to read this book."

"They can read it. Later, later, the words will stay."

Given Meme's apprehension about the end of his life, I think he found comfort in the fact that his words would be "staying" on after his death. His body, clearly, would not be. This learned lama spoke often of the fact that when humans die their *nam-she,* or souls, separate from their corporeal abodes, which are then cremated in a day or two, and they then must journey into death without the kind of bodily grounds that they were accustomed to while alive: "Our soul goes outside, it goes everywhere, but our body remains. It doesn't go. Our body's here, in this way . . . "; "It's not like we have a body then, after dying. There's no body then. Only the soul . . . "; "Only one's soul goes up. Everything is burned, even your body is burned . . . "; "This body won't be there, these hands won't be there. It's only the mind that goes away. . . ." Such a much-anticipated loss of bodiliness was presaged for Meme by the gradual erosion of his physique through the latter part of his life: in the past few years his body had, to him, become increasingly weaker, smaller, less visible; it had grown "down, down, down." It took him longer to walk places, and he often had to use a cane: "My body has died, my speech hasn't," he told us. Once, when showing his grandson and me a photograph of him taken years before when he was in India with some friends, he noted, "Before, before, among my brothers, I was the one with the big body. The rest of them had small bodies. Nobody's clothes matched me, not even my sons' clothes. Only my youngest son's clothes matched me; he's also big. Now, then, I'm already 81. Where has it gone? Where, where?" He spoke the last words while gesturing toward his torso.

There was an optical dimension to this vanishing body. Like a waning moon, Meme's physical form was becoming absent to the eye. He was becoming a ghost of himself, his body now a faint echo of its former size and strength. The texts that we were producing, in turn, could possibly shore up the forms of his life and fix something of that life within a durable, visible materiality. While his body would be reduced to ashes in death, it is as though he would in some sense remain present after death, in the subtle, echoic form of a text. "As though" is a crucial phrasing here, for in speaking of such matters we are dealing not with the principles of real souls or tantric practices but, rather, with questions of mimetic

echoes, of ghostly possibilities and wistful, momentary imaginings—questions, notably, from which anthropologists usually shy away, which means that our conceptual tools for thinking through such imaginings tend to be rather poor ones. I very much doubt that Meme thought that his soul or consciousness would continue in any vital form within a set of pages like these. But there is nevertheless something in the formal logic of Yolmo actions and ways of meaning—of residual traces and itinerant spirits—that suggests that some kind of conversion from body to text was at stake in an imagined, "as though" way.

In reflecting on my potential role in this dreamlike conversion, I read with some seriousness Veena Das's observation on the reconstruction of symbolic bodies during Hindu funeral rites that "it is the task of men to ritually create a body for the dead person and to find a place in the cosmos for the dead" (1996:78, see also 1986; Parry 1994). By *men* here she means primarily the sons of the deceased. Because Yolmo funeral rites require a similar set of ritual effigies that work to represent the deceased and embody that person's soul, though the direct role of sons is not so important, I ask myself if in some way I am performing a comparable task in Meme's case, either as a surrogate son or not, with his life story becoming a kind of "second body" that will linger after his body vanishes in death. Perhaps so. But then I also find that talk of a reconstructed body per se is a bit too overt and specific, that when it comes to Meme's life story what is really in question is a kind of materiality, a tangible afterimage, a kūra, or matter or talk, wherein visible, durable traces of his life could remain.

Ultimately, I think, it was a question of "transferring" certain traces or qualities of a life from one domain to another. "Dying does not mean dying. It means moving," Meme told us. Although he was speaking for the most part in Yolmo during this conversation, he used the Nepali word *sareko* here, which, when in the form of an infinitive transitive verb *(sārnu),* means "to move, to shift, to transfer." Yolmo wa often consider movement from one entity or spatial domain to another as a "transfer" of this kind, and I have heard people talk, in either Yolmo, Nepali, or English, of transfers of the dharma from teacher to student, of transfers of property and land between generations, of transfers of money between men, of transfers of family households from one place to another, of transfers of "empowerment" *(wang)* from a lama to his patrons, and, on one occasion, of transfers of young women to Bombay to work as prostitutes. Such transfers often assume a spatial form, in which something is transferred out of the body, from self to other or to some domain external to the body. When a person is dying, a lama, or a group of lamas, performs a ritual act of *phowa,* a "transference of consciousness," which works to transport the dying person's "soul" out of the body and deliver it to a heavenly realm. *Bombo,* or shamans, in turn, are said to "transfer" harm and evil forces from a client's body to an effigy or an animal, which is then sacrificed. Meme drew from the same word when talking about copies he made of religious texts: "I wrote, I made transfers/copies [n. *sārti*]," he told Nogapu and me when asked if he had ever written Tibetan texts. To "make transfers" in this way was to copy the letters and meanings found in one sacred text into the new one he was inscribing. Such an act—which is generally thought to accrue great merit for the copier—implies a direct carryover, in which everything supposedly remains the same and no changes are to be made in replicating the original.

Given that inscription for Meme typically entailed the idea of a mimetic transfer from one domain into another, it makes sense to consider that, within the imaginative frame of his own metaphysics, our work together implied the possibility that something of his life could be "transferred" or "translated" from a corporeal body into a textual one. Somewhat akin to the "transference of consciousness" that can occur at the moment of death, there was a sense at times of a transfer of Meme's voice and life from his body to the texts that we were producing. The old man alluded to such a textual reincarnation one day when, in the course of a conversation, he spoke of the fact that I was taking with me the set of transcripts of our taped conversations when I returned to America. "I myself feel," he said to Nogapu in my presence, "that when he takes this and goes there, I'm also going there, even though I haven't reached there." The textual presence of his life story appeared to involve a set of anticipated transfers, each of which took imaginative form at different, passing moments in our talk and in our thoughts. Along with the passage of his "talk" from Nepal to the United States, the texts variably implied, or so it impressed me, transfers from transmitter to scribe, from teacher to student, from a "grandfather" to a surrogate son or grandson, from high to low and inside to outside, from voice to print, from a life to an afterlife, from past to present and the present to the future, and from a soon-to-vanish body to a set of words that would "stay."

"Write That"

It was highly significant that Meme's words were being rendered into print. Speech for him was largely a matter of breath and wind. A person's voice was "like the wind," moving about, fleeting, impermanent, easily extinguished. Certain comments of his hinted that, for him, human speech was closely linked to human vitality. On one occasion he noted, "If our bodies did not have enough fire and water, we could not talk. There is fire and water in our bodies. The water is our blood. Because of the flame we can speak. Otherwise, how could we speak? We would be as dead." Life, for him, apparently came with breath and voice, all of which were ephemeral in their makings and easily extinguished.

Print, in contrast, tends to connote something lasting and permanent for many Yolmo wa, especially those involved in lamaic practices, which often rely on the oral reading of sacred religious texts. Written texts, as well as other kinds of physical inscriptions in the world, such as the footprints of great saints cast in stone, can serve as powerful bits of evidence and as "proof" of someone's existence or actions in the world. To see something in Yolmo is often to confirm its existence; when it comes to knowing things definitively, vision typically assumes priority over hearing or any other sensory faculties.[12] Whereas speech is of breath and wind, and so is fleeting and unreliable, words printed on a page are commonly invested with connotations of vision, truth, and permanence.[13]

Politically charged understandings such as these might help to explain why the tape recordings of our conversations seemed to interest Meme less than any writings that would result from those conversations, although he and his family did seem to appreciate a set of cassette copies that I gave him upon leaving Nepal in 1998. Indeed, when Meme said he was pleased that his talk would be "staying" after he died, he probably had in mind the understanding that his words would be put into print and that this print would, by its very nature, convey both truthfulness and durability. Implicit here was a quiet but fundamental metaphysical play, common to many Yolmo lives and influenced by Buddhist perspectives, of ideas of stasis and movement, presence and absence, truth and illusion, and permanence and impermanence.

Many Tibetan texts speak of the difficulty of humans leaving a "trace" behind after they die. Milarepa, for instance, rues the death of his father in these terms:

> Today, my good father, Mila Banner of
> Wisdom, is no more, no trace remains. [1977:106]

A short inspirational poem penned by the Seventh Dalai Lama, entitled "Meditations on the Ways of Impermanence," includes the following lines:

> . . . A young man, with teeth for the future,
> With plans for months and years ahead, died,
> Leaving but scant traces. Where is he now?
>   Gone!
> My mind turns to thoughts of death. [Mullin 1986:220]

Many biographies of Buddhist sages, in turn, remark that the only thing that remains of the sages after they die are their biographies. While an overt purpose of such biographies is to detail exemplary religious lives in order to illustrate to others how to attain salvation, a message rooted in many is that everything, including the lives and bodies of great religious masters, is ephemeral and impermanent. As one Nyingma lama suggests, "You can then meditate on impermanence by thinking about holy persons such as Buddha and his famous disciples, Shariputra and Modgalyayana. All that is left of them now are stories. . . . All we have of them now are impoverished biographies. . . . Of that famous adept Padmasambhava only his biography remains" (Khetsun Sangpo Rinbochay 1982:58). And then there is the great sage Milarepa, contemplating the loss of his mother:

> My mother . . .
> Is nothing but crumbling bones.
> This, too, is an example of ephemeral illusion,
> An example which summons me to meditation. [1977:106]

Yet an oblique implication of such assessments is that, while the subjects of such biographies are soon reduced to ashes, their words need not perish if transferred into writing. Legible traces can remain. Like the "cult of relics" that followed in the wake of the Buddha's death or the symbolic architecture of stūpas, which are said to represent simultaneously the presence and absence of the Buddha,[14] such texts signify at once themes of continuity and discontinuity, impermanence and intransience. So it is with Meme's biography. With his life story, there is the possibility of a (foot)print of sorts, even after he dies: it can entail a lasting residue, an imprint of his existence, a visual echo that lasts beyond the materiality and livelihood of his own body or voice. "My body has already died. My speech hasn't," he once told Nogapu and me. Yet, because his breath and voice might also soon perish, his speech would cease to be heard, as speech for Yolmo wa is usually tethered to the moment of its utterance.

If printed, the old man's words could also serve at times as evidence for actions he had undertaken in life—what he did, where he traveled to, how he had labored. The prospect of evidential truths seemed especially important for Meme when it came to the hardships and sorrows he felt he had suffered in life. And suffer he did, he detailed on numerous occasions: he had worked terribly hard; he had toiled in the rain and cold; he had traveled long distances barefoot; he had worn tattered clothes; he had carried heavy loads; and then, when his first wife died, he had struggled alone to maintain his lands and household because his sons had gone off in search of work in India—"I can say that I've had a lot of hardship [n. *dukha*] in my life." Hardships of this sort, his words imply, were more or less suffered by other members of his generation, and he and his peers often said as much. But they were not generally encountered by those of his grandchildren's generation, many of whom were able to attend school, eat good food, wear good clothes, and avoid the physical labor associated with "carrying loads." "The children of today haven't done any dukha," he told his grandson and me. "We have seen a lot of dukha. The children of today were in India [in boarding schools], they didn't do anything. We carried loads!" One reason for Meme's concern about the absence of suffering among "the children of today," including his own grandchildren, was that many Yolmo wa find that physical hardships can be quite valuable, especially when faced by young people, because the hardships can toughen them up and prepare them for the inevitable difficulties of life; one needs to "know dukha," it is said.

Yet, because the sufferings of Meme's generation were of a past time and could not be "seen" or witnessed but only spoken of in the present, their existence would always remain in question, especially when an elder was trying to convey them to a younger generation that did not know, or appreciate the significance of, such hard work. Meme seemed to have such thoughts in mind when he spoke one day of the hardships that occurred when his first wife died and his sons were away from home: "My first wife died 34 years ago. Before, it was a very desperate situation. I had many animals. I had to cut grass [to feed the animals]. So many troubles." He then nodded toward me and said to Nogapu, "Maybe he thinks I was always like this before. Rich and not working. I wasn't. I was in a desperate situation before. I had to work a lot, with all the animals. A ba ba!" A minute later he added, "Maybe people like you think, 'Now this man is staying like this.' They don't know how much I suffered." To "stay like this" meant that burdensome movement and physical labor was largely unnecessary, making for a life of leisure that was greatly at odds with (but perhaps the karmic fruits of) the toils of the past.

It is true. His interlocutors did not quite know how much he suffered, and any hard work that today's children (including, and perhaps especially, his own grandchildren) faced paled in comparison, he thought, to what people of "his time" undertook. But by telling us of his hardships, and especially by having them converted into print, there could be a trace of them in the present and future. If written down, the cultural logic went, they could gain an aura of truthfulness. His sufferings could echo in writing. He therefore found it important to tell us, among other things, of the hardships of his body and encouraged us to record in writing what he took to be the historical reality of such hardships. "Write that," he instructed his grandson Norbu and me early on during our talks, when he was detailing the exhausting set of prostrations and contemplative austerities that he performed in a month's time when he was 12 or so in order to "cleanse" any sins he had accumulated and begin a life of religious practice: "*Chag bum.* That means one hundred thousand prostrations. That should be written." Heeding his instructions, I dutifully jotted the words down in my notebook, and we soon moved on to other topics as the tape recorder continued to register our talk.

To write about a lama's initiations or other cultural practices served not simply to substantiate one man's sufferings, however. It also said something about how life in general was lived *tangbu,* many years before. As such, any writings helped to address another concern of Meme's: that much of "the old ways" could soon be lost, especially because Yolmo society seemed to be changing so quickly and so many Yolmo youths in Kathmandu were unable to speak Yolmo well. "Slowly everything will be forgotten," he told Norbu and me in reflecting on the waning use of the Yolmo language and traditional Yolmo customs. Others thought much the same. Writing about a life, in turn, could serve to counter the erosion of memory through the use of a medium that was known to work well against the possibility of forgetting. One Yolmo man—the president of the Yolmo Foundation, an association established in the late 1980s to promote and preserve Yolmo culture—expressed this idea upon learning in detail about my attempts to record the life stories of several elderly Yolmo wa. "This is very good. This is important," he said. "Because though we might not be able to read English well, our children and grandchildren will be able to, and they'll be able to know about the things that would otherwise be forgotten." An older generation's knowledge and memories could transfer, in writing, to a younger generation.

An intergenerational transmittal seemed particularly likely to occur in the case of Meme and his grandchildren. Norbu and his siblings conveyed to me that, because they had spent much of their childhood in India, they were not particularly close to their grandfather and, because he was, by nature, a "quiet" man, they knew little of the details of his life. They were quietly intrigued by my talks with him, however. While Norbu said he wanted to help me because, in part, he could learn about his grandfather's life, his sisters and brother, admittedly "reserved" themselves, read with interest the transcripts of the conversations I was translating into English when I offered them a chance to take the texts for a few days to read through them. "Last time, you had given us the book," Norbu's sister Tashi later told me, "and many things which we knew from there we didn't know before." She then went on to say that her grandfather could "be remembered from that book you're writing. Our children's grandchildren can read that book and know about him." I suspect that Meme held the possibility of such oblique communications in mind when talking with me.

Prospects of permanence and truthfulness (always tricky at best, any good Buddhist will tell you) thus took imaginative form once we began to transcribe the lama's words. His voice, various recollections of his life and "time," and perhaps something of his spirit could be cast into a set of physical inscriptions that would remain beyond the voice itself. At the same time, writing about his life could transfer oral accounts of that life and its opaque sufferings into a medium of "print" that many members of his society would find to be relatively evidential and truthful. While I am sure that Meme would admit to the unreal, illusory nature of such echoes, what seemed to win out for him over any such thoughts was the idea that fleeting speech could resound in a more durable record—and a scant trace could remain. "This book will come soon, and people will look at it," he observed toward the end of our conversations in 1998. "What we've been saying will come out in the book. . . . If we can't read, then other people will read, and they will think, 'It was this.' "

People Will Say

Meme knew well that anyone who might have the occasion and skills to "look" perceptively at his life story would also generate a sense that "he was [like] this," and he clearly sensed that the contents of any account of his life would affect his family's reputation once it was published and people had a chance to read, hear, or talk about it. Such an awareness is a terrifically important one among many Yolmo wa, for one's *min,* or name, is forever tied up with how one (and one's family) acts in life and what people say about those actions.

"People talk," Yolmo friends have often told me. They talk, in either critical or laudatory tones, about the "work" one does, good or bad, and of how well one talks or performs certain actions. Many activities that Yolmo wa engage in, or think of engaging in, therefore have an intersubjective air (and ear) to them from the start—subjective consciousness often implies an awareness of the consciousnesses of others—for there is always the chance that others will comment on those activities, sometimes in quite critical terms. Such *gyap-tum,* or back talk, which quickly spreads from household to household, does not apply to just oneself but, rather, to a person's entire family. If a person acts in what others consider a shameful or sinful manner, it can "cut the nose" of other family members, causing them to lose face, as it were, and find themselves to be similarly disgraced. "It sounds like Yolmo society is a whole world of people talking," I suggested once to a friend. "Oh yes. Oh yes," he answered. "It's like that. It just spreads—poooh! It just spreads." Good talk also regularly occurs, but it is the gossip that seems to spread most quickly. Something of the anticipatory, consequential logic of karmic principles resounds in both forms of commentaries, for the moral implications of one's actions can echo in what others later say about those actions: bad actions inevitably incur critical talk, the cultural logic goes, while good actions result in praise.

Such talk can have powerful consequences. Along with gossip leading one to feel "ashamed" or "shy" around others, and therefore hesitant to "show one's face" in public arenas, a person can lose the respect of others, who will then be reluctant to associate with or marry into that person's family. It therefore becomes crucial for children to maintain the reputations and good names of their parents and thus to "save" or "hold" their noses. People say that sons need to work well, marry spouses from good families, and hopefully "do something with their lives," as Meme put it once, while daughters need to be known as skillful, hospitable, chaste women. Many try to lead skillful, morally good lives and encourage or insist that other family members do so as well, in part to gain the respect of others and avoid any "cutting" talk.

Meme's family, respected by other Yolmo wa, has so far been free of the scabrous talk that has fallen on a few families. And while he and his family are, like other Yolmo families, forever worried about the possibility of such gossip, the old man appeared confident in what others might say or know about him, and he approached our conversations with a certain degree of comfort and candidness. It struck me that he thought his words and actions (and candidness) would bear out that he was, in fact, a good man, and he tried to convey as much when talking with us. "I say that I and my sons are very good," he asserted on one occasion. The phrase "I say that . . . " ("Nai mai . . .") characterizes well his stance in many of our exchanges, for his words had the effect, usually indirectly, of "saying" what he and his sons were like: namely, good people who faced a lot of hardships but who continued to practice dharma and act in morally good ways.

What troubled him more, apparently, was how much "prestige" he and his family might carry through the years. Ultimately, this was a question of what others might "say" about him and his family, especially if his sons or grandsons acted or failed to act in certain ways, as he noted on several occasions:

> Now, afterwards, some [of my family] are that way, others are that way [they live in different places]. Now there is a worry about what they are doing, whether they are fighting with people. If something happens, people will say he's so-and-so's son, so-and-so's grandson. With this, won't there be sorrow, won't there be worry?

> Now our relatives' children [Norbu and his siblings] don't speak our language. When we talk to them, they talk to us in Nepali. After going above [to the Yolmo region], they will say, "These people are not Yolmo."

Among other things, the old man worried over the fact that his grandsons could not speak Yolmo well, and so would not be considered Yolmo by other

Yolmo wa, and that they had little interest in learning to become knowledgeable priests, as he, his sons, and his revered ancestors had done. When, for instance, he told Norbu and me that he hoped that his grandsons would take up "lama work," he said it was a question of the family's *ijjat,* a Nepali word that can transfer into English as "honor," "prestige," or "good reputation" (see McHugh 1998; Schmidt and Mani Dahal 1993:47).

"So what do you want us to do?" asked Norbu, who on other occasions told me that he has had, to date, little interest in being a lama or in the prestige that usually comes with that role.

"Yes, lama," his grandfather replied. "If you continue the work done by your forefathers, the people will say you have continued the tradition. If you don't do anything, then ours [n. *hāmro*] will be forgotten."

"So, why do people say, 'Some things are good or bad'?"

"Well, they will say that, why not? You haven't followed your tradition. So they will say that. . . . People will talk about the things you all do, about what a family is doing. So it's a case of honor [ijjat]. If you do lama work, then people will say such and such families are doing lama work—and that [work] will be dharma also."

Such eventualities, good or bad, could be traced back to Meme's life and character, for Yolmo wa commonly understand that the moral consequences of a person's actions can eventually "affect" that person's children or grandchildren, such that a son's violent or drunken demeanor, for example, can indicate wrongdoings or spiritual failings on the part of that man's father. I first took note of this idea when I asked Meme how it is that children often assume the habits of their parents—and heard in his response something quite different than the "like father, like son" psychology that I knew. "Some children become good," my instructor replied,

> some become very bad, some become like murderers, some become like thieves. . . . If their grandfathers and fathers are doing good dharma, then that will help the children become good. If we don't do good before, then later our grandchildren will be negatively affected *[ne kalgen].* These days we're also saying, if someone is affected—if his head is funny or if he steals—we say, "Oh, his grandfather committed sins, so that's why he's like that."

Meme understood that a bad son or grandson can result from a bad father or grandfather, and he worried over the possibility that the demise of his family might indicate, to some, moral flaws on his part. This was one of the scenarios implied when he expressed his concern that people might say, "She's that lama's granddaughter," or, "He's so-and-so's son," if his descendants ran into trouble, for some might say that he was the distant source of such misfortunes.[15]

Faced with these potential legacies, Meme seemed to sense that the life story could effect a good echo and so help to shore up the genealogy of his family's "name." Nogapu and I once asked him what he thought about the fact that his great grandchildren would be able to read the book. "What do I think?" he replied. "It will become very good. Because my grandchildren will say, 'Our grandfather did this work, told all these stories.' Our name will come *[min ongin].*" A good name can result, that is, from what people read and know about Meme's words and actions—and from the simple fact that such a record exists. Still, the future cannot be predicted, the voicings of others cannot be fully determined. There is an air of slippage and unpredictability in these sorts of echoes: "I'm not the one to decide what people will say about me," Meme's son Latul once told me when asked what he thought others would say about him when he died. Any account of a Yolmo life would, to use Jacques Derrida's (1985) phrase, entail an "otobiography," destined for the ears of others, requiring others to later "countersign" or counterspeak in that person's name.

Given all this, it has become a question of which doings and tellings to stress in writing the life story, which could influence what people might "say" about Meme and his family later on. The more I learned of the potential implications of our talk, the more I became embedded within it; I wanted to ask Meme what he thought the focus of his life story should be. Nogapu helped me to pose the question one day in March 1998.

"Inside this book, Meme, people will read. What kind of good things should we write inside? Should 'a good household man' be written? Or should 'good dharma' be written? or 'good friendships and relations with all the relatives'?"

"For a good read," our elder replied, "you should tell about the good friendships and that there's good dharma. Also, about being close with my family, in the house. Also, that there's good dharma."

Because so much of Meme's talk circled about themes of sorrow and hard work in his life, themes that I thought would prove crucial in any account of his life, I wanted to know what he thought about including them in the book: "If we talk about suffering *[dhukpu],* should we put the sorrowful things? What do you think?"

"Why should the sorrowful words be put? What's the point? Suffering is a pain [*dhukpu mandi dhukpu*; literally, 'suffering means suffering']. Why put it in the book? Only talk about the pleasant talk. Then it's good for the book."

"It's good if dharma and the good friendships are put, yes?"

"Oh, that's it. If you talk about the dharma and the good friendships, that would be good, for sure. People will say, 'That man did dharma. He was a good man. But he's dead.' "

Because this assessment still left in question the accounts of Meme's hardships in life, accounts that I guess I was unwilling to part with, Nogapu and I pressed the matter: "All three should be put together, Meme," Nogapu said in conveying the gist of my thoughts. "Because you're a man who did hardship, and later you did a lot of dharma. Then, with dharma having been done, happiness now comes."

"Okay, okay. That's also good. Then people will think, 'This man suffered before. Now he has become like this.' "

At first, it seems, Meme balked at the idea of including his "sorrowful words," for he apparently felt that reading about suffering would inevitably (and perhaps mimetically) induce further suffering;[16] who would want to read a book of hardships? Accepting our logic, however, Meme changed his mind and decided, apparently, that the inclusion of hardship would make for a morally instructive biography, attesting to the principle of karma: a comfortable, merit-rich life is the eventual fruit of hard work and religious effort. Such a biography, faintly reminiscent of the moral teleologies implicit in the autobiographies of many great Tibetan saints, would speak well of him. People would say that, despite the hardships and sorrows he faced, he was a good man.

Much was riding, in short, on what people might say about the life and actions of this hardworking man. His afterlife will correspond in many ways to his afterimage. That afterimage will emerge, in part, from how others speak of him. For my part, any words I might write about his life and circulate among others could very well feed into such back talk in as-yet-undetermined ways. At the least, I find I need to write well of Meme's life, to say that he was a good man, which, I should say for the record, is an easy, straightforward thing to do because, like his children and grandchildren, he is, in fact, a good and virtuous man, without significant sins or moral failings to speak of.[17]

"The Poor Man"

"He was a good man. But he's dead"—as was often the case when we spoke, Meme anticipated what might occur after his death and how his life might echo in his afterlife. In his estimation, one that closely accorded with what many Yolmo wa think about the implications of acts-in-time, his reputation and social identity will be defined even more by what others say about him once he passes from his body and so can no longer speak or act on his own. His appreciation of the lasting legacy of people's talk, and of how people can be remembered in death, was evident in how he described his father and mother to us when asked what they were like:

> . . . My father was a hard man. He was hard. People said he was a hard man, but his heart was good. People also said that he was a good man, my father.

> . . . All the Tamang people [another ethnic group that lived in the same region] were saying that she [my mother] was a very good woman. They said this because she would cook food for them.

In characterizing people who had died, he related what others said about them. Voices again persist beyond a body's life. Meme expected people to talk about him as well after he died. Although it remains to be seen how others will speak of him and whether that talk will maintain the good name of his parents, he did seem to anticipate what they might say.

"How will people remember your life after you die?" Norbu and I once asked him.

"Even today villagers remember me," he answered. "They say, 'Don't stay in Kathmandu, come to the village.' For good people, people will always speak good of them. For bad people, people will always say bad things of them."

"After you die, do you think people will say good [things] about you?"

"I think they will. Because I have never done bad to anyone, never ruined anyone, never talked rudely to anyone. Everyone says I am a straight lama. The Tamangs say I am a straight lama *[teka lama]*, even today."

In effects similar to the cause, people speak good of good people and bad of bad; because of his actions, people will continue to say that Meme is "straight"—upright, honest, direct. Yet, for Meme at least, when it comes to talking about a recently deceased person, the import of such words does not simply shape that person's "name" or reputation. As with so many other kinds of talk among Yolmo wa, such as curses and the mantras of lamas and shamans, this kind of eulogistic, postmortem talk entails a physical force that can have powerfully real consequences in the world. As Meme explained it, what people say about a person after he or she dies influences where that person is reborn, for the gods listen to and heed such talk, which can then affect one's fate. "After people die," he told us, "if the people talk good about the person, then he reaches heaven because the gods also hear the people talking." He then pointed at the tape recorder and said, "This thing picks [up] when we talk. Similarly, the god picks [up] when people talk about us. It's like that, above."

On another occasion, with the tape recorder rolling on, Nogapu and I asked him where a person's soul travels to once it separates from the body in death. "If people did good things," Meme said,

> then the soul will go to a good place. If people did bad things, the soul will go to a bad place. If people do really good, then the Buddha will take them. If they've done sins, then they'll be taken down to hell. If they've done good, performing good rites [n. *pūjā*], talking well of others, then they'll go to heaven. That is our thinking. . . . If someone is bad, ah!, and the people say, "He should die because he's bad!" then he reaches hell because many people are saying that about him. If someone is good, people will say good things, and then he reaches heaven.[18]

"By oneself it's not enough," Meme told us, implying that a person cannot reach "heaven" by his or her efforts alone. Though a person travels alone and friendless in the "death-betweens," others need to help from a distance. As with the vocalizations of grief that can disturb a person's death if too intense, the voicings of others can, for Meme, powerfully influence the nature of one's journey and existence after death. The lamas who perform the funeral rites need to guide the soul toward a good "way," and the deceased's family and friends (and enemies even) have to act and speak on the dead person's behalf. Death and the fate of the deceased are immanently social affairs. There are, in fact, several activities that people can undertake on behalf of a dead person in the weeks following a death. Along with performing the funeral rites well, mourners can light candles to help illuminate "the way" after death; they can accept food distributed in the deceased's name; and they can participate in the group chorusing of prayers, known collectively as *mani,* that occurs at various times in the ritual process—the prayers and the wealth distributed increase the deceased's store of karmic "merit" *(gewa)* and so increase the chances of a good rebirth. Meme also noted that it is important for people to speak well and compassionately of the deceased: "We need to say 'nyingjua' to the person who is dying, even if he's our enemy."

Nyingjua, or *snying-brtse-ba* in Tibetan, literally means "compassion" (Jäschke 1995:198). In contexts such as these, however, its pragmatic import can perhaps be best heard in translation as "O the poor man" or "poor, unfortunate one" (cf. Jäschke 1995:198; Ortner 1978:43). As such, the phrase, often used when speaking of deceased loved ones or acquaintances, designates the respectful compassion one feels for a suffering or dying person. "It means he's a good man," Nogapu said when asked what the word meant.

The old man continued,

> We need to do some mani [prayers] and pray to the gods—we need to do this. We shouldn't cry. Everyone needs to die. Our enemies also need to die. If we say "poor, unfortunate one" [nyingjua] to our enemy when he's dying, he can get the nice place. If everyone says, "He's a bad person," then he goes down, down. If one or two people say he's good, then it helps a bit. If everyone says he's bad, then the gods also believe this. If people say he's a very good person and everyone says, "He's dead," then he can go to the Buddha. If one person tries to pick up a heavy stone, it won't rise. But if many people try to pick it up, it can be lifted. It's the same with saying mani.

There was a lot on the line for Meme when it came to the voicings of others. What people say about him after his death, he understood, and the extent to which they collectively voice mani prayers, will help to determine the nature of his rebirth. He seemed to anticipate that any writings about him would contribute to such a judgment. He mused, for instance, that people reading certain aspects of his life story, such as his sufferings and his dharmic career, might voice the mournful, nyingjua-like statement, "He was a good man. But he's dead." Notice how these words closely echo his observation, expressed a month later and noted above, "If people say he's a very good person and everyone says, 'He's dead,' then he can go to the Buddha." His words anticipated the mourning to come, as well as how an account of his life might help to shape any laments voiced on his behalf.

One reason Meme invested in the recording of his life, in short, was to convey that he was an important, morally good person—and so to effect good talk about himself before and after he died. Like the many texts he read daily in preparing for death, this, too, was "work for later." "A good read" might prompt people to speak compassionately about him; divine beings would ultimately be listening. As it is, the presumed consequences of such talk lead me to wonder if, and to what effect, the present chain of words will be heard by the gods. Such are an ethnographer's concerns and responsibilities when local realities and interests are taken seriously. For what it is worth, I do not take my responsibilities here lightly, in part because my life has become greatly interwoven with the

lives I wish to write about, and certain ethical duties come with those ties. At the same time, through the course of my engagements with Yolmo lives, some recesses of my mind seem to have acquired, in rather visceral, preconscious ways, many of the sensibilities toward action, time, and meaning that I have been trying to understand, such that when I put pen to paper the metaphysics of Yolmo lives echo powerfully in the soundings of my own thoughts. One consequence of this is that what, and how, the life history work apparently means for Meme has been converging at points with what, and how, that work means for me. Another related consequence, one in accord with a logic of karmic echoes, is that I have come to appreciate a wealth of potential long-term "pragmatic effects" resulting from our engagements together, effects that I would not have anticipated before getting involved in such work, given that the inhabitants of my Euro-American world, including its theorists of language, tend to conceive of the significance of acts-in-time in ways quite different than Yolmo wa do. For the record, then, and to help with the burden to come, nyingjua.

Attachments

The prospect of something tangible staying on after Meme's death was unusual as it stood, for one of the main messages of Buddhist teachings and practices is that a person's life and body are fleeting and impermanent. Yolmo funeral rites drive this message home in forceful terms. To begin with, the deceased's body is quickly cremated. Then, at the dramatic climax of a merit-making funeral ritual known as gewa, or "merit," often held around the 49th day after a person dies, a date that is thought to coincide with the end of the bardo death-betweens, a lifelike effigy of the deceased's body is built out of the person's clothes, along with a funerary "crown" and a white cloth for the face. People then carry the effigy out of the deceased's house into a lamas' temple in order to consummate the transmigration of the deceased's soul into the heavens "above." A series of rites is then performed once the effigy is set up in an appropriate place in the temple. After the head lama summons the deceased's soul to reside within the effigy, family members offer foods to the deceased, but with arms crossed at the wrists, perhaps to signify the constraints on exchanges between the living and the dead. They then perform prostrations to absolve the deceased of any "sins" or "vices" *(dikpa)* committed while he or she was alive. Such sins are further "cleansed" by having a man pour water from a vase over the image of the effigy as reflected in a mirror. Several family members then talk to the deceased, as embodied by the effigy, explaining that he or she is dead and can no longer remain among the living.

After these activities conclude, the head lama sets on the table before him a sheet of rice paper supported like a flag on a stick. This paper, known as the *chang par* or "purification paper," is inscribed with a human figure on one side and prayers to a deity on the other; the deceased's name is written in an appropriate place in these prayers. The head lama then purifies the sins of the deceased by holding a small flame to the paper and burning it. Just before the paper burns, it is thought, the deceased's soul journeys into the land above.[19] As the paper vanishes to a dramatic charge of lamaic music, the effigy is quickly dismantled into a pile of loose clothes.

These rites establish several ephemeral images of the deceased's body: the effigy, the effigy's image in the mirror, and the figure of a human body on the purification paper. While this series of quite subtle bodies suggests one way that a Yolmo wa might at least imagine the extension of his or her life after dying, it must be kept in mind that each of the images is dissolved through an act that conveys the end of a life. The inscriptions on the purification paper themselves embody a graphic trace of a person's life—and so a biography in the strict sense of the term. For many, the incineration of this paper signifies the final death of the deceased, the cessation of a singular identity, and the end of a living, public biography. "They burn the dead man's name," a friend said with a nervous laugh in summing up the rite.

Many in fact hold that after this paper is burnt, and after the conclusion of the funeral rites in general, one should no longer mention the deceased's name. As Meme's son Latul explained it to me, "There's no use in saying such names. A name is only for the living, not the dead." When I asked one man about this taboo, he said, "We do say that also: 'With death the name is lost.' *Min torsin.* We say that. To say, 'Min torsin,' means, 'His name is lost,' which means he's dead." The word *torsin* apparently relates to the Tibetan verb *'tor-ba,* which Jäschke translates as "to be scattered, to fly asunder, to be dispersed, to decay" (1995:246).[20] The lost name implies that its owner's social identity disperses and flies asunder. "So nothing is permanent. Everything is lost," the man went on to say, underscoring one of the Buddhist lessons of the rite: that not even a person's name lasts after death.[21] This, at least, is the message conveyed; more private, familial memories of the deceased readily continue.

When it comes to writing Meme's life story, I find that there is a similar engagement of paper and a life. It is as though his "name," if not his soul, is being transmitted into the paper of a text (again, we toil in a bhaja-esque logic of "as though"). But in contrast to the usual turn of events at Yolmo funerals, wherein so much goes up in flames, Meme's "name," and his life as cast in print, will carry on in the markings of a text. "Dying is not good," he told us. "How much one can live, that is good." Given that he was afraid of dying and wished to live longer, the texts we were producing together could enable him to extend the duration of his life and his "name" in an uncommon way. Any remainder would imply a middle way between immortality and complete annihilation. Dying would not quite be dying.

And yet I wonder about all this (and about my hand in all this) because Meme's desires were in tension with what many Buddhist teachings, and he himself, advocate: that one should not become too attached to one's life, especially when that life is ending. One reason for this creed is that attachments limit the possibility of any spiritual transcendence from a world of suffering and desire. Another reason, more commonly advanced by Yolmo wa, is that if strong attachment arises at the moment of death, a person risks becoming a ghost, a

lingering bhaja that, stuck between lives, haunts its former loved ones and possessions.

Most often Yolmo wa refer to such attachment as *semjha,* as a "clinging" or "keeping" of the sem, or heartmind, among others. As Meme himself explained it to us,

> If one gives semjha to anything, then he or she becomes a ghost *[shindi].* "Before I had this thing, I had this much of that"—the person who thinks like this becomes a ghost. *Semjha* means that. "I have this much money, I remember this, I have my children, I have my family"—that kind of attachment [semjha] comes. If one has attachment like this, one might return as a ghost.

When bereaved family members talk at the gewa to the spirit of the deceased, as represented by the effigy, they often tell it not to leave a semjha behind. "We talk to it," to quote Meme again: "We say to it, 'Don't give the semjha to many things, don't think about this, don't think about that. Think only about your gods and your lama.' The lamas say this."

What concerns me here in thinking about Yolmo attachments is that, while Meme himself was aching for a good death, one free of attachment and longing for the world, he also appeared to desire that something of his life "stay" on after he died. While there are significant and perhaps irresoluble tensions here, what I have come to understand is that, by converting his speech into print and leaving something tangible behind after he dies, he could, in fact, become less attached to the world. Something he once said, while talking about the need to die in the presence of one's family and to "see their faces" for the last time, helps me to comprehend this:

> It's better to die with one's family nearby. Then your semjha won't stay with them. If one dies in a different place, just alone, then he thinks, "I have this thing, I have that many children." Then the semjha gets attached to the house. So then the lamas need to tell him, "Don't keep the heartmind, don't do like this." If the children are not there, or if they're in a foreign country, then the attachment [semjha] comes. If the children are away when the person dies, then they return after the death and say at the gewa, "Don't do the semjha to me. I was away before, but now I'm here."

If one's children are absent when one is dying, there can be undue attachment because one longs for the missing, wished-for loved ones. If they are present, however, there is no need for any ghostbound attachments to occur because there is no one absent whose presence is desired. In much the same way, Meme's life story might diminish, rather than add to, his attachment to the world. The fact of its occurrence might lead him to become less attached to his present life, in part because he would no longer worry so much about his death and no longer need to long so much for a world that he must soon leave behind. With something longed for made present through writings about him, he can be at peace upon dying, and his spirit will need not linger as a ghostly bhaja.[22]

Responses

What I have come to gather, then, is that any written accounts of Meme's life will likely effect diffuse and as-yet-undetermined remainders/reminders that will work through a complex nexus of local semiotic principles to establish certain absences, presences, identities, and remembrances. Traces of "the old ways," of Yolmo history and culture, of a lama's deeds and sufferings, and of skillful, virtuous ways to live and die might transfer to and remain among others. Particular, and heavily coauthored, understandings of Yolmo engagements with life and death might also echo through texts such as this, much as novel ideas of biographic writing and its worldly (and otherworldly) consequences might resound in the minds of non-Yolmo authors and readers. And yet, while it now seems clear that writings about Meme will instantiate an array of echoes for different readers, it remains to be seen if some of these writings will function in more ghostly ways. For some time, in fact, I have been worried that any meanings invested in writings about him could potentially effect, or be understood as, bad disturbing bhaja among some Yolmo wa, including his family members. This is not an easy question to think through, for there are some representations of deceased loved ones, such as photographs, that people usually welcome and there are others, such as ghosts, that are greatly feared. Five months after leaving Nepal I sent an e-mail note to Karma Gyaltsen Lama, a Yolmo artist and friend who has helped me on many occasions to understand better the intricacies of Yolmo lives. Karma had just then purchased a computer to aid him in his artwork, and I took this opportunity to send him an e-mail letter in which I detailed my concerns to him and asked him to clarify, if possible, the difference between good and troublesome bhaja in Yolmo lives. "Why is it," I asked among other things, "that people don't want a deceased loved one to come back as a haunting bhaja, but will still keep photographs and other objects that help them remember their relation to that person?" His response, in English, included the following observations:

> Regarding your question on bhaja, I don't see any clear demarcation between a good and a bad bhaja. It's the same as distinguishing between good and bad dreams through the different meanings you can best make of images and the way you are involved. Maybe I can say it is psychological. When we talk about the photographs or other things of the deceased, they bring memories of the deceased physically and therefore can bring emotional moments. . . .
>
> Speaking of Meme Lama's life story, the book itself won't be a bhaja, but reading what he had to say will carry meanings[,] and therefore his words, sayings, will be his bhajas; these interpret into some meanings and as long as they don't mean anything evil, irritating, or bad, they cannot be his bad bhajas. However, if one sees nightmares with the book or what is written there after reading or seeing the book, it will be considered (as any other book) a bad bhaja, meaning it carries some bad meanings with it.
>
> I hope all this makes some sense to you.

These words do make sense. The implications of any bhaja, whatever their origins, reside largely in the mind of the beholder. But while that message is clear to me, my mind is not any more at peace for it. The ethnographer of bhaja is soon troubled by the meanings that bhaja "interprets into." I feel I can speak well of Meme and so help to effect good echoes of his life, however illusory they might ultimately be. I therefore plan to continue to write about that life and in more direct ways than I have done here. Still, in thinking about what and how this work might mean for Meme and others, I find myself increasingly entangled within the meanings emerging from that work. I worry about the potential effects of my writings. I am now accountable to a set of lives powerfully geared to the voicings of others. I listen to the tapes. Caught within a particular engagement with time, bracing for a death, I am haunted, at times, by the words of this good man.

Notes

Acknowledgments. The present article draws from ethnographic research I conducted among Yolmo people in 1988–89, 1997, and 1998. The most recent field studies were supported by grants from the American Philosophical Society and Sarah Lawrence College (SLC); earlier research was supported by grants from the Wenner-Gren Foundation for Anthropological Research and the University of California at Los Angeles. Special thanks go to Meme Lama, Latul Lama, Norbu Yolmo, Nogapu Prakash Sherpa, Pramod Lama, and Karma Gyaltsen Lama for their generous help on this particular project, as well as to Tracy McGarry, Theresa O'Nell, Joao Biehl, Susan Thames, members of the SLC faculty writing group, and three anonymous reviewers for comments on earlier drafts.

1. The first two words of Meme's quoted utterance, "Shi mandi . . . ," were in the Yolmo language, followed, after a brief pause, with the remaining words, all in Nepali (". . . mareko hoina. Sareko ho"), as though the inequation noted by the utterance (dying does not mean dying) prompted or necessitated a transfer from one language to another. Foreign words in the text prefaced by "n." denote words in Nepali; other foreign terms most often denote Yolmo words. For details on social, historical, and cultural dynamics among Yolmo wa (usually pronounced nowadays "hyer-mu wa," with an aspirated "h" quietly leading into "yer-mu"), see Bishop 1998; Clarke 1980a, 1980b, 1985, 1990; and Desjarlais 1992.

2. In general, then, conversations with Norbu present were conducted in Nepali, whereas those with Nogapu as translator were conducted in Yolmo. I usually spoke to Meme in Nepali, both during our formal interviews and during my visits alone to his home.

3. The works of Behar (1993), Crapanzano (1980), and Ortiz (1985) come close to these concerns, however, as do the contributors to an issue of the *Journal of Narrative and Life History* (2:1, 1992) devoted to what Margaret Blackman identifies as "the afterlife of the life history" (1992:1). See Peacock and Holland 1993 for a recent review of life history research in anthropology.

4. See Crapanzano 1994 and Haviland 1991 for exemplary accounts of the pragmatics of particular life history interviews.

5. "Om mani-padme hūm" is a merit-producing Buddhist mantra often heard among Tibetan peoples. Said to invoke the Bodhisattva Avokeiteśvara—known as Che Renzi in Yolmo—it can be rendered in English as "O you who hold the jeweled [rosary] and the lotus [have mercy on us]" (Lopez 1997:14).

6. See, for instance, Adams 1996, 1997; Desjarlais 1992; Maskarinec 1995; O'Flaherty 1984; Samuel 1993; and Smith 1989.

7. In this regard, Yolmo understandings of mimetic principles appear to differ from many so-called postmodern attitudes that contend that everything is simulation and, thus, that nothing is more or less authentic, original, or unreal than anything else (see, for instance, Adams 1996; Baudrillard 1983). While some well-trained lamas, including Meme at times, contend that everyday life is itself illusory, most Yolmo wa, Meme included, nevertheless live in a quite real world where important distinctions are made between fakes and originals: echoes, for instance, can be unreal repetitions of real sounds; Kathmandu, some say, offers "duplicate" foods that are pale, poor-tasting imitations of more authentic foods found in the foothills; "true stories" are sometimes contrasted to "false" ones; and people often distinguish between "true" and "untrue" lamas—"born lamas," that is, who inherit the role through patrilineal lineages, and "reading lamas," who cannot claim such divine inheritance but nevertheless learn to read sacred texts. The latter idea, bolstered by the former ones, carries important political implications, for "born lamas" are seen as more authentic than "reading lamas" and so incur more respect from others. In a land of illusions, some things are more unreal than others.

8. H. Jäschke's 19th-century Tibetan-English dictionary notes that *brag-cha* can also stand figuratively "for something insubstantial, shadowy, not existing" (1995:380).

9. In fact, the word *bhaja* sometimes serves as a colloquial grammatical structure that perhaps has most affinities with the English phrase "it appeared as though":

Milum du, nombu yimba bhaja	dream–appears to be, real–is–as though: "[It] is apparently a dream, [but] it seemed as though real."
Milumla tongdu, tempang tondan bhaja	dream–in–is/was seen, really–met–as though: "It was seen in a dream, [but] it appeared as though we really met."

Yolmo wa often voice such phrasings when speaking of dreams of the dead: friends or family members will appear in dreams "as though" they were real or "as though" a dreamer was actually meeting and talking with them.

10. According to Chökyi Nyima Rinpoche, a bodhisattva is someone who has developed "jang chup sem ba" or "bodhicitta," "the aspiration to attain enlightenment in order to benefit all sentient beings" (1991:170). Meme understood much the same, although for him and other Yolmo wa the term *jang chup sem ba* also entails the idea, simply, of a spiritually pure heartmind.

11. Che Gyalbu, the "Lord of Dharma," also known in Nepali as Yama Raj, the "Lord of Death," is for many Yolmo wa a personified, omniscient deity who observes and records all the actions a person commits when he or she is alive. When a person dies, he or she is brought to the heavenly domain of this lord, who then interrogates the shocked and frightened person about the acts, good and bad, that he or she undertook while alive. After listening to the person's responses, which might include attempts to lie or hide the truth, the Lord of Dharma reveals a singularly powerful mirror, known as the *leki melong* or "mirror of karma," which displays in detail all of the person's actions as they occurred in the course of the life that just ended. After this presentation concludes, with every good and bad deed revealed and weighed collectively on a scale, Che Gyalbu decides what the punishment must be for any sins committed and thereby determines to which realm that person is to be sent in rebirth.

12. This is often the case in cases of wrongdoing. When one man complained to another that money for a local school was being "eaten" by members of that village, for example, the second man said that he had not "seen anything" and so could not do or say anything about it. Without direct, visible evidence of theft, he was unable and unwilling to take action. To see something with "one's own eyes," in turn, can make for a powerful form of witnessing. "I saw it with my own eyes," one elderly Yolmo man, pointing a finger toward his eyes, said of the hanging of four martyrs by the Rana regime which he witnessed in Kathmandu several decades before: "It was a terrible thing that I saw."

Meme's various takes on knowledge often heeded a similar rule of vision. When the subject of "heaven" (n. *swarga*) came up once during our conversations, he observed, "Well, nobody has actually seen heaven, nobody has actually seen hell. It's just that people say that after we die, we go to heaven or to hell. But who has seen it?" During our conversation, we asked him if it was true that deities enter into a shaman's body when the shaman is healing. "Well, they say such a thing," he quickly replied. "We haven't seen, we cannot say." What remained unseen could not be spoken of definitively.

13. The differences presumed by many to hold between speech and writing are evident in tensions between lamaic and shamanic forms of knowledge among Yolmo wa. Many Yolmo wa, lamas in particular, contend that the oracular divinations of a shamanic bombo, in which tutelary deities "fall" into the bombo's body to orally "reveal" the causes and nature of human maladies, are "like the wind," fleeting and unstable. Lamas, in contrast, base almost all of their religious practice on the recitation of Tibetan texts understood to be eminently sacred and truthful. Said to be the inscribed talk of various buddhas, bodhisattvas, and religious saints, these texts convey a brand of knowledge and meaning at odds with (and, some would say, superior to) a shaman's speech-based divinations. Meme, who is known as a skillful reader of divinatory texts founded on astrological principles, put it well when he once explained to us why his text-based divinatory practices were more reliable than a shaman's oracles. "There are so many bombos," he said. "People don't believe in their predictions. They only come to me. The bombos just say it with guessing. But this thing [a divinatory text] has been written by a deity many, many years ago." A powerful ideology of speech, writing, and religious practice was being asserted here: whereas a lama reads texts "written by a deity" years before, a bombo "just says it" without conclusive knowledge. "He can't read. How can he know what is right, what is the truth?" one village lama said caustically of a bombo's defense of the ritual sacrifice of animals, such as chickens and goats. He then defended his own Buddhist-based aversion to such sacrifices by noting, "It's the deity's word. It's written in the holy books. So it's true, isn't it?"

No other kind of script in the Yolmo universe carries the aura of sacredness and truthfulness that Tibetan religious writing does. But many writings of various sorts, be they in Nepali, Hindi, or English, nevertheless convey for many Yolmo wa an air of truthfulness that few mediums of speech do. Certain kinds of writings authored by "Westerners" have, in particular, recently acquired a certain presumed veracity to some. When I returned to Nepal in the winter of 1998, I took with me several of the published writings of Graham Clarke, a British anthropologist who wrote on the social and religious orders of Yolmo life in the northeastern part of Helambu as he came to understand them while conducting fieldwork in the 1970s and 1980s. When I gave copies of these writings to a Yolmo friend who could read English, he said, "Ah, this will be really good." He immediately read through several passages with great interest and located discussions of his family's lama lineage. Later he said, "This will be really good. Now, when we talk to people about 'Yolmo,' we can say that even the Westerners have written this, and we can show them this. When people see something written, they believe it to be true. That's the way they think. Especially with things written in the West—or in the lama scripts."

14. See Gombrich 1988:123–124 and Strong 1995:34–41 on the cult of relics, for example, and Robinson and Johnson 1997:80–81 on the symbolism of stūpas.

15. Along much the same lines, Meme said, when asked, that the most important thing that had happened in his life was that his sons had done better financially than he had: "My children have done better than me, that is the most important." His children's success, his words imply, indicates that they bore the fruits of his good dharma.

16. It is also possible, though he never said anything to suggest such an interpretation, that Meme hesitated to include details of his hardships because they could also be understood locally as a consequence of bad karma incurred in previous lives. Indeed, an elderly Yolmo man told his grandson that he would not want to relate his life story to me because, if he did, he would feel compelled to tell of the many sufferings he faced in life, and because those sufferings could be perceived as the karmic "fruits" of previous bad deeds, they could also indicate, his grandson related, that he was "lesser" than others. Be that as it may, Meme might not have himself worried about potential assessments of this sort in part because, unlike this man's, his later years were ones of relative comfort, leisure, and high status.

17. Vincanne Adams (1996, 1997) has written insightfully about the potential reality-effecting karmic consequences of ethnographic writing as understood by another Tibetan Buddhist people, the Sherpas of the Solu-Khumbu region of northeastern Nepal. Drawing from her ethnographic research among these people, she has found that Sherpas understand that the ways in which anthropologists write about them can, in accord with Buddhist principles of karma and mimesis, have a powerful, determining effect on their welfare and personhood. Much as photographs of people dressed, by chance, in ragged clothes can result in a future of poverty for the subjects of those photographs, so, it is understood, certain ethnographic representations of Sherpas can become the reality for those portrayed. Some people that Adams spoke with, for instance, were concerned that a book that claimed that Sherpa society was in decline "could actually have produced that very situation for Sherpas" (1997:92). The means and consequences of such reality effects appear to be quite different among Yolmo wa: a negative representation of something or someone could be seen as an unwelcome omen-like "indication" *(preda)*—but not quite the cause—of a negative karmic consequence to come, and the voicings of self and others, spoken or written, tend to substantiate identities and destinies in everyday life more than anything else. And yet I do find, as Adams does, that a heavy accountability comes with any writings one might author in such a world. This accountability can ultimately work in positive, meaningful ways, however, for I, too, can speak well of Meme and so help to effect good echoes of his life, both now and in his death.

18. From what I understand, Meme's understanding of the soteriologic force of people's talk about a person is not shared by all Yolmo wa. Yolmo wa commonly say that if people say good things about a person, then that person will have a good afterlife. But the implication for many is not that the gods listen to such talk in judging a person or that people saying good things about that person in effect causes a good afterlife. Rather, it is that the talk itself is, like a good rebirth, a karmic consequence of a morally good life and so simply *foretells* a good rebirth to come.

19. Some Yolmo wa understand that the lama transfers the deceased's soul into the chang par paper before he burns it; others say that the paper is "just for show," with the real departure of the soul taking form in the lama's mind.

20. Meme once told me, in contrast to what most others advised (see also Fürer-Haimendorf 1964:236 on Solu-Khumbu Sherpa), that all the talk about "the name is lost" was misguided, for the original and correct phrase was not "min torsin" but, simply, "mi torsin": "the man is lost." The original became something else when re-sounded. His stance on the matter suggested that he was less attached to the idea that one's identity must be obliterated after death. It has also made me feel more comfortable invoking his name and presence both now and later.

21. The message is much the same as that which takes form in most Hindu funeral rites in Banaras, India, wherein, to quote Jonathan Parry, "the complete obliteration of the physical remains of the deceased is accompanied by an almost equally radical effacement of his personal characteristics and biography" (1994:210).

22. It is also possible that our talks enabled Meme to take the measure of his life and so helped him to come to better terms with the ending of that life.

References Cited

Adams, Vincanne

1996 Tigers of the Snow and Other Virtual Sherpas: An Ethnography of Himalayan Encounters. Princeton: Princeton University Press.

1997 Dreams of a Final Sherpa. American Anthropologist 99(1):85–97.

Baudrillard, Jean

1983 Simulations. New York: Semiotext(e).

Behar, Ruth

1993 Translated Woman: Crossing the Border with Esperanza's Story. Boston: Beacon Press.

1996 The Vulnerable Observer: Anthropology that Breaks Your Heart. Boston: Beacon Press.

Bishop, Naomi

1998 Himalayan Herders. New York: Harcourt Brace and Co.

Blackman, Margaret

1992 Introduction: The Afterlife of the Life History. Journal of Narrative and Life History 2(1):1–10.

Chang, Garma Chen-Chi

1977 The Hundred Thousand Songs of Milarepa. 2 vols. Boulder: Shambala.

Chökyi Nyima Rinpoche

1991 The Bardo Guidebook. Hong Kong: Rangjung Yeshe Publications.

Clarke, Graham

1980a A Helambu History. Journal of the Nepal Research Centre (Humanities) 4: 1–38.

1980b Lama and Tamang in Yolmo. *In* Tibetan Studies in Honor of Hugh Richardson. Michael Aris and Aung San Suu Kyi, eds. Pp. 79–86. Warminster, UK: Aris and Phillips.

1985 Equality and Hierarchy among a Buddhist People in Nepal. *In* Contexts and Levels: Anthropological Essays on Hierarchy. R. H. Barnes, Daniel de Coppet, and R. J. Parkin, eds. Pp. 193–209. Oxford: Journal of the Anthropological Society of Oxford Occasional Papers, 4.

1990 Ideas of Merit *(bsod-nams)*, Virtue *(dge-ba)*, Blessing *(bying-rlabs)*, and Material Prosperity *(rten-'brel)* in Highland Nepal. Journal of the Anthropological Society of Oxford 21:165–184.

Crapanzano, Vincent
1980 Tuhami: Portrait of a Moroccan. Chicago: University of Chicago Press.
1994 Kevin: On the Transfer of Emotions. American Anthropologist 96:866–885.
Das, Veena
1986 The Work of Mourning: Death in a Punjabi Family. *In* The Cultural Transition: Human Experience and Social Transformation in the Third World and Japan. Merry White and Susan Pollock, eds. Pp. 179–210. Boston: Routledge and Kegan Paul.
1996 Language and Body: Transactions in the Construction of Pain. Daedalus 125(1):67–91.
Derrida, Jacques
1985 The Ear of the Other: Otobiography, Transference, Translation. Texts and Discussions with Jacques Derrida. Lincoln: University of Nebraska Press.
Desjarlais, Robert
1992 Body and Emotion: The Aesthetics of Illness and Healing in the Nepal Himalayas. Philadelphia: University of Pennsylvania Press.
Fürer-Haimendorf, Christoph von
1964 The Sherpas of Nepal: Buddhist Highlanders. London: John Murray.
Gombrich, Richard
1988 Theravada Buddhism: A Social History from Ancient Benares to Modern Colombo. New York: Routledge.
Gyatso, Janet
1997 Apparitions of the Self: The Secret Autobiographies of a Tibetan Visionary. Princeton: Princeton University Press.
Haviland, John
1991 "That Was the Last Time I Seen Them, and No More": Voices through Time in Australian Aboriginal Autobiography. American Ethnologist 18:331–361.
Jäschke, H. A.
1995[1881] A Tibetan-English Dictionary. Delhi: Motilal Banarsidass Publishers.
Khetsun Sangpo Rinbochay
1982 Tantric Practice in Nying-Ma. Jeffrey Hopkins, trans. London: Rider.
Lopez, Donald S.
1997 Introduction. *In* Religions of Tibet in Practice. Donald S. Lopez, ed. Pp. 3–36. Princeton: Princeton University Press.
Maskarinec, Gregory
1995 The Rulings of the Night: An Ethnography of Nepalese Shaman Oral Texts. Madison: University of Wisconsin Press.
McHugh, Ernestine
1998 Situating Persons: Honor and Identity in Nepal. *In* Selves in Time and Place: Identities, Experience, and History in Nepal. Debra Skinner, Alfred Pach, and Dorothy Holland, eds. Pp. 155–174. Lanham, MD: Rowman and Littlefield.
Melberg, Arne
1995 Theories of Mimesis. Cambridge: Cambridge University Press.
Milarepa
1977 The Life of Milarepa. Lopsang Lhalungpa, trans. New York: Arkana.
Mullin, Glenn, ed.
1986 Death and Dying: The Tibetan Tradition. Ithaca: Snow Lion.
O'Flaherty, Wendy Doniger
1984 Dreams, Illusions, and Other Realities. Chicago: University of Chicago Press.

Ortiz, Karol
1985 Mental Health Consequences of Life History Method: Implications from a Refugee Case. Ethos 13:99–120.
Ortner, Sherry
1978 Sherpas through Their Rituals. Cambridge: Cambridge University Press.
Parry, Jonathan
1994 Death in Banaras. Cambridge: Cambridge University Press.
Patrul Rinpoche
1994 The Words of My Perfect Teacher (Kunzang Lama'i Shelung). Padmakara Translation Group, trans. San Francisco: HarperCollins.
Peacock, James, and Dorothy Holland
1993 The Narrated Self: Life Stories in Process. Ethos 21:367–383.
Robinson, Richard, and Willard Johnson
1997 The Buddhist Religion: A Historical Introduction. Belmont, CA: Wadsworth Publishing Co.
Samuel, Geoffrey
1993 Civilized Shamans: Buddhism in Tibetan Societies. Washington, DC: Smithsonian Institution Press.
Schmidt, Ruth Laila, and Ballabh Mani Dahal, eds.
1993 A Practical Dictionary of Modern Nepali. Kathmandu: Ratna Sagar.
Smith, Brian
1989 Reflections on Resemblance, Ritual, and Religion. New York: Oxford University Press.
Strong, John
1995 The Experience of Buddhism: Sources and Interpretations. Belmont, CA: Wadsworth Publishing Co.
Thurman, Robert
1994 The Tibetan Book of the Dead: Liberation through Understanding in the Between. New York: Thorsons.

Part 4:
Religions in Japan

OMEGA, Vol. 33(4) 279-302, 1996

ANCESTOR WORSHIP IN JAPAN: DEPENDENCE AND THE RESOLUTION OF GRIEF

DENNIS KLASS
Webster University, St. Louis, Missouri

ABSTRACT

Ancestor worship in Japan is ritual, supported by a sophisticated theory, by which the living manage their bonds with the dead. Differing cultural values on autonomy/dependence create differences in interpersonal bonds, thus different dynamics in breaking and continuing bonds after death. This article defines ancestor worship and places in its historical/political context, discusses autonomy and dependence as cultural values in terms of expressions and resolutions of grief, and describes ancestor worship as processes similar to the resolution of grief in the modern West.

Nearly three decades ago Yamamoto, Okonogi, Iwasaki, and Yoshimura suggested that grief might be different in Japan because ancestor worship was such a central part of the culture. They said:

> The main point of our research was to observe the natural process of mourning in a culture where the religious beliefs and institutions permit the "cultivation of the idea of the presence of the deceased" as ancestors [1, p. 1663].

They noted that the beliefs underlying ancestor worship directly contradict psychological theory in which the "work of mourning" is to assimilate the "reality" that the person is permanently absent. They noted that pathology in the West is defined in terms of attempts to maintain contact with the dead person. Speaking circumspectly as Japanese do when they wish to avoid the appearance of directly opposing another's view, Yamamoto and his colleagues suggested that cultural differences fostered different mourning processes. To the best of my knowledge, no Western scholars with a grounding in Western studies of bereavement have followed-up on Yamamoto and his colleagues' ideas. This article is an attempt to continue the cross-cultural dialogue Yamamoto and his colleagues invited so long ago.

The psychological theory to which Yamamoto and his colleague objected has now been severely questioned by Western scholars. Stroebe, Gergen, Gergen, and Stroebe, for example, have recently reminded us that the concept of "grief work," one of Freud's ideas, is really an artifact of modernity and that modernity is itself a reaction against romanticism which valued long-term sentimental attachment to the deceased [2, 3]. Data from many populations in Western culture show that, in fact, survivors seldom sever the bonds, but rather that survivors maintain an active role for the inner representation of the dead in their ongoing life [4]. Thus, it would seem, the healthy resolution of grief in the West has many similarities to the phenomena seen in Japanese ancestor worship.

The thesis of the article is a variation on that of Yamamoto and his colleagues. They said that the process of mourning would be different in Japan because rituals of ancestor worship provide for a continuing presence of the dead. But, as we have noted, Yamamoto et al.'s diplomatic suggestion is unnecessary. Rather, this study seems to indicate that ancestor worship has many similarities to the healthy resolution of grief found in the West. The place of autonomy/dependence and the value each culture places on autonomy/dependence, however, is a major difference between Japan and the West in the way interpersonal bonds are structured. Because the autonomy/dependence issue creates differences in bonds among people, it creates somewhat different dynamics in transforming the bond with the dead.

In this article, we will first, briefly define ancestor worship and put it into its historical socio-political context. We will show how Western theories about and social forms of grief have a similar socio-political context. Second, we will discuss the cultural value given to autonomy and dependence in Japanese and modern Western cultures and discuss ways in which those values affect the tasks survivors must accomplish in their grief, and how the values affect the expressions of grief and the continuing bonds with the deceased. Third, we will describe the beliefs and rituals of ancestor worship and show how the resolution of grief works out in this system.

DEFINITION OF ANCESTOR WORSHIP

The Japanese term which is translated "ancestor worship" is *sosen suhai.* Virtually all authorities agree that the translation is misleading but no good alternative has emerged [5, 6]. The term divides into parts. The word *suhai* means a deep, respectful feeling toward another person; it may be translated: admiration, adoration, idolization, or veneration, as well as worship. *Suhai* may be used to refer to respect toward highly esteemed living persons as well as toward the dead. *Sosen* are the objects of veneration. For any particular individual or family, the

sosen can be a rather large and inclusive group. Some are lineal ancestors, that is individuals from whom the family is descended. But also included are deceased children, relatives outside the formal hereditary line (including those by adoption or marriage), and non-relatives such as a respected teacher, friend, or lover. Deceased people who have no one else to care for them, that is, no family to perform the rituals, may also be included among a family's ancestors. Other *sosen* are ancestors of origin, that is the mythical deity from which the family is descended, as the emperor's family is descended from the Sun Goddess. There is, however, not a clear line between those kinds of ancestors, for mythical deities may once have been extraordinary humans now long deceased, and as we shall note, the goal of the rituals of ancestor worship is to transform the deceased human (*shirei*) into a god (*kami*).

SOCIAL FORMS OF GRIEF IN CULTURAL AND HISTORIC CONTEXT

All cultural forms have a socio-political context. Ancestor worship is intertwined with some important issues in Japanese political power and family structure. There has been a link between ancestor worship and Buddhism and with socio-political power at least since the Nara era (8th century) when there was a fusion of indigenous gods (*kami*) with Buddhism which had been imported from China and when the reverence for imperial ancestors was linked with reverence for one's own ancestors.

Two historical/political symbol systems are important. First, at the beginning of Tokugawa period (1603-1868), as a way of insuring there were no Christians in the country, everyone was required to register as a parishioner of a Buddhist temple where the main emotional and ritual connection was the ancestor rites. That historical connection continues as people return to their family's historic temple for funerals and subsequent rites. Second, in the Meiji Restoration (1868) an attempt was made to establish Shinto as the national religion, that is, State Shinto. That was not successful, partly because Buddhism's ancestor worship was so deeply integrated into the social fabric. But at that time, there was a direct link made between Shinto emperor worship *tenno suhai* and Buddhist ancestor worship *sosen suhai.* State Shinto ended in 1945, though it remains as a conservative political idea. When World War II dead were enshrined as *kami*, there was a great deal of controversy. Perhaps the closest Westerners can get to the linkage of political power and grief for the dead is the feeling we have in our bond with soldiers who have died in war. Lincoln's Gettysburg Address or the Vietnam Memorial both evoke the presence of the dead and make that presence a part of membership in the nation.

Ancestor worship was important in kinship bonds in Japan because the ancestors defined family connections. A common way of dividing Japanese households was into "succeeded houses" and "created houses." A succeeded house was headed by a successor to the previous head, usually the oldest son. The successor inherited the property as well as the duty to care for the ancestors. A created house was headed by a non-successor such as a second son. When someone in the created house died, that person became the first ancestor of the new house, setting the stage for further divisions in successive generations. So ancestors defined the individual's place in the family system as clearly a psychotherapist's genogram.

Japanese society underwent a series of radical changes after World War II, so the meaning of ancestor worship is now more ambiguous. At the end of World War II the tie between ancestor worship and loyalty to the emperor was officially severed. The end of the war also signaled a change in the family patterns as households were replaced by conjugal families, that is families based on the marriages with self-chosen partners. Yet the rituals continue to be observed in virtually all families. The historical meanings remain latently present much as the idea of heaven, hell, and judgment remain latently present for secular Westerners.

The historic centrality of ancestor worship should remind us that the theories about grief and the social forms in which grief is expressed is never apart from larger cultural mythology or from economic and political power [7]. The concept of the individual as a collection of temporary attachments, which are mourned and broken when they no longer instrumentally meet the individual's needs in the present, is just as integral to the social power of business corporations in consumer capitalism as was ancestor worship to imperial power. Just as we are defined in consumerism by the temporary satisfactions of products we buy, the dominant theories of grief in modernity define us by the attachments which serve us in the present. Just as advertisements define true living as the gusto of the purchasable moment, contemporary funerals "celebrate an individual life on earth rather than transport a soul into heaven" [8, p. 245]. Modern Western theories of grief and the social forms by which grief is expressed are as connected to the nuclear family and serial monogamy that characterizes the modern family system as was ancestor worship to the traditional household system. We wish to cut the bonds with the dead in the same way we wish to cut the bonds with our family of origin in order to found our own family which consists of a pair bond and dependent children. Taggart subtitled his report on his father's death "On saying goodbye to a deceased *former* (emphasis added) parent" [9]. We sever the bonds with a spouse after both death and divorce so we can enter a new monogamous pair bond which comprises the basic economic consumption unit and the success of which is supposed to provide life's personal meaning.

WESTERN PSYCHOLOGY AND JAPANESE PRACTICE

It is difficult at present to assess the meaning of ancestor worship in its changed historic context. But ancestor worship remains central to people's lives. Kaneko found that belief in the soul and ancestor worship were the most heavily loaded factors among those he found to be "pro-religious" [10]. Kazunari Yamamoto, a hospice physician in Osaka, told me that almost all families keep the forty-nine-day ritual described below, and that in the countryside most people do the full rituals, though in the urban areas about half the people now observe many ancestor rituals. He reports that in urban areas, about half the homes he visits have the buddha altars described later, but the absence of an altar may not indicate the degree the ritual is followed, because for those living in apartments, the altar may be in the home of parents or older siblings.

In this article we will trace the personal meanings of ancestor worship because we are comparing it to Western grief. Yanagawa and Abe note that Japanese religion has traditionally been communal, with the core of the religion being rituals which symbolically reinforce kin group interactions and national identity [11]. At the same time, however, there is also a strong personal element. Individuals undertake the disciplines of Buddhist meditation and people put their individual concerns on the prayer papers at Buddhist temples or buy charms for their personal problem at Shinto shrines. Most studies of Japanese religion focus on the communal. We can, however, for this discussion, bracket the communal and historical for just as there is an individualistic element in religion, there has always been a more personal element in ancestor worship. This personal element has received far less attention from scholars because the community-oriented aspect is much easier to observe, and allows Japanese people to talk about their similarities not their differences. But with the demise of the household system and imperial symbols, it would seem that the personal would remain the driving force in keeping the rituals.

The personal element is, however, difficult to study in Japanese culture because one is supposed to be so tuned to the other person that important meanings need not be spoken. To ask the Western question "How do you feel about that?" or "What is going on inside you?" is only to prove that the questioner cannot understand. To ask the direct question is to invade privacy most impolitely. It is especially impolite to ask about matters having to do with religion. There is a great deal of diversity in the various Japanese religions and talk of religion may bring out conflicting opinion, which is uncomfortable to Japanese. It is understandable, therefore, that researchers have studied kinship by asking what tablets are in whose altars and about cosmology by asking about folk beliefs, customs, and rituals. But we can use beliefs, customs, and rituals to understand the personal sphere on which Western studies of grief have focused. As Jung said, what is now internal and psychological in modern societies is, in traditional societies, external and objective in symbols, myths, and rituals [12]. That which the Japanese acted out, as a whole community, is in modernity played out in the individual psyche. So, perhaps we can gain some insight by looking for individual meaning in the ritual forms of ancestor worship, even though we cannot politely ask the Western questions directly. Kaneko makes the same point with consummate tact when he says that perhaps the rituals of Japanese religion comprise "a more complicated and differentiated extrinsic religiosity than that seen in the West" [10, p. 3].

AUTONOMY AND DEPENDENCE: CULTURAL VALUES AND GRIEF

The values and relationship patterns which undergird ancestor worship are as central to Japanese culture as are the values and relationship patterns which are the unexamined assumptions of modern theories of grief. Yamamoto and his colleagues diplomatically suggested that the presence of ancestor worship made Japanese grief different from Western grief [1]. The thesis of this article differs from that of Yamamoto and his colleagues. It appears that the dynamics of autonomy and dependence in Japanese and Western cultures are very different, that those dynamics are central in the different interpersonal bonds in the two cultures, and because bonds have different dynamics, grief has somewhat different features. But within that difference, we will find much in common between the rituals of ancestor worship and the dynamics of Western grief.

Western psychology assumes that individual autonomy is a good thing, that self-esteem is important to healthy functioning, and that both the body politic and the family system will function best when individual rights and satisfactions are maintained. The opposite of autonomy is dependence. In Western developmental theory, independence from parents is seen as normative ("separation anxiety disorder" was retained in DSM IV; the onset of the disorder may be up to 18 years old). Dependence is discouraged and negatively valued politically (welfare recipients are "dependent," but social security recipients have an "entitlement") and psychologically ("dependent personality disorder" remained a psychopathology until DSM IV; "autonomous personality disorder" has never been an official diagnosis) [13, 14]. Dependency is so undesirable in Western culture, that a few years after the introduction of the term, "codependency" became popularly regarded as one of the most widely distributed psychopathologies.

Dependence has been one of the defining conditions of "pathological grief" in Western grief theory [15, pp. 488-495; 16]. For example, while admitting her lack of data, Raphael assumes that dependent personalities are more prone to pathological grief:

> Although no specific risk factors have been demonstrated, it may be suggested that people with personal characteristics that lead them to form dependent, clinging, ambivalent relationships with their spouses are at greater risk of having a poor outcome [17, p. 225].

Parkes and Weiss are more certain:

> Some people may feel compelled to engage in perpetual mourning as tribute to the dead or to make restitution from some failure or sense of guilt. . . . There is some confirming evidence from systematic studies that both ambivalence and over-dependence predispose individual to chronic grief [18, p. 19].

Neither Raphael nor Parkes and Weiss find any grief pathology which is predisposed by over-autonomy.

In Japan, dependence, not autonomy is valued. Doi finds that *amae*, that is feelings and valuing of dependence, first known in the emotional state of the infant toward the nurturing mother, is the central feeling and cultural value in Japanese culture [19]. Thus membership (in the family, in the company, or in the nation), not individuality, defines the self. Watanabe [20], a Japanese child psychiatrist connects the psychology of Japanese culture to Western developmental concepts:

> Winnicott has said that there is no such thing as a baby; a baby is always a part of someone—the mother. His words remind us of the way the Japanese people feel deep at heart. Specifically, that there is no such thing as a man, as he is always a part of someone or something, be it his mother, his family, his motherland, or nature and the universe [21, p. 399; 22].

The bond individuals feel with ancestors is within the sense of dependence. The ancestors remain members of the family for the bonds are not severed.

Autonomy in the West and dependence in Japan are both held ambivalently. The independence of the solitary individual is maintained by not fulfilling the need to belong. The way out of loneliness is sought in the grandiose hope for "unconditional love" which was known in infancy, but does not exist in adult relationships. Thus, in the West, death is defined as "loss" from the point of view of the individual, and "grief work" is defined as accepting our essential separateness [23]. In the same way, dependence in Japan is held ambivalently. Anger at helplessness and guilt at the constant pressure of obligation can turn to rage which is undifferentiated or is directed against the self. Watanabe notes that dependence turned to rage and fear is expressed in a folk tale of a nurturing mother figure transformed into a murderous mountain witch [21]. She notes that this theme is similar to the idea of the castrating mother found in Freud's critique of the dependent relationships in the Victorian age. We will see that in the dependent bond with the ancestors, there is a constant fear that if the rituals are not maintained, the ancestors may turn against the living.

The sense of transcendence which is part of religious responses to death is defined by dependence in Japan and by autonomy in the West. Suzuki Diasetsu points out that whereas:

> at the basis of the ways of thinking and feeling of the Westerner there is the father, it is the mother that lies at the bottom of the Oriental nature. The mother enfolds everything in an unconditional love without difficulties or questioning. Love in the West always contains a residue of power. Love in the East is all-embracing. It is open to all sides. One can enter from any direction. One might see this as nothing other than a eulogy to *amae* [24, p. 77; 25, 26].

The Western religious response looks for more definition and more of a sense of otherness. The religious feeling of intimate belonging is, in Western transcendence, defined as "creature conscious" which is found at the depth of the experience of the "mysterium tremendum," that is, awe in the face of the "wholly other" [27]. Buber, writing about the Western transcendent moment, refutes Buddhist doctrine of no-self; he says that true transcendence maintains both the "I" and the "You." The individual self always remains, Buber says, half of the dialogic union.

> God embraces but is not the universe; just so, God embraces but is not my self. . . . there are I and You, there is dialogue, there is language, and spirit whose primary deed language is, and there is in eternity, the word [28, p. 143].

Hence in the West lines are more clearly drawn: You/me, God/human, earth/heaven, good/evil, living/dead.

With dependence the relationship of freedom and death, which is so central to western thinking, takes a quite different turn in Japan. The Japanese word *jiju* is usually translated freedom, Doi says, but it is never freedom from *amae*. In the West, the idea of freedom began with the distinction between free man and slave in ancient Greece. So freedom meant an absence of enforced obligation to another person and became tied to such ideas as the rights and dignity of man. Thus, the idea of freedom in the West serves as the basis of the precedence of the individual over the group, an idea that is impossible in Japan. The connection between freedom and death is central to Christianity.

> It is precisely here, I suspect, that the central message of Christianity lies. On this score Paul, the first Christian thinker, said: "Christ set us free, to be free men. Stand firm, then, and refuse to be tied to the yoke of slavery again."
>
> The possibility of man's being free, as is signified by the expression "freedom in Christ" arose, of course, because Christ himself was completely free. One might say that it was because he was too free that he was killed, and the faithful believe, moreover, that he even won freedom over death itself [19, p. 92].

Hence, in the West, death has come to mean freedom from human pain, but it also has meant traditionally the radical individuality of the last judgment. Doi notes that as Christianity lost ground, freedom had to be centered more and more

in the individual, so that "modern Western man is troubled by suspicion that freedom may have only been an empty slogan" [19, p. 94; 29, pp. 77-115]. As grief work has come to mean the freedom of the individual from the bonds to the deceased, it becomes one more element in the *anomy* which characterizes Western grief [30].

In Japan, on the other hand, the relationship of freedom and death works out differently. Since *amae* is the denial of the infant's separation from the mother, death is the reality which negates the denial. Thus, Doi says, the first time a Japanese person is experienced as an individual is when they die [19, p. 62]. But in such freedom remains obligation. Thus, the ancestor is free from obligation, but the survivor is not. So long as the survivor performs the rituals, the ancestor can continue the process of gaining independence from the living. Survivors, on the one hand are free to make the bond with the dead serve whatever purposes the survivors need, be that companionship, protection, or moral guidance. On the other hand, the survivor is not free to let go of the dead. If the survivor does not perform the prescribed rituals, the dead will turn into a harmful spirit, causing bad things to happen in the world of the living. Western psychological theory might find the dead's animosity toward the living to be a projection of the living's resentment toward the dead.

THE SPIRITS OF THE DEAD, NATURE AND LOCATION

The ancestors are those who can be reborn, though rebirth is not a personal matter in Japanese Buddhism, that is, there is not a particular set of past lives which can be identified for an individual. The point in the various meditation practices of Buddhism is to escape rebirth. The aim is nirvana, which means "to be blown out," as the wind blows out a candle. Nirvana in esoteric practice is achieved in life, for example, to be enlightened in Zen. Rebirth can cease because there is no karma left to pass on. If one is not to be reborn, it will be known within seven days after death. If one, however, is to be reborn, it will happen within forty-nine days after death. In Japanese Buddhism, the elite strive for nirvana in this life. But ordinary people become a buddha only when they die.

> "This gave a new and appealing meaning to the concept of nirvana, and the Japanese began to conceive of their ancestors as living in peace in the Pure Land or Western Paradise of the Amida Buddha" [5, p. 51].

Hence, the largest Buddhist sects are now Pure Land, relying on the merit and compassion of Amida Buddha to insure the individual's entrance into the Pure Land after death.

What is the nature of these spirits? The basic Japanese map of unseen reality in which the spirit of the dead is a buddha which is like a god (*kami*) may be difficult to grasp for those unfamiliar with Mahayana Buddhism. In this branch of

Buddhism, there are many buddhas. A god (*kami*) in the Japanese context is quite different from the Western idea. There are the *kami* of the place, such as a village, and the tutelary *kami* often of a family, and also the *kami* of the dead. Within this map of the unseen, neither buddhas, *kami*, nor spirits of the dead have substantial existence. That is, in the West, the soul has traditionally been a substance, an entity which after death exists independent of the body that once housed it. (So also God has a substance which could transubstantiate in the ritual of the Mass.) Long notes that Sakyamuni Buddha redefined reincarnation from a substance that passed through various lives.

> The human being or personality, therefore, is not to be understood essentially as an integral and enduring mind-body organism, but rather the manifestation of a highly complex succession of psychosomatic movement propelled along the temporal continuum by the force of *karman* [31, p. 141].

The individual is an interaction of the five skandhas, hence the teaching is "There is nothing that transmigrates and yet there is rebirth." How can this be? The question grows out of a misconstruing of the nature of *karman* which:

> is not a unified and independently existing entity that moves from life to life as a traveler might go from place to place. Rightly understood *karman* is the life process itself, the blending of energy, and form that coordinates an unending flow of life moments [31, p. 142].

Hence, when the individual who has died gradually merges with the generalized dead in the family—or as the *kami* of the individual melds into the family *kami*, and the family *kami* is part of the larger *kami* of the clan, community, and finally nation. It is as if we in the West were to understand the spirit of a dead person in the same way we understand "school spirit."

Where are these spirits? In common speech, *ano yo* (that world), as opposed to *kono yo* (this world) is the place of the ancestors and the *kami*. "That world" is the world on the other side of the *torii* (the orange gate in front of a Shinto shrine) or the other side of death.

> The world beyond cannot be described in any but equivocal phrases. Spatially it is both here and there, temporally both then and now. The departed and ancestors always are close by; they can be contacted immediately at the household shelf, the graveyard, or elsewhere. Yet when they return "there" after the midsummer reunion they are seen off as for a great journey. They are perpetually present. Yet they come to and go from periodic household fore-gatherings [32, p. 308; 33].

Some Japanese spirits are in a Pure Land, some in a kind of hell, but most spirits are still near the earth, available for interaction. Ritually they are thought

of as at the grave or on the altar where they are venerated. So the spirit may be contacted by addressing the stone or tablet, and may be called back in the *Bon* festival. Some of the dead go on to become *kami*. To some extent this is a function of where and by which rituals they are venerated (Buddhist or Shinto). The easiest way to become *kami* is to die in war or be a Shogun or emperor. But for others, the movement is slower and occurs at the end of the funeral rituals, which is either the thirty-third or fiftieth anniversary of death.

DYNAMICS OF GRIEF IN ANCESTOR WORSHIP

Transition from Person to Buddha

> The death of a person sets in motion a series of rites and ceremonies that culminates in the observance of a final memorial service, most commonly on the thirty-third or fiftieth anniversary of the death. Between a person's last breath and the final prayers said on his behalf, his spirit is ritually, and symbolically purified and elevated; it passes gradually from the stage of immediate association with the corpse, which is thought to be both dangerous and polluting, to the moment when it loses its individual identity and enters the realm of the generalized ancestral spirits, essentially purified [5, p. 69].

The names by which the dead are called shows this progression [5, p. 56]:

shirei (or *shir'yo*)—spirits of the newly dead
ni-hotoke—new buddhas
hotoke—buddhas
senzo—ancestors
kami—gods

The initial transformation from the newly dead to a new buddha is usually accomplished in the first set of rituals which takes forty-nine days. Much of what happens during this time would be described in the West as resolving grief. The dead are installed in their new status and there is a restructuring of the relationship between the survivor and the dead person.

Installing the Dead in Their New Status

During the forty-nine days there is very little time when people are left alone. There is lots of activity including: the service the night they die, the service during the cremation, and continual services and activities. So people are coming into the house all the time. People come in, go to the shrine, and bow and say whatever they are going to say in front of the shrine. Then they talk to the family members. There is a flurry of activity for forty-nine days, and at the end of that forty-nine days the dead person has safely become a *hotoke*. In an objective sense, the initial funeral rites are to help the dead to their new place. A woman told me that her mother said to her after her grandfather died, "Now you go to the funeral and you be good so we make sure that he gets over on to the other side."

A central part of the ritual is to inform the person that he/she is dead. As one Japanese person described it to me, the person is told, "You are dead, you have to go away now. We regret that you have to go away, but you can't stay here any more." If the dead continues hovering around because of some unfinished business, for example if the dead wish to get married and have children because it was not done before, the survivor will have to kindly tell the dead person "Well you can't do that now, it's time for you to go away. You need to go to the other side of that river." And if the dead person continues to hover around, then a priest might be called in and the priest will say: "You have to go away now." I asked in what other situations might someone be given a similar announcement. I was given the example of the message that might be delivered to a daughter after she gets married. She is told by her father or other members of the family "You're not a member of this family any more. You have to go away. You have to go to somebody else's house." And if she came back because she was in trouble, the father would say to her "Well you're not a member of this family any more." In other words, the social status change is told to the person so the person will know how to act appropriately. In this case, the dead are informed that they are dead and so they are to act appropriately.

People who attend the funeral do not offer condolence in the way Westerners do. Each person says, "Now you are experiencing how the end of life is."It is a formalized expression, used only on this occasion. In effect it is an announcement of the status. Thus, the issues of denial and acceptance of reality which are often a problem in modern American discussions of death is handled directly in a ritualized way. The dead are told, "You are dead now. You must go away. I am sorry." The living are told, "You are now experiencing what the end of life is." The ritual begins with reality orientation.

The cremation (in Japanese no euphemism is used; they say "burned") and placing the bones in the grave also provides a strong dose of reality. Cremation used to be restricted to the wealthy and powerful because it was expensive, but with Japan's present wealth, everyone can be cremated. The cremation is within a day or two after death. Within the first week after death, the family gathers and the bones are brought out on a tray. Two people, each with a set of chopsticks, pick up the bones together and put them into a pot. The pot is then taken and put in the family grave. As we will note in the section on graves, the bones of all family members are in the same pit, so the symbolism of the dead joining the other dead of the family is strong.

The forty-nine-day period may be extended if the death is not settled in the society. If, for example, the person died as a result of a crime or in an airplane accident, until the investigation is complete, the person cannot truly rest and

become a *hotoke*. In those cases people say, "My forty-nine days is not over." I observed an extreme example when I was in Japan. In a case that received wide national attention, a boy committed suicide because the school authorities were cooperating with other children to bully the child. Classmates held a mock trial and a mock funeral, and did other abusive acts. The mother fought for seven years until the national minister of education said the school was at fault and issued new guidelines. I was watching the news when the mother came on and said that now her son could rest because now justice had been done in this world.

Restructuring the Relationship

The issue of regret, which we saw as central to the dependence that structures interpersonal relationships in Japanese culture, is critical in the restructuring of the relationship between the dead and the survivors during this forty-nine days. In Japan, when a guest leaves instead of saying "Thank you for coming," the host apologizes, "I'm sorry. I should have done more for you." In other words, the core feeling is "I am not good enough in my relationship with you; I am never enough." Regret is a part of every dependent relationship, for the sense of obligation is never satisfied.

In his discussion of Freud's essay "Mourning and Melancholia," Doi [19] notes that Freud does not adequately account for the sense of sadness. The sadness of grief, he says, may not be for the loss, but may be regret at unsatisfied obligation and also regret that the mourner does not have the power to satisfy those obligations. Because dependence includes a sense of resentment, Doi says, the mourner feels guilt for feeling this way. Thus, Doi says, the reason Freud had a hard time making clear the place of self-reproach in depression and mourning is that he did not have a good idea of the positive place of dependence in relationships [19, pp. 124-125]. The survivor in saying good-bye to the dead, as in every good-bye, is saying "I'm sorry I should have done more for you." The survivor ends up with a feeling of sadness, which is not just sadness at being left, but it is the sadness of self-blame, that the relationship which was full of ambivalence did not get resolved so the survivor remains in the deceased's debt.

There are many folk beliefs about the newly dead as harmful wandering spirits. Indeed, *shirei* (newly dead) can be translated as ghost, in the sense of spook. Until the dead are safely *hotoke*, they may cause harm to the living, though most Japanese I talked to are reluctant to say what the harm might be, or to say why a person to whom they were so close would now harm them. Part of the reason for the ritual is to make sure the dead to not remain wandering spirits, dead spirits wander when no ritual is performed for them. One of the acts of compassion a person can do is to take in a spirit, that is perform rituals for spirits who have no one to care for them. At many Buddhist temples there are places where the stones of families with no survivors are kept. In front of the stones, is a place where rituals can be performed.

During the forty-nine days there is some sort of a reconciliation that takes place. I was told that it is very common for the dead to return in a dream and say, "It's OK, you did your best." In effect, the dead forgive or say the relationship is now even. If it is not in a dream, a person just feels at some point during that forty-nine days that "It's OK, that the deceased is happy and has forgiven me." When the survivor lets go of the ambivalences in the relationship, the deceased is free to go on and become a *hotoke*. Thus, for the first time the mutual obligation of *amae* is no longer in effect. Doi says that after the deaths of his parents that, "I became aware of them for the first time as independent persons, where hitherto their existence was real to me only insofar as they were my own parents" [19, p. 62].

Continuing Interaction with the Deceased

Once the deceased become a *hotoke*, he or she is available for active interaction. Very often when people are troubled apparently they feel the sense of *hotoke* to be near them. Often the dead come in a dream to comfort and to just be with the living. There is an expression which pictures the *hotoke* as "standing by the dream pillow." I was told a story of a very old family which badly wanted a son to carry on the family name. They kept having girls. When a son was finally born the mother reported that she knew it would be, because the night before her child was born, her father came to her in a dream and told her it would be a boy.

Ritual Places

Such interaction with the dead, however, is not simply a spontaneous event, springing, as we might describe it in the West, from the person's unconscious or from their wishes. Rather interaction with the deceased is regularized and ritualized. Indeed, properly ancestor worship is the ritual interaction with the dead.

Home Altars and Memorial Tablets

The focal points for ancestor worship in the home are the *butsudan*, the buddha altar and *kamidana*, the Shinto god shelf in the home, and the grave. The buddha altar is a cabinet with the implements of a Buddhist temple, incense burner, bell, candles, in which the *ahai*, (memorial tablets) for departed spirits are placed. In traditional homes, each morning Buddhist worship is performed in front of the buddha altar. Even though the central image on the altar is a more famous buddha, usually Kannon, Goddess of Mercy, the basic reason for having a buddha altar in the home is veneration of spirits of dead. The god shelf is the household shrine before which Shinto worship is performed. Worship before the buddha altar tends to be more intimate and personal, including memories of the dead.

When the dead becomes a *kami*, in some places the tablet is moved from the Buddha altar and some substitute for it is placed on the god shelf.

Traditional memorial tablets are upright lacquered wood plaques four to six inches high. Another type of tablet is unlacquered wood in a small container shaped like a small altar. Recently, rather than having tablets, some families keep a book on the altar with all the names of the deceased family members. Tablets are not always made for children and other minor members of the household. Sometimes temporary tablets for children are set adrift or burned; but some people keep tablets for children on the altar for many years. Written on the tablet is a posthumous name (*kaimyo*), death date, an indication of the age group the person belonged to when they died, and an often stereotyped, but occasionally highly personalized, reference to the person's qualities. The reverse side has the person's name in life and age at death, and often includes the relationship of the person to the head of the household. The tablets are counted as the most important family possession. There is a formula in newspaper reports of fires that the flames spread so quickly the residents only had time to save the memorial tablets [5, p. 84].

What is going on in the lives of people as they are in the presence of their ancestors on the buddha altar? The first answer is that they are engaged in a non-verbal ritual.

> The importance of ritual in religion is like the importance of performative acts in social life. If I am walking along the street and see a friend, I wave. I do this out of friendship, so my act helps both to express my warm friendly feelings and to reinforce the bond between the other person and myself. It is an act of communication, but I am not communicating information. Rather I impart a feeling and reinforce a relationship [34, p. 122].

The bell is rung, the hands are clapped, and the head is bowed. The ritual, the act, is the communication. A Japanese psychologist told me that she often prayed with her family to the ancestors. I asked what prayer means. She said that prayer for the Japanese is not like prayer for the Christians because Christians are asking for something. Prayer, even for the Japanese Christians, she said, is just being there and being with and feeling together. The Western concept of prayer is grounded in the distance between God and humans. But in Japan the people are never really separated from other people. Because, the psychologist explained, we are never really separated from other people, we are with the ancestors much as we would be with them when they are alive. It is not what we say to them as much as just being with them.

The question of the reality of the spirits and the ontological reality of the messages or presence communicated by the spirits seems to be more of a problem in Western culture than in Japan. In the West, the strong inner truth that the survivor is interacting with the dead usually calls forth the claim that the spirits are "real," that is, in some way, objectively present. We can understand the western difficulty if we look at the different communication styles that are part of the cultural value autonomy and the value of dependence.

> Westerners value directness. The sender of the message is basically responsible for its success. Skills of clarity and range of expressiveness are distinguishing points of good communication in Western culture. . . . Japanese place more emphasis on indirect, implicit communication. . . . It is a *high context* culture, meaning the situation, hierarchy of relationships and countless other factors are more important to the communication than the actual words being exchanged. Meanings are seldom conveyed explicitly, it is more or less the responsibility of the listener to interpret the meaning. Successful communication depends on skills of intuition and empathy, assets in a society where the priority is on integration, not differentiation among people [35, p. 13].

Thus, in Japan the survivor uses intuition and empathy in communications with the dead, but those are the same faculties which they have always used to communicate with the living. It may be that in the West such communication with the dead is more based on the survivor's skill in receiving communication than the deceased's skill in sending communication, but since Westerners are less adept at the former, they confuse it with the latter.

In an attempt to get inside the non-verbal ritual, Offner did a survey asking the purpose and motivation of the people performing the rites before their buddha alters [36]. Results are:

	An important element	Most important element
Comforting/cheering	81%	44%
Expressing gratitude	65%	29%
Maintaining tradition	34%	10%
Reporting	31%	
Showing respect	30%	8%
Sense of personal satisfaction	23%	6%
Fulfilling responsibility	12%	
Petitioning for favors	12%	
Apologizing	7%	
Averting punishment	5%	

The survey list was designed by a Christian and some respondents added elements not on his survey:

—eliminating one's own evil karma
—self-reflection
—opportunity for family fellowship

Expressing gratitude, showing respect, and fulfilling responsibility, and probably reporting are expressions of *amae*. Comfort and cheering would seem to be similar to the Western idea of solace or consolation. I have shown elsewhere that one of the functions of the continuing bond with the dead is solace [36, 37].

A Japanese woman whose two-year-old daughter had died seventeen years earlier, talked about the daughter's tablet: "I have it because I want to keep her near at hand" [5, p. 139]. And a woman visiting the succeeded family home said it was good to be back. The researcher asked her why; the building was new, not the one she grew up in, and all her siblings were gone.

> She turned to the *butsudan* and said it was because of all the people in there, especially her father. Then she turned to another wall of the room and began pointing out photographs of the ancestors, explaining to me which of them had tablets in the butsudan. She obviously felt warm and close to the altar and to the tablets it contained [5, p. 131].

Plath quotes a novel about an illegitimate daughter who returned to her father's house as a widow, for there was nowhere else for her to go. She was treated badly. She comforted herself with the dreamy memory of her father and would sometimes speak to his photograph which was on the buddha altar [32, p. 309].

Yamamoto et al. said the altar with its tablets was a transitional object [1, p. 1664; 22]. The phrase was first used to describe things like a child's security blanket. Volkan noted that such transitional objects are common in grief [38]. He called them "linking objects." But the concept of transitional or linking objects does not convey the lively, personal relationship between the living and the dead which takes place before the buddha altar. Yamamoto and his colleagues give us a sense of the interaction:

> If you would for a moment give up your Judeo-Christian beliefs and attitudes about one's destiny after death and pretend to be a Japanese, you might be able to feel how you are in direct daily communication with your ancestors. The family altar would be your "hotline." As such, you could immediately ring the bell, light incense, and talk over the current crisis with one whom you have loved and cherished. When you were happy, you could smile and share your good feelings with him. When you were sad your tears would be in his presence. With all those who share the grief he can be cherished, fed, berated, and idealized, and the relationship would be continuous from the live object to the revered ancestor [1, p. 1663].

The dead are addressed in the same language and with the same emotion as when they were living. Smith tells of old man who was nearly deaf with whom he often passed time [5]. Smith was away when the old man died and when Smith returned, he asked if he could burn incense at family altar. The wife of the house put one of the cakes Smith had brought on a dish and took it to the altar. She knelt and said loudly, "Grandfather, Mr. Smith is here" [5, p. 143].

Many of the interactions in front of the buddha altar are continuations of the bond which was there before the person died. Offerings on the altar are often foods or flowers that the deceased liked [32, p. 308]. Smith gives a report of a widow at an anniversary ritual, who had a chocolate cake—her husband's favorite—with decorative inscription saying "Happy Anniversary." The first slice was placed at his tablet on altar and the rest served to guests. Smith [5, p. 141] constructs a composite story of a young man about to take college entrance exams going to the altar where his mother's tablet is and there he may ask for her to look after him as he takes the exam. If he passes, he may say, "Thanks to you, everything went well. Thank you." If he failed, he will apologize and promise to try harder next time. Smith notes that these interactions are entirely within the developmental phase-appropriate son-mother relationship, for if the mother were living, getting him to pass the exams would be the central focus of their relationship at that time in his life.

The dead still care for the living, not by granting favors like Western saints, but in the sense that the dead share joys of any positive achievement of a family member, and indeed may be given credit for the success. In a TV drama about a recently widowed woman and her twenty-year-old daughter, the daughter waits for letter telling her she has been hired for a job she really wants. When the letter arrives, she opens it,

> clasps the letter to her breast, beams tearfully to her mother, and hurries into the living room. There she kneels before the altar, opens its doors, holds up the letter to her father's photograph and tablet, and bows low. The camera pans to the mother's tear-streaked face [5, p. 142].

Some differences between how Japanese and Westerners relate to the dead include the differences in child-rearing techniques based on dependence and shame and those based on autonomy and guilt. Plath quotes a sociology textbook written in the early sixties which assumes it is a common experience to be:

> dragged by dad or mom to the front of the household shelf and asked "Do you think you can give any excuse to the ancestors for doing that?" The shelf is associated with the household and with society, so that rebelling before it is like rebelling against the whole world [32, p. 312].

A Japanese psychologist told me that when children have been bad, instead of being sent to their room as an America, they may be sent into the room with the buddha altar and told to sit there and reflect on their behavior in the presence of their ancestors. When I asked one Japanese woman about this discipline technique she said it happened to some of her friends, but, "My mother was modern."

Other cultures, of course, make use of the ancestors in child rearing. When I told a colleague about children being shamed in front of the shrine, he put his hands in the air, imitated his grandmother's accent, and said, "It is good your grandfather died that he should live to see this day."

Graves

Although the stones in the *cemeteries* around Buddhist temples or among the rice fields remind us of Western graveyards, they are quite different. Each grave is for a family. There is a wide variation in the complexity of each grave, but each has an upright stone on which is carved the family name. Names of individuals may be inscribed on the side or back of an upright stone, or on stones set along the sides of a small area in front of the upright stone, but sometimes only the family stone marks the place. Near the front of the grave is a stone incense burner. Behind each grave there is a stand for holding *stupas*, boards about eight feet high with the top cut in the shape of a Buddhist *stupa*, on which are written the name of the recently dead and the date, and on the back, who gave the board. *Stupas* are placed at the grave when the dead person is installed there. The *stupas* clacking in the breeze, together with the birds, create the soundscape of a cemetery.

Bodies are cremated. In old-style cemeteries, no bones are in the graves. In the newer style there is a large pit in which bones of all the family members are put. Thus, the dead join the ancestral dead in the physical sense as well as in a spiritual sense. The grave is a ritual site. This is where visits are made and where prayers are said for the soul. The grave is cleaned at *bon* and at the equinoxes. Ordinarily flowers are offered and water is poured over the stone.

As I walked through a cemetery attached to a temple, my guide whose grandmother had died a few months earlier pointed to the stone slab in the ground and said her grandmother was "here." She then bowed with her hands together in the ritual gesture of prayer.

Although the graves are the focal points at *bon*, the festival described below, at the temple where we stayed, there was a steady stream of visitors to the cemetery. People would take a bucket from a rack, fill it with water, and wash the grave, described in Japanese as "cooling the spirit." Then they would bow and burn incense. Usually they brought a gift or flowers. As are the offerings on the buddha altar, the gift on the grave is often something the person liked when alive. Canned drinks ranged from beer to carrot juice. Most of the burners at the graves had stubs of incense sticks and many had gifts and flowers, evidence, it seemed, of recent visits. An old woman explained:

> For us old people, visiting the graves is like going to the pictures and so on for the youngsters. You go and meet your dead; you can see their faces in your

> mind's eye and you can talk to them—you don't get any reply, of course, but it feels good [32, p. 309].

Ritual Time: *O Bon*

O Bon, the major summer festival in Japan, celebrates the temporary return of the dead to visit the living. The rituals all have as their purpose the welcoming of spirits of the dead into the village. Spirits of people who have died since the last *bon*, have a special place in the ceremony. The newly dead are welcomed back in some places with "You must be very sad," indicating that the family understands that it is as hard for the dead to leave the world of the living as it is for the survivors who are left behind.

> The periodic merging of the two worlds (living and dead) strengthens the sense of continuity of the house and reassures the dead of the living's continuing concern for their well being. Neither death nor time can weaken or destroy the unity of the members of the house [5, p. 104].

Smith quotes answers to a survey on peoples thoughts at *bon:* A sixty-three-year-old woman said, "Maybe they come and maybe they don't: I feel that they are here." A sixty-seven-year-old man said, "I live in their presence and make a welcoming fire early and a sending-off fire late at *bon*, so that the ancestors will stay longer" [5, p. 150]. When I asked Kazunari Yamamoto, the hospice physician, what I should understand about ancestor worship he said he feels the presence of his ancestors, especially at *bon* and at New Year. Of their presence he said: "I don't feel so lonely."

As with other parts of ancestor worship, it is difficult to define the meaning of *bon* in the modern world. To the extent that the public parts are not celebrated, the *bon* ceremony has become privatized. That means that the ceremony takes on a more psychological character, because the remaining reason for the rituals are in the personal relationship with the dead. In the countryside, the traditions are kept by almost everyone. In many urban areas, the public parts of *bon* are hardly celebrated now, or have become simply summer activities. Some of the younger generation now use the days to travel abroad. Yet, virtually everybody who lives in urban areas, especially Tokyo, thinks of themselves as from somewhere else. At *bon* there are huge traffic jams as people go back to their ancestral home towns. Kazunari Yamamoto estimated that 50 percent of the people living in urban areas keep the *bon* ritual, either by celebrating it in their own home or by going back to their home town.

In smaller towns these days it is a more informal family gathering. Some family members have come from the big city, and some have come from the realm of the dead. Neither are ever really far away. Different varieties of squash are brought into the house, and chopsticks are stuck into them so that they can be

put together as a decoration. That is a sign that the ancestors can come. Then the ancestors come onto the buddha altar and are made welcome. Candles are lit and the food is offered. It feels good, a person told me, to have them around.

Especially around *bon*, the TV programs and the newspapers are full of stories about the dead coming back. In a TV program which was described to me, a man whose wife had died described how sad he was and that he was unreconciled to the death until he came home one day to find his house had been cleaned. And after that every day when he came home his house had been cleaned and it was obviously the spirit of his dead wife who was coming back to clean his house for him. He said that he felt that now she was happy. As is typical on Japanese television, part of the program was devoted to audience comments. The audience responded that it was a very good thing because now the dead person was happy and he was happy.

Even though the public festival has largely fallen into disuse, we will describe the traditional ceremonies, as a way of understanding what now seems more internal and psychological. There is a great deal of local variation, but we can give the typical, though not a normative, description (the following relies heavily on Gilday [33] and Smith [5]).

The festival takes place over three days in late summer. After sunset on the first day, lanterns at the family grave sites are lit and incense burned to invite the spirits home. The color of these lanterns varies depending on whether a family has lost a member during the preceding year, if so, white, otherwise, red or blue/green. There is one lantern for each deceased member still remembered by someone in the household. Fires are lit at the doorway of the house to guide the spirits. In some areas the entire village forms a torchlight procession, singing and dancing through the village to those homes that have lost a member in the previous year.

In some places a temporary spirit shrine is built outside the house as a shelter for these spirits during their visit. In other places this temporary shrine is placed inside the home, or in some families, the buddha altar is thought to hold and shelter the spirits. In early evening family members gather to welcome back the spirits of the dead who are greeted very formally, just as honored guests would be.

On the second day of *bon*, people visit graves again, and may go to temple. A Buddhist priest makes rounds to each family in the parish, and offers a brief prayer at each house, but the day is a family affair and the priest may not even be invited in.

On the third day, the spirits depart. There is a large gathering and a dance in which the spirits are entertained before their departure. "Many of the songs that accompany the dance are laments, expressing the community's regrets that the visit is drawing to a close" [33, p. 296]. And then the spirits return to the *kami* realm. In some places, the gathering just disbands, so it seems, the dead can find their own way back. In other places lanterns are lit by individual families to send the spirits off. Formal farewells are said with expressions such as "Come back next year." In some areas, a candlelight procession moves

> toward the river where one by one representatives of each household place small boats, bearing the candles, into the current. As far as the eye can see the flickering flotilla plies on. When the candle goes out, it is said, the spirit has been released to the other world [33, p. 296].

CONCLUSION

Japanese ancestor worship provides sophisticated theory and ritual to accomplish what is described in the West as the "resolution of grief." Yamamoto, Okonogi, Iwasaki, and Yoshimura suggested that grief might be different in Japan because ancestor worship encouraged the "cultivation of the idea of the presence of the deceased" as ancestors [1, p. 1663]. But Yamamoto and his colleagues accepted that the "work of mourning" in the West is to assimilate the "reality" that the person is permanently absent. They note correctly that pathology within that idea of grief work is defined in terms of attempts to maintain contact with the dead person.

The psychological theory to which Yamamoto and his colleague objected has now been challenged by Western scholars. There appears to be an emerging consensus among scholars that survivors seldom server the bonds, and that survivors maintain an active role of the inner representation of the dead in their ongoing life. Thus, the healthy resolution of grief in the West has many similarities to the phenomena seen in Japanese ancestor worship. The thesis of this article is a variation on that of Yamamoto and his colleagues. We have found that the place of autonomy/dependence and the value each culture places on autonomy/dependence, creates differences in the way each culture constructs interpersonal bonds and the way each culture defines personal identity. Because the autonomy/dependence issue creates differences in bonds among people, it creates somewhat different dynamics in transforming and then continuing the bond with the dead.

Yet, even though we have seen differences between the dynamics of ancestor worship and those of Western grief, many of the interactions and feelings we have seen in ancestor worship are very similar to those in the West. The reason for the similarity, I would venture, is that instead of the "either/or" we in the West find between autonomy and dependence, it is "both/and." Perhaps in practice we in the West are not so autonomous as our psychological theory would have us, and when we are dependent, we are not so pathological as clinical diagnoses would make us. Perhaps what we see in Japan is grief where the balance is tipped toward dependence and what we see in the West is grief where the balance is tipped toward the autonomy. But those are only guesses. More detailed study of contemporary Japanese individual and family meanings in their relationship to the dead

and more detailed study of autonomy/dependence in grief in the West should clarify the cross-cultural similarities and differences in grief. If in examining Japanese ancestor worship, we can see our own understanding and practice of grief more clearly, and if in doing so, we can help the Japanese to appreciate the psychological acuity of rituals that seem old-fashioned to many in the younger generation, I hope other scholars and clinicians will find reason enough to accept the invitation to intercultural dialogue that Yamamoto and his colleagues extended nearly three decades ago.

REFERENCES

1. J. Yamamoto, K. Okonogi, T. Iwasaki, and S. Yoshimura, Mournings in Japan, *American Journal of Psychiatry, 125*, pp. 1661-1665, 1969.
2. M. Stroebe, M. M. Gergen, K. J. Gergen, and W. Stroebe, Broken Hearts or Broken Bonds: Love and Death in Historical Perspective, *American Psychologist, 47*, pp. 1205-1212, 1992.
3. M. Stroebe, Coping with Bereavement: A Review of the Grief Work Hypothesis, *Omega, Journal of Death and Dying, 26*, pp. 19-42, 1992.
4. P. Silverman, D. Klass, and S. Nickman (eds.), *Continuing Bonds: Understanding the Resolution of Grief*, Taylor & Francis, New York, in press.
5. R. J. Smith, *Ancestor Worship in Contemporary Japan*, Stanford University Press, Stanford, California, 1974.
6. C. B. Offner, Continuing Concern for the Departed, *Japanese Religion, 11*:1, pp. 3-16, 1979.
7. P. J. Geary, *Living with the Dead in the Middle Ages*, Cornell University Press, Ithaca, New York, 1994.
8. T. Walter, Natural Death and the Noble Savage, *Omega, Journal of Death and Dying, 30*:4, pp. 237-248, 1994-95.
9. M. Taggart, Salvete et Valete: On Saying Goodbye to a Deceased Former Parent, *Journal of Marital and Family Therapy, 6*:2, pp. 117-122, 1980.
10. S. Kaneko, Dimensions of Religiosity among Believers in Japanese Folk Religion, *Journal of the Scientific Study of Religion, 29*:1, pp. 1-18, 1990.
11. K. Yanagawa and Y. Abe, Cross-Cultural Implications of a Behavioral Response, *Japanese Journal of Religious Studies, 10*:4, pp. 289-307, 1983.
12. C. K. Jung, *Psychology and Religion*, Yale University Press, New Haven, Connecticut, 1938.
13. S. Coontz, *The Way We Never Were: American Families and the Nostalgia Trap*, Basic, New York, 1992.
14. M. Lerner, *Surplus Powerlessness: The Psychodynamics of Everyday Life . . . and the Psychology of Individual and Social Transformation*, Humanities Press, Atlantic Highlands, New Jersey, 1 991.
15. T. A. Rando, *Treatment of Complicated Mourning*, Research Press, Champaign, Illinois, 1993.
16. E. K. Rynearson, Psychotherapy of Pathologic Grief: Revisions and Limitations, *Psychiatric Clinics of North America, 10*:3, pp. 487-499, 1987.

17. B. Raphael, *The Anatomy of Bereavement*, Basic Books, New York, 1983.
18. C. M. Parks and R. Weiss, *Recovery from Bereavement*, Basic Books, New York, 1983.
19. T. Doi, *The Anatomy of Dependence*, J. Bester (trans.), Kodansha International, Tokyo, 1973.
20. H. Watanabe, Establishing Emotional Mutuality Not Formed in Infancy with Japanese Families, *Infant Mental Health Journal, 8*:4, pp. 398-408, 1987.
21. H. Watanabe, Difficulties in Amae: A Clinical Perspective, *Infant Mental Health Journal, 13*:1, pp. 26-33, 1992.
22. D. W. Winnicott, Transitional Objects and Transitional Phenomena, *International Journal of Psychoanalysis, 34*, pp. 89-97, 1953.
23. P. Reiff, *Freud: The Mind of the Moralist*, Viking, New York, 1959.
24. D. T. Suzuki, Toyo Bunmei No Kontei ni Aru Mono, *Asahi Shimbun*, December 22, 1958.
25. D. T. Suzuki, *Studies in Zen*, C. Humphreys (ed.), Delta, New York, 1955.
26. D. T. Suzuki, *An Introduction to Zen Buddhism*, Grove Press, New York, 1964.
27. R. Otto, *The Idea of the Holy*, J. W. Harvey (trans.), Oxford University Press, New York, 1923.
28. M. Buber, *I and Thou*, W. Kaufmann (trans.), Charles Scribner's Sons, New York, 1970.
29. R. F. Baumeister, *Meanings of Life*, Guildford, New York, 1991.
30. E. Durkheim, *Suicide: A Study in Sociology*, J. A. Spaulding and G. Simpson (trans.), G. Simpson (ed.), Macmillan, New York, 1951.
31. J. Bruce Long, Reincarnation, in *Death, Afterlife, and the Soul*, L. E. Sullivan (ed.), Macmillan, New York, pp. 138-145, 1987.
32. D. W. Plath, Where the Family of God is the Family: The Role of the Dead in Japanese Households, *American Anthropologist, 66*:2, pp. 300-317, 1964.
33. E. T. Gilday, Dancing with the Spirit(s): Another View of the Other World in Japan, *History of Religions, 32*:3, pp. 273-300, 1993.
34. N. Smart, *Worldviews: Crosscultural Explorations in Human Beliefs* (2nd Edition), Prentice-Hall, Englewood Cliffs, New Jersey, 1995.
35. P. Howe, Speaking a Different Language, *Kansei Time Out*, pp. 12-14, 1994.
36. D. Klass, *Parental Grief: Solace and Resolution*, Springer, New York, 1988.
37. D. Klass, Solace and Immortality: Bereaved Parents's Continuing Bond with Their Children, *Death Studies, 17*, pp. 343-368, 1993.
38. V. Volkan, *Linking Objects and Linking Phenomena: A Study of the Forms, Symptoms, Metapsychology, and Therapy of Complicated Mourning*, International Universities Press, New York, 1981.

Direct reprint requests to:

Dennis Klass, Ph.D.
Webster University
470 E. Lockwood Ave.
St. Louis, MO 63119-3194

Buddhism and Abortion in Contemporary Japan: Mizuko Kuyō *and the Confrontation with Death*

BARDWELL SMITH

Facts of publication: *Smith, Bardwell. 1992. "Buddhism and Abortion in Contemporary Japan:* Mizuko Kuyō *and the Confrontation with Death," from* Buddhism, Sexuality, and Gender, *65–89. Edited by José Ignacio Cabezón. Albany: State University of New York.* *This article revised from an article published in* Japanese Journal of Religious Studies *15(1) (1988). Reprinted with the permission of* Japanese Journal of Religious Studies, *Nanzan Institute for Religion and Culture.*

Drawing on the research of a psychologist (Robert Jay Lifton) and anthropologist (Victor Turner), Bardwell Smith considers the psychosocial processes of grief, guilt, and healing after abortion in contemporary Japan. The mizuko kuyō, *a memorial service for unborn children, is one means of facilitating this process. Smith shows how it can function as a redressive rite in dealing with an experience that evokes considerable shame, isolation, and suffering among Japanese women.*

Compare this account with that of William R. LaFleur in Liquid Life: Abortion and Buddhism in Japan *(Princeton, NJ: Princeton University Press, 1992).*

About the author: Dates: *1925– , Springfield, MA, U.S.A.* **Education:** *B.A., Yale University; M.A., Yale University; Ph.D., Yale University.* **Field(s):** *religious studies; anthropology of religion; Buddhism and society.* **Career:** *Professor of Religion and Asian Studies, 1960–present, Carleton College.* **Publications:** *with Frank E. Reynolds and Gananath Obeyesekere,* The Two Wheels of Dharma: Essays on Theravada Buddhism *(American Academy of Religion Monograph Series, 1972); editor, with John C. Perry,* Esssays on Tang Society *(Brill, 1976); editor,* Religion and the Legitimation of Power in Sri Lanka *(Anima, 1978); with George Elison,* Warlords, Artists and Commoners: Japan in the Sixteenth Century *(University of Hawaii, 1981); with Holly Reynolds,* The City as a Sacred Center: Essays on Six Asian Contexts *(Brill, 1987); editor,* Essays on Gupta Culture *(Motilal Banarsidass, 1993).* **Additional:** *American Council of Learned Studies research grant in Buddhist Studies, School of Oriental and African Studies, London University, 1972–1973; Fulbright research grant, Kyoto University, 1986–1987; National Endowment for the Humanities Collaborative Research Grant, 1991–1994; Memberships: American Society for the Study of Religion; American Academy of Religion; Association for Asian Studies. "Since 1986 I have been doing collaborative research with Elizabeth Harrison of the University of Arizona on the problem of child loss for Japanese women and Buddhist responses to abortion. We are hoping to complete a book on this subject. The topic involves much attention to ritual, though we seek to put the problem of ritualistic approaches to it in a larger social and religious context with Japan."*

The fact of death is the central human preoccupation. Other preoccupations are often skillful diversions from coping with one's mortality. In Reinhold Niebuhr's words, the human problem is not that we are finite but that we have trouble living with our finitude. To put the matter more directly, the central problem of life is not death but learning how to die. This chapter is about the confrontation with death set within the context of present-day Japan. It deals with the reality of death in the form of abortion, miscarriage, or stillbirth. It is not about abortion or infant death *in general*, but about the experience of mortality in personal terms. In particular, it is about the mother's experiencing of death, whether or not this death has been willed by her. And, it is also about factors within Japanese society that contribute to the dilemma surrounding abortion specifically.

Second, this chapter deals with various Japanese Buddhist reactions to the widespread modern phenomenon of abortion and raises questions about these responses. The primary response to this phenomenon is known as *mizuko kuyō: mizuko* meaning water child or children, referring normally to an aborted fetus (induced or spontaneous) but also to stillborn infants and those who died soon after birth. *Kuyō* itself is a memorial service conducted in most cases by Buddhist priests for the spirits of *mizuko* and intended in part as consolation to the mother, as the one most directly affected, but often with other members of the family in mind as well. Understanding the many features of this widespread movement throughout Japan provides one example in the modern period of how diversely Buddhism and gender are found to be interrelated.

Although based on research that began intensively in 1986 and . . . extend[ed] through 1994, this [essay] is not primarily a report on that research but an initial attempt to view the contemporary phenomenon of *mizuko kuyō* against a wider socioreligious background in modern Japan. . . .[1]

The primary research is of several kinds. It includes extensive interviews with temple priests and women who have experienced the loss of a fetus or child. We have also distributed over 3000 questionnaires to worshippers who have participated in memorial services (*kuyō*) for aborted or stillborn children (*mizuko*). Beyond this, we have access to data being collected on *mizuko kuyō* by sociologists at two major Japanese universities and to more than 1500 questionnaires completed by women at an important temple in Kyoto. Finally, we have collected sizeable amounts of published materials in Japanese that deal with abortion and *mizuko kuyō* directly or seek to relate those to wider social and religious issues of both a contemporary and historical nature. These materials will be analyzed in the projected volume based upon this research.

THE GENERAL CONTEXT

In the *Japanese Journal of Religious Studies*, published by Nanzan University in Nagoya, two articles on *mizuko kuyō* have appeared in recent years, one by Anne Page Brooks (1981) and, in December 1987, a translation of an essay published two years before in Japanese by Hoshino Eiki and Takeda Dōshō.[2] Surprisingly, this is the extent of serious research on the subject yet to appear in English. The article by Anne Brooks is a good overview of the scene. The essay by Hoshino and Takeda is helpful in placing *mizuko kuyō* within the general conceptual framework of Japanese attitudes toward the spirits of the dead, in providing reasonably current statistics on abortions in Japan, and particularly in making careful distinctions between the meaning of abortion or infanticide (*mabiki*) within traditional life in Tokugawa Japan (1603–1867) and the meaning of *mizuko kuyō* today. This paper is addressed to the contemporary scene. Although the differences between traditional and contemporary Japanese social systems are complex, among the major assertions of the Hoshino article is the following: that with the gradual devolution of the traditional family system in modern urban areas the responsibility for abortion, which used to be shared by the local community in Tokugawa or Edo Japan, must now often "be borne in secret completely by the individual."[3]

It is precisely this "broken connection," as Robert Jay Lifton uses the term, that needs examining, not only with respect to earlier family systems and communal forms of support but also compared with former ways of relating death to life.[4] Arising out of his extensive interviews with survivors from several contexts (including Hiroshima, the Chinese cultural revolution, and the Vietnam War), Lifton's studies have focused on the importance and difficulty of grieving, on the process by which one confronts death (or "death equivalents"), and on symbols relating death to the continuity of life.

> Images of death begin to form at birth and continue to exist throughout the life cycle. Much of that imagery consists of death equivalents—image-feelings of separation, disintegration, and stasis. These death equivalents evolve from the first moments of life, and serve as psychic precursors and models for later feelings about actual death. Images of separation, disintegration, and stasis both anticipate actual death imagery and continue to blend and interact with that imagery after its appearance.[5]

Lifton's research makes clear the importance of psychoanalytic studies that take seriously the human life process as well as an individual's feelings, such as anxiety, guilt, rage, and violence, which often accompany the confrontation with death or any of its equivalents. At the same time, his research indicates the equal importance of images of continuity, or life equivalents such as connection, integrity, and movement. Whereas modern existence is frequently the experience of broken connections of various sorts, Lifton believes that life-promoting connections are possible *provided* one confronts and learns to handle factors within human community that resist the facing of death, or death equivalents, such as injustice, collapse of communal order, profound disillusionment, and the like. Lifton's twofold approach (that is, of realism in the face of death equivalents and hope if these are seriously encountered), is central, implicitly, to the theme of this [essay] and the issue of Buddhism and gender.

Thus far, no attention has been paid to the implications of these sorts of findings on the widespread modern social and religious phenomenon known as *mizuko kuyō*. This seems ironic, because at the heart of this phenomenon lies both the experience of death and difficulties encountering this death. Lifton's research confirms my own suspicion that the problems experienced with abortion in Japan are not only more serious than often is acknowledged, but that complex factors exist within Japanese society related to abortion which are rarely discussed. It is part of this [essay]'s purpose to identify some of these.

As is commonly done by the media, one can easily dismiss the phenomenon of *mizuko kuyō* as another form of *shōbai* or business enterprise. Without question, there has been the tendency for it to become commercialized in many circles. Along with this there has been the inclination of some priest-practitioners to capitalize on feelings of guilt and fear that women frequently experience following abortion and to attribute many subsequent personal and family problems to the decision to abort. Our findings also reveal the problematic nature of economic support for many temples, thereby forcing some priests into activities even they may question. The present economic basis of temple support in Japan thus, in our estimation, is an important subject on which careful research needs to be done. As far as we are aware, no systematic studies exist.

But on whatever grounds one can legitimately question certain forms of *mizuko kuyō* practice, one quickly encounters the emotional problems that significant numbers of women attest to following abortions (in some cases years afterward). Our interviews reveal both the diversity of these experiences and the varied ways in which temple priests and sympathetic lay people have responded. The more deeply one looks, the more evident it becomes not only that widespread abortion creates genuine problems within Japanese society but that this society in fact has made it almost inevitable that these problems exist. Whereas problems connected with abortion are hardly unique to Japan, there are peculiar features here that one does not find elsewhere, or in earlier times within Japan. Hoshino and Takeda are right, for instance, in stressing that although early death was common in previous times there are new ingredients in the modern experience: for one thing, the very number of abortions today; for another, the more private nature of the experience and hence the greater emotional burden upon individuals. In Lifton's sense, the experiencing of this death becomes even more difficult within the framework of a vastly broken religious and cosmological world-view. The old connections are more problematic today. And this raises the interesting question as to whether the extraordinary public attention being paid to *mizuko* (whether aborted or stillborn) in Japanese society has arisen partly because the "image" of *mizuko* itself may have become yet another symbol of the broader social sense of disconnection.

The basic thrust of this [essay] therefore is to begin raising questions about what lies behind the complex phenomenon of *mizuko kuyō*. First, it will discuss the anomalous situation of birth control in Japan, in which abortion is the most effective of the widely used methods, with the result that the number of abortions is unusually high for a society like Japan. The very lack of significant procreative choices for most Japanese women contributes to the many problems not being adequately faced by the medical profession or other segments of Japanese society. Therefore, the [essay] also looks at the emotional needs women frequently have following abortion and asks what these represent. Third, as the *kuyō* or memorial service is the most common response offered by Buddhist temples, its general nature is examined briefly. Furthermore, because ritual and cosmology are necessarily related, the [essay] discusses certain forms of traditional Buddhist cosmology, especially the omnipresent Jizō figure and the concept of the six paths (*rokudō*) and asks about the appeal of these ancient ideas within a modern and "broken" era. Finally, the [essay] concludes by questioning whether the present Buddhist response addresses itself to certain deeper and often unstated grievances felt by Japanese women. In the context of this discussion other forms of ritual that seek to confront resentment and anger in particular will be mentioned. A concern of this kind is akin to Lifton's conviction that the life-cycle process and the rituals related to it help to create forms of renewal, with social as well as personal meaning, *only* when they address the pervasive experience of broken connections, in Japan or anywhere else.

THE PARADOX OF ABORTION: A WORLD OF NECESSITY AND SORROW

To enter the world of abortion is to observe a scene of resolution undermined by doubt, a scene of both conflict and relief. As one perceptive viewer of this world has put it: "This is the heart of the struggle. The quality of life pitted against life. Whichever we choose, we lose. And that, too, is part of being human. That too is the dilemma of abortions."[6] It is no longer surprising to hear American or European women, who have gone through an induced abortion and who affirm a woman's right to do so, express the emotional difficulty of such an experience, even to hear them reliving spiritual or psychic pain for years after the fact. It is clearly more anguishing still to absorb, through miscarriage or stillbirth, the death of a child one wished to have, let alone the death of an older child. Each instance is unique, though support from those who have encountered similar sorrow helps in offsetting isolation. The pain of grieving, inevitably personal, becomes more bearable when it can be shared, when it becomes less private.

In modern Japan the world of abortion is both similar to that of some other countries and very different. Although abortion has been legal in the United States only since 1973, Japan passed the Eugenic Protection Law in 1948 (with revisions in 1949 and 1952), making abortion legally possible for the first time. And yet, approaches to birth control exist here that are radically different than those found in most modern societies. As many studies reveal, there are but three primary methods of birth control practiced in Japan. *One* is the rhythm method, which lacks reliability. The *second* is the condom, which can be reliable if used properly, but this means of contraception frequently keeps the woman in a position of dependence on the male partner. The *third* method is by far the most effective, namely, abortion, thereby setting the stage for widespread emotional unrest—especially when adequate contraceptive alternatives are minimal. It therefore is accurate to say that the procreative choices available to Japanese women are remarkably slight.

Because of fears about side effects, oral contraceptives are not normally available; and because of their reluctance to be fitted by male gynecologists, Japanese women do not commonly use the diaphragm. It is possible that some form of abortificant (preventing the fertilized egg from becoming implanted in the uterus) may be available on the Japanese market in a few years if it proves free of serious side effects. The result would be a considerable lowering of the incidence of abortions and thus should be welcomed. The present conservative estimate of abortions per year is about 1 million, which is twice the officially reported number. More liberal estimates put the figure at close to 1.5 million. At any rate, obstetrician–gynecologists (Ob-Gyns) have a tremendous economic stake in abortions, deriving a large share of their income from this practice. The fewer reported, the less income declared. A clear conflict of interest exists: abortions pay off for the profession.

The most thorough analysis of birth control and abortion in Japan is by Samuel Coleman, *Family Planning in Japanese Society*, the data for which goes through 1976.[7] Although written in English, this study uses primarily Japanese sources along with the author's own research conducted over a period of twenty-eight months in Tokyo. This analysis spells out the inadequacies of family planning methods and sex education in Japan. The consequences of this situation appear not only in the general unavailability of modern contraceptive means but in the continued lack of reliable information provided to men and women regarding safe and effective methods of family planning. "Few private practice Ob-Gyns provide contraceptive counseling and methods for their patients. The most striking omission of this service appears among abortion cases, where contraceptive counseling should be a matter of routine."[8] The topic of sexual relations remains a taboo subject for discussion in most schools and in family circles (even between husband and wife, at least in early stages of marriage, let alone between parents and children). The result is naivete, embarrassment, misinformation, and an alarming rate of unwanted pregnancies within marriage and, increasingly in the past ten years, outside of marriage as well. It is common for women to have had at least two abortions by the time they are forty years old. Coleman speculates about what might alter this picture and believes that change will be prompted only from the bottom up, not from government or from the medical profession (primarily men in this case) with its vested interests.

Other, even more fundamental, differences in the Japanese social and cultural scene compound the problem of whether to keep or abort a pregnancy. It is perhaps true that the average relatively young, politically liberal Japanese professional woman, married or not, might have few qualms about an abortion if she wishes not to have the child. That category of person in Japan, however, is a tiny minority. As is well known, the vast majority of women are family bound, normally getting married in their middle to late twenties. For them, this path is deeply imbedded in their self-image and in social expectations. Within this customary pattern are two children, with a family beginning as soon as possible. For the married woman who does not wish to work full-time, therefore, the issue of abortion is not one she faces at the start. *Before* she is married, however, or *after* her complement of two children, the issue is real. At these times the lack of adequate family planning methods makes abortion a statistical probability if pregnancy occurs. The fact that women often have small procreative choice contributes not only to frustration but to considerable resentment, however diffused or obliquely expressed. Our findings reveal that women, trapped in this fashion, have strong feelings, even if these are seldom voiced in public. Indeed, frustrations mount precisely because so few contexts exist in which to discuss such matters.

At the most basic level, therefore, Japanese women possess insufficient procreative choice. Huge numbers become pregnant against their wishes or because of ignorance of adequate family planning methods. Husbands and wives rarely discuss matters of this kind in ways that help to open up communication on such issues, let alone correct the problem. As a result, women experience considerable frustration, and only after one or two abortions do they begin to assert their needs and rights in this arena. Japanese society does little to help in the areas of family planning and sex education. The medical profession would seem to be notably recreant in its responsibility to serve the needs of women who may neither want to get pregnant nor wish abortion to be their primary option. Often one hears the rationalization that more contraceptive means are not made available because this would simply encourage teenagers to become sexually promiscuous "like their Western counterparts." (Actually, women frequently express the same fear about their husbands: the safer sex becomes, the more he will play around.) As the statistics given in the Hoshino article make clear, the teenage years are one of two age brackets in which there have been sharp increases (almost double) in the number of abortions during the period 1974–1981, which simply means that more unmarried people are having sexual relations but without adequate birth control protection.

A SPECTRUM OF REACTIONS TO THE ABORTION EXPERIENCE

Even if a woman favors having an abortion, it does not mean she will go through this experience unscathed. Even with perfect assent she may later, much to her own surprise, encounter feelings of guilt, and if not that, then often a sense of sadness, brought about by something deeper than hormonal adjustments. Thoughts of "what might have been" surface in almost every person. The experience, in other words, is rarely simple relief, as though the object removed were an intruder, with no connection to the woman.

At a still-deeper level is the unexpected awareness that one's need to mourn this loss is very real and not unnatural. This is not simply because Buddhism teaches that human life begins at the instant of conception. Actually, it is more likely the reverse: Buddhism's teaching may be the endorsement of a profoundly human experience, namely, that nothing less than a human life is at issue. One question revolves around the symbolic nature of what are called *mizuko*, for in the case of *mizuko* there is obviously a fundamental inversion of the typical and expected sequence in the ancestor-descendent continuity. A child here dies before its parents. This naturally raises religious questions in Buddhism about what happens to the *mizuko*, as well as psychological questions as to how one experiences the loss, how one grieves. Even this prospective experiencing of family bond becomes an avenue for discovering hidden connections in life (in Lifton's sense) and a source of deep meaning. If so, whenever ambivalence exists in the decision to abort, mourning becomes the acknowledgement that something of consequence has occurred, that one is never quite the same again. It is therefore to acknowledge death, even a death which one has willed. Once more, therefore, in the words of Magda Denes, "That . . . is the dilemma of abortions."

At a still more painful psychic and spiritual level, there is the encountering of a reality so filled with sorrow that much deeper healing is required. One experiences a rupture or brokenness that tears at one's inner nature. Many Japanese words convey this quality of affliction: *nayami, kurushimi* and *modae,* each of which suggests anguish, ache, torment, agony. Perhaps the most appropriate term would be *kumon,* incorporating the Japanese *kanji* of *kurushimi* and *modae,* doubling their intensity. An apt Western equivalent might be Kierkegaard's "sickness unto death"; that is, a form of spiritual malaise for which there is no remedy without cost. There remains only the possibility of healing through deep suffering.

The earliest Buddhist example of this may be the story of Kisa Gotami who lost her only child, a young son. Her grief was such that she could not face the reality and refused to bury the child. Days ensued and the neighbors became alarmed, urging her to visit the Buddha. Although sympathetic, he advised her to make the rounds of each house in the village, requesting a grain of mustard seed from any family where death had not occurred. At the day's end she returned, with no mustard seeds. The universality of pain suddenly hit her. In Lifton's sense, she had in some authentic way confronted mortality itself. She could then bury her son and, although continuing to mourn his passing, became able to release her attachment to grief. As this happened, her own capacity for compassion emerged.

It is appropriate now to provide some sense of what the Buddhist memorial service called *mizuko kuyō* entails. To begin with, the term *kuyō* literally means "to offer and nourish." In this sense, it is the offering up of prayers for the nourishment of the spirit of the aborted or stillborn child. Also, as mentioned earlier, it is intended to console the parents, especially the mother, though not infrequently one finds fathers coming with the mother or even by themselves. This service may take place once, or once every month, or it may occur annually on the anniversary of death. Also, one may request a private service or include one's suffering with a service for many *mizuko.* This latter is more common. As one would expect, in Japanese Buddhism, because of the sectarian variety, there is no one pattern to this service. And, because the very existence of a memorial service for an unborn child had no precedent until the past three decades in Japan, one finds considerable variation in content and emphasis. Although debate occurs in denominational circles among priests about all aspects of the *mizuko kuyō* phenomenon and about the service in particular, no official stated policy exists nor any recommended form of service.

On the other hand, the number of common elements are significant, as the general pattern that is followed bears some resemblance to what is used in regular services for the recent dead and even more to the memorial services for ancestors known as *senzo kuyō.* In general, priests conduct the service on behalf of those requesting it and face the altar during most of the service. At the beginning, the names of one or more forms of the Buddha and various bodhisattvas are invoked. Parts of several Mahāyāna *sūtras* are chanted, often including the *Heart Sūtra* (*Hannya-shin-gyō*) or the *Kannon Sūtra* (or *Kanzeon Bosatsu Fumon-bon* from the *Lotus Sūtra*), as well as selected *wasan* or songs of praise in behalf of figures such as Jizō Bosatsu. Frequently, the congregation joins in this chanting, but not always. Central to these services is the offering of light, food, flowers, and incense to the Buddha in behalf of the child and as tokens of the larger offering of one's life. In most cases, some sculpted representation of Jizō or of an infant symbolizing a *mizuko* is bought by the family and left in a specially designated place within the temple grounds. Quite frequently a *kaimyō,* or posthumous Buddhist name, is given the child; and this is inscribed on an *ihai* or mortuary tablet, which is left in a special chapel within the temple or taken home and placed in the family *butsudan,* or Buddhist shrine.

Clearly much more is involved in the memorial and grieving process than the externals of ritual. Often, for instance, a sermon is given, which tries to put the experience of those who attend into a wider human and Buddhist context. Furthermore, normally, a certain amount of counseling precedes and also may follow the service. In some cases there may be contact with other women who have already gone through a similar experience. On the other hand, for reasons of privacy, it is common for people to have these services performed at a temple where their identity is not known. Again, this supports the claim made by the Hoshino article that here we are dealing with a phenomenon in which there often is little, if any, communal support.

To provide another example both of the sorrow of losing one's child and of a *kuyō* in the child's behalf, a look at a well-known Noh play, *Sumidagawa*, is instructive. Written by Jūrō Motomasa (1395–1459), son of Zeami Motokiyo, this play is in the genre called *kyōjo-mono* or "mad woman" piece. The scene is set at the banks of the Sumida River in what is now Tokyo. A ferryman is about to take an unnamed traveler to the other shore when an obviously distraught woman appears, also seeking passage across. Unknown to the others, she is the widow of Lord Yoshida of Kita-Shirakawa in Kyoto and the mother of a twelve-year-old boy who was abducted the year before by a slave trader. Ever since, she has searched with "frenzied longing" for her lost son, Umewaka-maru. As the boat makes its way across, the woman divulges her mission, and the ferryman realizes that she is the mother of the boy whose death anniversary is just then being memorialized on the opposite shore by villagers who remember well his valor in the face of sudden illness and death.

One needs to see this play to appreciate the emotion portrayed by the mother as she takes part in the memorial service for her son.

> Before the mother's eyes the son appears
> And fades away
> As does the phantom broomtree.
> In this grief-laden world
> Such is the course of human life . . .
> Now eyes see how fleeting is this life.

On stage, the ghost of Umewaka-maru emerges from the burial mound, disappears, and reappears again. Each time the mother tries to touch him, but she cannot cross the boundary of life and death. The child speaks to her and echoes the villagers' chanting of the *nembutsu*. She reaches for his hand again.

> The vision fades and reappears
> And stronger grows her yearning.
> Day breaks in the eastern sky.
> The ghost has vanished;
> What seemed her boy is but a grassy mound
> Lost on the wide, desolate moor.
> Sadness and tender pity fill all hearts . . .

One is struck by how effectively the play creates in the viewer genuine feelings of loss and grief. The play not only incorporates a *kuyō* service but in a dramatic sense becomes one itself. By its very length on stage it draws out these feelings of grief in extended catharsis. The tragedy of the child's death remains, but of central importance is the way in which this has been faced in full, not glossed over or denied. A grief not encountered is a grief denied, and one thereby retains the "frenzied longing" in one guise or another. Only through realizing that the apparition is a ghost can she begin to accept his death and regain her sanity.

CONFRONTATION WITH DEATH AND DEATH EQUIVALENTS

Alongside the direct encounter with grief is the necessity of confronting feelings such as anger, guilt, or despair which frequently accompany the experience of another's death. For, as Lifton's research makes evident, these feelings may derive from significant exposure to what he calls *death equivalents*; that is, the sense of profound separation, fragmentation, and immobility or stasis. Sigmund Freud, in his rich essay "Mourning and Melancholia," makes a related point in distinguishing between two conditions whose symptoms often appear alike. "In mourning it is the world which has become poor and empty; in melancholia it is the ego itself. The patient represents his ego to us as worthless, incapable of any achievement and morally despicable."[9] As Freud knew, a gradation exists between these, not a sharp line. The clearest distinction is that the symptoms of mourning fade in time whereas the low esteem of melancholia persists. Freud also observed that in melancholia is a strong ambivalence toward the person who has died; an inner struggle occurs "in which love and hate contend with each other." Indeed, he correlates "obsessional self-reproach" with this ambivalence, regarding it as "the motive force of the conflict."

With Freud's thesis in mind it is reasonable to suggest that women who become pregnant against their wishes and who may also feel guilty over having to abort are prime candidates for a type of inner conflict that includes not only diffused resentment but self-reproach as well. This combination of repressed anger, guilt, and diminished self-esteem has many ramifications in the lives of women. This is not to imply that they are caused mainly by the problems over birth control and abortion. If anything, it is the reverse, namely, that problems arising there are attributable to less than satisfying relationships between men and women in so many areas of Japanese social life. The literature on women and the Japanese family is filled with portrayals of tensions within the home. The reality may be better or worse than the image, but it is certain that the widely read novels of Enchi Fumiko, Ariyoshi Sawako, and other women writers present a bleak picture.[10] In them one finds vivid portrayals of the kind of fragmentation and disconnectedness Lifton cites as death equivalents. Although the absence of realistic procreative choices discussed earlier, often leading to the necessity of abortion, is sufficient cause for frustration, the deeper causes are rooted within the whole social structure in which women have little opportunity to participate in the decision making that affects important areas of their lives. It must be acknowledged that Japan is hardly alone in this, as the women's movement, in its various forms throughout the world, makes clear.

A recent anthropological study by Takie Sugiyama Lebra, *Japanese Women: Constraint and Fulfillment*, provides a view different but not opposed to that of the Japanese women novelists just mentioned.[11] Her discussion of the well-known phenomenon of the close mother-child relationship is pertinent here. Referring to the mother's existence as filiocentric, in which she tends "to see a mirror image of herself in the child," Lebra calls the relationship one of "double identity" (herself and the child as one entity).[12] The most vivid expression of this relationship is suggested by the term *ikigai*, or that which is worth living for. In this case, the mother's worth is inherently related to her child. On one level this can mean genuine caring; on another level it suggests preoccupation, which is the usual connotation. What I am proposing here is that a correlation may exist between this heavy investment of self-esteem in her child and the ambivalence and dissatisfaction so many women feel (even if rarely expressed publicly) about their situation within Japanese society in general and their subjection to frequent abortion in particular. It would not be surprising if considerable melancholia (in Freud's sense) were present in the psyche of Japanese women, arising from a high level of ambivalence about their status in a male-governed society, a situation in which they develop various strategies to compensate for a sense of relative powerlessness. If so, Japanese women would not be alone, but they may have devised unique ways of approaching their dilemma. In another paper I have discussed this subject.[13]

At this point I turn to the concept of *redressive ritual*, as one means of confronting situations of frustration caused by broken connections of one sort or another. My thesis is that rituals of this kind can assist in providing imagery not only of death and death equivalents but also imagery of life's continuity, as Lifton uses these terms. In the process, people are assisted to confront threatening situations or broken connections both more deeply and more constructively.

In his last few years the anthropologist Victor Turner wrote at length on the topic of performative ritual and its relation to four phases of social drama (breach, crisis, redressive action, and outcome). His basic assumption is that society and social dramas are combative, filled with conflict, "agonistic," yet not yet settled, indeterminate.[14] Breach and crisis are chronic possibilities, not exceptional circumstances. The third phase, redress, implies the possibility of encountering conflict and moving through and beyond it, either to resolution or to recognition of stalemate. Although the latter may be unsatisfactory, it is at least honest. The phase of redress "reveals that 'determining' and 'fixing' are indeed processes, not permanent states or givens. . . . Indeterminacy should not be regarded as . . . negation, emptiness, privation. Rather it is potentiality, the possibility of becoming. From this point of view social being is finitude, limitation, constraint."[15] Turner sees ritual (and theater) as able "to mediate between the formed and the indeterminate" for these especially entertain the subjunctive mood, thus employing a serious engagement of new visions of reality.

There is a distinct similarity between the Turner thesis of ritual's potential within conflictive situations and Lifton's psychoanalytically based research into how one copes with life's broken connections. In both, there is the recognition of the commonness of conflict and of situations of fragmentation. In both, there is the stress on encountering these and learning how to experience them anew. In Lifton's words, there is a "three-stage process available to the survivor of actual or symbolic death encounter, consisting of confrontation, reordering, and renewal."[16] Within the second of these stages one discovers the possibility of "converting static to animating forms of guilt" or anger or despair. Using an anthropological approach, Victor Turner elaborates a theory of the therapeutic nature of "rituals of affliction" (as distinguished from the "prophylactic rituals" of life crises and seasonal festivals) and thereby takes his notion of redress a step further. Central to rituals of this kind is "divination into the hidden causes of misfortune, conflict, and illness (all of which in tribal societies are intimately interconnected and thought to be caused by the invisible actions of spirits, deities, witches, or sorcerers)," along with curative rituals that seek to move the afflicted person through and beyond the causes of this affliction.[17] As Turner well knew, these phenomena were not limited to tribal societies, and he had plans to study their presence in Japanese life before he died.

One could place *mizuko kuyō* precisely in the genre of rituals of affliction, for the sources of anguish are not only within each person's experience but within a larger cultural and social environment. Again and again, our research reveals how frequently women in Japan, in seeking explanations for repeated illness, financial troubles, or tensions within the family, begin to attribute these to an earlier experience of abortion. This search for causation is entirely understandable and analogous to Western explanation of evil from Job to Camus (questions of theodicy). One is struck, however, by how often abortion is cited as the cause for personal and social misfortune in Japan today. The simplest form of this is to view such misfortune as the punishment or evil spell (*tatari*) caused by the spirit of an aborted child. As the Hoshino and Takeda article states, "In traditional society the spirits of the children were not considered as possible purveyors of a curse, whereas in contemporary society the spirits of children are considered as the same as the spirit of an adult, and thus have the potential for casting a curse."[18] Although this is but *one* way of explaining the diverse phenomenon of *mizuko kuyō*, it is a common explanation offered by some proponents and cited by most critics.

It is our judgment, however, that behind the attribution of misfortune to abortion is a much larger issue, namely, the attempt to understand what underlies the confusions and fragmentation of a culture whose connections with its past are simultaneously broken and yet in many ways still alive. For this reason one needs to look at the forms of ritual and cosmology that are resorted to repeatedly in Buddhist temples and to ask whether these are potentially means of enabling men and women to confront the deeper and more systematic causes of what Lifton means by death equivalents. One problem, of course, is that in the modern period men and women live with several, often conflicting world-views. On the other hand, world-views are always in process and traditional forms of cosmology and ritualistic expression respond in various ways to newly experienced human needs. This is again to put the anguish so often experienced after abortion into a larger cultural framework and to seek for more complex factors behind this widespread phenomenon.

PATHS TO HEALING THROUGH COSMOLOGY AND RITUALS OF AFFLICTION

In an essay on Thai Buddhist healing, Stanley Tambiah discusses the inevitable relationship between ritual and cosmology. "In the rituals we see cosmology in action. Ritual is symbolic action that has a telic or instrumental purpose—to effect a change of state. The cosmology and ritual are closely connected because the cosmological concepts and categories are translatable into an action medium that employs symbols of various kinds—verbal, visual, auditory, graphic, tactile, alimentary, and so on."[19]

To anyone familiar with Japanese Buddhist ritual that will be an apt description. Of particular importance here is ritual's instrumental purpose in effecting a change of state. In the case of some worshippers, the cosmological symbols as experienced in a ritual setting will be taken with a certain literalness. The ritual state is the real state. For most, the symbols will refer to something else, imperfectly understood but also real in some sense. For any one, their meaning in an age of broken connection becomes problematic. And yet, this happens frequently in history.

Within all forms of Buddhism, for instance, both Theravāda and Mahāyāna, there is reference to the six worlds or paths or destinies known as *rokudō* in Japan. These are paths within the realm of desire (the ego world), far removed spiritually from the realms of buddhas and bodhisattvas, and are composed of six graduated levels: the world of gods or heavenly beings, humans, *asuras* (warlike spirits who can also protect the Buddha Dharma), animals, hungry ghosts, and those who inhabit the many hells. Even if not taken literally as places, their meaning is metaphorically symbolic of real states of existence which all beings experience in one way or another. In the language of Japanese proverbs: "the Six Roads are right before your eyes"; "Hell and Heaven are in the hearts of man"; and "there is no fence to the Three Realms, no neighborhood to the Six Roads" (meaning "beyond there is only *nirvāna*; and short of that there is nowhere to escape"). In modern parlance, Sartre's play *No Exit* or Arthur Miller's *Death of a Salesman* might serve to convey analogous visions of entrapment, the central difference being that none of the six worlds or paths is a permanent place of residence. Each person is reborn or finds himself or herself in one or another because of previous karma, remaining a pilgrim in these realms until all sense of a separate independent self (what the French call *la moi*, the idea of "me") is extinguished. Because progress along these paths is slow and arduous, Buddhism provides symbols of hope and sources of grace. Foremost among the bodhisattvas who have vowed never to rest until all beings are rescued are Kannon and Jizō. Because Jizō is especially central to *mizuko kuyō* he will be singled out here.[20]

Jizō is omnipresent in Japan, from now-deserted but once-used mountain trails, to crossroads throughout the land, to tiny neighborhood shrines, to chapels and main altars in larger temples. He is the foremost protector of children, particularly those who have died early. As such, he is intimately identified with those who have been aborted, who never came into this realm of existence. Jizō Bosatsu is therefore the single most important figure in the drama of young children, infants, and unborn fetuses in Japanese Buddhist cosmology, and in ritual related to this. He is known as *migawari*, one who suffers in behalf of others, one who can transform his shape infinitely to rescue those in dire straits. He is the only bodhisattva who is associated with all six worlds, being present in each simultaneously, though he identifies especially with those in the three unhappy conditions (*san-akudō*): the realms for animals, hungry ghosts, and those in hell.

In other words, Jizō identifies with those in any kind of suffering. He is an apt paradigm for worlds where strife, discouragement, and passion reign. In such a world he represents the possibility of hope; he is the epitome of compassion in a realm where this is rare. In Turner's language he is the liminal figure par excellence; he is the androgyne who represents male and female equally. He is in the midst of life and death, present symbolically in the womb and tomb alike. Moreover, he is the alternative to chaos, but challenges all forms of order implicitly by his compassion, settling for nothing less than rescue from defeat and ultimate liberation. He thus is both antistructure *and* the hope for communitas (in Turner's words) beyond all present structures. In Lifton's sense, Jizō assists in the confrontation of death and death equivalents. Serene in appearance, he nonetheless confronts demonic and other forms of hellish experience.

He is thus potentially a symbol toward which all redressive action points. Within pan-Buddhist cosmology he is said to be the connecting link between Gotama (the last historical buddha) and Maitreya (*Miroku*), the buddha to be. This in-between age typically is depicted in Buddhism as one devoid of buddhas. It therefore epitomizes a time of broken connection; it is separation, disintegration, and stasis per se. It is the time once called *mappō*, the last days of the law, when conditions worsen, when hope seems impossible, and skillful means of rescue have powerful attraction. For these many reasons, Jizō's symbolic importance to the believer is clear. *Mizuko kuyō* needs to be viewed partially within this cosmological context, ancient but still alive. On the other hand, these are the words of conventional piety, and they may not reach those whose sense of broken connection is more than personal and who view the disorder of the modern world with greater seriousness.

As one seeks to understand a phenomenon as widespread and complex as this, is it possible that the Jizō and *mizuko* figures can be viewed as opposite yet virtually inseparable symbols at this point? And, in their dialectical relationship as life-death paradigms respectively? If Jizō is clearly the salvific boundary figure between all forms of life and death, one symbolic meaning of *mizuko* lies in its representation of radical isolation, a figure with no connection to anything living or dead, one whose "spirit" remains in limbo unless freed ritualistically to reenter, to be reborn within this world.

A traditional term in Japanese Buddhism for someone who has died without relatives is *muenbotoke*, one who has lived but who dies with no connections. This term was used for anyone who died without descendents to make offerings for his or her spirit. It was regarded as the ultimate desolation and also as a potentially dangerous circumstance because the person's spirit had not finally been put to rest. Its very restlessness was highly threatening, a concept that has been pervasive throughout East Asia, as well as elsewhere, since ancient days. As Emiko Ohnuki-Tierney has expressed it: "The freshly dead hover at the margin of culture and nature, the point at which the latter threatens the former . . . the world of the ancestors and the world of the living."[21] They therefore are in a condition of limbo, which always has been seen as both polluting and dangerous to the Japanese. Whereas it would be too simple to equate the *mizuko* with the *muenbotoke*, there is a sense in which they are genuinely homologous. Each represents a radical disconnection from its origins, and the departed spirit of each has not received proper treatment in the ancestral tradition. Indeed, in the case of the *mizuko* the point is precisely to put them *into* the ancestral lineage. It is also the function of ritual to assist in the process of transforming potentially malevolent or demonic forces into ones capable of being protective and benevolent to the living. In the classical Buddhist sense, all mortuary ritual has this continuing transformation as central to its purpose.

It is but one step of the imagination to propose further that the condition of *muen*, or not-relatedness, is a pervasive experience in the modern world and certainly within Japan. In this vein, the symbolic power of the *mizuko* or the *muenbotoke* lies in the fact that they are not metaphors abstracted from living human existence, but indicators of what that existence commonly experiences. Perhaps only in this sense can one come to understand the rather extraordinary preoccupation with abortion manifested by so many Japanese women and with the various ways to encounter the meaning of this experience (as illustrated in *mizuko kuyō*). Further, this may also help one to understand the immense weight put upon the mother-child relationship, in which the average woman seeks to find her deepest identity. Without disparaging this bond, it is ironically a tie that tends to undermine the sense of wider, more corporate relationships with others within a pluralistic world. The price paid for forging a relationship so potentially narcissistic is not only that it may backfire (in cases of failure) but also that it fails to encourage broader, transpersonal bonds across lines of social difference. In other words, its very limited nature contributes paradoxically to the world of broken connection instead of helping to heal this condition in more basic ways. The current privatism of urban Japanese family life may be an attempt to construct connections of a closely personal sort, but most evidence suggests that this is rarely the outcome, either for parents or for children, and that it serves primarily to increase the sense of brokenness and isolation from a larger social fabric.

This, of course, is what Lifton is arguing on a more general level, and what he means by the term *broken connection*. His discussion of this condition is on many levels. Fundamentally, it deals with images of death and life and the symbolically broken connection between them. "Much more elusive is the psychological relationship between the phenomenon of death and the flow of life. Psychological theory has tended either to neglect death or to render it a kind of foreign body, to separate death from the general motivations of life. Or else a previous deathless cosmology is replaced by one so dominated by death as to be virtually lifeless."[22] It would be gratuitous to claim that a condition of nonrelatedness is the only experience men and women have in Japan or anywhere else. In fact, one might observe the very high premium put on relationships, especially close emotional relationships, in modern society. Again, there are innumerable forms of this within Japan. Yet it would be plausible to say that this emphasis exists, to a significant degree, precisely because so many of the old connections in traditional societies lack compelling power. This is not to romanticize these connections, but, in Lifton's words, "something has gone seriously wrong with everyone's images and models."[23]

In our research on *mizuko kuyō* we have come to realize that what is of central importance in any analysis of nonrelatedness or broken connection in Japan is the steady deterioration of traditional ancestral bonds. This cannot be overemphasized. Although these still exist in many forms and in certain circumstances they remain powerful, they are not strong enough to offset the more powerful experience of a people's increasing deracination from its past. Again, this phenomenon is worldwide. Half a century ago Walter Lippmann labeled this process as *the acids of modernity*. This is not to suggest that new forms of ancient traditions are not possible, only that the condition of disconnection is extreme. At the core of his research on survivors in many important contexts Lifton has observed a factor that has no precedent in history and that certainly affects the Japanese mind deeply, more so than that of any other people except perhaps the Jewish community (because of the Holocaust experience). The following words are telling:

> The broken connection exists in the tissues of our mental life. It has to do with a very new historical—one could also say evolutionary—relationship to death. We are haunted by the image of exterminating ourselves as a species by means of our technology. Contemplating that image as students of human nature, we become acutely aware that we have never come to terms with our "ordinary"—that is, prenuclear—relationship to death and life-continuity. We seem to require this ill-begotten imagery of extinction to prod us toward examining what we have steadfastly avoided.[24]

I wish to conclude this section by suggesting that many ingredients within the Japanese world-view are potential catalysts in this confrontation with both death and its equivalents and with the continuity of life and its equivalents. If the imagery of benevolent grace is powerfully expressed within Japanese religions, so too is the dark side of human existence with imagery of fury and malevolence. Although scarcely unique in this respect, the Japanese consciousness has managed to keep alive (whether in traditional or modern form) the awareness that these elements within the human and nonhuman scene (in worlds visible and invisible) are constants within psychic and spiritual existence. Japanese art and mythology are rich in depicting demons (*oni*), ghosts (*yurei*), raging deities (*araburu kami*), ferocious guardians at temple gates, and menacing divinities like Fudō-san who epitomizes sternness in the face of evil. In fact, Jizō and Fudō are often seen as complementary figures, two seemingly opposite forms of encountering tough reality. At least two features about these "dark" portrayals of the spirit world are central. First, they attest to the ambiguity of all existence, which clearly can be malevolent but is not *inherently* so. And second, intrinsic to all Buddhist mythology is a transformationist motif, meaning that (for those who seek wisdom and compassion) the most malign of forces can be transmuted into benevolent protective figures. Metaphorically, all of these forces suggest an august realism about the basic Japanese world-view; that is, an absence of sentimentality about the destructive potential within all existence, and at the same time, a basis for believing that even the most painful forms of nonrelatedness or separation are not the final or deepest expression of human experience. The key question here, of course, is how this might relate to the issue of abortion in modern Japanese society.

REDRESSIVE RITUAL AND SOCIAL DISORDER: A CONCLUDING PARADIGM

If the symbols of *mizuko* and *muenbotoke* have a homologous relationship, and if these represent human experience in some universal sense, then the question naturally arises of how ritual in particular can assist persons and communities to confront obstacles to the possibility of transformation and renewal. When one considers the full ritualistic process, as Arnold van Gennep did in his classic work *The Rites of Passage* (1909), one typically sees it as a movement from symbols of discontinuity to those of transition to those of continuity (or reincorporation).[25] In this final section my focus is on the first phase only, in part because I see it as crucial to the others and as frequently neglected in much modern expression of ritual. I have in mind *mizuko kuyō* in particular, for I also believe this same ritual has the potential to effectively help persons to face forms of *social* disconnection as well as the inner anguish they may feel personally after having lost a child or experienced deeply negative feelings following abortion.

For this purpose I return to Turner's idea of redressive ritual as one way to understand the deeper potential of a phenomenon such as *mizuko kuyō.* Central to any redressive ritual is its attempt to "include divination into the hidden causes of misfortune, conflict, and illness."[26] It is one thing to settle for the same explanation for all personal turmoil or family problems (attributing these to "vengeful spirits"), and it is another to allow for, even to smoke out, multiple interpretations. In the case of *mizuko kuyō* a major problem is to get society to conceive of a wider diagnosis. To pursue this wider diagnosis is to encounter the complexity of real existence. As Victor Turner writes, this openness to plural interpretation is evident "in ritual procedures, from divination to shamanistic or liturgical curative action, in which many invisible causes of visible afflictions are put forward by ritual specialists as they try obliquely to assess the main sources of discord in the communal context of each case of illness or misfortune."[27]

Such a diagnosis takes more time, though its value lies not only in inviting a richness of contending interpretations, but even more in its involvement of a wider community of people who then puzzle about their own implication in the misfortune at hand. As a way of gaining a certain perspective on the Japanese scene I wish to provide an example along similar lines from another culture with which I am familiar.

An eloquent discussion of this process is given by Bruce Kapferer in *A Celebration of Demons: Exorcism and the Aesthetics of Healing in Sri Lanka.*[28] More often than not in cases of spirit possession it is unclear why someone has become possessed or who the possessing spirit is. In other words, the diagnosis is part of the cure, is even intrinsic to the cure. It becomes a means of widening the circle of involvement both sociologically and cosmologically. In Śrī Laṅkā, "demonic spirits" are not viewed as foreign to the natural or human realms but permanent ingredients within a more universal sphere. Demons, so-called, are allowed their place. Symbolically, they personify the possibility of disorder, confusion, and injustice, but they are seen within a deeper framework of social and cosmic order, not as independent of this order. The demonic element therefore is recognized as inherently present within a world of pain, not some intrusion into it.

This recognition is identical with Turner's view of existence as conflictive and agonistic. The demonic element may be found anywhere within the social and natural order, but its existence is not granted free play. It too is part of contingent reality. Demonic possession thus symbolizes the inversion of true order, somewhat like the death of a child represents a fundamental inversion of typical expectation. Also, this demonic possession manifests itself within normal human contexts of family and neighborhood. And, exorcism (which is one form of redressive ritual) is designed as the means of reestablishing harmonious order, but only *after* the roots of disharmony have been confronted and displaced. The relationship of order to disorder (the demonic) thus is ritualistically the same as that of life to death, for unless the threats of fundamental disorder and death are confronted (personally and communally) in symbolic, psychological, and liturgical ways one is avoiding the dark side of existence and hence the situation remains paralyzed by it.

In the process of encouraging over many days multiple diagnoses of the illness at hand, the Śrī Laṅkān exorcist invites those close to the victim (family, neighbors, friends) to assess *why* so-and-so has become afflicted. In the hands of a skillful practitioner, the speculations grow more and more complex and many plausible explanations are rehearsed. There are even acknowledgments by those who perceive how they may have contributed to a poisoned and disordered climate (not unlike what can happen in group counseling if candor emerges). At a certain point, the exorcist deems the time ripe for the ritual itself to begin; without that preparation, diagnosis would be premature. It would have settled on causes within the patient alone, raising no questions about the social environment in which he or she exists. All possibility of confronting the wider picture would have been neglected, and the ritual's impact would be severely limited. Whenever the social roots of the disease or of the broken connection are ignored, the communal involvement in healing is also diminished.

There are important implications in the preceding example for how one may approach the anguish of losing a child and the ritual of *mizuko kuyō* in Japan. Although afflictions take infinite shape there is a clue here in how one tries to assess what lies beneath the surface and who else may be involved in creating the situation at hand. On one level, through *mizuko kuyō* thousands of women are being helped to go through the mourning process after the turmoil of abortion, miscarriage, or stillbirth. That certainly has great value. On the other hand, there remains a need to address the specific factors that make abortion so frequently necessary. These are rarely being addressed, in part because doing so would reveal other sources of conflict and pain; but their very avoidance may also contribute to what Freud called *melancholia* and to diminished self-esteem. Although women can become skilled in coping with difficult aspects of a male-oriented society, the very strategies they employ successfully may serve to perpetuate the basic problems.

As mentioned earlier, this [essay] is not intended as a descriptive report on our research. Although admittedly speculative, it is one effort to see the *mizuko kuyō* phenomenon within a broader socioreligious background than is normally done. It is also an attempt to place it in the context of other research, notably that of Robert Jay Lifton and Victor Turner, as theirs has been concerned with issues very similar to what I find here. If one adopts the metaphor of social drama, as Turner and others do, then what one finds in relations between men and women in Japan is precisely what Michel Strickmann intriguingly calls a *theatre for the unspeakable* when discussing an ancient Taoist ritual in which resentment and anger against a dead parent are expressed, though obliquely through a priest. Thus the *form* of filial piety is maintained, but very unfilial emotions are given expression. The ritual is therapeutic, though not basically redressive.

It is a truism that whenever deep feelings cannot be expressed either with sufficient candor or in some effective ritualistic manner, then anger and frustration go underground. If indeed this is true, then the important phenomenon of *mizuko kuyō* must finally be seen within a larger context. When analyzed in this fashion, it illuminates more aspects of Japanese society and religion than one would initially suspect. The significance of any ritual and its healing powers usually will vary with the level of depth at which affliction is perceived and the extent to which the social fabric is seen as connected to the suffering of individuals, particularly when the extent of that suffering is so widespread. This [essay] represents the first stage of trying to outline certain connections between the momentum behind this movement and various features of the present Japanese social system and its economic values. It helps to illuminate also some of the very real tensions that Japanese Buddhism needs to address as it exists in an increasingly gender-conscious period of time.

NOTES

1. This research is being conducted collaboratively with Elizabeth Harrison who has a Ph.D. from the University of Chicago in Tokugawa intellectual history. For several years, while living in Kyoto, she was a research associate at Ryūkoku University. Currently, she is teaching in East Asian Studies at The University of Arizona. The project has been funded by grants from the Fulbright Commission and the Faculty Development Fund, Carleton College.
2. See Anne Page Brooks, "Mizuko Kuyō and Japanese Buddhism," *Japanese Journal of Religious Studies* 8, nos. 3–4 (1981); and Hoshino Eiki and Takeda Dōshō, "Indebtedness and Comfort: The Undercurrents of *Mizuko Kuyō*," *Japanese Journal of Religious Studies* 14, no. 4 (1987).
3. Hoshino and Takedo, ibid., p. 314.
4. Robert Jay Lifton, *The Broken Connection: On Death and the Continuity of Life* (New York: Basic Books, 1983).
5. Ibid., p. 53.
6. Magda Denes, *In Necessity and Sorrow: Life and Death in an Abortion Hospital* (New York: Penguin Books, 1976), p. 245.

7. Samuel Coleman, *Family Planning in Japanese Society: Traditional Birth Control in a Modern Urban Culture* (Princeton, N.J.: Princeton University Press, 1983), pp. 38–41.
8. Ibid., p. 40.
9. Sigmund Freud, "Mourning and Melancholia," *The Standard Edition of the Complete Psychological Works of Sigmund Freud*, trans. James Strachey in collaboration with Anna Freud (London: Hogarth Press, 1964), vol. 14, pp. 247–268. This quote is from p. 254.
10. See Fumiko Enchi, *Masks*, trans. Juliet Winters Carpenter (Tokyo: Charles E. Tuttle, 1984); and *The Waiting Years*, trans. John Bester (Tokyo, New York, and San Francisco: Kodansha International, 1980). Those by Sawako Ariyoshi are *The Doctor's Wife*, trans. Wakako Hironaka and Ann Silla Kostant (Tokyo, New York, and San Francisco: Kodansha International, 1981); *The River Ki*, trans. Mildred Tahara (Tokyo, New York, and San Francisco: Kodansha International, 1981); and *The Twilight Years*, trans. Mildred Tahara (Tokyo, New York, and San Francisco: Kodansha International, 1984).
11. Takie Sugiyama Lebra, *Japanese Women: Constraint and Fulfillment* (Honolulu: University of Hawaii Press, 1984).
12. Ibid., p. 165.
13. Bardwell Smith, "The Social Contexts of Healing: Research on Abortion and Grieving in Japan," . . . in Michael A. Williams, et. al., eds., *Innovation in Religious Traditions: Essays in The Interpretation of Religious Change* (New York and Berlin: Mouton de Gruyter, 1991).
14. Victor Turner, *Dramas, Fields, and Metaphors: Symbolic Action in Human Society* (Ithaca, N.Y., and London: Cornell University Press, 1974), pp. 38–44.
15. Victor Turner, *From Ritual to Theatre: The Human Seriousness of Play* (New York: Performing Arts Journal Publications, 1982), p. 77.
16. Lifton, *Broken Connection*, p. 177.
17. Victor Turner, "Dewey, Dilthey, and Drama: An Essay in Anthropology of Experience," in *The Anthropology of Experience* (Urbana and Chicago: University of Illinois Press, 1986), p. 41.
18. Hoshino and Takeda, "Indebtedness and Comfort," p. 316.
19. Stanley Jayaraja Tambiah, *Culture, Thought, and Social Action: An Anthropological Perspective* (Cambridge, Mass.: Harvard University Press, 1985), pp. 103–104.
20. Jizō is the Japanese name for this figure. In Chinese he is known as Ti-tsang; in Sanskrit, Kṣitigarbha.
21. Emiko Ohnuki-Tierney, *Illness and Culture in Contemporary Japan: An Anthropological View* (Cambridge: Cambridge University Press, 1984), p. 70.
22. Lifton, *Broken Connection*, p. 4.
23. Ibid., p. 3.
24. Ibid., p. 5.
25. Arnold van Gennep, *The Rites of Passage* (reprinted Chicago: University of Chicago Press, 1960).
26. Victor Turner, "Dewey, Dilthey, and Drama," p. 41.
27. Victor Turner, "Liminality and the Performative Genres," in *Rite, Drama, Festival, Spectacle*, ed. John J. MacAloon (Philadelphia: Philadelphia Institute for the Study of Human Issues, 1984), p. 25.
28. Bruce Kapferer, *A Celebration of Demons: Exorcism and the Aesthetics of Healing in Sri Lanka* (Bloomington: Indiana University Press, 1983).

Apologizing to the Babies

Joan Frawley Desmond

Japan has been called "abortion heaven." The Ministry of Health and Welfare reported 364,350 abortions in 1994, though that figure does not include abortions by the private physicians whose lucrative business has reportedly blocked distribution of the birth control pill. In a 1982 survey conducted by the Kyodo News Service, about 60 percent of women in their forties with college degrees and executive-level husbands admitted having had one or more abortions.

No one in Japan seems willing to speak about the moral brutality of the Japanese custom of abortion used as birth control. Even a Jesuit missionary, residing there for half a century, cannot recall a single homily on the subject. Japan's abortion industry appears to drift along by itself, an anomaly in a relatively nonviolent society, graced by intact families and safe streets.

And yet, though there is no public debate, the unborn have not been forgotten. With no prompting, Japanese couples have begun acknowledging their role in the death of their own unborn child. They have done this not through talk-show therapy, but in a ritualized, thoroughly Japanese, manner. While couples bow to the necessity of abortion—saying, *shikata ganai*, "there's nothing to be done"—millions have been drawn to a Buddhist cult devoted to Jizō, the protector of aborted, miscarried, and stillborn children. Once a minor bodhisattva in the Buddhist pantheon, Jizō has revived the fortunes of local temples that perform *mizuko kuyo*, the ritual designed to assist in the peaceful resettlement of "returned" children who cannot pass alone across the river separating the living from the dead.

The Jizō figurines crowd hillside cemeteries, coastal promontories, and city temples. In Kamakura, just to the side of the famous Hasedera Temple, is an area devoted to a flourishing Jizō cult, with a large covered statue of the bodhisattva surrounded by a battalion of small Jizō figures, some of them decorated with traditional red capes or bibs, a few even accompanied by toys. A message board stands next to the bodhisattva, allowing parents to leave signed apologies and prayers. The Jizō figurines (which cost about $80), fresh flowers, and other gifts can be purchased at the main temple. The statues remain in place for some time, after which a formal offering is made for the soul of the aborted child. At the site, a short, printed explanation of the plight of "returned" souls—known as *mizuko*, or water children—suggests that they will remain in limbo if parents neglect their religious obligations.

There is just a hint of coercion here, but it is enough to provoke accusations of extortion from feminists and others who believe the cult manipulates guilt-ridden parents. The Hasedera Temple skirts the threat of *tatari*, or retribution, from the souls of aborted children. But some new temples and cemeteries devoted to the Jizō cult have gained a reputation for both questionable theology (the *mizuko kuyo* ritual becoming an implicit kind of exorcism), and, occasionally, even criminal blackmail for money to forestall bad luck.

Buddhist scholars, too, are uncomfortable with the Jizō phenomenon, which borrows heavily from medieval Japanese folk practices and Shinto beliefs. But it is significant that Buddhist thinkers avoid the moral issues that preoccupy Western societies. Rather, scholars bemoan the cult's accommodation of *tatari*, as well as the garish commercial trappings. Within Buddhism, few seem prepared to address the ambiguous, even mysterious motives of Jizō devotees. Yet Buddhist leaders have not blocked the cult. Temple priests understand that this grassroots movement plays an essential role in Japanese culture, filling the moral vacuum that organized religion has left untouched.

Jizō began to attract followers in the 1970s, after a decade of steadily rising abortion rates. The cult defies simple explanations, and Westerners should not shrug off this memorial service as a peculiar, if haunting, foreign custom. Its importance lies in its revelation of the damaging consequences of abortion. Despite the lack of moral guidance, Japanese parents want to admit wrongdoing. At the same time, however, the narrow scope of the ritual (which promises purification without conversion of the heart) serves as a warning of what the West could become: a society that goes on without a thought of redemption.

In the past, even when abortion was officially illegal, the Japanese exhibited a pragmatic approach to new life that threatened the survival or prosperity of the family. Many feudal peasants—along with wealthier Japanese—practiced infanticide as a method of "spacing" children in medieval times. And while Japanese Buddhism officially frowned on such practices, local monks sympathized with the plight of overburdened peasants. The thorough penetration of Confucianism and Shintoism into Japanese Buddhism produced a patchwork religion that shrank from moral absolutes, including the commandment against killing. It may be true that infanticide was occasionally practiced in medieval Europe, but Catholic theology never condoned the destruction of developing human life. In contrast to medieval Catholicism, writes William LaFleur—author of an important, if partisan, study, *Liquid Life: Abortion and Buddhism in Japan*—Japan's Buddhists "saw life as a kind of ontological chess; its movements could be forward, lateral, or backward on the board. This opened up a wider range of possibilities."

The moral force of Japanese Buddhism was also stunted by another trend in the nation's development: organized religion's submission to political power. This pattern of church-state relations eventually resulted in the ascendance of "Japanism" (described by Karel van Wolferen in *The Enigma of Japanese Power* as a "surrogate religious force"). As secular authority became fundamental, Buddhism lost its moral force. Today most Japanese view Buddhism as a funerary component of an undifferentiated Japanese religion, characterized by a preference for ritual activity over transcendent spiritual and moral beliefs.

During the early modern era, political leaders, not temple priests, challenged the "culling" of unwanted children. The Meiji Restoration of the 1860s paved the way for the criminalization of abortion, though a penal code largely imported from France could not dislodge the feudal vision of human life as ontological chess. Much later, in the years preceding the Second World War, Tokyo sought to increase birth rates to fuel its war effort. Abortion was viewed as a political crime, and state Shintoism applauded parents who produced large numbers of children. After the war, a baby boom spurred a dramatic return to illegal abortions, leading the government to introduce the 1948 Eugenic Protection Laws that opened the door to abortion-on-demand by the following year.

The democratic, affluent Japan of the 1990s has moved beyond the political and economic conditions that shaped the nation during the thirties and forties. Yet, wartime and even medieval Japan surface in unpredictable and surprising ways. Certainly the past has tainted any attempt to carve out a political solution to the problem of abortion. While Catholics quietly provide anti-abortion counseling and services for unwed mothers, only the neo-Shintoists occasionally denounce abortion publically—and Japan's steeply declining birth rate may be the prime reason for this concern.

While political-legal intervention remains unlikely, the Jizō cult has emerged as a stopgap response to abortion. Some observers contend that Japanese parents participate in the ritual as a way of affirming their essential goodness. According to LaFleur, prayers, gifts, and financial donations reverse the impression that one's child has been treated summarily and dehumanized. Possibly, the affluence of modern Japan has deepened distaste for abortion, which can no longer be explained away as a necessity for family survival. Or perhaps Japanese women want to move beyond both the moral passivity and the childlike dependence on physicians' directives that have fed the high abortion rate. Whatever the reasons, the number of abortions is falling among younger married women.

Abroad, the popularity of the Jizō cult has provoked a mixed response from activists on both sides of the abortion debate. Citing the cult, American pro-lifers argue that even non-Christian cultures recognize that abortion involves the destruction of human life. But feminist writer Naomi Wolf, in a 1995 *New Republic* cover story, "Our Bodies, Our Souls," noted the Jizō ritual and seemed to imply that a Westernized form of the memorial service might sooth consciences troubled by abortion guilt. The appearance of *mizuko kuyo* in Wolf's article seems a sign of desperation within pro-choice ranks. Most Americans, whatever their view of abortion, have been shaped by a notion of developing human life as unique and unrepeatable. Even if a Westernized memorial service shed the original Buddhist trappings, few participants could consciously embrace two colliding positions: the acknowledgment of abortion as the killing of an unborn child, and the decision to abort one's own child.

In Japan, the landscape is quite different. The nation's guiding ethical principles remain largely situational, and almost infinitely pliable, tranquilizing the conscience while providing an easy target for political manipulation. The weakness of organized religion has permitted a hodge-podge system of morality and ritual to establish itself, one that provides a primitive form of consolation despite its internal contradictions.

Joan Frawley Desmond *is a writer and teacher who recently returned to the United States after four years in Japan.*

On International Government. Nobody can be a citizen of the world as he is the citizen of his country. . . . The very notion of one sovereign force ruling the whole earth, holding the monopoly of all means of violence, unchecked and uncontrolled by other sovereign powers, is not only a forbidding nightmare of tyranny, it would be the end of all political life as we know it. Political concepts are based on plurality, diversity, and mutual limitations. A citizen is by definition a citizen among citizens of a country among countries. . . . Philosophy may conceive of the earth as the homeland of mankind and of one unwritten law, eternal and valid for all. Politics deals with men, nationals of many countries and heirs to many pasts; its laws are the positively established fences which hedge in, protect, and limit the space in which freedom is not a concept, but a living, political reality. The establishment of one sovereign world state, far from being the prerequisite for world citizenship, would be the end of all citizenship.

—Hannah Arendt, *Men in Dark Times* (1968)

Part 5:
Religions in Africa

WOMEN'S ROLES IN THE MOURNING RITUALS OF THE AKAN OF GHANA

Osei-Mensah Aborampah
University of Wisconsin-Milwaukee

Akan women play central roles in the care and disposal of the dead and the management of bereavement. Mortuary rituals provide members of the society with adaptive means of mourning the dead, and the expressions of grief ensure a systematic adjustment to human loss. Funerals and mourning rites include music and dance, which capture so many aspects of Akan transitional rituals. The funeral celebration has become a perfect medium for not only understanding Akan traditional and popular culture, but also for appreciating the impact of social changes on Akan society. (Akan, women, funerals, culture, change)

From birth through puberty, marriage, maturity, and old age, Akan[1] lineage members pass through various rites and rituals binding them spiritually and culturally to others in their communities. Because of the inevitability of death and belief in an active life after death, the Akan of Ghana have developed elaborate rituals to ease the pain of physical separation and to guide the dead into the spiritual world of the ancestors. The patterns and processes of grieving among the Akan appear to be similar to those reported elsewhere. According to Platt and Persico (1992:xi-xii), four significant variables tend to influence the human response to grief. These are the social meaning of death, the relationship between the deceased and the survivors, the significance of the mode of death, and the nature of the support network available to the bereaved. The notion of the social meaning of death relates to various definitions that members of a society attach to the nature of death, the origin of death as a cultural concept, and the survivors' prior experiences. Relevant issues addressed in this area include a group's conception of the universe and humankind's place in it, as well as its relationship with nature and its religious beliefs.

Questions about the relationship between the deceased and survivors seek an understanding of the positions occupied by the deceased and the bereaved family in their community. Types and extent of social, economic, political, and religious relationships that prevailed between the deceased and survivors also are relevant. The third factor (the significance of the mode of death) entails comprehension of the manner of death experienced by the deceased and the social meaning that a group attaches to that form of death. For example, a group's response to suicide or death from retaliatory sorcery may be different from how the group responds to death from an illness or from old age or to death attributed to the work of witchcraft. Finally, according to Platt and Persico (1992:xii), the nature of the social support network available to survivors includes the social definitions associated with the role of the bereaved and the expectations for family and community members to share in supportive behavior to aid the grieving individuals. The relative importance of each of the variables is difficult, if not impossible to ascertain, but collectively they appear

ETHNOLOGY vol. 38 no. 3, Summer 1999, pp. 257-71.
ETHNOLOGY, c/o Department of Anthropology, The University of Pittsburgh, Pittsburgh PA 15260 USA

to account for most of the cross-cultural variations in human response to and management of death.

However, Platt and Persico (1992:xiii) deplore the fact that anthropological inquiry on death and grief responses has been conducted largely in Western societies and that "very little comparative examination of the determinants of grief responses in non-Western societies has been undertaken to date." Their edited volume attempts to fill this gap by presenting case studies from non-Western societies. This essay seeks to contribute to the attempts to broaden the knowledge base for cross-cultural understanding of death and responses to grief. More specifically, this essay is concerned with the general meanings of death and the roles of women in funeral celebrations of the Akan of Ghana. While much of the presentation is focused on Platt and Persico's concern with the social meanings of death that influence grief responses, their other three factors will be examined as well. To do so, the first section presents an interpretive understanding of the social meaning of death to the Akan through a review of the socioanthropological approaches to issues of death and mortuary rituals, highlighting only the aspects germane to the present project. The second section provides a description of women's roles in Akan funeral celebrations. In effect, this section addresses an aspect of the nature of the social support network available to survivors. Here, emphasis is placed on the different kinds of work performed by women for the management of death and the successful resolution of grief, including the poetic speeches and literary qualities contained in mourning and funeral dirges performed by women. These funeral dirges, along with the mortuary rituals, beliefs about life after death, the culturally determined ways of disposing the mortal remains, and the ritual and popular responses of survivors, constitute what I call Akan death culture. The third and concluding section examines the impact of the industrializing process on the Akan conception of death and its accompanying mortuary rituals and grief responses/The main argument of this essay, then, is that Akan culture provides members of the society with a highly adaptive means of mourning the dead and that various mechanisms and emerging opportunities for the expression of grief ensure a systematic and positive adjustment to human loss✓

THEORETICAL APPROACHES TO DEATH AND AKAN MORTUARY RITUALS

According to McCaskie (1989:420), social anthropology has provided us with the fullest discussion of the cross-cultural meanings of death and mortuary rituals. In McCaskie's view, two approaches from the socioanthropological tradition are relevant to the Asante (Akan) death culture. The first approach focuses on the constructions placed on death and mortuary rituals and their link to reproduction and sexuality. This approach has more relevance for an understanding of the social meaning of death pertaining to (Asante) kings. Therefore, its explanation will be rather brief.

In its simplest treatment this approach pertains to the symbolic relationship between the killing of a divine king and the belief that subsequent agricultural production or hunting would be bountiful. McCaskie (1989:421) finds aspects of this symbolic relationship built into Asante oral history in the sense that the creation of Asante society and culture involved the arduous task of taming a huge and threatening natural forest. Mastery over, and thus the "death" of the forest connoted sustenance of human life. Since the power of the *Asantehene* (king of Asante) was equated with *odum* (the largest tree in the forest of Asante), its destruction was taken to mean increase in the fertility of the land and people. McCaskie alludes to Rattray's (1927:127) characterization of the festival of *Odwira* as "the feast of the dead" to underscore the link between the commemoration of the deaths and mortuary rituals of all past Asante kings, and the future fertility of crops and people. Here again, the idea is that the two events of the Odwira festival and mortuary rituals (i.e., funeral celebrations) brought people together in cultural performance that assured the future growth of crops and the anticipated prosperity of the Asante nation. In effect, McCaskie employs the metaphor of the coolness provided by large trees in the forest region of Asante and the festival of Odwira to explain the vital role of the Asantehene in the defense and regulation of the social order, the propitiation of the royal ancestors, and the cleansing of society from defilement. The explanation thus far is sufficient for our purposes since this theoretical approach to death and mortuary rituals is not directly relevant to the present analysis. With regard to the drama associated with the disposal of the corpse and the behavior of the bereaved and the community, mortuary rituals are treated as rites of passage in which sociological dramas centered around corpses are enacted. McCaskie (1989:426-27) explains it as follows:

> Typically, this drama had two significant, enabling acts separated by an interval. In the first act, the deceased individual was ritually detached from the social, often by means of "**primary**" burial or some other alternative form of temporary disposal of the corpse. In the second act, the corpse was given final or "**secondary**" burial, the social role of the dead individual was reallocated, and society moved on from its temporary dialogue with mortality. The interval between the two acts was liminal period, distinguished by mourning, and characterized by a recognition that the departed, lingering ambiguously somewhere between the end of biological existence and a full incorporation into the afterlife, might intervene in human affairs in malicious and dangerous ways.

This rightly points out that the notions of primary and secondary burial are relevant to understanding Akan mortuary rituals. Implied in the primary and secondary burials are the processes of grieving and mourning. It is these two dramas that are of immediate concern here. Lindemann (1963:703) defines grief as "the state of pain, discomfort, and often physical or natural impairment that in most persons follows from the loss of loved ones." Lindemann (1963) suggests that grief seems a particularly personal emotion. Nonetheless, its onset and course can only be understood in their social and cultural context. The latter point was emphasized in Hertz's (1960) treatment of mortuary rituals. He argued that the intensity of grief expended by any individual or group was dependent on a socially constructed formula, rather than an innate or natural feeling. For example, the mourning of an infant or the first-born child to an Akan was always cursory, while the mourning of an elder was not. The longer a person has lived, the more protracted the period of mourning tends to be. The extended mourning derives from, among other things, the loss of shared experiences, and the loss of the sense of stability and well-being provided by the presence of the deceased.

The implication here is that culture affects grief and therefore Akan culture influences what sort of loss a death will involve. In traditional Akan societies, the belief was that the deceased elder would transit into the afterworld where he or she could transform into a postmortem jural authority over his or her living lineage members. An elder's death was deemed to pose a crisis in the group's life, and required an elaborate ritual and funeral to ensure his or her comfort in the afterlife. This type of management provided an avenue for the deceased to reclaim himself or herself after death. In this regard, the deceased gained by death. To the extent that this interpretation is acceptable, it seems to explain the past attitudes of Akan people to death. An old Akan enjoyed the status of an elder and contemplated death with very little or no anxiety. He or she never pretended to be younger and knew that when he or she died, members of his or her lineage in particular, and the community in general, would assemble to sing stirring memorial dirges and odes to his or her character and achievements, and to introduce him or her to the ancestors with a lavish funeral celebration (Antubam 1963). These beliefs and presumed practices linger in Akan communities in Ghana today.

Culture also affects who experiences a loss by death. Every Akan belongs to an *abusua* (matriclan or matrilineage). The idea of oneness among members of the abusua is expressed in the collective responsibility for organizing the secondary burial of a departed member. The mourning group is organized by matrilineal descent. Also, the death of a member of the minimal lineage (*yafunu*) has a relatively higher grief potential than a member of the individual's patrikin group.

Hertz (1960) also suggests that through mortuary rituals grief is controlled and distributed. Among the Akan the control and distribution find expression in public mourning or funeral celebration, which provide institutionalized opportunities to express displaced or delayed grief. The premise here is that grief is an inevitable response to death among those for whom the deceased was a valued or loved person. Visible expressions of grief take conventionalized forms such as the dirges already alluded to and occur in predictable contexts, as will be explained later. Alternatively, funerals provide opportunities for individuals to express grief over their own impending deaths; that is, the felt uncertainty about the nature and types of death that await them. The Akan expression, "*mesu me wu da mu*" (I am weeping over the day I will die), underscores this point. In relation to the primary burial mentioned earlier, funerals may serve as conduits for the physical removal of the body. In the past, as is often the case at present, elderly members of Akan matrilineages were secretly buried at designated places other than the public cemeteries. In those instances, public mourning by bereaved lineage members provided convenient avenues to distract public attention from the disposal of the corpse.

Perhaps the most important aspect of the public mourning or funeral celebration (i.e., in the context of the secondary burial) is to secure the happiness of the departed on its journey to the spirit world. Relying on insights provided in the work of Rattray (1927:103-04, 182), McCaskie (1989:428) explains this point rather succinctly:

> Birth was a suspenseful drama of management into life. Children might elect to run from whence they had come, and accordingly were not named until eight days after birth. Puberty marked their full acceptance of the fact of biological existence. At death, by direct analogy, the indestructible spirit component of the human individual had to be managed back into the continuity from whence it had emanated. Properly transacted mortuary rituals were the indispensable instruments of that process of management. Imperfectly performed or neglected mortuary rituals left the departed in anxious uncertainty of limbo. The dead responded to this offensive status by harassing the living, and by exacting retribution from them.

It follows from McCaskie's explanation that rites performed during the funeral celebration also served to repair the potential breaches in the fabric of the community that could be caused by a death. The deceased as a corpse and spirit was perceived as a potential source of danger. The perceived threat explains, in part, the elaborate sequence of rituals followed to secure the happiness and safe passage of the deceased into the spirit world.

This interpretive summary has been offered to clarify the social meanings Akan people attached, and in many instances continue to attach, to mortuary rituals. The rituals and grief responses, central to the psychological health of the Akan in light of the social disruption caused by the departing member, are discussed below in relation to women's roles in Akan funeral ceremonies. The question of gender in the production, circulation, consumption, and reproduction of various cultural dramas is complex. In the next section, it is examined in relation to three key areas: women's roles in Akan funeral ceremonies and their prominence in accompanying secular and ritual dramas; the operation of the principle of consanguinity during these ceremonies; and presentation of women's respectability, which stands in sharp contrast to the male-dominated culture of silence during the phase of public mourning and the accompanying rituals.

WOMEN'S ROLES IN AKAN FUNERALS

Kinship structure among the Akan is matrilineal. This means that an individual, from birth to death, remains a component of a matrilineage. Upon death, the body remains the property of the matrilineage, whose responsibility it is to provide the deceased member with a decent funeral in relation to the purposes articulated in McCaskie's (1989) explanation. The roles of female lineage members is critical in several areas of funeral rites. For example, women play a vital role in protecting a widow or widower from the deceased. This is achieved through the observance of the widowhood ritual. In the case of a widow, female affines deal kindly or harshly with her depending on the way and manner she treated her husband while alive. During the first 40 days after the death of her spouse, the widow is considered to be in an impure state, and until she is purified her actions are to be governed, regulated, and dictated by an attendant. She is not to do anything that is not ritually sanctioned by this attendant. The matrilineage of the deceased usually selects an experienced female member as an attendant to the widow. The widow is supplied with a charm to wear in order to repel evil forces, particularly the spirit of the dead spouse that would otherwise haunt her. The female attendant makes sure the charm is properly secured during the entire 40-day funeral celebration. The attendant also supervises the grieving, eating, drinking, conversation, and public seating of the widow. The widowhood ritual, according to Kyei (1992:82), is performed to meet three basic needs. First, it protects the widow or widower from misfortune, including economic loss. Second, it preserves the mental balance of the widow or widower. Third, the charm is intended to keep all bodily organs, genitals in particular, unimpaired. These ends could be attained only with the crucial role of the female attendant, and by undergoing this ritual both privately and publicly, a widow is given the support needed in the process of adjustment to normal life.[2]

Another area of responsibility is preparation of the body for lying in state. The corpse is washed by the older women of the matrilineage. Since the departed spirit is believed to journey to the spirit world, it is important for the deceased to be provided with the necessities of a traveler, including food. Until the recent past, it was quite common for special dishes to be prepared by female lineage members and set on a table in front of a corpse that lies in state. This responsibility to feed and equip the spirit of the deceased on its long journey to the spirit world falls on female members of the matrilineage. In the past, an elderly woman also prepared handmade beads to be placed in a brass pan before the corpse of a fellow elderly woman and later buried with her to allow free passage into the ancestral realm (Warren 1975:39). This particular ritual is rarely performed these days. According to Warren (1975), a deceased's son's daughter would also sit next to the corpse to fan away flies (if necessary).

As Goody (1975:5) points out, funerals have a dramatic quality and incidents in the past life of the deceased are often dramatized in various Akan communities. Women, at special moments of the funeral celebration, could become the channel or medium of communication with the deceased. At high points of the celebration, any female celebrant, usually not of the deceased's matrilineage, could be possessed by the spirit of the deceased. She then dramatizes the life experiences and desires of the deceased. These could include dress and speech or a dance imitation of the deceased. She also could transmit messages, instructions, advice, etc., to the bereaved family or community, could forecast impending fortunes or disasters, and prescribe possible measures for forestalling them. Misfortune could befall surviving family members or the community as a whole if these messages and instructions were not duly acted upon. As seers, women in trance at funeral celebrations rose to the position accorded the community's priests and priestesses, and were thus treated not only with respect but with awe as well. More important, through these mediums, an otherwise very difficult family or lineage conflict could be resolved. Akan people trusted such mediums as oracles to resolve difficult cases for which satisfactory adjudication by the living was deemed impossible. Vestiges of these types of mortuary rituals prevail in the rural areas of Akan communities.

Women also play an indispensable role in the perpetuation of the matrilineage or matriclan within the context of the tripartite role of social construction involving the living, the dead, and those yet to be born. An Akan had, and to a large extent still has, a deep-rooted sense of belonging, loyalty, and emotional attachment to his or her matriclan. This is succinctly articulated by Danquah (1928:194):

> If you would know what an Akan regards as most sacred and inviolable, attempt to make distinctions between him and members of his clan, or worse still, his family. The family being more or less the unit personality in society an individual tends to regard himself as out of touch with all existence when divorced from his family. Hence the sacredness of the family tie.

In practical terms, the matriclan serves as what Davidson (1969:113) calls instruments of collective lineage welfare. This partly explains the premium placed on having many children in Akan culture. One of the measures of the strength of an Akan matriclan was, and to a large extent still is, its numbers, and of course it is the female members whose reproduction ensures lineage continuity. Their numbers come alive during funeral celebrations of deceased members. Public mourning sums up the past history of a matrilineage and represents an affirmation of the contributions of female members for the survival of the lineage.

There is yet another important responsibility that female members of a lineage assume during funeral celebrations. Akan funeral celebration is marked by sanctioned displays of behavior that would seem unusual to a stranger. To an Akan, a funeral with large numbers of mourners and wailers is a sign of the worthiness of one's existence here on earth. So it is important to bewail the dead aloud and openly. However, since men should not shed tears in public, women do most of the crying and weeping.[3]

As indicated earlier, funerals constitute legitimate occasions not only to express grief, but also to pay tribute to the dead. According to Kamerman (1988:66), the symptoms of normal grief include bodily distress, a preoccupation with the image of the deceased, guilt, hostility, and alteration or loss of normal patterns of conduct. While the symptoms are present among the Akan, especially the women, their expressions are conventionalized and artistic in the sense of the oration and the poetic gestures that accompany them. For example, a woman would mourn by repeatedly saying "*Ahia me*." (I am impoverished by this death), with both hands clasped on top of her head. Or, she would cry out, "*Aka me nko o*!" (I have become lonely by this death), with both arms stretched up and forward pointing to the corpse lying in state. Several other grieving gestures are discussed in Antubam (1963:64-65).

The oral literary aspect of Akan mourning finds expression in the libation before the corpse and in singing stirring memorial dirges to the character and achievements of the deceased. Singing funeral dirges is a major function of women, while elderly men usually, but not always, pour the libation. Unfortunately, many of the dirges cannot be associated with the individual women who created them with much intellectual and aesthetic genius. Nonetheless, it is important to note that for the audience at a funeral ceremony, the performance is much like a poetic recital. Many of the texts have been composed by nameless individuals and handed down from one generation to another by word of mouth. The singing is not an organized performance. Bereaved mourners, friends and sympathizers can join in the wail by singing a dirge of one sort or another. Singers are supposed to sing well and use appropriate gestures and steps where necessary. Regarding performance, Nketia (1969:9) offers the following observation:

> A good singer wins in emotional appeal: She moves her audience. Nevertheless, a funeral is not the occasion for mere display, though the temptation is great and many succumb to it. One of the requirements of a performer is that she should really feel the pathos of the occasion and the sentiments embodied in the dirge. Pretense is condemned and mock-sadness is discouraged. A tear should fall, lest you are branded a witch and a callous person. If a tear is physiologically difficult to shed, you must induce it by some means; but if it is physiologically impossible for you, it would be better to have the marks of tears on your face than nothing at all.
>
> The singers of the dirge rarely sit down: they pace up and down the place of the funeral, flanked on all sides by members of the lineage, friends and sympathizers seated on stalls, raised planks, chairs or on the ground. Each circuit brings them in front of the corpse or where the lineage head or the bereaved father, mother, husband or wife sits. Some walk out then come in again.

An effective combination of excellent choice of text, poetic recital, and appropriate gestures is sure to captivate the audience and the bereaved lineage. The dirges themselves cover the whole spectrum of social life, including kinship, marital and familial relations, economics, political activities, and societal values. Below are selected examples of dirges usually sung in praise of the deceased. The selections are taken from Nketia (1969) and McCaskie (1989). While no attempt has been made to adjust the Twi renditions or the English translations, the ordering has been rearranged to facilitate comprehension of their import.

An Expression of the Extent of Loss

Ahunu mu nni me dua bi na maso mu	There is no branch above which I could grasp
Asuo ayiri me oo, na Otwafoo ne hwan?	I am in flooded waters. Who will rescue me?
Agya behu me, na onhu me yie bi	When father meets me, he will hardly recognize me.
Obehu me, na meso ketego ne nwansena	For he will meet me carrying all I have: a lorn sleeping mat and a horde of flies.
Mene womma bewe ananse oo,	Your children and I will feed on the spider;
Na akura dee, obopou	The mouse is too big a game
Praa e, mene wo mma oo	Your children and I (what will become of us!)
Ena e, me nko m'anim	I am done for
Ayya e, ahia me	I am destitute
Praa e, ahia me	Your children are looking for you
Wo mma rehwe w'ano	The night is fast approaching, where the orphan is dying to see its mother
Onwunu redwo oo, dee awisiaa afe ne na	

(Nketia 1969:47-48)

An Expression of Desire for Continued Fellowship and Love

Obi reba a, mane me	Send me something when someone is coming
Mane me na mene wo di mane	Send me something for you and I exchange gifts
Eye a, mane me denkyemmoo na	Send me parched corn so that I can eat it raw if I am unable to find fire to cook it on
mannya gya a, mawe no mono	
Wore mane me a mane me	When you are sending me something, I would like a a big pot that receives strangers
sen kese a egye ahohoo	

(Nketia 1969:49)

For a Deceased Mother/Father

Eno, nko nnya me akyire oo	O, mother do not leave me behind
Eno, nko nnya me akyire oo, Osiantan	O, mother, please do not leave me behind
Ena awu agya me oo:	Mother has died and left me alone:
Na mene hwan na ewo ha yi?	With whom am I now here?
Agya e, aka me nko	Father, I am here alone
Mene wo beko	I shall go with you
Agya e, befa me ko	Father, come and take me away
Eye a, ma yenko yen dee mu	Let us go back together to the place where we came from
Na enyé yen tenabere ne ha	We do not belong here

(Nketia 1969:45-46)

For a Deceased Priest

Obosomfoo Kosekose oo:	Farewell, thou priest
Ohene ni, nkumankuma brebre	Fare thee well, mother of the king
Woko a, duom oo, ohene ba	When you start, do not tarry, Prince
Gye due na duom oo!	Receive condolences and proceed on
Wo duru Kurotia a, bo wodin ma abrane	When you reach the outskirts of the town,
mma wo so na wodi amantire nu	mention your name so that strong
	men carry you shoulder high for you rule two worlds.

(Nketia 1969:44-45)

For a Deceased Asantehene (Asante King)

Nana atu ne kyinie	Nana (the Asantahene) has removed his umbrella
Awia na ebeku yen.	We shall be scorched to death by the sun.
Womim dee wo gyaa me	You know the condition in which you have left me
Ya ma nsuo nto na ma so bi anom.	See to it that there is rain so that I can collect some of it to drink.
Se womane me a, mane me denkyembrebo	If you are sending me parcel
Mannya gya a mawe no mono.	Send me a crocodile's liver

Which I can eat raw failing to get fire with which to
cook.

(McCaskie 1989:424-25)

Singing a dirge in the past usually signaled the commencement of the funeral ceremony and remained its mainstay for a long time, until it was reinforced and eventually overshadowed by music and dance (Nketia 1969:17). The very enactment surrounding singing dirges is a clear testimony to the artistic endowment of Akan women. The themes of the dirge, music and dance, and literary and popular cultural expressions existing today are elaborated in the section that follows.

AKAN FUNERALS AS POPULAR CULTURE

Many elements of contemporary Akan death culture may be viewed as popular culture in the sense that the food, clothing, music, dance, gestures, specialized language, and the commercial advertisements on display during funeral celebrations constitute "distinctive moments in the production, circulation, consumption, and reproduction of cultural forms" (Adjaye 1997:6), which are readily accessible to and affectionately embraced by a wide spectrum of members of various Akan communities. In this regard, the death tradition has become a festival that combines solemn ritual with joyful celebration. Because music and dance capture so many aspects of Akan transitional rituals, including death, funeral celebration has become a perfect medium for not only understanding Akan popular culture, but also for appreciating the centrality of women in the entire drama.

As already indicated, death is framed in religious terms even though secular dimensions are apparent. Given the belief in reincarnation, with biological existence believed to represent a corporeal episode in an unending continuity and the unborn child understood to exist in the spirit world (McCaskie 1989:427), mortuary rituals have been developed accordingly. The patterns and processes of mourning in the past may be summarized here. First, when an Akan lineage member died, the body was prepared and displayed at home. Death customs like washing and dressing the deceased, watching, and waking were observed scrupulously. Neighbors, relatives, and friends were informed of the death and came to provide support. Mourning dresses, usually red and/or black, were worn. Fine gradations of dress marked the different social statuses and categories of those assembled. Finally, the deceased was buried with grave goods such as food, kente or other types of cloth, trinkets, farm implements, and gold dust to ensure an uneventful journey to the spirit world. All these practices constituted cardinal ritual facts of Akan death culture. The festive celebration represented an important occasion for the expression of familial, lineage, and community solidarity, and women played as central a role as in the ritual dimension.

Although many of the traditional ritual practices have been discontinued, much of the popular culture comes alive in the pomp and pageantry of the funeral celebration. In specific forms, popular culture is reflected not only in the dirges and odes sung to praise the deceased, but more importantly in music and dance. During the public funeral celebrations, traditional singing and drumming groups may provide entertainment for those present. The most popular of these traditional dance ensembles are *adowa, nwonkoro, adenkum, kete, asaadua,* and *bosee,* in most of which women are the lead singers. Some of the accompanying musical instruments, such as the *firikyiwa* or *nnawuta* (bells) and *donno* (gong), are played by experienced women. Many of the women singers learn the art of singing early in their youth and an accomplished performer is very pleasing to listeners' ears. A person will be roused to join a singing group or dance if the song reminds him or her of a series of events in his or her life. As in the case of the dirges, the lead singers learn to be adept at manipulating those present by drawing on the direct and indirect experiences of people in the community and by being acutely sensitive to the reactions of the sympathizers and celebrants of the funeral. In this regard, a mutually supportive relationship between the traditional singer and the dancer is established. The singer can work the dancer to high frenzy and the dancer can do the obverse. Both depend on each other for the desired outcome. Until recently, the traditional dance ensembles were rarely paid for their performance at funerals.

An entertaining element of Akan funeral celebration comes alive in the realm of dance movements as well. Men and women frequently dance in separate spaces, moving back and forth toward each other where appropriate. Dance to traditional (or lately highlife) music can be exhausting, involving rapid movements and sometimes leaping to the furious rhythm of the African drum. An exquisite execution draws approval from those present. Nonetheless, the ultimate goal of the performance is always borne in mind: to allow people to pay tribute to the dead. Thus the mortuary ritual and the funeral celebration, in effect, constitute a balancing act. Respect for the deceased is complemented in the display of popular culture with an understanding that the customary care given to the body and the public celebration will somehow safeguard both the dead and the living.

Traditional rituals no longer provide the support they once did. The meaning of a traditional libation today is lost upon a person who holds no beliefs in the traditional religions. The contemporary celebration of death has become largely secularized and/or Christianized, but also a major showcase for conspicuous consumption. A ceremony that invites all to mourn a death has become an avenue for the bereaved to not only express their sentiments for the deceased, but also to openly display the deceased's and bereaved's social class standing. Monetary expenditures serve the latter purpose. Funeral professionals and entrepreneurs have become secular substitutes for family and relatives in the handling of the dead. Many elements of funeral services may be purchased nowadays. For example, refrigeration of the corpse allows time for elaborate funeral preparations. Popular orchestras, church choirs, or traditional music and dance troupes may be hired to provide the best entertainment possible. Local announcers equipped with loudspeakers mounted on taxis or private cars may go around to make funeral announcements in poetic language. These announcements may be aired on the regional or national television and radio stations. In the course of the funeral services, public announcers may be engaged by sympathizers to present their respective donations to the bereaved families. Female representation in Akan death culture, however, remains central even as new features are introduced.

DISCUSSION

Profound social changes are taking place in Ghana as in other developing societies of Africa, and mortuary rituals have not been immune to these changes, but have come to reflect a new meaning of death. The dread once held for the spirit of the deceased has waned. Christian interpretations of death have come to supersede traditional ones for Akan Christians. Respect for the dead and the bereaved is now partially conferred by the quantity and quality of material trappings. These changes are themselves a reflection of processes of modernization and Westernization, which purportedly foster the ascendancy of new beliefs and commercialism over tradition.[4]

Much of contemporary Akan popular culture that has crept into funeral ceremonies can be viewed as commercial exploitation. Where palm wine and *Akpeteshi* (local gin) used to be the principal drinks at funerals, imported liquor, various brands of beer, and mineral water have become substitutes. In many instances, fanciful and very expensive caskets placed in hearses have replaced the wooden caskets constructed by local carpenters and carried shoulder high to burial places. Gone are the days when Akosombo red and black prints served as important markers for distinguishing the social hierarchies of those involved in a funeral ceremony. Distinctions are partly made on the basis of who wears the best Dutch wax and other imported prints.

In the past, contributions in kind to funeral ceremonies constituted the norm. Nowadays, cash is collected to spend on a variety of items required to conduct a public funeral ceremony, including remodeling or repairing the lineage base compound, preparation of burial place and food, hiring local or professional musicians and dancers for the entertainment of guests and participants. Cash donations have become a mark of social distinction in many Akan communities. A sympathizer not only has to put on the best funeral clothing, but also has to present a donation of considerable value to the bereaved family. The creeping commercialization is transforming bereavement into a largely monetized venture. Some Akan communities, including many in the Ashanti and Brong Ahafo Regions, have reacted to this process of change by imposing upper limits on the amount of money donated at funeral ceremonies held within their jurisdictions.

Nonetheless, the competition for status in an industrializing society like Ghana has given death much prominence with the accelerated incorporation of business norms into bereavement practices (Pratt 1981). It is now possible to give wide publicity to the deceased's achievements in terms of culturally accepted criteria of success. This is achieved through the use of media channels available in the country.

Not only that, wide publicity also enhances the status of the living members of the deceased's lineage, especially if an elaborate and expensive funeral is provided. By directly or indirectly imposing business norms on bereavement, Akan funeral ceremonies have become social security systems, as well as fashion and entertainment for many participants, especially women. Writing about the ceremonial duties of Kumasi market queens (*Ahemma*), Clark (1994:269) observes:

> The scale of funeral attendance marks structural divisions within the market. When a commodity group member dies, her Ohemma leads all the group members to attend her funeral en masse. The individual ahemma also attend funerals of group members' close relatives, accompanied by several elders and near neighbors of the bereaved, presenting a group contribution. . . . Many traders also belong to church women's groups and choirs that attend members' funerals in uniform, singing. They gain further prestige by fundraising and attending church services together in uniform. Asantes value group membership as such, since for many ceremonial purposes groups are virtually interchangeable. At one funeral I attended, a middle-aged woman remarked appreciatively that the dead woman had belonged to four *ekuo*, or groups: Two church choirs, a commodity group, and a benevolent society. All four groups attended en masse to make a grand funeral such as anyone might aspire to.

Another social change can be discerned from the passage just cited. Within the context of contemporary ceremonies, nonkin bases of social alignment have emerged to supplement kin relations. Market women's and church choir groups have become significant celebrants in Akan funerals. As can be inferred from the passage, social realignment provides one more avenue for the infusion of popular culture into Akan mortuary rituals, and the prominence of women in this process is clearly apparent. This process of change underscores Giddens's (1991:10) observation that "in struggling with problems, individuals help actively to reconstruct the universe of social activity around them." The point here is that even though death may be viewed as a form of social disruption, it nonetheless offers opportunities for self and group development and future happiness.

In the midst of the rapid social changes, business innovations by women have converged with other social forces to reshape Akan, and for that matter Ghanaian, mortuary rituals and bereavement customs. For example, it is quite common nowadays for the corpse to be elaborately dressed for the wake by professional women. It is also common for women in the clothing business to design and sew special dresses for bereaved families, church choirs, and commodity groups for funeral celebrations. Often these preparations are funded by relatives (both men and women) residing in the cities and abroad.

Those aspects of popular culture infused into the contemporary expression of Akan funerals provide an opportunity for both men and women to make public statements about their own social worth. Given the increasingly hierarchical social order, the competition for status is rendering the need for observing many of the death rituals less significant. Past practices concerning property transfers (i.e., cocoa farm or home ownership) in the course of Akan funeral ceremonies tended to perpetuate gender difference. Since respectability and reputation have come to be associated increasingly with women's educational status, wealth in terms of landed property, money, and Christian religious participation, among others, strict observance of widowhood rituals is waning. The acquisition of these status symbols provides women much latitude in the construction of their own life course, and it is likely that a change in the balance of decision-making concerning mortuary rituals will favor the more affluent. Among the largely illiterate masses of women, the traditional mortuary rituals will continue to offer them legitimacy in their management of and responses to death.

Throughout this presentation emphasis has been placed on how Akan culture affected and continues to affect the management and disposal of the dead. Primary and secondary burials are the processes by which these acts are accomplished. Women's roles in the ritual and popular drama have been assessed. The different kinds of work performed by women make death a reality which demands a community's reorientation toward life. Affirmation of the social status of the deceased and the bereaved family is achieved through the joyous celebration of the funeral, marked by the display of institutionalized behavior. In general, honor and respect for the dead and the bereaved family come from a large turnout of mourners, music, and dance. The large turnout is achieved not only through the numerous descendants of the deceased's matrilineage, but also through the social connections accumulated over the deceased's lifetime.

Akan mortuary rituals are undergoing dramatic changes. The processes of change have resulted in the emergence of an immense and varied amalgam of sentiments, attitudes, and community responses to the funeral celebration which, in its contemporary form, also reflects an expression of popular culture as well as women's increasing importance. Contemporary expressions of grief help to reinforce Akan communities and, as Giddens (1991:10) points out, while the changes taking place may produce anxieties for many, those changes may also help mobilize more adaptive responses and novel initiatives to death and grief.

NOTES

1. The Akan of Ghana comprise the forebears and succeeding generations who occupied the present Ashanti, Brong Ahafo, Central, Eastern, and Western Regions of the country. Akan cultures include more than a dozen ethnic groups, speaking mutually intelligible dialects. Among these groups are Asante, Fante, Bono, Akyem, Akuapem, Kwahu, Akwamu, Asen, Denkyira, Twifo, and Wassa. Another cluster of Akan people occupy southeastern Ivory Coast.
2. This interpretation may be regarded as one of many possible interpretations where there are multiple layers of meaning. If the widowhood ritual should be interpreted as an example of female oppression in Akan societies (Oduyoye 1995), then the source of the oppression may also be attributable to the increasingly monetized economy in which the accumulation of material, rather than social, wealth has gained in ascendancy and thereby exacerbated marital and other interpersonal tensions.
3. This behavior has been interpreted as an instantiation of the tyranny of the system of patriarchy prevailing in Akan society (see Oduyoye 1995 and Dolphyne 1991).
4. For a full treatment of the economic implications of this transformation in Akan culture, see Arhin (1994).

BIBLIOGRAPHY

Adjaye, J. K. 1997. Introduction. Language, Rhythm, and Sound: Black Popular Cultures in the Twenty-First Century, eds. J. K. Adjaye and A. R. Andrews, pp. 1-16. Pittsburgh.

Antubam, K. 1963. Ghana's Heritage of Culture. Leipzig.

Arhin, K. 1994. The Economic Implications of Transformations in Akan Funeral Rites. Africa 64(3):307-21.

Clark, G. 1994. Onions Are My Husband: Survival and Accumulation by West African Market Women. Chicago.

Danquah, J. B. 1928. Akan Laws and Customs. London.

Davidson, B. 1969. The African Genius. Boston.

Dolphyne, F. A. 1991. The Emancipation of Women: An African Perspective. Accra.

Giddens, A. 1991. Modernity and Self-Identity: Self and Society in the Late Modern Age. Stanford.

Goody, J. 1975. Death and the Interpretation of Culture: A Bibliographic Overview. Death in America, ed. P. Aries, pp. 1-8. Philadelphia.

Hertz, R. 1960. Death and the Right Hand, transl. R. Needham and C. Needham. Glencoe.

Kamerman, J. B. 1988. Death in the Midst of Life. Englewood Cliffs.

Kyei, T. E. 1992. Marriage and Divorce among the Asante. Cambridge African Monographs 14.

Lindemann, E. 1963. Grief. Encyclopedia of Mental Health, Vol. 2, eds. A. Duetsch and H. Fisherman, pp. 703-06. New York.

McCaskie, T. C. 1989. Death and the Asantehene: A Historical Meditation. Journal of African History 30:417-44.

Nketia, J. H. 1969. Funeral Dirges of the Akan People. New York.

Oduyoye, M. A. 1995. Daughters of Anowa: African Women and Patriarchy. Maryknoll.

Platt, L. A., and V. R. Persico, Jr. (eds.) 1992. Grief in Cross-Cultural Perspective: A Casebook. New York.

Pratt, L. 1981. Business Temporal Norms and Bereavement Behavior. American Sociological Review 46:317-33.

Rattray, R. S. 1927. Religion and Art in Ashanti. London.

Warren, D. M. 1975. The Techiman-Bono of Ghana: An Ethnography of an Akan Society. Dubuque.

3. The Ontological Journey

"In a muddy land, a person slips and falls easily. Those who follow behind beware." These were the words of wisdom spoken to Ọrunmila when he was traveling in a strange land called Ejibọnmẹfọn.

Before he set out, his diviners warned him to perform a sacrifice [*erubo*] so that he could be disgraced only to be later blessed. He sacrificed animals, birds, yams, palm oil, and all sorts of foodstuffs. The diviners put everything in a clay bowl, instructing Ọrunmila to carry it on his journey. He followed their instructions. Thank goodness he made the sacrifice. On the way, he first passed through the market on the outskirts of the town. There, Ẹṣu decided to humiliate him.

Causing it to rain heavily, Ẹṣu made the land slippery, but Ọrunmila persevered. As he reached the marketplace he slipped and fell down. The animals' blood, the palm oil, the food splattered all over his body. It was not pleasant to be so dirty. When the women and children in the market saw what happened, they began to laugh and ridicule him.

Ọrunmila did not know anybody. Ashamed and disgraced, he sat down feeling sorry for himself. That night when the marketwomen and their children went to sleep, Ẹṣu made them dream of blood spilling over their bodies. They were startled. Some woke up in fright, some became ill, some fell unconscious. Their husbands and fathers worried. Ẹṣu suddenly appeared inquiring:

What happened?

Husbands: The women woke up frightened and now they are ill.
Ẹṣu: Oh! You must consult a diviner.
Husbands: But there is no diviner around.
Ẹṣu: Yes, there is. You don't know? He is in the market.
Husbands: Take me to him.
Ẹṣu: Well then, bring a ram, a cow, some fish, a he-goat, a she-goat, and plenty of money.

Everybody went, one-by-one, each taking the prescribed animals and cash. Ọrunmila received everybody and helped them. In addition to the wealth he accumulated in that strange land, he also became famous.

Ọrunmila decided to thank the diviners who had advised him on his journey. During his thanksgiving service, he described how his beloved, learned diviners, in interpreting Ifa for him so wisely, had given him the words of wisdom that slippery land slips people up. Those who follow behind take note and be cautious.

But Ọrunmila's diviners said they were not to be thanked, that they themselves had to thank Ifa for giving them their wisdom. Then Ifa interjected that he is with God and God is with him.[1] Thus he too must not be thanked, but he must thank God Almighty.

In celebration, Ọrunmila's diviners summoned *apere* musicians from Ilara, *apesi* musicians and dancers from Ikija, and *iṣẹrimọlẹ* dancers from Kijikiji, gathering them from different quarters.[2] As they played, Ọrunmila sang:

I fell down and everybody saw me.
They ridiculed me.
Who knew what the result would be?
I fell down and everybody saw me.
They ridiculed me.

***

Mo ṣubú, wọ́n rí mi ò.
Ẹ̀ lí sì mù'gbè yìn.
Ẹ̀ lí sì mù'gbèhìn eti mi o?
Mo ṣubú o, wọ́n rí mi ò.
Ẹ̀ lí sì mù'gbè yìn.
(Ọṣitọla #86.75)

Stories such as this often narrate the experiences of ancient diviners or animals on their distant journeys. "Words of wisdom" begin the verses, framing the story, teaching lessons about life. But these words require interpretation and contemplation. Thus the wisdom of the story above is not to beware of slipping and falling, but has to do with humility, humiliation, and reciprocity. Ọrunmila withstood humiliation only to be blessed with fame and wealth. He thanked his diviners, who thanked Ifa, who in turn thanked God. Who slipped—Ọrunmila or those who ridiculed him? And who gained most from the humiliation? Ọrunmila learned humility through the experience of humiliation, while the ones who humiliated him suffered most and in the end paid the greater price. This journey is only one among the many represented in Ifa literature that posit uncountable life situations. Such stories are always told in relation to an individual's personal problem.

Ọṣitọla, my diviner friend who lives in the town of Imodi only a few kilometers outside Ijẹbu-Ode, told me this story in relation to a personal experience of mine, so that I would not feel discouraged. Things had been going amiss; it was

one of those kinds of days that is often associated with the workings of Eṣu, the unpredictable trickster/messenger, who in the story was instrumental in transforming Ọrunmila's disgrace into fame and fortune. According to his family history, Ọṣitọla is a seventh-generation diviner as well as a drummer and a member of the Oṣugbo society, formerly the indigenous judiciary in Yoruba communities (M. Drewal and H. Drewal 1983). He and I have been working together since 1982, tape-recording more than one hundred fifty hours of conversations (fig. 3.1). Our talks, mostly in English, but interspersed with key concepts and discussions in Yoruba, covered religious and ritual topics.

Trained in the two hundred and fifty-six sets of divination texts (Odu Ifa), each with uncountable verses (*ẹsẹ*), Ọṣitọla has a keen memory.[3] In 1986, he remembered details of our discussions from 1982, sometimes reminding me that I was being redundant. When I responded that I was merely cross-checking, he retorted, "no, you are double-crossing." He always looked forward to "wonderful" questions, that is, ones that made him wonder. They were not always easy for me to produce; Ọṣitọla thinks analytically and by his own account used to pester his father and grandfather quizzing them incessantly on the whys and wherefores of various ritual acts. He learned divination as a young boy simply by accompanying them during ritual, and at recess in primary school he used to divine for classmates on the ground. By the age of ten he was already taking leading ritual roles. From his grandmother, who was a priest of the deity Oriṣanla, he learned how to prepare shrines and care for the deities.

Nicknamed Abidifa (A-bi-di-Ifa, "One who teaches the ABC's of Ifa"), Ọṣitọla can go on at great length naming the segments that make up the rituals he performs, describing the action associated with them, and explicating their meanings. In interviews, after exhausting all my questions, he would usually end by telling me what I had failed to ask. This eventually developed into an almost structural feature of our interviews. My most "wonderful" questions by his standards were the ones for which there were no ready answers, the ones that required thought and sometimes left him momentarily blank.

We discovered that the best method of working was simply for him to narrate what he does—step by step—and for me to ask questions for clarification. The Ijẹbu Yoruba term for a discrete ritual segment is *aito*, which is related to the noun *eto*, an order or program, the root word for *letoleto*, implying "in an orderly fashion one after the other." The serial form of performance is evoked in the very terms Yoruba use to characterize it (M. Drewal and H. Drewal 1987). Therefore, not only are participants' experiences of ritual fragmented, but the form itself is segmented.

During our many discussions of various kinds of rituals Ọṣitọla performs, he kept referring to the "journey" as a way of conveying the experiential impact that ritual has on its participants. Finally I asked him explicitly, "are all rituals journeys?" He explained,

> the whole life span is wonderful. And even the actors are wonderful, I mean, the human beings. They are the main actors. The two are wonderful.

3.1 Diviner Kọlawọle Ọṣitọla and his three sons, together with the author. Ijẹbu area, village of Imodi, 1 November 1986.

> One proverb says, when a young child falls, he looks to the front, but if an elder is falling he will always turn to look back in search of what befell him. Nowadays, the elders don't look back to see what has befallen them.
>
> It is a sort of wisdom to reflect on past events to make a good decision on where we should try to go or what should happen. And this makes a journey. But it seems to me as if everybody is contented, everybody is satisfied, everybody has already completed their journeys. No more journeys. Then I get worried. The actors want to end the journey. Or the journey wants to end. But to my knowledge the journey ends not. That is one of the things that makes your question wonderful to me because I know you are one of the actors. And I wondered how you could even ask, are they all journeys. (Ọṣitọla #86.75)

Ọṣitọla does not use the word "actors" in the Western sense of "players of roles." Rather, he means people of action. I perceived the significance of his use of the metaphor of the journey only after I began to realize just how many Yoruba rituals are actually constructed as journeys.

JOURNEYING IN ORATURE AND RITUAL

Divination verses tell of the journeys of ancient diviners and of deities and witches, "when they were coming from heaven to earth" (*nigba ti wọn n t'ọrun*

bọ w'aye). The journey (*irin ajo*, or simply *ajo*) is an important organizing metaphor in Yoruba thought.[4] The verb *rin*, "to walk," when compounded means "to travel" (*rin irin* or *rinrin*). More than simply a movement forward, the act of traveling implies a transformation in the process, a progression.

Rituals in the form of masking displays travel in the sense that trained specialists "bring them into the world" from their otherworldly domain and send them away again through their performances of spectacle (H. Drewal and M. Drewal 1983:2–4). The deities journey into the world, too, by mounting the heads of their priests, who go into states of possession trance (M. Drewal 1986, 1988). Elaborated transitional stages mark the deity's arrival and withdrawal.

Wherever Yoruba religion thrives—Brazil, Cuba, the United States—this practice of journeying through possession trance has been maintained. Cast in a myriad of ways—in narratives and in ritual performances—the journey as a metaphor highlights the experiential, reflexive nature of day-to-day living. Nowhere is this more explicit than in the oral tradition and performance of Ọṣugbo, the traditional society of elders that historically formed the judiciary in communities throughout southern Yorubaland.[5] Ọṣitọla recited the following Ifa verse as the foundation of Ọṣugbo (taped discussion #86.83):

A small child works his way off the edge of his
  sleeping mat.
A bird soars high above it all.
They divined for our elderly people,
When they were preparing to leave heaven to go to the
  world.
They said, what are we going to do?
They asked themselves, where are we going?
We are going in search of knowledge, truth, and justice.
In accordance with our destiny,
At the peak of the hill
We were delayed.
We are going to meet success.[6]
We will arrive on earth knowledgeable.
We will arrive on earth in beauty.
We are searching for knowledge continuously.
Knowledge has no end.

***

Ọmọ ilé tí a gbà gbé l'órí ẹní, yí o já bọ́.
Òkè l'ẹyẹ fò wún.
A diá fún àwọn àgbàgbà,
Tí wọ́n ti ìkọ̀lè ọ̀run bọ̀ wá ilé ayé.
Wón ní kíni wón ńlọ ṣe?
Ènyìn ọ̀rọ̀, níbo lò ńlọ̀?
À ńlọ wá ìmọ̀, òtítọ́, àti òdodo.

Kádàrá àyànmọ̀,[7]
L'órí òke
Àti pẹ̀tẹ́lẹ̀.
À ńlọ sí ààfin ọba réré.
A ó dé ilẹ̀ mímọ̀.
A ó sì dé ilẹ̀ tó l'ẹ́wà.
À ń wá ìmọ̀ síi l'ójo júmọ̀.
Ìmọ̀ kò ló'pin.

Ọṣitọla's gloss on this verse was as follows:

"A small child works his way off the edge of his sleeping mat. A bird soars high above it all." These were the words of wisdom spoken to some wise elders when they were leaving on a journey from heaven to the world. The classic meaning is just that a person should not be elevated unless he is prepared to fly above and search more.

Ifa told the elders to make a sacrifice. He told every one of them to carry along a walking stick for themselves, because their journey was far and they would feel tired. They did, and their path was blessed when they grew old.

These people in youth had the power to do things; in middle age the spreading world still had power;[8] then they moved to the elderly age. Their sacrifice was the staff, their assistant.

The elders thought. They started to search. They felt uncomfortable in their positions. They wanted to know more throughout the world. They decided to search for more, more, more. Because they were getting old, they felt worn out. That is why they were assisted by their staffs. Then their minds struck and asked them, "you, where are you going?" *Enyin ọrọ, nibo lo nlọ?* It started changing their conscience. Then they remembered what Ifa had told them. On their journey they are searching for truth, wisdom, and knowledge. *A nlọ wa imọ, otitọ, ati ododo* in obedience to their *kadara ayanmọ*, destiny. In accordance with our destiny, we are searching for true knowledge and the facts. Then their conscience told them to continue with the search.

A person still searches with a staff in his hand after he has labored. Then the elders quickly remembered that their conscience told them that if they search for knowledge and wisdom, it will be through all the rough paths, *ori oke on pẹtẹlẹ*. That means, if they want to fulfill their destiny, they have to walk the path through the land, the hills, the water, the thorns, the troubles. They have to pass all troubles so that they can fulfill their destiny. And if they can afford to do this, they are sure to land at a holy place. *L'ori oke, ati pẹtẹlẹ, a nlọ si aafin ọba rere, a o wa dẹlẹ mimọ, a o si wa a dẹlẹ to lẹwa.* That means, if we can continue to search, to search,

the end of our journey will be a cooler place where we have a good head, where it is holy, where it is smooth. This story is in Ifa.

Why I am telling this story is that it is related to Ọṣugbo. That is their guidance or their foundation. When you are a member and you are upgraded to a point, that is your foundation—that Ifa verse relates to the behavior, the belief, the thinking, and the reasoning of the Ọṣugbos. That was why you saw me nodding when we concluded that the journey continues, the search continues.

You know Ogboni means elderly people. You think that you still start, you feel that you still begin. And even at your dying point, you will feel that you will decide you will still continue. You will not be sure whether you have searched enough. And even on your death, after you have found yourself at the resting place, at the cooler place, then you will feel you are leaving the search to be continued with those who will take it from you. They will bid you bye, and say you are expected to continue. That is why you see me so serious that night when we are trying to agree that, oh, the search continues.

This story may not be so interesting, but it is a true picture of our discussion, and it is a true picture of Ọṣugbo. It relates to the research of the elders and why elders are still searching. You know nowadays elders get contented, even at [age] forty.

The reason why I am trying to translate or transcribe it or share the view with you to digest is because it is very serious. That is one of the foundations of our family. Their foundation is the search continues. That is one of the motives behind our continued inheritance of Ifa and Ogboni in our family. We want the search to be continued. Even my grandfather wants me to continue; my father wants to continue; I want to continue. Since Ọṣijo [the father seven generations back] we want the search to be continued.

The verse is one of the important things my grandfather gave me. And I have been graduating on it. He didn't elaborate it to such an extent, but when I became a staunch member of Ọṣugbo and I learned more, I found more, I could get what he was really concerned with deeply from my initiation, going through some rituals, and I found out that, oh, the search continues in fact. In my family circle, it is my life.

Ọṣitọla's explanation was an improvised narrative based on a preformulated verse. As he commented, his grandfather "gave" him the verse, but did not elaborate it. Only later—Ọṣitọla claimed—after going through rituals did he come to understand his grandfather's deep concerns. The verse served as a precedent for the narrative and to some extent guided it.[9] He contextualized both the verse and the improvised narrative within our conversations, regarding the latter not only as a "true picture" of what it means to be a member of Ọṣugbo, but as a "true picture" of our own conversations. By that time, I had in fact gone through a preliminary initiation into Ọṣugbo at Imodi so that the story was meaningful for me on two levels. The narrative also reflected Ọṣitọla's perception of my work as a researcher, which he correlated with the "journeying" of Ọṣugbo elders and Ifa priests.

At Ọṣugbo meetings during the annual festival—I attended six in three different society lodges (*iledii*) between October 11 and December 1, 1986—each of the titled elders danced solos from one end of the enclosed space to the other, giving concrete expression to the idea of the journey. Their performances were improvised. Each dance was a personal condensation of life's journey (*ajo l'aye*), performed to the drum language of music called *ẹwẹlẹ*, an ideophonic word implying an assortment of rhythms considered good for dancing. As an Ọṣugbo drummer, Ọṣitọla says he changes the rhythms according to the particular dancer's concentration. By approximating the tonal patterns and rhythm of spoken Yoruba, Ọṣitọla weaves into the music praise epithets (*oriki*) particular to each dancing elder. For Akọnọrọn—to take one example—the titled elder who acts as the defense counselor in criminal cases, Ọṣitọla sometimes plays:

Teacher of the art of speaking
The one who teaches how to state a case
Pleads for the innocent

***

A kóni ní oro
A kó-ni lẹ́jọ́
Àwí jàre

In and around the praise epithets, Ọṣitọla weaves dance instructions—one-liners that are mixed and repeated to form a free rhythm, each alluding to life's journey. One tells the dancing elder in effect to watch where he or she is stepping. It alludes to life's potential pitfalls—"the thorns, the troubles" and the value of reflecting on the past in order to guide present action:

Elder, watch the ground

***

Àgbà wolẹ̀

Improvisationally in step with the *agba* drums, the dancer enacts "checking up" the ground (fig. 3.2), visibly watching where she or he places the foot. Or, in another example:

Carry on]stepping[on the ground

***

Ǹṣó n'lẹ̀

The *lẹ* in both verses above refers to the ground or earth, *ilẹ*. To the latter rhythm the dancer is supposed to step lively and confidently on the earth. How the rhythm is interpreted spatially and stylistically is left to each dancer's discretion. The latter verse, Ọṣitọla explained to me, is an assertion that the elders have authority over the earth; therefore, the drummers direct them to "carry on" with the business at hand. Their authority is rooted in the precolonial, gerontocratic government of Yorubaland.

It was with his experience of this kind of ritual performance described above that Ọṣitọla said he came to understand his grandfather's deep concerns. On the surface, the verbal content of the drummed messages does not say much. It is only in living, or "journeying," that elders begin to read meaning into such esoteric words and actions. My own understanding comes from Ọṣitọla's explanations, and only then after my initiation, which entitled me to enter Ọṣugbo lodges to participate in certain performances.

In many kinds of Yoruba ritual, the performance processes embody all of the characteristics of a journey: 1) travel from one place to another, and a return—sometimes actual, sometimes virtual, 2) new experiences, 3) joys and hardships along the route, 4) material for further contemplation and reflection, and 5) presumed growth or progress as a result of the whole experience. Rites of passage that scholars mark in a tripartite movement from separation and liminality to reaggregation (Turner 1977a:94) are in a very real sense journeys. But transition is not merely social, not simply a collective adjustment to internal changes or an adaptation to the external environment.

Like journeys, rites of passage are fundamentally transformations of experience, a deepening and broadening of each individual's understanding in relation to his or her prior experience and knowledge. If this were not so, how would participants *feel* social transition? Or, from another point of view, why is it that social transition cannot often simply be legislated or ordained? Even in our own society, rituals often attend legislated transitions. Thus what constitutes a marriage legally has little to do with what getting married means performatively. The latter in most cases constitutes the greater part of the experience of transition. Both in rituals and in journeys, participants operate at different levels of understanding and also have different capacities for making meaning.

As Ọṣitọla argued for a ritual he conducts:

> All people who go to the sacred bush]*igbodu*[benefit from it. They may be observers; they may be priests; they may be the initiate. Only we concentrate on the initiate most. Yet everybody is involved, particularly the priests, for there is a belief—and it's an agreement between ourselves and Odu]the deity[within the sacred bush—that we are reborning ourselves. Even we priests, we are getting another rebirth. At every ritual, we are becoming new because we have something to reflect upon. We have something to contemplate during the journey, at the journey, after the journey. Our brains become sharper. We become new to the world. We

think of everything. We *do* there, and we *see* there. And even more simply we pray for everybody. (Ọṣitọla #86.134)

With each restoration of behavior, even the ritual specialist is transformed and "becomes new to the world." This is also true for me as I experience Yoruba ritual repeatedly. Through a process of observation/participation, conversations with participants, contemplation, and reflection, I too become a ritual traveler in Ọṣitọla's sense, although what I derive from the experience will not necessarily be the same as what anyone else derives from the same experience. This is so not only because of differences in cultural and personal experience, but because of differences in the motives and motivations of the various participants. Most important is the idea that the sojourner may return to the same place physically, but not experientially.

Rituals attend both birth and death and serve as temporal articulation points of ontological transformation analogous to the spatial point of articulation represented by the crossroads. Such rituals are the focus of the remainder of this chapter and the next. As a member of Ọṣugbo, Ọṣitọla narrated to me a detailed outline of funeral ritual from the practitioner's point of view, designating the names of the various stages of performance. Ọṣitọla's outline is an individual's normative account of what he knows from personal experience, not a presentation of dogma. Whether or not a funeral *always* happens just this way is not my concern here, although his descriptions of the public portions do correspond to what I have observed.

My intention is threefold: 1) Ọṣitọla's account illustrates how Yoruba practitioners conceptualize, order, and explicate ritual. Both the doing and the talking about the doing derive from the same stock of performance knowledge (Giddens 1986:29). 2) His specialist's view is also revealing about the concept of the ontological journey. This is critical at the end of the chapter for a reevaluation of the notion of cyclical time in Mircea Eliade's sense (1959:77–78).[10] 3) Equally important, Ọṣitọla's conceptual model underscores the centrality of play in Yoruba ritual, a topic I explore throughout the rest of the chapters. It is apparent throughout that Ọṣitọla is conscious that ritual specialists are engaged in acts of interpretation and representation. Although I have not always quoted him verbatim, I have preserved his language, descriptions, and explanations quite literally, restricting my own comments to footnotes.

THE FUNERAL PASSAGE

There are many different kinds of funerals. The circumstances of death, its perceived causes, the age and social as well as religious affiliations of the deceased all are taken into account as a family decides what type of funeral to perform. Here Ọṣitọla narrates the structure and content of the funeral he claims everyone hopes to have—the desired one—except if the deceased is Muslim or Christian.[11] These funerals (*isinku*) are for those who have died of old age. They are not simple matters of burying the corpse; rather, they involve seven days of ritual (*etutu*) performed to convey the spirit of the deceased to its otherworldly realm, where it remains along with other ancestral spirits. Friends of the deceased's family experience a funeral primarily as a time of dancing and feasting in celebration of the elder's long successful life. For the family, however, a funeral demands great effort and an enormous expense to ensure the continued beneficence of the elder's spirit toward those still on earth. A funeral is a critical time when the deceased's spirit lingers in the world, disembodied. There is also the expectation that the spirit will eventually return in newborn children. A funeral in this way marks an ending as well as a new beginning.

The actual interment of the corpse is conceived only as a preliminary event to the funeral process. The performances that follow are more critical for the family. After the interment, family members gather to decide on a date for the performances that complete the *isinku*, the funeral. Since the *isinku* entails great expense, it is incumbent on the family to set a date far enough in the not-too-distant future to give them time to gather sufficient resources. The funeral may therefore occur anywhere from a month to a year, or more, after burial. What follows interment, according to Ọṣitọla, is a seven-day program in which certain days are set aside for celebration: the first, or "main," funeral day of ritual (*ọjọ isinku*); the third day, for feasting (*itaoku*); the fourth day, a public celebration or day of play (*irenoku*, literally "playing on the deceased's behalf"); and a seventh and final celebration day (*ijeku*).[12] Funerals are in this way elaborated with feasting and public performances, part of the sacrifice to the deceased.

Most of the rituals that revolve around interment are exclusive. They are the prerogative of the Ọṣugbo society, whose membership in the past was restricted to those whose parents were dead. Prior to the colonial period, Ọṣugbo included the senior members of each family in a community. Because of their age, accumulated knowledge, and power, they comprised the segment of the community that was indeed closest to the ancestors by virtue of their proximity to death.

INTERMENT (*IFẸHIN OKU-TILẸ*)[13]

"Washing the corpse" (*Iweku*): A cosmetologist (*ọnatonise*, "one skilled in the art of restoration"), who is a member of Ọṣugbo, prepares the corpse by first sacrificing a cock or a hen, depending on whether the deceased is male or female. In the case of a female, for example, it is said that the voice of the hen follows the deceased to the otherworld.[14] The sacrificial blood, together with a preparation of water and herbs, is used to wash the corpse.

"Rubbing chalk on the deceased's palms" (*Ikẹfunlọwọ*) and "Rubbing camwood on the palms" (*Ikosunlọwọ*): After washing the corpse, the eldest living offspring of the deceased rubs chalk (*ẹfun*) and then camwood (*osun*) on the deceased's palms. This means that the child who was nurtured is now nurturing the deceased parent in return. Or, in other words, as a parent brings a child into the world so must the child assist in the parent's passage into the otherworld. As the eldest applies the chalk, the children say to the deceased, "you put chalk in my hand for me" (*ikẹfun lọwọ fun mi*).[15]

"Wrapping the corpse of the wise elder" (*Idiku Ologbon*): Relatives and other supporters of the deceased each bring cloth for the Oṣugbo members to wrap around the corpse. The cloth expresses their gratitude to the deceased for his or her good deeds. The sheer volume of the wrapped corpse is indicative of the social significance of the deceased. The word *ologbon* literally means "a wise person." In this context it refers both to the deceased elder and to a colorful, highly patterned cloth known as *aṣọ ologbọn*—a trademark of elders (fig. 3.3). The importance of wrapping the deceased in cloth is expressed in the adage "the corpse of the elder should not be thrown away; it is white cloth that I wore from heaven to the world" (*oku ologbọn ki s'oko; ala mo fi b'ọrun w'aye*). The idea is that the elder should leave the world in a similar manner as the child is born into it.[16]

The multipatterned cloth represents the accumulation of the deceased's experiences while on earth. Hence—to quote directly:

> We bury them with these kinds of cloth to make them more concerned. You know they have gotten experiences. They have lived in hot weather—all sorts of weather—they have mixed with all sorts of people. They will be settling differences between people when they quarrel. They have been seeing women with good characters, with bad characters, and men with good characters and bad characters. They have moved with the elders, the youths, the ancestors. Now they have combined many experiences. This cloth contains within itself their many experiences with animals, with human beings, up and down the hills, with dangerous creatures, with non-dangerous creatures. Experiences make you more open to life and death.[17]

"Washing the coffin" (*Iwegi*): Later in the evening, a representative from both the father's and the mother's sides of the family join the cosmetologist to sacrifice a goat to the coffin, blessing it for the deceased by putting some of the blood in their hands and a little in the coffin. The three of them then wash the coffin inside and out with herbal water: together they dip balls of cotton wool into the water, the left hand washing inside as the right washes outside. Then reversing the process, they cross their arms and use the right hand on the inside and the left on the outside. After working their way around the coffin in this manner three times, the cosmetologist removes the sacrificial goat, whose meat is part of his remuneration for work.

"Laying the back of the deceased on the earth" (*Ifẹhinkutilẹ*):[18] This occurs in the evening when it is cool. Starting around eight o'clock, the cosmetologist arranges the body in the coffin in preparation for the next stage of the ritual, when the elders gather and feast with the deceased throughout the night.

"Entertaining with the deceased" (*Ibokuu-yaju*): When an elder dies, her or his contemporaries, normally the Oṣugbo members, celebrate with the deceased after they have wrapped the corpse. The high-ranking elders go with their drums

before it is too dark and send the naive people away—the youth, the untrained, and the uninitiated. They lay the deceased out on a handwoven mat (*ẹni fafa*), and all sit down with him or her to feast. This ritual is conceived as a kind of "send-off party" to bid their comrade farewell. The elders wine, dine, and discuss, reaffirming their camaraderie in the deceased's presence.

As Ọṣitọla put it, "now that the soul is going to join the ancestors, they must present themselves in the same spirit as the deceased and the other ancestors, who may have gathered to receive him, in order to bear witness that they are still loyal. They still love him. Their mind is still open to him." Each time they put the wine to their lips, they also open the cloth and put it to the deceased's lips to express their cooperation. The cosmetologists then dance as the drums are beaten.

This ritual segment tests the honesty and sincerity of Oṣugbo members. Thus those among them who do not show up are assumed to be dishonest,

> because he[19] will not be able to lead himself between life and death. Because he cannot live to the death point, it means he is not supposed to be among them. That is a test, and it is a belief among Yorubas in the olden days that somebody who cannot go through *ibokuu-yaju* has in his mind that he has not been behaving openly. Hence he must be sure to eat and dine with the dead because it is they who join the ancestors. And the ancestors' spirits are supposed to be ruling the community and guiding the community right. Somebody who cannot join somebody who is joining the ancestors is not for the good of the community. He is not open. He may be a sort of liability. He is not a good asset because nobody will be able to believe him.

This ritual is the deceased's initiation by the society of elders into the group of the ancestors.

"Sending away the spirit of the deceased" (*Ikanku*): After the lid of the coffin is closed, the eldest child takes the cosmetologist's brass staff and raps it three times near the corpse's head. The knocking dispatches the soul of the deceased. Finally, the cosmetologist sees to it that the coffin is placed in the grave, completing the interment of the corpse.

The Main Funeral Day (Ọjọ Isinku)

"Collecting money for the deceased" (*Owoetiwẹku*): During the main day of the funeral, family members first of all collect money from all the relatives to buy gin and arrange for food. Formerly bean cakes were most desirable. The relatives contribute money in proportion to their closeness to the deceased. The more distant the relations, the less they are expected to contribute.[20]

"Playing for the funeral" (*Ereisinku*): The first public ceremony is a spectacle of playing and dancing in honor of the deceased. Relatives of the deceased hire music groups and accompany them around the town dancing and singing the praises of the family (fig. 3.4).[21] Family members also try to hire music groups that reflect the stylistic tastes of the deceased. Ọṣitọla told me of the funeral of his father, Ọṣinẹyẹ, when his father's junior brother attempted to attract musicians from his senior brother's group so that he could personally provide the deceased's favorite musical style. Any style is appropriate as long as the group is mobile, for it is essential to parade throughout the community.

The social importance of the deceased is measured by the amount of *ere,* or "play," going on throughout the town. Forty-three musical groups paraded around for Ọṣitọla's father's funeral. The number of groups became a topic of discussion among townspeople. They asked, "How many groups played for Ọṣinẹyẹ's funeral?" (*Ere meloo ni wọn ṣe l'ọjọ ti Ọṣinẹyẹ ku?*)

The parades of music and dance independently working their ways through the town are a formal ritual segment (*aito*) that is meaningful beyond the display for its own sake. As Ọṣitọla expressed it,

> they think dancing and enjoying after the death will depict the deceased's achievements on earth, how he or she was able to behave to the community. [. . .] It is not that they are extravagant. They do it for a meaning. If they don't do it, then the deceased who is joining the ancestors will be concerned and unhappy—and be wandering—because he has not been remembered. The deceased will have to answer queries [that is, from the ancestors]. "Why are you not properly initiated, or sent to us? Perhaps you have not performed well, have not achieved well? If you have performed well, why is posterity forgetting you?" The only way for us on earth to judge the deceased is to know how much honor was given to him by his descendants.

"Taking the achievements of the deceased" (*Imoran Oku, Imu ọran oku*): The main day ends around eight or nine o'clock at night with a more elaborate ceremony to send the deceased's soul to the ancestors. By "taking" the achievements of the deceased, the family this time introduces the soul into heaven. The cosmetologists lead a representative of both the father and mother of the deceased to the grave site. They carry with them a piece of white cloth, a *fafa* mat, and some of the deceased's personal possessions. There they call the soul of the deceased and offer a goat to his or her inner head in a ritual segment known as *ikankuolowo.*

"Invoking the soul of the deceased" (*Ikankuolowo*): Holding the mat by the corners and dancing to the outskirts of the town to the major crossroads (*orita*), the relatives send the soul to join the other spirits. They do so simply by mutual agreement that the soul is happy to be sent away honorably. On the road, they chant declaratively that the elaborateness of the ceremonies befits the departed ("it befits him," *o yẹ ọ*). By extension, then, he or she is presumed worthy to dwell with the ancestors. The mat, the piece of cloth, and other materials are

divided up so that a portion can be used for the next ritual stage. This ends the main funeral day. After performing the first two parts of the main funeral day, the family feels that they have contributed to the deceased's successful journey to heaven.

The Third Day of the Funeral (Itaoku)

The third day is reserved for feasting; at night there is a sacrifice at the grove of Oro (*igbo Oro*).[22] Children of the deceased and other relatives share their favorite foods with their friends throughout the entire day. During that night the caretaker of the Oro bush sacrifices a ram to the ancestor. Those who hold the title of caretaker (*atẹjumole*) are among the kingmakers (Agba Oke, or Iwarefa) within the Ọṣugbo society.

"Opening the voice of the deceased" (*Ilakuoun [Ila oku oun]*): The new ancestor's voice will be heard for the first time.[23] People say, "Oro is crying." The voice of Oro on that night is presumed to be the spirit of the newly buried deceased coming to endorse the funeral performances of his children and other relatives. After the *atẹjumole* has opened the deceased's voice, he will ask the deceased to follow the male family members into the town to bless the relatives who have provided an honorable burial. Women must close themselves inside their rooms and lock the doors, for it is strictly forbidden for women to witness Oro. They hear only the sound.

Playing on Behalf of the Deceased (Irenoku)

During this fourth day of the funeral, the children and friends parade through the town and feast once again, this time principally to affirm their own success in providing a proper burial, but also to celebrate their ancestor's endorsement of their efforts.[24] It is the second day devoted strictly to dancing and enjoying, a formal ritual segment of play (*aito ku mere muṣe*) that is simultaneously a sacrifice performed willingly and very elaborately at the expense of the deceased's descendants. The children arrange for musicians, just as they do on the main funeral day, only more elaborately. "By dancing around the town, everybody can see from their own places how many plays have been done, how the drummers beat respect, how the children finish the ceremony happily." Again, they also count the number of groups, or plays, on that date as a sign of the seriousness of the descendants. The various groups stop at different places, particularly the compounds of relatives, where it is believed the new ancestor's spirit will stay. "You know the spirit of the father will be going around his children's houses. And he will stop at the marketplace and at important junctions on the outskirts of the town."

Seventh Funeral Day for the Deceased (Ejeoku)

Four days following the play day the children offer the new ancestor pounded yam and fish soup at home (*ibọ oṣi*). After the descendants perform this sacrifice, and another in the Oro grove, the ancestor becomes manifest once more, this time together with Oro music played on *agba* drums, in a ritual segment known as *asipelu*. Thus the deceased comes to receive the sacrifice "in the Oro mood."[25] Oro society members as well as male relatives of the deceased follow the ancestor's voice, which thanks and blesses all the family members. Once again women must close themselves inside their rooms and lock the doors.

This outing of the spirit voice is the final act of transference, the incorporation of the spirit of the deceased into ancestorhood. An incantation affirms, "the deceased who possesses wisdom will not be deaf" (*oku ologbon ki ṣeti*), that is, will attend his or her descendants in the world in return for their attention during the funeral. In celebrating the deceased, friends and relatives of the family pay homage to the ancestors broadly as a collective. As the living send off the deceased, so too the deities prepare the deceased's place in the otherworld. When somebody dies, it is said, "the deities establish the father who sleeps" (*oriṣa tẹ ni fun, baba o sun*).[26]

In Oṣitọla's account of how funerals should be performed, both play and competition were built into the structure of performance. Not merely a display of wealth for its own sake, the funeral literally constructs the social significance, power, and prestige of the deceased and his or her family at the same time that it constructs for the family and community a representation of the quality of the deceased's existence in the otherworld. The family and the community in this way judge themselves by the spectacle they create, and by extension judge the spirit's acceptance by the ancestors. Strong support for a deceased family member at the same time expresses the power of the corporate group.

VARIATIONS ON THE THEME

In the periods designed for play, especially on the main and the fourth days, funerals for the elderly take on other dimensions, in addition to those described by Ọṣitọla, when the deceased has other kinds of affiliations. If, for example, an elderly man was a hunter, blacksmith, drummer, or brasscaster, the funeral will typically include a send-off known as *iṣipadẹ* or *ipadẹ*, literally, the act of opening the way for the hunter (*a nṣi ipa ọdẹ*). This ceremony is reportedly conceived to send the spirit of the deceased to join all the other ancestors who during their lifetimes worked specifically with metal implements requiring strong, direct, powerful action—the killing of animals, the forging of iron, the beating of drums (cf. M. Drewal 1989). They include devotees of Ogun, the deity of iron and war, and of Ọbalufọn, the deity of artists.

The members of the funeral party wear old worn-out clothing. If the deceased was a hunter, for example, they carry guns and knives and create havoc around the town. As the drummers play, the spirit of the deceased mounts and possesses the hunter's comrades. The spirits of those in such professions are necessarily brave, fierce, and, above all, active. The participants thus fire their guns, lash and cut themselves, and tear each other's clothes as they engage in mock combat. In the process their clothes become even more ragged.

After parading around the town three times, they then process to a main crossroads on the outskirts. There they remove their clothes and place them at the junction, hanging some on a stake with a crossbar that is reminiscent of a scarecrow (fig. 3.5). This accumulation at the crossroads is the trace (*ipa*) of the hunter, from which the *ipadẹ* derives its name; more literally, *ipa* refers to the translucent trail left by a snail as it moves along the ground. In this way the participants create an impression of the deceased standing at the crossroads. The clothes are also evidences of the tremendous physical energy that the deceased's supporters have expended on his behalf. Their actions also dramatize the ethos of hunters and those who work with metal.

Such special performances woven into the fabric of funeral rites serve to distinguish groups and group affiliations. "You know everybody has his own group in the ancestor world," I was informed. Different affiliations are marked differently. Special funerals are accorded to diviners, as well as to priests of the deities, whose heads have been ritually prepared for possession trance.[27] Likewise, Egungun masks perform as part of the *isinku* of deceased Egungun society members (see chapter 6), Ẹfẹ and Gẹlẹdẹ masks sing and dance for the *isinku* of deceased Gẹlẹdẹ society members (H. Drewal and M. Drewal 1983:59–61, 156, 193), and Agẹmọ masks come out during the *isinku* of Agẹmọ society members (see chapter 7). These performances are part of the public displays on the days set aside for play. There are many other variations along these same lines, both public and private.

The funerals of kings are also special, because their rites of installation elevate them to a sacred status. Thus, kings are hailed, "the king with metaphysical power is second only to the gods" (*ọba alaṣẹ, ekeji oriṣa*). Since Agẹmọ priests are also the headmen of their own communities, their funeral rites combine components of those rites performed for kings, priests of deities, and Agẹmọ society members, including the appearances of Agẹmọ masks.

Multiple affiliations give rise to heterogenous funerals that can incorporate many distinct traditions and styles of performance. In 1978 in a western Yoruba town just outside Ilaro, the funeral of a deceased elder included performances of both the Egungun and Igunnuko masking societies. Igunnuko is an imported tradition, introduced into Yoruba country by Nupe emigrants, who are maintaining their own cultural identities and at the same time being assimilated into Yoruba culture. The deceased's affiliations were multiple, reflecting this heterogeneity.[28] The relationship of one Igunnuko mask to the deceased was explicitly drawn when the mask went to stand on the ancestor's grave just outside the house (fig. 3.6). The two columns that decorate the foot of the grave depict the mask in miniature, while a Muslim writing board with Arabic script is set in relief on the front. Both reflect the deceased's identity as masked performer and Muslim, or at least they reflect the way the family wanted to remember him. The two masking societies to which he belonged worked it out between themselves so that the Igunnuko masks performed in the afternoon, and the Egungun masks performed overnight that same evening.

The competition among families, and even within families, to put on the largest displays around the town—some say—encourages people in the community to perform better in life with the idea that their funerals will "befit" them. Since funerals are evaluated, elders fear appearing comparatively insignificant, especially after it is too late to do anything about it. If the dimension of public display seems extravagant, even relentless, it is because it is considered a sacrifice. Approval comes back directly from the deceased spirit's voice through the instrumentality of the elders, whose age, special training, and ritual roles make them living representations of the ancestors. That is the essence of the elders' wining and dining the deceased, as Ọṣitọla expressed it. It is the power of public display to proclaim the enormity of the family's concern throughout the town and even into the otherworld.

Ọṣitọla did not elaborate the play segments of music and dance since they are highly variable. Instead, what he stressed was the quantity of the performing groups. The choice of styles, it was suggested, is based primarily on the perceived music tastes of the deceased, his or her social affiliations with performing groups such as Ifa or Agẹmọ, and the tastes of the sponsors. Such funerals incorporate different styles and traditions of performance.

CYCLICAL TIME AND THE OTHER

Ritual journeys have a synecdochic relationship to the greater ontological journey of the human spirit in that they are nested in "life's journey" (*ajo l'aye*). Not conceived as cyclical in the sense of beginning time over or returning to the world the same each time, journeying is always a progression, a transformation. The idea of transformation is implicit in a divination text given by Wande Abimbọla (1976:132), which narrates how three men, before leaving heaven to come to earth, chose their heads. When two of them, Oriseeku and Orieemere, compared the success of the third, Afuwape, with their own failures, they remarked:

> I don't know where the lucky ones chose their heads,
> I would have gone there to choose mine.

Afuwape answers, concluding the verse:

> We chose our heads from the same place,
> But our destinies are not identical.

Every time spirits return to the world, they choose different heads or personalities (*ori inu*), different bodies (*ara*), and different destinies (*ayanmọ*).

One of the projects of the functionalist-structuralist approach, according to Johannes Fabian (1983:41), was to contrast "Western linear Time and primitive cyclical Time, or [. . .] modern Time-centeredness and archaic timelessness." Ritual tends to be placed in the latter category, even so-called secular rituals

(see Moore and Meyerhoff 1977:8). But does this really reflect Yoruba thought?[29]

If in Yoruba thought life on earth is merely a temporary segment in a human spirit's journey, then all time would have to be classified as cyclical, not just ritual time. What Benjamin Ray (1976:41) terms "ordinary linear time" would not exist in Yoruba consciousness, since, conceptually, the human spirit is always coming into the world and returning in one unending cycle. On the other hand, since nothing ever repeats itself, and since from this ontological perspective there is always change and transformation—of body, of personality, of mission, of destiny—then existence in time would be more appropriately conceived in spatial terms as a spiral—neither cyclical, nor linear. There is no time-out-of-time, properly speaking that is, if I have understood the concept as Ọṣitọla expressed it:

> The whole life span of a man or a woman is a journey. That is our belief. *Ajo l'aye* [literally, "journey of life"]. When you are going to start your life, you go through a journey. Even when you are coming to the life, you go through a journey. And if you want to develop on the life, it is a journey. So it is just journey, journey, journey all the while.
>
> Me: When people go on a journey, what does that mean?
>
> Ọṣitọla: I have told you, the whole life span of a human is a journey. What we are doing now is a journey. All movements are journeys. We are progressing, we are moving. (taped discussion #86.77[I])

3.2 The Akọnọrọn of Ọṣugbo Imodi watches where he places his foot as he dances. Ijẹbu area, village of Imọsan, 1 December 1986.

3.3 In a dance facing the *agba* drums, the Apena of Ọṣugbo Ikan wears a highly patterned "cloth of the elders." The complexity of the designs alludes to the complexities of life itself and the elder's mastery of them. Ijẹbu area, village of Imọsan, 14 October 1986.

3.4 A funeral "play" (*ere*) travels about the town. A member of the family carries aloft a photograph of the deceased. Ijẹbu area, village of Imosan, 13 September 1986.

3.5 The accumulation of clothes placed at the crossroads represents the "trace" (*ipa*) of a deceased hunter, created during the *iṣipadẹ* ritual. Ijẹbu area, village of Imọsan, 13 September 1986.

3.6 An Igunnuko mask stands on the deceased's grave. In the foreground, two masks in miniature and a Muslim writing board with Arabic script decorate the concrete tombstone. Ẹgbado area, village of Olute, 3 December 1977.

Part 6:
Mexico: Day of the Dead

Iconography in Mexico's Day of the Dead: Origins and Meaning

Stanley Brandes, *University of California, Berkeley*

Abstract. This article analyzes the origin and meaning of artistic representations of death—principally skulls and skeletons—in Mexico's Day of the Dead. It challenges stereotypes of the death-obsessed Mexican by tracing mortuary imagery in the Day of the Dead to two separate artistic developments, the first deriving from religious and demographic imperatives of colonial times, the second from nineteenth-century politics and journalism. Now generally perceived as belonging to a single, undifferentiated iconographic tradition, cranial and skeletal images of death have become virtually synonymous with Mexico itself.

Artistic Representations of Death in the Day of the Dead

In Hayden Herrera's biography of Mexican painter Frida Kahlo (1983), there appears a photograph of the artist lying on her sickbed, looking straight into the camera and holding in both hands a colorfully decorated sugar skull with her name scrolled on the forehead. Although the photograph bears no date, we may assume that it was taken on or around 1 and 2 November, when Mexican shops and street stalls are filled, as one traveler put it (quoted in Haberstein and Lamers 1963: 587), with "gleaming gay skulls, sugary-white and with splendid gold trimmings." It is common at this time of year for sugar skulls with people's names written on them to be sold in stores and on street corners. A similar product is made out of chocolate as well. People present these candy skulls to friends or relatives just as short, satiric literary verses known also as *calaveras* (skulls) are given to colleagues, compadres, and family members.

Representations of skeletons are also common at this time of year. Perhaps the most prevalent skeletal form is the soft, spongy, shapeless kind

Ethnohistory 45:2 (spring 1998). CCC 0014-1801/98/$1.50.

fashioned out of bread dough and known as *pan de muerto*, or, humorously in American English, as "dead bread." In Tlaxcala, for example, there is a wide range of such breads, many of which "are representations of human males and females" (Nutini 1988: 170–71). But there is also throughout the republic an enormous variety of skeleton toys of all sizes and plastic materials, with the skeleton displayed as naked or clothed, holding a recognizable object like a pipe or musical instrument, and usually giving some indication of age, gender, occupation, and the like. During the end of October and beginning of November, too, the newspapers are filled with images of political or other well-known personalities, anatomically drawn as skeletons but draped with the recognizable trappings of their office. The skeleton figures might also be grouped into little scenes taken from everyday life and installed in tiny painted boxes like dioramas; or they might assume the form of a party of funeralgoers, bus riders, or mariachi musicians (Figure 1).

Other than skulls and skeletons, the most common death-related toys are small caskets, usually made out of chocolate or sugar, and decorated with multicolored icing. Like the skulls, these caskets might or might not contain an individual's name inscribed in sugar icing. A popular type of casket has a little plastic window at the top through which you can view a little sugar cadaver, set prone at the base. When a string is pulled, the cadaver sits up, as if resuscitating.

Probably more than any other single element, it is the prevalence of skulls and skeletons and caskets of all types that has made the Mexican Day of the Dead famous throughout the Western world. The ornamentation on these figurines and funerary objects is almost always colorful; it is occasionally detailed and aesthetically pleasing as well. Far from evoking morbid feelings, the Day of the Dead toys and candies are filled with charm and humor. Like other Mexican artisan crafts—for that is what in essence they are—Day of the Dead figurines have awakened tourists' interest in the holiday. Among foreigners, they invariably appeal to the collectors' instinct. They are transported back to the United States as evidence that Mexicans really are different from mainstream Americans. These toys and candies have been taken to reflect a peculiarly Mexican view of death—an "acceptance of death," as Patricia Fernández Kelly (1974: 535) puts it. Fernández Kelly sums up the meaning of Day of the Dead folk crafts: "These complex and diversified folkloric traditions—the poetry and songs, the masks and sculpture—inevitably suggest the enormous tenacity and wisdom of a people and a culture whose oppressed situation has not been an obstacle for the expression of a unique and creative philosophy of life and death."

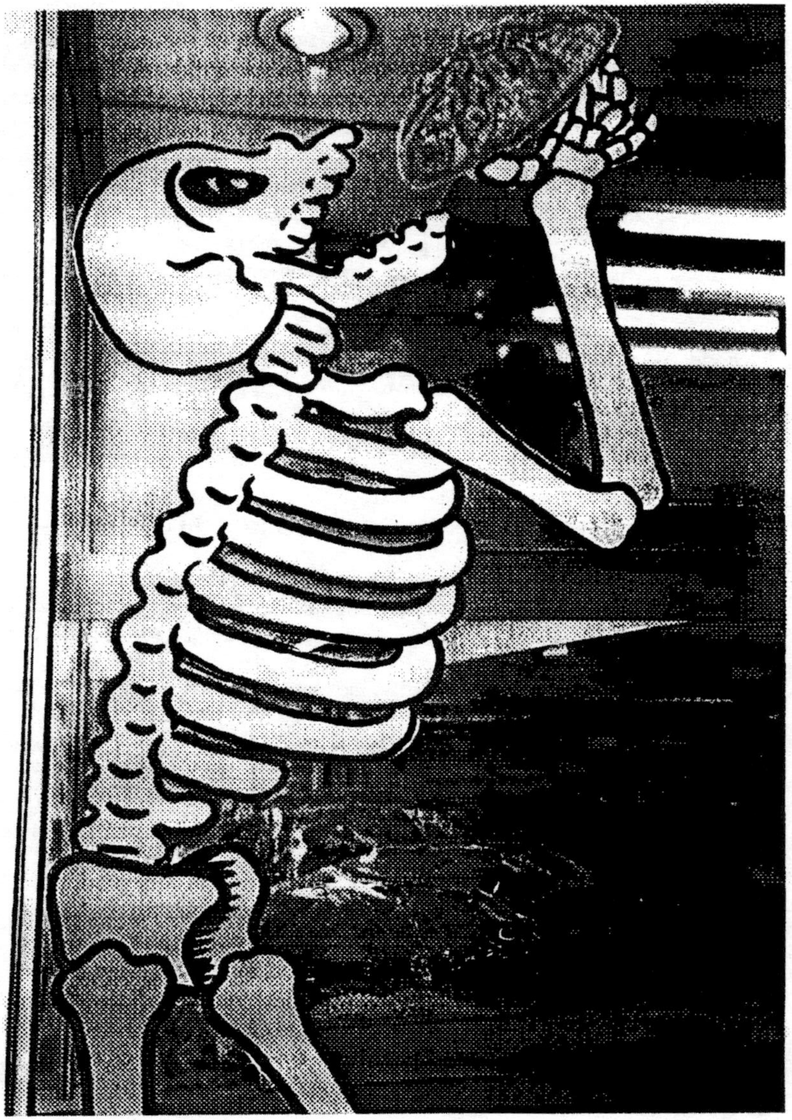

Figure 1. Bakery shop window with *pan de muerto* for sale displayed behind the glass. Cuernavaca, October 1995. Photograph by Stanley Brandes.

For Paul Westheim (1983: 9), too, the ubiquitous presence of skulls, skeletons, and the like is a supreme manifestation of the enormous difference between Mexican and Western attitudes toward death. Describing the reaction in Paris during the early 1950s to an exhibit of Mexican art, he says:

> The skull as an artistic motif, a popular fantasy that for millennia has found pleasure in the representation of death. . . . this was a tremendous surprise and almost traumatic for visitors to the Exposition of Mexican Art in Paris. They stopped in front of the statue of Coatlicue, goddess of the earth and of death, who wears the mask of death; they contemplated the skull of rock crystal—one of the hardest minerals—carved by an Aztec artist, during innumerable hours of work, with an impressive mastery over his craft; they looked at the engravings of the popular artists, Manilla and Posada, who resorted to skeletons in order to comment on the social and political events of their times. They found out that in Mexico there are parents who on the second of November give their children presents of sugar and chocolate skulls on which are written the children's names in sugar letters, and that these children eat the macabre sweet, as if it were the most natural thing in the world. They were fascinated by a popular art, made of very simple materials like cloth, wood, clay, and even chicle, dolls in the form of skeletons . . . common toys loved by the people.

Mexicans, in their popular arts, display an undeniable fascination with skulls, skeletons, and other representations of death, items that elsewhere cause a sensation of unpleasantness or even dread.

This article explores the nature and origin of death imagery related to the Day of the Dead. In my reading of the Day of the Dead literature, I find that much of the meaning of these objects to Mexicans and foreigners alike lies precisely in their presumed uniqueness, a uniqueness that Fernández Kelly and others take to signify a kind of folk wisdom and collective recognition of humanity's inevitable fate. I wish first to ask just how singular these toys and candies really are, then to explore their similarities and differences with related phenomena in ancient Mesoamerica and early modern Europe, and finally to speculate why they have assumed such prominence in the Mexican Day of the Dead.

The Cultural Continuity Model in Day of the Dead Art

In Mexico the literature on death, and the Day of the Dead in particular, invariably incorporates a cultural continuity model to explain religious beliefs, practices, and iconography. Consider, for example, Patricia Fernández Kelly's article "Death in Mexican Folk Culture" (1974), which is structured almost paradigmatically. Fernández Kelly begins by talking about the centrality of death to humanity in general and to Mexicans in particular. She proceeds to a lengthy examination of death-related artifacts in pre-Columbian Mexico and what they express about the meaning and importance of death to those people. The author's stated purpose here is to point out "the permanence of some traits and in general the sense of continuity of the idea of death within contemporary Mexican folk culture" (ibid.: 526). There follows a brief section on the European conquest, which the author summarizes thus: "The polytheistic religions were replaced by Christianity and the voice of the indigenous Mexican was dimmed forever. Its former power was lost, but a murmur was to remain." Fernández Kelly fails to identify explicitly the precise nature of that murmur, although it is possibly revealed in her psychological association concerning the origin of sugar skulls: "When looking at them in the showcases of the sweet shops," she says (ibid.: 527), "one cannot help recalling the ancient Aztec tzompantlis, special stone structures where the skulls of the men who had died in sacrifice were exhibited." Whatever else that preconquest murmur may consist of, it presumably accounts for those aspects of contemporary Mexican funerals and Day of the Dead ceremonies that seem unfamiliar to Westerners. The murmur represents the exotic.

Fernández Kelly concludes her article with a description of funerals and the Day of the Dead. Like the vast majority of scholars who have written on this issue, she rightly believes that the attitude toward death in present-day Mexican folk culture is the product of a combination of pre-Hispanic with Spanish beliefs and practices: "Without doubt, the Christian tradition has left Mexico a priceless collection of artistic and literary testimonies which document its own interpretation of death. But the fusion of the European cultural patterns with the pre-existing beliefs offers a third and perfectly individualized complex of practices and ideas" (Fernández Kelly 1974: 526).

As an overall formulation of Mexican culture today, it would be hard to dispute this fusion model. It is important to note, however, that embedded within the model is a reification of culture. Culture has an existence of its own. It is passed down from generation to generation and blends with alternative, coexistent traditions to create a new cultural product. The role of historical events and socioeconomic circumstances in producing particular beliefs and customs is vague at best. Above all, those who express and carry on these traditions—that is, the people themselves—are missing from this type of narrative. The story is essentially Kroeberian; culture is implicitly portrayed as superorganic. The actual mechanisms of continuity and change are missing from the account.

A similar point of view comes from *The Skeleton at the Feast: The Day of the Dead in Mexico*, a scholarly and beautifully illustrated exhibition catalog written and compiled by Elizabeth Carmichael and Chloë Sayer (1991). The book starts with a detailed description of Day of the Dead activities, especially (befitting a museum catalog) as they incorporate the visual arts. There are reproductions of sugar skulls, papier-mâché skeletons, decorated tombs and home altars, storefronts painted with animate skeletons, and the like. The following chapter, "The Pre-Hispanic Background," is illustrated with diverse pre-Columbian stone sculptures of deities and humans with skull-like faces; with pages from various codices (Borgia, Laud, Borbonicus) showing skull-like and skeletal-like drawings of supernatural beings; and with the *tzompantli*, or skull rack, at the Mayan site of Chichén Itzá, among other death-related representations from pre-Hispanic Mesoamerica. The accompanying text focuses on the cosmology, deities of death, beliefs in the afterlife, artistic imagery related to death, and death-related rituals of the ancient Aztecs and related peoples. Carmichael and Sayer make no explicit connection between these phenomena and the Day of the Dead. Rather, they summarize with a noncommital statement: "To what extent these pre-Hispanic festivals and their associated rituals were transmuted into the Christian festivals remains a matter of keen debate" (1991: 33). Carmichael and Sayer formulate their neutrality with utmost caution. However, the sheer length and detailed elaboration of their textual and artistic presentation related to pre-Hispanic customs, art, and beliefs lead readers to assume that these phenomena are in fact precursors of Day of the Dead arts and crafts.

The next chapter in Carmichael and Sayer 1991, "The Spanish Conquest," tells the story of the imposition of Catholicism on Mesoamerica and briefly describes the Day of the Dead in colonial Mexico. The chapter is illustrated mainly with Mexican death images: an eighteenth-century painting of a deceased nun, contemporary masked death and devil dancers, an ancient decorated skull, a toy Day of the Dead altar, and the nineteenth-century artist José Guadalupe Posada's image "The Grand Banquet of Skeletons," among other pictures. There are no European images save a reproduction from a 1972 Mexican printing of Fray Joaquín Bolaños's book, *La portentosa vida de la muerte* (The portentous life of death). As in the chapter on pre-Hispanic background, this exposition avoids explicit analysis of European origins, with one exception (Carmichael and Sayer 1991: 42–43): the citation from Foster 1960 of the Castilian custom, transferred to Mexico, whereby a large funeral bier covered with a black cloth is erected in churches during All Saints' and All Souls' Days.

The authors also include in the chapter a general statement about the syncretism that occurred between the religion of the Aztecs and Catholicism during the first century after the conquest (ibid.: 40–41). Their example is the classic one—nowadays seriously challenged (Taylor 1987: 198)—of the image of the Virgin of Guadalupe as representing the pre-Columbian goddess Tonantzin and functioning in colonial times as a saint to whom Indians had particular devotion. Although there is no explicit statement of syncretism in the Day of the Dead, the authors do state that "where there was some possibility of combining an Aztec fiesta with a feast day in the Catholic calendar, this was done" (ibid.: 40). The organization of chapters in *The Skeleton at the Feast* clearly implies a syncretic process without openly stating which elements of the festival were ancient Mesoamerican and which European. However, insofar as European origins go, Carmichael and Sayer are willing to say of the Day of the Dead: "*Nominally* this is the Christian feast of the All Saints' and All Souls', but it is celebrated in Mexico as nowhere else in the Catholic world" (ibid.: 14; italics added).

Scholars find it difficult indeed to minimize the role of the Aztecs in the Day of the Dead or, conversely, to emphasize European origins. Much of the justification for pre-Columbian antecedents comes from the iconography of ancient Mesoamerica, with its undeniable plethora of skulls and skeletons, as well as from the equally prevalent presence of skulls and skeletons during the contemporary Day of the Dead. What is missing from most accounts is an analysis of the context in which skulls and skeletons appear. Hence, the first step in assessing origins is to examine the essence of Day of the Dead skulls and skeletons, that is, their intrinsic characteristics and how these skulls compare with skulls and skeletons incorporated in related religious traditions.

Day of the Dead Art: Some Basic Characteristics

In order to trace the possible origins of Day of the Dead art, we must first identify some of its essential features. As George Kubler (1969) pointed out, artistic form and function, content and meaning, must be differentiated. For our purposes, this means that the mere repetition of skulls and skeletons as a motif does not necessarily indicate cultural continuity. The function and meaning might well vary enormously from one historical epoch or ethnographic context to another.

Mexican representations of skulls and skeletons during the Day of the Dead display at least nine intrinsic characteristics:

1. They are *ephemeral* art. Pan de muerto (dead bread), sugar skulls and coffins, drawings of skulls and skeletons on storefront windows, death images made of straw and cut into colored paper: all

of these items are made for momentary consumption. They tend to be constructed from flimsy, nondurable material. For the most part, at the popular level in Mexico, they are not saved for display or enjoyment. They exist to celebrate the moment.

2. They are *seasonal* art. Artistic images are specifically connected to the celebration of All Saints' and All Souls' Days. Representations of death that appear at this time of year are decidedly not incorporated into funerals or the permanent decoration of family tombs. When these images are sold at other times of the year, they tend to occur in a touristic context and, in any event, refer to the specific holiday known as the Day of the Dead.

3. They are *humorous* in content. For the most part, the skulls, skeletons, caskets, and other death-related images that appear during the Day of the Dead evoke laughter rather than sadness, enjoyment rather than pain.

4. They are *secular*. The iconography of death holds virtually no sacred meaning either for its producers or its consumers. True, the sugar caskets with little cadavers inserted inside are sometimes decorated with a simple, colored sugar cross. But aside from that one symbol, it would be difficult to discover religious imagery in the Day of the Dead iconography. Skulls and skeletons, be they made of bread or sugar, are generally eaten. Paper, straw, or clay toys are played with and quickly fall apart unless handled with the utmost delicacy. Little or no sacred significance attaches to the objects themselves, although they are incorporated into the celebration of a sacred holiday.

5. This iconography is *commercial*. It is made by skilled artisans to be purchased and can be found for sale around the time of the Day of the Dead at virtually all marketplaces throughout Mexico. Urban shopkeepers use drawings of skulls and skeletons to decorate their stores and attract customers.

6. Day of the Dead art is *designed for living people*, not for the deceased. It is true that this art occasionally decorates tombs and home altars, but it is employed in this fashion solely during the Day of the Dead. Never does it accompany funerals, nor are the recently deceased buried alongside any artistic objects related to the Day of the Dead. The objects and artistic representations associated with the Day of the Dead tend mostly to be purchased by and exchanged among the living as a way of reinforcing social relationships. They are also used for purposes of commercial advertisements as well as political and social satire.

7. Day of the Dead art is *ludic*. The toys and candies are often

designed for play. They have moving parts. The skeleton marionettes and puppets are fixed with flexible joints that make them come alive when manipulated. The coffins, crafted with plastic windows allowing a view of little cadavers inside, come laced with strings that allow the cadavers to resuscitate. Much of this art, then, is meant to be handled and manipulated.

8. Day of the Dead art is *small, light, and transportable*. You can hold this art in your hand; you can lift it and move it around. Even the altars are assemblages of numerous small pieces that can be mounted and unmounted easily by a single person.

9. Much of Day of the Dead art is *urban and shared among Mexico's cultural elite*. It is manufactured and created in the city for consumption by city people, although there is a rural artistic tradition associated with this holiday as well.

In examining the origins of Day of the Dead art, all these characteristics should be taken into account. Day of the Dead art is integrated into social and cultural life in particular ways. Any discussion of how and why this art exists, and the reasons for its preeminence in contemporary Mexican life, must recognize that function is as important as form. Two images that look alike might differ greatly in the ways they are employed and interpreted, thereby casting doubt on common origins. It is important to bear this point in mind when comparing Day of the Dead art to similar representations in ancient Mesoamerica and Europe.

Pre-Columbian Skull and Skeleton Representations

In assessing the possible contribution of ancient Mesoamerica to the iconography of the Day of the Dead today, we must bear in mind the essential fact that the ancient world was diverse, complex, and long-lived. We cannot speak of the pre-Columbian world as if it were, artistically and symbolically, a single undifferentiated entity. Even where symbols appear, they might have well operated socially according to different principles. Scholars are fond of pointing out that "the image of death is everywhere in the arts of pre-Hispanic central Mexico" (Childs and Altman 1982: 6). Along with Gombrich (1972: 20–21), what we want to ask about, however, is "the institutional function of images" as well as "to which genre a given work is to be assigned." As for the ancient Maya, who flourished in southeastern Mesoamerica, it has been said that although they seemed less obsessed with death than the Aztecs, "this is compensated for by a greater presence of death in abstract form, especially in symbols, which appear with high frequency" (Coe 1975: 92).

Let us first consider these Mayan symbols of death. Among them are the ubiquitous human skulls and bones, often crossed. At Toniná, for example, located near Palenque in eastern Chiapas, there survives a spectacular stone panel carved with skull bas-reliefs. In fact, practically all ancient art in the Mayan area and in Veracruz shows crossbones and fleshless mandibles (Winning 1987: 55). Human skulls and bones are, of course, nearly universal iconographic representations of death. However, the ancient Maya also employed a unique iconography of decomposing corpses, symbolized by black spots or blotches on the cheeks of the victims or by a sort of division sign—a horizontally oriented squiggle with a dot above and below—also situated on the cheek of the deceased (ibid.: 92–93). At Palenque there is a vase in which death is represented not only by the skeletal state of the victim but also by long, black hanks of hair in the shape of a bow tie, as well as by disembodied eyes affixed to the skulls (Robicsek and Hales 1988: 267). Throughout the Mayan region, too, death was represented by the closed eyes and open mouth of the victims (ibid.). Except for the human skulls and bones, none of these Mayan death symbols can be found in present-day popular Mexican art, including that associated with the Day of the Dead.

Turning now to central Mexico, the iconographic representation of death varies markedly from one culture to another. At Teotihuacán, which flourished during the first seven centuries of the present era, skulls and skeletons as a design motif are relatively insignificant (see, e.g., Berrin 1988). Although Winning (1987: 58) briefly describes two monuments at Teotihuacán that display skulls, he states that overall skull representations at this site are "rare" (ibid.: 61). Instead, Teotihuacán artists represented death by a simple iconographic sign: "They added a pair of perforated disks, or rings, above the eyes on the forehead" (ibid.: 60). Cultures that flourished about the same time as Teotihuacán, in the present states of Colima, Jalisco, and Nayarit, show similarly rare skeletal representations (Fuente 1974), although the first Mesoamerican skull rack, containing sixty-one human heads, was erected prior to the Christian era in southern Mexico, at Coyotera, in connection with Zapotec expansionist warfare (Hassig 1992: 42).

At the Toltec capital of Tula, however, there exist the first indications in central Mexico of a real fascination with skulls and skeletons. Tula flourished from the ninth until the thirteenth century A.D. The site includes the decimated remains of a tzompantli, or skull rack, which once displayed multiple rows of stone-carved skulls adorning the sides of a broad platform upon which the actual skulls of sacrificial victims were publicly exhibited (Hassig 1988: 206, 1992: 112). The tzompantli appeared during the final

phases of civilization at Tula, which was destroyed around 1200 (Davies 1977). Chichén Itzá, almost contemporaneous with the Toltecs and located far to the southeast in the heart of Yucatan, contains a better-preserved tzompantli. Says Diehl (1983: 149) of this structure: "The platform sides are covered with grisly carved stone panels showing human skulls strung up on upright posts like beads on a necklace. These probably symbolize the real skulls which once covered the platform summit." In the Mayan area, too, Uxmal displays a tzompantli, with skulls and crossed long bones.

In addition to the tzompantli, there is a freestanding wall at Tula known as the *coatepantli*, or Serpent Wall, which formerly enclosed the north side of the pyramid, on which stand tall, rigid warrior figures, the famous *atlantes*. This wall, probably associated with the cult of Tlahuizcalpantecuhtli (the supreme god Quetzalcóatl in the form of Venus the morning star), is decorated with a series of carved stone panels that show feathered serpents devouring human skeletons (ibid.: 64). The most remarkable feature of these skeletons is their lanky limbs and prominent joints, which allow for corporal flexibility; they are surprisingly like large, lithic versions of the wooden and clay toy skeletons found in markets all over Mexico around the time of the Day of the Dead. Like small toys today, these stone skeletons appear animate, with their awkwardly crossed legs and outstretched arms. However, their artistic design and execution were considerably removed in time from the Spanish conquest at the beginning of the sixteenth century. It thus appears unlikely that these lifelike skeletons, today an isolated archaeological find, would have themselves survived into the colonial and postcolonial eras in Mexico in the form of figurines associated with All Saints' and All Souls' Days.

Since the Aztecs were the leading power holders at the time of the Spanish conquest, it is reasonable to suppose that their iconography—rather than that of their predecessors—was what carried over into the art of colonial Mexico and exerted a long-term influence over folk art associated with the Day of the Dead. There are at least three elements of Aztec art that scholars point to repeatedly as demonstrating the indigenous focus on death. First is the well-preserved tzompantli, found at the site of the Great Temple at the Aztec capital of Tenochtitlán. On each side of this structure there are five horizontal rows of sixteen stone skulls, which form a tightly knit design that completely covers the base of the platform. Second are the numerous prominent stone sculptures of deities who are represented with skull-like features. Among the most famous is the image of Coatlicue, also known as Ilamatecuhtli, goddess of the earth, life, and death, whose face usually appears as a skull. The fleshless face is sometimes itself decorated above the brow and below the neck with a row of smaller skulls (see, e.g., Anonymous 1963–64: 209–10; Spranz 1973: 83–85). Similarly, stone sculptures representing Mictecacihuatl, goddess of the underworld and of the dead, also show the face in the form of a skull (Matos Moctezuma 1992). One of the most famous artifacts from the Aztec Great Temple is an enormous circular monolith, 3.25 meters in diameter, showing Coyolxauhqui, the moon goddess, decapitated, with limbs spread across the entire stone slab; she bears a skull-shaped back ornament typical of earth deities. Finally, the Aztecs left skull offerings that were found at the Great Temple (Carrasco 1992: 116–17). These are actual human skulls, decorated with shell and pyrite eyes and sacrificial flint knives, which were inserted into the skulls to represent tongues and noses.

If we examine the art associated specifically with pre-Hispanic burials in central Mexico, we discover almost no representation of skulls and skeletons anywhere. At Teotihuacán, for example, "a large variety of pottery vessels were made for everyday use and for burial with the dead, but none bear elaborate imagery" (Pasztory 1988: 54). The multitudinous clay funerary offerings found in western Mexico, dating from 100 to 300, contain no skeletal or skull-like representations whatsoever. They instead include lively sculptures of musicians, warriors, water carriers, people sitting, and people drinking (Fuente 1974). At Tula, burial sites occasionally contain a few undecorated pots, but nothing else (Diehl 1983: 90). Tenochtitlán shows offerings of skulls and skeletons, although not necessarily funerary offerings. Contreras (1990: 407) describes an offering found at the Great Temple that contained three skulls with some perforations above the forehead and with incrustations of shell and of a material similar to red clay placed within the eye sockets. A ceramic funerary urn from Offering 14 at the Great Temple of Tenochtitlán shows a nonskeletal representation of the deity Tezcatlipoca but no skulls.

As far as ancient Mayan burials are concerned, there, too, we find principally nonfigurative art. Death themes do appear among the polychrome vessels associated with elite burials, but most mortuary art reflects various human activities in the context of life, not death. Consider two contrasting Late Classic (c. 600–900) burials at the Altar de Sacrificios, Palenque. Burial 128, belonging to a nobleman, shows that the priests placed the deceased in a large clay urn, together with offerings of mantles, mats, gold, silver, food, and charcoal. At Burial 7, that of a poor commoner, "the only offerings were two plain, inverted bowls, one placed over the head and the other near the pelvis" (Coe 1988: 223). In no case do we have skulls or skeletons—except those of the actual deceased—associated with Mayan burials. To the contrary, iconic representations tend to symbolize affirmations of life. To Eduardo Matos, the great tomb at Palenque represents an "allegory of life in the vicinity of death" (quoted in Museo universitario 1974–75: 15). In the case of another funerary artifact, the famous polychrome vase at the Altar de Sacrificios, Palenque, iconographic representations include animals, dancers, canoes, flowers, and serpents, with no skulls or skeletons at all (Schele 1988).

What general points might be derived from this brief survey of skull and skeletal art in ancient Mesoamerica? First, however extensive this art might have been, it was unevenly distributed through time and space. Teotihuacán and western Mexico seem to have incorporated this kind of iconography sparingly, if at all, whereas the Maya, Toltec, and Aztec civilizations made important use of it. The Aztecs show representations of skulls but no full-length skeletons. Their predecessors, the Toltecs, used both. As a rule, skull and skeletal iconography in Mesoamerica is not associated with mortuary ritual as such. It is also stiff and stylized. There are two notable exceptions: the skeleton tablets at Tula, described above, and a ceramic codex fragment from Palenque, known as the Sacrifice of Xbalanque (Robicsek and Hales 1988), in which there appear death figures represented in animated skeletal state.

The archaeological remains that seem closest in feeling and spirit to contemporary Day of the Dead skulls and skeletons are the stone bas-reliefs at Tula and the representations of death on the ceramic codex from the Palenque Sacrifice of Xbalanque. And yet these two artifacts are far removed in space, time, and function both from one another and from the Spanish colonial regime. These remains are also very different stylistically from one another. It would be difficult to make a case for continuity of iconographic representation dating from these pieces to the present. At Tenochtitlán, on the other hand, we have an abundance of skulls and skeletons, both real and representational, that might very well have exerted a direct influence on church and folk art in colonial and postcolonial Mexico. However, skull iconography at Tenochtitlán displays stylized rigidity and seriousness that diverge enormously from art associated with the Day of the Dead. These archaeological remains display nothing of the playfulness and humor so essential to contemporary Mexican skull and skeletal representations.

And how could they? Consider Hassig's (1988: 121) graphic description of Aztec tzompantli:

> Captors did not kill their captives but brought them as offerings to the priests, who carried out the sacrifices, dragging them to the sacrificial stone if they faltered, and sacrificing them to Huitzilopochtli. After they were killed, the bodies were laid by the skull rack, and each warrior identified the one that he had captured. Then the body was taken

> to the captor's home, where it was eaten; the bones were hung in the house as a sign of prestige. The heads of those who were sacrificed were skinned, the flesh was dried, and the skulls were placed on the skull rack, the *tzompantli.*

Contextually, the use of skulls among the Aztecs could not be further removed from that among Mexicans in today's Day of the Dead celebration.

Given the diversity and complexity of skull and skeletal representations in ancient Mesoamerica, it is impossible to discount their cumulative impact on colonial and postcolonial art. Nor can we state that any one culture or civilization contributed to contemporary skull and skeleton representations more than any other. At the same time, it is impossible to draw clearly defined lines of stylistic and thematic influence from ancient times to the present day. Mesoamerican cultures were varied, and each in its own way showed a concern with death. But that was true, too, of Europe at the time of the Spanish conquest.

Christian Representations of Death in Europe and New Spain

As noted, skulls and skeletons were only a few of the means by which the peoples of ancient Mesoamerica represented death. The archaeological record in this part of the world, as everywhere, is discontinuous and incomplete. Hence it is impossible to say whether skulls and skeletons were the most common symbols of death or, if not the most abundant, whether they were the most powerful and salient. It is all too easy to read back into the historical record that which seems to display the most evident continuity.

Similar doubts arise when we turn our attention to Europe at the time of the Spanish conquest and after. José Moreno Villa's essay "The Death Theme in Spanish and Mexican Arts" (1986: 113–37) offers a survey of the topic from the fifteenth through the twentieth centuries, with an emphasis on Spain. There is nothing either in the text or in the numerous artistic reproductions that bears the least resemblance to a skull or skeleton. We are presented with stone sarcophagi of well-dressed nobles and clerics; paintings of delicate toga-clad damsels collapsing in the arms of muscular protectors; and, of course, sculpted and painted figures of the deceased Christ hanging on the cross, cradled in the arms of his mother, lying prone in his casket, and the like. From Moreno Villa's vision of Spanish and Mexican representations of death, it would seem that the skull and skeleton are negligible images at best. In the words of another

author (Bialostocki 1987: 15), it was "the cruel death on the cruciform gallows" that dominated Christian thought and artistic imagination: "From the Early Medieval times down to the Late Baroque sculpture and to the naturalistic painting of XIXth century the image of the dying God in the shape of a suffering man constitutes the main subject of Christian art."

This does not mean that the artists of early modern Europe confined themselves to the motif of the dying Christ. Skulls and skeletons were, in fact, important features of European iconography during colonial times and after. Bialostocki (ibid.: 28) points out that "the great period of the skull and skeleton ornamentation is the period of the Baroque"—that is, a period coinciding with much of the Spanish colonial era—"which introduces an inflation of these elements." Consider, for example, the no-longer-extant tomb of the Good King René of Anjou, which shows the deceased monarch as "a wobbly skeleton, sitting on his throne, his crowned head powerlessly inclined and his scepter and royal globe having slipped from his hand to the ground" (ibid.: 28). This description is reminiscent of the holy image of San Pascual, King, a saint venerated throughout Latin America, especially Guatemala (Luján Muñoz 1987). The cult of San Pascual emerged during the middle of the seventeenth century. He almost always wears a crown on his fleshless skull. Sometimes he is represented as a full skeleton, holding a scythe, with scepter and other accoutrements of his office lying at his feet; sometimes he is clothed in cape and gown. In folk art, he is a full-bodied skeleton wearing no clothing and carrying no identifying objects but a crown. Although San Pascual is principally a Guatemalan image, portraits of him can be found for sale outside churches all over Mexico as well. San Pascual and the Good King René of Anjou are not isolated cases. Death heads, sometimes combined with the hourglass, sometimes with bat wings, became a popular design motif. Gian Lorenzo Bernini carved skeletons on two of his most well-known papal tombs. That of Pope Urban VIII shows a skeleton emerging from beneath the sarcophagus; the skeleton is portrayed as inscribing on the tablet the name of the deceased.

In eighteenth-century New Spain, as throughout Europe, allegorical portrayals of the ages of man often included a skeleton as the image of death. Life was represented typically as a two-sided staircase, ascending on the left side and descending on the right. Upon each stair was drawn a person representative of a particular age, starting at the lower left-hand side with a picture of a baby representing infancy and ending, at the lower right-hand side, with a skeletal figure symbolizing death (e.g., Museo Nacional de Arte 1994: 254–55). Another common eighteenth-century motif was the *arbol vano* (tree of vanity) or *arbol del pecador* (sinner's tree), generally portraying a young man, the sinner, reclining or seated at the base of a tree, completely spent from sensual excesses (ibid.: 256–63). Invariably, there are otherworldly figures surrounding the sinner, often a devil, occasionally an angel, but always a menacing skeleton, wielding an ax or a scythe. Apparently, the tree of vanity in New Spain derives from the engravings of the sixteenth-century Flemish artist Hieronymus Wierix, who directly influenced artists working in the New World during the baroque era (ibid.: 256).

In eighteenth-century New Spain, too, elaborately decorated funeral catafalques portrayed animated skeletal figures (ibid.: 271–88). Two of the most elaborate can be observed today in the Museo de Bellas Artes in Toluca and the Museo de Arte Virreinal in Taxco. The catafalque of El Carmen, displayed in the museum at Toluca, shows multiple scenes of the skeletal death figure. In one panel the skeleton fires a cannon at a fortress; in another the figure helps a nun card wool; in a third it rides a fancy carriage. Other panels portray the skeleton walking hunched over with a cane, writing while seated at a small table, and of course wielding a scythe. Several of these panels show the skeleton wearing some article of clothing; most of them, too, portray the skeleton talking, an act symbolized through white banners, strung with Latin words, streaming from its mouth (ibid.: 272–76). The catafalque of Santa Prisca, housed in the museum at Taxco, displays equally animated skeletons. One is seated on a tree stump in contemplative mode, legs crossed and head resting on one hand. A scythe and bow and arrow are at the skeleton's feet. Another panel shows the skeleton actually shooting the bow and arrow; in another it is walking by a lakeside, holding an hourglass; in another, toppling a castle; and so forth (ibid.: 277–80). Death is as alive in these figures as it is in Day of the Dead iconography today (Figure 2).

It is clear that even in the pre-baroque era skulls and skeletons were characteristic features of European art. The cloister at the Augustinian monastery in Malinalco, dating from 1540, contains an alcove dominated by a painted fresco of a friar and a skeleton with scythe standing next to one another (Peterson 1993). Consider, too, the open-air chapel at Tlalmanalco, on the road to Amecameca, east of Mexico City, constructed by Franciscans in 1550–60. The chapel portrays dozens of skulls lining the upper reach of its graceful arches, all of them alternating with diverse plants. On each of the central columns there are representations of human figures, dressed in Renaissance garb and holding hands. According to Curiel Méndez (1987: 156), the entire ornamentation at Tlalmanalco is designed to demonstrate "the Triumph of Death over humanity." The figures on the open-air chapel suggest different states of decomposition; in the

Figure 2. Panel from an eighteenth-century catafalque, housed in Toluca. The angel declares, "Death runs with time" (i.e., death is inevitable). Photograph by Stanley Brandes.

words of Curiel (ibid.: 156–57), "There are skeletons, skulls with remains of flesh and intact heads, all with distinct expressions of horror before the inevitable triumph of death." Curiel interprets the figures on the open-air chapel at Tlalmanalco as a version of the Dance of Death. His main evidence (ibid.: 156) is that some of the carvings represent people holding hands, as is the case with the Dance of Death. This feature, together with the alternation of skulls with plants, makes the entire sculptural ensemble reminiscent, if not an exact replica, of the Dance of Death.

The Dance of Death was popular in Europe for several centuries from the second quarter of the fifteenth century onward. It even had important reverberations in the nineteenth century (Goodwin 1988), and possibly up to the present time in the form of Day of the Dead iconography. Most frequently, the Dance of Death appeared as both literature and drawing. In searching for origins, art historian James Clark (1950: 90) maintains that "whether our starting point is in England, France, Germany, Switzerland, Denmark, Italy or Spain, we find all the signposts pointing in the same direction," that is, to the Cemetery of the Innocents, located in Paris and dated 1424. For others, the Dance of Death motif is much older, in that it is a textual and artistic elaboration of old Germanic mythology (American Art Association 1922: prefatory note).

There exist innumerable versions of the Dance of Death; collector Susan Minns amassed over seven hundred separate items, dating from the fifteenth through the nineteenth centuries, all of them European (American Art Association 1922). The first known printed edition was published by Guy (or Guyot) Marchant in Paris in 1485 (Chaney 1945: 6). Oddly, the Spanish versions, from the early fifteenth century onward, contain text alone, with no pictorial art (Clark 1950: 41–50; Whyte 1931). Probably the forty-one woodcuts published in Lyons in 1538 by Hans Holbein the Younger (1971) constitute the most famous rendition of the textual and pictorial Dance of Death. Literary and artistic versions of the Dance of Death vary enormously. However, it is possible to describe a prototypical dance. Robert Wark (1966: 8–9) offers an excellent, succinct description:

> Normally the pictorial side of the work consists of a series of human figures each accompanied by a skeleton or cadaver that came to symbolize Death. The figure of Death is frequently represented as if in a grotesque dance to which he is leading his human companion. The human figures are drawn from the various strata of society in more or less descending order: Pope, Emperor, Cardinal, King, Bishop, Duke, and so on, down to the Parish Priest and the Laborer. The order and number of figures vary a great deal from one rendition to another, but the general theme of Death leading away members of the various ranks of society remains the same. The pictures usually are accompanied by a text which takes the form of a series of brief conversations between the human figures and Death. The meaning behind the presentation is clear enough: Death visits all ranks and conditions of men; he is the great leveler before whom all worldly distinctions crumble.

As in the funeral catafalques of eighteenth-century New Spain, Dance of Death pictography during the late Middle Ages and the Renaissance portrays highly animated skeletal figures. The most artistically meritorious versions of the Dance invest the skeletal figure with a wide range of human emotions: hostility, glee, insolence, furtiveness, haste, and the like. These skeletons symbolize the deceased and yet interact with the living and occupy their world.

Art historians agree that the Dance of Death was above all didactic. As James Clark (1950: 105) puts it, "The equality of all in death is the theme, with the further conclusion that man must repent before it is too late." Death was, of course, a daily presence for Europeans in the late Middle Ages and the Renaissance. The Black Death was within living memory, and people lived in daily contact with death. "The mortality rate

was high," Werner Gundersheimer (1971: xiii) reminds us, "and the infant mortality rate was such that a family might well confer the same Christian name on several successive children. Funerals were frequent and public, and . . . executions were performed in public places." The Dance of Death, in addition to portraying the inevitable and demonstrating death as a great leveler, was a manner of "realizing graphically, and thereby perhaps of somewhat domesticating, the dreadful fatality that hovered over even the most sheltered lives" (ibid.).

Christian art at the time of the Conquest was replete with skeletal representations of death in the abstract. In Europe and in New Spain, drawings of both the tree of vanity and the allegories of the stages of life regularly incorporated skeletal figures as representations of death. Clark (1950: 108–11) concludes that the Dance of Death was not designed to portray individual deceased people in skeletal form. Rather, he says (ibid.: 111), "The dance is a symbol of death, nothing more. Poet and artist alike intended to portray in allegorical form the inevitability of death, and the equality of all men in death. . . . The motive was at first didactic. John Lydgate put it in a nutshell: 'To shew this world is but a pilgrimage.'"

The Dance of Death is the one prominent antecedent of Day of the Dead art that contains an element of humor, although it is hardly the whimsical, spontaneously generated humor of the sugar skulls and toy skeletons sold in Mexican markets during October and the first days of November. In Holbein's woodcuts, the most widely disseminated versions of the Dance of Death, the skeleton usually mocks "the living person while summoning him to die" (Gundersheimer 1971: xii). Since Holbein's woodcuts were published during the first generation after the Conquest, they might easily have influenced popular art in early colonial New Spain.

And yet much argues against any sort of direct influence, at least in the first two centuries following the Conquest. For one thing, the earliest example of what is possibly the Dance of Death in New Spain is the sculptural ensemble at the open-air chapel of Tlalmanalco. Certainly there is nothing humorous in this ensemble, nor, as sculpture, is it executed in the medium through which the European Dance of Death appeared. Second, it is by no means definite that the chapel at Tlalmanalco represents the Dance of Death at all. In fact, much argues against it: the portrayal of skulls at Tlalmanalco in lieu of the usual skeletons; the stone in lieu of paint or print; and plants, rather than humans, in sequential alternation with the death figures. Added to this evidence is the complete absence of graphic versions of the Day of the Dead from Spain, the country that provided the most immediate influence on Mesoamerica for generations after the Conquest (Figure 3).

Further, Day of the Dead skeletons vary noticeably from Dance of

Figure 3. Detail from the open-air chapel at Tlalmanalco. Photograph by Stanley Brandes.

Death skeletons in one critical way: In the case of the Day of the Dead representation, skeletons do not interact with live humans. In toys and quotidian scenes, all the Day of the Dead figurines are skeletons—dressed as humans but entirely fleshless nonetheless. In the Dance of Death, the skeletons almost invariably interact with portrayals of live humans. They interrupt their daily activities to carry them off; they tug at the humans, poke them to get their attention, pull them away to their inevitable demise. Death figures in the Dance of Death do assume a mocking expression, but they clearly ridicule the living victims about to die, who frequently belong to the social elite, for example, the clergy and nobility.

In the case of Day of the Dead figures, death itself is mocked rather than any specific human victims. At the countless cemeteries where daytime or nighttime vigils are held in honor of relatives during the Day of the Dead, humorous iconography is scarce or absent. Mexicans do not mock the real death of their loved ones. And apart from Day of the Dead vigils, Mexican tombstones rarely display representations of skulls or skeletons. The humor about death is most prevalent in anonymous contexts, like stands and markets where death figures and colorful paper cutouts are sold (Sandstrom and Sandstrom 1986), as well as in newspapers, where the weaknesses of living public figures, portrayed in skeletal form, are exposed publicly. Artistic humor comes out, too, in the labeling of sugar skulls with the names of living persons, never with the names of the deceased. In Mexico the funerals of very young children—those classified as *angelitos* (little angels) because they are said to pass directly to heaven after death, without having to go through purgatory—are often lively affairs accompanied by music. But there is no special humorous iconography associated with these funerals, as there is with the public celebration of the Day of the Dead.

Mexicans, like people virtually everywhere, take the death of friends and relatives seriously. Humorous iconography is a product of and is appropriate to a single celebratory moment, the Day of the Dead. For this reason, most of this iconography can be classified as ephemeral art. It need not last beyond that one occasion.

Artistic Humor in the Day of the Dead

It is fair to say that no other predominantly Catholic country in the world celebrates All Saints' and All Souls' Days with the artistic exuberance and humor that Mexico does. In Spain, which brought this holiday to the Americas, the celebration is thoroughly somber. In New Spain, at some still indeterminate date, All Saints' and All Souls' Days began to assume a humorous cast. However, we can be pretty certain that it was sometime during the first two centuries after the Conquest. By the mid-eighteenth century, the holiday already had acquired its unique Mexican name, the Day of the Dead. By that time, too, humorous figurines had appeared. We may thus deduce that the Day of the Dead at this time took on its present-day flavor, at least in the Valley of Mexico.

Contrary to reports that sugar figurines are documented "only to the 1840s" (Green 1980: 71), there is excellent evidence that they appeared a full century earlier. In the 1740s Capuchin friar Francisco de Ajofrín (1958: 87) wrote:

> Before the Day of the Dead they sell a thousand figures of little sheep, lambs, etc. of sugar paste [today called *alfeñique*], which they name ofrenda, and it is a gift which must be given obligatorily to boys and girls of the houses where one is known. They also sell coffins, tombs and a thousand figures of the dead, clerics, monks, nuns and all denominations, bishops, horsemen, for which there is a great market and a colorful fair in the portals of the merchants, where it is incredible [to see] the crowd of men and women from Mexico City on the evening before and on the day of All Saints.

Note that this passage, the earliest account of secular objects being sold during the Day of the Dead, makes no specific mention of skulls or skeletons. Significantly, however, it does report death imagery in the form of "coffins, tombs and a thousand figures of the dead." Moreover, it is implied that these and associated objects served as children's toys; hence, they were probably humorous or at least whimsically conceived objects, not unlike those of today. The friar goes on to explain (ibid.) that sugar figurines and other "cute little things" [*monerías*] are made in rapid succession by "clever" artisans who sell them cheaply. However, he warns the consumer not to pay in advance, which would result, he says, in the receipt of second-rate, tardily delivered items.

The most explicit precursors of the humorous popular art found in today's Day of the Dead comes from the last half of the nineteenth century. It was at this time that broadsides, known as *calaveras* (skulls), began appearing in significant numbers. Childs and Altman (1982: 54) view this development as a consequence of the freedom of the press that arrived with Mexico's independence from Spain in 1821. Technical advances in newspaper printing and the emergence of illustrated newspapers were also partly responsible. The first illustrated newspaper in Mexico was called *El Calavera*, which began publication in January 1847. Through drawings, verse, and essays, *El Calavera* specialized in satirizing political currents of the day and particularly in poking fun at the new nation's leaders. After thirty-one issues, it was suppressed by the government and its leaders were imprisoned for trying to incite rebellion (ibid.). Yet the long-term impact of this newspaper was considerable.

Shortly thereafter, journalist Antonio Vanegas Arroyo hired illustrator José Guadalupe Posada (1852–1913) to illustrate his topical ballads, which he hawked around streets and fairs, pilgrimages, and public gatherings (Wollen 1989: 14). By the late nineteenth and early twentieth centuries, Posada was creating powerful calavera images each year on the occasion of the Day of the Dead; these "vivid and lively skeletons and skulls with grinning teeth [were shown] dancing, cycling, playing the guitar, plying their trades, drinking, masquerading," and doing dozens of other comical activities (ibid.: 14–15). Childs and Altman (1982: 56) correctly observe that "everyone and everything was a likely subject of his illustrations. There are calaveras of leaders of the 1910 revolution like Francisco Madero, who is depicted as a drunken peon, and another of Vanegas Arroyo, Posada's publisher. There are grand ladies and gentlemen of the aristocracy and coquettish barmaids, all in skeletal form. There are also scenes drawn directly from Días de los Muertos celebrations, such as the one of a cemetery picnic and another of a seller of sugar skulls." Probably the most famous of Posada's images is that of the *catrina*, the female dandy, portrayed as a fleshless skull, topped with a fancy, wide-brimmed hat replete with large billowing feathers and other decorations (Figure 4).

Posada's influence on Mexican art and culture is incalculable. Largely ignored by artists of his day, he was discovered and popularized through

Figure 4. Bakery window in Cuernavaca portraying Posada's *catrina*, who states, "Dona Blanca the baker has delicious *pan de muerto*. Go inside, passerby, and take away what you wish. R.I.P." Photograph by Stanley Brandes.

the zealous efforts of artists and writers, many of them non-Mexican. Peter Wollen (1989: 14) recounts the birth of Posada as a recognized genius:

> The painter Dr Atl, the most persistent early pioneer of modernism in Mexico, and the young French immigrant, Jean Charlot, one of the group of muralists around Diego Rivera, were the first to notice

> Posada's work in the new artistic context of the post-revolutionary years. Charlot, who first saw Posada prints in 1920, followed up his discovery, showed prints to other painters and wrote the first biographical and critical essays on Posada's work, in the early twenties. In time, other artists—including Rivera, José Clemente Orozco and David Alfaro Siquieros—took up Posada's cause, often in hyperbolic terms, and acknowledged their debt, direct or indirect, to the humble popular print-maker. The legend was born.

Folklorist Frances Toor and collaborators promoted Posada's reputation when in 1930 she published *Las obras de José Guadalupe Posada, grabador mexicano*. Diego Rivera, in an introduction to a book reproducing 406 of Posada's engravings, called him "an engraver of genius" and "the greatest artist" among those Mexicans who have produced popular art (quoted in Macazaga and Macazaga 1979: 21). In his famous mural *A Sunday Afternoon in Alameda Park*, Rivera reproduced Posada's catrina, placing both this figure, a parody of full bourgeois costume, and a portrait of Posada in the center of the huge painting, where they flank Rivera himself.

Posada was not the first or only great satiric engraver of his day. In fact, Manuel Manilla, among others, preceded him. And these Mexicans were themselves part of an international artistic movement. As Wollen maintains (1989: 19), Posada is part of the more general phenomenon of broadside artist, part of "the whole repertoire of nineteenth century urban popular art—catchpenny prints, peep-shows, panoramas, Punch and Judy, melodrama and fairground attractions." Like the rest of this art, Posada's addressed particular historical circumstances in the national arena in which he found himself: a new country with an unstable political framework in which the normal democratic means of criticism were highly restricted. Posada needed to make a living; his art had to sell. He found his market among an enormous restless urban populace dissatisfied with their political leaders and needing an outlet in which to criticize them. Posada's art became just one of numerous forms of popular resistance (Beezley et al. 1994) expressed throughout Mexican history. As William Beezley (1987: 98) puts it, the rhymed, illustrated obituaries "offered the common people the opportunity, without fear of censure or reprisal, to express their dissatisfaction with political and social leaders and to define their grievances, real or imagined."

Posada became nationally and internationally famous through the promotional efforts of famous artists and writers within and outside Mexico. Hence for a second time Posada's art was popularized, this time not by struggling journalists but by the country's artistic elite, who read into

his imagery the meaning of Mexico itself. Wollen (1989: 16) summarizes Posada's legacy thus:

> It is wrong to see Posada simply as an "influence." His name and legend were constitutive in the establishment of the Mexican renaissance; they symbolized both an alternative tradition and, crucially, a chain of succession. This particular role assigned to Posada was important both in relation to Mexicanism and in relation to Modernism. It gave credibility to claims to be part of an authentically Mexican artistic tradition, crossing both the class gap and the historic divide of the Revolution itself and, at the same time, guaranteed the modernity of the tradition by aligning it with the revival of popular imagery among the European avant-garde. It was a way of solving the classic dilemma of evolutionary nationalism—how to be popular, authentic, traditional *and* modernizing, all at the same time.

By the 1930s Posada and his calaveras had become symbolic of Mexico. The irreverence of the calaveras suited the revolutionary ideology of Mexico; yet the international art community had virtually declared these satiric skulls and skeletons a kind of high art. As analyzed by Liza Bakewell (1995: 31), Posada's work satisfied the needs of a "cultural nationalism" that started with the Mexican Revolution and persists to this day.

It is important to recall at this point that even though Posada's art has long been widely disseminated, reproduced, transformed, and mimicked in nonritual contexts, he himself used the Day of the Dead as a creative stimulus and, one supposes, a commercial opportunity. By his time it was an entrenched tradition. Artistically, as well, the sugar candies in the form of dead people, caskets, and related mortuary imagery—all of it humorous—had been a part of the popular celebration of the Day of the Dead for generations. It is not surprising, then, that Posada's satiric imagery, itself the immediate product of crucial developments in Mexico's political history and in the evolution of printing, should have been enthusiastically received in its day. Both his thematic material and humorous tone coincided with already-established artistic patterns in the celebration of this holiday. The imagery also responded to the desires of Mexican artists, who were in "full revolt against a tradition of dependence on European, especially Spanish, academic art. They wanted to replace it with an art whose genealogy would go back before the Conquest, which would be original to Mexico, popular and authentic" (Wollen 1989: 15).

Mortality, Politics, and the Convergence of Iconographic Traditions

To this point, the analysis of mortuary iconography in the Day of the Dead has focused on three possible artistic precursors: the death imagery of at least some pre-Columbian art; the sugar candies that appeared during the colonial celebration of the Day of the Dead; and the satiric engravings of Posada and others that became part of the popular celebration of this holiday during the last half of the nineteenth century and the beginning of the twentieth. To conclude, I wish to discuss the relationship among these separate but related phenomena, as well as the implications of popular art for the formation of Mexican national identity. As indicated earlier, it is insufficient simply to postulate that Day of the Dead iconography is the product of an uninterrupted tradition of images of skulls and skeletons, stretching from the ancient past to the present. Artistic styles and motifs are not merely transmitted across generations. The people who inherit these traditions retain them, transform them, or discard them according to particular historical circumstances. What we need is some indication—even a speculative indication—of how and why artistic features persist or disappear. We lack any convincing account of the mechanisms by which Day of the Dead iconography has been shaped into a Mexican national symbol. A processual treatment of the artistic dimension of the Day of the Dead is what has been missing from the literature.

The little we know about Day of the Dead figurines in the colonial era comes from Ajofrín. The friar tells us that by the mid-eighteenth century people in the Valley of Mexico were buying whimsical figurines made of sugar paste for this occasion. We also know that some of these figurines incorporated mortuary symbolism. How is the existence of these sweets related to pre-Columbian patterns? To begin with, the only evidence of humorous sugar figurines during the colonial era comes from the Valley of Mexico; hence we would do well to focus on the Aztec, whose presence dominated the Valley of Mexico at the time of the Conquest. The artistic imagery of other ancient Mesoamerican peoples, like the Maya, Toltec, and Totonac, are of possible interest. But these peoples varied so much from one another both in iconography and in space and time that their influence on colonial patterns in New Spain was remote at best.

It is significant that the mortuary imagery of the colonial era during the Day of the Dead was not, as with the Aztec, made of permanent material like stone and bone. This imagery took the form of sugar candy. If we are trying to establish lines of continuity between the ancient Aztec and colonial culture in the Valley of Mexico, it would be more fruitful,

in my opinion, to examine ritual Aztec foods than sculpture. The great sixteenth-century chronicler Fray Bernardino de Sahagún, who has rightly been called a "pioneer ethnographer" (Klor de Alva et al. 1988), provides the most telling evidence. According to Sahagún (1978 [1829]: book 3.5–6), the Aztecs made images out of wood, which they covered with *tzoalli*, or amaranth seed (*Amaranthus hypocondriacus*) dough, shaped in human form. Consider, for example, the account of what the Aztecs did with a tzoalli image of the great god Uitzilopochtli during Panquetzalitzli, the fifteenth month: "And when he died, they broke up his body, the amaranth seed dough. His heart was Moctezuma's portion. And the rest of his members, which were made like his bones, were disseminated among the people. . . . And when they divided among themselves his body of amaranth seed dough, it was only in very small [pieces] . . . the youths ate them. And of this which they ate it was said, 'The god is eaten.'" During Atemoztli, the sixteenth month, anthropomorphic amaranth seed images were made for a feast honoring the rain god, Tlaloc. Sahagún's account states (book 2.29) that "they made eyes and teeth on them and worshiped them with music." During Tepehuitl, the thirteenth month (ibid.: book 2.131–33), the Aztec amaranth dough figures took on a specific mortuary cast: "All the [wooden] serpent [representations] which were kept in people's houses and the small wind [figures] they covered with a dough of [ground] amaranth seeds. And their bones were likewise fashioned of amaranth seed dough. . . . And [for] whoever had died who had not been buried, they also at this time made representations of mountains. They made them all of amaranth seed dough. Thereupon they dismembered the amaranth seed dough [figures]. . . . little by little they went, taking some of it when they ate it." As indicated in this passage, these dough images commemorated only specific classes of deceased, namely, those who had drowned or who had died in such a way that they were buried rather than cremated. Food offerings were set out in honor of the images. Continues Sahagún (ibid.): "They . . . placed these images of the dead on . . . wreaths of grass, and then at dawn placed these images in their oratories, on beds of grass, rush, or reed; having placed them there they offered them food, tamales and mazamorra [a dessert made of maize gruel and fruit], or stew made of fowl or dog meat, and later burned incense to them in a pottery incense burner." It is tempting to interpret the anthropomorphic dough figurines as precursors of the molded sugar candy sold on the Day of the Dead in mid-eighteenth-century New Spain and up to the present day. It is likely, in fact, that the acceptance of anthropomorphic foods by residents of the Valley of Mexico in the colonial era can be traced to the prevalence of tzoalli images in Aztec ritual. After all, anthropomorphic foods are not automatically acceptable to everyone; in some parts of the world—France, for example—they are rejected as cannibalistic.

To the Aztec custom of consuming anthropomorphic sweets we must add the Spanish ritual practice of offering food at cemeteries in honor of the dead. Consider the province of Zamora, in Old Castille. From the 1500s on, All Souls' Day celebrations required a catafalque, situated in the main chapel of any given church; the catafalque was encircled by candles and "twenty-five rolls of bread" (Lorenzo Pinar 1991: 95). From late medieval Majorca there are several testaments that conclusively document the custom of situating bread on tombs during All Souls' Day. In his will dated 13 December 1344, Jaime Corbera stated: "I wish and arrange . . . that my heirs should give each year, on the Day of the Deceased [i.e., All Souls' Day], on my sepulcher, five *sueldos* of bread, candles, and other obligatory objects, in such manner as on this day is custom to do" (quoted in Gabriel Llompart 1965: 96–97). A century later this Majorcan practice was still flourishing, as witnessed in another will: "My . . . brother Pedro Juan shall be obliged for life on the Day of the Deceased each year to carry to the sepulcher of the 'Betnassars' . . . a *cuévano* of bread worth 10 sueldos, as well as a tall candle to burn while the holy office is celebrated, as is customary" (ibid.: 96).

There is evidence that by the seventeenth and eighteenth centuries sweets formed part of the All Saints' and All Souls' Days celebration in the Iberian Peninsula. A document from the Barcelona silversmiths' guild, dated 15 October 1671, stipulates that on All Souls' Day two *corteras* of *pa dels morts*—Catalan for "dead bread"—be offered to the deceased. What is astounding about this document, aside from references to dead bread, is the use of the term "Diada dels Morts," that is, Day of the Dead, to refer to All Souls' Day. This is the earliest such reference of which I am aware. Equally relevant is Joan Amades's (1956: 611) observation that in eighteenth-century Barcelona, during All Saints' Day, *panellets* and chestnuts "were combined and distributed in such a manner that they formed whimsical designs and figures." *Panellets* (little breads) are still the All Saints' Day sweet par excellence in Catalonia. For generations, they were made of marzipan—sweetened almond or walnut paste—and coated with pine nuts. Nowadays these ingredients are replaced by lemon, strawberry, pineapple, and the like, which, according to one Barcelona baker, are more in keeping with contemporary preferences for "light cuisine" than the rich nuts of times past.

These examples are a modest sample of the abundant evidence that in Spain, and indeed throughout southern Europe, bread and sweets formed an integral part of the celebration of All Souls' Day prior to and during

the colonial era in New Spain. (For a fuller account see Brandes 1997). Not only was bread carried to tombs and churches during All Souls' Day, but it was also distributed to the poor and handicapped (Llabrés Quintana 1925). We can safely assume that this tradition was carried to Mexico during the sixteenth and seventeenth centuries, when it must have been taught to the Indian converts. At the same time, Indians in the Valley of Mexico, at least, were accustomed to offerings of edible anthropomorphic figures, in the form of molded amaranth dough, during mortuary and other rituals. To reconstruct the precise sequence and combination of practices is risky. Nonetheless, we may postulate that when the Spaniards introduced All Saints' and All Souls' Days rites to the Indians, food offerings were an essential part of what they taught. The Indians, being accustomed to offerings of this nature, made such items an essential component of their gifts to ancestors and the saints.

What is unusual about the Mexican food offerings is that so many of them, from colonial times to the present, explicitly play on mortuary themes, including skulls, skeletons, and caskets. As far as we know, too, Mexico is the only country where sugar is the principal substance out of which Day of the Dead figurines are sculpted, rather than being combined with nuts and flour. The unique nature of sugar production and distribution in New Spain had a critical impact on ritual foods used during All Saints' and All Souls' Days (Brandes 1997). Because of the peculiar role of sugar in the economy of New Spain, Mexicans used sugar as Europeans used moldable, edible substances like bread and marzipan or as the ancient Mexicans used tzoalli.

In explaining the importance of skulls, skeletons, caskets, and the like, it is crucial to recall the prevalence of these images in the Valley of Mexico—the seat of pre-Columbian and Spanish power at the time of the Conquest and thereafter. We have seen that both the Aztecs and the Europeans were accustomed to these images as religious symbols, although the Aztec and European images lacked the humor that characterized and still characterizes these images in the Mexican context. Equally critical is the relation between the humorous Mexican images and the ubiquitous presence of death in early colonial Mexico. In the first century after European contact, numerous major and minor epidemics afflicted the indigenous peoples of the Valley of Mexico and their neighbors. The first major epidemic, a virulent attack of smallpox, came to Mexico from the island of Hispaniola and decimated Tenochtitlán; it is generally agreed that this decisive event favored the Spanish Conquest (McNeill 1976: 183–84). Severe and widespread disease recurred in the years 1545–48, 1576–81, and 1736–39, although, as Charles Gibson (1964: 136–37) points out, many lesser epidemics caused destruction in limited areas. Throughout the sixteenth and early seventeenth centuries, large-scale depopulation occurred both during and between epidemics. Although it is uncertain which pathogens were responsible for the three major epidemics, the most likely candidates are those that caused smallpox, measles, typhus, and typhoid (ibid.). Spanish methods of treatment, based largely on bloodletting, exacerbated the effects of disease. In the plague of 1576, for example, the viceroy distributed medical instructions to all affected towns; the principal method was prompt bleeding. The same remedy was applied during an epidemic in 1595 (ibid.: 499).

Although estimates of the population decline are by no means definitive, Sherbourne Cook and Woodrow Borah's are widely accepted and cited. Based on exhaustive research into the source of royal revenues, they calculate that from 1519 to 1532 the population of central Mexico shrank from 25.2 million to 16.8 million (Cook and Borah 1979: 1). In 1548 the population stood at about 6.3 million and in 1605 at 1.075 million. By the 1620s only about 730,000 Indians were left (ibid.: 100). John Super (1988: 52) refers to this loss as "a demographic catastrophe perhaps unequalled in the history of the world." Spanish observers of the era were understandably concerned about the population loss. A summary of the literature indicates that "excessive labor requirements, excessive tributes, mistreatment, drunkenness, the Indians' 'flaca complexión' [weak constitution], starvation, flood, drought, disease, and divine providence were all mentioned . . . as causes" (Gibson 1964: 136).

From the vantage point of a sixteenth- or seventeenth-century observer, however, the full extent and impact of this massive loss of life could not have been recognized. The one early chronicler who faced up to it was Fray Bartolomé de Las Casas (1992 [1552]: 58), who placed most of the blame on his countrymen: "The Spaniards have killed more Indians here in twelve years by the sword, by fire, and enslavement than anywhere else in the Indies. They have killed young and old, men, women, and children, some four million souls during what they call the Conquests. . . . And this does not take into account those Indians who have died from ill treatment, or were killed under tyrannical servitude." Whether through warfare, debilitation, or disease, the enormous destruction of life suffered by the Indians of sixteenth-century Mexico is nearly incomprehensible.

Under the circumstances, it seems reasonable to posit that the Day of the Dead became ritualistically elaborate in Mexico as a by-product of this loss of life. Not only did people die in staggering numbers, but they were also uprooted and resettled in unfamiliar territory. For purposes of taxation and civil obedience, they were herded into hundreds of new grid-

plan towns (Foster 1960: 34–49). The anguish that these changes must have wrought is incalculable.

During colonial times, sugar figurines with mortuary themes must have had a profound psychological impact. It is significant in this context that they are ephemeral. This quality is what enabled people simultaneously to confront and to deny the death that they celebrated ritually and that was a biological catastrophe of their times and those of their ancestors. The humor and whimsy of the figurines, too, must have assisted the inhabitants of New Spain in coping with dire demographic circumstances by mocking, and thereby implicitly denying, the tragic reality experienced by them and their forebears. In the colonial era, death figures, to be sure, were the combined iconographic offspring of Mesoamerican and European civilizations. However, the images no doubt took firm hold in New Spain because of the demographic collapse, the cruel, relentless, utterly public presence of death. The figurines were and always have been particularly available during, and appropriate to, the Day of the Dead, a community holiday in which the common fate of humanity is commemorated. They have never been associated with funerals, honoring the death of particular relatives. This distinction casts serious doubt on claims, summarized earlier in this article, that Mexicans display a unique relationship with death (Figure 5).

As Childs and Altman (1982: 58) have pointed out, the sugar skulls and skeleton toys that predominate in rural areas of Mexico during the Day of the Dead represent one artistic tradition. This article has demonstrated the origins of this tradition, which include the artistic and religious legacy of Aztecs and Spaniards at the time of the Conquest, as well as demographic circumstances during the colonial regime. There is a second artistic tradition related to the Day of the Dead that was initiated with the broadside illustrations by José Guadalupe Posada during the late nineteenth and early twentieth centuries. This second tradition, as we have seen, had a more overtly political and social mission than the first. It consisted mainly of satiric artistic commentaries, which could flourish because of the humorous license provided by the Day of the Dead.

Posada's art and its offshoots provided what has elsewhere been called a type of "peaceful protest" (Brandes 1977). Members of all social strata came under Posada's mocking eye, but there was an especially biting quality to the humorous portrayal of political leaders and other public figures, who could not ordinarily be ridiculed in public. There is an enormous anthropological literature, skillfully synthesized and summarized by Mahadev Apte (1985), that demonstrates the opportunities provided by religious ritual for humorous commentary on otherwise forbidden themes, as well as for mockery of social and political elites. This is essentially the theoretical

Figure 5. Sugar skull (about six inches high). Mexico City, October 1995. Photograph by Stanley Brandes.

mode in which Posada's art, and the literary and artistic offshoots of his art, must be understood. Posada could employ calaveras—skulls, skeletons, and other mortuary imagery—in part because a well-established artistic tradition in Mexican popular art allowed him to do so. His calaveras, too, were appropriate to the occasion for which they were produced. The Day of the Dead in essence provided Posada with a uniquely propitious artistic opportunity. However, the purpose and impact of his art were different from those of the sugar candies that emerged during the colonial era.

Posada's calaveras, through their popularization by famous artists who took up his cause, have influenced Mexican street and gallery art profoundly. Childs and Altman (1982: 58–59) provide several apt examples:

> The wire and plaster skeleton figures of the Mexico City artist, Saúl Moreno, are on the surface not very different from toys made in Oaxaca. But Moreno's work is not produced for friends and neighbors, but is made for and consumed by art collectors. A skeleton sculpture by Moreno is more likely to be found in a Berlin art collection than on a villager's altar in Tepoztlán. Another Mexico City artist, Pedro Linares, works in papier-mâché and has created Días de los Muertos objects which have no real counterpart in observances of the festival. He makes large skeleton figures which compare to the Judas figures commonly made for Holy Week. But whereas the Judas figures are made to be burned in a village fiesta, the Linares papier-mâché skeletons and skulls . . . have no such function and are intended *for a national and in fact international art market.*

The political and social commentaries that follow the Posada tradition continue to appear in newspapers throughout Mexico around the time of the Day of the Dead. But the art that his work spurned, through its validation by world-famous Mexican artists, now transcends Posada's immediate goals. It has become an important commercial enterprise and for this reason has acquired a life of its own. Mexican skulls and skeletons sell well to the international community of tourists and collectors. Judging from the Posada reproductions drawn annually on store windows and displayed in supermarkets, skulls and skeletons also stimulate business among Mexican consumers.

These two separate, albeit related, traditions of mortuary art—the first stemming from the religious and demographic imperatives of colonial times, the second from the political and journalistic developments of a new nation—are now generally perceived by Mexicans and outsiders as one undifferentiated phenomenon. They have virtually become emblematic of Mexico itself. As indicated earlier in this article, scholars interpret the skulls and skeletons that appear during the Day of the Dead as evidence of a peculiarly Mexican view of death. On the contrary, no special Mexican view of death, no uniquely morbid Mexican national character, has yielded this mortuary art. Rather, specific demographic and political circumstances originally gave rise to it, and commercial interests have allowed it to flourish in the twentieth century. It is above all the enormous proliferation of Day of the Dead art that has produced the all-too-familiar stereotype of the death-obsessed Mexican.

Note

I wish to give special thanks to the National Endowment for the Humanities and the John Carter Brown Library for providing me with the resources necessary for the completion of this project. Thanks also go to library staff members at the University of California, Berkeley; Harvard University; Brown University; the University of Seville; the Colegio de México; the Archivo de Indias; and the Escuela de Estudios Latinoamericanos in Seville. Individuals who have provided me with bibliographic and other valuable assistance include Liza Bakewell, Jorge Duany, John Graham, Javier Inda, Jorge Klor de Alva, James Taggart, and William Taylor. I am very grateful for all their help.

References

Ajofrín, Francisco de
1958 Diario del viaje que por orden de la sagrada congregación de propaganda fide hizo a la America septentrional en el siglo XVIII. Vicente Castañeda y Alcover, ed. Madrid: Real Academia de la Historia.

Amades, Joan
1956 Costumari català: El curs de l'any, Vol. 5. Barcelona: Salvat.

American Art Association
1922 The Notable Collection of Miss Susan Minns of Boston, Mass . . . Illustrative of "The Dance of Death." New York: American Art Association.

Anonymous
1963–64 Master Works of Mexican Art: From Pre-Columbian Times to the Present. Los Angeles: Los Angeles County Museum of Art.

Apte, Mahadev L.
1985 Humor and Laughter: An Anthropological Approach. Ithaca, NY: Cornell University Press.

Bakewell, Liza
1995 *Bellas Artes* and *Artes Populares*: The Implications of Difference in the Mexico City Art World. *In* Looking High and Looking Low: Art and Cultural Identity. Brenda Jo Bright and Liza Bakewell, eds. Pp. 19–54. Tucson: University of Arizona Press.

Beezley, William H.
1987 Judas at the Jockey Club and Other Episodes of Porfirian Mexico. Lincoln: University of Nebraska Press.

Beezley, William H., Cheryl Martin, and William E. French, eds.
1994 Rituals of Rule, Rituals of Resistance: Public Celebrations and Popular Culture in Mexico. Wilmington, DE: SR Books.

Berrin, Kathleen, ed.
1988 Feathered Serpents and Flowering Trees: Reconstructing the Murals of Teotihuacán. San Francisco: Fine Arts Museums of San Francisco.

Bialostocki, Jan
1987 The Image of Death and Funerary Art in European Tradition. *In* Arte funerario. Louise Noelle, ed. Vol. 1, pp. 11–32. Mexico: Universidad Nacional Autónoma de México.

Brandes, Stanley
1977 Peaceful Protest: Spanish Political Humor in a Time of Crisis. Western Folklore 36: 331–46.
1997 Sugar, Colonialism, and Death: On the Origins of Mexico's Day of the Dead. Comparative Studies in Society and History 39: 270–299.

Carmichael, Elizabeth, and Chloë Sayer
1991 The Skeleton at the Feast: The Day of the Dead in Mexico. Austin: University of Texas Press.

Carrasco, Davíd
1992 Toward the Splendid City: Knowing the Worlds of Moctezuma. *In* Moctezuma's Mexico: Visions of the Aztec World. Davíd Carrasco and Eduardo Matos Moctezuma, eds. Pp. 99–148. Niwot: University Press of Colorado.

Chaney, Edward F.
1945 La danse macabre des charniers des saints innocents à Paris. Manchester: Manchester University Press.

Childs, Robert V., and Patricia B. Altman
1982 Vive tu recuerdo: Living Traditions in the Mexican Days of the Dead. Los Angeles: Museum of Cultural History, University of California, Los Angeles.

Clark, James M.
1950 The Dance of Death in the Middle Ages and the Renaissance. Glasgow: Jackson, Son, and Co.

Coe, Michael D.
1975 Death and the Ancient Maya. *In* Death and the Afterlife in Pre-Columbian America. Elizabeth P. Benson, ed. Pp. 87–104. Washington, DC: Dunbarton Oaks Research Library and Collections.
1988 Ideology of the Maya Tomb. *In* Maya Iconography. Elizabeth P. Benson and Gillett G. Griffin, eds. Pp. 222–35. Princeton, NJ: Princeton University Press.

Contreras, Eduardo
1990 Una ofrenda en los restos del Templo Mayor de Tenochtitlán. *In* Trabajos arqueológicos en el centro de la ciudad de México. Eduardo Matos Moctezuma, ed. Pp. 403–14. México: Instituto nacional de antropología e historia.

Cook, Sherbourne F., and Woodrow Borah
1979 Essays in Population History: Mexico and California. Vol. 3. Berkeley: University of California Press.

Curiel Méndez, Gustavo
1987 Aproximación a la iconografía de un programa escatológico francis-

cano del siglo XVI. *In* Arte funerario. Louise Noelle, ed. Vol. 1, pp. 151–60. Mexico: Universidad Nacional Autónoma de México.
Davies, Nigel
1977 The Toltecs until the Fall of Tula. Norman: University of Oklahoma Press.
Diehl, Richard A.
1983 Tula: The Toltec Capital of Ancient Mexico. London: Thames and Hudson.
Fernández Kelly, Patricia
1974 Death in Mexican Folk Culture. American Quarterly 25: 516–35.
Foster, George M.
1960 Culture and Conquest: America's Spanish Heritage. Viking Fund Publications in Anthropology, No. 27. New York: Wenner-Gren Foundation.
Fuente, Beatríz de la
1974 Arte prehispánico funerario: El occidente de México. México: Universidad Nacional Autónoma de México.
Gabriel Llompart, C. R.
1965 Pan sobre la tumba. Revista de dialectología y tradiciones populares (Madrid) 11: 96–102.
Gibson, Charles
1964 The Aztecs under Spanish Rule: A History of the Indians of the Valley of Mexico, 1519–1810. Stanford, CA: Stanford University Press.
Gombrich, Ernst H.
1972 Symbolic Images: Studies in the Art of the Renaissance. London: Phaidon.
Goodwin, Sarah Webster
1988 Kitsch and Culture: The Dance of Death in Nineteenth-Century Literature and Graphic Arts. New York: Garland.
Green, Judith Strupp
1980 The Days of the Dead in Oaxaca, Mexico: An Historical Inquiry. *In* Death and Dying: Views from Many Cultures. Richard A. Kalish, ed. Pp. 56–71. Farmingdale, NY: Baywood.
Gundersheimer, Werner L.
1971 Introduction to The Dance of Death, by Hans Holbein the Younger. Pp. ix–xiii. New York: Dover.
Haberstein, Robert W., and William M. Lamers
1963 Funeral Customs the World Over. Milwaukee, WI: Bultin.
Hassig, Ross
1988 Aztec Warfare: Imperial Expansion and Political Control. Norman: University of Oklahoma Press.
1992 War and Society in Ancient Mesoamerica. Berkeley: University of California Press.
Herrera, Hayden
1983 Frida: A Biography of Frida Kahlo. New York: Harper and Row.
Holbein, Hans, the Younger
1971 [1538] The Dance of Death. Facsimile ed. of *Les simulachres & historiees faces de la mort.* New York: Dover.
Klor de Alva, J. Jorge
1988 Sahagún and the Birth of Modern Ethnography: Representing, Confessing, and Inscribing the Native Other. *In* The Works of Bernardino

de Sahagún: Pioneer Ethnographer of Sixteenth-Century Aztec Mexico. J. Jorge Klor de Alva, H. B. Nicholson, and Eloise Quiñones, eds. Pp. 31–52. Albany, NY: University at Albany, Institute for Mesoamerican Studies.
Klor de Alva, J. Jorge, H. B. Nicholson, and Eloise Quiñones, eds.
1988 Introduction. *In* The Works of Bernardino de Sahagún: Pioneer Ethnographer of Sixteenth-Century Aztec Mexico. Pp. 1–12. Albany, NY: University at Albany, Institute for Mesoamerican Studies.
Kubler, George
1969 Studies in Classic Maya Iconography. New Haven: Connecticut Academy of Arts and Sciences.
Las Casas, Bartolomé de
1992 [1552] The Devastation of the Indies: A Brief Account. Herma Briffault, trans. Baltimore, MD: Johns Hopkins University Press.
Llabrés Quintana, Gabriel
1925 Los panetets de mort. Correo de Mallorca, October.
Lorenzo Pinar, Francisco Javier
1991 Muerte y ritual en la edad moderna: El caso de Zamora (1500–1800). Salamanca: Universidad de Salamanca.
Luján Muñoz, Luís
1987 Contribución al estudio de la iconografía de la muerte en Guatemala: El rey San Pascual. *In* Arte funerario. Louise Noelle, ed. Vol. 1, pp. 161–70. México: Universidad Nacional Autónoma de México.
Macazaga, Ramírez de Arellano, and César Macazaga Ordoño, eds.
1979 Posada y las calaveras vivientes. Mexico: Editorial Innovación.
Matos Moctezuma, Eduardo
1986 Los dioses se negaron a morir: Arqueología y crónicas del Templo Mayor. México: Secretaría de educación pública.
1992 Aztec History and Cosmovision. *In* Moctezuma's Mexico: Visions of the Aztec World. Davíd Carrasco and Eduardo Matos Moctezuma, eds. Pp. 3–97. Niwot: University Press of Colorado.
McNeill, William H.
1976 Plagues and Peoples. New York: Doubleday.
Moreno Villa, José
1986 Lo Mexicano en Las artes plásticas. México: Fondo de cultural económica.
Museo nacional de arte
1994 Juegos de ingenio y agudeza: La pintura emblemática de Nueva España. México: Patronato del Museo nacional de arte.
Museo universitario
1974–75 La muerte: Expresiones Mexicanas de un enigma. Mexico: Universidad Nacional Autónoma de México, Dirección general de difusión cultural.
Nutini, Hugo G.
1988 Todos Santos in Rural Tlaxcala: A Syncretic, Expressive, and Symbolic Analysis of the Cult of the Dead. Princeton, NJ: Princeton University Press.
Pasztory, Esther
1988 A Reinterpretation of Teotihuacán and Its Mural Painting Tradition. *In* Feathered Serpents and Flowering Trees: Reconstructing the Murals of

Teotihuacán. Kathleen Berrin, ed. Pp. 45–77. San Francisco: Fine Arts Museums of San Francisco.

Peterson, Jeanette Favrot
1993 The Paradise Garden Murals of Malinalco: Utopia and Empire in Sixteenth-Century Mexico. Austin: University of Texas Press.

Robicsek, Francis, and Donald Hales
1988 A Ceramic Codex Fragment: The Sacrifice of Xbalanque. *In* Maya Iconography. Elizabeth P. Benson and Gillett G. Griffin, eds. Pp. 260–76. Princeton, NJ: Princeton University Press.

Sahagún, Bernardino de
1978 [1829] Historia general de las casas de Nueva España. 3 vols. Mexico: Alejandro Valdés.

Sandstrom, Alan R., and Pamela Effrein Sandstrom
1986 Traditional Papermaking and Paper Cult Figures of Mexico. Norman: University of Oklahoma Press.

Schele, Linda
1988 The Xibalba Shuffle: A dance after Death. *In* Maya Iconography. Elizabeth P. Benson and Gillett G. Griffin, eds. Pp. 294–317. Princeton, NJ: Princeton University Press.

Spranz, Bodo
1973 Los dioses en los códices mexicanos del grupo borgia: Una investigación iconográfica. México: Fondo de cultura económica.

Super, John C.
1988 Food, Conquest, and Colonization in Sixteenth-Century Spanish America. Albuquerque: University of New Mexico Press.

Taylor, William B.
1987 The Virgin of Guadalupe in New Spain: An Inquiry into the Social History of Marian Devotion. American Ethnologist 14: 9–33.

Toor, Frances, et al., eds.
1930 Las obras de José Guadalupe Posada, grabador mexicano. Mexico: Mexican Folkways.

Wark, Robert R.
1966 Introduction. *In* Rowlandson's Drawings for the English Dance of Death. Pp. 1–13. San Marino, CA: Huntington Library.

Westheim, Paul
1983 La calavera. 3d ed. México: Fondo de cultura económica.

Whyte, Florence
1931 The Dance of Death in Spain and Catalonia. Baltimore, MD: Waverly.

Winning, Hugo von
1987 El simbolismo del arte funerario de Teotihuacán. *In* Arte funerario. Louise Noelle, ed. Vol. 1, pp. 55–63. México: Universidad Nacional Autónoma de México.

Wollen, Peter
1989 Introduction. *In* Posada: Messenger of Mortality. Julian Rothenstein, ed. Pp. 14–23. Boston: Redstone.

STANLEY BRANDES

The Day of the Dead, Halloween, and the Quest for Mexican National Identity

Mexico's Day of the Dead is a version of the widespread Roman Catholic feasts of All Saints' and All Souls' Days. This article analyzes how the holiday has come to be perceived, both within and outside of Mexico, as a unique Mesoamerican legacy, hence a symbol of the nation itself. Tourism and international relations have been largely responsible for this development. The recent spread of Halloween within Mexico has given rise to a symbolic competition in which Halloween is associated with the United States and the Day of the Dead with Mexico. The presence of Halloween symbols within Mexico is interpreted throughout Mexico as symptomatic of U.S. imperialist aggression.

As David Kertzer has demonstrated, ritual, religious or otherwise, is "an important means for structuring our political perceptions and leading us to interpret our experiences in certain ways" (Kertzer 1988:85). "The symbols employed" in ritual, he says, "suggest a particular interpretation of what is being viewed" (1988:85). In Mexico, the Day of the Dead, celebrated uninterruptedly from colonial times to the present, is on the surface a conspicuously apolitical event, a communal occasion on which families honor their deceased relatives. Yet this holiday in recent years has assumed an increasingly political cast, linking the celebration specifically to Mexico and Mexican national identity. The Day of the Dead helps to create an interpretation of the world in which Mexico is unique, culturally discrete, and above all different from the two powers that have dominated the country throughout its long existence: Spain and the United States. Of special significance in this regard is the Mexican reaction to Halloween. Halloween and the Day of the Dead, with obvious common historical origins, have come to symbolize nationally discrete observances. The rapid penetration of Halloween symbols into Mexico increasingly evokes Mexican nationalistic sentiments, embodied in a campaign to preserve the country from U.S. cultural imperialism.

This article, then, explores the Day of the Dead as a political event, which expresses, among other things, the complexities of Mexican–U.S. relations. The article also reaffirms a phenomenological view of tradition as, in the words of

Stanley Brandes *is Professor of Anthropology at the University of California at Berkeley*

Journal of American Folklore 111(442):359–380.

Handler and Linnekin, "a model of the past . . . inseparable from the interpretation of tradition in the present" (1984:276). Linnekin herself put the matter wisely when stating that "tradition is a conscious model of past lifeways that people use in the construction of their identity" (1983:241).

Before proceeding, it is necessary to define just what the Day of the Dead is. The Day of the Dead is a specifically Mexican term referring to the Mexican version of pan–Roman Catholic holy days: All Saints' and All Souls' Days, observed on November 1 and November 2, respectively. Strictly speaking, the Day of the Dead—known in Spanish as el Día de Animas (Souls' Day), el Día de los Finados (the Day of the Deceased), or el Día de los Fieles Difuntos (the Day of the Faithful Departed)—refers to All Souls' Day, which normally falls on November 2. Only when November 2 happens to coincide with Sunday is All Souls' Day celebrated on November 3. The Day of the Dead includes such a range of interlocking activities that in colloquial speech it has come to denote not only November 2 but also, and more usually, the entire period from October 31 through November 2. The Day of the Dead is in actuality a sequence of Days of the Dead. Hence, we occasionally also encounter the term Días de Muertos, or Días de los Muertos—that is, Days of the Dead, in the plural.

Note that, despite the elaborate manner in which the Day of the Dead is celebrated, the Roman Catholic Church requires only the observance of special masses on November 1 in honor of all the saints and on November 2 in honor of the souls in purgatory. These masses, which originated as early as the 11th century (Cornides 1967:319; Smith 1967:318), assumed a permanent place of importance in the liturgical calendar (nearly equivalent in significance to Christmas and Easter) by the 14th century (Gaillard 1950:927–932). Today, the Church requires parish priests to recite one special mass on November 1 and another on November 2, although three masses on November 2 are more common: one in honor of the departed souls, a second in honor of a cause designated annually by the pope, and the third in recognition of a cause selected by the parish priest himself. These special masses constitute the only official part of All Saints' and All Souls' Days celebrations throughout the Roman Catholic world, including Mexico.

Most observers would agree, ironically, that Mass in Mexico is the least-salient part of the holiday (see Brandes 1981). Come the end of October, a multitude of foreign visitors descends upon Mexico to witness colorful—some would say carnivalesque—ritual performances and artistic displays. Decorated breads, paper cutouts, and plastic toys, most of them playing humorously on the death theme, are evident everywhere. Sculpted sugar candies in the form of skulls, skeletons, and caskets suggest an almost irreverent, macabre confrontation with mortality. During October 31 through November 2, Mexicans clear, decorate, and maintain watch over relatives' graves. Everything from expensive tombstones to simple earthen-mound burial sites are adorned with flowers, candles, and food, aesthetically arranged in honor of the deceased. In Mexico, most of the activities and artistic displays connected with this holiday—including special food offerings, cemetery vigils, altar exhibitions, and the like—are a folk elaboration entirely separate from liturgical requirements. The origin of these folk practices is a source of scholarly and popular debate. What is clear is that, for Mexicans, foreigners, and peoples of Mexican descent, the holiday has come to symbolize Mexico and Mexicanness. It is a key symbol of national identity.

Mexican national identity is no easy subject for discussion. It has long been the object of lengthy deliberation and passionate debate, philosophical, historical, and otherwise. Scholarly and literary reflections on Mexican national character include penetrating and influential portraits by Samuel Ramos (1962), Octavio Paz (1961), and Roger Bartra (1987), among others. The whole topic has recently received sensitive treatment in the writings of Matthew Gutmann (1993), who demonstrates that ideas about supposed Mexican distinctiveness undergo transformation from generation to generation in the face of the country's enormous cultural diversity. States Gutmann, "Analysts of a would-be uniform 'national character' (or culture) of Mexico often resort to origin myths, downplaying class, gender and ethnic divisions within the geographic boundaries of the nation state, and also discount the fact that new and significant cultural features have emerged since the Revolution and Independence" (1993:56).

The Mexican state has been confronted not only by a need faced by many other states, that is, the need to forge a national consciousness and unity among a multitude of diverse regions and peoples. It has also had to—or at least seen fit to—create a sense of national distinctiveness by contrasting itself to the two great powers to which it has been subject over the course of centuries: Spain and the United States. With respect to Spain, Mexico suffers particular difficulty in creating a sense of discreteness. Most analysts would agree, after all, that two of the most salient features uniting any people are language and religion. Mexicans, who overwhelmingly speak Spanish and practice Roman Catholicism, can claim neither of these features as a source of difference from the imperial conqueror. Insofar as Mexican relations with the United States are concerned, language and religion are indeed a potential cultural resource for forging a sense of national identity. More important in U.S.–Mexican relations, however, is Mexican suffering at the hands of the economically and militarily powerful neighbor to the north. From the 1840s, when newly independent Mexico lost approximately half its territory to the United States, to the present, which is characterized by overwhelming disparities in national wealth and the increasing presence of U.S. financial and manufacturing institutions in Mexico, Mexicans have had to struggle against all odds to maintain a sense of autonomy and equality. From one vantage point, Mexican dependency upon and domination by Spain and the United States have impeded the emergence of a fully autonomous nation. From another, however, Mexicans have been able to use these countries as ideological foils against which to emphasize their own undeniable uniqueness.

In its quest for a unique identity, Mexico has enjoyed one major resource: the Indian, past and present. Gutmann is correct to state that Mexican intellectuals tend to date Mexico today from the times of the Spanish conquest, "whether for the triumph of the Spanish in the case of Ramos, or for the defeat of the Aztecs in the case of Paz" (Gutmann 1993:53). Nonetheless, it is Mexico's Indian heritage, as demonstrated through archaeological and ethnographic evidence, that clearly separates the country from both Spain and the United States, and it is the Indian heritage that the Mexican state has chosen to elevate symbolically. One effective way to further a sense of discrete national identity is through art and museum displays (see Karp and Lavine 1991). In this respect, the National Museum of Anthropology in Mexico City may be considered a glorious monument erected in honor of Mexican uniqueness and authenticity. Its two floors are distributed to show, first, the archaeological record, as displayed chronologically on the ground story; and, second, contemporary indigenous presence, as displayed through rooms devoted to key Indian communities, on the top story. Taken as a whole, the National Museum of Anthropology is designed to exhibit, to nationals and foreigners alike, an official view of an authentic Mexico, unaffected by contaminating outside influences.

In Mexico, as elsewhere (see Hague 1981; Herzfeld 1982; Wilson 1976), folklore has been important in the quest for national identity. Folklore often reflects popular ideas about the origins of a people. It also is believed to penetrate beneath the superficial and culturally confounding layers of modern life to some authentic core, thereby representing the essence of a people, its principal style and values. Folklore, further, is often shared by a given group in contradistinction to other groups. In all these respects, folklore serves nationalistic goals.

Ritual and festival in general are of course among the most prominent forms of folklore in this regard. A people, be they national minority or state-defined nation, can reinforce their separate identity through reference to presumably unique ceremonials. These ceremonials come to be perceived as part of what makes the group unique and reflects the group's defining norms and values. It is within this ideological context that we must understand Mexico's Day of the Dead.

The Perceived Uniqueness of the Day of the Dead

The Day of the Dead is now and has long been a symbol of Mexico. But the nationalistic dimension dates from relatively recent times, probably no further back than the present century. Almost certainly, from the time of the Spanish conquest in 1521, Mexicans observed All Saints' and All Souls' Days, feasts that then as now were required of all Roman Catholics. Special masses, as part of the obligatory liturgy, were intrinsic to the celebration, as they still are. There is good evidence (Brandes 1988:88–109), too, that at the time of the conquest, All Saints' and All Souls' Days were occasions in Spain and elsewhere in Europe for visiting cemeteries; presenting offerings of flowers, candles, and food to deceased relatives; and soliciting or begging in ritualized form.

With regard to All Saints' and All Souls' Days in New Spain, however, so little written documentation exists that it is impossible to determine the precise ways in which Mexicans celebrated this holiday. We may assume that, whether through formal Church decree or informal processes of culture transmission (Foster 1960), All Saints' and All Souls' Days in colonial Mexico more or less followed European practices. However, the precise regional distribution of ritual activities and their relative acceptance among diverse linguistic communities and social classes are matters for speculation alone. We do know that in the 1740s, in the Valley of Mexico, All Saints' and All Souls' Days began to assume the flavor of the contemporary event. It is from this time that we first hear from a Capuchin friar named Francisco de Ajofrín (1958:87) of the commercial production and sale of whimsical figurines made of the sugar paste known in Mexico as *alfeñique*. Ajofrín's pivotal account, too, incorporates the first known use in Mexico of the term *Day of the Dead*. Both the existence of sugar-paste figurines and the reference to All Saints' and Souls' Days as "the Day of the Dead" are characteristic of the Mexican celebration (Brandes 1997).

The degree to which the overall celebration of the Day of the Dead is in reality unique to Mexico is a source of ongoing debate, a debate that cannot be resolved here. It is necessary to repeat, however, that key elements of the contemporary popular celebration of All Saints' and Souls' Days in Mexico—elements including family cemetery vigils; the erection of home altars; the preparation of special sweets; the presentation to the deceased of flowers, candles, and food; and the performance of ritualized begging or solicitation—can be found throughout much of the Roman Catholic world, including Latin America and southern Europe. Ritualized begging is even common on All Souls' Day among Indian pueblos in the Southwestern United States, pueblos conquered and influenced by Spain (Espinosa 1918; Parsons 1917). What seems to me unique to Mexico are three features of the celebration: first, the name *Day of the Dead;* second, the abundance and variety of whimsical sweet breads and candies; and third, the humor and gaiety that pervade the holiday.

Much of the reason for uncertainty about the origins of the Day of the Dead is an absence of adequate source material. The Day of the Dead, like Carnival, always presented a threat to the official political and religious establishment. Hence, during the colonial era, the Spanish rulers attempted to tone down, if not entirely eradicate, the popular celebration of All Saints' and All Souls' Days. Writes historian Pedro Viqueira,

> The nocturnal visit which village men, women, and children made to the cemeteries, the festivities and drunkenness that took place there, could only scandalize and above all horrify the illustrious elites, who looked to expel death from social life. This fiesta, which drew boundaries between the living and the dead and partially inverted their roles, showed up the presence of death in the midst of life in an era in which the elite of New Spain . . . tried to forget its existence. [Viqueira 1984:13]

It is not surprising, says Viqueira, that in October 1766 the Royal Criminal Chamber (Real Sala del Crimen) prohibited attendance at cemeteries and also imposed a prohibition on the sale of alcoholic beverages after nine in the evening (1984:13).

Nearly one hundred years later, following Mexico's independence from Spain, the Day of the Dead still seemed to pose a threat to public order and stability. In 1847, liquor stores were closed for all but two or three hours on November 1 and 2, as a security measure. *The North American Star,* a newspaper serving the U.S. community in Mexico City, declared on November 2 that "yesterday, the first day of the festival, went off with perfect quietness, with no disturbance of any kind, that we could hear, and we presume we shall be able to say the same to-day and to-morrow" (1847). Despite the observed calm, the holiday apparently caused some anticipation of social unrest. It is precisely this unrest, whether or not justifiably feared, that undoubtedly produced some degree of press censorship. Throughout the colonial era and the 19th century, Mexican newspapers and other popular sources provide only the most limited, sanitized coverage of Day of the Dead activities. From these sources we obtain the elite view of the event, which consists primarily of accounts of formal religious activity. Textured ethnographic detail, which might allow an assessment of which aspects of the holiday derive from Spain, which from ancient Mexico, and which from the colonial encounter, are virtually absent.

What is of main interest here is not, however, the actual historical derivation of the Day of the Dead but rather its *attributed* derivation and connection to Mexico. Consider, for example, that the second chapter of Octavio Paz's *Labyrinth of Solitude* (1961) is entitled "The Day of the Dead." For Paz, this ritual occasion shows that the Mexican "is familiar with death, jokes about it, caresses it, sleeps with it, celebrates it; it is one of his favorite toys and his most steadfast love" (1961:57). Paz believes that the Mexican looks at death "face to face, with impatience, disdain or irony" (1961:57). In this respect, the Mexican view of death is very different from either the North American or European views:

> The word death is not pronounced in New York, in Paris, in London, because it burns the lips. . . . The Mexican's indifference toward death is fostered by his indifference toward life. He views not only death but also life as nontranscendent. . . . It is natural, even desirable to die, and the sooner the better. . . . Our contempt for death is not at odds with the cult we have made of it. [Paz 1961:57]

Paz, one of the most widely read and penetrating Mexican men of letters, clearly uses the Day of the Dead as a lens through which to discern a peculiarly Mexican view of death. It is a perspective shared by numerous other Mexican intellectuals, including Caso (1953:122), Covarrubias (1947:390), Díaz Guerrero (1968:15), Fernández Kelley (1974:533), and Lope Blanch (1963:8). Foreigners, too, have long identified what is for them a specifically Mexican attitude toward death. For Soviet filmmaker Sergei Mikhailovich Eisenstein, this attitude is nowhere better displayed than during the Day of the Dead:

> At every step [in Mexico] life and death fuse constantly; so too do appearance and disappearance, death and birth. On the "Day of the Dead" even small children stuff themselves with crystalized *[sic]* sugar skulls and chocolate coffins, and amuse themselves with toys in the form of skeletons. The Mexican despises death. . . . Most important of all, the Mexican laughs at death. November 2nd, "Death Day," is given over to irresistible mockery of death. [quoted in Sayer 1993:45]

For Mexicans and the world at large, the Day of the Dead represents Mexico and things Mexican. Elektra and Tonatiúh Gutierrez sum up this attitude perfectly by stating that the only thing that the Day of the Dead has in common with All Souls' Day is that "both are cases of a day sanctified to honor the memory of deceased relatives" (1971:75). As indicated above, there are of course many other features shared by the European and Mexican celebrations. But these authors, like most, promote Mexico's Day of the Dead as a unique phenomenon. The Day of the Dead and the attitude toward death that it represents have come to symbolize Mexico itself.

The Day of the Dead and the Mexican Indian

Mexico's indigenous past and present, as I have stated, are what distinguish this country undeniably from both Europe and the United States. It is not surprising, then, that in the quest for national identity, the Indian should be closely associated with the Day of the Dead. This association appears explicitly throughout the literature. Perhaps more than any other Mexican ritual, the Day of the Dead has acquired the reputation of being either a basically preconquest Indian survival with a European Catholic veneer or a near-seamless fusion of preconquest and Roman Catholic ceremonial practices. Consider the statement of Haberstein and Lamers that "in Mexico everywhere the Day of the Dead celebrations combine a curious admixture of ancient Indian and Catholic beliefs and practices" (1963:592). The same goes for Childs and Altman, who claim that "the beliefs and practices associated with contemporary observances of Días de los Muertos, although not a direct and simple survival of pre-Hispanic ritual, have their roots in the ancient religions of Mesoamerica" (1982:6). They continue, "However successful the Spanish church may have been in the destruction of state cults, it is apparent on close scrutiny that much 'Catholicism' of contemporary Indian communities is pre-Hispanic in origin, especially the beliefs and customs related to death and the dead" (1982:6–7). Yet another expression of this viewpoint comes from Alan Sandstrom and Pamela Sandstrom, who claim that, at least for three indigenous linguistic groups in the central Mexican highlands (the Nahua, Otomí, and Pepehua), "even observances that clearly have a pre-Hispanic base, such as All Souls and Carnival, are syncretized with the Christian celebration of similar character" (1986:254).

The alleged pre-Hispanic base of All Souls' Day is indeed "clear" in the minds of many scholars. Unfortunately, this relationship never receives systematic demonstration. Rather, there is a presumption of pre-Hispanic survival, manifested in a casual association of the Day of the Dead with Aztec ritual, on the one hand, and contemporary Indian funerary ritual, on the other. In *The Skeleton at the Feast: The Day of the Dead in Mexico* (1991), Carmichael and Sayer compile an enormous amount of documentary and ethnographic information regarding the Day of the Dead. A full chapter is devoted to pre-Hispanic beliefs and practices regarding death and mourning, without the authors establishing an explicit connection between past and contemporary events. Although they state that "to what extent these pre-Hispanic festivals and their associated rituals were transmuted into the Christian festivals remains a matter of keen debate" (1991:33), they never actually discuss the content of this debate. Their chapter entitled "The Pre-Hispanic Background" remains an implicit endorsement of the idea that the Day of the

Dead can in fact be traced to pre-Hispanic ritual. In a popular anthology entitled *Mexico: The Day of the Dead* (1993), Sayer reproduces a chapter from Evon Vogt's description of funerals in Zinacantán, a Tzotzil-speaking community in the heavily indigenous state of Chiapas. Despite the fact that the Day of the Dead is decidedly not a funerary ritual, the inclusion of this chapter in the book implies that Zinacanteco ritual represents an exemplary indigenous expression of the Day of the Dead.

It is true that Mexican Indians have demonstrated, through both archaeological and ethnographic evidence, that they possess complex and subtle ideas about death and the dead. They also have always celebrated the dead through the performance of specific rituals. But the possession of elaborate ideas about death as well as the ritualized commemoration of the deceased are human facts, characteristic of all known societies past and present (see Metcalf and Huntington 1991). The celebration of death cannot itself be presented reasonably as evidence for an indigenous origin for the Day of the Dead. Nonetheless, Day of the Dead ceremonies are presented throughout Mexico as if they were unambiguously Indian. The alleged indigenous character of this fiesta means that it is automatically associated with Mexico and correspondingly dissociated from Europe and North America.

There are various mechanisms through which the Day of the Dead as an Indian holiday is publicly acknowledged and asserted. Among the most prominent is the popular belief that there exist a limited number of communities—all of these Indian communities—where the Day of the Dead is celebrated in its fully elaborate and authentic state. These towns include the Purépecha island of Janitzio in the state of Michoacán, the Nahua village of Mixquic in the state of Mexico, and the Zapotec village of Xococotlán in the state of Oaxaca. All of these communities, and others like them, share one major characteristic: they are famous nationally and internationally for their Day of the Dead celebrations and consequently draw enormous numbers of tourists from both Mexican cities and abroad. And yet anyone who visits cemeteries in Mexico City during the Day of the Dead can attest to the elaborate observance of this holiday in the country's immense, highly industrialized and commercialized metropolitan capital. The decoration of tombstones, flower and food offerings, presence of relatives respectfully guarding vigil over their deceased relatives, and the like are as elaborate in Mexico City's Panteón Jardín, Panteón Municipal, and Panteón Francés as can be found anywhere in the country. In city cemeteries such as these, however, the tourist presence is minimal. Middle-class Mexicans from Mexico City, Guadalajara, and elsewhere, searching for cultural roots, prefer to travel to the handful of Indian towns and villages that have become famous for the authenticity of their Day of the Dead celebrations. Often these Mexicans form part of international tour groups.

Mexican scholar Juanita Garciagodoy, who has carried out extensive research on the Day of the Dead (Garciagodoy 1994:33–34), decided for purposes of investigation to join two such groups that visited Day of the Dead ceremonies in Xococotlán in the state of Oaxaca. She reports as follows:

> We were each given a bouquet of flowers, two veladoras (votive candles), and torches which consisted of a candle set into a split bamboo shaft and protected by orange cellophane paper. Before the tour departed from the meeting point, we were given a short lecture (once in Spanish, once in English, the latter much more brief and simple) about the importance of Días de muertos. We were reminded that we would be guests at a spiritually important event and counseled to behave appropriately. And we were instructed to place our flowers and candles on graves that were unadorned and untended; we would gain spiritual merit this way and be rewarded in the hereafter. A majority of the people on the tour were from the United States; there were a few from Canada, Europe, and Mexico. The male and female, bilingual guides were Mexican. [1994:33–34]

I visited Xococotlán during the Day of the Dead in 1996, at which time I was lecturing to a group of Americans on a University of California Extension School study tour. Even without making a firm head count, it was clear to us all that there were many times more foreigners wandering around the cemetery of Xococotlán on the night of November 1–2 than there were inhabitants of the town itself (see Figure 1). Xococotlán, with its multiple food vendors and the throngs of visitors crowding its narrow streets, had taken on a carnival atmosphere.

The same occurs during the Day of the Dead in Tzintzuntzan, with the difference that most outside visitors are Mexicans rather than foreigners. Tzintzuntzan, a community of about 3,000 artisans, farmers, and merchants, is located several hundred miles northwest of Mexico City on the shores of Lake Pátzcuaro in the state of Michoacán. Tzintzuntzan is famous for having been the capital of the ancient Purépecha Empire, a political entity that successfully resisted Aztec domination. No doubt because of its illustrious past, Tzintzuntzan is perceived as a Purépecha settlement. Tzintzuntzan's reputation as a center of Purépecha culture, both ancient and contemporary, has been codified and propagated through an ethnological display occupying a full exhibition hall of the National Museum of Anthropology in Mexico City. This exhibit, a permanent installation, portrays Tzintzuntzan as the epitome of enduring Purépecha culture. The reality is that Tzintzuntzan is and long has been an overwhelmingly mestizo community, with only about 7% of villagers able to speak Purépecha throughout the 1980s and 1990s (Kemper n.d.). Even in 1960, the start of the decade that saw the construction and design of the National Museum of Anthropology, only 11.4% of the population could be identified as indigenous (Foster 1988:35). Yet the community's fame as a center of Purépecha culture has increased since that time, rather than abated.

One reason for this persistent misidentification is the governmental promotion of Tzintzuntzan's Day of the Dead ceremonies as an authentic indigenous religious ritual (Brandes 1988:88–109). Tzintzuntzan long celebrated the Day of the Dead exactly as did countless other rural communities throughout Michoacán and Mexico as a whole, that is, in relatively muted fashion. There were always special masses, of course. Families erected home altars in honor of the departed and visited the graves of recently deceased relatives, in whose honor they decorated the burial sites with flowers and candles. George M. Foster and Gabriel Ospina, who witnessed the event in 1945, describe activities on November 2 as follows:

Figure 1. Sign in a Oaxaca hotel lobby, October-November 1996. Photo by author.

> About four o'clock in the morning family groups begin to wend their way to the cemetery, carrying arcos [decorated latticework displays] and other offerings of food, to take up their vigil by the graves of departed relatives. Again yellow marigolds are scattered over all graves and candles are lighted. Toward dawn perhaps 40 tombs are thus arranged, and the twinkling of several hundred candles in the dark suggests will-o-the-wisps run riot. . . . After daylight other persons come, to talk with friends keeping vigil, to eat a little, and to see what is happening. By 11 o-clock most people have gone home and the graveyard is again deserted. [1948:220]

In 1971, governmental agencies intervened in such a way as to transform the event entirely. It was in that year that the Ministry of Tourism of the State of Michoacán, together with two state agencies—the Casa de la Cultura and the Casa de Artesanías—began a campaign to attract tourists to Michoacán. They selected 11 towns, among them Tzintzuntzan, as targets of tourism. Widely disseminated posters and radio commercials, directed at an urban, middle-class public, announced the traditional celebration of the Day of the Dead in Tzintzuntzan and elsewhere. Images on the posters show an indigenous woman, flanked by tall candles, kneeling at a gravesite. In Tzintzuntzan itself tourists received a brochure with a cover bearing the title "Noche de Muertos en Michoacán" [Night of the Dead in Michoacán], with the prominent Purépecha translation, "Animecha Kejtzitakua." In the period since the intervention of state agencies, Day of the Dead, as a denomination for this holiday, became known as Night of the Dead, in recognition of the fact that villagers en masse began to spend the entire night of November 1–2 at the cemeteries. The agencies had encouraged this transformation and, in any event, tourists had come to expect it. Tourists, who began to arrive by the thousands in large buses and long automobile caravans, had been led by publicity to anticipate the presence of certain ritual activities, which now began to be practiced in conformity to their needs.

Gradually, over the course of the 1970s and 1980s, massive tourism increasingly defined the contour of Tzintzuntzan's Night of the Dead. There was the all-night vigil, of course, although its potential picturesqueness was marred by the presence of television cameras recording the scene live for a national audience. Enormous, noisy electric generators were now strategically situated in the cemetery to provide illumination for the cameras. High above the town, on an esplanade spread out at the foot of five imposing pre-Columbian pyramids, the Ministry of Tourism established a "Festival of Dances and Pirekuas," *pirekuas* being Purépecha songs. Using an 18th-century open-air chapel as stage, state agencies also mounted a production of José Zorilla's 19th-century Spanish classic drama, "Don Juan Tenorio." Drama and dance performers alike were brought in from outside, and, because a substantial fee was charged for this entertainment, it was tourists and tourists alone who attended. Along the highway leading through Tzintzuntzan, tourists could now buy food and drink from any of the numerous temporary stands set up to accommodate their needs. They could seek medical assistance by visiting the temporary Red Cross station situated for the occasion near the town plaza.

By the end of the 1980s and beginning of the 1990s, the event began to change names yet again. It was now referred to commonly as "La Feria," the Fair. One middle-aged villager reported her opinion of the changes that had taken place: "The event has become shameful. People hardly talk about the Night of the Dead anymore. They say Feria, or '¡Vamos a la Feria de los Muertos!' [Let's go to the Fair of the Deceased!] It's practically scandalous!" This reading of the event probably reflected a minority opinion among townspeople themselves, who earned substantial income from the tremendous influx of tourists. In fact, young unmarried men, who used to toll church bells all evening and solicit contributions of food and drink from village households, now no longer played this time-honored role. They had become too busy helping their families run food stands for the tourists. "The event used to be so sad," reminisced one elderly man, as if this emotion were somehow inappropriate to the occasion.

Despite radical transformations, the event since 1971 has been billed by the government of the state of Michoacán as both traditional and indigenous. It has thus become famous nationally as a survival of ancient practices and hence a cultural treasure for the Mexican people as a whole. A similar process has occurred in indigenous communities—be they allegedly indigenous, as in the case of Tzintzuntzan, or actually so, as in the case of Xococotlán—all over Mexico.

The Day of the Dead versus Halloween

Any observer of Day of the Dead ceremonies in the 1990s would be impressed by the presence of Halloween symbolism. Prefabricated children's costumes, mainly witch, devil, and ghost costumes, are displayed for sale in traditional markets all over the country. There are diverse plastic and rubber masks, everything from comical likenesses of Mexican and U.S. political leaders to red-faced Satanic figures, apes, and a plethora of unidentifiable beasts (see Figure 2). One can also find plastic jack-o'-lanterns in every imaginable size. These items are mixed indiscriminately among the more usual Day of the Dead ware, including special seasonal sweet breads, colorfully decorated sugar and chocolate skulls and caskets, wooden and papier-mâché skeletons with moveable joints, as well as long-stemmed, bright orange marigolds and tall white candles destined to be used as offerings at burial sites and home altars.

On the face of it, the presence of Halloween symbolism should cause no surprise. For one thing, Halloween, which occurs on All Saints' Eve, has for centuries shared a close resemblance to the Day of the Dead. Jack Santino traces Halloween back to the Celtic (Irish, Scottish, Welsh) festival of Samhain, the New Year's Day of the Celts, celebrated on November 1. This pre-Christian holiday, says Santino, "was also a day of the dead, a time when it was believed that

Figure 2. Oaxaca market display of rubber masks, October-November 1996. Photo by author.

the souls of those who had died during the year were allowed access to the land of the living. It was a time when spirits were believed to be wandering" (1994:xv). Many of the beliefs and practices characteristic of Samhain survived to the Christian era. These include the belief that October 31 was a time of the wandering dead and the practice of providing food and drink to masked and costumed revelers on this night, known to Christians as the Eve of All Saints or Hallows Even, a term yielding the familiar contraction *Hallowe'en* (Santino 1994:xvi). Santino traces the incorporation into the celebration of All Saints' Eve of symbols of the dead, including skeletons, ghosts, and malevolent creatures such as witches and the devil. These figures, in a word, were the transmuted pre-Christian gods and goddesses, whom the early Christians used as a syncretic means to spread their new religion. "Because of these events," Santino concludes, "Halloween is associated with All Saints' Day and, by extension, with the church calendar" (1994:xvi).

Santino calls the Day of the Dead a "cognate" (1994:xviii) or, one might say, a functional equivalent of Halloween. Indeed, the historical origins of the two holidays, if not identical, are nonetheless closely intermeshed. For centuries, too, they have displayed an array of shared symbols of death, a kind of playing with death, including humorous replicas of skulls, skeletons, and souls, the latter taking the form during Halloween of ghosts and during the Day of the Dead of inanimate but ever present spirits. Special sweets are an important part of both Halloween, with its characteristic black and orange candies, and the Day of the Dead, with its *pan de muertos* ("dead bread"), and skulls and skeletons. Ritualized begging is significant in the two holidays as well. During All Saints' and All Souls' Days in Mexico as much as in Europe, bands of young men wander from house to house asking for food and drink. I myself have observed this custom in Tzintzuntzan, Mexico (Brandes 1988:94–95), and Becedas, Spain (Brandes 1975:135), although institutionalized begging and charity giving has been traditional everywhere in the Catholic world on this day (see Aguirre Soronda 1989; Brandes 1997; Espinosa 1918; Llabrés Quintana 1925; Parsons 1917). Halloween, of course, incorporates an especially aggressive form of begging known as trick or treat (Tuleja 1994).

These common origins and shared symbols by no means erase major differences between Halloween, on the one hand, and All Saints' and All Souls' Days, on the other. One major difference, of course, is that All Saints' and All Souls' Days remain a part of the sacred Roman Catholic calendar, while Halloween has long assumed a completely secular cast. Despite possible readings to the contrary, we might also say that All Saints' and Souls' Days are fundamentally occasions for adult ritual performance, while Halloween, at least as celebrated in the contemporary United States, is largely a children's holiday. Over and above this differentiation, a major symbolic cleavage has appeared in the representation of the Day of the Dead and Halloween: in Mexico, the Day of the Dead has come to symbolize Mexican identity and autonomy, while Halloween has become a symbol of the United States and its cultural imperialistic designs. The actual origins and meaning of ritual beliefs and practices during Halloween and the Day of the Dead are more or less irrelevant to the growing significance of these holidays for national identity.

In her Ph.D. thesis, Juanita Garciagodoy states,

> I cannot count how many informants have answered my questions as to the meaning of Días de muertos for them, their reasons for performing this or that aspect of it, their reason(s), for that matter, to celebrate it at all by saying, "Es muy mexicano," "It's very Mexican," or, "Porque somos mexicanos," "Because we're Mexican." [1994:28]

Then, speaking as a Mexican herself, the author continues:

> Many of us feel more patriotic during this celebration and because of it. This is partly because we think our way of relating to death and the dead—and by implication, to life—is unique in the world, setting us apart from (and at least a little above) everyone else. We are *más machos*, braver, and we have *más corazón*, more heart, than other cultures. [1994:28]

As an international scholar, Garciagodoy well understands how the Day of the Dead contributes to Mexican national identity. But as a Mexican, she cannot help but experience the nationalistic sentiments increasingly associated with the holiday. In fact, at one point in her discussion she includes herself among a group of "nationalistic Mexican scholars," as she calls them (1994:163). Nationalism leads Garciagodoy, like so many other Mexican intellectuals, not only to reaffirm the Day of the Dead as a symbol of Mexican national identity but correspondingly to reject Halloween; "Hallowe'en as a Threat to National Tradition and Identity" is in fact the title of one of her dissertation chapters.

Garciagodoy is hardly alone in her assessment. Consider the statement of Mexican physician and author Frank Gonzalez-Crussi (1993:36) that there are disquieting signs of Halloween's ascent. On a recent trip to Mexico City on the Day of the Dead, Gonzalez-Crussi found that

> the stores are stocked with objects intended for use at Halloween, many imported from the United States. In shop windows, hollowed-out pumpkins, most made out of plastic, with cutout holes that figure eyes, nose, and mouth, beam their ghostly smiles, abetted by the flickering light within. Groups of children come out of schools or private homes disguised as monsters, werewolves, vampires, and extraterrestrial beings. Have we come this far to see an imitation, in third-world gear, of the North American Halloween? [1993:36]

Exactly how has Halloween entered into the celebration of the Day of the Dead? Garciagodoy correctly identifies two main classes of Mexicans who now celebrate the Day of the Dead by drawing on symbols and customs more usually associated with Halloween. First are urban middle-class Mexicans, many of whom dress their children in store-bought, Halloween-style costumes. Judging from the costumes I have seen on sale at middle-class malls, as well as from what I have seen the children wear, I would say that almost all the costumes play on one of five themes: witches, ghosts, skeletons, vampires, and devils. Unlike in the United States, I have rarely seen a Mexican adult wear a costume—or even a portion of a costume. For example, in 1996 in the city of Oaxaca I observed a parade of hundreds of costumed schoolchildren, accompanied by dozens of teachers and other adults. None of the grown men and women donned so much as a witch's cap. The urban middle-class Halloween manifests itself, too, in disco dances, with advertisements and disco decorations based on icons like witches, carved pumpkins, ghosts, and the like, usually colored in black and orange. Newspapers all over Mexico display commercial advertisements aiming at a middle-class audience and incorporating Halloween symbols. Consider a computer store advertisement that appeared on 31 October 1996 in the national daily, *Reforma.* The advertisement appears with black background, white lettering, an orange jack-o'-lantern, and the silhouette of a cloaked death figure wielding a scythe. "Do our competitor's prices scare you?" reads the ad. A Goodyear tire advertisement that appeared on 30 October 1996 in *Reforma* is drawn in white against a black, nighttime scene. Bats fly high above, scraggly cats arch their backs, and jack-o'-lanterns grin at the readers. "Macabre nighttime sale on tires," the advertisement states. Expensive clubs all over Mexico City—Snob and The Men's Club, for example—use the press to announce Halloween parties and dances at this time of year.

For the working class, the Halloween appeal is somewhat different. For one thing, although some children might put on an inexpensive mask, for the most part they go uncostumed. Halloween for these children—and the participants seem uniformly to be boys rather than girls—means a money-making opportunity. Carrying any sort of small receptacle that they can find, everything from a battered cardboard box to a miniature plastic jack-o'-lantern with handle (the kind that U.S. children sometimes use to collect candy), the boys beg through the streets and among the graves, asking for their "Halloween" (see Figure 3). The word *Halloween* is even entering the Mexican Spanish lexicon, spelled phonetically, "Jaloüín." The children might also beg for *mi calabaza*—"my pumpkin." Other than this form of simple solicitation, the working-class Halloween seems limited to the purchase of orange-, white-, and black-colored candy in the shape of witches, ghosts, and jack-o'-lanterns. Also, the occasional carved pumpkin or plastic jack-o'-lantern rests on gravesites, along with the usual offerings, during the Day of the Dead.

Most middle-class Mexicans are well aware that Halloween symbols are part of U.S. culture and probably use Halloween symbols consciously as a means of elevating their status. It is unclear that this can be said of the working classes, for whom Halloween seems to have become seamlessly sewn within the fabric of Day of the Dead proceedings. I asked a Mixtec Indian fruit vendor and his mestiza wife, who run a small store in Mexico City, why they were selling Halloween candies and whether their customers complain about the recent introduction of Halloween. The wife just laughed. "We Mexicans are *muy fiesteros* [great merrymakers]. We like everything that adds to festivities!" While watching schoolchildren carry out their Halloween march in 1996 in the city of Oaxaca, I asked a couple of teenaged passersby to tell me when the march was initiated. They answered, "Maybe ten years ago, or 15 . . . or five." They did not know. They did say, however, that if I really wanted to learn about "these customs," I should go to the surrounding villages where they have been practiced as long as anyone can remember. Rural schoolchildren in Oaxaca do not participate in Halloween

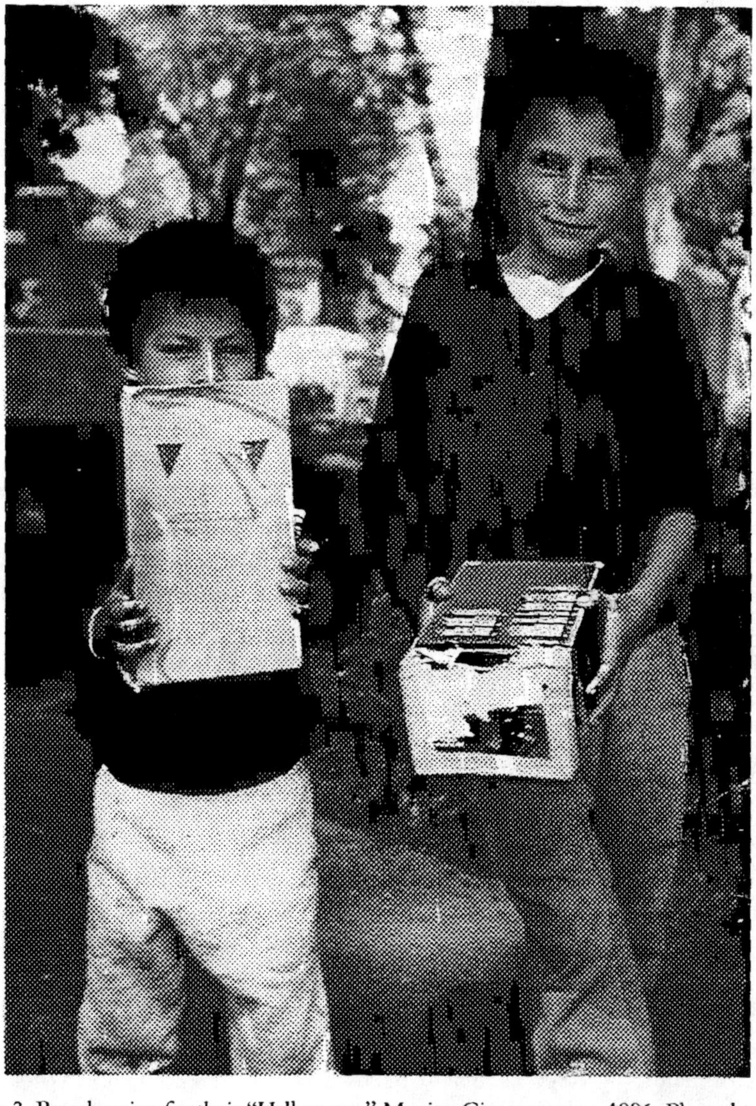

Figure 3. Boys begging for their "Halloween," Mexico City cemetery, 1996. Photo by author.

marches, nor do they dress as witches, ghosts, devils, and the like. These two teenaged boys simply confounded Halloween with the Day of the Dead. For them, as for most Mexicans in central and southern Mexico, there is one major holiday at the end of October and beginning of November. The distinction between Day of the Dead elements and Halloween elements does not occur to them.

In fact, there are parts of Mexico where celebration of the traditional Day of the Dead is relatively recent. The northern states of Chihuahua, Coahuila, and Sonora, for example, were places in which Halloween has long enjoyed a visible presence. A middle-class, middle-aged friend of mine from the state of Coahuila remembers celebrating Halloween and Halloween alone as a child. He claims that there was no Day of the Dead in the 1940s and 1950s in Coahuila. Occasionally around the end of October his family would take him to Mexico City to visit relatives. He remembers being horrified at the elaborate displays of skulls and skeletons he found there, attributing to the people of Mexico City a kind of morbidity lacking in his home state. In 1996, however, key clerics in the northern Mexican states actually prohibited the celebration of Halloween on the grounds that this holiday, which they declared secular and commercial, represented a threat to the sanctity and very existence of the Day of the Dead.

Numerically, there are probably few Mexicans who perceive Halloween as posing a threat to their national culture. But those who do are articulate and visible Mexicans, the intellectuals, representatives of the church and the state, and outspoken members of major cultural institutions. All over Mexico today, there appears evidence of formal and informal resistance to the Halloween invasion from the north. A large mural painted along a wall in Tepoztlán, in the state of Morelos, shows a soccer player kicking and knocking down an individual whose head is in the form of a jack-o'-lantern. The accompanying text reads, "No to Halloween. Preserve your cultural traditions" (see Figure 4). Also, town governments are beginning to mount competitions with prizes for best Day of the Dead altar. Among the contest guidelines for the city of Oaxaca competition is that "altars which present elements foreign to our tradition [elementos ajenos a nuestra tradición] will be automatically disqualified." Throughout Mexico, in fact, similar competitions are becoming an integral part of Day of the Dead celebrations. The competitions are becoming traditional. There can be no more dramatic proof of Handler and Linnekin's insightful statement that "one of the major paradoxes of the ideology of tradition is that attempts at cultural preservation inevitably alter, reconstruct, or invent the traditions that they are intended to fix" (1984:288). On 29 October 1996, the national daily *La Jornada,* famous for its photographic displays, showed a picture of a man out on a busy street dressed and masked in skeleton costume. The caption reads "Costumbre foránea," or "foreign custom." Ironically, the

Figure 4. Mural, Tepoztlán, Morelos, October 1995. Photo by author.

costume is not foreign to Mexico. Death figures don very similar garb in village dances, where they play the role of clown figures (Brandes 1979).

El Imparcial, a Oaxaca city newspaper, published a feature article on 31 October 1996 entitled "Halloween or No Halloween? A Fearful Dilemma." The term *fearful* was rendered here in Spanish as *de miedo*, which is such a clear reference to the scariness theme of Halloween that the article itself, which questions the validity of Halloween, actually reaffirms the influence of this holiday. The article describes a unified campaign by both Catholic and Protestant churches in Oaxaca to stamp out Halloween. A seven-year-old boy is quoted as saying,

> I don't know what to do. In church they told me that it's not good to participate in Halloween because it has to do with evil spirits, and that's why the stores choose witch and vampire costumes to wear in the streets. The bad thing is that my friends already have their costumes and I do want to accompany them, but I don't want to do anything sinful. [*El Imparcial* 1996:1]

The article also tells about a third grader who heard at Mass that he should not participate in Halloween. In school, he was told that it was all right to do so, "as long as he first familiarizes himself with the Mexican traditions of the Day of the Dead" (1996:1).

For many Mexican intellectuals, Halloween represents the worst of the United States. It is reputed to be excessively commercial. Garciagodoy declares that

> while Días de muertos is undoubtedly an occasion for extravagant spending, it does not enter the style of consumerism that characterizes US celebrants of Hallowe'en all year round. . . . As far as the inculcation of beliefs is concerned, I would speculate that the most important belief the exporters of Hallowe'en wish to inculcate is one in the acceptability of seasonal, disposable merchandise. [1994:131]

For Garciagodoy, as for other Mexican intellectuals, Halloween serves political interests as well. "I do not want to fuel the fires of xenophobia or cultural paranoia," she says,

> but I would not want to trivialize the cultural impact of the exportation of holiday traditions which, surely inadvertently, serve American interests not only economically, but also by cultivating a strong pro-US element that will continue to insure political and diplomatic harmony between two countries with an extraordinarily long and porous border. It is not impossible that such an effect is consciously desired by a few powerful people on one or both sides of the Río Bravo [Rio Grande]. Still, to me it seems more likely that the cultural impact is a side-effect of the principal objective of economic gain. [1994:129]

Economic gain is in fact close to the heart of the traditional Day of the Dead proceedings as well. Since at least the 18th century, there has been a brisk market in sugar-candy figurines. Consider the words of Francisco de Ajofrín, dating from the 1760s and mentioned earlier in this article:

> Before the Day of the Dead they sell a thousand figures of little sheep, lambs, etc. of sugar paste [alfeñique], which they call ofrenda, and it is a gift which must be given obligatorily to boys and

> girls of the houses where one has acquaintance. They also sell coffins, tombs and a thousand figures of the dead, clerics, monks, nuns and all denominations, bishops, horsemen, for which there is a great market and a colorful fair in the portals of the merchants, where it is incredible [to see] the crowd of men and women from Mexico City on the evening before and on the day of All Saints. [1958:87]

Ajofrín goes on to explain that sugar figurines and other "cute little things" *(monerías)* are made in rapid succession by "clever" artisans who sell them cheaply (1958:87). However, he warns the innocent consumer against advance payment; this practice, he says, often results in the receipt of tardy delivery or defective goods.

Clearly, even in colonial times, the Day of the Dead had a commercial cast. Nowadays in cities all over Mexico stores decorate their windows with humorous Day of the Dead icons. Newspapers are filled with advertisements playing on Day of the Dead themes, mostly skulls, skeletons, and the satiric verses that are themselves known as *calaveras*, or "skulls." Traditional artisans throughout Mexico have for generations supported their families mainly through the production of sugar skulls and figurines. Judging from contemporary testimony, they do not object to the introduction of Halloween symbols, so long as their handiwork sells. Witness the testimony of one such artisan, Wenceslao Rivas Contreras, from Toluca, the capital of the state of Mexico and a famous center of alfeñique production:

> I've often been told to stick to what's Mexican, yet I enjoy trying my hand at different things. Ten years ago I added skulls in pumpkins to my range. Pumpkins are a feature of Halloween in North America, but I'll make them if I can sell them, and witches as well! I want my displays to have variety, and my customers to have choice. In truth, although these various styles sell, skulls sell best—they belong to us, to Mexico! [quoted in Carmichael and Sayer 1991:115]

The Day of the Dead apparently has always incorporated a degree of commercialism. Even the most sacred portion of the fiesta, the special observance of Mass in honor of the departed souls, originally had an economic component. In colonial Mexico, for example, it was customary to give part of the food offering to the priest in return for the recital of these special masses (Carmichael and Sayer 1991:45).

Yet this aspect of the festivities, which has grown through time and persists in a major way to the present day, remains relatively unacknowledged in the collective mind of Mexican cultural nationalists. Cultural nationalists are comparable to those folklorists who, as Dan Ben-Amos states, identify and seek to purge so-called enemies of that which they themselves consider traditional (1984:107). For cultural nationalists in Mexico, Halloween is, in contrast to the Day of the Dead, a grossly commercialized and profane holiday. Halloween to these nationalists also contaminates the Day of the Dead by introducing foreign elements into otherwise ancient, sacred proceedings. In other words, Halloween and the Day of the Dead, holidays that stem largely from a common source and that still exhibit many similar features, have become metaphors for relations between the United States and Mexico, respectively. Halloween has become a symbol of gringo imperialism.

Given the long-term presence of U.S. communities within Mexico, as well as the lengthy border shared between the two countries, it is not surprising that Halloween symbols have been evident in Mexico over the past several generations. It is only recently, however, that the markers of Halloween—particularly costumes and jack-o'-lanterns—have become an obvious part of the end-of-October celebrations throughout central and southern Mexico. It is certainly only now, in the 1990s, that there have emerged vociferous reactions from Mexico's religious and intellectual elite and that there should be organized opposition to the incursion of Halloween symbols into Day of the Dead activities.

It is of course now, too, that the destinies of Mexico and the United States are closer than ever. The North American Free Trade Agreement (NAFTA), ratified in 1993, has increased the presence of U.S. citizens in Mexico enormously. Sanborn's, a gigantic department store chain located throughout Mexico and catering to the ever more prosperous middle and upper middle classes, has begun large-scale marketing of Halloween costumes and candies. As far as the working classes are concerned, the ever increasing migrant stream means growing numbers of Mexican returnees, who bring to Mexico an exposure and predilection for certain aspects of U.S. popular culture, including Halloween, which many of them learned about in U.S. classrooms, if nowhere else. This trend is fomented, too, through the omnipresence of U.S. programming on Mexican television, programming that familiarizes the Mexican public with typical U.S. holidays, like Halloween.

As a result of all these developments, Halloween has indeed become a palpable part of Day of the Dead proceedings. Mexicans who resent the growing U.S. influence over the Mexican economy and cultural scene respond effectively by focusing on a concrete, discretely defined event like Halloween. Halloween's success, to these Mexicans, represents Mexico's failure. In truth, the Day of the Dead has correspondingly become an important part of Halloween celebrations in the United States. Turner and Jasper demonstrate in vivid detail their assertion that "Mexican-derived Day of the Dead traditions are currently enjoying immense popularity in galleries and museums north of the border" (1994:133). The increasing presence of the Day of the Dead within the United States causes little competitive concern within our borders, however, because the power relations between the two countries clearly are in the favor of Anglo Halloween customs. Anglos in the United States probably perceive Day of the Dead celebrations as a quaint curiosity, related to Halloween distantly if at all. For the Anglo majority, Day of the Dead customs are no doubt seen as a holiday ritual to be adopted or abandoned at their will. The Day of the Dead on this side of the border is certainly not an imposed tradition, whether perceptually or actually. But that story, yet another in the centuries-old saga of All Saints' and All Souls' Days, still remains to be told.

Note

An earlier version of this article was presented on 3 March 1997 at the Watson Center for International Studies of Brown University. I wish to thank those who attended the presentation for their commentaries, which were useful in formulating the published article. I am also grateful to the John Carter Brown Library, the University of California at Berkeley, and the John Simon Guggenheim Foundation for the financial support necessary to carry out the research upon which this article is based. Friends, students, and colleagues provided encouragement and assistance for this project. These include Liza Bakewell, Suzanne Calpestri, Jorge Duany, Jonathan Xavier Inda, Jorge Klor de Alva, and Katharine Young. I take this opportunity to thank them all.

References Cited

Aguirre Soronda, Antxon. 1989. El fuego en el rito funerario vasco. In *La Religiosidad Popular,* vol. 2, eds. Carlos Alvarez Santaló, María Jesús Buxó y Rey, and Salvador Rodríguez Becerra, pp. 344–584. Barcelona: Anthropos.

Ajofrín, Francisco de. 1958. *Diario del viaje que por orden de la sagrada congregacion de propaganda fide hizo a la América septentrional en el siglo XVIII.* Madrid: Real Academia de la Historia.

Bartra, Roger. 1987. *La jaula de la melancolía: Identidad y metamorfosis del mexicano.* Mexico City: Grijalbo.

Ben-Amos, Dan. 1984. The Seven Strands of Tradition: Varieties in Its Meaning in American Folklore Studies. *Journal of Folklore Research* 21:97–132.

Brandes, Stanley. 1975. *Migration, Kinship, and Community: Tradition and Transition in a Spanish Village.* New York: Academic Press.

_________. 1979. Dance as Metaphor: A Case from Tzintzuntzan. *Journal of Latin American Lore* 5:25–43.

_________. 1981. Gender Distinctions in Monteros Mortuary Ritual. *Ethnology* 20:177–190.

_________. 1988. *Power and Persuasion: Fiestas and Social Control in Rural Mexico.* Philadelphia: University of Pennsylvania Press.

_________. 1997. Sugar, Colonialism, and Death: On the Origins of Mexico's Day of the Dead. *Comparative Studies in Society and History* 39:270–299.

Carmichael, Elizabeth, and Chloë Sayer. 1991. *The Skeleton at the Feast: The Day of the Dead in Mexico.* Austin: University of Texas Press.

Caso, Alfonso. 1953. *El pueblo del sol.* México, D. F.: Fondo de Cultura Económica.

Childs, Robert V., and Patricia B. Altman. 1982. *Vive tu Recuerdo: Living Traditions in the Mexican Days of the Dead.* Los Angeles: Museum of Cultural History, University of California at Los Angeles.

Cornides, A. 1967. All Souls' Day. In *New Catholic Encyclopedia.* New York: McGraw-Hill.

Covarrubias, Miguel. 1947. *Mexico South: The Isthmus of Tehuantepec.* New York: Knopf.

Díaz Guerrero, Rogelio. 1968. *Estudios de psicología del mexicano.* México, D. F.: F. Trillas.

El Imparcial. 1996. Halloween or No Halloween? A Fearful Dilemma. October 31:1.

Espinosa, Aurelio M. 1918. All Souls' Day at Zuñi, Acoma, and Laguna. *Journal of American Folklore* 31:550–552.

Fernández Kelley, Patricia. 1974. Death in Mexican Folk Culture. *American Quarterly* 25:516–535.

Foster, George M. 1960. *Culture and Conquest: America's Spanish Heritage.* Viking Fund Publications in Anthropology, No. 27. New York: Wenner-Gren Foundation.

_________. 1988. *Tzintzuntzan: Mexican Peasants in a Changing World.* Prospect Heights, Ill.: Waveland Press.

Foster, George M., and Gabriel Ospina. 1948. *Empire's Children: The People of Tzintzuntzan.* México, D. F.: Smithsonian Institution.

Gaillard, Jacques. 1950. *Catholicisme.* Paris: Presse Catholique.

Garciagodoy, Juanita. 1994. Romancing the Bone: A Semiotics of Mexico's Day of the Dead. Ph.D. dissertation, University of Minnesota.

Gonzalez-Crussi, Frank. 1993. *The Day of the Dead and Other Mortal Reflections.* New York: Harcourt Brace.

Gutiérrez, Elektra, and Tonatiúh Gutiérrez. 1971. La muerte en el arte popular mexicano. *Artes de México* 1:75–86.

Gutmann, Matthew. 1993. Primordial Cultures and Creativity in the Origins of "Lo Mexicano." *Kroeber Anthropological Society Papers* 75–76:48–61.

Haberstein, Robert W., and William M. Lamers. 1963. *Funeral Customs the World Over.* Milwaukee: Bultin.

Hague, Abu Saeed Zahurul. 1981. *Folklore and Nationalism in Rabindranath Tagore.* Dacca, Bangladesh: Bangla Academy.

Handler, Richard, and Jocelyn Linnekin. 1984. Tradition, Genuine or Spurious. *Journal of American Folklore* 97:273–290.

Herzfeld, Michael. 1982. *Ours No More: Folklore, Ideology, and the Making of Modern Greece.* Austin: University of Texas Press.

Karp, Ivan, and Steven D. Lavine, eds. 1991. *The Poetics and Politics of Museum Display.* Washington, D.C.: Smithsonian Institution Press.

Kemper, Robert V. N.d. Tarascan Speakers in Tzintzuntzan, 1945–1990. Paper presented at the Annual Meeting of the American Anthropological Association, November 1996.

Kertzer, David I. 1988. *Ritual, Politics and Power.* New Haven, Conn.: Yale University Press.

Linnekin, Jocelyn. 1983. Defining Tradition: Variations on the Hawaiian Identity. *American Ethnologist* 10:241–252.

Llabrés Quintana, Gabriel. 1925. Los panetets de mort. *Correo de Mallorca,* October.

Lope Blanch, Juan M. 1963. *Vocabulario mexicano relativo a la muerte.* México, D. F.: Universidad Nacional Autónoma de México, Centro de Estudios Literarios.

Metcalf, Peter, and Richard Huntington. 1991. *Celebrations of Death: The Anthropology of Mortuary Ritual.* Cambridge and New York: Cambridge University Press.

North American Star. 1847. *North American Star,* November 2.

Parsons, Elsie Clews. 1917. All Souls' Day at Zuñi, Acoma, and Laguna. *Journal of American Folklore* 30:495–496.

Paz, Octavio. 1961. *The Labyrinth of Solitude: Life and Thought in Mexico.* Translated by Lysender Kemp. New York: Grove.

Ramos, Samuel. 1962. *Profile of Man and Culture in Mexico.* Translated by Peter G. Earle. Austin: University of Texas Press.

Sandstrom, Alan R., and Pamela Effrein Sandstrom. 1986. *Traditional Papermaking and Paper Cult Figures of Mexico.* Norman: University of Oklahoma Press.

Santino, Jack, ed. 1994. *Halloween and Other Festivals of Death and Life.* Knoxville: University of Tennessee Press.

Sayer, Chloë, ed. 1993. *Mexico: The Day of the Dead.* Boston: Shambhala Redstone.

Smith, C. 1967. Feast of All Saints. *New Catholic Encyclopedia.* New York: McGraw-Hill.

Tuleja, Tad. 1994. Trick or Treat: Pre-Texts and Contexts. In *Halloween and Other Festivals of Life and Death,* ed. Jack Santino, pp. 82–102. Knoxville: University of Tennessee Press.

Turner, Kay, and Pat Jasper. 1994. The Day of the Dead: The Tex-Mex Tradition. In *Halloween and Other Festivals of Life and Death,* ed. Jack Santino, pp. 133–151. Knoxville: University of Tennessee Press.

Viqueira, Juan-Pedro. 1984. La ilustración y las fiestas religiosas populares en la Ciudad de México (1731–1821). *Cuicuilco (Revista de la Escuela Nacional de Antropología e Historia)* 14–15:7–14.

Wilson, William A. 1976. *Folklore and Nationalism in Modern Finland.* Bloomington: Indiana University Press.

Part 7:
Brazil

6 Everyday Violence

Bodies, Death, and Silence

What's true? What's false? Who knows how to evaluate anymore?

Seu João Gallo, *morador,* Alto do Cruzeiro

This chapter takes my various reflections on nervous hunger, delirium, and the mindful bodies of *Nordestino* sugarcane cutters to their final and logical conclusion. I ground my discussion in the problem of the "disappeared," for the specter of missing, lost, disappeared, or otherwise out-of-place bodies and body parts haunts these pages even as it haunts the imaginations of the displaced people of the Alto do Cruzeiro, who understand that their bodies, their lives, and their deaths are generally thought of as dispensable, as hardly worth counting at all. In this context even the most interpretive and qualitative of ethnographers becomes an obsessive counter, a folk demographer, her function that of the village clerk, the keeper of the records recording and numbering the anonymous dead and disappeared.

And yet short of a theological meditation on the passions of the soul, what meaning have these empty spaces, these missing and disappeared bodies? I hope to show the difference they make when the everyday, lived experience of a large number of threatened people is introduced into current debates on the state, the politics of fear, and the problem of the disappeared.

The Breakdown of Consensus

The multiple and contradictory social realities of Bom Jesus and its surrounds contribute to fleeting perceptions of the community as a ruthless, unstable, amoral place. There is a sense of almost desperate vitality and of chaos threatening to unleash itself, so that Bom Jesus sometimes feels like a place where almost anything can happen. If there are rules to discipline and govern public interactions, they appear to exist only in the negative, to be violated, scoffed at. Only fools would obey a stop sign; never mind that the slow and fussy *solteirona* (old maid) of the Chaves family was knocked down

by a speeding Fiat as she tried to cross the main *praça* of Bom Jesus on her way home from Mass. The obvious contradictions do at times rise to the surface and threaten a social consensus that is, at best, tentative and fragile. The guise of civility is rent by sudden explosions of violence, some apparently calculated, others merely reactive.

In 1986 the children of one of the wealthiest landowners in Bom Jesus were kidnapped in front of their home in broad daylight by masked *desperados*—angry "social bandits" from the interior of the state—who later demanded, and received, a huge ransom. The band of unemployed field hands then declared "war on the greedy *latifundiários.*"

During the 1987 drought hungry rural workers throughout the *zona da mata* began looting stores, warehouses, and train depots, thereby forcing the governor of Pernambuco to send emergency rations to divert the looters. In an interview with the press the governor blamed the looting on the expulsion of rural workers from their *roçados,* which led to a "savage, violent, and disorderly urbanization" (Riding 1988:1-A4), an "occupation and siege" mentality evidenced in the social geography of shantytown "invasions" and squatter camps throughout the state.

Several young men of the Alto do Cruzeiro, each of them black, young, and in trouble with the law for petty theft, drunkenness, vagrancy, glue sniffing, and other infractions, were seized from their homes just after Christmas in 1987 by unidentified men "in uniform" and were "disappeared." A few weeks later two of the bodies were found slashed, mutilated, and dumped between rows of sugarcane. The police arrived with graphic photos for family members. "How do you expect me to recognize *meu homem* [my man] in this picture?" Dona Elena screamed hysterically. Similar events were repeated in 1988 and 1989. Finally they came late one night for the teenage son of Black Irene, the boy everyone on the Alto knew affectionately as Nego De. The existence of paramilitary "death squads" with close ties to the local police force is suspected, but on this topic people are generally silent; if and when they do speak, it is in a rapid and complicated form of sign language. No one else wants to be marked.

In February 1987 Evandro Cavalcanti Filho, a young lawyer for the Pernambucan rural workers syndicate, representing 120 peasant families in dispute with local landowners in the area of Surubim, was shot dead in front of his wife and children on the patio of their home. One of the gunmen (a suspected informant) was shot and killed by military police.

One year later, in February 1988, a small group of *posseiros,* traditional squatters using the abandoned and marginal fields of a local plantation called the Engenho Patrimônio, a few miles outside of Bom Jesus, were ambushed by *capangas,* hired gunmen in the employ of the *senhor latifundiário.* The peasants were quietly tending their *roçados* when the gunmen opened fire without warning. One peasant was maimed; another, a twenty-three-year-old father of a small family, was killed.

In 1989 rumors surfaced concerning the disappearance of street children, *meninos da rua* and *moleques,* several of whom lived in the open-air marketplace, took shelter at night in between the stalls and under canvas awnings, and helped themselves to bits of produce from crates and baskets. Even though many of the vendors were tolerant of the hungry street urchins, others enlisted the help of the local police in a local "pest control" campaign.

Throughout all, Bom Jesus da Mata continued to perceive itself as a quiet, peaceable interior town in the *zona da mata,* far from the violence and chaos of the large cities on the coast. As the initial excitement of each incident blew over, life resumed its normal course. The kidnappers were apprehended and the frightened children returned to their parents, but only a fraction of the ransom money was recovered. The sacking and looting of markets continued throughout the *zona da mata,* and a state of emergency was declared just before Holy Week in 1988, when suddenly the skies opened and torrential rains swept many Alto residents from their homes, which disappeared down rushing ravines of the shantytown. The *castigo* of drought was replaced by the *castigo* of floods. "Life is harsh. Man makes, but God destroys," said the *moradores* of the Alto do Cruzeiro philosophically.

The hired gunmen from the Engenho Patrimônio were arrested and then freed immediately on bail. The owner of the *engenho* was never cited or brought to trial. As of 1989 three ex-military police officers were in prison awaiting trial for the murder of Evandro Cavalcanti, but the special investigator appointed to the inquiry had resigned from the case, and another one had not been appointed. The disappearance of young black men continues on the Alto do Cruzeiro and in other poor *bairros* of Bom Jesus and is treated as a nonissue, not even thought worthy of a column in the mimeographed opposition newspaper of Bom Jesus. "Why should we criticize the 'execution' of *malandros* [good-for-nothings], rogues, and scoundrels?" asked a progressive lawyer of Bom Jesus and a frequent contributor to the alternative liberal newspaper. "The police have to be free to go about their business," said Mariazinha, the old woman who lived in a small room behind the church and who took care of the altar flowers. "The police know what they're doing. It's best to keep your mouth shut," she advised, zipping her lips to show me exactly what she meant.

Padre Agostino Leal shook his head sadly. "Is it possible that they murdered Nego De? What a shame! He was in reform. I trusted him. He even attended my Wednesday night Criminals' Circle." Then, after a pause, the good padre added ruefully, "I guess it was just too late for Nego De."

Violence and the Taken-for-Granted World

> The tradition of the oppressed teaches us that the "state of emergency" in which we live is not the exception but the rule. We must attain to a conception of history that is in keeping with this insight. . . . One reason why Fascism has a chance is that in the name of progress its opponents treat it as a historical norm.
>
> Walter Benjamin (cited in Taussig 1989b:64)

Writing about El Salvador in 1982, Joan Didion noted in her characteristically spartan prose that "the dead and pieces of the dead turn up everywhere, everyday, as taken-for-granted as in a nightmare or in a horror movie" (1982:9). In *Salvador* there are walls of bodies; they are strewn across the landscape, and they pile up in open graves, in ditches, in public restrooms, in bus stations, along the sides of the road. "Vultures, of course, suggest the presence of a body. A knot of children on the street suggest the presence of a body" (9). Some bodies even turn up in a place called Puerto del Diablo, a well-known tourist site described in Didion's inflight magazine as a location "offering excellent subjects for color photography."

It is the anonymity and the routinization of it all that strikes the naive reader as so terrifying. Who are all these *desaparecidos*—the unknown and the "disappeared"—both the poor souls with plucked eyes and exposed, mutilated genitals lying in a ditch and those unidentifiable men in uniform standing over the ditches with guns in their hands? It is the contradiction of wartime crimes against ordinary peacetime citizens that is so appalling. Later we can expect the unraveling, the recriminations, the not-so-guilty confessions, the church-run commissions, the government-sponsored investigations, the arrests of tense and unyielding men in uniform, and finally the optimistic reports—Brazil, Argentina (later, perhaps even El Salvador) *nunca mais.* Quoth the raven, *"Nunca mais."* After the fall, after the aberration, we expect a return to the normative, to peacetime sobriety, to notions of civil society, human rights, the sanctity of the person (Mauss's *personne morale*), *habeas corpus,* and the unalienable rights to the ownership of one's body.

But here I intrude with a shadowy question. What if the disappearances, the piling up of civilians in common graves, the anonymity, and the routinization of violence and indifference were not, in fact, an aberration? What if the social spaces before and after such seemingly chaotic and inexplicable acts were filled with rumors and whisperings, with hints and allegations of what could happen, especially to those thought of by agents of the social consensus as neither persons nor individuals? What if a climate of anxious, ontological insecurity about the rights to ownership of one's body was fostered by a studied, bureaucratic indifference to the lives and deaths of "marginals," criminals and other no-account people? What if the public routinization of daily mortifications and little abominations, piling up like so many corpses on the social landscape, provided the text and blueprint for what only appeared later to be aberrant, inexplicable, and extraordinary outbreaks of state violence against citizens?

In fact, the "extraordinary" outbreaks of state violence against citizens, as in Didion's *Salvador*, during the Argentine "Dirty War" (Suarez-Orozco 1987, 1990), in Guatemala up through the present day (Paul 1988; Green 1989), or in the harshest period following the Brazilian military coup of 1964 (Dassin 1986) entail the generalizing to recalcitrant members of the middle classes what is, in fact, normatively practiced in threats or open violence against the poor, marginal, and "disorderly" popular classes. For the popular classes every day is, as Taussig (1989b) succinctly put it, "terror as usual." A state of emergency occurs when the violence that is normally contained to that social space suddenly explodes into open violence against the "less dangerous" social classes. What makes the outbreaks "extraordinary," then, is only that the violent tactics are turned against "respectable" citizens, those usually shielded from state, especially police, terrorism.

If, in the following ethnographic fragments, I seem to be taking an unduly harsh and critical view of the "state" of things in Brazil, let me hasten to say at the outset that I view this interpretation as generalizable to other bureaucratic states at a comparable level of political-economic "development" and in a different form to those characterized by a more "developed" stage of industrial capitalism such as our own. Violence is also "taken for granted" and routinized in parts of our police underworld operating through SWAT team attacks on suspected crack houses and crack dealers in inner-city neighborhoods. And state terrorism takes other forms as well. It is found in the cool jargon of nuclear weapons researchers, our own silent, yet deadly, technicians of practical knowledge. Carol Cohn (1987) penetrated this clean, closed world and returned with a chilling description of the way our nuclear scientists have created a soothing and normalizing discourse with which to discuss our government's capacity for blowing populations of bodies to smithereens. "Bio-power," indeed.

I share with Michel Foucault his suspiciousness of the state as a social formation that spawns what Franco Basaglia (1987a) called the official and legalized "institutions of violence." Yet Foucault (1979) believed that public spectacles of torture and execution had gone the way of the ancien régime. The use of torture by the state, associated with criminal proceedings, was abolished throughout the Western world in the eighteenth and nineteenth

centuries, so that Victor Hugo could confidently announce in 1874 that "torture has ceased to exist" (Peters 1985:6). In Foucault's analysis, the mutilated body as the icon of state repression and control gave way to the more aestheticized and spiritualized character of public discipline, regulation, and punishment. The retreat from the body allowed for new assaults on the mind and the moral character of citizens. The new objects of discipline and surveillance were the passions, will, thought, and desire.

In advanced industrialized societies and in modern, bureaucratic, and welfare states, the institutions of violence generally operate more covertly. A whole array of educational, social welfare, medical, psychiatric, and legal experts collaborate in the management and control of sentiments and practices that threaten the stability of the state and the fragile consensus on which it claims to base its legitimacy. We can call these institutions, agents, and practices the "softer" forms of social control, the gloved hand of the state. But even the most "advanced" state can resort to threats of violence or to open violence against "disorderly" citizens whenever the normal institutions for generating social consensus are weakening or changing. I think that this is the situation we are rapidly approaching today in the United States with respect to the general tolerance of violent police actions in our urban inner cities on behalf of combating the "drug war."

The Brazilian state has been thrown into considerable turmoil in recent years by the democratic "awakenings" of previously excluded and alienated populations to new forms of political praxis and mobilization in the proliferation of highly politicized shantytown associations, mothers clubs, squatters unions, rural workers defense leagues, and so on, many of these supported by the clergy and hierarchy of the "new" Catholic church. The changing allegiance of the Catholic church, which, following the Latin American Bishops' Conference at Medellín withdrew much of its traditional support from the traditional landowning and industrial political-economic elite of Brazil, produced a crisis. Bishops and clergy throughout the country have in the last decade increasingly taken the side of peasants, squatters, Indians, and small landholders in disputes with *latifundários* and multinational companies, and they have publicly denounced the use of violence in extracting forced labor from plantation workers and in evicting peasants from their traditional holdings. In 1980 the Brazilian National Bishops' Conference released a statement that implicated not only landowners and hired *pistoleiros* in perpetrating the violence but also the state itself: "There is ample proof that such violence involves not only hired thugs and professional gunmen, but also the police, judges, and officers of the judiciary" (cited in Amnesty International 1988:3). The result was a stepped-up campaign of police-initiated harassment culminating in the murder of priests and religious sisters associated with rural trade unions, land rights claims, and shantytown associations throughout Brazil.

Northeast Brazil is still at a transitional stage of state formation that contains many traditional and semifeudal structures, including its legacy of local political bosses (*coroneis*) spawned by an agrarian *latifundista* class of powerful plantation estate masters and their many dependents (see Lewin 1987). To this day most sugar plantation estates are protected by privately owned police forces or at least by hired *pistoleiros*. The web of political loyalties among the intermarried big houses and leading families of the interior leads directly to the governor and to the state legislature, which is still controlled by a traditional agrarian oligarchy. Consequently, civil police, appointed by local politicians, often collaborate with hired gunmen in the employ of the plantation estates owners and sometimes participate themselves in the operations of the "death squads," a widespread and pernicious form of police "moonlighting" in Brazil.

One could compare the semifeudal organization of contemporary Northeast Brazil with Anton Blok's (1974) description of the state and state terrorism in Sicily in the early decades of the twentieth century. In both cases state power is mediated through a class of landholding intermediaries and their hired guns: the *coroneis* and their *capangas* in the Brazilian case and the *gabelotti*, the wealthy leaseholders and landlords who supported the rural mafia, in the Sicilian case. The Sicilian mafia evolved in the late nineteenth and early twentieth centuries when the modern state superimposed itself on a marginal peasant society that was still feudal in its basic features. The mafia served as a kind of modus vivendi mediating the claims of the new state apparatus with traditional landowners and big men. Acts of graphic public violence underscored the authority of the traditional power elite and of the newly emergent state as well.

Similarly, Northeast Brazil has not yet produced the range of modern social institutions, scientific ideologies, or specialized "technicians of practical knowledge" (a term first used by Sartre) to manage and individualize (and so contain) public expressions of dissent and discontent. The health and social welfare agencies, psychiatric clinics, occupational therapies, or varieties of counseling that help to bolster a wavering consent to the prevailing order of things are not yet completely in place. Clinical medicine in the interior of Brazil is, as we have seen, fairly brutal and unsophisticated in its goals and techniques. In the interior of Northeast Brazil there are only the police, a judiciary that has generally failed to prosecute cases of police brutality, the prison, the FEBEM federal reform schools for criminalized or simply marginalized youth, and the local death squads, all of them violent institutions.

There are three public security and law enforcement institutions in Brazil: the federal, civil, and military police. The federal police, under the jurisdiction of the Ministry of Justice, supervises immigration, protects the national frontiers, and investigates the black market and drug contraband in the country. Civil police are generally under the jurisdiction of the *município*, and the chief of police (*delegado de polícia*) is usually appointed by the mayor and is financially dependent on him and the town councilmen. In addition to the officially appointed civil police, a large number of ex-officio *vigias* (night watchmen) are nominated or tacitly approved by the chief of police. *Vigias* patrol virtually every *bairro* of Bom Jesus and are supported by weekly "dues" collected (or extracted) from each household on their beat. All *vigias* and most civil police have no formal training, and most are recruited from the poorer social classes. Often civil police and *vigias* are difficult to distinguish from thugs and vigilantes. In addition to these is the military police, which, under the jurisdiction of both the army and the state, is responsible for maintaining public order and security. It is the military police that is usually called on to enforce, often with violence, the evictions of traditional squatters. Throughout the years of the dictatorship (1964–1985), military police officers were heavily implicated in the disappearances, tortures, and deaths of suspected subversives in Bom Jesus as elsewhere in Brazil. The process of democratization has been painfully slow and has yet to challenge the local presence and the fearful psychological hold of the military police over the poorer populations (Amnesty International 1988, 1990). Consequently, poor *Nordestinos* have been living for many years with state violence and threats of violence. The alternative to "softer" forms of persuasion and control is direct attack on citizens: arrest and interrogation, imprisonment, disappearance, and, finally, torture, mutilation, and killing.

At certain levels of political-economic development—and the sugar plantation zone is one of these—violence and threats or fear of violence are sufficient to guarantee the "public order." In any case, violence is the only technique of public discipline available to a military government such as the one that ruled Brazil for twenty-one years and that still plays an important role in the state today. The military is not an educational, charitable, or social welfare institution; violence is intrinsic to its nature and logic. Violence is usually the only tactic the military has at its disposal to control citizens even during peacetime (see also Basaglia 1987b:143–168).

One of the ways that modern military dictatorships have legitimized the use of violent acts against citizens is through the legal loophole of the *crimen exceptum*—that is, the "extraordinary crime" that warrants extraordinary and often cruel punishment. The concept may be extended to extraordinary situations warranting extraordinary measures to protect the state. And so, paradoxically, during an era of expansion and centralization in which the Brazilian state commands great strength and power to mobilize vast resources, state policy is nonetheless based on a concept of extreme vulnerability. The fear of subversive or simply of criminal activity can become obsessional (see Suarez-Orozco 1987), and torture may be used in an attempt to assert, as Elaine Scarry put it, the "incontestable reality" of a particular state's control over the population. "It is, of course," she continued, "precisely because the reality of power is so highly contestable, the regime so unstable, that torture is being used" (1985:27). And so I have borrowed Franco Basaglia's notion of "peacetime crimes" as a way of addressing the routinization of violence in everyday aspects of contemporary *Nordestino* society.

What, then, is the rationale for turning a military, wartime arsenal against private citizens. What crimes have they committed (or do they threaten to commit)? What makes some citizens assume the character of "threats" or "dangers" to the state so as to make violence an acceptable form of social control, the legitimate "business" of the police? (Remember the words of Mariazinha, the religious spinster: "The police have to be free to go about their business.") The "dangerousness" of the poor and marginal classes derives directly from their condition of desperate want. Hunger and need always pose a threat to the artificial stability of the state. Following Basaglia (1987a:122), we can say that the marginals of the Alto do Cruzeiro are guilty of "criminal needs."

In the specific instance of the *posseiros* (peasants who, by Brazilian law, acquire *legal* tenure in unused, though privately owned, plantation lands) who were ambushed by hired gunmen working for the owner of Engenho Patrimônio, the squatters were "executed" by criminals who were never brought to trial. The "crimes" of the poor, of the desperate—of the *posseiro* whose very way of life stands as a negation of "modern," bourgeois notions of property rights or of Nego De, whose petty thievery helped maintain his mother and siblings after the murder of his father—are understood as "race" crimes and as "naturally," rather than socially, produced. Nego De and other poor, young black men like him steal because it is thought to be in their "nature," "blood," or "race" to steal. They are *malandros*, and they are described in racist terms as *bichos da Africa*. Their crimes can be punished with impunity and without due process. *Posseiros*, with their precapitalist notions of "the commons," are viewed as dangerous retrogrades, and the gunmen contracted to kill them do so with the full, often explicit, understanding and tacit approval of the local police. Those few gunmen who are apprehended usually escape from jail with the help of local prison guards.

Meanwhile, the violent crimes of the wealthy classes are understood and

forgiven as socially produced. Landowners must "protect" their patrimonies; politicians are "put into" totally corrupting situations. Lies and bribes are endemic to politics; they are part of the "game" of power. People are surprised to find an honest political leader or a fair and just employer. There is no such cultural and political immunity for the peasant squatters who occupy lands because they have no other way to survive or for Nego De, who was better able to sustain a large and desperate household by stealing than by "honest" work for one dollar a day in the cane fields. Although these are crimes of need, they are neither excused nor understood in social terms. Instead, they are seen as base, instinctual crimes that are natural to an "inferior" and "mulatto" population.

Increasingly today race and racial hatred have emerged as subliminal subtexts in the popular discourses that justify violent and illegal police actions in shantytown communities. Remnants of the older racial "harmony ideology" of *Nordestino* plantation society still render it "impolite" for the powerful and educated classes to comment in public on racial differences (while in private and behind closed doors racist discourse is rampant and particularly grotesque and virulent). But this same "polite" society can thereby fail to see, fail to recognize, that police persecution is now aimed at a specific segment and shade of the shantytown population. Even my radical black friend, João Mariano, was profoundly embarrassed when I raised the question of the racial nature of Alto disappearances at a study group formed by the small, literate, leftist intelligentsia of Bom Jesus, and the discussion was tabled.

Here we can begin to see the workings of a hegemonic discourse on criminality/deviance/marginality and on the "appropriateness" of police and state violence in which all segments of the population participate and to which they acquiesce, often contrary to their own class or race interests. How is this extraordinary consensus forged, and how is it maintained in the face of living (and dying) contradictions? Why is there so little expressed (or even submerged and seething) outrage against police and death squad terrorism in the shantytown? Why is there no strongly articulated human rights position among even the most progressive forces and parties of Bom Jesus? What has made the people of the Alto so fearful of democratic and liberal reforms?

In an attempt to answer these questions my analysis proceeds in two directions: ideology and practice. The first, relying heavily on the writings of contemporary Brazilian social scientists, concerns the political ideology of democracy, the state, and citizenship in Brazil. The second, based on my observations of everyday life in Brazil, explores the mundane rituals and routines of humiliation and violence that assault the bodies and minds of the *moradores* as they go about the complicated business of trying to survive. Both tend to reinforce an acceptance of "terror as usual."

Citizenship and Justice in Brazil

We tend to think of the Western political traditions and concepts of democracy, citizenship, and the modern state—as well as the necessary preconditions for their existence—as universally shared among modern nations. But as the recent events in Eastern Europe indicate—especially the difficulty with which newly liberated citizens are attempting to "reclaim the public" and recreate civil society following the "fall" of repressive and totalitarian communist regimes—the concepts of democracy, equality, and civil society may have very specific and different cultural and historical referents. In Eastern Europe the relationship between civil society and the state was perceived not in terms of collaboration and consensus but rather in terms of mutual hostility and antagonism (see Kligman 1990:394).

In Brazil the political traditions of republican democracy and equality, influenced by both the French and American revolutions, have always been mediated by traditional notions of hierarchy, privilege, and distinction. The Brazilian constitution, like the American constitution, was adopted before slavery was abolished, and by the end of the nineteenth century the public sphere had been constituted exclusively for a very small, elite group (Schwartz 1977; Caldeira 1990). Liberty and democracy became the exclusive preserves of the dominant minority, those educated and landed men (and, later, women) of breeding, culture, and distinction. Civil liberties and human rights were cast as "privileges" and "favors" bestowed by superiors on subordinates within relations structured by notions of personal honor and loyalty. "Favors" included everything from personal protection, material goods, jobs, and status to the right to vote. Consequently, up through the first half of the twentieth century in the Northeast, votes and elections were controlled by a few local big men and their clients.

Roberto da Matta pointed out that although Brazilian law is based on liberal and democratic principles of universalism and equality, its practice often diverges from theory and it "tends to be applied in a rigorous way only to the masses who have neither powerful relatives nor important family names." He went on to state that "in a society like Brazil's universal laws may be used for the exploitation of labor rather than for the liberation of society." Those who are wealthy or who have political connections can always manage to "slip under or over legal barriers" (1984:233).

Brazil's system of criminal justice is a "mixed system" containing elements of both the American and the European civil law tradition (Kant 1990). Contrary to the American system, there is no common-law tradition whereby precedents and jury verdicts can actually participate, in conjunction

with the legislature, in making the law. And in addition to many modern, egalitarian, and individual rights protected by the Brazilian criminal justice system (such as the right to counsel and to *ampla defesa*—that is, the right to produce any possible evidence on equal footing with the prosecution), there are other, more traditional, and less liberal traditions. First among these is the tradition of progressing from a position of "systematic suspicion," rather than from an assumption of innocence, and, relatedly, the judge's "interrogation" of the accused relying on information produced by prior police investigations that are "inquisitorial" in nature. In the words of one police chief interviewed by Roberto de Lima Kant, police interrogations entail "a proceeding *against everything* and *everyone* to find out the *truth* of the facts" (1990:6). Within this inquisitorial system, "torture becomes a legitimate—if unofficial—means of police investigation for obtaining information or a confession" (7). In all, "Brazilian criminal proceedings are organized to show a gradual, step by step, ritual of progressive incrimination and humiliation, the outcome of which must be either the confession or the acquittal. The legal proceedings are represented as a punishment in themselves" (22).

Within this political and legal context, one can understand the *moradores'* awesome fear of the judicial system and their reluctance to use the courts to redress even the most horrendous violations of their basic human rights. And, as Teresa Caldeira (1990) noted, the first stirrings of a new political discourse on "human rights," initiated by the progressive wing of the Catholic church and by leftist political parties in Brazil in the late 1970s and early 1980s and fueled in part by the international work of Amnesty International, was readily subverted by the Right. Powerful conservative forces in Brazil translated "human rights" into a profane discourse on special favors, dispensations, and privileges for criminals. Worse, the Brazilian Right played unfairly on the general population's fears of an escalating urban violence. These fears are particularly pronounced in poor, marginalized, and shantytown communities. And so, for example, following a 1989 presidential address broadcast on the radio and over loudspeakers in town announcing much-needed proposed prison reforms in Brazil, the immediate response of many residents of the Alto seemed paradoxical. Black Zulaide, for example, began to wail and wring her hands: "Now we are finished for sure," she kept repeating. "Even our president has turned against us. He wants to set all the criminals free so that they can kill and steal and rape us at will." It seemed to have escaped Black Zulaide that her own sons had at various times suffered at the hands of police at the local jail and that the prison reform act was meant to protect *her* class in particular. Nevertheless, Zulaide's fears had been fueled by the negative commentary of the police, following the broadcast, on the effects these criminal reforms would have on the people of Bom

Jesus but especially on those living in "dangerous" *bairros* such as the Alto do Cruzeiro and needing the firm hand of the law to make life minimally "safe."

Similarly, Teresa Caldeira offered two illustrations of right-wing ideological warfare that equated the defense of human rights with the defense of special privileges for criminals. The first is from the "Manifesto of the Association of Police Chiefs" of the state of São Paulo, which was addressed to the general population of the city on October 4, 1985. The manifesto takes to task the reformist policies of the then-ruling central-leftist political coalition, the PMDB:

> The situation today is one of total anxiety for you and total tranquility for those who kill, rob, and rape. Your family is destroyed and your patrimony acquired with much sacrifice is being reduced. . . . How many crimes have occurred in your neighborhood, and how many criminals were found responsible for them? . . . The bandits are protected by so called human rights, something that the government considers that you, an honest and hard working citizen, do not deserve. (1990:6)

Her second example is taken from an article published on September 11, 1983, in the largest daily newspaper of São Paulo, *A Folha de São Paulo,* written by an army colonel and the state secretary of public security:

> The population's dissatisfaction with the police, including the demand for tougher practices . . . originates from the trumped up philosophy of "human rights" applied in favor of bandits and criminals. This philosophy gives preference to the marginal, protecting his "right" to go around armed, robbing, killing, and raping at will. (6)

Under the political ideology of favors and privileges, extended only to those who behave well, human rights cannot logically be extended to criminals and marginals, those who have broken, or who simply live outside, the law. When this negative conception of human rights is superimposed on a very narrow definition of "crime" that does not recognize the criminal and violent acts of the powerful and the elite, it is easy to see how everyday violence against the poor is routinized and defended, even by some of the poor themselves.

Mundane Surrealism

In Mario Vargas Llosa's novel *The Real Life of Alejandro Mayta,* the Peruvian narrator comments on the relations of imagination to politics and of literary fiction to history:

> Information in this country has ceased to be objective and has become pure fantasy—in newspapers, radio, television, and in ordinary conversation. To report among us now means either to interpret reality according to our desires or fears, or to say simply what is convenient. It is an attempt to make up for our ignorance of what is going on—which in our heart of hearts we understand as irremediable and definitive. Since it is impossible to know what is really happening, we Peruvians lie, invent, dream, and take refuge in illusion. Because of these strange circumstances, Peruvian life, a life in which so few actually do read, has become literary. (1986:246)

The magical realism of Latin American fiction has its counterparts in the mundane surrealism of ethnographic description, where it is also difficult to separate fact from fiction, rumor and fantasy from historical event, and the events of the imagination from the events of the everyday political drama. The blurring of fiction and reality creates a kind of mass hysteria and paranoia that can be seen as a new technique of social control in which everyone suspects and fears every other: a collective hostile gaze, a human panopticon (see Foucault 1979), is created. But when this expresses itself positively and a state of alarm or a state of emergency is produced—as in the epidemic of *susto* discussed in chapter 5—the shocks reveal the disorder in the order and call into question the "normality of the abnormal," which is finally shown for what it really is.

Peacetime Crimes

The peoples' death was as it had always been:
as if nobody had died, nothing,
as if those stones were falling
on the earth, or water on water. . . .
Nobody hid this crime.
This crime was committed
in the middle of the Plaza.
  Pablo Neruda (1991:186–187)

What makes the political tactic of disappearance so nauseating—a tactic used strategically throughout Brazil during the military years (1964–1985) against suspected subversives and "agitators" and now applied to a different and perhaps an even more terrifying context (i.e., against the shantytown poor and the economic marginals now thought of as a species of public enemy)—is that it does not occur in a vacuum. Rather, the disappearances occur as part of a larger context of wholly expectable, indeed even anticipated, behavior. Among the people of the Alto, disappearances form part of the backdrop of everyday life and confirm their worst fears and anxieties—that of losing themselves and their loved ones to the random forces and institutionalized violence of the state.

The practices of "everyday violence" constitute another sort of state "terror," one that operates in the ordinary, mundane world of the *moradores* both in the form of rumors and wild imaginings and in the daily enactments of various public rituals that bring the people of the Alto into contact with the state: in public clinics and hospitals, in the civil registry office, in the public morgue, and in the municipal cemetery. These scenes provide the larger context that makes the more exceptional and strategic, politically motivated disappearances not only allowable but also predictable and expected.

"You gringos," a Salvadorian peasant told an American visitor, "are always worried about violence done with machine guns and machetes. But there is another kind of violence that you should be aware of, too. I used to work on a hacienda. My job was to take care of the dueño's dogs. I gave them meat and bowls of milk, food that I couldn't give my own family. When the dogs were sick, I took them to the veterinarian. When my children were sick, the dueño gave me his sympathy, but no medicine as they died" (cited in Chomsky 1985:6; also in Clements 1987:ix).

Similarly, the *moradores* of the Alto speak of bodies that are routinely violated and abused, mutilated and lost, disappeared into anonymous public spaces—hospitals and prisons but also morgues and the public cemetery. And they speak of themselves as the "anonymous," the "nobodies" of Bom Jesus da Mata. For if one is a "somebody," a *fildalgo* (a son of a person of influence), and a "person" in the aristocratic world of the plantation *casa grande,* and if one is an "individual" in the more open, competitive, and bourgeois world of the new market economy (the *rua*), then one is surely a nobody, a mere *fulano-de-tal* (a so-and-so) and João Pequeno (little guy) in the anonymous world of the sugarcane cutter (the *mata*).

Moradores refer, for example, to their collective invisibility, to the ways they are lost to the public census and to other state and municipal statistics. The otherwise carefully drafted municipal street map of Bom Jesus includes the Alto do Cruzeiro, but more than two-thirds of its tangle of congested, unpaved roads and paths are not included, leaving it a semiotic zero of more than five thousand people in the midst of the bustling market town. CELPE, the state-owned power and light company, keeps track, of course, of those streets and houses that have access to electricity, but the names the company has assigned to identify the many intersecting *bicos, travessas,* and *ruas* of the Alto do not conform to the names used among the *moradores* themselves. The usual right of the "colonizer" to name the space he has claimed is not extended to the marginal settlers of the Alto do Cruzeiro.

The people of the Alto are invisible and discounted in many other ways. Of no account in life, the people of the Alto are equally of no account in death. On average, more than half of all deaths in the *município* are of shantytown children under the age of five, the majority of them the victims of acute and chronic malnutrition. But one would have to read between the lines because the death of Alto children is so routine and so inconsequential that for more than three-fourths of recorded deaths, the cause of death is left blank on the death certificates and in the ledger books of the municipal civil registry office. In a highly bureaucratic society in which triplicates of every form are required for the most banal of events (registering a car, for example), the registration of child death is informal, and anyone may serve as a witness. Their deaths, like their lives, are quite invisible, and we may as well speak of their bodies, too, as having been disappeared.

The various mundane and everyday tactics of disappearance are practiced perversely and strategically against people who view their world and express their own political goals in terms of bodily idioms and metaphors. The people of the Alto inhabit a world with a comfortable human shape, a world that is intimately embodied. I have already suggested that the *moradores* of the Alto "think" the world with their bodies within a somatic culture. At their base community meetings the people of the Alto say to each other with conviction and with feeling, "Every man should be the *dono* [owner] of his own body." Not only their politics but their spirituality can be described as "embodied" in a popular Catholicism, with its many expressions of the carnal and of physical union with Jesus, with His mother Mary, and with the multitude of saints, more than enough for every day of the year and to guide every human purpose. There is a saint for every locale, for every activity, and for every part of the body. And the body parts of the saints, splintered into the tiniest relics, are guarded and venerated as sacred objects.

Embodiment does not end with death for the people of the Alto. Death is itself no stranger to people who handle a corpse with confidence, if not with ease. ("When you die, Dona Nancí," little Zefinha used to say affectionately, "I'm going to be the first to eat your big legs," the highest compliment she could think of to pay me.) On the death of a loved one, a local photographer will often be called to take a photo of the adult or child in her or his coffin. That same photo will be retouched to erase the most apparent signs of death, and it will become the formal portrait that is hung proudly on the wall. The deceased continue to appear in visions, dreams, and apparitions through which they make their demands for simple pleasures and creature comforts explicit. As wretched *almas penadas,* "restless souls" from purgatory, the dead may request food and drink or a pair of shoes or stockings to cover feet that are cold and blistered from endless wandering. Because the people of the

Alto imagine their own souls to have a human shape, they will bury an amputated foot in a tiny coffin in the local cemetery so that later it can be reunited with its owner, who can then face his Master whole and standing "on his own two feet."

Against these compelling images of bodily autonomy and certitude is the reality of bodies that are simultaneously discounted and preyed on and sometimes mutilated and dismembered. And so the people of the Alto come to imagine that there is nothing so bad, so terrible that it cannot happen to them, to their bodies, because of sickness (*por culpa de doença*), because of doctors (*por culpa dos médicos*), because of politics and power (*por culpa de política*), or because of the state and its unwieldy, hostile bureaucracy (*por culpa da burocracia*).

I am not going so far as to suggest that the fears of mutilation and of misplacement of the body are not shared with other social classes of Brazil, which also "privilege" the body in a culture that prides itself on its heightened expressions and pleasures of the sensual. What is, however, specific to the marginal classes of the Alto do Cruzeiro is a self-conscious sort of thinking with and through the body, a "remembering" of the body and of one's "rights" in it and to it. The affluent social classes take for granted these rights to bodily integrity and autonomy to the extent that they "go without saying." The police oppressors know their victims all too well, well enough to mutilate, castrate, make disappear, misplace, or otherwise lose the bodies of the poor, to actualize their very worst fears. It is the sharing of symbols between the torturer and the tortured that makes the terror so effective (see Scarry 1985:38–45; Suarez-Orozco 1987).

The unquestionability of the body was, for Wittgenstein, where all knowledge and certainty began. "If you do know that here is one hand," he began his last book, *On Certainty,* "we'll grant you all the rest" (1969:2e). And yet Wittgenstein himself, writing this book while he was working with patients hospitalized during the war, was forced to reflect on the circumstances that might take away the certainty of the body. Here, in the context of *Nordestino* life, I am exploring another set of circumstances that have given a great many people grounds to lose their sense of bodily certitude to terrible bouts of existential doubt—"My God, my God, what ever will become of us?"—the fear of being made to vanish, to disappear without a trace.

It is reminiscent of the situation described by Taussig with reference to a similar political situation in Colombia: "I am referring to a state of doubleness of social being in which one moves in bursts between somehow accepting the situation as normal, only to be thrown into a panic or shocked into disorientation by an event, a rumor, a sight, something said, or not said—

something even while it requires the normal in order to make its impact, destroys it" (1989b:8). The intolerableness of the situation is increased by its ambiguity. Consciousness moves in and out of an acceptance of the state of things as normal and expectable—violence as taken for granted and sudden ruptures whereby one is suddenly thrown into a state of shock (*susto, pasmo, nervios*)—that is endemic, a graphic body metaphor secretly expressing and publicizing the reality of the untenable situation. There are nervous, anxious whisperings, suggestions, hints. Strange rumors surface.

The Disappeared: Traffic in Organs

And so the *moradores'* feelings of vulnerability, of a profound sort of ontological insecurity, are manifested in a free-floating anxiety and in rumors (that are never publicly squelched or denied) about the disposability, anonymity, and interchangeability of their bodies and body parts. They imagine that even their own chronically sick and wasted bodies may be viewed by those more powerful than themselves (by *os que mandam,* those who give the orders) as a reservoir of "spare parts." I am referring to a rumor that first surfaced on the Alto do Cruzeiro (and throughout the interior of the state) in the mid-1980s and that has been circulating there ever since. It concerns the abduction and mutilation of young and healthy shantytown residents (especially children), who are eyed greedily for their body parts, especially eyes, heart, lungs, and liver. It was said that the teaching hospitals of Recife and the large medical centers throughout Brazil were engaged in an active traffic in body parts, a traffic with international dimensions.

Shantytown residents reported multiple sightings of large blue or yellow vans, driven by foreign agents (usually North American or Japanese), who were said to patrol poor neighborhoods looking for small stray children whom the drivers mistakenly believed no one in the overpopulated slums and shantytowns would ever miss. The children would be nabbed and shoved into the trunks of the vans. Some were murdered and mutilated for their organs, and their discarded bodies were found by the side of the road or were tossed outside the walls of municipal cemeteries. Others were taken and sold indirectly to hospitals and major medical centers, and the remains of their eviscerated bodies were said to turn up in hospital dumpsters.

"They are looking for 'donor organs,'" my clever research assistant, Little Irene, said. "You may think that this is nonsense, but we have seen things with our own eyes in the hospitals and in the public morgues, and we know better."

"Bah, these are stories invented by the poor and illiterate," countered my friend Casorte, the new socialist manager of the municipal cemetery of Bom Jesus, in August 1989. "I have been working here for over a year," he said. "I arrive at six in the morning, and I leave at seven at night. Never have I seen anything. Where are the bodies or even the traces of blood left behind?"

When overnight the life-sized body of Christ disappeared from the huge cross that gives the shantytown of Alto do Cruzeiro its name, the skeptical and the irreverent wondered aloud whether the same kidnappers were responsible. They suggested that community leaders search the dumpsters of the local hospital to find out if the Christ had had His organs removed. But among the devout and the more simple, the "missing Cristo" of the Alto increased people's sense of threat and physical vulnerability. Dona Amor wiped a stray tear from her wrinkled cheek and confided in a hoarse whisper, "They've taken Him, and we don't know where they have hid Him." "But who?" "*Os grandes*," she replied. "But why?" I persisted, and she answered in a word: "*Política*." Dona Amor was referring to the politics of power, to all the inchoate forces summoned by the poor to explain and account for the misery of their lives. Whereas for us politics is something remote that happens elsewhere and in a separate discourse with its own vocabulary and etiquette, for the *Nordestino* peasant-workers *política* is imminent and omnipresent. It accounts for and explains everything, even the size of one's coffin and the depth of one's grave.

The body-snatching rumors were so widespread in the *favelas* and poor neighborhoods of Pernambuco that local journalists soon picked up the story and went to great lengths to expose the credulity of the population, sometimes cruelly satirizing people's fears as bogeyman stories. But to the illiterate, or partly literate, the newspaper and radio coverage only added further validity to the rumors. "Yes, it's true," insisted Dona Aparecida, pacing anxiously in front of her house on the Rua do Cruzeiro. "I heard it on the radio yesterday. They are reporting it in Recife. Now what will become of us and our poor children?" And she started to cry.

The stories had reached such proportions that my attempts one morning to rescue little Mercea, Biu's perpetually sick and fussy three-year-old, backfired when I attempted to get her into the back seat of a taxi, even as she was carried in the arms of Xoxa, her older sister. As soon as I gave the order "To the hospital and quick!" the already terrified little toddler, in the midst of a severe respiratory crisis, began to choke, scream, and go rigid. "Does she think I'm Papa-Figo [the Brazilian bogeyman]?" the annoyed cab driver asked.[1] No amount of coaxing could convince Mercea that her tormented little body was not going to be sold to the ghoulish doctors. Biu had instructed her little girl well: "Don't let *anyone* take you outside the house."

Even more children than usual were kept out of school during this period, and others were sent away to live with distant kin in the *mata*. Meanwhile, small children, like Mercea, who were left at home while their mothers were at work in the cane fields or in the houses of the wealthy found themselves virtual prisoners, locked into small, dark huts with even the wooden shutters securely fastened. On several occasions I had to comfort a sobbing child who, through a crack in a door or shutter, would beg me to liberate her from her dark and lonely cell.

As a result of these organ theft rumors, there are a fascination and horror with autopsy, plastic surgery, and organ transplant operations, which are sometimes understood quite fantastically. "So many of the rich are having plastic surgery and organ transplants," offered an older Alto woman, "that we really don't know whose body we are talking to anymore." As the people of the Alto see it, the ring of organ exchange proceeds from the bodies of the young, the poor, and the beautiful to the bodies of the old, the rich, and the ugly and from Brazilians in the Southern Hemisphere to North Americans, Germans, and Japanese. The people of the Alto can all too easily imagine that their bodies may be eyed longingly as a reservoir of spare parts by those with money.

It was just this perceived injustice of unfair and unequal exchange of organs and body parts that kept Dona Carminha in search of extraordinary medical help for her only living son, Tomás, who was blinded when he was eight years old because of a poorly treated eye infection. Secondary scar tissue had grown over the cornea of both eyes, and the boy, entering adolescence, lived in a world of impenetrable blackness to which his mother refused to let him make the slightest adjustment or accommodation. She was convinced that the boy's blindness was temporary and would someday be reversed through an eye transplant. The obstacle, as she understood it, was that the "eye banks" were reserved, like everything else in Brazil, for *os ricos*, those, she said, who could afford to pay "interest." She had taken the boy to Recife and then by bus, to Rio, where she lived in a *favela* with distant relations while she relentlessly pursued one impossible option after another. Although she could not read and was terrified of the city, she learned to make her way, she said, and went from hospital to hospital and clinic to clinic until she finally exhausted all possible options there. Yet she persisted in her belief that there was still hope for her son, that somewhere she would find a doctor of conscience, *um doutor santo*, who would be willing to put his hands into the till and come up with a new pair of eyes for her son. (Her story put me in mind of the images I knew as a child of Santa Lucia, with her plucked eyes resting on a dish held in her hands.) Didn't they give new eyes to the rich? Carminha asked me. And wasn't her own son *gente* (a good person) just like them and equal before the "eyes" of God? How could the doctors not "see" what they were doing, she continued. Were they so "blind"? Her husband, patient and long-suffering Seu Evanildo, sighed, shaking his head at me.

"Maybe," I said gently, "maybe, Carminha, it *is*, as the doctors have told you, too late for your son's eyes. Maybe he will have to learn how to walk in the shadows." "Never," she said, "I will never give up as long as I have the strength to walk the streets and I have a mouth to speak. I will take him to Texas if that is the only solution."

The rumor that the "rich are eating us" or "eating our children" is not exclusive to these impoverished *Nordestinos*. One can find similar stories in other places and historical periods—for example, in the "blood libel" stories that European Catholic peasants spread against Jewish merchants, who were accused of using the blood of Christian babies for Passover rituals, and in the contemporary Pishtaco myths found among Andean Indians. The Andean version, held widely from the colonial period to this day (see Oliver-Smith 1969; Taussig 1987b:211–241), maintained that sugar mills could not be started up at the beginning of the milling season without being greased with human fat, normally Indian fat and preferably Indian children's fat. The mills ran by feeding on human bodies, an apt enough metaphor. The Indians mistrusted all aspects of the milling industry—the factory with its heavy machinery, electric power plants, and engineers who managed them. The Indians had reason enough to be suspicious because mill and factory owners had both exploited the labor and mistreated the bodies of the Indian population since the beginning of the conquest.

There are modern versions of the Pishtaco tale. In the 1950s Peruvian villagers told Eugene Hammel (personal communication) that airplane jet engines could not be started up without human fat and that Indian children were stolen to provide it. It was also rumored during a famine in the southern highlands of the Andes in the 1960s that U.S. grains and other surplus foods that were being sent to Peru through the Food for Peace program were designed to fatten up Andean babies for the U.S. Air Force. When USAID programs began to provide Andean children with a nourishing school lunch, the Indians stopped sending their children to school altogether. Finally, in the 1980s Bruce Winterhalder, a biological anthropologist from the University of North Carolina, found his attempts to study the physiological effects of high altitude on Andean Indians stymied by the rumor that the anthropologist and his team of assistants were modern-day Pishtacos. They believed that the researchers were measuring the fat folds of adults and children with calipers to select the fattest for their nefarious, cannibalistic purposes.

The *Nordestino* rumors about kidnapped children and organ theft for medical procedures are more complicated than the blood libel or Pishtaco myths. Even though beliefs about greasing the engines of sugar mills and jet planes with human fat vividly express people's fears of exploitation by the rich and powerful, they remain metaphorical, speaking only to symbolic, not to actual, truths. *Nordestino* fears and rumors of body and organ snatching by medical institutions are grounded in a historical reality going back as far as Renaissance anatomists and surgeons (see Lindburgh 1975) and in a new biomedical technology that is real and in some respects monstrous enough. The "Baby Parts Story Just Won't Die" (see *San Francisco Sunday Examiner and Chronicle*, September 30, 1990, B-7) because the "misinformed" shantytown residents are onto something. They are on the right track and are refusing to give up on their intuitive sense that something is seriously amiss.

Certainly the scarcity of organ donors for transplant surgery and the development of new techniques for the medical use of fetal tissues have created a gruesome market for human "organ harvesting," one with international dimensions. There are several sources of human organs and body tissues for transplant surgery and for basic medical research. The primary source of "spare parts" comes from "neomorts"—that is, brain-dead hospital patients whose vital organs may be kept "alive" and "available" for days, even weeks, via machines that can push and pull oxygen out of lungs, electrically shock the heart into beating, and keep the blood warm and circulating through body tissues. This process of maintaining life-in-death is fairly routinized today in American hospitals. Another source is from still living, yet doomed, anencephalic infants, and a third comes, relatedly, from the brain tissue taken from aborted fetuses. In Berkeley, California, the Hana Biologics Company is currently developing techniques to produce insulin-producing cells from aborted fetuses to transplant into patients with diabetes. The company hopes to accomplish the same for Parkinson's disease. Craig McMullen, the president of the company, deals with the ethics of this procedure rather cursorily: "We take a waste product of society and use it to find a cure for diseases affecting millions of people" (*San Francisco Chronicle*, October 6, 1987, 6).

Information and disinformation about these and other seemingly magical medical innovations are rapidly picked up by the media and disseminated worldwide. Consequently, the organ theft rumor has spread rapidly throughout the Third World, even in the absence of literacy, newspapers, and television sets. Perhaps the medical practice that most reflects the anxieties underlying the organ theft rumors is the use of living, healthy, unrelated donors who are paid to "donate" a spare organ, most commonly a kidney. The business of organ transplants is conducted today in a multi- and transnational space. For example, between 1984 and 1988, 131 patients from three renal units in the United Arab Emirates and Oman traveled of their own accord to Bombay, India, where they purchased, through local brokers, kidneys from living donors, most of them from impoverished shantytowns outside Bombay. The donor's "extra" kidney was surgically removed for transplant, and the "donor" was compensated between $2,600 and $3,300 for the missing body part.

This subject was treated in a recent issue of *The Lancet*, perhaps the premier medical journal in the world. A. K. Salahudeen et al. (1990) analyzed the high mortality among the Arab recipients of the purchased kidneys. There was no parallel follow-up or discussion, however, of the possible adverse effects on the health and mortality of the organ donors. The authors did, however, comment on the ethics of organ sale. While they condemned the practice of "rampant commercialism" in Bombay (without mentioning the rampant commercialism of the Arab participants), they considered ethically "acceptable" the practice of "rewarded gifting" or "compensated gifting" whereby living, unrelated donors are "rewarded" for the inconvenience of the procedure and for the loss of earnings during the period of recovery. Citing studies by C. T. Patel (1988) and K. C. Reddy et al. (1990), *The Lancet* authors concluded that financial incentives for living organ donors may be considered "moral and justified" on the grounds that "kidney donation is a good act. It is a gift of life" (1990:727).

The language of *The Lancet* article evoked an early and formative essay by Talcott Parsons, Renée Fox, and Victor Lidz in which the authors drew on religious imagery and the biblical idea of self-sacrifice as the ethical basis underlying the then still very experimental medical technology that made heart transplants possible. The donation of an organ, they wrote, was the most literal gift of life that a person could offer or receive:

> The donor contributes a vital part of his (her) body to a terminally ill, dying recipient, in order to save and maintain that other person's life. Because of the magnitude of this gift exchange . . . participating in a transplantation can be a transcendent experience for those involved. . . . It may epitomize for them man's highest capacity to make the sacrificial gift of life-in-death, that is supreme love, commitment, and communion. In this sense . . . deep religious elements, some of them explicitly Christian, are at least latently present in the transplant situation. (1972:412)

Obviously, there are many ethical and political dilemmas involved in the question of organ transplants that are being creatively addressed by shantytown residents. While Western Europeans and North Americans persist in thinking of organ transplants as "gifts" donated freely by loving and altruistic people, to the people of the Alto, whose bodies are so routinely preyed on by the wealthy and the powerful (in economic and symbolic exchanges that have international dimensions), the organ transplant implies less a gift than a commodity. In place of the gift of life, there is a suspicion of a theft of life in which they will serve as the unwilling and unknowing sacrificial lambs.

The body parts rumor is so persistent and widespread today among poor and vulnerable people living in urban shantytowns on the fringes of modern social life that in November 1988 the European Parliament passed a resolution condemning the "traffic" in Central and South American children for international adoption, an undersupervised commercial as well as a charitable activity that sometimes involves such children in prostitution and pornography and possibly even, as the rumor suggests, in a covert traffic in baby parts (see R. Smith 1989; Raymond 1989).

At the very least the organ theft rumor should give pause to those medical technicians and political leaders in the United States who have sometimes made indecent proposals for the acquisition of scarce donor organs.[2] The Brazilian rumors express poor people's perceptions, grounded in an economic and biotechnomedical reality, that their bodies and the bodies of their children may be worth more dead than alive to the rich and the powerful.[3]

And so the rumors of the "medically" disappeared and mutilated bodies continue unabated, coexisting, of course, with actual cases of politically motivated abductions and mutilations of Alto men and young boys, about which people are too afraid to speak, so that when touching on *this* subject *moradores* are suddenly struck mute. The rumors of "what can happen next" express, albeit obliquely and surrealistically, the *moradores'* implicit and intuitive understanding that something is amiss.

The Disappeared: Traffic in Children

Por este pão pra comer	For this good bread to eat
Por este chão pra dormir	For this hard ground on which to sleep
Por me deixar respirar	For letting me breathe
Por me deixar existir	For letting me exist
Deus lhe pague!	God reward you!

Chico Buarque, popular song (cited in Pires 1986:39)

The anxious stories of shantytown children snatched up for their organs may also be a reflection of the active roundup of small street urchins, thousands of whom disappear each year into Brazilian prisons and federal correctional and education reform facilities that are viewed with suspicion and horror by shantytown residents (see Fonseca 1987). But the stories of physical and sexual abuse of children detained in Brazil's correctional institutions are matched by equally horrible stories of abuse, battering, mutilation, and death on the streets (see Allsebrook & Swift 1989). Benedicto

Rodrigues dos Santos, the head of the Brazilian National Street Children's Movement, reported the violent deaths of 1,397 street children between 1984 and 1989 alone. Many of these were the victims of one version of "urban renewal," and similar to the death squad assassinations of adult marginals, the bodies of some of these "lost" street children were also mutilated.

It is curious to note how the official public discourse about street children has changed in Brazil (and more widely in Latin America as well) over the past two decades. In the 1960s street urchins were accepted as a fairly permanent feature of the urban landscape, and they were referred to affectionately as *moleques,* that is, "ragamuffins," "scamps," or "rascals," or any small black child. *Moleques* were "streetwise" kids, cute, and cunning, sometimes sexually precocious, and invariably economically enterprising. They tried to make themselves useful in myriad small ways, some of these bordering on the deviant. Think of Fagin's "boys" from *Oliver Twist,* especially the Artful Dodger, and you have it. Many *moleques* survived by "adopting" a particular affluent household, where they often ate and slept in a courtyard or patio. Hardly a Peace Corps volunteer in Brazil in the 1960s didn't have a special *moleque,* who attached himself or herself to the volunteer for the duration of the stay. A few of these "loose" and "excess" children were adopted and brought back to the United States.

Today, street children in Brazil tend to be viewed as both a public scandal and public nuisance. They are now referred to either as "abandoned" children or as marginals. The first connotes pity for the child (and blame for the neglectful mother), whereas the second connotes fear. But both labels justify radical interventions and the removal of these all too public "pests" from the landscape of modern, congested cities in Brazil. Yet today's abandoned and criminalized street children seem no more neglected and no more (or less) dangerous than yesterday's playful *moleques.* Most of the children are today, as they were in the 1960s, "supernumerary" children of impoverished single mothers. And although they may be quite on their own economically, most are still emotionally and socially attached to a larger family unit. In fact, street children, most of them boys, are quite sentimental on the topic of mothers, their own mothers in particular. When asked why they begged, stole, or lived in the streets, the children often replied that they were doing it to help their mothers. Most shared a percentage of their earnings with their mothers, whom they visited each evening. "Fifty-fifty," said Giomar proudly with his raspy, boy-man voice. "Oh, *chê!*" his nine-year-old friend Aldimar corrected him. "Since when did you ever give your mother more than a third?" (I was more impressed, however, with the math skills of two street children who had never been to school.)

Self-portrait of Luiz: "Begging." Happy to be alive!

A band of street children who had attached themselves to us in 1987 liked nothing better than to be invited indoors to use our indoor toilet, to wash up with soap and water, and, afterward, to flop on the floor and draw with magic marker pens. Their sketches were curious. Given free hand to draw whatever came into their heads, most drew self-portraits or conventional nuclear family portraits, even when there was no "papa" living in the house or when the child himself had long since left home. The street children also liked religious themes, the crucifixion in particular, colored in with lots of bloody red. But their self-portraits tended to be smiling and upbeat, like the one that eleven-year-old Luiz sketched of himself, posing with his beggar's sack.

The main shadow that is cast over the lives of street children today is their fear of the police and of the FEBEM children's asylums in Bom Jesus and in nearby Recife. "You won't ever turn me in to FEBEM, will you, Nancí?" I was made to answer many times over. "They kill children there," Luiz insisted. The more I denied that this could be so, the more the children ticked off the names of friends who had been "roughed up" or hurt at one of the Federal Schools for the Well-Being of Minors, as the FEBEM institutes are misnamed. "Why do you think that they built the FEBEM school so close to the cemetery of Bom Jesus?" asked José Roberto, aged 12, with a quiver of fear in his voice. No one can tell these experienced street children that their fears for their physical safety are groundless.

By the same token, one cannot suggest to Alto women that their fears of child snatching are fantastic and groundless in light of the active domestic and international black market in Brazilian children (see Scheper-Hughes 1990). The thriving trade in babies has affected the lives of a dozen or more Alto women with results that are complex and ambiguous. In the absence of any formal child protective service, with the exception of the punitive FEBEM asylums, child arrest, child stealing, and child saving are hopelessly muddled. When coercion, bribery, and trickery are involved in Brazilian child adoption, the humanitarian gesture is easily unmasked as little more than institutionalized reproductive theft that puts the bodies of poor women in the Third World at the disposal of affluent men and women in Brazil and elsewhere. But regardless of the form it takes, the trade in babies has contributed to the chronic state of panic that I am describing and to Alto residents' perceptions of bodily destinies that are out of their control.

When Maria Lordes, the mother of five sickly and malnourished children living in a miserable hovel on the hillside path called the Vulture's Beak on the Alto do Cruzeiro, was approached by her wealthy *patroa,* the woman for whom she washed clothes for less than one dollar a week, who asked to "borrow" her pretty little four-year-old *galega* (fair-haired, fair-skinned child), Maria readily agreed. The woman said she would keep the child overnight just for amusement and would return her in the morning. Maria sent her little girl off just as she was: untidy, barefoot, and without even a change of clothes or her little pink comb with its missing teeth.

That night passed and then another. Maria was worried, but she assumed that her child was happy and having a good time, and Maria did not want to anger her boss by appearing anxious or mistrustful. After almost a week had gone by, Maria's husband, Manoel Francisco, came home from the plantation several hours to the north where he had been working as a sugarcane cutter. When he returned to find that his favorite daughter was missing, he pushed Maria against the wall of their hut and called her a "stupid woman." He went frantically in search of the little girl, but on arriving at the house of his wife's *patroa,* he learned it was already too late: the little girl had been sent by bus to Recife to an "orphanage" that specialized in overseas adoption.

"I did your wife a favor," the *patroa* said to Manoel. "Leave your daughter alone and soon she will be on her way to America to become the daughter of a rich man. That pretty *galega* of yours had no future in your household. Don't be selfish. Give her a chance." The woman would give no further information, and when Manoel became insistent, she called on one of her houseboys to have him forcibly removed from her patio.

Had they lodged a complaint with the police? I asked. "And do you think that the police would take a complaint from us, Dona Nancí?" I was told. No, said Maria, adding that although she was still very angry at having been tricked, she had come to accept what had happened, to *se conformar* (adjust) to her and her daughter's fate. Marcela was most certainly better off where she was now. Later Maria withdrew into the little back room where the members of the family slept crisscrossed in hammocks of various sizes and colors, and she emerged with a small plastic basket that contained all her daughter's earthly possessions: a couple of tattered cotton shifts, her chewed-up pacifier on its string, a pair of plastic flip-flops, the comb, and a tiny mirror. "Marcela was so vain, so proud of her blond hair and fair skin," her mother said wistfully, "and look what happened to us because of it." Maria's oldest daughter picked up the objects and turned them over. There were tears glistening in the corners of her eyes. "Does she miss her little sister often?" I asked. "Don't mind her," Dona Maria replied, pushing the girl away roughly. "She's only crying for herself, that it was her bad fortune *not* to have been stolen!"

"But do you still miss your little girl?"

"I don't think of her too often now. But when I go into her things, it makes me sad. I feel so bad to see the little bit that she left behind, and I think to myself, 'Why don't you just throw the things out? Even if by some miracle she would walk through that door, she could never use them anymore.' When Manoel catches me looking at her things, he starts up again, arguing about my stupidity. But now I yell back at him: 'What are you saying? Do you want Marcela back here amid all this want, all this abuse and maltreatment? Let her escape! What can we do with another child when we already have too many? Don't cry for her. *We* are the ones to be pitied, the ones who were left behind.'" Later Maria added that sometimes when she was alone, she could get really wound up and she would curse the American who changed her life, saying, "Damn that rich woman! Why doesn't she come back and get the rest of us as well!"

Each year close to fifteen hundred children leave Brazil legally to live with adoptive parents in Europe (especially Italy, Scandinavia, and Germany), the United States, and Israel. But if one counts the more clandestine traffic that relies on the falsification of documents and political and bureaucratic corruption at the local, state, national, and international levels, the number of children leaving Brazil has been estimated at three thousand per year, or about fifty children per week. The clandestine and black markets work through murky channels by relying especially on employers and *patroas* to put pressure on female workers and to exploit the ignorance of poor, rural women, like Maria, whose children are living in a state of real poverty and neglect. On what grounds could Maria defend herself? She was afraid of the police and received no sympathy from her *patroa,* who dismissed her complaint by saying, "You already killed two of your children by neglect; did you want to finish off your pretty little blonde as well?"

Child protection, such as there is on the Alto do Cruzeiro, often takes the form of child theft. And even where a radical intervention may be justified to save a child's life, the unpredictable form it takes attacks women at the core of their fragile existence and increases their feelings of hopelessness and powerlessness. The bad widow Maria José came within a hair's breadth of losing her youngest child, a fair-haired and rosy-cheeked little cherub. Although the little tyke was generally filthy and often left to play with stray goats and in the rubbish pile behind the unfinished mud lean-to where the family lived, he was healthy enough and better fed than many Alto toddlers. He was also better cared for than his lice-infested older sister and scarecrow-skinny brother. The brunt of scarcity falls in disequal proportions on children in any given Alto household, and this one was no exception.

The Franciscan sister, Irmã Juliana, made a visit to the young widow only to find her smoke-filled hovel empty, save for a couple of pigs rooting about in a pile of dirty rags near the twig fire. Fearing a possible fire hazard, Juliana kicked the pile of rags away from the flames only to have them respond with a howl. When she realized that inside the bundle was a little boy covered with dirt and feces, the nun scooped him up and was about to leave with him when his older sister arrived home and begged Juliana not to take her baby brother away, for her mother would surely "kill" her for having left him unattended. Juliana relented when the girl promised to wash the baby and take better care of him. When the nun returned the next day, she argued with Maria José to give her child to a Franciscan home for abandoned children in a nearby town. The widow adamantly refused; threats followed. Sister Juliana vowed she would do nothing more for the widow, not help her with weekly food baskets or with bricks and cement to construct a proper home. The widow replied angrily, "I may be a poor and miserable cur, but I am not so depraved as to trade my beautiful baby for a basket of food and a roof over my head."

Stories like these circulate wildly among the *moradores* of the Alto, who take from them the lesson that they are powerless before the big people of Bom Jesus, who can dispose of them and their children as they wish. True, the women of the Alto agreed, Maria José was not a particularly doting mother, but it was "wrong" of the nun to force the widow to choose between food and a house *or* her child.

Nonetheless, each year many thousands of children change parents in Brazil. Some of this "circulation of children" is traditional and voluntary, as in the pattern of the informal fosterage of *filhos de criação* discussed in chapter 3. Some of it is formal and bureaucratized, but much of the exchange, as we have seen, remains coerced, illegal, and covert. One of the reasons that *moradores* so fear the asylums of FEBEM is that these institutions also serve as intermediaries in the domestic adoption process, transferring poor and "abandoned" children from their neglectful birth mothers to adoptive mothers elsewhere in the country (see Fonseca 1987:22). Meanwhile, temporary and informal fosterage is problematic because of the ease with which any middle-class woman can go to a civil registry office and *limpar a certidão*—that is, be issued a new birth certificate with her own name listed as the child's natural parent.

One young Alto mother told of the unfortunate day when, on her way to the post office, she stopped at the front gates of a big house in town to ask for a cup of water for herself and her one-year-old daughter. The *dona da casa* requested that the child be brought inside for a few moments. The cup of water was brought out to the thirsty woman, but her baby was not. The mother cried out in protest, but the wooden door and the gates were slammed in her face. The woman was told to leave or the police would be called. Before the week was out the mistress of the big house had registered the child in her own name. The wealthy woman had taken advantage of a Brazilian law that allows for the transfer of legal rights in a child from its birth mother to another woman at the *latter's* request (see Código Civil 1916; Lei 4655, 1965; Código de Menores 1979). Local courts in Brazil favor the rights of the middle class to adopt, almost at will, the needy and often neglected children of the poor.

And so these incidents feed bizarre rumors, such as the organ theft stories, and the rumors feed a culture of fear and suspicion in which ambiguity contributes to the experience of uncertainty and powerlessness, which then present themselves as a kind of "fatalism" and despair. The privileging of rumor over reality, of the fear of what can happen over the reality of what has already come to pass, may be seen as a kind of collective delirium. Or by way of another analogy, it is not difficult to drive people crazy by telling them that their fears or beliefs are groundless or that they are "paranoid" when, in fact, everyone is actually talking about them behind their backs. The elements of reproductive trafficking in poor women and children that I describe here contain, as Janice Raymond recently put it, "all the worst elements of human rights violations" (1989:245). This trafficking involves the barter and sale of human beings, coercion, and the uprooting of children from their homes and sometimes from their cultures and countries of origin. Finally, we cannot eliminate the suspicion, kept alive in the form of a strange and outrageous rumor that refuses to die, that within the clandestine international black market in babies, there are some violations resulting, more often than we may know, in the medical abuse or death of such children.

Everyday Violence: Hospital Clinics

The body and organ theft rumors also have their basis in poor people's mundane encounters with a clinical and medical reality that does view and treat their bodies and body parts and those of their children as "dispensable." When Seu Antônio, a rural cane cutter from the Alto do Cruzeiro, appeared in a local clinic following a series of small strokes that left his eye damaged and his vision impaired, the clinic doctor said, without even bothering to examine the afflicted eye, "Well, it's not worth anything; let's just have it removed." While the wealthy indulge themselves in the very latest medical technologies—plastic surgery and body sculpting are now almost routine among the middle-aged and middle class in this region—the frequent accident victims among the cane cutters and mill workers on the plantations return home from the hospital with grotesque scars and badly set bones that leave them permanently disfigured or disabled.

Seu João Gallo was one of the young leaders of the shantytown association in the 1960s. He was spirited and lively, known as a particularly good dancer of the *Nordestino forró*, a sexy version of the two-step. Often in those days João would try to teach me to dance after UPAC meetings, and I would stumble along to everyone's amusement except my own. My feet and hips simply would not move to the complicated and smooth steps he so effortlessly made. "Is that you, João, truly?" I asked the defeated-looking man with deep furrows cut into his brow. He was seated uncomfortably on a chair outside his hut set into a niche of the Alto that looked out over the *mata*. He greeted me with the taunt that perhaps I was now altogether "too grand" a person to recognize an old beau who today was a "cripple." His story was a not uncommon one. While away working in São Paulo on a road construction gang, he'd been knocked down by a car that came speeding out of nowhere. He never knew what hit him. As a temporary worker without proper documents, he had been treated as a "charity" patient in the general hospital, which explained the ugly and botched repair work on his leg that left it both useless and ugly. Not even minimal cosmetic surgery had been attempted to hide the brutal effects of the trauma, although Brazilian plastic surgeons practicing in Rio de Janeiro and São Paulo are considered among the finest in the world.

The frequency of sudden and violent death in this vulnerable population leads to a confusion between killing and dying so that the people of the Alto speak routinely of relatives "killed" by pharmacists who prescribed, knowingly or not, the wrong medication or by surgeons in Recife whose steady hands slipped fatally during the course of otherwise routine operations. It is hardly surprising, then, that one encounters among the poor a nagging and persistent anxiety about what can happen to their bodies, anonymous enough in Bom Jesus, once they leave the *município*. No one from the Alto travels beyond Bom Jesus, especially not to the capital city of Recife, without his proper identification papers. There are too many stories of *companheiros* and family members who were transported to Recife for medical treatments and then were "lost" in the web of exchanges of charity patients among public, private, and teaching hospitals. On several occasions I was recruited in the search for a "missing person," a hospitalized patient who had gotten lost, as people say, "in the bureaucracy" and discovered that it was next to impossible to trace "anonymous" bodies attached to "generic" interior names such as José or Maria da Silva.

I think of Nilda Gomes, who in 1982 suddenly found herself mother to four grandchildren after their mother "disappeared" into a hospital in Recife. "And now these poor children are orphans," sighed Nilda as the two youngest ones put their heads in their grandmother's lap and cried pitifully. In her desperation Nilda had "arranged" some money from the *prefeito* to cover her bus fare into Recife, where she went to find her missing daughter or at least, she said, to find out what had been done with her body. ("I am afraid they gave her up to the medical students. She was burned all over her body from the house fire, and she would certainly be a great curiosity to them," Nilda commented sadly.) But when she arrived at the Hospital das Clínicas in Recife, the old woman was made to wait many hours. Finally Nilda was told that there was no record of her daughter ever having been registered at the hospital. "Liars!" Nilda accused the nurses. "Murderers!" And for her troubles she was physically pushed out into the street.

"It's always like that with the poor," said Nilda somewhat philosophically. "Our lives and our deaths are very cheap. The nurses and doctors look at us and they say, 'Well, what does it matter, one more or one less?' And when we arrive in the city in our ugly clothes without knowing how to speak properly or how to behave, they make us wait and tell us nothing. It's for this reason that we are so afraid of hospitals and why we fight with the *prefeito* to let us travel in the ambulance with our family members."

Maria Luiza, the "good widow," would most certainly have agreed. Maria's husband, Cosmos, was a popular handyman on the Alto. When a badly infected sore on his leg failed to heal ("It was so deep," Maria said, "that you could see to his bones"), Cosmos went to the local hospital, where Dr. Francisco gave him a half dozen ill-advised injections, one each week. "But he didn't get any better," the patient little woman said without a trace of rancor. "Cosmos would scream at night with the pain so it would freeze your blood." Finally, they took Cosmos by ambulance to the Hospital das Clínicas in Recife, but he was rejected by admitting staff that did not want to take responsibility for a man who was so close to death. Later, Cosmos was taken to the Hospital de Restauração, where his leg was amputated. Nonetheless, a few days later Maria received an order from the hospital to get her husband's body if she did not want him sent to the Medical-Legal Institute, the ML, as people called the public morgue in Recife. The *prefeito* refused to send the municipal ambulance. "You are entitled to only *one* trip," Seu Félix scolded the widow, "and the municipal ambulance is not a hearse"—a phrase I was to hear on several occasions.

"Cosmos died screaming and banging his head," Maria Luiza continued. At least, that is what a nurse offered her for consolation when she arrived at the hospital in a battered, rural taxi cab with a recalcitrant taxi driver who did not want to carry a "stiff" back into the interior. "But I was firm," the widow concluded. "I told him that a deal was a deal and that he had already agreed to the fare in Bom Jesus." "But you didn't tell me about *him*," the driver muttered. "And if I had," replied the stoic little woman, "would you ever have agreed to take me?"

Because the poor believe that those who arrive deathly ill to public hospitals, without medical insurance, official documents, or without family members to identify and protect them, often become fodder for medical experimentation and organ theft, it is hardly surprising that so many *moradores* resist hospitalization altogether. Above all, the poor fear dying in the charity wards of urban public hospitals where their remains may be "donated" to medical students as a way of canceling their unpaid medical debts. "Little people like ourselves," Little Irene cautioned, "can have *anything* done to them." Stories like the following one, told by a washerwoman from Recife, confirm some of those suspicions.

"When I was working in Recife," she began, "I became the lover of a man who had a huge, ugly ulcer on his leg. I felt sorry for him, and so I would go to his house and wash his clothes for him, and he would visit my house from time to time. We were going along like this as lovers for several years when all of a sudden and without warning, he died. The city sent for his body. I decided to follow him to make sure that his body wouldn't be lost. He didn't have a single document, so I was going to serve as his witness and as his identification papers. But by the time I got to the public morgue, they had already sent his body to the medical school for the students to practice on. So I followed him there, and what I saw happening at the school I could not allow. They had his body hung up, and they were already cutting off little pieces of him. I demanded the body back, and after a lot of arguing they let me take it home with me. It's true, he was only a beggar, a *tirador de esmolas*,

who sometimes did magic tricks on the bridge in Recife to amuse people. But I was the one who washed his clothes and took care of his wound, and so you could say that I was the owner of his body."

And when Biu's little girl, Mercea, who had been sick for a very long time, finally died in late February 1988 just as they arrived at the emergency room of the hospital, Biu and her half-sister Antonieta wisked the child's body away despite the protest of the clinic staff. They buried Mercea hurriedly that same day, as is customary. I accompanied Biu to the *cartório civil*, where she and Antonieta registered the child as having died at home unattended that morning. I was asked to sign as a "witness." I did so but later asked for an explanation. "We were afraid of the state," Antonieta said simply. "We didn't want an autopsy or Mercea's body tampered with. She is *our* child, and we are the *donas* of her body."

But Mercea, like most of the more than three hundred children who die in Bom Jesus each year, was buried in an unmarked grave, although in her own little coffin purchased on credit. In less than six months her grave was cleared to make room for another "little angel," and her remains were tossed in the deep well that is called the "bone depository" (*depósito de ossos*). And so Mercea's older sister, Xoxa (who was away working on a plantation at the time of her baby sister's death), could not on her return home locate the little grave. This made it difficult for Xoxa to offer her sister the pretty white stockings that Mercea told Xoxa in a dream that she wanted. "Your vision was a true one," Biu told her eldest daughter. "In our rush to bury Mercea we had to put her into the ground barefoot."

Everyday Violence:
The Social World of the Cemetery

Alas, poor Yorick!

William Shakespeare, *Hamlet*, Act V, Scene I

Nenhum dos mortos daqui	None of the dead from here
vem vestido de caixão.	are carried in a coffin. They
Portanto eles não se enterram	are not so much buried as
são derramados no chão.	dumped into the ground.

Cemitérios Pernambucanos (cited in de Castro 1966:vi)

While going throughout the death registry books in the *cartório civil* in Bom Jesus, I came across the following handwritten entry. There were many others just like it. It encapsulated something about the violence of hunger, exclusion, and marginality in this community:

Died: September 18, 1985, Luíza Alvez da Conceição, female, brown, aged thirty-three, unmarried

Cause of Death: Dehydration, acute malnutrition
Observations: The deceased left behind no living children and no possessions. She was illiterate. She did not vote.

I was later able to determine that she died in the municipal hospital, that she was carried to the graveyard in a borrowed coffin, and that she was put in her shallow grave wrapped only in a worn hospital sheet. Within the year her remains, too, would be exhumed, and she, too, would be permanently disappeared.

Nowhere, perhaps, is the anonymity and disposability of their bodies and their lives made more explicitly clear to the peasant-workers of Bom Jesus than in the symbolic violence directed to their remains in the municipal cemetery, a social space that in microcosm reproduces the social and political structure of the community. The bodies of their loved ones accumulate in unmarked graves and in the municipal graveyard's bone depository, while the wealthy and middle classes build family vaults and elaborate marble tombstones that are privately owned, permanent, and inviolate, even when fallen out of use for many generations.

"It's bad enough for the poor who die in the hospital," said Seu Jaime, a hospital orderly and servant. "Their families have to come and pick them up and wake them at home. But those who are hurt on the highways or on the plantations and are brought here without any documents, *coitados,* they are just thrown outside on the stones in the back of the hospital. After a few days the *prefeito*'s men come with the *bandeja* [a tin-lined coffin that is returned to the *prefeitura*] and take the body to the cemetery. They won't even have a grave. Those who are too poor to buy their own plot, and all the 'unknowns' are put together in the same place. Their bones are all mixed together." Lordes interrupted Jaime to ask anxiously, "Do you think that Jesus will be able to sort all of them out on the day of the Last Judgment?"

Although the bodies of the poor have, as Thomas Laqueur (1983:109) noted, always been treated with less care and buried with less splendor than the bodies of the rich, it is only in fairly recent times—if Laqueur is correct, between 1750 and 1850—that the idea of a proper and well-appointed burial came to signify the sum total of a person's social worth (see also Aries 1974; Urbain 1978; Rodrigues 1983). With the advent of bourgeois society and values, death—rather than the great "equalizer" of men and women—became the ultimate discriminator. Eventually, the social distinctions that separated the living were brought to bear on the architecture and geography concerning the disposal of the dead.

The social history of the Brazilian funeral begins in the colonial plantation *casas grandes* of the Northeast with the extravagant displays of splendor with which the feudal patriarchs and their family members were put to rest. The masters and mistresses of the great estates were buried in "silks, religious robes, decorations, medals, jewels; the babies all painted with rouge, clusters of blond hair, angel's wings; the virgins dressed in white, a garland of orange flowers and sky-blue ribbons" (Freyre 1986a:440). Their remains were placed in family vaults in private chapels, with their portraits kept in glass cases in the sanctuary among the images of Christ and the saints. Votive lamps and fresh-cut flowers were offered to both. A dead woman's braids or an infant's curls might be preserved in the chapel as if they were holy relics. Freyre interpreted these practices as a cult of the dead that put him in mind of the ancient Greeks and Romans. Of course, for the plantation slaves there were no elaborate funerals, and *their* bodies were simply wrapped in palm leaf mats and buried in the space reserved for slaves in the small graveyard outside the chapel.

By the mid-nineteenth century the competing domains of *casa* and *rua,* the world of the traditional rural aristocracy and of the modern town, came into direct conflict over the treatment and disposal of the dead. The traditional elite of the feudal *casa grande* began to lose out to the new, liberal, progressive bourgeoisie of the town, which sought to "modernize" and "rationalize" all aspects of social life, including burial customs. This new class drew for support on the rhetoric of medicine and public hygiene. The traditional customs of burying the elite in partly opened vaults and catacombs in family chapels or churchyards and the disposal of the urban poor in pauper trenches were both condemned as unsanitary. "How long can the dead continue to enjoy the unhappy perogative of poisoning the lives of living persons?" asked Jose Martins da Cruz Joabim rhetorically on the occasion of the installation of the Medical Society of Rio in 1830 (cited in Freyre 1986a:439). At about this time the first cemeteries for slaves, paupers, and heretics were founded by the Misericórdia, but a public health report prepared by the Medical Society of Rio de Janeiro (1832) considered these charitable ventures to constitute a veritable public health hazard. The corpses "were thrown in heaps in a huge trench . . . barely covered over with earth, the layers of earth being poorly pressed down . . . so that the bones would come out with the ligaments and membranes still clinging to them" (cited in Freyre 1986a:441, n. 92).

Eventually, even the remains of the elite that were once preserved as precious family relics came to be viewed as dangerous sources of contamination through the emissions of foul airs and gasses called "miasmas" that were believed to cause sickness when inhaled. And so new municipal codes were passed that regulated the disposal of the dead, introducing death certificates, mandating the construction of walled public cemeteries, and in general transferring power and control from religious to secular authorities. Every *município* was ordered to construct a public cemetery enclosed by high, white walls at the outskirts of town (see Rodrigues 1983).

These new cemeteries were truly "public," and *all* citizens—including heretics, paupers, and unbaptized babies—were to be buried there under law. Forced to rub shoulders with the public, the wealthy and middle classes sought to distinguish their resting places from those of the common lot. Those who could afford to do so purchased private spaces within the public cemetery for the construction of elaborate family catacombs reminiscent of the plantation mausoleums. Those who could not afford either a catacomb or a modest individual grave were buried at the expense and at the mercy of the *município*. In this way the cemetery became the final arbiter of one's individual, family, and social identity.

The Good Death: "Six Feet Under and a Coffin"

Essa cova em que estás com palmos medida é a conta menor que tiraste em vida	This grave you lie in, measured by hand, represents the small space you occupied in life
É de bom tamanho nem large, nem fundo, é a parte que te cabe deste latifúndio.	But it's a good-sized grave, neither wide nor deep. It's all you'll ever get from this plantation
É uma cova grande para tua carne pouca mas a terra dada não se abre a boca.	It's a large enough grave for your small bit of flesh. When it's a pauper's grave, you can't complain.

João Cabral de Melo Neto, "Morte e Vida da Severina" (as recited by Dona Amor, Bom Jesus da Mata)

And so the cemetery became a mirror world, a symbolic representation of the social world that the dead had presumably left behind. And the image of the handsome burial (*o bom enterro*) came to play on the popular consciousness against the abhorrent image of the "ugly" or mean burial, the *enterro dos pobres*, the "poor people's funeral." "It is to die," said Dona Amor, her voice quivering with emotion, "*no pior desprezo do mundo*, in the greatest contempt in the world."

The good burial was equated in the popular mind with the idea of the "happy death," one that liberated the soul from its wretched sufferings on earth. No matter how mean or miserable the conditions of one's earthly existence, the "good" Catholic who lived and died in the state of grace was

guaranteed a "good death" and an eventual reunion with Jesus, Mary, and the saints. But even the best Catholics might die with some debts to be squared with the Almighty, requiring a period of "detention" in purgatory. All the more important, then, to be served a "decent" burial in a well-marked grave where loved ones could light a candle and offer a prayer to help liberate the soul from purgatory. But the proper burial also had its social referents as well, and to "go into the hole without a coffin" represented the worst kind of social stigma: "Abandoned in life, abandoned in death," again noted Dona Amor.

But before the people of the Alto had come to live in the *rua*, they lived and died in the *mata* and were usually buried there as well. Dona Xiquinha, a local "praying woman" (i.e., an older woman who cures minor ailments by prayer) who also prepares the dead for burial, explained how it was when she was a little girl living on an *engenho*.

"In the old days, the dead were put back into their *redes* [hammocks] when they died. In those days it took only two people to carry a man to his grave: one took hold of the cords in front, and one took the cords at the other end. For an adult the *rede* was closed, the sides were thrown together, but if it was a *moça* or a *moço* [i.e., virgin, male or female, young *or* old, as in the case of some elderly women], the *rede* would be open because they had no sins to hide.[4] Babies always had open *redes*, of course, and their eyes were left open because soon they would be able to see God. Those who could would put their loved ones *no chão* [into the ground] wrapped up in their *redes*. But if the need was great, the body would have to go into the ground wrapped only in a sheet, and the *rede* would go back to the family, poor things."

The rural people of the *zona da mata* always struggled to assure for themselves and their loved ones a decent burial, and eventually this came to mean, in the words of Zé de Souza, a founding member of the Peasant Leagues, "six feet under and a coffin of one's own" (de Castro 1969:7). This slogan became the rallying cry of the Peasant Leagues, which adopted as one of their first projects a rural mobilization around the burial needs of the dead: land rights for the dead, rather than for the living. "Before the leagues," Zé de Souza explained, "when one of us died the coffin was lent by the *município*, and after the body had been carried to the common grave, the coffin went back to the municipal warehouse." He continued, "Today the [Peasant] League pays for the funeral, and the coffin is buried with the dead. That's what the League did for us, *meu filho*" (cited in de Castro 1969:12).

In fact, funeral societies have been common in Northeast Brazil throughout this century. They were formed in rural communities so that people might avoid the humiliation of a poor people's burial. The horror of the pauper's funeral in which the coffin stopped at the mouth of the grave remained strong among the people of the Alto. The travesty of the poor people's burial was the supreme humiliation, a mortification that seemed to the peasants to carry over into eternity.

One of the reasons for the relative popularity of Seu Félix, an otherwise much criticized mayor, was his inauguration of the municipal coffin factory and coffin distribution program in the 1960s, which local radicals had satirized as "a baby for every hovel and a coffin for every baby." Until that time, however, there was only the despised *bate-queixo*, the unadorned and unlined (hence, "chin-knocker" or "jaw-breaker") borrowed municipal coffin, or a more elaborate charity coffin donated by some local benefactor. Dona Clarice recalled the latter custom well: "When I was a girl there were always a few rich patrons in Bom Jesus who would request in their wills that they be buried like paupers in the ground and that their own coffins be left at the cemetery and loaned out to those poor souls who had no one to bury them. It was a blessing for the poor to be carried to the cemetery in grand style, but it was still shameful to have to dump the body in the ground without its coffin. Today, thanks to our 'godfather,' Seu Félix, we all go into the ground, each with his own, proper box. Only babies are sometimes buried without a coffin because their parents think that a coffin is wasteful for a little angel."

Anxiety about a "good burial" was keen enough to appear as a common theme in Alto children's drawings as well as in their TAT stories. When ten-year-old Giomar was asked to draw a panoramic scene of Bom Jesus, he sketched the three shantytown hills that encircle the town, but he neglected to draw the "downtown" of Bom Jesus. Instead, he drew the municipal graveyard located on the outskirts of town. Similarly, in his response to card 13MF (the picture of a man turning away from a partly nude woman in bed), Giomar told this story: "This man in crying because 'his woman' just died. He's worried about a lot of things. He is wondering if he can find enough money to bury her good."

I wondered how so young a boy had come to be so preoccupied with death and burial. It did not take very much probing to learn that Giomar's father had been shot by nameless people as they were breaking into his mother's house one night. The *município* had sent for the body, and it was buried in a "charity" coffin. "But in a pretty spot under a mango tree," Giomar assured me, fiercely wiping the tears from his dirt-stained face. Later that day Giomar and I went to visit his father's grave, but when we got there we could not locate the place where he had been buried. "They even took the *mangueira* away," said Giomar angrily. On our way home Giomar "slipped" me to scale the wall of a private, enclosed garden. He refused to respond to my calls. He was "picking mangoes," he told me. I made the Brazilian gesture

Dona Amor: "If our sweet Savior could come into this world resting in hay, my sweet mother can leave this world in a pauper coffin lined with paper."

for washing my hands of the matter and went home thinking about the boy's anger in the cemetery.

Laqueur wrote that in nineteenth-century England "the pauper funeral had become perhaps the dominant representation of vulnerability, of the possibility of falling irrevocably from the grace of society. . . . It was an image which worked on the poor . . . who would sell their beds out from under them sooner than have parish funerals" (1983:125). Indeed, much the same could be said of the *moradores* of the Alto. Black Irene, for example, admitted that the only thing capable of forcing her back into domestic service for her bad boss, Dona Carminha, was her even greater fear of dying a pauper. "Even a bad and abusive boss," said Irene, "must still, in the end, act like a mother and bury her miserable child. Yes, I would go back to my *patroa* and die with her if there was no other solution in the end."

But it was Dona Amor, herself nearing ninety years, who perhaps had the most to say on the subject of the good burial, and she took up the better part of a long rainy afternoon in 1988 to record for me, in her grand oratorical style, the story of the death and burial of her mother. What follows is a much reduced and edited transcription of that narrative.

"My mother, may Jesus and His angels embrace her, lost a bunch of children. Only a few of us survived. We suffered a lot in growing up, until everyone left and there was only me working to keep my mother housed and fed in her old age. We went on and on like this until finally one day, I walked out of the house and I prayed, 'My Heavenly Father, excuse the weakness of my flesh for saying this to You—if I sin it is only because of the misery I am living in—but if I have to live only to see my old mother slowly die of hunger, I would prefer her to die now. The future is in Your hands. You have the power. Do with me whatever it is I deserve, for I am a miserable sinner.' I cried some more, and I said, 'Take her or take me; take her or me. It's in Your hands. But as a matter of fact, if You take her, it would actually be a little bit better for me because I am still strong and I can work for a living. She, poor thing, can no longer live without me.'

"Well, it turned out that it was only a week before my mother suffered the terrible fall that was to claim her life. . . . She called me to her side and said, 'My love, I am not going to escape death this time, so don't forget about the little brass box where I have hidden away the money for my funeral.' She wanted me to go and order her coffin and her *mortalha* [burial clothes and coffin decorations]. 'My God,' I thought, 'what will I do now?' You see, my little saint, I had to spend a long time nursing Mama after the fall, and during that time I could not work. So from time to time I had to take out a few notes and coins from the brass box. I took out only what was needed, not a penny more. I could recognize the value of the bills from their colors. After all, was I going to let her and me die of hunger, *querida,* knowing all along that there was money set aside?

"I was always a long-suffering woman, and all the suffering I accepted with goodwill as sent by God. It often fell to me to take care of sick people on the Alto, not only my mother but anyone who needed a prayer recited or a sponge bath. All these things I did with pleasure and satisfaction. But I have to confess, I *did* take that money without telling my mother.

"When mother's end grew near, my brothers and sisters came home from the *mata* to be with her. While I was out she told them, 'It gives me some satisfaction to know that the money for my burial is carefully put away. Before I die I would like to see my coffin.' When I came home my sisters asked me, 'Where is mama's money for her funeral?' 'Well, let's get it down and see,' I said. When we opened the box there were only three or four mil reis [worth about $2]. My sisters accused me of hiding the money to keep for myself after mother died. Then I explained what had happened, but they refused to believe me.

"I felt very bad after this, and I walked the streets all that afternoon. When I came home my mother was very, very weak. I said to her, 'Mama, I am not going to be seeing you very much any more.' And we both cried. And all I could think of was that my mother would die without anything put aside for her burial. But I lied to her: 'Don't worry, Mãe. I will go down into the street and order your funeral things.' 'That's a good girl,' she said. My mother was a simple person. It never would have entered her head that I could have spent the money from her special brass box.

"I went to my old boss's house. 'What is it?' he said. 'Has your mother died?' "

" 'Not yet,' I said, 'but she is at the portals of death, and I'm here to borrow the money I need so I can arrange her funeral.'

" 'I don't have any money here,' he said. Imagine that! And he was the manager of a big bank! But he said, 'Just take this check, and with it you can buy what you need.' Well, *minha santa,* ignorant race that I am, did I understand anything about bank checks? I thought my patron was tricking me, and so I took the check from him, but outside I tore it up and threw it away. Before I left the house of my patron, his wife said to me, 'Now run off quickly to the coffin shop, and pick out everything that you need.' But I thought to myself, 'How could I ever do that with my mother still alive in her bed? God deliver me!'

"On the way home I was full of agony. What was going to happen to me after my mother died? Who would be left to worry about how *I* went into the ground? I thought of my unmarried cousin who died a pauper *no pior desprezo no mundo,* in the worst kind of neglect and disregard. How much worse off was myself, who had nothing and no one left in the world!

"Finally the night arrived when my mother died in my arms, just like a little baby. She didn't weigh very much anymore. When the end finally came, I was calm. God finally brought some peace into my heart, and I decided that I would make the best of it. So I made up a good fire of twigs, and I sent a neighbor's child to borrow a plastic pan. Imagine! I had to wash my mother with a borrowed basin. Excuse me for telling you, but I washed every part of her body. I washed her good and with nice hot water. I straightened her up and warmed up her feet, and I combed her hair. I even put a little cologne on her head. I took out her own best clothes, which I had washed, mended, and ironed, and I dressed her up. Then I wrapped her up nice and tight in her covers. I did everything without the help of a single person.

"I left her in the bed, and I went to look for someone to help me move her out into the front room. As my luck would have it, there was a gravedigger's apprentice who was passing along the street. 'Hey, hey,' a neighbor called to him. 'Go inside that house because Amor's mother has died and she needs help bringing her bed into the front room.'

"The boy thought that my neighbor was making fun of him because he worked at the cemetery, and so he came into the house full of jokes. Well, he was plenty surprised to see my mother lying there all right! But he was a good boy, and he helped me move her, and he sat up with me until very late that night.

"I was waiting for the coffin to arrive. I had sent for one from the old folks home run by the *Vicentinos*. It was very late by the time the assistant came carrying the coffin on his head up the hill. And the shameless boy greeted me saying, 'Come and look at the piece of crap the *Vicentinos* have sent you!'

"*Porcaria*, nothing!" I replied. He was talking about *my mother's* coffin, and I told him that anything the *Vicentinos* sent us was good. But he insisted that it was a piece of rubbish because it was a charity coffin, decorated with paper and not with fabric and ribbons.

" 'Mother's coffin has nothing wrong with it,' I said. 'It is just the way she wanted it to be. Didn't she tell me before she died that she wanted to be buried the same as my own father had? And his coffin was just like this one. So I am content. If our sweet Savior could come into this world in a manger lined with hay, then my mother can surely leave this world in a coffin lined with paper!'

"The boy said, 'Well, is she going to be buried in her old tattered clothes, then?' At this I began to *me endoidar* [go mad]. 'No,' I thought to myself, 'I *can't* put her into the ground with her old, patched clothes.' So I told him to wait, that the *mortalha* was coming. I ran to my sister-in-law and I said, 'Hey, there, do you have five mil reis to loan me until tomorrow?' 'I have,' she said. 'Well, give it to me then so that I can bury my mother properly.' With the money in my hand I ran to a woman who cut out the cloth to put in the coffin, and she quickly sewed some new clothes for my mother. She even came and helped me dress her in the coffin.

"Finally, everything was just right. But my brothers and sisters said that I had fooled everyone and that I still had my mother's funeral money hidden away. Poor things! Poor things! God above forgive them! God Almighty save them! For I am the victor! I am still walking around on this earth, and long ago they have left it!"

I did not ask Amor how she would be buried or whether she had a nest egg with her funeral money squirreled away. But I do know that Amor, like the other *moradores* of the Alto do Cruzeiro, does not remember the dead—not even her own mother—by visiting the local cemetery. There is no point in doing so, not even on November 2, All Souls' Day, the universal Day of the Dead in Latin America. The local cemetery, like Potter's Field in New York City, is a place to be avoided. It stands as a forceful reminder of the fragile *inexistência* of the poor, their socially constituted being and nothingness.

Pauper Funerals, Misplaced Bodies, and the State

Today in the small, compact, walled enclosure of the municipal cemetery of Bom Jesus, the conflicting social realities of *casa, rua,* and *mata*—the colliding worlds of the feudal *casa grande*, of the "streets" of the modern town, and of the peasant countryside—and their accompanying definitions of person, individual, and anonymous nonentity are graphically reproduced. In the municipal cemetery of Bom Jesus one is immediately struck by its density. At the entrance is the *vila nobre*, as Casorte refers to the aristocratic section of the graveyard with its huge, white stone mausoleums, family homes that are miniature reproductions of the plantation society's *casas grandes*. Here the coffins rest on cement benches *above* ground, the preferred form of burial in Bom Jesus, as throughout Brazil.

People in Bom Jesus have a marked fear, as they say, of "going into dirt" or "going into a hole" and being eaten by bugs, and so they prefer above-ground entombment. They also fear being buried alive. These fears are shared with the people of the Alto. Dona Xiquinha, the elderly praying woman of the Alto who prepared bodies for burial, offers, "Those who can afford to, have their own catacombs. Nobody wants to go into the hole, into the dirt, to be eaten by insects. But the poor, *coitados*, they have no choice." On the fear of being buried alive Xiquinha had this to say: "We became afraid after the time of the cholera, the sickness that took so many people there were hardly any living left. They buried so many and so quickly that they even buried some people who were still alive. So for this reason we like to leave the coffin unnailed, and we want to have a *velório* [wake] for one night. It is prohibited to bury a person on the same day he dies, but infants can go into the ground right away."

Some of the mausoleums are constructed to look like family chapels complete with altar and votive lamp. With the passage of time the disintegrated remains are swept into an urn or pottery container and placed to the side, making room for a new occupant. The family remains are treated collectively but are never removed from the family vault. They are the property of the family. With the transformation of rural society and the consolidation of family plantations into large industrial sugar mills and refining factories, many of the original big families of the sugar estates have left the *município*, and their family vaults have fallen into a state of disuse and disrepair, thereby projecting the image of aristocratic families now fallen on hard times.

Leaving the *vila nobre*, one comes on the graveyard's *rua burguesa*, a representation of the modern town with a paved street alongside of which are individual graves with personalized tombstones. At once the traditional

"Look, corn decorates the graves of *matutos*."

The Bone Depository: "They have counted my hands and feet; they have numbered all my bones."

notion of the "person" gives way to the modern notion of the "individual" freed from familistic constraints. These new marble niches are also built above ground, and some carry air vents.

Beyond the *vila nobre* and the *rua burguesa* of the cemetery lies the *mata,* the field where small mounds of earth cover the new graves of the anonymous poor, which are marked, if at all, by small white wooden crosses and decorated with stalks of corn rather than with fresh or plastic flowers. No individual or family names grace these graves. Anonymous in life, they carry their *inexistência* (as Casorte puts it) with them into the grave. Into the looking glass that is the funeral space, the poor and humble classes are destined to be unreflected.

For the poor of Bom Jesus and of the Alto do Cruzeiro, who are buried at the public's expense, their graves are not their own. Because of overcrowding, they can expect to keep their spaces only for a year for an adult, six months or less for a child. Pauper graves are shallow—two feet is common for a child—and when the site is needed again, the order is given to exhume the remains. The partly disintegrated coffin, made of plywood and cardboard, is tossed over the west walls of the cemetery, where it is burned. What remains ("hair and all"), says Casorte, making an evil face, is tossed into the deep well that is called the *depósito dos ossos.*

The rapidity of the transfer from shallow, individual grave to collective bone depository is understood by all as a necessary (i.e., a hygienic) evil, one

Angel graves: two feet under and a cardboard coffin.

that entails a certain violation of the bodies of the deceased. "It's not ugly," Casorte says, trying to persuade me to come closer to the bone well, to overcome my reluctance to "examine" its contents as he pulls off the stone cover to expose the multitude of the anonymous dead of Bom Jesus. "They have counted my hands and my feet"—the words of the Easter psalm returns to me—"they have numbered all my bones." My eye catches sight of cloth, and I turn away. "Socks," Casorte says, "socks last forever. It's because they're synthetic." And I think back to little Mercea and her bare feet.

"Shall I jump in?" Casorte offers teasingly. And then he pulls out a small fibula that must have belonged to a very young person. "Enough, Casorte," I say, and we return to his "office" at the back of the cemetery to go over his books to see if his burial figures matched the deaths recorded that year at the *cartório civil.* I ask Casorte how many of the 162 children buried in the cemetery in the first six months of 1989 (it was July of that year) were "bourgeois" children, falling into his preferred usage. Only two babies, he replies, were *not* buried as paupers that year. The others would all soon join the multitude of skeletal angels in the bone depository. "Is that any way to treat angels?" I ask, for we have both descended into a devilish sort of gallows humor, united by our politics and by our anger.

As we speak a middle-aged, working-class woman raps on the open door of the office. She enters apologetically, explaining that this is her fifth attempt to talk to Casorte about a "personal matter" of great importance. She asks to purchase the space where her father and husband are both buried so that no one could "mess" with their remains. She adds, "I don't want anyone to *arrancar eles* [drag them up, as though by the roots]." Casorte is gentle with the woman and asks her to fill out a form, reassuring her that her wishes can be arranged. She leaves, with relief evident on her careworn face.

As Casorte accompanies me out to the front gate of the cemetery, he offers to show me the antique *bate-queixo* or *quebra-queixo* (jawbreaker), as the old borrowed pauper coffin is called because of the way the bones rattled on its hard surface without so much as a piece of felt or cloth under the body. But just then Seu Cristavão, a local coffin maker, appears. Sweating profusely and mopping his face, he stops to lean on a tombstone. Next to him he places a tiny child's coffin that he has been carrying in the crook of his arm. The shoe-box-size coffin is decorated in a dark blue fabric, with silver paper stars glued across the top. "It looks like the American flag," quips Casorte, and then he adds, "Here's another little angel going into the pit." "But where," I asked, "was the procession of the angels?" Sometimes, Casorte explains, the mother or father will pay Seu Cristavão or another owner of a *casa funerária* to deliver the coffin for them. And once in a while a cab driver will "deliver" a baby in his or her coffin as a favor to the mother, who was, perhaps, too ill to arrange a proper funeral. "But the saddest thing of all," he says, "is to see a *matuto,* dressed in his one good suit, arrive from the country in the back of a hired cab, with the baby coffin resting on his knees." Seu Cristavão and I have crossed paths on many other occasions. "Why the *pesquisas* [research]?" the coffin maker taunts. "Just put down that they all died of hunger." I promise to quote him.

I return the following morning to complete the count of child burials for 1989. Casorte is late, and while I am waiting for him at the front gates, a municipal truck pulls up quickly, and two stocky young men jump out of the cab, slamming its doors. They immediately engage the disabled gravedigger in a mock fist fight and then ask him to run and get the *bandeja* (serving plate), a euphemism for the tin coffin that is used to pick up and deliver unidentified bodies. "This one," says the older of the two men, "is a real mess, a *morte desastrada,*" the victim of a "violent assassination." His remains had been found in the fields of an *engenho* outside of the town. He had been shot and mutilated. The body had lain unclaimed for two days in the "morgue" of the local hospital. The mayor now requested that the body, which was "already beginning to offend the hospital workers," be brought to the cemetery and kept there for another few days. If by the weekend no one showed up to claim it, the judge would give the orders for it to be buried as a *desconhecido,* an "unknown person."

"Is it possible," I ask, "that *no one* really knows who the man was?" The municipal workers look away, offering no reply. Later, Casorte explains that with assassinations like these, in which no one knows exactly what is involved, the relatives and friends are afraid to show their faces or to have anything to do with the body. "They are afraid"—and here Casorte brings the conversation to a hurried conclusion—"that they could be the next ones marked."

The Public Morgue / Bureau of Missing and Disappeared Persons

But what the *moradores* of the Alto fear most of all is the police summons to appear in Recife at the ML to identify the body of a loved one who met a violent or precipitous end. Here the bodies of the unknown, the unregistered, and the pauperized rub shoulders with the bodies of the assassinated, the murdered, and the disappeared. Of the two—the unknown and the violently killed—the latter are more stigmatized because theirs were "sudden deaths," *mortes de repente,* and by definition "bad deaths" as well. People say of them that they died alone, *sem dizer aí Jesus,* "without calling on Jesus."

As Casorte says, it takes a considerable amount of courage to appear in

the morgue of the local hospital, the holding space in the back of the municipal cemetery, or the dreaded cavernous underworld of the ML in Recife to identify and claim a lost, unknown, or disappeared body. It is not a job for the faint of heart or the weak of stomach. Among the *moradores* of the Alto do Cruzeiro it is a job for women, for wives and mothers in particular.

Elena Morena did not want to go to the ML for a second time when notified by her sister in August 1989. Elena rocked back and forth on her little stool with her arms crossed and beat her fists against her hard, small breasts. The tears rolled down her cheeks, but not a word escaped from lips pressed together so tightly they seemed to lose all their color. Two years before Elena's husband had been murdered by local policemen. "In uniform," she said. They came to Elena's door in the dead of night, dragged her husband, Sérgio, from the house, and murdered him, dumping his mutilated remains on a country road. A few days later more police officers appeared with photos, asking Elena to identify the body as it was when it was found, and they carried the collapsing, grieving woman to the morgue, where she was forced to make the identification in person. She was given no explanation for the assassination by the police, but it was widely rumored on the Alto do Cruzeiro that Sérgio was a thief.

Sérgio was, in fact, a local guard, a *vigia* chosen by the *delegacia* of Bom Jesus to police his immediate vicinity near the top of the Alto. He was murdered within a few days of having given up guard duty to work for himself. Sérgio was not the first *vigia* to die on the Rua da Cruz of the Alto in 1989. He had come into his position following the murder of the previous *vigia* during an argument with some off-duty policemen on the street at the base of the hill where pineapples were sold at Saturday *feira.* The shots could be heard halfway up the Alto.

After Elena reported the murder to the judge of Bom Jesus, demanding not justice but merely the widow's pension that had been denied her, police harassment of the family continued. Elena began to fear for the safety of Jorge, her eldest son. She urged Jorge to take up residence with her sister, who lived in a poor neighborhood in Recife. On a quiet Wednesday night, just a few days after Jorge had moved to Recife, he went to a corner stand to buy a Coke and talk with some of the local boys. Two men rushed up to him, hit him across the head, and shot him twice in the back. They left him lying in the street. Within minutes children and stray dogs formed an agitated circle around him. Jorge was dead before the ambulance arrived.

As soon as her sister sent word, Elena rushed to the city to identify and claim her son's body, which meant another descent into the hades of the ML. Elena shuddered in the telling: "It is a place, Nancí, that no human wants to enter, not even once in her life. But *two* times. . . ." Her one consolation was that her friends had taken up a collection so that Elena could get the body from the morgue and back to Bom Jesus for a proper burial, one fitting a handsome youth, the joy, she said, of her "old" age. Elena was forty-two at the time.

"And what would have happened if you hadn't the money?"

"Those who can pay for the burial get to take the body home with them. Those who can't, lose it."

"Where does it go?"

"The doctors get it, and they can take from it what they want."

"And the rest?"

"Who knows what they do with the bones? Maybe the *urubus* [vultures] get them. This is the fate of the poor, Nancí. *Nem donos do corpo deles, eles são* [They don't even own their own bodies]."

It is no coincidence that the Brazilian filmmaker Marcel Camus retold the Orpheus legend around the magical disappearance of Orpheus's beautiful lover, Euridice, during *carnaval* celebrations on a hillside shantytown, a *favela,* of Rio de Janeiro. In the 1959 masterpiece *Black Orpheus* (*Orfeu Negro*), Orfeu searches frantically for his "disappeared" lover amid the frenzied crush of Rio's streets during the four days of the festival. He is directed to the Department of Missing Persons on the thirteenth floor of a modern high-rise building. But, of course, during *carnaval* the corridors are deserted, except for a minor clerk—poor, black, and illiterate—who is sweeping up pieces of shredded and discarded paper. Confetti? Reports of missing persons?

"Is this the Missing Persons Department?" Orfeu asks anxiously.

"It is," replies the old man, "but I have never seen a missing person here." And he opens the door to an office that is stacked with papers.

"Here are your missing persons. You see? Nothing but paper. Fifteen floors of it, and all for nothing. Can you read? I can't, but you may look through them if you like. But if you ask me, you'll never find a lost person in papers. That's where they get lost forever. . . . Do you think that papers are ever sorry for a man?"

From the Missing Persons Bureau, Orfeu goes to a Xangô meeting to contact his dead lover through spirit mediums. He fails, and from there he must go to the public morgue, where, like Elena Morena, Black Irene, and many other women of the Alto do Cruzeiro who have had to face the same, he is met by a cold, unfeeling functionary who tries to dissuade Orfeu from carrying the body of his loved one away.

"You know a body is always useful for science. And if you just left it here, it would save you a lot of money."

Orfeu roughly pushes the functionary aside and kisses the cold lips of his beloved Euridice, who is lying on a stone slab among the anonymous dead still in their *carnaval* costumes, here in the underworld of Rio.

These brief, potent scenes evoke, even thirty years later, some key themes of shantytown life: the anxious, ontological insecurity of the *favelados* and their worst fears—separation, loss, disappearance, and violent, inexplicable physical assault on the body. Camus also captured the images of an indifferent bureaucracy that turns a deaf ear to the cries of the people, transforming their misery into mountains of paper that are discarded and swept away by the illiterate custodian to whom the words are meaningless.

Postscript

On the last day of the liberation theology missions in mid-August 1989, on the evening of the ritual bonfire into which effigies and images of the "social sins" of the community were thrown and burned, the Alto women whose husbands or adult sons had disappeared were called forward. Tentatively, a half dozen women made their way to the front of the makeshift altar under the still empty gaze of the crucifix of O Cruzeiro. One of the women was Black Irene, whose scream on the night that the men came to take away her eldest and favorite son, Nego De, was heard up and down the length of the Alto and all along the Rua da Cruz. It is said to reverberate there still.

But on this night Irene was silent, stunned by her own daring in coming forward to make her dangerous loss public. The simple prayers recited, an Ave Maria, a Pai Nosso, the deeds silently recorded, the people of the Alto returned to their homes, mulling these events over in their hearts.

Later that same night a little street urchin, a *moleque* known to everyone on the Alto as Pitomba (after a fruit he frequently stole and then resold in the marketplace) disappeared from the steps of the church where he normally slept. The next morning it was said that someone reported seeing his body, eviscerated and tossed outside the west wall of the cemetery, in the place where the partly disintegrated coffins of recently exhumed infants were burned. The Franciscan nuns of the chapel of Santa Lúcia, who occasionally ministered to the street children of Bom Jesus, fervently prayed that the boy's itinerant soul might be received, indeed welcomed, by his heavenly Father.

But the boy's body, like that of the missing Cristo, was never recovered, and the story remains unverified.

6. EVERYDAY VIOLENCE

1. The *papa-figos* of Brazilian folklore are the "liver-eating" monsters that are used throughout Brazil to frighten badly behaved children, especially those who refuse to go to sleep at night. Papa-Figo comes by stealth and grabs the child away to devour in secret her tasty liver. This is obviously a traditional form of the organ-stealing rumor. Freyre (1986a:339) recounted the widespread Papa-Figo story in Pernambuco told of a certain rich man who could eat nothing but children's livers. He had his black servants go out everywhere with gunny sacks to look for young, fat ones.

2. In May 1990 Anthony Zielinski (*New York Times*, July 19, 1990 [AP]), a young member of the Milwaukee County Board of Supervisors, proposed that the county government sell the organs of dead welfare recipients to private medical companies, without their prior consent, as a way of reducing the county's public burial expenses. The supervisor introduced his bill by saying, "If these people can't help society while they're alive, maybe they can help it when they're dead." Criticism from welfare rights and homeless organizations forced Zielinski to drop the proposed bill and to apologize. Nevertheless, another proposal—that welfare recipients be invited to sign forms permitting the county to donate their organs after death—is still under consideration.

3. "Until recently," wrote Emmanuel Thorne and Gilah Lagner, "it was possible to joke that the value of the body, based on its chemical constituents, was about $1.98. Now its value exceeds $200,000 and is rising. Tissue is being harvested for transplantation, research and diagnostic and therapeutic products. . . . However repugnant the idea, the body now has economic value that cannot be wished away or ignored" (1986:23).

4. See also Kligman (1988), for a fascinating discussion of virginity and death in Transylvania.

Part 8:
Death in Hindu Traditions

9

CITY OF DEATH AND LIBERATION

No other city on earth is as famous for death as is Banāras. More than for her temples and magnificent *ghāts,* more than for her silks and brocades, Banāras, the Great Cremation Ground, is known for death. At the center of the city along the riverfront is Manikarnikā, the sanctuary of death, with its ceaselessly smoking cremation pyres. The burning *ghāt* extends its influence and the sense of its presence throughout the city. Entering Banāras from the villages to the south, one sees, leaning against the walls of the shops on Lankā Street, stacks of bamboo litters for carrying the dead. Along the main roads of the suburbs or in the dense lanes of the city one suddenly hears the familiar chant of a funeral procession on its way to Manikarnikā: *"Rāma nāma satya hai! Rāma nāma satya hai!"* "God's name is Truth! God's name is Truth!"

In Kāshī, life is lived in the perpetual presence of death. One of the most popular couplets of the poet Kabīr, painted upon the walls of buildings throughout the city, reminds the passerby of death's inevitability:

Seeing the grinding stone turning, turning,
Kabīr began to weep.
Between the two stones, not a single grain is saved!

The verse is often accompanied by a vivid folk art depiction of a woman turning the simple domestic grinding stone, throwing not

grains but people into the mill, where they are sure to be crushed between the two stones. Death is as common, as certain, as the grinding of wheat once it is thrown into the mill. Rounding the corner of a narrow lane, or glancing up from a streetside market, one will see this famous couplet, next to the advertisements for the newest movie, or the slogans of the latest political campaign. The rickshaw-pullers and vegetable vendors know it by heart. Kāshī is comfortable with the fact of death.

For death in Kāshī is death transformed. As the saying goes, "Death in Kāshī is Liberation"—*Kāshyām maranam muktih.* It is dying that unleashes the greatest holy power of Kāshī, the power of bestowing liberation, *moksha* or *mukti.* Death, which elsewhere is feared, here is welcomed as a long-expected guest. Death, which elsewhere is under the terrifying jurisdiction of Yama, is free from that terror here, for Yama is not allowed within the city limits of Kāshī. Death, which elsewhere is polluting, is here holy and auspicious. Death, the most natural, unavoidable, and certain of human realities, is here the sure gate to *moksha,* the rarest, most precious, most difficult to achieve of spiritual goals

"Bound for Moksha"

Kāshī's greatest gift is the bestowing of *moksha*—the final fording of the river of *samsāra* to the far shore, beyond birth and death. Here, as the Purānas put it, "the ferryboat is set for the crossing." But the fare cannot be purchased with any of the other *purushārthas.* No amount of wealth, no accumulation of *punya,* no perfection of *dharma* can qualify one for *moksha.* Only that wisdom that completely floods one's consciousness with light will enable one to make that final crossing.

Moksha is the fourth of the *purushārthas,* but as an aim of life it constitutes a qualitative break from the others. *Kāma, artha,* and *dharma* are pursued by those who still consider this world to be their home—students, householders, even retired people. But *moksha* and the wisdom by which it is gained are pursued only by those who have "left behind" *(sannyāsa)* their worldly home. These renouncers may be seen in the streets of Banāras, dressed in faded orange garments, car-

The "*burning* ghāts" *at Manikarnikā.*

rying only a wooden staff and a coconut husk water vessel. Although they may belong to an order of *sannyāsins* and live in a *matha,* they are, strictly speaking, homeless in this world. They are called *mumukshus,* those "bound for *moksha.*"

Since the era of the Upanishadic sages and the Buddha, Banāras has been a gathering place for those who have renounced the world. They have come to the groves of the Forest of Bliss to practice asceticism, to pursue disciplines of yoga, and to strive toward wisdom. For them, Banāras is famous as the "Bestower of *Siddhi*"—the spiritual attainments, the perfections, which are the goals of those who devote themselves totally to spiritual disciplines. It is called the "Birthplace of *Siddhi.*"[1]

Jaigishavya is one of the ancient legendary yogis in the Hindu tradition, and it is well known in the Purānas that his yogic practice was brought to fulfillment in Kāshī, by the grace of Lord Shiva. His story is taken as a paradigm for the fulfillment of spiritual goals in Kāshī. It is said that when Shiva left Kāshī to dwell on Mt. Mandara, during the reign of Divodāsa, Jaigishavya established a *linga* and vowed that he would neither eat nor drink until Shiva returned. Jaigishavya sat in meditation until his limbs withered. When Shiva returned, entering the city from the north, he went immediately to Jaigishavya's place of meditation and bestowed upon this yogi a much-deserved boon:

"I give you the wisdom called *Yogashāstra,*" said Shiva, "which is the means to *nirvāna.* May you be the teacher of yoga to all yogis. O sage, rich in ascetic practice, you will know the whole secret of yogic knowledge, by my grace, and by that knowledge, you will reach *nirvāna*."[2]

Shiva pledged to dwell in the *linga* which Jaigishavya established in order to bestow *siddhi*, "fulfillment," upon all who practice yoga.

The *linga* of Jaigishavya may still be seen today. Its temple is in a small, peaceful monastic compound in the northeastern sector of the city. Here the ancient traditions of the yogi Jaigishavya continue. The *linga* in the temple is striking: an enormous, rounded stone some five feet tall.

There are many renouncers who have emulated Jaigishavya's severe ascetic practice, the most radical being those called the Aghorīs, who not only renounce the world for a life of asceticism, but turn the values of the world upside down and fasten upon the reverse side, so to speak. Their name is euphemistic, meaning "Not Terrible," but in truth they are the most terrible of all from a worldly point of view. They haunt the cremation grounds and sleep upon graves. They drink wine, sever and cure a human skull to use for collecting food, and cook their food on the embers of cremation pyres. Like Shiva, who is also known by the name Aghora, they seem deliberately to adopt the things the world scorns, following a path of spiritual tempering that ensures their liberation from the values of *dharma*. If all, indeed, is Brahman, then one must not spurn any aspect of life or death. It is no coincidence that a modern Aghorī, Bābā Bhagavān Rām, has established the most active center for the treatment of lepers in Banāras.

The goal of the renouncer, whether the ordinary yogi or the radical Aghorī, is to become "liberated-in-life," a *jivan mukta*. Such a person has transcended the tensions, the dualities, the anxieties of life and of death, even while living on "this shore." When he dies, he will make that final crossing, never to return.

Renouncers, of course, are not the only ones bound for *moksha* in Kāshī. In a sense, this city, while it is famous for its ascetics, yogis, and renouncers, constitutes a challenge to their labors, for everyone here is bound for *moksha*. We have already heard that sleep is yoga in Kāshī, and it is said that what is discovered by studying the Vedānta and all the Upanishads may be learned playfully in Kāshī, with no effort at all. The Purānic *māhātmyas* are filled with the radical juxtaposition of the hard path of the ascetics and the easy path of those who do nothing more than meet their death here in Kāshī.

Here why should a man dwell in a solitary place?
And what is the use of turning from the pleasures of sense?
And what is the use of practicing yoga or sacrificing to the gods?
For without these one gets mukti *easily in Kāshī.*[3]

Not only is living in Kāshī as good as the ardent seeking of the professional *mumukshus*, but it is a more certain path. The yogi may not reach his desired goal in this lifetime, perhaps not in many lifetimes. But the rickshaw-puller, haggling over the price of a ride, peddling through the streets all day, waiting for a few late customers at night, is following a spiritual path that leads directly to *moksha*.

People come from all over India to live in Kāshī until they die. They come for *Kāshīvāsa*—"living in Kāshī." Having come to Avimukta, they never leave. For them, this is the final stop on a pilgrimage that has lasted for many lives, through birth and death and birth again. Dying in Kāshī, they make the final crossing which ends the pilgrimage of this life, and of all lives.

Through the ages, Banāras has been colonized in its various sectors by these Kāshīvāsīs. The Madrāsīs have settled at Hanumān Ghāt, the Bengālīs in Bengālī Tolā, the Mahārāshtrians near Rāma Ghāt and Panchagangā Ghāt. Some have come here to retire. Some are widows, who are left without recourse in their old age. They have been the pillars of their family religious life for decades. They have gone barefoot on more pilgrimages, observed more fasts, sung more devotional hymns than either their husbands or their sons. And now, thin and almost invisible in their plain white *sārīs*, they are among the most pious of the Kāshīvāsīs.

In addition to the Kāshīvāsīs, there are others who have come to Kāshī at the eleventh hour. They come for what is colloquially called Kāshī Lābh—"The Benefit of Kāshī." They make it just in time. They are brought to hospices such as Kāshī Lābh Mukti Bhavan, near Godauliā crossing. Here they may die in peace, for dying a good death is as important as living a good life.

Entering the Kāshī Lābh Mukti Bhavan from the street, one passes into a garden compound where the two-story hospice building is located. There are sacred *tulsī* bushes on either side of the path, with little signs set amidst the plants saying "Rām, Rām—Remember the name of Rām." Entering the hospice, there is a *pūjā* room, with an altar and many deities. There are attendants and employees of the

The Kāshīvāsī, "bound for moksha."

hospice who take turns chanting "Hare Krishna! Hare Rāma!" throughout the day and night. And if the attendants are all busy at other duties, there is a record player which carries the sound of sacred *mantras* softly through the quiet building. Around the center courtyard are the small, bare rooms where the dying may be cared for by their families. There is no conventional medicine here, however, for the patients have come, not to recover, but to die in an atmosphere in

which their final thoughts may be directed toward God. Every few hours they are given some *tulsī* leaves and Ganges water, the finest medicine there is for the dying. On the wall of the hospice, as one enters, the rules of the house are painted. Here are the first few: (1) Only those sick people who are dying and who believe in liberation in Kāshī and have come especially for "The Benefit of Kāshī" may stay here. The ill who wish to get well by taking medicines should stay elsewhere in a hospital. (2) Those good people who are followers of the Hindu *varnāshrama dharma* may stay in this place. (3) One may stay here for fifteen days. After that, one may stay, if there is special necessity, by the permission of the director.

The praises of dying in Kāshī are well known to those who have come here to die. There are thousands of verses, any two or three of which they may know by heart:

> Where else does a creature obtain liberation as he does here, simply by giving up the body, with very little effort at all!
>
> Not by austerities, not by donations, not by lavish sacrifices can liberation be obtained elsewhere as it can be obtained in Kāshī simply by giving up the body!
>
> Even the yogis practicing yoga with minds controlled are not liberated in one lifetime, but they are liberated in Kāshī simply by dying![4]

Shiva, the Teacher at Death's Door

"THE PLACE where Shiva himself, the Great Lord, teaches the *tāraka mantra* at the time of death—that is Avimukta."[5]

When one dies in Kāshī, they say, it is Shiva himself who whispers in one's ear the *tāraka mantra,* the "ferryboat *mantra,*" or the "*mantra* of the crossing." In the Hindu tradition, it is the guru who ordinarily bestows the *mantra* upon a qualified student, and the *mantra* is the means of wisdom. The guru mediates the kind of wisdom that cannot be learned from books but is conveyed in personal instruction from one generation to the next. Here in Kāshī, Shiva himself is the guru. The light of wisdom here is shed by no human teacher but communicated directly from God to the human ear and the human heart.

Shiva's personal role as bestower of salvation is one he chose in the beginning. Remember how Shiva and Pārvatī stood in Kāshī, before the world was made, and decided to create Vishnu precisely so that Vishnu could take over the task of sustaining and governing the rest of the universe, freeing Shiva to spend his time doing that in which he most delights: bestowing liberation. Shiva became the ruler of Kāshī, the place of light and wisdom, and he pledged:

This land, bounded by the Panchakroshī, is dear to me. My rule will prevail here, and no other rule will have power. O Vishnu, no other shall teach the creatures who live in Avimukta, even if they are sinners. I alone shall be their teacher.[6]

Hindus have portrayed Shiva, the merciful deathbed teacher, with great tenderness. In his posture of granting liberation, Shiva has a very personal form, bending down to the ear of the dying to whisper the secret of wisdom. It is said that when the great saint Rāmakrishna came to Kāshī in the late nineteenth century, he went into a deep trance of meditation as he passed Manikarnikā by boat. He later described what he had seen in his moments of vision: The goddess Annapūrnā held in her lap the body of a dead man, while Shiva knelt to whisper the *tāraka mantra* in his ear. It is little wonder that death is said to lose its terror in Kāshī, for Shiva will be present and will speak into one's ear all one needs to know.

The Tāraka Mantra

Creatures are released by the knowledge of Brahman, and never in any other way. I am that knowledge of Brahman for those who die in Kāshī. I teach the *tāraka* at the time of death, and they are released at that moment.[7]

WHAT is this "ferryboat" *mantra* which Shiva whispers in the ear of the dying? Our curiosity is aroused as with any whispered secret. The word *tāraka,* like *tīrtha,* comes from the Sanskrit root meaning "to cross over." *Tāraka,* however, is from the causative form of this root, meaning "to carry over" or "to rescue, save." Since a boat carries one across the flood, it is also called a *tāraka.* Like a boat, the *mantra* saves one from the waters of *samsāra.* In one work on this subject, the *Kāshī Moksha Nirnaya* ("The Discussion of Liberation in Kāshī"), the author explains the meaning of *tāraka:* "It is the boat, which carries one over

the sea of *samsāra.* And that [boat] is Brahman. Thus it is called the Tāraka Brahman."[8]

In the classical tradition of the Upanishads, the *mantra* that *is* Brahman is *Om*—the verbal symbol of the Supreme Reality. According to some, *Om* is the *mantra* Shiva utters at the time of death. Others claim it is the mantra "Rāma, Rāma" that is spoken. The scholar Nārāyana Bhatta in his sixteenth-century digest, the *Tristhalīsetu,* cites scriptural evidence for both views.[9]

On one level, of course, Rāma is the hero-*avatāra* of the *Rāmāyana.* But over the centuries in North India, the name Rāma has gathered so much weight and significance that it has come to mean God, with no sectarian connotations: the Supreme, and yet personal, Lord. It is Rāma's name they chant as they carry the dead to the burning *ghāt.* And so the poet Tulsī Dās has said, voicing the hope of many Hindus:

What instruction does the great lord Shiva give the dying
Upon the banks of [the] Ganges in Kāshī, the land of Dharma?
Hara tells them of the glory of Rām's Name, and he himself recites it,
From age on age this universe has known it and the Vedas too describe it.[10]

Whatever the uttered word of the *mantra* is, however, is quite beside the point. When Shiva speaks in person it is a revelation of God, from God.

"Death in Kāshī *is* liberation." This is the great religious claim of the City of Light. But an objection may be raised by those who stand firmly upon *shruti,* the "revealed scriptures." It is this: According to the Upanishads liberation comes only from wisdom—*jnāna.* This is the one prerequisite for release: the deep, transforming knowledge of *ātman,* the soul, and of Brahman, the one Reality. How, then, can liberation come from merely dying? How can this claim be justified in the light of the revealed tradition?

Both Sureshvara, the author of the *Kāshī Moksha Nirnaya,* and Nārāyana Bhatta, the compiler of the *Tristhalīsetu,* have taken on these objections, and many others, in their discussions of liberation in Kāshī. Both authors emphasize that it is not the physical act of dying that occasions liberation, or the word of the *mantra* itself. Rather, it is precisely the wisdom one receives at the time of death, when the *mantra* is imparted. Nārāyana Bhatta explains, "There is no liberation in the absence of wisdom—that is clear from statements in both the revealed and remembered tradition, such as 'From wisdom alone comes liberation.' Therefore, knowledge of the *ātman* arises here from the *tāraka,* which is taught by the guru Vishveshvara." He goes on to quote the *Kāshī Khanda* on the matter: "Creatures are released by knowledge of Brahman and never in any other way. *I am* that knowledge of Brahman for those who die in Kāshī. I teach the *tāraka* at the time of death, and they are released at that moment."[11]

The author of the *Kāshī Moksha Nirnaya* takes the strictly "nondualist" point of view in discussing this matter. The soul, *ātman,* and Brahman truly are "not different" one from the other, but the soul is shrouded with dark veils of ignorance and subject to a mistaken perception of the nature of reality. Death in Kāshī does not "cause" liberation, but is the occasion of liberation. It is the time when the veils of ignorance are lifted, and the light of day shines:

> Receiving knowledge from the Great Lord Shiva at the time of death, all creatures, bound by beginningless ignorance, are liberated.
>
> Liberation for them means absolute unity, like the unity of the air that is inside a pot with that that is outside the pot. There remains no cause at all for the creation of another body.
>
> God, the Supreme Lord, destroys ignorance . . . merely by rising, just as the sun destroys darkness, merely by rising![12]

"All Creatures"

"Whatever is known as a 'creature'—from Lord Brahmā down to a blade of grass, in the four categories of beings—gets liberation in Kāshī."[13]

One might ask, "Who is liberated in Kāshī? What is meant when it is said that all creatures are liberated here?" I posed the question to a number of Banāras pandits, including one very learned man nearly eighty years old.

"There is liberation for all creatures," he replied. "Not only people, you see, but birds and animals reach *moksha* here as well."

"Birds?"

"Yes, *moksha* for birds too." One could tell by the twinkle in his eye that the notion delighted him. "Dying here is sufficient, that is all.

Dying here is sufficient, even for a mosquito," and he added with a mischievous smile, "even for the tiniest germ." There was a long silence. *Moksha* for mosquitoes stretched the imagination. "You see," he went on, "living beings are always *mukta*—liberated, free. When Shiva gives the *tāraka mantra* at the time of death, he tells creatures what has been true all along: they are free, *mukta. Aham Brahmāsmi. Tat tvam asi.* 'I am Brahman. That thou art.' "

"He says this to all creatures?"

"Yes, even donkeys." He smiled again.

"How about Muslims and Christians?" came the foolish question.

"Of course! They are more worthy than donkeys!"

The poignant image of Lord Shiva whispering wisdom into the ear of the dying is here shattered by an even more challenging claim—that Shiva enlightens not only human beings, but all creatures in the "four categories of beings": those born from moisture, such as insects; those born from seeds, such as plants; those born from eggs, such as birds; and those born from the womb, such as humans. The chain of life extends "from Lord Brahmā down to a blade of grass."

A substantial scriptural tradition supports the claims of this pandit. There are dozens of verses in the Purānic texts that take that same apparent delight in confounding the religious imagination with the saving power of Shiva:

> Brāhmanas, kshatriyas, vaishyas, shūdras, *and even bastards,*
> *And others who are worms, or foreigners, who are impure and born to a sinful estate,*
> *And insects, and ants, and animals, and birds*
> *Hear, O Beloved, when they reach a timely death in Avimukta*
> *They* all *wear the crescent moon in their hair, have eyes in their foreheads, and become bull-bannered Shivas!*[14]

Brahmins to ants all in one breath: this is the continuum of life that animates the universe as perceived by Hindus. All life is qualitatively one. The same life breath unites "mobile creatures" *(jangamas)* like ourselves and the birds, with the "stable ones" *(sthāvaras)* of the plant kingdoms that are unable to move about. For Hindus, life is not "one" in any simple sense. Life is infinitely diversified and stratified. Even human beings are not all born into the present lifetime with the same maturity of spirit and self-awareness, and these human differences are reflected in the *jātis,* literally "births," which we call castes. Despite the elaborate stratification, there is an undergirding unity that links all life together into one coherent whole. The individual life spirit, the *ātman,* moves through the various realms of the living until it realizes its true nature and its true home, in oneness with Brahman.

All the levels of life can therefore be given a common name as creatures. They are called *jantu,* those "born," or *prānin,* those with "breath," or *bhūta,* those "existent" ones. All these Sanskrit terms refer to living beings by their common denominators: they are born, they have breath, they come into being. When it is said that all "creatures" are liberated in Kāshī at death, these are the creatures included.

Naturally, the stories of the Kāshī literature are filled with examples of the salvation of great and small creatures. There are stories about animals or about people who have been reborn as animals in Kāshī. It is assumed, of course, that to dwell in Kāshī as a donkey or a bird is far superior to living elsewhere as a king. In one story, a flock of birds speak of their past lives. Once they were gods, enjoying the delights of heaven. Once they were heavenly musicians and dancers. In the earthly realms, they were born in every rank of being from fishes to kings. They lived in forest and town, they were beggars and donors, wise and foolish, winners and losers. They had happy births and sad. From all this they learned one thing: that everything in this world and in the worlds above and below is forever changing and cannot bring lasting happiness. Now at last, having lived so many lives, they have become birds in Kāshī, for the final crossing, from this shore of birth and death to the far shore of immortality.[15]

Finally, according to most Banāras pandits and priests, "all creatures" means people of all religious persuasions, including Christians, Muslims, and atheists. Karpātrī, the scholar *sannyāsin,* has written that just as poison will poison anyone who drinks it, so will the nectar of immortality, called *amrita,* impart immortality to anyone who drinks it. "In this same way," he said, "from dying in Kāshī everyone will get liberation, whether he be Muslim, or Christian, or an unbeliever." While some pandits would quibble that non-Hindus may live in the earthly Banāras, but do not truly live in "Kāshī," most would agree with one priest who exclaimed to me, "God knows that, according to our faith, you will also get *mukti* if you die in Kāshī!"

If everyone is liberated by death in Kāshī, how can there be justice among people? What of those who appear to be shameless scoundrels,

and yet they die here? And what of those who have been very pious and yet, perchance, die elsewhere? This issue has perplexed thoughtful Hindus, just as the issue of evil and the apparent prosperity of the wicked has perplexed people the world over. According to some, the scoundrel simply will not die in Kāshī. Something will happen at the last moment, and the scoundrel will die on the road to Allahabad or on a business trip to Calcutta. After all, running the undeserving out of the city is the job of the divine sheriff, Dandapāni, along with his two deputies, Confusion and Doubt. Who dies in Kāshī, then, is not a matter of chance. As one priest put it, "A really great sinner will not die here, but will leave. Not all of the millions of people in India can die in Kāshī. Many will come, but 'accidentally' or through the conspiracy of the Lord, some will leave before they die."

Just as the flock of birds had come to Kāshī at the end of a long pilgrimage through countless lifetimes, so the saints and sinners of Kāshī have come to this city in the course of a journey through many lives. It is also true, then, that from our limited perspective in this lifetime we cannot begin to say who is a saint and who is a sinner. The law of *karma,* operating inexorably as it does through life after life, does not permit us to say that the beggar or the swindler is undeserving of death in Kāshī. Sureshvara addresses just this point when he writes in the *Kāshī Moksha Nirnaya:* "Some people say, 'Such and such a sinner dies in Kāshī while the doer of good dies outside.' People who really understand should not think along these lines. In this lifetime, we are the ones who discriminate our good and evil deeds, but the Great Lord is the one who discriminates what good and evil we have done, by thought, word, and deed, from time immemorial."[16]

The Punishment of Bhairava

THERE is another answer to this question of justice, however, and that is that the scoundrel will be severely punished before attaining *moksha* here. This punishment, meted out by Bhairava, is called the *bhairavī yātanā,* the "punishment of Bhairava."

The *bhairavī yātanā* is the product of a religious imagination as complex and legalistic as that which produced the notion of purgatories in the West. Indeed, *bhairavī yātanā* is a kind of purgatory and serves something of the same purpose, as a way station between this world and the bliss of heaven.

The question to which *bhairavī yātanā* is the answer is, in part, the question of justice: How can the apparent scoundrel get off without punishment and, what is more, attain liberation here? In part, it is also the question of *karma:* How can liberation in Kāshī be squared with the law of *karma,* by which the results of one's previous actions are experienced? *Karma* in the Hindu view operates as inexorably as the natural law of gravity, and that portion of *karma* that is in the process of being worked out cannot be destroyed by wisdom. It is like an arrow shot from a bow, they say. It cannot be retrieved until it has reached its destination. Similarly *karma* cannot be destroyed. It must reach its destination, and this means one must experience its results, both good and bad.[17]

The mechanism by which all this *karma* is experienced is the *bhairavī yātanā.* Because it is called a "punishment" one can only conclude that it applies especially to the experiencing of bad *karma.* Bhairava's punishment is brief, lasting but a moment, and very intense. It is a kind of compression chamber of experience in which the *karmas,* which might ordinarily land one in hell or in countless difficult births and rebirths, are experienced completely in a split second. As one of the *pandās* at Manikarnikā Ghāt put it, "The punishment that Yama, the God of Death, would deal out in a thousand years is experienced here in one second of *bhairavī yātanā.* That is how intense it is. After the punishment one is pure, and then one sees Shiva himself."

Sureshvara compares the experience of this punishment with the experience of dreaming.[18] Just as in a dream one might experience a whole lifetime of activity in a very brief moment, so in *bhairavī yātanā* one might take on many bodies, one after another, and live through many lives, in one moment. In explaining this time chamber, Sureshvara recalls the famous story of Nārada, a tale used to illustrate the nature of *māyā:*

Once Brahmā told the sage Nārada to take a dip in a nearby river. When he did so, Nārada emerged from the water as a lovely woman of a good family. She was given in marriage by her father and, in time, she had many sons and grandsons. Ultimately a war broke out between her father and her husband, and in the course of the battle both were killed, along with many of her sons. Mourning, she mounted the funeral pyre that had been laid for her husband, and as she began to burn, engulfed in flames, she suddenly felt cool, as if she were in the water. And indeed she, as the sage Nārada, was still in the water, taking that dip recommended by Lord Brahmā.

Sureshvara also tells the tale of King Lavana in which the king, under the influence of a court magician, experienced a lifetime of adventure and anguish, only to wake up and find that but a moment had passed. Commenting on these stories, Sureshvara says, "Remembering stories like this, one should understand that it is after the manner of *māyā* that certain people [who die] in Kāshī enter into other bodies and experience the punishments of Kāla Bhairava."[19]

There is one further mechanism in the Hindu universe for dispatching the sins of the scoundrels who die in Kāshī: they become *pishāchas* of Rudra for a vast number of years and only then will they be granted *moksha.* This fate is apparently worse than the *bhairavī yātanā* and reserved especially for those who have sinned grievously within the bounds of the sacred city.

A *pishācha* is a "fiend" or a "goblin." One scholar describes them as "eaters of raw flesh," "evil elves," "half-fabulous, half-human."[20] *Pishāchas* are also the unsatisfied spirits of the dead, especially the spirits of those who have died violent or unnatural deaths, or whose death rites were improperly performed. Being a *pishācha* is a wretched in-between state of being, neither in this world nor in the world of the ancestors. In a cosmological system in which there are so many "worlds" and "heavens," so many compartments of the universe, there is nothing worse than being neither here nor there. The *pishācha* is doomed to be perpetually thirsty, to eat food mixed with blood, to be roped to Kāla Bhairava's post for punishment, and to roast on Kāla Bhairava's fire. His *mukti* is hard won, for the scriptures agree that the miserable fate of the *pishācha* lasts for 300,000 years.[21]

Yet even the claims of Bhairava's terrible punishments for the sinful are countered in Kāshī by equally strong attestations of Kāshī's grace. After all, Bhairava's punishment is said to endure but one terrible moment. For those fated to become *pishāchas,* there is Pishāchamochana, "Where *pishāchas* are set free." There one may be released from that condition. And according to some, if one dies in the Kedāra Khanda of the city, one cannot be touched by any punishment, and one reaches *moksha* directly. As quickly, it seems, as the brahminical imagination could concoct the most fearsome and ferocious of punishments and purgatories, it could invent the means of mercy to avoid them or to circumvent their effects.

In the last analysis, there are many who believe in no punishment at all in Kāshī. The City of Light is a place of pure grace. There Shiva pours the nectar words of immortality into the ear of the dying without asking after their good and bad deeds.[22] There people who die become pure by the power of the City of Light, just as wine poured into the Ganges becomes the Ganges.[23] "This Vārānasī is the divine embodiment of mercy," they say, "where, leaving one's body, one enters happily into the brilliance of the Universal Lord and, with one's own form, attains formlessness."[24] "In Kāshī," they say, "the great tree of *samsāra,* which grows from the seed of desire, is cut down with the axe of death, and grows no more."[25]

The Last Sacrifice

At Manikarnikā cremation ground, there is a sacred fire which is said to have burned constantly for as long as anyone can remember. It is kept by the Doms, the untouchable caste that cares for the cremation ground and tends the pyres. With the flame of this sacred fire, the cremation pyres are lighted, although some groups of mourners may bring embers from home.

The cremation rite is called the "last sacrifice"—*antyeshti.*[26] The rite is, indeed, a sacrifice, having a certain structural continuity with all fire sacrifices in India, from the most complex to the most simple. What is prepared, ornamented, and offered into the fire is, in this case, the deceased. When the body arrives at the cremation ground, after the chanting procession through the lanes of Banāras, it is given a final dip in the River Ganges. It is sprinkled with the oil of sandalwood and decked with garlands of flowers. The deceased is honored as would

befit a god, and in Kāshī it is said that the dead take on the very form of God.

The word for a dead body is *shava,* and Hindus have often underlined the phonetic relation between *shava* and Shiva. The identification of the dead with Shiva is suggested by the brahmins in their *māhātmyas* of Kāshī. In the great cremation ground, they say, the dead receive the form and emblems of Shiva. They become three-eyed, wearing the crescent moon in their hair, carrying the trident. Little cares Shiva for the pollution usually associated with death, and here in Kāshī he takes up his post on the cremation ground and transforms the dead into his very likeness. In the fire of the "last sacrifice," the *shava* is a holy offering indeed.

It is the chief mourner, usually the eldest son, who takes the twigs of holy *kusha* grass, flaming, from the Doms' eternal fire to the pyre upon which the dead has been laid. He circumambulates the pyre counterclockwise—for everything is backward at the time of death. As he walks round the pyre, his sacred thread, which usually hangs from the left shoulder, has been reversed to hang from the right. He lights the pyre. The dead, now, is an offering to Agni, the fire. Here, as in the most ancient Vedic times, the fire conveys the offering to heaven.

After the corpse is almost completely burned, the chief mourner performs a rite called *kapālakriyā,* the "rite of the skull," cracking the skull with a long bamboo stick, thus releasing the soul from entrapment in the body. Now, truly, nothing but ash remains. The chief mourner takes a large clay pot of Ganges water, throws it backward over his left shoulder upon the dying embers, and walks away without looking back. "These living have turned back, separated from the dead," they say; "this day our invocation of the gods became auspicious. We then went forward for dancing, for laughter, firmly establishing our long life."[27] The members of the funeral party do not grieve openly, for it is said that many tears pain the dead.[28]

The rites for the dead that follow the cremation last for eleven days and consist of daily offerings of rice balls, called *pindas,* which provide a symbolic, transitional body for the dead. During these days, the dead person makes the journey to the heavens, or the world of the ancestors, or the "far shore." As a whole, these rites are called *shrāddha,* or *pindadāna,* the "offering of *pindas.*" The rites also include the providing of feasts for a group of brahmins, who take nourishment on behalf

The riverfront at Manikarnikā Ghāt.

of the dead. On the twelfth day, the departed soul is said to reach its destination and be joined with its ancestors, a fact expressed symbolically by joining a small *pinda* to a much larger one.

Death is dangerous because it is a time of transition. It is a liminal or marginal time, a space between life and life. In this transitional period, the soul is called a *preta,* literally one who has "gone forth" from the body but has not yet arrived at its new destination.[29] The rites following the cremation enable the *preta* to become a *pitri,* an ancestor, or more precisely, a "father." Without such rites, one might remain a homeless *preta* for a long time. For those who are very great sinners or who have died hideous deaths, this transition from life to new life might be obstructed by becoming a *pishācha.*

But death is not only a time of danger, for it is also held to be a time of great illumination. At death, they say, the light is very intense, and what separates this shore from the far shore is almost transparent. The time of death, therefore, is a time of clear seeing, of vision, of insight. One's thoughts are to be on God at such a time, for what one thinks and sees at the time of death directs one's first steps toward the next life. Those close to the dying should whisper the name of God in that person's ear. While death may be the final event in one life, it is also, in a sense, the first event in the life beyond. For Hindus, death is not the opposite of life; it is, rather, the opposite of birth.[30] The great transition which death occasions is not from life to death, but from life to life.

In Kāshī, rites for the dead are enacted with great care. One might ask, since such rites are intended to see the soul safely to the heavens or the world of the ancestors from which ultimately the soul will take birth again, "Why are such rites necessary in Kāshī?" Here, after all, the dead merit liberation: freedom from this endless journeying through the various compartments of the universe, through life after life. According to the very cautious, the rites do no harm and one can never be too careful. According to the very thoughtful, these rites and the sense of ongoing connection with the loved one that they engender are as much for the living as the dead. For most Hindus, however, the question of this seeming contradiction does not arise. One always does these things, for they are the right things to do, even in Kāshī. It is the *dharma* of the living to perform rites for the dead. It is one of the debts a Hindu man must honor, not only for the sake of his own father and mother recently deceased, but for the sake of all the ancestors who have gone before.

Kāshī promises much more than a good life. This city promises a good death. Here death comes as no surprise. Every day the processions pass, bearing a corpse toward Manikarnikā. Every night the fires burn on the riverbank. The procession of life includes the procession of death. Here death is not denied. Perhaps that is why they can say that death is not feared, but welcomed as a long-awaited guest.

The promise of a good death takes the danger out of the transition, the crossing, death occasions. The very sick or the distressed may lose consciousness as death approaches and be unable to place their thoughts upon the name of God, but Shiva himself will be there, they say, to whisper wisdom into the ear of the dying. Yama, the God of Death, may not approach the dead here, noose in hand. Kāla Bhairava takes charge of the dead, and he is Shiva's own servant, indeed, Shiva's own self. Even if there is some terrible punishment to be meted out, it is guaranteed to be short-lived and to be followed by the bliss of liberation. Here even as one dies, the boats are ready for the crossing.

Kāshī draws into powerful focus the greatest symbols of Hindu culture—its gods, especially the Great Lord, Shiva; its sacred geography, especially the Heavenly River, Gangā; and its vision of transcendence, *moksha*. For over 2,500 years, the people of India have come to this place, which they have described as both the Great Cremation Ground and the Forest of Bliss. Here they have built temples and ashrams, palaces and homes, schools and businesses, transforming the ancient groves and pools of the *yakshas* and *nāgas* into one of the most awesome cities in the world. It is a city of wealth, exuberance, and life. It is also a city of poverty, confusion, suffering, and death. But the City of Light, they say, extends one's vision across the river of life and death to the far shore of immortality. "It is called Kāshī, for here the light shines."

3

Perfection and Devotion: Sati Tradition in Rajasthan

LINDSEY HARLAN

Although English defines the term *suttee* as an act, the self-immolation of a widow on her husband's funeral pyre, the Sanskrit and Hindi term *sati* literally means "a good woman," a woman who has become capable of self-immolation. This distinction reveals a crucial presupposition: whereas suttee as an act is something one commits at a particular moment, *sati* as a person is something one becomes gradually through good behavior. This chapter examines the personal ideal of sati espoused by certain Rajput women—those belonging to the erstwhile aristocracy of Rajasthan. It then articulates two often interrelated ways in which those Rajput women practice good behavior by keeping in mind (that is to say, by remembering) those who have died as satis.[1]

My observations are based on fieldwork concentrated in the southwest portion of Rajasthan, particularly around the Udaipur area, where I lived for a year and a half in 1984–1985. When I arrived in Rajasthan, I had not expected to find sati veneration a thriving tradition. I had supposed that, because there was only passing mention of contemporary sati worship in the scant secondary literature available on religious tradition in Rajasthan and because self-immolation had been made illegal by the Indian government, the tradition of veneration would have largely disintegrated. My supposition turned out to be false: although very few women end their lives as satis these days in Rajasthan, sati veneration is a major aspect of the religious lives of Rajput women. It shows no sign of diminishing.[2] To fulfill the terms of my proposal to study the religious traditions of Rajput women, I had to find out what this was all about.

One of the first things I learned is that, from the traditional Rajasthani Rajput perspective, a woman becomes a sati through the acquisition of virtue or goodness—that is, *sat*. Acquiring *sat* is thought to be the consequence of a personal transformation that comprises three conceptual stages, recognized in Rajput tradition as *pativrata*, *sativrata*, and *satimata*. The first is the *pativrata* stage. Rajput women assume that a sati who immolates herself has been a *pativrata*, a devoted wife. In fact, dying as a sati is said to prove that a Rajput woman has been a good wife. It demonstrates to all concerned, including the woman herself, that she has developed appropriate and admirable character.

The notion of *pativrata* is not the exclusive property of Rajput women. The Rajput women I came to know in Rajasthan, however, tend to understand their Rajput constitution as enabling them to be particularly good *pativratas*. Often in conversation Rajput women point out that the ethos of sacrifice with which Rajputs, soldiers by tradition, have been inculcated has enabled wives to sacrifice personal or selfish desires in order to serve their husbands better. This is why, the logic continues, the Hindu tradition of dying as a sati has been primarily practiced by (and so associated with) Rajput women. Self-sacrifice throughout life has predisposed Rajput women to sacrifice themselves at the time of their husbands' deaths.

The term *pativrata* has often been used to refer to any married woman. Even in this basic sense, however, it bears an ideological nuance, for it literally means someone who has made a vow (*vrat*) to her husband (*pati*). The substance of this vow is protection. If a wife is devoted to her husband and therefore protects him, he will prosper. If not, he will suffer and perhaps die.

A *pativrata* protects her husband in two basic ways. First, she serves him: she attends to his personal needs and encourages him to perform his duties. In other words, she both attends him as he is and helps him to become what he ought to be. This is clear not only from women's testimony, but also from the many Rajput stories that celebrate women who have driven their husbands from cowardly retreat into heroic battle. Second, she performs ritual vows (*vrats*), most of which involve fasting. By fasting she pleases various deities, who compensate her by protecting her husband and by helping her to be a better *pativrata*, thus increasing her personal capacity to protect her husband.

According to the traditional point of view, if the *pativrata*'s husband predeceases her, she is culpable. She may be suspected of insufficient or

insincere devotion. She can escape suspicion, however, if she takes yet another vow—a *vrat* to die as a sati. If she does so, she enters the second sati stage. She goes from being a *pativrata* (one who has taken a *vrat* to protect her husband) to a *sativrata* (one who has taken a *vrat* to join her husband in the afterlife).

When a woman utters her sati vow, she places herself in the context of a vivid temporal fiction. Time is condensed, so that she becomes a *sahagamini*, "one who goes (*gamini*) together (*saha*) with one's husband." Hence, even though technically her husband has died before she has, she is absolved from blame if she burns herself during his cremation ceremony. Indeed, she is even absolved if she burns herself after his cremation, if his cremation occurs before she learns of his death.

The Rajput *sativrata*'s death is thought to be a manifestation of her goodness, her *sat*. The sacrifices she undertook as a *pativrata* built up in her stores of *sat*, which is a moral heat not unlike *tapas* (ascetic heat). It is said that when the *pativrata* learns of her husband's death, this heat begins to consume her body. So the woman who has taken a sincere *vrat* of *sati* quite literally becomes too hot to touch. Therefore, anyone who tries to restrain her will be burned in the process. When the *sativrata* mounts her husband's pyre, her body explodes into flames, and these cremate her own body and the body of her husband. In the process, the ashes of the two bodies become intermingled, which symbolically affirms the unity of husband and wife that was established at their wedding fire.

During the period between the *sati vrat* and the sati's death, a woman is considered extremely powerful. Because she has renounced life, she has in a sense progressed beyond life. She possesses special powers, among them the power to curse and the power to establish prohibitions, the nature of which will be explored shortly.

In the process of dying, the *sativrata* becomes transformed once again, this time into a *satimata*. The term *mata* (mother), often used as an epithet denoting female divinity, indicates the understanding that a *satimata* cares for the family amidst which she lived quite as a mother cares for children. As a *satimata*, the wife shares her husband's fate while continuing to protect her earthly household.[3]

As a transcendent being, the *satimata* personifies *saubhagya* (good fortune), for she remains married to her husband eternally. As wives live their lives day in and day out, and try to realize the *pativrata* ideal, they look to the *satimata* as a moral exemplar and they pray to her to help them acquire the fortitude essential to achieving the virtue she represents, the virtue that will make them better *pativratas*.

The notion of the *satimata* as a moral ideal and model is so prominent in the minds of her *pativrata* devotees that, however many satis might have taken their lives in a particular family, these satis are almost invariably referred to in the singular. What is important is not the individual woman who dies on a pyre but the transformative reality that her death symbolizes. Thus, generally speaking, in the context of each Rajput family, all satis eventually become *hamari satimata*, as it is said: our *satimata*.[4] Particular features associated with individual satis come to be associated with the amalgamated, condensed, singular sati personality. Instead of many satis with many stories, there is one sati who possesses many aspects.

While reflecting *pativrata* morality, the *satimata* functions as a powerful, transcendent being. She protects by warding off or curing family sickness and financial misfortune. Often, however, she intervenes in family life by issuing warnings to women that, unless they faithfully and sincerely perform domestic and religious rituals—rituals she knows they have been slighting—they and their families will suffer great misfortune. To put women on notice, the *satimata* appears in their dreams, gives them visions, or sends them bad omens.

Rajputs understand the sati tradition I have described as being overwhelmingly *their* tradition: they believe Rajput women to be uniquely capable of possessing the motivation required for a woman to become a valid sati. Of course, non-Rajput women have immolated themselves on their husbands' funeral pyres. Consequently, although all non-Rajputs understand the Hindu sati tradition to have originated with the Rajputs, and although they concede that most satis have in fact been Rajput, they claim that non-Rajput women have also become satis.

On the whole, Rajput women dismiss these supposed non-Rajput satis as insincere and pretentious women. Many imply that most non-Rajput women who have died on their husbands' pyres were only emulating Rajput satis in hopes of gaining status, prestige, and upward mobility for themselves, their families, and their *jatis* (castes).

Rajputs often point out that members of various lower castes have adopted other Rajput customs, including wearing Rajput dress, using Rajput names, and even eating meat and drinking wine, activities that Rajasthani custom specifically designates as Rajput privileges. Given the prevalence of these multiple forms of emulation, Rajput women find it unsurprising that non-Rajput women have also taken to immolating themselves, hoping to elevate their caste position and perhaps eventually allow their caste members to infiltrate Rajput ranks through marriage. Thus Rajputs say that such non-Rajput women have immolated themselves not out of devotion, but for ulterior motives; they cannot, therefore, be considered legitimate satis.

This point is crucial. According to Rajput women, merely immolating oneself does not guarantee that one will become a *satimata*. One has

to have the proper motivation, which must be selfless. The aspirant must have no desire except to share her husband's fate. Because a Rajput woman naturally has this single-minded desire, she makes her *vrat* to die as a sati spontaneously. When she learns of her husband's death, she automatically (without consideration and without calculation) utters a *vrat* of sati, and so becomes a *sativrata*. Her intentions are selfless and her motives pure. Therefore, the Rajput *sativrata*'s death becomes a direct reflex of her character (*charitra*) and a manifestation of her goodness, her *sat*. This goodness or *sat* is presumed to build up easily in Rajput women because they have an inherent, caste-derived inclination to realize the role of the *pativrata*.[5] Being Rajput means knowing how to sacrifice; being predisposed to sacrifice makes Rajputs the very best wives.

This is especially significant in light of the primary meaning Rajput women attach to the sati's death: they believe that is serves as proof to the sati and to others that the sati has successfully led the life of a *pativrata*, a good wife. This proof is necessary because status as a *pativrata* is more or less uncertain during a woman's lifetime. Every wife and mother must make decisions that are unpopular. Many times a woman is unsure whether the course of action she is taking is right, particularly if it draws family criticism. By dying as a sati, however, she can be confident—and others can be confident—that she has, on the whole, made correct decisions and lived selflessly as a *pativrata*. Hence, the sati's death serves an important validating function.[6]

In the case of non-Rajput satis, however, immolation has not in and of itself served this function. For non-Rajputs, say Rajput women, validation requires additional evidence. This evidence is provided by the observed emergence from within a *sativrata*'s body of flames, which have been ignited by the fervor of moral goodness, *sat*. Here, one can see clearly that Rajputs understand goodness as being both a moral quality and a physical substance—moral fiber in the literal sense, "the right stuff." This substance manifests itself as virtue during life and as fire at the time of death.

The qualification that the wifely virtue of non-Rajputs must be seen to be believed raises an interesting practical problem. Usually a *sativrata* mounts a pyre that is already burning or is lit soon thereafter. Of course, if the *sativrata* is a Rajput, the presumption is that the fire that consumes her is not the fire lit by someone else's hand, but the internal fire of *sat*. If the *sativrata* is not a Rajput, such an assumption is not made. In that instance the flames of *sat* must be visibly distinct from the lit fire. This is a tall order, and an order seldom filled; hence, few instances of non-Rajput satis occur in Rajput tradition. There are occasional exceptions, however, and I will soon refer to one of them.

To summarize, the fundamental idea Rajputs have of the sati's death is that it represents a manifestation of the virtue of *sat*, a moral and substantive quality that is inherent but latent in the Rajput *pativrata. Sat* causes the *pativrata* to become a *sativrata* if her husband predeceases her, and it manifests itself in flames, which prove that the woman has been a *pativrata* even as they transform her into a *satimata*.

With this schema in mind, let us return to examine more extensively the liminal stage in the sati scenario, the *sativrata* stage. During this period a sati sets the terms of the relationship she will share with the family members whom she will later protect; she also teaches that the sati's will must be respected, and her desires remembered.

The Srap

The first way in which a *sativrata* may express her feelings is by issuing a curse. A *sativrata* pronounces a curse (*srap* or *shrap*) if she becomes angry while preparing to die. By cursing, she makes it known that some person or persons have behaved badly and that behavior of such a nature is unacceptable to her. The curse, which hangs over a family for a number of generations, usually seven, serves to encourage within it proper attitudes and activities. Some examples, stories drawn from my interviews with Rajput women in 1984–1985, follow.

The first illustrates a situation quite common in sati mythology: a situation in which someone misbehaves by interfering with a woman who has manifested her intention to die as a sati. The *sativrata* makes it clear that intervention is unacceptable, and in fact dangerous:

> There once was a *sativrata* whose relatives failed to provide her with a horse and a drummer for her sati procession. Every *sativrata* is supposed to proceed from her home to her husband's pyre in grand style. A horse and a drummer are absolute essentials. Enraged, the slighted *sativrata* cursed her husband's family to the effect that for seven generations whenever it might require a horse or drummer for ritual purposes, neither would be available.

The consequences of this *srap* were far-reaching. Both horse and drummer have always been essential to many important rituals, among them marriage and Dashara rituals.[7] Thus the sati's curse subjected the family to hardship, ableit justifiable hardship.

Besides stories that demonstrate the perils of interfering with a *sativrata*'s intentions, there are stories that tell of the fury that may be unleashed if bad behavior by a family member, even a husband, has been the reason that the *sativrata* has had to become a *sativrata*. The following narrative serves as an example:

> There once was a woman whose husband was fond of liquor. Rajputs are allowed to drink liquor. This husband, however, abused his prerogative by

> overindulging regularly. This caused much unpleasantness within the family. One day while inebriated he fell off a roof and died. At that time his wife took a vow of sati. Before immolating herself, she pronounced a curse that from then on no male in the family would be allowed to drink liquor.

This story illustrates what might be called a conditional curse. It curses the family to be deprived of alcohol *or else*. Here the "or else" is an inexplicit, though apparently effective, threat. Family members say that, since the curse was pronounced, no one in their household has dared to drink. Like the first curse I described, this curse pronounces a punishment that teaches a lesson, but it is a lesson that promises further punishment if ignored or forgotten.

The third example involves a curse that is violated. As will soon be apparent, the secondary or conditional punishment implicitly established by the curse turns out to be quite severe. The story goes like this:

> There once was a Rajput king who decided to get married. Not long after his wedding, he found that he liked being married so well that he wanted a second wife. When he returned home from his second wedding, however, his first wife, full of jealousy, sprang on him from behind the entryway and stabbed him to death. At that time the second wife, livid, took a vow of sati. Then later, before mounting her husband's pyre, she pronounced a curse. She said that from then on no king from that kingdom would ever be able to be married to more than one woman at the same time. Several generations later, however, a king from that family took a second bride while his first wife was still living. Not long after the wedding, he died. Since that time the curse has not been breached.

Ultimately this curse's consequence is serious: the foolhardy transgressor dies. Actually, the curse's impact is harsh even when the *srap* is not breached. Polygamy was an accepted practice, which even Rajput women today feel was necessary in times past to ensure that there would always be an heir to the throne. Back then, they say, wars, disease, and court intrigues (including not a few poisonings) depleted the population of royal heirs.

One particularly notable feature of the three *sraps* described here is that all had a major impact on women, whether or not the women were the direct cause of the sati's ire. In the first case, the absence of a horse and a drummer meant that future satis would be deprived of these. In the second, the prohibition on drinking by men caused women, although technically allowed to drink, to abandon the habit, lest their enjoyment of alcohol tempt their husbands to partake of it. In the third, the remarriage ban meant an increased possibility that adoption, one of the major sources of disharmony, intrigue, and general unpleasantness within the *zanana* (women's quarters or harem) of a traditional Rajput household—would be necessary.

Thus, the curse is not simply aimed at punishing men for what they have or have not done. It is also designed to instruct and influence women, because, as the sati paradigm teaches, a woman must always share her husband's fate. By way of further illustration, one could point to the fact that the most common curse pronounced by *sativratas* upon men with whom they are angry is infertility, yet Rajputs understand infertility as biologically a woman's problem. The result is that, however many times a cursed husband might marry, if he produces no offspring, his wives are deemed infertile. Regardless of who is targeted by sati curses, then, the lives of women are inevitably affected.

Usually when a sati utters a curse, she, targets her husband's family. In the three curses described earlier, the husband's family was targeted. Occasionally, however, satis aim their curses at other relatives. Sometimes a sati curses her husband's sisters or daughters. For example, in one royal estate, a sati cursed the daughters of her husband's family never to have both happiness and children. When the daughters married, their misfortunes traveled with them and plagued their husband's families.

Other times, a sati curses her father's family. A story that comes readily to mind is that of young girl, engaged to a prince of Mewar. Unfortunately, just after her engagement ceremony, her fiancé died. When the girl learned of his fate, she asked her father to take her to her fiancé's pyre. The father, however, was reluctant. He did not want his little girl to die.

The father and daughter argued with one another until finally the father, exasperated, said, "Very well, go ahead and kill yourself!" Then he rigged his bullock cart with a curtain so that the daughter could travel to Udaipur while maintaining *parda*, seclusion. By the time he had finished preparing the cart, however, his temper had cooled down and he was once again heavy-hearted. He simply could not bring himself to drive his daughter to Udaipur. Miraculously, however, the cart started up of its own accord and proceeded without a driver to the daughter's destination.

When the girl arrived in Udaipur, she dismounted the cart and circumambulated her fiancé's funeral pyre seven times. In this way she married her intended. Afterward, she ascended his pyre, sat down, and took her husband's head in her lap. As she did so, her body ignited spontaneously. Flames of *sat* consumed both her body and the body of her husband.

As the sati burned, she pronounced a curse on her father's family. Today no one in the family recalls the nature of that curse: family members simply say that it lasted seven generations and then lapsed. Evidently it no longer matters to them what the curse was. The important thing is that it instituted a tradition of venerating the *satimata* and of receiving the *satimata*'s protection, for the *satimata* has become its guardian.

In sum, while *sativratas* usually curse their husband's families, they may curse other related families if given cause. In either case, the *sativrata*'s curse is taken to be benevolent, instructing those whom she loves. Her curse discourages future bad behavior that would only cause the family greater heartache in the long run.

Thus, by cursing, the sati may well assume a permanent role as a protector of family health and welfare. Nevertheless, when a sati curses persons to whom she is not related it is understood that she punishes without providing protection. To outsiders, she is malevolent and vengeful. This point is illustrated beautifully by the following story told by women in one Rajput family about a Gujar woman who was a consort of one of their ancestors. When that nobleman died, the Gujar woman prepared to die as a sati. Skeptical, the daughters of the consort's family scoffed at her and said, "You won't go through with it. You're no Rajput." In effect, they felt that she lacked the requisite *sat*. Adding further insult to injury, the family priest, drummer, and barber also taunted her and refused to join her procession as they would a Rajput sati procession.

When the Gujar woman reached the *mahasatiyan*, the cremation ground, she cursed all who had ridiculed her, beginning with the daughters. She said that neither they nor daughters born to them would possess any of the three happinesses a woman wants: sons, wealth, and a decent husband. The crowd that had gathered to watch the sati's immolation was shocked by the severity of the Gujar's curse. It pleaded for mercy on behalf of the princesses. Moved, the sati reduced the sentence so that if a woman had two of these happinesses, she would be deprived of the third.

Today her family says that so far this curse has held true for six generations. It also points out that, although its daughters have suffered from this, both they and the entire family have benefitted from the sati's protection. The sati has been a good mother (*mata*) to them.

The sati also pronounced curses on the priest, the barber, and the drummer. She tailored each curse to fit its target. To the priest, who was a Brahmin, she said, " In each generation, your family will have one son and he'll be half-cracked." Brahmins are supposed to be intelligent; their traditional tasks required that they be learned if not wise. A halfwit Brahmin is thus worthless, professionally speaking.

To the barber she said, "Your family will have no sons." Many of the barber's chief ceremonial functions have to do with childbirth and its rituals. Hence once again, the curse is particularly appropriate to its target. Finally, to the drummer the sati said, "If you or your descendants are playing your drums at one end of the village, nobody will be able to hear your music at the other end of the village." All of these curses remain in effect today. The Rajput family says that it has received protection along with its problems, but the nonfamily targets have received only problems.

The last sati account is notable not only because it demonstrates the benevolence or malevolence of the sati according to the nature of her target, but also because it provides a rare example of a non-Rajput woman who is ultimately (although not easily) accepted by Rajputs as a legitimate sati. Thus the story is careful to record the witnessing of the Gujar consort's death by the crowd, who saw flames erupt from her body. Because of this testimony, the Rajput family venerates the Gujar woman as their sati. One might think that the undesirable consequences of the curse would be enough to convince the Rajputs of the Gujar's transformation, but here, as usual, the witnessing of *sat* flames is shown to be essential.

The explanation family members give of the Gujar woman's success in becoming a true sati accords with that given by Rajputs of all verified, non-Rajput satis. The Rajput family says that because the Gujar lived as part of their family and behaved as a Rajput wife—that is, as a woman selflessly devoted to her husband's welfare—she was able to improve her character, accumulate *sat*, and die as a sati in the Rajput fashion. Living in a Rajput environment, the Gujar became so "Rajputesque" that she acquired the power to die as a sati and thereafter to protect her Rajput family as a Rajput sati would. Her intentions were shown to be honest, her curse effective, and (for Rajputs) her power of protection real. Others whom she cursed were not protected. It was as if she had been adopted as a Rajput.

From these observations some conclusions can be drawn. First, we cannot understand the sati as malevolent simply because she utters a curse. We have to look at her intentions as they are understood by her protegés. In their view, the sati is malevolent toward outsiders who anger her; but she is benevolent toward insiders, relatives, for she is their mother and a mother is benevolent even when she punishes. The sati punishes to instruct her family and to correct its behavior. Her curses demonstrate her love.

Second, we must take into account the extraordinary extent to which intention is stressed by participants in the tradition. Even if a putative sati pronounces a curse that appears to be effective, the curse will not be deemed effective unless the *sativrata*'s motivations are demonstrated to be pure, either by her possession of Rajput blood or by her eruption into flames of *sat*. In short, according to the traditional perspective of Rajput women, a sati is a person impelled by virtue (*sat*) to follow her husband in death. Any other source of inspiration is thought to

contaminate a woman's intentions and prevent her from becoming a true *satimata*.

The Ok

While not every *sativrata* becomes angry and pronounces a curse, every *sativrata* establishes an *ok*, which proscribes certain practices or possessions. By establishing an *ok*, a *sativrata* marks a household for protection. So long as the terms of the *ok* are remembered and respected, the sati, now a *satimata*, will ward off and dispel bad fortune.

Widespread *oks* include the following : (1) bans on the wearing of traditional colors that women wear as brides (red, rose, and magenta) and colors women wear after giving birth (bright yellow speckled with red); (2) prohibitions against certain types of jewelry associated with marriage, such as jingly ankle bracelets (*chaurasi*) and various other bracelets and bangles; (3) rules against using baby cradles. The objects that are prohibited by *oks* are almost always associated with being a wife and mother. Each of them connotes female auspiciousness, *saubhagya*. They represent marriage, sexuality, fertility.

Paradoxically, however, the observance of an *ok* is considered auspicious, for it brings a woman and her household under the protection of the *satimata*, who is, as we have seen, a paradigm of auspiciousness. On the one hand, observing an *ok* helps a woman be a *pativrata*, because worship of the *satimata* is an essential part of a woman's duty as a wife. Women are generally responsible for performing rituals that honor the *satimata* and for observing *oks*. On the other hand, observing an *ok* also causes the devotee to grow in goodness, *sat*, ultimately enabling her to become a sati should her husband predecease her.

This notion of giving up the auspicious to gain in auspiciousness is aptly illustrated by the following sati story, which combines the imposition of an *ok* with the pronouncing of a *srap*; the two are frequently, though not always, found in combination. As the tale goes, there once was a woman who, having learned of her husband's death, took a vow to die as a sati. She tried to persuade a co-wife to die as a sati with her. The co-wife replied, "I'd love to, really, but you see I have all these dishes to do, and we both know a good wife never leaves dishes undone."

The sati found this a weak excuse. She cursed the co-wife and all daughters-in-law that, from then on, no one would be able to do dishes after dinner. Here, obedience to the *srap* is also the observance of an *ok*. Doing dishes is a wife's task; it is auspicious work and an integral part of caring for a husband's family. Yet when an auspicious activity such as this becomes so important in and of itself that it interferes with a woman's vow (*vrat*) of loyalty and service to her husband, its status changes. What would have been auspicious becomes inauspicious.

The prohibitions demonstrate the assumption that items and activities associated with *saubhagya* (auspiciousness) are auspicious only if they reflect a woman's desire to fulfill her vow as a *pativrata*. If these items or activities, supposedly symbolic of *saubhagya*, are used or performed by a woman without sincere motivation to be a good wife, they become wholly inauspicious.

It is not that the items and activities themselves are inauspicious. Only their use or performance is so, for it reflects bad intentions, a lapse in the vow of total service to one's husband (*pativratya*). This distinction, subtle as it may seem, is illustrated candidly in the tradition: many items that are flatly prohibited by *oks* may actually be used if a woman's intention to revere her *satimata* is demonstrated in related way. Thus women whose families are not supposed to possess baby cradles almost always borrow baby cradles from others. The borrowing is understood as a tribute to the *satimata*. In borrowing rather than buying a baby cradle, the woman shows that she remembers her obligation to the *satimata*, and thus displays the purity of her motivation to be a good *pativrata*.

In a similar practice, women who are not allowed to wear certain kinds of jewelry may actually wear such jewelry if they receive it as a present from someone outside the conjugal family. In not buying the jewelry but waiting to receive it from her parents, say, a woman shows that she respects the jewelry *ok* and the *satimata* who imposed it and that she intends to be faithful to the ideal that the *satimata* represents.

In sum, the traditions of *srap* and *ok* require that family members remember and respect the sacrifices that satis have made. When I speak of sacrifice in this context, I do not refer simply to the *balidan* itself—"suttee," the ritual sacrifice in which a woman immolates herself. True, self-immolation is the central event that sati tradition celebrates, but it is not the only sacrifice venerated within the tradition. The act of self-immolation is really only the culmination of a series of sacrifices performed throughout life by a *pativrata* who has thus built up stores of explosive moral substance, *sat*. Similarly, through a network of *sraps* and *oks*, it creates occasions for many other sacrifices to be performed.

By remembering the sacrifices that satis have made, Rajput family members seek to imbibe the spirit of sacrifice that has encouraged men and women to perform their duties properly. Not only does the sati influence family fortune through direct intervention in its affairs, she also serves as a paradigm of selflessness. Thus, like the hero who falls in battle, the sati stands for a way of life, a way of life informed by values that are only slowly changing to suit changing social norms and circumstances.

Notes

1. More extensive treatment of traditional sati veneration in Rajasthan can be found in Harlan, *Religion and Rajput Women: The Ethic of Protection in Contemporary Narratives* (Berkeley: University of California Press, 1992).

2. The self-immolation of the Rajput village woman, Roop Kanwar, on her husband's funeral pyre in September 1987 has brought international attention to the ongoing veneration of *satimatas*, as in the present volume.

3. David Mitten has discussed a parallel dual locality of familial spirits in ancient Greek conceptions of the afterlife. See Mitten, "Aspects of Meaning in Greek Burial Customs," paper presented at the conference, "Representations of Death," Harvard University, November 4, 1988. For similar reflections on Maharashtrian tribal culture, see Günther-Dietz Sontheimer, "The Religion of the Dhangar Nomads," in Eleanor Zelliot and Maxine Berntsen, eds., *The Experience of Hinduism* (Albany: SUNY Press, 1988), p. 115.

4. Similar observations are made about other classes of ancestors in rural Rajasthan by Ann Grodzins Gold in *Fruitful Journeys: The Ways of Rajasthani Pilgrims* (Berkeley: University of California Press, 1988), p. 91. This collectivization of spirits does not occur in the case of aristocratic Rajput hero spirits (*jhunjhars* and *virs*). See Harlan, *Religion and Rajput Women*, p. 178.

5. For a general discussion of caste norms understood as being transmitted genetically, see McKim Marriott and Ronald B. Inden, "Towards an Ethnosociology of South Asian Caste Systems," in Kenneth David, ed., *The New Wind: Changing Identities in South Asia* (The Hague: Mouton Publishers, 1977), pp. 227–38.

6. For further discussion of the probative value of death scenarios, see Harlan, "Abandoning Shame: Mira Bai's Bad Behavior," paper presented to the Association for Asian Studies, Washington, D.C., March 17, 1989.

7. Dashara is a holiday celebrating the defeat of the demon Ravana by Rama, the hero of the *Rāmayāṇa*. The principal rituals performed on this day by Rajputs are the cleaning of weapons and the veneration of horses.

Comment: Good Mothers and Bad Mothers in the Rituals of Sati

KAREN McCARTHY BROWN

In September of 1987, thousands gathered to watch Roop Kanwar, an eighteen-year-old Rajput woman, burn to death on her husband's funeral pyre. A shrine, built on the site in the town of Deorala, was for a time, at least, the center of intense devotional and political activity. The shocking nature of the event, as well as its obvious social and religious power, demands explanation. The sati of Roop Kanwar may be understood variously as an expression of Rajput chauvinism during a period of social and economic flux, an assertion of Indian traditionalism and nationalism against the forces of modernity and Westernization, and a handy means of enforcing social norms and keeping women in their place. Somewhat on the side, the revivification of the sati cult allows Marwari businessmen to make a profit, build important networks between their urban business centers and their rural homelands, and share in the machismo glory of the warrior caste, an increasingly important ingredient in the generalized male image in modern India. Thus sati is not simply a religious ritual; it is a confluence of religious, political, and social ideologies.[1]

Setting Roop Kanwar's death in a complex matrix of social, political, and economic forces, and then placing that in conversation with Rajput gender roles and certain Hindu beliefs appropriately demystifies the event. It sweeps away much of the smoke and shadow (often rank with sentimentality) and allows the rawer dynamics of the event to emerge. It makes Roop Kanwar's immolation an event within its time and place, but it does not explore the reasons for the gender roles and religious beliefs that allow a sati to function as the organizing metaphor for such varied problems and issues.

I am an outsider to Indian Studies. I have never visited India, let alone carried out field research there. Yet the first time I heard Roop Kanwar's story, it was not lack of understanding I experienced but an instant stab of recognition. Cultural relativity and the importance of understanding context are key principles for me in my own fieldwork situation in the Caribbean. I am much more flexible and tolerant with Haitians than I am, for example, with my own family or my university colleagues. I withhold judgment longer and work harder to understand the cultural context of actions that, on the surface, I find offensive. Yet there have been times when this carefully cultivated attitude could not staunch a rush of judgment. It happened once in Haiti when I witnessed a brutal instance of domestic violence. I reacted without a second's analytic pause. My reaction was equally quick when I read the *New York Times* account of Roop Kanwar's sati. I immediately saw it as an instance of a people acting out its deep-seated hatred and fear of women. While I never felt that the context was irrelevant, I did not think I needed to know much about it to make such a diagnosis.

Therefore, as the nonspecialist in this group, I have chosen to respond to Lindsey Harlan's rich phenomenology of sati in Rajasthan by addressing sati on common human ground. I want to consider it as an extreme example of misogyny—the cultural component that comes as close as any I know to being a human universal.

There is another way to describe what I propose to do here. I want to ask why and how the burning of a young woman could come to be a powerfully articulate symbol, one capable of drawing to itself—like a

magnet—a diverse collection of social, political, and economic agitations and, in turn, making each of them more articulate. Answering this question requires beginning at a level of human universality. It requires looking at the special vulnerability that accrues to women because they bear and, for the most part, rear children. The specifics of childbearing and childrearing in India will then emerge as variations on a common human theme, variations that help explain the particular tone and direction misogyny takes in modern India.

We human beings, unlike other animals, are born almost entirely unprepared to deal with our environment. Our entry into the world is marked by a long period of profound and mute dependence, and a woman presides over this fearsome vulnerability. Dorothy Dinnerstein describes it this way:

> The mother is in a literal sense, not just a figurative one, . . . in charge of the most intimate commerce between the child and the environment: the flow of substances between the flesh and the world. The infant gets from her the stuff that goes into its body and gives to her the stuff that comes out of it. And the sense of her presence—carnally apprehended in rocking and crooning, in cuddling and mutual gazing—is what makes the world feel safe. Separation from the touch, smell, taste, sound, sight of her is the forerunner of all isolation, and it eventually stands as the prototype of our fear of the final isolation. . . . In the body's pain, which it is up to the mother to prevent, is all the terror of annihilation. The sinking sense of falling—loss of maternal support—is the permanent archetype of catastrophe.[2]

The mothers we all carry within us are, by definition, both good mothers and bad mothers:

> It is in interaction with woman that the child makes another basic carnal discovery: that the body's love of pleasure, and its vulnerability to deprivation and pain, can subject the person who inhabits it to the dominations of another person's opposing will. The least coercive of mothers must sometimes restrain an infant's movements, or make it wait against its wishes. . . .[3]

And from such inevitabilities, when experienced in the oceanic space of infancy—a timeless, wordless world of unbounded emotion—comes the image of mother as rapacious, polluting, and death-dealing.

A human being's attitude about the basic safety of the world is thus shaped in an intimate, fleshly, preverbal conversation with a woman's body. The maternal presence is, furthermore, so thoroughly enmeshed with the infantile world that a child's first experiences of pain and loss are, by default, experiences of her. As adults, we carry the inchoate memories of these primal moments of safety and panic, consolation and loss within us. They are the deep waters rushing through the basements of our carefully constructed edifices of culture and self.

It is not that these currents are more important than all others in shaping adult life. Most of the time we manage to stay on dry ground and act out of places in ourselves that can be influenced by later experiences, as well as by reason and personal and communal values. Yet, when stress mounts sufficiently, when fear grows and generalizes itself, and most of all when need for reassurance is profound enough, we plummet into these chaotic waters and the problems of the moment assume an aura of boundless infantile need and fear. At such times, something must be done about the Mother, and no other solution will suffice.

In the Marwari businessman's envy of the accouterments of *kshatriya* manhood; in the loss of Rajput hegemony as the larger world encroaches on Deorala; in the precarious jockeying for power characteristic of the nationalist arena; and in the disorientating incursions of Western culture and modern life—in such things begin the "sinking sense of falling" that Dinnerstein argues is always, at some level, felt as a loss of maternal support. When the immediate circumstances that cause those feelings cannot be controlled, there are always women around who can be. When it seems as if catastrophe might be lurking around the next corner, keeping women in their place—doing what they are supposed to be doing—can make the world feel safer.[4]

It is every woman's special vulnerability to carry (at least potentially) for every other human being in her world something of an aura of the mythic good and bad mothers. This is what makes women the frequent scapegoats of individual and social pathology. Turning women into scapegoats for needs and fears whose roots drink from the deep waters of helpless infancy produces complex ritual forms in which the victim is forced to act out good and bad mother roles simultaneously. Just as devotees insist that a widow's pure devotion to her husband propels her toward sati (if it is a "true sati"), so rapists frequently insist that their victims express pleasure and arousal. Yet both rituals are patently punitive at the same time. Just as a Hindu woman may be held morally responsible if her husband predeceases her, so the victim of rape is told by the rapist (and too frequently also by the general public) that she brought it on herself. The two-sided nature of both these "rituals" allows for punishing the bad mother while, at the same time, calling on the good mother to give assurances that the world is ultimately safe and the raging infant still lovable.

While sati and rape may share some basic psychodynamics, they are also profoundly different. Sati is a public event, a type of ritualized theodicy, a religious drama called into being by the most threatening of human realities, death itself. As such, the rare occurrence of sati can speak meaningfully about many different types of loss and do so to large numbers of people. A religious event, unlike a political or social one, directly addresses our multilayered selves. With touch and taste, sound and smell, image and act, religion can give solace to the screaming, preverbal infant as well as to the frightened adult. Religion binds the whole together. The richly sensual character of Hindu ritualizing adds an important nuance to this picture and suggests that Hinduism may be especially proficient at addressing the preverbal levels of psyche and society.

The particular forms of childbearing and childrearing in India add further nuances. In *The Inner World: A Psycho-analytic Study of Childhood and Society in India,* Sudhir Kakar argues that the bond between Indian mothers and children is especially intense and long-lasting for several reasons. First, the mother–child bond is strong because, in India, a woman's worth tends to be defined by her ability to bear children. The arrival of a child, particularly a son, saves a young bride from the suspicion and even open hostility that are frequently occasioned by her arrival in her husband's extended-family home. Women thus hold tightly to their children, because, to some extent, they experience them as saviors.[5] The second *reason* for such strong mother–child bonding is the prolonged period of infancy characteristic of Indian childrearing. Kakar says that the Indian child does not experience any significant separation from the intense, intimate, and exclusive bond it has with its mother until the age of four or five. These early years are characterized by the nearly constant presence of the mother and by large amounts of physical interaction with her. During this same period, according to Kakar, the father generally plays "no significant caretaking role."[6] The third reason concerns Indian women's attitude toward developmental tasks. Kakar says that Indian mothers tend to be relaxed and accepting of the vicissitudes of childhood, following the child's inclinations in such things as weaning and toilet training, rather than imposing rules and limits of their own. Indian children, Kakar reports, routinely breastfeed until the age of two or three, but "it is not uncommon to see a five or six year old peremptorily lift up his [sic] mother's blouse for a drink."[7] Kakar concludes: "the Indian infant's experience of his [sic] mother is a heady one, his contact with her is of an intensity and duration that differentiate it markedly from the experience of infancy in western worlds."[8] From this configuration of the infant's world, Kakar sees strong images of both the good mother and the bad mother emerging, and he traces each type to multiple locations in Hindu mythology.[9]

In India, the expectations placed on women to offer selfless nurturance are great. The Hindu ideal of the *pativrata,* the self-sacrificial wife, mythologically represented through such characters as Sita and Parvati, is an especially potent expression of this expectation. And as might be expected, the fear that the mothering one will not give food but, instead, turn others into food for herself (think of the rapacious Kali) is equally great.

When viewed from a psychological perspective, such as the one I have suggested here, the symbolic language of sati opens up in a new way. A dialectical tension between images of woman—nurturer on the one hand, devourer on the other—reveals itself to be at the heart of sati practice. The drama of sati is shown to take place in the midst of a dense choreography of images of the eaters and the eaten, the consumers and the consumed. These images are transparent to the sort of infantile vulnerability experienced by all human beings; but they also gain specificity and intensity from the prolonged breastfeeding and strong mother–child bonding characteristic of India. The data in Lindsey Harlan's paper offer abundant illustrations in support of this analysis. Harlan has provided a text that makes it possible to read this subtext clearly.

The good wife, the *pativrata*, stands at the center of the sati drama. According to Harlan, the good wife offers her husband two kinds of protection: service and ritual austerities. The latter are vows, "most of which involve fasting." Through these dual activities—giving to him and withholding from herself—the wife assures her husband (and herself) that she is a self-sacrificing nurturer, one who has no hunger, need, or will of her own that could interfere with her caring for him. In other words, she shows herself to be a good mother.

But the good wife becomes frighteningly anomalous without her husband. Whereas before whatever she consumed, literally and figuratively, could be understood as fuel for further acts of self-sacrifice, as a widow she threatens to become a consumer of family resources, literally and figuratively, in her own right and for her own purposes. Whereas before her will (another form of hunger) was contained by being subject to that of her husband, there is now a danger that it may break loose, untempered by larger family agendas.

And this is exactly what happens during the liminal period in the sati rituals when a woman is a *sativrata*, one who has taken a vow to commit sati but has not yet carried it through. For the short period of time during which she is a *sativrata*, the woman gains a power and autonomy she knew at no other point in her life. "During this period," Harlan says, "a sati sets the terms of the relationship she will share with the family members whom she will later protect; she also teaches that the sati's will must be respected, and her desire remembered." In the transformation that occurs when a woman becomes a *sativrata*, a powerful social secret is briefly vented. Good mothers can also be bad mothers. Women have wills of their own. The *sativrata* becomes dangerous (she is said to be literally too hot to touch) and punitive. Against anyone who angers her, she delivers a curse (*srap*). Furthermore, she is expected to place prohibitions (*oks*) on the activities of the very family that until recently confined and restricted her. But the secret of the bad mother is like a scary truth whispered quickly through a small crack in the ritual process. The bad mother fully emerges only for a brief moment and in ways that are ritually contained (she dies shortly after issuing her curses and proscriptions) and later rationalized (her curses are said to be blessings in disguise). As Harlan puts it, "a mother is benevolent even when she punishes."

On rare occasions a woman takes a vow to commit sati and is prevented from going through with it. This might happen because a family fears breaking the law or, in a few cases, because the woman is needed in the home. When the family prevents her sati, the woman may nevertheless become a "living *satimata*." Harlan tells a story about such a woman who proved her virtue by miraculously needing to consume no food. This widow, confined to a tiny room, resolutely refused to eat any of the food offered to her, but did give blessings to all who came to see her.[10] The woman earned the title of living *satimata* by acting out the part of a good mother. She denied herself but served others; she never took but always gave; she never consumed but nourished all who came to her.

When the sati event is actually carried through, as the *sativrata* mounts the funeral pyre, the dialogue between consumer and consumed, devourer and devoured becomes more convoluted and more highly charged. The bad mother, who made a brief appearance through the curses and prohibitions of the *sativrata*, has now retreated from the foreground. Her rapacious presence is still felt, however, beneath the increasingly intense images of beatific female self-sacrifice. For example, from the moment a woman takes a vow of sati, a process of self-devouring is said to begin. Harlan notes the belief that when a woman, on hearing of the death of her husband, utters the spontaneous vow that she will die with him, her *sat* (virtue) begins to heat up and "consume her body." This same *sat* is believed to ignite the funeral pyre and finally consume both husband and wife. But this does not happen until, as the devotional images of Roop Kanwar show, she mounts the funeral pyre and takes the body of her husband into her lap, in a breastfeeding posture. Then, as Harlan characterizes it, "her body explodes into flames, and these cremate her own body and the body of her husband."

As he feeds on her, she eats him up and, most important, devours herself as well. The nurturing woman and the devouring woman become one through a process in which fire transforms the rapacious, willful bad mother (who made an uncharacteristically direct appearance lest anyone should miss that she was there) into a self-devouring good mother. When woman's power is safely turned back against herself, the net result is that the bad mother gets burned up while the good mother survives. But the good woman who survives is very different from the one who mounted the funeral pyre.

The flames purge the actual woman of any blame in her husband's death. He did not die because her *sat* was insufficient. On the contrary, they both burned because her virtue was so great. Yet even as the good mother triumphs, the individual woman, who momentarily incarnated her, disappears. As Harlan reports, "satis are almost invariably referred to in the singular. What is important is not the individual woman who dies on a pyre but the transformative reality that her death symbolizes." The flames transform the untrustworthy, fallible, particular human woman into a safe, infallible, generalized, transcendent mother called Sati.

While much more detail could be added to this analysis, I think the point has been made: whatever else the rituals of sati are about, they are surely about "Mommy" and about putting Mommy in her place.

Notes

1. Sudesh Vaid and Kumkum Sangari, "Institutions, Beliefs, Ideologies: Widow Immolation in Contemporary Rajasthan," *Economic and Political Weekly* 26:17 (April 27, 1991), especially pp. WS-14–16; also, Madhu Kishwar and Ruth Vanita, "The Burning of Roop Kanwar," *Manushi* 42–43 (1987), pp. 15–25.

2. Dorothy Dinnerstein, *The Mermaid and the Minotaur* (San Francisco: Harper & Row, 1976), p. 131.

3. Dinnerstein, *Mermaid*, p. 132.

4. To some extent women, as well as men, support this maneuver. Women and men gathered to watch Roop Kanwar burn, and women are often eager devotees at sati shrines. Women have mothers just as men do, and they too hold deep in themselves a view of woman as a combination of a pure goddess, totally selfless and nurturant, and a polluting, rapacious witch. But women do not write the culture script (empathy alone might have prevented them from including the chapter on sati), even though they have to live (and sometimes die) on its terms.

5. Sudhir Kakar, *The Inner World: A Psycho-analytic Study of Childhood and Society in India* (Delhi: Oxford University Press, 2d ed., 1981), p. 79.

6. Kakar, *Inner World*, pp. 79–80.

7. Kakar, *Inner World*, pp. 80–81.

8. Kakar, *Inner World*, p. 80.

9. Kakar makes a connection between mythic images of the good mother and the extraordinary degree to which Indian women conform their lives to their children's needs. He also argues that these same childrearing practices create generalized Indian personality traits, principally trust in the world and openness to others. But Kakar attributes mythic images of the bad mother to a destructive pattern in which frustrated women overwhelm their children with needs that could more appropriately be met by their husbands, if it were not for the dense extended-family context in which marital life must be negotiated. While I find Kakar's connections between women's social roles and mythic images generally quite enlight-

ening, because of the near universality of the bad mother image, I find Dinnerstein's argument for the etiology of this image more convincing; it stresses the inevitability that a child will experience pain and frustration with even the best of mothering.

10. Lindsey Harlan, personal communication, September 27, 1988.

Part 9:
Indigenous North American Traditions

CHAPTER
9

Death and Grieving among Northern Forest Hunters: An East Cree Example

Richard J. Preston
and
Sarah C. Preston

The chapter by Richard and Sarah Preston focusses on the Cree people living east of James Bay in the Province of Quebec in Canada. The chapter is an example of collaboration by researchers coming from different perspectives after more than a quarter century of research and residence among the Cree. Their perspectives differ because Richard began his sojourn among the Cree as a trained anthropologist whose primary interest was in mental culture, values and symbolism. Sarah first accompanied Richard in her role as wife, and came to know the Cree as neighbors and friends. She has since taken an undergraduate and graduate degree in anthropology and followed her own independent work among Cree with a special interest in women's work and life histories. The Cree place great value on personal autonomy and competence and do not intervene in each other's lives. Their restraint, even in the face of death, is a hallmark of their culture. The Prestons, after so many years of residence among the Cree, also speak of their own grief at the death of their friends.

* * *

INTRODUCING THE CREE

The patterns of death and grieving we represent here are, we believe, characteristic of the native people living on the Quebec side of the coast of James Bay, Canada. Our interpretations are derived from experiences shared during sojourns between 1963 and 1984, and from narratives of events which we take to be true to life and of value as they provide a guide for living. It is a simple but difficult fact of human mortality that some of our friends would meet their deaths over this twenty-year-period. These deaths would have been difficult for us to discuss a few years ago. We are comfortable now presenting these events with some objectivity derived from some years' passage of time, and with the social distance of this volume's comparative research.

The cultural events we discuss in this chapter were considered to be traditional by Cree adults in the 1960s. By traditional we mean a recognition of continuity with the past which gives people a feeling of authenticity. Eastern Cree traditional culture is characterized by an ideal of personal autonomy, with pervasive attitudes, themes, and values of interpersonal composure and reticence. They attend to subtle cues in interpersonal relations, but have a remarkable capacity for non-interference in the personal autonomy of others (R. Preston, 1976, n.d.; S. Preston, 1986). The Cree cultural focus or premise is an ideology of egalitarian personal autonomy. The authority of the individual person is primary; giving orders to another is insulting, for all are responsible for their own actions. Most perceptive sojourners in this area are impressed, first with the superficial similarities to, and later with the fundamental differences from, our own ideology of individualism.

For many Cree people, the 1970s and 1980s have seen a turning away from traditional attitudes and sensitivities, a diffidence towards listening to narratives for guidance, and the adoption of more cosmopolitan values (J. Blythe, P. Brizinski and S. Preston, 1985). We doubt our ability to make a precise assessment of the effect of these changes on the topic of dying and grief, so we focus on the not too distant 'traditional.' On the other hand, the last grieving we were a part of occurred in 1984, on the death of Malcolm Diamond, an exemplar of tradition and the old chief at Waskaganish. We were aware at that time that grief was powerfully felt and expressed in traditional mourning, while concern for the behavior of the departing spirit seemed to be much less evident. The death of the old chief may have signalled the end of an era, but some of the events and feelings we shared at that time were certainly traditional.

We wish to emphasize three main themes from Cree Culture:

1. People can and should control themselves in sustained synchrony, or cultural coordination, both with human others in personal community, and with non-human others in an inclusive community of human, spiritual, and animal persons;
2. Living and dying are full of contingencies that are only partly predictable and to which human beings must adapt by trying to meet them competently.
3. Life is viewed metaphorically as a journey. All who make this journey in its various aspects—from the daily following of trails, to longer hunting trips, to seasonal periods of camp movement through a hunting range, to movement through the life course—are guided by paths. The narrative is such a path.

Our presentation centers on several narrative texts which provide primary evidence for our discussion of cultural aspects of Cree dying and grieving. By providing examples of what others have done and the consequences of their

actions, Cree narratives traditionally offered guidance for living one's life competently and wisely. Stories are intended to draw the listener into vicarious participation with the narrator and with the persons involved in the events recited, so that one can learn not only to tell the story but also to guide one's life accordingly.

CREE BASIC ATTITUDES, NOTIONS, AND CONCEPTIONS

Death is at once a commonplace event and one with much significance. Hunters chronically pursue, cause, and perceive death of the animals that are their food as part of the ordinary process of living. Cree believe that animals give themselves to humans gladly (or they would never let their whereabouts be known) and yet, somehow, not willingly (because they try to escape). That is, it is the purpose of animals to give themselves, so that humans can obtain their food and live. The human who is capable, once given a clue to the location of the animal, of playing out the strategy and action of the hunt, and who then is competent in the respectful use and disposition of the remains, is destined to continue to be the recipient of these covert gifts of love (R. Preston, 1975:198-234). The consequences of incompetent hunting or disrespectful acts toward the animals through the casual disposal of their remains are expected to be failure and hardship.

Human death, in contrast to the death of an animal, is an intensely emotional event, and dangerous in its potential for difficult consequences. It is not necessarily a crisis, but it *may* become one. Like birth (S. Preston, 1982), a person's death is an occasion for unusual effort at self-control. As with the person in the act of giving birth, self-control is expected of the person who is dying, and it is hoped that others present will not give way to fear. If you are dying, a controlled death is the ideal for your own composure and for the composure of those around you. If others are dying, you hope that they will not only die well, but will continue to manifest composure in their activities after death, and that they will soon depart.

Death is normally regarded as a letting go of the body, and a subsequent departure of the spirit. In some narratives, this is given the explicit metaphor of a voyage or journey, when the person goes out to meet his or her death, perhaps not much interrupted from life's voyage. There is an ideal of a good death, one that maintains human and other-than-human relationships much as they were before death. This emphasis on continuity constitutes a moral pattern for the subsequent behavior of spirits of the deceased, both human and other-than-human. The behavior of the spirit is the final test of that person's true character and attitudes towards the living. On the occasion of a human's death, people watch for signs of the person's final intentions. At the same time, people watch to see the animals' intentions towards the human survivors. The animals may leave the region that was used by the deceased, requiring the survivors to move elsewhere or starve, or they may choose to make themselves available for hunting and eating to the surviving humans. Cree say that the deceased human may influence these animals' decisions to make themselves available. Belief in the ability of the spirit of the deceased to influence animal behavior is dramatically illustrated in the following recollection by an Anglican priest:

> An old Indian woman . . . died about the middle of April, when the snow was beginning to melt. . . . This was my first funeral and it had a somewhat surprising climax. After the service I walked at the head of the funeral procession with her husband, the chief mourner, who had his capote over his head. It was very solemn. As he and I walked together in front of the coffin towards the graveyard, a flock of Canada geese returning from the south suddenly appeared over the trees. A person who has never lived in the north could not realize the thrill of the first wild goose call in the Spring. Often it means the end of hunger. It always means fresh meat.
>
> The whole procession dropped on its knees. The pallbearers crouched and the bereaved husband dashed back to his tent for his gun. Meantime the whole congregation were answering the call of the geese. As they came overhead, Manitoshans raised his gun and brought down two geese with a shot from each barrel. One dropped on the coffin. A smile came over his face as he handed the geese to his daughter. "I knew she'd bring me luck," he said (Renison, 1957:31-32).

The man's words speak for themselves, with the same kind of mystical certainty that the arrival of the geese expresses. If it seems odd to us that only the widower ran for his shotgun, we may wonder what restrained the others. Were they simply afraid of scaring the geese by their movement, or did they recognize who sent the geese, and to whom?

SOCIAL DEATH CONTRASTS WITH DYING IN COMMUNITY

"Social death" is an awkward concept in the Cree case, because ostracism is such an extreme measure, and because it is normally an individual's autonomous action that brings it about. The most extreme form is the mythic windigo condition, a person's transformation into a monstrous, damaging state of being. Windigo is thought to be the dying of a person's humanity through a loss of self-control, a giving up of community, and becoming a hunter and eater of humans (R. Preston, 1980).

The Cree consider death to be natural more than social or symbolic. It may be rendered premature by sickness, by accidents, by errors in judgement or actions, or by hardship or sorcery. Nonetheless we suspect that the Cree think that even a death by sorcery is primarily a natural death with social and symbolic causes, as Evans-Pritchard explains for Zande witchcraft (Evans-Pritchard, 1937). There is a notion of fate, at least to the extent that no one, not even a powerful conjuror can give himself more days than he was allotted (perhaps at birth). While anyone may be caught earlier by one of life's many hazards, we are not aware that the Cree think of this as unfair. They do understand, certainly, that premature death is an

unfortunate event that requires some effort to accept; it is not considered an imposition of fate. This understanding seems to us to emphasize the essential contingency of the Cree world.

People differentiate between good and bad deaths largely on the basis of what we currently call 'cognitive control.' For the traditional Cree the good death is a well composed act of 'going out to meet one's death.' We are not certain whether we can say confidently that people—like the animals they hunt—seek the ideal of dying a good death, not willingly, but gladly, but the idea has an intuitive fitness to it. That is, a person ideally goes to meet his or her death with composure and an acceptance that he or she may engage with, but not delay, this event, since this mysterious meeting implies a human destiny that will lead to some further experience.

The following narrative is an example of meeting one's death with composure. The understanding that death is a continuation of life's journey is implicit in the behavior described. Also implicit in the narrative is fore-knowledge and acceptance of an event which could not be delayed. The preparation for further experience on the part of the man making the transition from life into death is explicit in the way he chose to dress. Dressing in one's best clothes for this journey is the means through which one shows respect for the relationships one may be about to enter into, and one hopes that this respect will be reciprocated.

THE DEATH OF PHILIP DIAMOND (REMEMBERED BY MALCOLM DIAMOND)

> I'm going to tell you the story about when my brother died. That morning we were supposed to go out to cut some wood. We had some snares over there and we were going to check those snares. That morning he got up very early. I wasn't even out of bed yet and he was all dressed, all ready to go. He came and stood by the doorway of the bedroom and he asked me when we were leaving. My wife had made a new pair of moccasins and new mittens for him and he'd never worn them before. That morning he dressed up, he wore those moccasins and the new mitts she had made for him. He was all ready to go by the time I got up. Then the old lady got up too, to make some breakfast for us. My brother never used to do that. This was the first time I knew that he was up so early and so anxious to go.
>
> While I was eating my breakfast, the telephone rang. It was the chief, asking me if I could be here that day. He told me he wanted me to be here because they were bringing two men in from the trapline. Their mother had just recently died and he wanted me to meet the plane to tell them about the death of their mother.
>
> When we left here on the skidoo my brother was sitting on the sled, behind. He seemed OK. He didn't look like he had any problem at all. He used to carry this stick that he used as a cane, and as we drove along over there where those small islands are, up the river, not too far from here, he threw his stick ahead of the skidoo to alert me. When I stopped and looked back he said, "I see some white birds on the island." When we stopped near the island the white birds flew off to the other side where there were small willows and bush. So he told me to go and get our snowshoes. We usually leave our snowshoes when we come down the river, and hang them up in a

> tree. I told him, "We can't waste time too long here because we have to get back soon." My brother said, "You shouldn't say that. If we get those white birds, then the old lady will have something to eat. We catch rabbit and she doesn't eat rabbit. She doesn't have any other kind of meat except what you can buy that she can eat." I guess he was thinking of my wife, that she won't have anything to eat even if we catch some rabbit in our snares, because she didn't eat rabbit. That's the last time he talked to me. Those were his last words.
>
> I decided to leave him there and go with the skidoo to get our snowshoes. I'm sure it was only about a 15 minute ride and then I would be back again. I told my brother to wait there and look for the white birds in case they fly somewhere else. I left the gun and said, "If you see them out in the open away from the willows maybe you can go and shoot them." That's when I left him there, and he was OK. He didn't say he was feeling sick or anything like that.
>
> When I was on my way back from the bush, I saw another man on his skidoo. He didn't have anything else with him. He waved and I stopped and he stopped too. I asked if he saw my brother over there where I had left him. He said, "I saw him and I gave him a ride a little ways. He said he wasn't feeling very well." So we both started back. We didn't drive very long and we could see where my brother was. He wasn't sitting up anymore. He was lying on the small sled and he had his face down. He didn't even look up and show he could hear the skidoos coming. I was thinking to myself, "He doesn't even move. He must be in great pain, why he doesn't move when he hears the skidoos coming." Then we stopped and still he didn't move. The other man didn't get off his skidoo. He waited for me to go and see what was happening. He said, "I don't think he's breathing anymore." I guess he could tell because he wasn't moving at all. When I got closer I pulled the hood (of his parka) up because it covered his face, and right away I knew he wasn't breathing anymore, he was gone. I said, "He's gone. He's not breathing anymore." And the other man said, "What are we going to do?" I said, "We have to go back. You drive the skidoo and I can sit at the back." So we came back to the village on one skidoo.

When Sarah asked Malcolm if he thought Philip knew this was to be his last day, Malcolm answered, "I'm sure there was a way that he knew this was going to be his last day, because when he got dressed, he dressed just like he was going somewhere." Although Philip Diamond met death deliberately, with self-knowledge and composure, it is possible that his departure from this world took place more quickly than he had anticipated; an event which he was prepared to meet, but could not postpone. It would seem that he had hoped to speak to his brother one last time, but the expected journey began before he could say his farewells to his relatives. When he was buried, his family left him dressed as he was, assuming that he had prepared himself for this journey by wearing the new moccasins and mitts.

Because they cannot know the future, either in this life or the next, Cree do not know when or if departing loved ones may be seen again. Unforeseen death may intervene. It is, therefore, important to say farewell before leaving on a journey of lengthy duration or distress. Saying farewell affirms relationships and is a recognition of friendship. It is important for those who are dying as well as those who are living to be able to make this statement. Even though people may be afraid, it

is considered strange and unfriendly to fail to make their goodbyes when there is the chance to visit the dangerously weak or dying person. Dying persons share the attitude that it is important to say farewell. Ideally, even in the extremity of dying, Crees will make their goodbyes in a way that comforts the survivors.

Accidental or conjured death may pre-empt composure, but we do not know whether the Cree think that the manner of death influences or determines experiences in the afterlife. It is our impression that the afterlife, being unseen, is necessarily left vague in Cree beliefs. If the character of spirits is known at all, it is known only vaguely. Spirits speak only rarely or indirectly (as in the gift of the geese noted in Renison above) before they depart for good. Most people would be skeptical of claims of knowledge based on mere surmise. Following the example of the Cree, we prefer to leave our consideration of the spiritual realm indefinite.

Successful hunters have to be practical, to see tangible signs in order to know the character of a person, animal, or spirit. In the contingent universe of the Cree there are no guarantees. A person does not know what might be found at the end of a track. There may be caribou there, but one may never catch up with them. It is up to the hunter and to the animals who are unseen.

In the same way, one may not know what is on the other side of death, but the following near-death experience of a nine-year-old girl provides some indication of what Cree might expect. The narration suggests that the dying may enter into relations with spirits whom they encounter on their journey. These may be spirits with whom one already has a reciprocal relationship or they may be spirits with whom one hopes to establish new relationships.

A CHILDHOOD VISION (REMEMBERED BY ALICE JACOB)

> I was so sick, it seems like a dream, but at the same time, I thought I went away. I thought I was walking in the clouds. I came to a large house with a door in the middle. When I came to the door it opened and I went inside. Straight ahead of me I didn't see anyone, but on either side I saw a fence and a stairs. And I saw children, just children, very happy children.
>
> During this vision Alice thought she was met by a tall man dressed in white. She laughed as he came toward her and she felt happy. But the man told her she was going to go back to her mother. When she was told this, instead of turning to go, she waited. She was given a small dish which she thought contained food which she was told to take home to her parents. Then she turned to go. She turned again to see the man hold his hands up to her. . . . When she woke she was told she had not been sleeping, her eyes had been open and she had been gazing upward. She had tears in her eyes and she felt as if she had just returned from being away. "I just went out and came back again." She tried to give to her mother the food she thought she had brought with her, but her mother had only been aware of her illness, not of her 'journey,' and did not understand what she was talking about.

In Alice's near-death narration, she meets a spirit person who is generous to her, but does not let her stay in this happy place. She had no foreknowledge of this meeting, or indeed of her travel to another realm and return to this world. She follows a new path, discovers what is there, and then returns with this new knowledge. There is no certainty that she or anyone else will again take this path, or encounter the man dressed in white. But it might happen, or another path might be taken, and other spirits might be met. As with their hunting, the Cree cannot know the outcome in advance, but only have some idea of what has happened in previous hunts, and a sense of how to conduct oneself along the path to discovery.

The following narrative provides an illustration of foreknowledge and preparation for death. The events exemplify a good death. Although these events may have been experienced by relatives as sudden and unexpected, they were experienced by the dying man with composure, self-control, and understated competence.

I'M ALMOST FALLING OFF MY CHAIR THE DEATH OF JIMMY MOAR (REMEMBERED BY ALICE JACOB)

Near the time when my foster father would die, I knew about that. I really loved him, like a father. . . .

Late one evening, I went to see him. He knew I came into the house because he heard me talking. He was sitting in a chair and he said to me, "What are you doing?" And I said, "Nothing, I just came by, dropped in for awhile." He said, "How is my grandchild?" I told him, "I already put her to bed." The he said, "Take care of my granddaughter all the time. Take good care of her. I'm almost falling off from my chair. That's all I can sit here. I'm very tired. It's quite awhile since I was blind. I really love you because we brought you up. I always stopped Maggie from beating you or spanking you. I am very happy we never hurt you."

Then I said to him, "Why are you talking like this to me?" I felt in my heart there was something I didn't like, the way he was talking to me. I felt like crying when he said all this to me. His wife said to him, "Don't talk that way." Then he said, "I wanted to tell you so you would be ready." I never even sat down. I was standing when he was talking to me. So I decided to go outside because I was wondering about what he said to me. I told him, "I'm leaving now." I said, "Good night" to him, and he said, "I love you, my child." Then I went home.

As soon as I went out from their house, he started to sing a hymn from the hymn book. He sang in English and he stood up while he was singing. Then he felt for the string, (which was about the house for him to get around on his own) and started walking while he was singing. After he finished singing, he asked for his suit-coat. Then his wife asked him, "Why do you carry on like this?" He acted very different, and he didn't tell her why. Then he went to bed; he lay down on the bed with his suit on. My foster mother thought he had gone to sleep.

My foster mother went to bed too, and when she touched him on the bed, she thought she couldn't hear him breathing. There was another old woman there with them, my foster mother's sister. Then she made sure, she looked at him and watched him to see if he was already gone. He wasn't breathing any more. And my foster

mother told her sister, "Go and get Alice;" When I got there I checked and he had no pulse. So I believed what he told me (S. Preston, 1986:71-72).

When Jimmy Moar told Alice he was almost falling off his chair, his meaning went beyond the literal statement that he was so tired that he felt as if he might fall out of the chair. He was also stating, indirectly, that his death was near, and he was preparing himself and his family for his leave-taking. He made every effort to create a disciplined experience; expressing his respect and concern for those persons closest to him, saying his goodbyes, and reaffirming his relationship to his daughter and her child. He also expressed his respect for those persons he might be expected to meet on his journey from this life into the next through singing and dressing in his best clothes.

It is the rare individual who can both create and sustain the balance between the ideal and action achieved by Jimmy Moar. Others strive to achieve this ideal through their efforts to meet death as one should meet life: with equanimity and conscious deliberateness imbedded in reticence, friendship, and as much self-reliance as possible. The response of the old man's wife to his words and actions is a reminder that subtle cues are not always readily understood, or accepted, even among Crees. She seemed to avoid sharing his foreknowledge, refusing his cues or teasing about them instead of taking them into composed acceptance and acknowledging his indirect message that he was about to leave them. Although Alice was reluctant to act on the basis of what she knew in her heart, she did not avoid the foreknowledge, but went outside to keep her composure. Both women were in some sense avoiding a recognition of loss and a premature expression of grief. Although this may not be the ideal response, the measure of disengagement allows the women to maintain emotional control.

BEHAVIOR FOLLOWING A DEATH

The body of the deceased is carefully washed, usually by older relatives. New moccasins and sometimes new or fancy clothing is put on. In cases like that of Philip Diamond, however, where it was thought that the person had dressed himself for his journey, people would not interfere, assuming that the person had chosen those things to be buried in.

The place at home, where the deceased spent his/her final days, is scrubbed down, and some personal things of little value to others may be burned by spouse, parent, child, or other close relative. In one instance even a small house was demolished. Useful personal property of the deceased is stored away by immediate family for a year, then distributed to relatives. The family puts possessions away partly to keep from being reminded of the death, and partly as a sign of respect for the deceased. This is also a demonstration that family members are not anxious to claim these possessions. One man who did not wait a full year to claim the rifle that a brother might have claimed was the focus of gossip censuring his possessiveness.

Delaying a burial is not good for the dying person or for those who grieve. Delay may interfere with the forthcoming journey and result in unusual activity by the departing spirit. Delay may also result in over-long and intense expression of grief and a loss of emotional control on the part of the bereaved. The death of a person whose body is lost or a death which occurs while a person is 'outside' (and so may be casually disposed of), is a cause for real concern. Whenever possible, a person who dies 'outside' (for example, in hospital) is brought home for burial.

In this century a funeral service conducted by an Anglican priest in the church building and burial in a marked and decorated grave in the churchyard are considered to be appropriate, but burial in the bush is also acceptable and sometimes necessary. Graves in the graveyard are visited, tidied and decorated, especially on an annual day set aside by the Anglican Church for that purpose. Graves in the bush may be visited, especially when they are located within a family hunting territory. After some years, however, feelings of grief are let go in favor of acceptance and remembrance; prolonging grief or brooding is unhealthy for the mental well-being of the living. The following narrative provides an example of the continued love and respect which is expressed to the deceased through the care of the gravesite.

A STORY OF A MAN FROM EASTMAIN (RECOUNTED BY MALCOLM DIAMOND)

The man and his family were out on their trapline and they were very short of food. The man's older brother went hunting and was gone for two days. When he didn't return, the man told his mother, "I think we should follow his tracks and check on him, to see what happened." They walked all along the lake shore. The wind had shifted from the north and there had been quite a snow storm. Finally they came to a hump, partly buried in the snow. They discovered this was the man's brother and they gave him a burial.

What they used to do to identify where the burial site was, they just removed the bark (from a tree). The only thing is, every year you do that. Every time you pass the grave, you peel it or cut it more, so it's bare on that side.

Every time he went to the bush, if he was near the grave, he always removed the bark. He said, "That's just to show respect for my brother, that I loved him. But now that site is where they were going to put the Eastmain River Dam, so it's under water. Of all the things that happened as far as all that damming around here, that's what hurt me the most. Seeing that grave under the water like that. Even though my whole trapline is under the water, I think that showing that respect for my brother, marking that tree like that, is what I really feel bad about. I feel bad about losing my land to trap on, but I feel worse about losing the site of my brother's burial."

Death, being so much a part of the hunter's world, is also associated symbolically with some categories of animals. For example, the stuffed and decorated head

of the first goose that a boy killed, was kept as a tangible sign of the continuing relationship of a hunter to geese, and finally was hung on the hunter's grave pole. This may be symbolic of a transformation of the relationship of the man with the geese into an unknown but hoped for continuity.

To our knowledge, people do not make any associations between death and particular categories of person. Old women, usually family members, prepare the body for burial and an older man, either family member or respected elder of the community, will probably coordinate the burial activities, but this is not necessary. After a lifetime of experience older people are willing to assume a leadership role, making decisions about what is to be done in a variety of situations, including preparations for burial. They have acquired both the knowledge of what needs to be done and the ability to handle the stress which accompanies death and grief.

Cree characteristically accept death rather than deny it. We are aware of no mandatory or ritual behaviors to ensure acceptance of death, but the attitude seems to be strongly and generally held. We think that it is accurate to say that people may be able to bring their attitudes and actions into accord with the process of their dying, as indicated by the narratives we have cited above. The dying person knows that death is close at hand and makes an effort consciously to act in a manner reflecting the deeply held, unconsciously patterned, beliefs about appropriate social behavior.

Hardship and death may be brought about through the incompetent actions or the poor judgment of a person within the group. Two narratives of the same events illustrate death as a consequence of misjudgment. In the first an old woman recalled her daughter's death in the bush.

REMEMBERED BY MARY DIAMOND

I want to tell you about when we were in the bush when my daughter had a baby who was just about two months old when the mother got sick. It was too late to come (to Waskaganish) to get the airplane. My daughter got sick very suddenly and she was nursing the baby, and then, she died. I didn't have any milk and there were two women in the same tent that were still nursing their year-old children, so they had to breast feed the baby. And I had to boil some oatmeal and take the juice out of the porridge, that's what I used to feed the baby before I put him to bed. I think it was about two weeks those women had to breast feed the baby. Then at last there were people coming down the river and they had a little bit of powdered milk with them. One of the women had a nursing bottle which she gave me, so I boiled the milk and that's the way I fed baby. Then we came down to the village and I raised the baby. Now he's grown and I am staying with him.

Another woman's account of these same events suggests that the loss of the daughter was so great that Mary was able (or willing) to recall and retell only the story of the infant's survival and not the story of her daughter's death. Her omission may be the result of her grieving over this death and her regret at having misjudged the situation. Silda's account tells us, among other things, why one should listen carefully to what others have to tell, as well as why one should always say goodbye when leaving.

REMEMBERED BY SILDA DIAMOND

The next fall, in September, we went out on the trapline by canoe and we stopped at Middleton Island. Walter Diamond and his son and son-in-law and all their families were camped there, but when we left to go up the river, they stayed. Walter Diamond's youngest daughter, apparently liked my little boy, Joey, very much. When we left we didn't go to see them (to say goodbye). She didn't even see the baby, my little boy, before we left their camp. After we were gone, she said she didn't know (we were leaving) and she was sorry she didn't get to see my little boy. She told her mother, "I guess they are so sure that we're going to live until we see them again, is the reason why they don't even come to shake hands and say good-bye to us when they leave." She wasn't very old, this woman, she'd just been married two years at that time. She acted as if she really wanted to be friends and she really loved us, because she used to come to see us all the time, before she was married, and after too. Then, they came up the river after us (to go to their camp). We had to go farther up than they did.

Everything went fine at the camp for us, nobody was sick out there, and we were there all winter. The men did very well with trapping and hunting. We had meat all the time, all through that winter. Later on, some of the families that were with us went down to Waskaganish for the spring and some stayed behind with us. We spent spring out there and came down the river after breakup. Sometimes Walter Diamond and his family would come to our camp and we were surprised when he didn't come that spring, because we could hear their shots. We could hear them shooting at something and Malcolm wondered what happened, why they didn't come to see us. So we decided we should go and check on them, to see what happened. Before we reached their camp—they were already quite a ways down river—we found a letter they had written telling us their daughter had passed away. And then Malcolm told everybody we should go and camp where they were camping.

Walter Diamond's daughter had a baby boy, born on March 6, and she died on April 19. She had been breast-feeding this baby, and after her death they didn't have a bottle to use to feed the baby. One of the women told us that after the baby was born, the young mother got worse. She got very sick and then she started to lose weight very fast. She got worse and worse. She used to complain to her mother that she was losing weight very fast, and her mother would just say to her, "That's because you're nursing the baby, you're going to lose weight." Louisa Diamond (the young mother's sister-in-law) told her husband, "I think your sister is very sick. I think you should go to Waskaganish and try to find a way for her to be taken back to the settlement."

Louisa told us the parents didn't seem to notice or pay any attention to the fact that their daughter was sick. They weren't worried at all, because they thought it was the effect of the birth that was why she's losing weight. Then, she really was sick, and they didn't seem to notice that she was that sick. They weren't really worried about her. Louisa was very surprised, because Mary really worries about what happens when somebody is sick. But, that's the way, I guess. They didn't worry about their daughter, but that's the way things went.

About a month after the baby was born they were moving to another place, and Mary told her daughter, "Get your baby on the toboggan and pull the baby on the toboggan while we're traveling." Not too long after they left the camp, they were behind all the others, she told her husband she wanted to stop and rest because she felt very tired. It hurt her chest when she walked and she told her husband, "Let's sit down and rest for a while." So that man told his wife, "Never mind, don't pull the baby, just take some of our stuff off my toboggan and I'll pull you on with the baby. I'll pull you on the toboggan."

When they got to the camp they were already putting up the tent. When Mary saw her daughter bundled up on the toboggan with her husband pulling her she asked why did she have to ride on the toboggan. Her daughter said, "I didn't feel well at all, I couldn't walk." Then Mary told her, "You would feel better if you had walked for quite a while, but it was just the beginning when you're trying to walk that you felt like that." All of a sudden the daughter was unconscious, and that's when they started to wake up and begin to worry about her. Then it was hard to come down to Waskaganish because it was thawing already, it was spring. She was unconscious for three days before she died. So it was very hard on them, what happened, and Mary tried to look after the baby herself. After we moved to the camp with them, we tried to help her with the baby and we came down the river all together.

The baby didn't have very much milk when we saw them and we were able to give them nipples and bottles and milk, too. Everybody would give them some. Mary wasn't well after that, that spring, after we came back. She went to see the doctor here when he came, but he said she wasn't sick. It was because she was taking her daughter's death so hard, that's why she thought she was sick. They took her to the hospital in Moose Factory, but apparently after they did all the tests that they did on her, the doctor told her the same thing again, that it was because she was taking her daughter's death very hard, that's why she though she was sick.

Mary had only two children, one girl and one boy. Apparently that girl was always well, before she was married, she was never sick. This was an arranged marriage and then she got sick after she was married.

Silda's narrative presents the events in their full complexity, with a sense of the tragic fate of a young woman to whom people did not pay enough attention. Silda is a very competent, wise and graceful person, and we can see from her story that she recognizes the mistake, accepts the tragic consequences, and forgives Mary's uncharacteristic lapse of competence. Silda's group, after all, also made a serious mistake. They did not say their goodbyes, and the young woman's comments carry a foreboding of what is to happen. Mary's error of judgement is twofold: she is too ready to interfere and direct the actions of her daughter, and she does not perceive her daughter's fatal illness until it is too late. She is not the cause of her daughter's death, but she did not respond to the illness quickly enough.

COMMUNICATION WITH THE DYING AND THE BEREAVED

The first person to realize that death is approaching may be the dying person, or an astute observer, or someone who has received the knowledge in a dream. Cree do not normally tell a person directly that he or she is likely to die, for such a statement probably would be taken as a personal insult or as a threat instead of as a diagnosis. A person may, however, make such a statement if care is taken to avoid implications of threat or sorcery. Alternatively, the person who discerns that another is dying might show concern by some caring inquiry or action. In contrast, if a white man with authority, such as a trader, missionary, or medical practitioner informs a person of oncoming death, the diagnosis usually does not imply ill intent.

The news that someone has died should be told simply, directly, and promptly so that grief may be expressed quickly and fully. The consequences of delaying the report of a death may be difficult and unpredictable. Part of the reason for this has to do with the pattern of quick, full venting of grief. Adult women do not cry often, though they may do so when hunters return, long overdue, with needed food, or when sharing a sad story, or in remembrance, while in the security of a church service. The event of the death of a relative is perhaps the only time that an adult man will cry openly. This brief expression of grief is followed by the appearance of fully regained composure, even when the inner feelings are still troubled. Part of the reason is that the strong emotions may lead to a misconstruing and misreporting of events, if they are not already known clearly and quickly. But mistaken understanding is not so risky as unpredictable actions.

If the death is accidental, badly managed, or complicated in some other way, the details may be discussed as gossip by those only distantly related, and cause implied. For instance, a reputed sorcerer had a severe stroke and survived for many months in a distressed and disorganized way, shouting profanities and in other ways being out of control. This was widely regarded as an awful way to die.

In the 1960s we observed several times that no one went out the night after a death. A candle or lamp was set into the window of a house or kept in a tent to discourage the spirit from entering. It is possible for a spirit to remain for up to seven days, before continuing on his or her way. In a few troublesome cases, this departure may take even longer. There is an assumption that the spirit of a dying person will visit those persons for whom he or she had strong feelings, whether positive or negative. Those who are visited may be at risk of being taken by the dying one. On the other hand the visitor may be mischievous, or may simply wish to say farewell, as a good person should.

The death of a woman who had been involved in an affair with a philandering widower was preceded by a premonitory dream in which the man's deceased wife was seen to call to the indistinct image of another woman, "Come on, ______." The situation was regarded as one of considerable risk for the philanderer who was advised to keep his food covered up against poisoning. In another case, which was regarded as less ominous and more mischievous, and old man finally shot his rifle at an old woman's spirit to hurry her away. This unusual step was taken only after she repeatedly disturbed her belongings, which first had been put away at home, then later in the Hudson Bay Company warehouse. In a much less troublesome case of simple farewell, another departing spirit was unexpectedly heard by a man to say to him, "Boy! I didn't come to tease you."

EXPRESSIONS OF GRIEF

What expression of grief is appropriate? The immediate, open expression of personal, spontaneous grief by relatives and friends is expected, accepted, and normally is expressed by both publicly and privately. People cry freely and are quickly supported, comforted, and encouraged to carry on with their lives by those less affected. This support is part of the lifelong process of renewing and strengthening the bonds of friendship and kinship. The outpouring of grief will be repeated in spells until the burial. Cree hope that the mourners soon will be able to let go of their grief, for to hold it and brood for a long time is unhealthy, and may lead to madness.

The following vignette demonstrates that the appearance of equanimity after the burial can be disconcerting to an outsider and can contribute to the outsider's brooding and social isolation. (See Figure 9.)

Figure 9. Death and grieving among northern forest hunters: an East Cree example.

THE DEATH OF WILLY WEISTCHEE (REMEMBERED BY DICK PRESTON)

I was present at the death of a good friend in 1964. The events are still vivid. Willy was my first good Cree friend, my advisor ("Never get excited; never lose your nerve."), practical helper, interpreter, and teacher about life in this Cree settlement. We were the same age. He had been out to the Hamilton Sanatorium for five years as a teenager in the 1940s, with tuberculosis of the spine. Consequently, he was fluent in English as well as Cree, and could swear in Hungarian and Chinese. He had few relatives in the settlement where I knew him. His parents were dead, and some brothers lived in mining towns to the south. He was aware that, as a cripple, he could probably never marry; however, he held the hope that with his intelligence and fluency, he might be chief someday.

At the time of his final sickness, his old Aunt Maria and a girl who lived in their tent were gone to a fishing camp, so he was alone. I knew that he had a persistent feeling of something stuck in his throat, and we had delayed a trip inland until it would clear up. I also knew that he had been concerned about telling me some things about an old man whom he believed to be dangerous. The throat did not clear up. A traditional healer made an herbal concoction for him, but it didn't help. I asked if he wanted to go to the nursing station, but he declined. Then, one night, I had a premonitory dream in which my friend died.

The next morning I went next door to his tent, and he said, "Boy, I almost died last night." He showed me a teaspoon that was strangely blackened, and told me he had got up in the dark and used the spoon to take some Emo laxative salts, and then felt much worse. He looked quite ill, and I urged him to go to the nursing station, only a few hundred yards away. He balked again, this time saying that he was not sure he could walk that far. I interfered a little, saying that if he could not make it, I could carry him.

He made it, and the nurse put him in bed and seemed reassuring. Next morning I went there and she said he was doing well, and had eaten a little porridge. I went in his room and was shocked at how wasted he looked. When I told the nurse that I thought he looked much worse, she became concerned and radioed for a plane to take him to hospital. Willy gave me the key to his tent, and asked me to get him a few personal items, and to "tell someone that I am leaving, Lawrence maybe."

I told Lawrence, brought the things, and sat with him. He was sweating and wanted fresh air, but I was afraid he would chill. Time seemed to go too slowly for him. Then he wanted a bedpan, so I went for the nurse. She put it under him, and came out into the hall, where we talked for a minute. I thought I heard him call, but could not be sure. Then he rang the hand-bell. The nurse went in, and when she came out she was crying. She said she just picked him up from the bedpan, and he died in her arms.

Willy had a married sister, Emily, living with Rosie and Anderson, her in-laws. I went straight to their house and in the door, holding my grief. Emily was pregnant and in a bed in the corner. I walked halfway to her, and she pulled the blanket up closer to her. I stopped and said, "I am sorry to tell you this, but Willy is dead." She and others started to cry right away, and I stood there, choked up. Then Rosie came and put her arms around me to help me to cry. I can't recall for sure, but I think I did. Then I sat down with Anderson, and he started to tell me about Charlton Island, the land where he trapped, how good the water was to drink there, and how many kinds of berries grew there in the fall. I was confused by this. It seemed to make no sense to try to listen to these things in such a situation. After a while, I went to my cabin.

The plane came, with a young doctor. I went to speak to him at the Nursing Station. He wanted to do an autopsy right there. I sensed his inexperience and arrogance, and spoke strongly against this, saying that if an autopsy was to be done, it must be done fully and properly, at the hospital. He resented my skepticism of his ability, but I saw that the nurse also did not respect him, and insisted. He said that if he agreed to that, then the Indians would expect the Northern Health Service to pay to return the body for burial. I told him that I would pay the charter. He was unhappy with this, but accepted it. The nurses' aide told me she wanted to help pay, but had a debt still from her father's funeral. I went back to get Emily's permission for the autopsy, and then he was taken out.

That afternoon, or perhaps it was the next day, the chief came to tell me that some of the men were saying they would put some money to pay for the charter, and he heard that I said that I would do that, too. He said that he just wanted to know how much money I wanted to put in. I told him whatever was needed. My vague answer was not helpful, he wanted to know an amount. I did not know what to estimate for an amount, and repeated my first answer. They went away.

Northern Health Service paid the charter. I went to the funeral, and one of Willy's friends made room for me and showed the places in the hymnal. We went outside and the casket was put in the grave. I did not know, or try to find out, how to be a part of any of the work of preparation or burial.

Following the funeral, I withdrew to my cabin. The night after the burial, it was extremely quiet; even the dogs were silent. The next morning, a neighboring boy opened my door to ask if I had been in my cabin that night. "Yes, it was pretty quiet."

The board walls and floor of Willy's aunt's tent were scrubbed twice. Some small things were burned, and others gathered and put away. Willy's missing pliers were, for some reason, a problem, and I was asked for them three times although I explained that I did not have them. It is unusual to persist in requests for something; the death may have made their location more urgent for someone, or perhaps they thought I was lying.

I remained withdrawn and brooding. I thought that Willy had been ensorceled by the old man. I then thought that the old man would wish me the same ill condition, since I had learned about him from Willy, and he might somehow know about this. I wondered if my questions about sorcery had been a cause of Willy's dying. I wanted to pack up and run away from the situation and from anthropology. I was afraid to eat. I felt terribly alone. Then I determined that I would pit my will power against the old man's, so that he would not beat me.

Old John Blackned took a unique initiative and came to see me. He came with an interpreter, to tell me "The Beaver Wife," a particularly entertaining story. I wrote it down carefully, but it was difficult to get it straight because the interpreter was not competent. Some days later, with a good interpreter, I checked it with John.

The first day or two after the burial, when I went out to the store, I looked depressed, and people seemed to avoid eye contact. When, in a few days, I shook off my depression and began speaking in a normal, casually friendly fashion, the avoidance disappeared, and with it my sense of isolation. After a few days, someone told me, "We feel badly, too, even if we don't show it." I asked if anyone had been visited by his spirit on the night after the funeral. Maybe one or two people; it wasn't certain. There was no trouble, I didn't ask anyone else. He was a good man.

At the burial, grief is openly shown in crying, but, so far as we know, is not expressed in more violent actions. Indeed, while the relation of hunters to animals routinely includes bloody injury, human interaction emphatically should not be violent and rarely is this stricture broken. Similarly, one should not inflict violence on oneself. It would, for example, be wrong to gash oneself in grief. After the burial, close relatives go into formal mourning, with an arm band of black or some other visible sign, for a year. Gaiety, flirting, or remarriage are inappropriate during this period. These outward expressions of mourning may have been introduced by Anglican missionaries in the 19th century. In a culture where emotional reticence is a distinctive characteristic, the brief period of open grief is particularly striking, and perhaps particularly effective as a catharsis. It may be that a mourner's expression of deep feelings of grief is directed not to those around him, but directly to the person of the deceased, now only present as spirit.

Relatives and friends of the deceased will differ in the strength of their feelings of grief, according to the strength of the love they feel for him or her. We would not be confident, however, in differentiating the kinds of feelings experienced or shown to others, and we intuitively resist the notion of categories of loss value. Social categories are resisted by the Crees, even when they manifestly exist. In our experience, people may help the bereaved by simply being present, by talking about the deceased, or by talking of other, seemingly irrelevant and distracting things, according to their leading.

A RECENT DEATH

In 1984, when we received the phone call that the old chief, Malcolm Diamond, had died, Dick was away giving a lecture at a university in New England. Sarah, responding to many years' close friendship with the old man's wife and daughters, as well as her great respect for him, felt the need to return to Waskaganish for the funeral. Sarah made hurried and complicated travel arrangements which she thought she had fully organized. On our arrival at Timmins, however, we met Diamond family members who were being brought in from the bush by charter, as well as those who were arriving from Manitoba. These relatives had been told that we would be arriving in Timmins also and they expected us to join them for the last portion of the journey.

It was a solemn meeting and trip, but open expression of grief did not take place. We flew into Waskaganish late in the evening and were met by the deceased man's sons who took us immediately to their parent's home. One of the daughters, with whom we normally would have stayed, arranged for us to stay at the Anglican mission, because her house was filled with family. When we entered the Diamonds' house, we came into the front room filled with relatives, friends and neighbors, sitting together, weeping. (See Figure 10.)

Figure 10. Death and grieving among northern forest hunters: an East Cree example.

THE FUNERAL OF MALCOLM DIAMOND (REMEMBERED BY SARAH PRESTON)

I went immediately to Silda to hug her and join the weeping—then I remember shaking hands and greeting all those in the room, hugging and weeping with all the women I knew. Then I sat beside Silda's daughter Annie, who has been like a sister to me. I continued to weep and to hold Annie's hand—or perhaps Annie was holding my hand. I remember experiencing intense sorrow, not only because I considered many of those around me, who were weeping, to be close friends and I shared their grief—but also, over the years in and out of the household, the old man had begun to treat me as another daughter. I felt the loss as I might have felt the loss of the father I never knew.

I was able eventually to control my weeping as those around me were doing, but at the funeral service the following day I clung to Annie's hand and continued to weep. Finally, because I was aware that Annie was beginning to control her tears, I tried to also. After the burial service I visited with sisters exchanging family news and cheerful small talk. One of the sisters told stories about her adventures with their father when she was young. We shared in the cooking and child care and household duties which continue even in the face of grief.

I greeted Alice Jacob with Annie, and the weeping was part of the greeting, then there was effort to encourage each other and to cheer each other up. I visited in Silda's house also, where all the relatives gathered and exchanged family gossip, cheerful memories and encouragements. Silda remained in her room most of the time, but I had the opportunity to visit with her there and tell her of my respect for the old man, and that my feelings were those of a daughter for a father. She acknowledged my expression of care and I joined the relatives in the front room.

The second day, signalling the ending of open grieving, Silda, with sons and son-in-law, was in the basement putting away Malcolm's tools. Finally, when we came to say our goodbyes before returning home, Silda and I hugged and wept together for a moment, no doubt both of us wondering if we would ever see each other again.

Dick recalls the evening that we arrived: "Malcolm's oldest son, with whom I had travelled and camped, held onto my hand for what seemed to me a very long time, and Malcolm's closest brother came and spoke at length, firmly and gently, to Silda, offering her encouragement and guidance rather than tears."

CONCLUSIONS

In this chapter we have sought to craft a balance of text and discussion, and have ordered these nine texts with our audience in mind. We began with a text that would have a familiar cultural style, that of an early sojourner with the Crees, an Anglican priest (and later bishop) of the James Bay region. The core of the chapter is six Cree texts, which we hope conveyed something of their cultural style. The final texts are ours, recent sojourners who brought to their experience of dying and grieving an earned measure of bicultural empathy. We found this chapter a chance to objectify our experience, and offer these for the reflexive goals they may serve.

The 1980s are a point in history when we can expect to find that we share some bicultural empathy with most contemporary young Crees, with one critical difference. They have experienced and internalized substantial parts of Western civilization's youth culture and protest politics, while we have experienced and internalized substantial parts of Cree "old ways" and reticence. In some of this we are facing in opposite directions.

Some of the young Crees are impatient with the Cree past and with its value of patient quiet composure that is maintained by traditionalists despite chronic failures of fairness by white men. For our part, we tend to be impatient with the Euro-Canadian present and with the barrage of words used for advantage rather than for community; whether it is the strategic use of ordinary language for persuasive marketing, the strategic use of technical vocabulary by social methodologists, or the strategic rhetoric of competition between ethnic group identities. We could use a bit more reticence in our lives, and solitude (not loneliness, which is endemic, but solitude, which is rare), and patience. And we could use friends. As one Cree lady told a departing anthropologist guest who had not stopped to say goodbye, "Don't you realize that the only thing we have in front of death is friends?"

And so to summarize. The ideal for Cree dying combines 1) harmony with others and with the process of dying, 2) maintaining competence in the face of this, the greatest of life's contingencies, and 3) setting out on a journey to a little known domain of the after-life. These three themes emphasize the importance of self-reliance, preparing one's self and one's friends, and going out, solitary and with composure, to meet death. This ideal is close to our somewhat narrower, technical concept of cognitive control. If it is the ideal way to set off on a next voyage, it is also only realistically a very solitary trip.

The ideal for Cree grieving is an immediate, shared, emotional release, with mutual support for those most at loss and perhaps at risk. But the release of crying and support is soon followed by a return to outward self-reliance and composure, though the inward, private feelings may still be strong. Realistically, much of Cree life, too, may be a solitary journey.

The Crees are not primitive existentialists, but this abstract comparison is not a trivial one. Their emphasis on an egalitarian, individual autonomy was nurtured not by a European-style interior struggle with the question of faith and hierarchies of sacred and secular power, but by unknown centuries of hunting for a living in the great Circumpolar Boreal Forest. They had few other humans for company, and periodic starvation as certain, though as contingent on the whims of nature as anything else in life.

Depending upon our culture and particular circumstances, we may meet death with equanimity or with anger, rage, and fear. Through the process of grieving we are brought face to face with our own mortality. These culturally defined attitudes toward death may reflect our attitudes toward the value of life. For the Cree, grieving is an intense expression of bonding between those with whom one shares a community. It is reestablishing community with those still living and at the same time reaffirming a relationship with the deceased, now transformed into spirit. Anger is out of place here.

We find that the Cree deal with death as well as anyone we know.

ACKNOWLEDGEMENTS

"Good Death, Bad Death (1): In Other Times and Places"
Kastenbaum, R.
On Our Way: The Final Passage Through Life and Death, Kastenbaum, R.
Copyright (C) 2004 ** University of California Press - books
This material has been copied under licence from Access.
Resale or further copying of this material is strictly prohibited.

"Living with the Dead: Exiting Gracefully"
Grimes, R.L.
Deeply into the Bone, Grimes, R.L.
Copyright (C) 2000 ** University of California Press - books
This material has been copied under licence from Access.
Resale or further copying of this material is strictly prohibited.

"Rites of Passage"
Bell, C.
Ritual: Perspectives and Dimensions, Bell, C.
Copyright (C) 1997 Oxford University Press (US)
This material has been copied under licence from Access.
Resale or further copying of this material is strictly prohibited.

"Territorial Passage and the Classification of Rites"
Van Gennep, A.
Readings in Ritual Studies, Grimes, R.L.
Copyright (C) 1996 Prentice Hall Inc.
This material has been copied under licence from Access.
Resale or further copying of this material is strictly prohibited.

"Forms and Attributes of Rites of Passage"
Turner, V.
The Ritual Process: Structure and Anti-structure, Turner, V.
Copyright (C) 1969 ** Aldine Transaction Publishers
This material has been copied under licence from Access.
Resale or further copying of this material is strictly prohibited.

"Introduction: Grief and a Headhunter's Rage"
Rosaldo, R.
Culture and Truth: The Remaking of Social Analysis, Rosaldo, R.
Copyright (C) 1989 ** Beacon Press
This material has been copied under licence from Access.
Resale or further copying of this material is strictly prohibited.

"Death Rituals and Life Values: Rites of Passage Reconsidered"
Huntington, R. and Metcalf, P.
Celebrations of Death: The Anthropology of Mortuary Ritual, Huntington, R. and Metcalf, P.
Copyright (C) 1979 ** Cambridge University Press US
This material has been copied under licence from Access.
Resale or further copying of this material is strictly prohibited.

"The Structure of Chinese Funerary Rites: Elementary Forms, Ritual Sequence, and the Primacy of Performance"

Watson, J.L.

Death Ritual in Late Imperial and Modern China, Watson, J.L. (ed.)

"Ghosts and Ancestors in Medieval Chinese Religion: The Yu-Lan-P'en Festival as Mortuary Ritual"

Teiser, S.F.

History of Religions, Vol. 26, 1986

"The Journey Through the Bardo: Notes on the Symbolism of Tibetan Mortuary Rites and the Tibetan Book of the Dead"

Corlin, C.

On the Meaning of Death: Essays on Mortuary Rituals and the Tibetan book of the Dead, Cederroth, S. et al. (eds.)

"Echoes of a Yolmo Buddhist's Life, in Death"

Desjarlais, R.

Cultural Anthropology, Vol. 15, 2000

"Ancestor Worship in Japan: Dependence and the Resolution of Grief"

Klass, D.

Omega: Journal of Death and Dying, Vol. 33, No. 4, 1996

"Buddhism and Abortion in Contemporary Japan: Mizuko Kuyo and the Confrontation with Death"

Smith, B.

Readings in Ritual Studies, Grimes, R.L.

"Apologizing to the Babies"

Desmond, J.F.

First Things, No. 66, October 1996

"Women's Roles in the Mourning Rituals of the Akan of Ghana"
Aborampah, O.M.
Ethnology, Vol. 38, No. 3, 1999

"The Ontological Journey"
Drewel, M.T.
Yoruba Ritual: Performers, Play, Agency, Drewel, M.T.

"Iconography in Mexico's Day of the Dead: Origins and Meaning"
Brandes, Stanley
Ethnohistory, Vol. 45, No. 2, Spring 1998

"The Day of the Dead, Halloween, and the Quest for Mexican National Identity"
Brandes, Stanley
Journal of American Folklore, Vol. 111, No. 442, 1998

"Everyday Violence: Bodies, Death and Silence"
Scheper-Hughes, N.
Death Without Weeping: The Violence of Everyday Life in Brazil, Scheper-Hughes, N.

"City of Death and Liberation"
Eck, D.L.
Banaras: City of Light, Eck, D.L.

"Perfection and Devotion: Sati Tradition in Rajasthan"
Harlan, L.
Sati: The Blessing and the Curse, Hawley, J.S.

"Death and Grieving among Northern Forest Hunters: An East Cree Example"

Preston, R.J. and Preston, S.C.

Coping with the Final Tragedy, Counts, D.R. and Counts, D.A.